Antarctic Challenge III

VERÖFFENTLICHUNGEN
DES INSTITUTS FÜR INTERNATIONALES RECHT
AN DER UNIVERSITÄT KIEL

Herausgegeben von

Jost Delbrück · Wilhelm A. Kewenig · Rüdiger Wolfrum

105

Antarctic Challenge III

Conflicting Interests, Cooperation
Environmental Protection, Economic Development

Proceedings of an Interdisciplinary Symposium
July 7th - 12th, 1987

Organized by the Institut für Internationales Recht an der Universität Kiel
and the Alfred-Wegener-Institut für Polar- und Meeresforschung, Bremerhaven

Edited by

Rüdiger Wolfrum

Assistant Editor:
E. A. Michos-Ederer

Duncker & Humblot / Berlin

The organization of the symposium and the publication of this volume have been made possible by generous grants from:
Bundesministerium für Forschung und Technologie, Bonn
Dr. Otto Bagge-Gedächtnisstiftung

CIP-Titelaufnahme der Deutschen Bibliothek

Antarctic challenge: conflicting interests, cooperation, environmental protection, econom. development; proceedings of an interdisciplinary symposium / organized by the Inst. für Internat. Recht an d. Univ. Kiel and the Alfred-Wegener-Inst. für Polar- u. Meeresforschung, Bremerhaven. Ed. by Rüdiger Wolfrum. Assistant ed.: E. A. Michos-Ederer. — Berlin: Duncker u. Humblot.
Literaturangaben
NE: Wolfrum, Rüdiger [Hrsg.]
3. July 7th - 12th, 1987. - 1988
(Veröffentlichungen des Instituts für Internationales Recht an der Universität Kiel; 105)
ISBN 3-428-06550-6
NE: Institut für Internationales Recht <Kiel>: Veröffentlichungen des Instituts ...

Druck: Vollbehr u. Strobel, Kiel
Printed in Germany
ISBN 3-428-06550-6

Contents

Abbreviations

AFDI	Annuaire Français de Droit International
AJIL	American Journal of International Law
ANS	Astronomical Netherlands Satellite
APG	Antarctic Policy Group
ASEAN	Association of South East Asian Nations
ASOC	Antarctic and Southern Ocean Coalition
ATCM	Antarctic Treaty Consultative Meeting
ATCP	Antarctic Treaty Consultative Party
ATPs	Antarctic Treaty Parties
BAPS	Baseline Air Pollution Stations
BGR	Bundesanstalt für Geowissenschaften und Rohstoffe
BIOMASS	Biological Investigation of Marine Antarctic Systems and Stocks
BSR	Bottom Simulating Reflections
BYIL	British Yearbook of International Law
CCAMLR	Convention on the Conservation of Antarctic Marine Living Resources
CATSA	Cooperative Air Transport System Antarctica
CEOS	Committee on Earth Observation Satellites
CFR	Code of Federal Regulations (U. S.)
CHM	Common Heritage of Mankind
CMG	Commission for Marine Geology
C.O.N.D.	Centennial of Nansen's Drift
COPUOS	Committee on the Peaceful Uses of Outer Space (UN)
COSOD II	Conference on Scientific Ocean Drilling (Strasbourg 1987)
CZCS	Coastal Zone Colour Scanner
DDT	Dichloro-diphenyl-trichloro-ethane ($C_{14} H_9 Cl_5$)
DFA	Diesel Fuel Additive
DMSP	Defense Meteorological Satellite Program (U. S.)
DOD	Department of Defense (U. S.)
DSDP	Deep Sea Drilling Program
DVDP	Dry Valleys Drilling Project
EDF	Environmental Defense Fund
EEZ	Exclusive Economic Zone
EFZ	Exclusive Fisheries Zone
EIS	Environmental Impact Statement
EPA	Environmental Protection Agency (U. S.)
ESMR	Electrically Scanning Microwave Radiometer
F. 2d	Federal Reporter (U. S.)
FAO	Food and Agriculture Organization
Fed. Reg.	Federal Register (U. S.)
FIR	Flight Information Regions
Friendly Relations Declaration	Declaration on Principles of International Law concerning Friendly Relations and Co-operation among States in Accordance with the Charter of the United Nations
FUND	International Convention on the Establishment of an International Fund for Compensation for Oil Pollution Damage

GDR	German Democratic Republic
GEBCO	General Bathymetric Chart of the Oceans
GYIL	German Yearbook of International Law
HEW	Department of Health, Education and Welfare (U. S.)
IAGP	International Antarctic Glaciological Project
IBEA	International Biomedical Expedition to Antarctica
ICAO	International Civil Aviation Organization
ICL	Inter-Union Commission on the Lithosphere
ICSU	International Council of Scientific Unions
IGBP	International Geosphere Biosphere Programme
IGY	International Geophysical Year
IHO	International Hydrographic Office
IIED	International Institute for Environment and Development
ILC	International Law Commission
ILM	International Legal Materials
ILO	International Labour Organisation
IMCO	Intergovernmental Maritime Consultative Organization
IOC	Intergovernmental Oceanographic Commission
ITT	International Telegraph and Telephone
ITU	International Telecommunication Union
IUCN	International Union for the Conservation of Nature
IWC	International Whaling Commission
IUGG	International Union Commission of Geodesy and Geophysics
IUGS	International Union of Geological Sciences
JOIDES	Joint Oceanographic Institutions for Deep Earth Sampling
km	kilometers
kw	kilowatts
LDC	The Convention on the Prevention of Marine Pollution by Dumping of Wastes and other Matter (London Dumping Convention)
LOSC	United Nations Convention on the Law of the Sea (1982)
m	meters
Ma	million years before present
MAF	Ministry of Agriculture and Fisheries (New Zealand)
MARPOL	The International Convention for the Prevention of Pollution from Ships
MARPOL 73/78	The Protocol of 1978 Relating to the International Convention for the Prevention of Pollution from Ships
MIT	The Massachussetts Institute of Technology
MNAP	Managers of National Antarctic Programs
MODIS	Moderate Resolution Imaging Spectroradiometer
MSR	Marine Scientific Research
MSS	Multi-Spectral Scanning
my	million years
NARE 85	Norwegian Antarctic Research Expedition (1985)
NASA	National Aeronautics and Space Administration (U. S.)
NCPs	Non-consultative Parties
NEPA	National Environmental Protection Act (U. S.)
NGO	Non-Governmental Organization
NOAA	National Oceanic and Atmospheric Administration (U. S.)
N-ROSS	Naval Research Oceanographic Satellite System (U. S.)
NSF	National Science Foundation (U. S.)
NSFA	Naval Support Force Antarctica (U. S.)
N. Z.	New Zealand
OCI	Ocean Color Imager
ODA	Ocean Dumping Act (U. S.)
ODP	International Ocean Drilling Program

para.	paragraph
PCB	polychlorinated biphenyl
RIAA	Reports of International Arbitral Awards
RTA	Return to Australia
RV	Research Vessel
RdC	Recueil des Cours (Académie de Droit International)
SAR	Synthetic Aperture Radar
SAR Convention	International Convention on Maritime Search and Rescue
SCAR	Scientific Committee on Antarctic Research
SCOPE	Scientific Committee on Problems of the Environment
SCOR	Scientific Committee for Oceanic Research
sect.	section
SMMR	Scanning Multichannel Microwave Radiometer
SOLAS	International Conference for the Safety of Life at Sea (London 1960)
sonar	sound navigation ranging
SPA	Specially Protected Area
SSM/I	Special Sensor Microwave Imager
SSSI	Sites of Special Scientific Interest
TIAS	Treaties and Other International Acts Series
UIR	Upper Information Region
U.K.	United Kingdom
U Miami L. R.	University of Miami Law Review
UN	United Nations Organization
UNCLOS	Third United Nations Conference on the Law of the Sea (1973—1982)
UNDP	United Nations Development Programme
UNEP	United Nations Environmental Programme
UNESCO	United Nations Educational, Scientific and Cultural Organization
UNGA	United Nations General Assembly
UNJYB	United Nations Juridical Yearbook
UNTS	United Nations Treaty Series
U. S.	United States of America
USAP	United States Antarctic Program
USARP	United States Antarctic Research Program
USC	United States Code
USGS	United States Geological Survey
USSR	Union of Soviet Socialist Republics
WG	Working Group
WMO	World Meteorological Organization
WOCE	World Ocean Circulation Experiment
WQB	Winter Quarters Bay
WWSP	Winter Weddell Sea Project
WWW	World Weather Watch
Yale JIL	The Yale Journal of International Law

Preface

With interest in Antarctica and Antarctic resources continuing to grow apace, the Institute of International Law at the University of Kiel and the Alfred Wegener Institute for Polar and Marine Research in Bremerhaven organized a third interdisciplinary symposium on the scientific, environmental, legal and political challenges of the Southern Continent, which took place in Kiel from July 7th—12th 1987.

This volume, part of the publication series of the Institute of International Law at the Christian Albrecht University of Kiel, containing the presentations, comments, and discussions of the Symposium, is the third volume (together with volumes 88 and 95 of the Institute's publications) of the Antarctic Challenge series.

Over 70 scientists, diplomats, international lawyers and environmentalists from 24 nations met in their private capacity to discuss legal and administrative aspects of the Treaty System, both as it stands now and with a view toward necessary or likely changes; the nature of both pure and applied scientific research, together with its impact on living resources and the environment; and the question of the legitimacy of both the interest of the greater international community, represented by the UN, and that of the Consultative Parties to the Antarctic Treaty, in regulating the affairs of the continent.

During the time of this volume's publication, the Convention on the Regulation of Antarctic Mineral Resources is open to signature to the Antarctic Treaty Parties. This Convention, together with the ones already in force — namely, the Convention on the Protection of Antarctic Seals and the Convention of the Conservation of Antarctic Marine Living Resources — represent elements strengthening the Antarctic regime. This legal development, together with the perhaps incremental, yet nonetheless continual technological progress of humankind in the exploitation of the Earth's natural resources, as well as the environmental dangers thus posed, are evidence enough for the increased interest in Antarctica.

The Institute of International Law and the Institute of Polar Research are greatly indebted to the Federal Ministry of Research and Technology for funding this Symposium, as well as the publication of its proceedings. The publication of the proceedings have been further supported by the

Dr. Otto Bagge-Gedächtnisstiftung. Our sincere thanks also go to the Government of the Land of Schleswig-Holstein and the Rectorate of the Christian Albrecht University of Kiel for their involvement. My personal thanks to the staff of the Institute of International Law, whose efforts made the Symposium possible, with special gratitude to *Ingrid Jahn*, the research assistant responsible for the organization and functioning of the Symposium, and hence, its success.

Rüdiger Wolfrum

Welcoming Address

*Jost Delbrück**

Excellencies, *Herr Minister*, dear Colleagues, Ladies and Gentlemen:

On behalf of the Christian Albrecht University I have the great honour and pleasure to welcome you as participants of Antarctic Challenge III. Since 1983, this is the third time that a great number of eminent experts in the fields of Antarctic policies and research have assembled here in Kiel as guests of this University, and in particular of the Institute of International Law, as well as the Alfred Wegener Institute at Bremerhaven. We thank you for accepting our invitation so numerously. We consider this a vote of confidence in the conference facilities, environment and follow-up, as provided for in the past.

The Christian Albrecht University endeavours to strengthen its research programs in the marine and polar sciences, which have traditionally been, and still are, a stronghold of this University, situated as it is in a state between the Baltic and North Seas. Since our last meeting in 1985, our plans have become more concrete. We have received a full grant to establish a new Institute of Geomarine Research, which will be a welcome complementary institution to the established and highly recognized Institute of Marine Research. With the Institute of International Law being able to serve both, it is a fairly unique setting for our research activities in the future. I should like to wish for cooperation with its growing center of marine and geomarine and, particularly, Antarctic research in the years to come.

The programme of the present Conference is very rich. I congratulate *Rüdiger Wolfrum* that he has been able to persuade such a great number of eminent experts to contribute papers to the deliberations of the Symposium; I thank you all for your intellectual inputs into this effort. I also thank the Ministry of Research and Technology, as well as the State Government, for their material and spiritual support of the Symposium.

In one of the oldest marine research papers written here in Kiel in 1697 the author, a scientist named *Möbius*, mentioned that he could not

* Prof. Dr. *Jost Delbrück*, Rector of the Christian Albrecht University of Kiel, Director of the Institute of International Law at the Christian Albrecht University of Kiel.

have attacked his problem without the support of a sponsor — a well-to-do citizen of Kiel.

In our times it is mainly governments which have to act as sponsors, and we thank you for your help. I am confident that the funds will be spent well during these conference days. And I wish you a successful meeting. Welcome to Kiel, again.

Welcoming Address

*Roger Asmussen**

Verehrter Herr Präsident, Professor Delbrück, meine sehr verehrten Damen und Herren,

es ist mir eine große Freude und zugleich auch Ehre, das Symposium Antarctic Challenge hier in Kiel zu eröffnen und die hochqualifizierten und berühmten Antarktis-Fachleute aus allen Teilen der Welt im Namen der schleswig-holsteinischen Landesregierung herzlich willkommen zu heißen.

Your Excellencies, Ladies and Gentlemen:

On behalf of the State Government of Schleswig-Holstein I want to extend a warm welcome to all the participants. When my predecessor, *Dr. Westphal*, spoke to you on the same occasion in 1985 he mentioned that it might be yet too early to talk of "new tradition" of Antarctic conferences in Kiel. Now, however, I take the liberty of saying that a new tradition has successfully been established. Our sincere thanks go to all those who made this meeting possible: above all, to our distinguished guests, who by their presence, by their devotion to Antarctica, and by their profound expertise provide the intellectual basis for this conference. In particular, I am pleased to mention that this time the number of delegations from Latin American, Asian and African states is remarkably higher than during the first two conferences. I take this as a positive signal — in Schleswig-Holstein and, in a wider context, in Northern Germany; public institutions and private enterprises oriented towards marine and polar problems and applications have assembled such a large concentration of scientific and technical expertise.

Such institutions in Kiel include the fifty-year old *Institut für Meereskunde*, a new Institute for Polar Ecology, and the Kiel Institute of International Law. A new national center for Marine Geosciences (GEOMAR) complemented by a privately operated company for marine technology and services and a training center will start its work by the end of this year. Polar research vessels and other scientific equipment is being manufactured in this part of Germany. While all this is being sponsored

* Mr. *Roger Asmussen*, Minister für Finanzen und Minister für Wirtschaft und Verkehr des Landes Schleswig-Holstein.

by the State Government of Schleswig-Holstein, this is not necessarily a limiting factor. On the contrary, we are well aware that we must be prepared to expand our commitment to meet urgent needs of scientific research, environmental management and education which face the global community. Also, I can assure you that the Federal Government in Bonn, in particular the Ministry for Research and Technology, which so generously funds and coordinates all German activities, will continue to support this sector of research.

Against this background, I want to stress that we are prepared to take on our share within the framework of the Antarctic System and contribute to the growing task in Antarctica. This includes the scientific and environmental activities as well as a closer cooperation among interested states.

If discussions reveal the necessity for new fields of activities, for instance, more exchange of information, joint activities and central services, we are seriously interested in providing all kinds of help and services which may be required in the future. We are convinced that the Federal Republic of Germany and Kiel University in particular, is a good place for this purpose. You may be well aware that German universities are independent of "too much" state influence. At the same time, they have the organizational capabilities and the flexibility which are necessary to maintain international projects and to host conferences like this.

Again, let me tell you how happy we are to welcome you in Kiel. I hope that the deliberations of the next four days will be successful, and I look forward to seeing all of you again tonight, at the reception hosted by the Government of Schleswig-Holstein. Thank you very much.

Opening Address

Rüdiger Wolfrum[*]

Magnifizenz, Your Excellencies, *Herr Minister*, dear Friends, Ladies and Gentlemen:

On behalf of the Institute of International Law at the Christian Albrecht University of Kiel, and the Alfred Wegener Institute of Polar and Marine Scientific Research, we warmly welcome you to our third symposium concerning Antarctica. We are particularly grateful that so many of you have responded positively to our invitation — it is nice to think that some of you start to feel at home here in Kiel. It is my hope that the Symposium fosters presentations which are of interest to each one of you and equally addresses the core problems that the Antarctic legal and political regime, as well as the scientific activities undertaken in Antarctica, are faced with at present. We shall discuss matters concerning the interpretation and workings of the Antarctic Treaty, from the point-of-view of effectiveness. We shall hear about the results of research activities recently carried out in Antarctica, we shall speak about how to secure the interests of all mankind in administering Antarctica, and last, but not least, we shall deal with the question of the protection of the Antarctic environment.

As you all know, the progressive development of the regime in Antarctica has come to a crossroads, making it more important that every opportunity for discussion among the various groups interested in Antarctica be used. As I have indicated earlier, this Symposium is meant to serve as a neutral scientific forum for a thorough and open discussion on Antarctic matters. I shall deem it to be successful if a better understanding of the various positions could be achieved. Although we all have different backgrounds, and may pursue different interests, we are unified in the belief that Antarctica should continue forever to be used exclusively for peaceful purposes and should not become the scene or object of international discord. Furthermore, to me the principle seems to be accepted that the unique Antarctic environment and its dependent ecosystems are to be protected. Divergent approaches, however, exist as to how these goals are to be achieved. Whether or

---

* Prof. Dr. *Rüdiger Wolfrum*, Director of the Institute of International Law at the Christian Albrecht University of Kiel.

not we come to a better understanding will very much depend upon the openness of the discussion. In this respect, I would like to assure you that according to established practice, you will have the opportunity to review your contributions before the publication of the proceedings of this Symposium. Nothing will go to the printer and nothing you have said will leave this circle without your express consent.

I draw your attention to the exhibition here on marine and polar research. Some of the scientists who are very active in this field are among us. Please, ask them if you want additional information, although you will get further exposure to their fields in Bremerhaven on Thursday.

Finally, may I take this opportunity to thank all those who have made this Symposium possible, namely the *Bundesministerium für Forschung und Technologie, die Landesregierung von Schleswig-Holstein*, which is represented by *Minister Asmussen, das Rektorat der Christian-Albrechts-Universität* and the staff of the Institute of International Law. The members of the Institute, whom you will recognize by the red dots on their name tags, will try their best to solve any organizational problem which may arise during the meeting. Please address them, or myself, if you have any questions.

The Role of Scientific Advice for the Decision-Making Process in the Antarctic Treaty System

John A. Heap[*]

Mr. Chairman, I must own to feeling in something of an exposed position as the first speaker in this, the third in the series of Kiel conferences on the Antarctic and, more particularly, on the challenges that the Antarctic presents.

I take heart, however, Mr. Chairman, from the fact that what I am asked to speak about relates to science. The pursuit of knowledge in the Antarctic is, after all, the activity which gives the Consultative Parties to the Antarctic Treaty their position regarding the making of decisions.

It has often been said that science is the main export from Antarctica and is likely to remain so for the foreseeable future. It is therefore not unreasonable to expect, with such a wealth of scientific capacity available, that scientific advice should play an important part in the decision-making process in the Antarctic Treaty System.

What I want to do is to look at the relationship between the decision-making process and scientific advice in three fora: firstly, the regular Consultative Meetings, secondly, in the Commission for the Conservation of Antarctic Marine Living Resources and, thirdly in the Antarctic minerals negotiations.

I. The Consultative Meeting Forum

Of the 154 Recommendations that have been adopted in Consultative meetings up to and including the XIIIth, 71 refer in one way or another to the Scientific Committee on Antarctic Research — known familiarly throughout the Antarctic Treaty System as SCAR.

In these 71 Recommendations, the references to SCAR fall broadly into four main groups:

(i) Straight-forward requests for advice on a particular matter;

---

* Dr. *John A. Heap*, Foreign and Commonwealth Office, London. The opinions expressed in this volume are the personal view of their authors only.

(ii) Acknowledgements of the responses to such requests that have been received from SCAR, usually, but not always, followed by some sort of action in the light of the response;

(iii) Making use of initiatives of SCAR which have not resulted from a direct request; and

(iv) Encouragement of activities that are already being undertaken by SCAR.

Anyone reading through these 71 Recommendations would, I think, be struck by four things. The first is the reluctance of governments to take recommendatory action on any issue which relates directly to what is done or not done in the Antarctic without first seeking the views of SCAR. The second is the strict recognition by governmental representatives of the need to respect the autonomy of their National Antarctic Committees affiliated to SCAR: requests are not made to SCAR directly but through National Antarctic Committees and the advice comes back from SCAR through the same channel. At no time can a National Antarctic Committee or its Government reasonably claim ignorance of the content of the relationship between SCAR and the Consultative process. The third point is the strong element of pragmatism in the relationship between SCAR and the Treaty. It is very much a relationship between equals. SCAR is, formally, a non-governmental body of the International Council of Scientific Unions, despite the fact that most of the scientists who compose it are supported by governments. While it is not clear to me that SCAR needs the Treaty, it is very clear that the Treaty mechanism would be very much the poorer if it did not have SCAR to turn to.

The fourth point relates to the rarity, the extreme rarity, of a request from the Treaty for advice from SCAR which imposes on SCAR a requirement to use the scientific method of observation, measurement and prediction.

The relationship between the Consultative mechanism and SCAR does not, except very rarely, in the strict sense, involve the provision of *scientific* advice to the Consultative decision-making mechanism. While it cannot be denied that the advice from SCAR is formulated, for the most part, by scientists, the dominant characteristic of the advice is that it comes from people who earn their daily bread and butter in the Antarctic — who know what they are talking about.

Another important characteristic of the advisory relationship between SCAR and the Consultative process is the clear separation of the advisory function, in SCAR, from the decision-making process of the Consultative mechanism. SCAR presents its advice without fear or favour. The Consultative mechanism takes the advice for just what it is and then feeds it, as one of many factors, into the political context of the decision to be made. That is just as it should be; there is no doubt amongst representatives of governments in the Consultative mechanism that it is they, not SCAR, who have the responsibility for making the decisions.

II. The CCAMLR Commission

Let me turn now to the second forum of the Treaty System in which scientific advice is called for, the Commission for the Conservation of Antarctic Marine Living Resources — CCAMLR Commission. It is a common feature of international fishery agreements that any measures taken to restrict the freedom of fishermen to catch however much they can are to be "on the basis of the best scientific evidence available." The International Whaling Convention is an example of an agreement which contains such a provision; there are others, including CCAMLR, but I will return to that later. It would not, I believe, be going too far to suggest that those nine words, which look so right and proper on paper have, in the event, constituted the kiss of death for the fisheries they were intended to protect.

I can see eyebrows rising. Is he, you may be asking, decrying the proposition that science is an indispensable tool in coming to decisions about how a fishery should be regulated? I am not, far from it. But I want to draw attention to a serious, almost fatal, drawback involved in such an advisory and decision-making system. It is this. It has allowed the decisions-makers to divest themselves of the responsibility for the decisions which should be theirs, and theirs alone, to take and has pushed that responsibility onto the scientific method. I submit that the scientific method cannot sustain such a responsibility.

The use of the phrase "the best scientific evidence" raises in the mind the notion of advice which is consistent, elegant and admits of no element of doubt. "These are the facts," it seems to say, "act accordingly." But natural science, and more particularly biological science, is rarely like that. How much more so must this be the case in relation to a natural distribution hidden within the sea. It stretches the bounds of credibility to the point of absurdity to believe that advice, based on inevitably imperfect knowledge, should be without doubt.

Scientists, called upon to offer advice on the basis of the best scientific evidence available, and feeling that the responsibility is theirs to give clear and unambiguous advice to the decision-makers, take one of two ways out of what is, I believe, an impossible situation. They either exaggerate the different interpretations that can be given to the evidence, or whatever sides there may be in the argument seek a single compromise solution to their dilemma.

Thereafter, it is virtually humanly inevitable that the decision-makers take either the compromise or note the divergent interpretations being placed on the evidence and opt for the more optimistic of them, in the hope that there might be more fish than the pessimists think. No decision-maker likes to put fishermen out of work on the basis of the pessimistic advice of a bunch of scientists. Experience has shown almost universally that the decision-makers have thus shirked their responsibility.

The question before us now, against such a background of unhappy experience, is whether CCAMLR provides differently.

The relationship between the CCAMLR Commission and the Scientific Committee is described in three Articles in the Convention. Article IX places the responsibility for the formulation and adoption of conservation measures firmly on the Commission and it has to do it "on the basis of the best scientific evidence available" — there are those dreaded nine words again. Article IX also says that "In exercising its functions . . . the Commission shall take full account of the recommendations and advice of the Scientific Committee." Up to this point it looks as though the relationship between scientific advice and the decision-making process in CCAMLR is virtually the same as relationships which have failed in other fishery agreements.

Articles XV and XVI, however, give some room for an expectation that the relationship in CCAMLR should not work out in that same unhappy way. Article XV sets out a number of functions or tasks which the Scientific Committee is to carry out quite independently of any requests or questions that might be addressed to it by the Commission. Article XVI, in speaking of the Scientific Committee's Rules of Procedure, says that "The rules shall include procedures for the presentation of minority reports."

It is vital, I believe, that the Scientific Committee and Commission should work out the implications of the independent functions with which the Convention tasks the Scientific Committee and the implications for the Commission that the advice it gets from the Scientific Committee is to represent all the main arguments relating to any particular issue. Beneath working out these implications, however, there is an even more vital question. That is, that the Commission should not expect to be told by the Scientific Committee what it, the Commission, should do in any particular case. Let me try to explain what I mean by a couple of examples based on problems that are current within CCAMLR.

Let us use as the first example that of *Notothenia rossii* — that famous species which makes such excellent eating and which has virtually disappeared from some Antarctic fishing grounds. So much so that one fisherman said, "Well, we don't often see them but if we do catch one we send it straight to the galley for the cook to serve up for lunch!" The Scientific Committee tells the Commission that the stocks of the species are well below the level at which Article II of the Convention requires that action be taken to protect them. The Commission has to do something but it is unclear as to what it should do. Among the questions that might occur to it are the following: is it sufficient to protect the inshore areas where juveniles live? Can whatever stocks there may be of fish of breeding age be protected by restricting fishing in certain areas or at certain times of year? Will it do simply to prevent a directed fishery on the species? Or, is the situation so serious that the risks of by-catches cannot be tolerated and therefore the fishery in the area has to be stopped altogether?

Back might come the Scientific Committee, in response, saying that protection of the inshore habitat of juveniles is vital and is not likely to have a significant effect on the fishing of other species; that they do not know enough to be able to say whether protection by spatial or temporal restriction would help very much; that any by-catch of *N. rossii* should not be sent to the cook before it has produced as much scientific data as it can provide; that they are unclear about the effectiveness of prohibiting a directed fishery but it might help and that, lastly, they cannot answer the last question about whether the situation is sc serious as to warrant total closure of the fishery unless the Commission give it guidance as to what the Commission wants. Is the top priority, for example, the recovery of the stocks of *N. rossii* in the minimum time; would it, alternatively, be acceptable that the recovery of *N. rossii* should be in slower time? And so on.

At the end of such a dialogue the Commission should have before it a series of management options which it can judge against the requirements of the Convention and other relevant facts of the fishery in the area concerned.

The important thing throughout such a dialogue should be that the Commission should not attempt to pass to the Scientific Committee the bulk of the responsibility for the final management decision and that the Scientific Committee should be asked for advice on things where its advice admits of doubt and which are within its capacity to answer without prejudicing its scientific virtue.

Let us take as the other example, krill. It is the common view that there is so much krill in the Antarctic that there is no current need for protection. It would, I should have thought, be prudent for the Commission to check this out with the Scientific Committee. I could imagine that the Scientific Committee might come back with something along the following lines: "Yes, we agree with you that there is no current evidence which suggests the need for restriction but we ask you to consider the implications of the fact that the scientifically based estimates of the longevity of krill appear to be increasing; that means of knowing whether krill is being taken from a stock at rates which would indicate the need for protection are in their infancy and are not likely to be developed quickly and that the consequences of overfishing krill could be disastrous, not only for the species dependent on krill but also for investments made in krill-catching capacity.

The message would be fairly clear. At the very least it is that it would be prudent to take steps to protect investment. Such steps could take a number of different forms such as intensified data collection, scientific research dedicated to contemporaneous work alongside krill-catching fleets, independent research on the biology of krill and precautionary effort limitation. Taken together, steps such as these, and others like them, would amount to a strategy for the steady development of krill catch on a course and at a rate intended to avoid the necessity for the imposition of draconian economically damaging restrictions at a later stage.

Again, as in the case of SCAR and the Treaty, the relationship between the Scientific Committee and the Commission would be one in which the separation between their respective responsibilities and capacities were clearly maintained.

III. Antarctic Minerals

I should now like to turn to the negotiations of an Antarctic minerals regime and to try, if I may, to look at the role of what is currently known as the Scientific, Environmental and Technological Advisory Committee or, for short, as the Advisory Committee. It is not my intention to open up drafting of the present informal text but rather to underline the importance of maintaining what is currently there.

Much time in these negotiations has been expended on the nature of the relationship between the Advisory Committee, on the one side, and the Commission and Regulatory Committees on the other. Does the preceding discussion have any lessons for us in connection with the role of the Advisory Committee in relation to the decision-making functions of the Commission and Regulatory Committees?

Let me digress for a moment to consider what appear to me to be the main lessons for the role of scientific advice in decision-making that have appeared from discussion of the Consultative mechanism of the Treaty and of CCAMLR. They are:

(i) that the independence of the advisory functions is essential; as it is,

(ii) that the advisory body must have functions which enable it to build up its own information base and methods of work;
(iii) that the separation of the responsibilities and capacities of the advisory and decision-making bodies must be clearly stated and then be maintained;
(iv) that the development of a habit of dialogue between the advisory and decision-making bodies is an important means of ensuring that the advisory body is not put into a false position in which it is tempted into offering advice which is beyond its capacity to give;
(v) that it is important for the decision-making body to make clear to the advisory body what is expected of it.

Returning now to the minerals negotiations, it is, I believe, reasonable to underline how important it is that the Advisory Committee should not be a decision-making body (except in relation to its own internal affairs) and should have the capacity to present all the main views on a point at issue. These points have already given rise to debate in the negotiations and are now settled in a reasonable manner. There is, however, one aspect which I would like to discuss a little further. It relates to the point, to which many parties attach considerable importance, that all the main views on a matter at issue in the Advisory Committee should be represented to the decision-making body. Others of our colleagues believe that this is a recipe for a Tower of Babel, with as many views being represented as there are parties to hold them.

I must say that I have never seen this as in any way a real probability. The pressure within the Advisory Committee to provide a single piece of advice on a question at issue will be considerable. The majority and minorities on any issue will seek to convert the other side to its view. Indeed, I see the opposite danger — of creating situations in which consensus advice is called for — as being far more potentially damaging to the regime. In the search for consensus vital elements of the argument tend to get lost; instead of differences being clearly stated there is blurring and fudge which does not help the decision-makers to discharge their responsibilities properly.

Let me try to give a concrete example. For argument's sake, the question at issue is one of transferring oil from an off-shore well to an on-shore storage facility. The majority take the view that it is preferable to do this by pipeline, the minority want to use small ice-breaking tankers but their arguments for tankers are not making much headway in the debate and they begin to spend their time looking more seriously at the pipeline option rather than spending it, apparently fruitlessly, arguing the virtues of tankers. One of the minority, taking a hard look at the pipeline specification notes that although it deals in some detail with what is widely acknowledged as "the permafrost problem," it makes no distinction between continuous and discontinuous permafrost which, he suspects, is likely to give rise to engineering problems which have not been adequately dealt with. He makes known his fears that the stresses exerted on the pipe in discontinuous permafrost could exceed the design limits. He is not sure, but he has a real worry. The proponents of the pipeline, sensing victory because of the apparent collapse of the pro-tanker group, put enormous pressure on our poor doubting Thomas to forget his fears which, they say, are baseless anyway.

If the ground rules for the conclusion of this debate were to be consensus advice the pressure on our lone representative would be overwhelming and the temptation in the majority to avoid taking a serious look at the objector's stress calculations would be very great indeed. Do not desert the ship now would be the cry. But as our poor man holds his ground, while knowing that he is heading inexorably towards crucifixion, someone in the majority with an instinct for fair play offers him a way out, a form of words which fudges the real issue. Our objector feels he can retire with honour and join the consensus. He has achieved something, and, after all, he tells himself, he might be wrong. The rest of the story is, of course, that the decision-making body misses the point of fudged wording or takes a rosy view of it; the pipeline is built to specification and after some years have gone by it fails. Enquiry shows that it failed in an area of discontinuous permafrost. No one is to blame — all the majority have forgotten the argument. But our poor objector's wife finds her husband has hanged himself leaving a note saying that if only he had had the courage of his convictions there would still be seals left in the Ross Sea.

Not a bad scenario for an *Arthur Hailey* novel, you will say?

Let us now take a look at how the story might develop in a situation where the ground rules allow for minority reports. Put briefly it might be this. Our objector's fears are looked at seriously. He gains some support. A minority view is written which appended to a majority report. The Regulatory Committee makes it clear to the operator that they need to be satisfied on this point. The specifications are improved, the pipeline is built and does not fail. *Arthur Hailey*'s hopes of writing his Antarctic blockbuster entitled "Pipeline" have disappeared.

Mr. Chairman, the main conclusion that I draw from this brief survey of the relationship between scientific advice and the decision-making process in the Antarctic Treaty System is twofold — two sides, in fact, of the same coin. Firstly, advisers must not be put into positions which encourage them to exercise powers which are not theirs to exercise. And, secondly, that decision-makers must not be put in positions which encourage them to take less than full responsibility for the decisions they must make.

General Discussion

R. Wolfrum, Chairman:

I would now like to open the discussion of the presentation given by *John* (*Heap*). As I see it there is no need for me to structure the discussion as the presentation very clearly indicated the highlights to be dealt with. *Mr. Delbrück*, please.

J. Delbrück:

Thank you. Before I let the experts dive into the details, I would like to underline a few points that *Mr. Heap* has raised here. I think that the problem he has posed is a serious one. A first element relates to consensus as a device for arriving at decisions. I have always been rather apprehensive about it because on the one hand the majority is always tempted to somewhat rephrase the majority opinion in order to achieve consensus. This results in a deviation from what the majority actually is about. But even worse, the minority, for consensus' sake, is under pressure to not only rephrase but also to give up the main point of their original thoughts about a particular issue, thus obscuring the true picture of opinions. Therefore, I have always been much more in favour of clear-cut voting, majority versus minority. The second sub-problem is the question of what is the role of scientific advice in decision-making. *Dr. Heap* has touched upon a very fundamental problem of all modern societies. Science is being misused and it is misusing itself on many points, in that a so-called "scientific opinion" is one that is couched in absolute terms. Its pronouncer is considered to be in the possession of truth and therefore political decisions have to tie in — conform with these scientific findings — and if that gets mixed up with "consensus decision-making processes" then we really are at odds. I am very grateful to you for having raised this so clearly. My hunch is that we will be better off if we restrict scientific advice to raising all the doubts scientists are actually not only likely to hold, but also those that they are obliged to have, because we as scientists know that there is nothing like absolute truth. If we try to get at some kind of a balanced perception of the respective roles of the political decision-makers and scientists, and keep the decision-making process in that kind of a

---

The opinions expressed in this volume are the personal views of their authors only.

delicate balance when heading for decisions, it will be much more helpful in the long run, rather than the somewhat blurring and muddling-up types of processes that we encounter today — not only in the areas that you have touched upon, but everywhere, I think, where we are confronted with the relationship between political decision-making and science. Thank you.

R. Wolfrum, Chairman:

Thank you. *Pat Birnie*, please.

P. Birnie:

Thank you. I was very interested in *John Heap*'s remarks about the role of scientific research, in view of my experiences of this role in the operation of the International Convention for the Regulation of Whaling, where a lot of similar problems have been experienced. There are two kinds of problems to which I would particularly like to draw your attention. One is the problem that there are constantly certain objectors on the scientific committees when it comes to a question of setting stock quotas or making comments on any problem that has been addressed to the committees by the Commission as such.

One of the things that arises is the general credibility of particular schools of scientific advice and particular research methods that are adopted by different countries, thus I am not sure that *John*'s conclusion that the Commission itself would be able to take account of those kind of objections and build them in will necessarily work out. I doubt whether there will be sufficient caution: certain kinds of objections recur and get discounted over the years.

The other problem that has arisen is that, in the light of disagreement on scientific advice occurring on a permanent basis, the Commission, instead of always taking a wise, balanced decision, tends to put off taking a decision at all if it possibly can, rather than face up to the dilemma it is confronted with, that of conflicting advice. So, although they are supposed to review and evaluate the state of stocks and give advice on the catch and so on, the Whaling Commissioners prefer, if possible, to leave things as they are and postpone these decisions, which is certainly not very good for the health of stocks. Another aspect which you did not touch on at all but which occurs in some of the Antarctic Treaties, under the Agreed Measures and in CCAMLR and the Seals Convention and so on, is that exceptions can be made to some of the measures adopted. For example, in the Whaling Convention exceptions exist for the issue of scientific permits or special permits for purposes of scientific research, and this has raised questions about definitions of scientific research, which is a hugely difficult problem. *Professor Delbrück* has just touched on one aspect of this; he has offered his own definition of it, but very many different definitions of research can be offered.

Now, in attempting to offer some guidelines and criteria for what is understood by "scientific research," great problems have arisen in the Whaling Commission — as I am sure everyone here knows, as it has received quite a lot of publicity in the last few weeks. The problems concern the fact that, as particular stocks become depleted — perhaps the species to which you made particular reference — the particular stock concerned can be seriously affected by the issue of scientific permits. This has much more significance for depleted stocks than it would otherwise have. It is now open to the IWC's Scientific Committee to express a view on these prior to their issue, but this has raised a great deal of objection from individual states, because they regard it as an invasion of their rights under the Convention to issue such kinds of permits. It is not a matter that falls within the powers of the Commission itself. However, the Commission has, just in the last couple of weeks, decided to review the advice of the Scientific Committee on these permits, and this has raised even more questions about whether this is, in fact, within the scope of the Convention, whether it invades the individual sovereignty and thus discretion of states concerned to issue such permits. I wondered if *Mr. Heap* might like to comment on the possibility of some of those problems raising their ugly head within the framework of the Antarctic Treaty System.

R. Wolfrum, Chairman:

Thank you, *Pat*. The next speaker will be *John*.

J. Heap:

I am grateful to *Pat Birnie* for raising those points, however, she is much more expert than I am on questions that have arisen in the International Whaling Commission. I would, however, like to return the ball to your court, *Pat*, and ask you whether you think that the International Whaling Commission is now a prisoner of its inability in its early days to to get this relationship right: between scientific advice on the one hand, and the Commission on the other, for it has always seemed to me that the problem with the International Whaling Commission has been just that it has been unable to separate the powers of the Scientific Committee properly from the powers of the Commission. In fact, the scientists have been put in the position of being tempted to make decisions, which are not within their power to make, and the Commission has been tempted to avoid taking decisions in the way that you have mentioned, and in other ways of making decisions, which they should make. Before actually passing that buck back to you, I would say that the problems of the taking of resources for scientific purposes in a manner and on a scale which gives rise to doubt as to whether the purpose is really scientific or maybe something else is indeed something which, I think, is going to arise within the Antarctic Treaty System quite soon.

R. Wolfrum, Chairman:

Thank you. I have *Alberto* as the next speaker.

A. Davérède:

Thank you very much, *Rudi*. I would like to thank *Dr. Heap*. I found his lecture most enlightening and challenging, so I have a few comments and a question. I took it from his speech that one of the main features of within the Antarctic Treaty System has been the independence of the one group from the other, through a pragmatic relationship in which the group from the other, through a pragmatic relationship in which the scientists have not participated in the decisions. He gave as an example the relationship between the Consultative Parties and SCAR which, of course, I fully agree has been a most productive one, and this relationship, as he very truthfully said, has taken place through national committees. Now as you know, in the Fourteenth Preparatory Meeting in Rio de Janeiro in April, a decision *ad referendum* of the next Consultative Meeting has been taken to allow the president of SCAR as well as the president of CCAMLR to participate as observers in the meetings of the Consultative Parties. This will mean that in some way the SCAR president will be involved in the political maneuvering, let us say, or in the decision-making process. Even if observers do not participate in that process, or in decision-taking in the Consultative Meeting, we know that decisions are usually or always taken by consensus. He will be present in the meetings, he will influence delegates and he might be influenced by delegates. And this might be a matter of concern, perhaps, in light of what *Dr. Heap* has mentioned as the main features of the traditional relationship between the scientific community and the political decision-makers, the diplomats. The same might happen with the participation in the Consultative Meetings of representatives of international organizations in general, because the decision was somehow enlarged in the last preparatory Consultative Meeting and always *ad referendum* of the final decision, which will be taken in the Consultative Meeting next October. International organizations will be able to participate as experts in those meetings, to present their views on certain points in the agenda — provided that they are invited and according to the rules that will be set up in each meeting. This will give another opportunity to the scientists to be present in this decision-making process. I would like to know *Dr. Heap*'s views on this and how this might change those traditional rules of procedure that have been so beneficial in the past. Thank you.

J. Heap:

I think that *Alberto Davérède* has touched upon a real point. I did indeed stress in what I said, the separation between SCAR and the Consultative process. However, I think there are two problems, or two questions, which we had in mind when making the decision at the Brussels Consultative Meeting to go down this path, towards a situation in which the president of SCAR would be present to give a report on the proceedings of SCAR to the Consultative Meeting.

The first, I think, is to say that the Consultative process perhaps does need to know, in the formal sense, what SCAR has been doing in the previous year. It does not need to discuss it, it just needs to know it. That, I think, is best achieved by providing the opportunity for a report to be given by SCAR to the Treaty-Consultative mechanism. Now, I agree that you could get a situation, where you have the representatives of international organizations involved in the Consultative mechanism and present at a Consultative Meeting, whereby the technical advice, the technical views, which they are there to represent, would indeed influence the political process. There would also be an influence which went the other way, between the political process and the technical process. I see this as an information exercise in which both sides are learning, as it were, from the other. I do not think that the question of influence is one which, either way, needs to undermine the principle of separation between the scientific side, as it were, and the decision-making side. Thank you.

R. Wolfrum, Chairman:

Thank you, *John*. Our next speaker on my list will be *Mr. Finn Sollie*.

F. Sollie:

Thank you. Well I, too, must say that I like *John*'s approach to his subject. I do not want to raise a question, rather, I would like to emphasize one or two points and to put in a little comment. First of all, it is quite clear that science in Antarctica plays a quite unique role, both as an instigator of international cooperation in Antarctica and for its role *vis-à-vis* the Consultative process. An I think fundamentally it is important to maintain the role of science in the conduct of Antarctic affairs, and it seems that the SCAR set-up works beautifully in this respect, provided of course, that it will not be corrupted. So, my comment is rather along the lines of *Delbrück*'s comment, of what you could call scientific honesty. The scientist, or in this example that *John* gave, the technician, who found that he could agree to a consensus statement on the risks of technical installations under certain natural conditions, was in a sense corrupting himself, and he was corrupted by the system and he was cororupted by management. This, I think, is a major danger, and we see it in all types of examples and connections.

I talked to *John* earlier today, and I mentioned one particular matter, for instance that of sealing. I agree thoroughly that in the Whaling Commission, science is sometimes corrupted and the mix between politics and science in the Commission is very difficult to sort out. Now in regard to sealing, we have had a very strong move where the scientific value of advice has been claimed by a number of protagonists of protection. The example I gave *John* was this: that last season in Norway something like 120,000 or more seals suffocated in the fishing nets along the coast, because of scientific advice, and other movements — the corruption of science into politics, into causes. We have had a ban on sealing, primarily, in the northern region, with the result that you submit the poor seals to massive growth and also then to massive suffering. I think one of the things that it is essential to do in Antarctica is to maintain the previously very strong and independent and uncorrupted role of scientific advice in that organization, through SCAR, and to prevent politicians from entering into these affairs. And there I come back to you, *Dr. Delbrück*: the honesty of the scientists and the absence of consensus, the mix of the consensus system on the political and legal side in Antarctica, with the strict requirement for honesty and uncorruptibility on the part of the science is, I think, the most unique feature of that system.

J. Heap:

Could I just thank you very much, sir, but also simply point out that science always advances because there is an odd man out.

R. Wilson:

Yes, I just have a couple of observations about *John Heap*'s presentations and some comments relating to CCAMLR, which I notice is not on the agenda as a specific item, and so perhaps this is the appropriate place to address CCAMLR. *John* observed that governments were often reluctant to act without advice from SCAR, and I would say that this is absolutely true. It is equally true, however, that governments are sometimes reluctant to act on the advice that SCAR gives them, and I think that a most recent example of this is the question of environmental impact assessment under the Antarctic Treaty. This is, in my view, a very pressing concern and one on which SCAR's advice was sought, and an issue on which SCAR performed, I think, very creditably in providing a very serious and well thought-out response to the request made by the Antarctic Treaty System. It may again be on the agenda in Rio de Janeiro in October, but there is no guarantee that there will be a consensus, even at that meeting, to permit such proposals to go through unscathed. There is a distinct possibility that it may be emasculated, and it may well emerge in a form quite different to that which SCAR intended. I think that this also highlights the slow speed of the decision-making process, something which other people might hopefully be able to address in the next few days.

Second, I would observe, from the contacts I have had with people in SCAR, that it may not be so much a relationship of equals, as many of them feel that they are quite at the mercy of the Antarctic Treaty System when it comes to actually getting decisions made.

Third, I would just like to address the question of CCAMLR. *John* highlighted the problems in CCAMLR, although I would myself have used somewhat stronger language. The fact is that in the case of CCAMLR, Article II is not being complied with, even though the Commission has adequate scientific advice to the effect that Article II is not being complied with. It is not a scientific problem but it is a political, diplomatic problem. It is clear that a small number of countries in CCAMLR, to take a charitable view, have a different interpretation of what Article II actually means. I think it is urgent that there be a clear understanding on the part of all CCAMLR member-states as to the meaning of Article II, and that there should be some kind of renewal of commitment to the provisions of that Article, so that some real progress can be made. Otherwise, I fear that CCAMLR's failure will severely damage the credibility of the entire Antarctic Treaty System. Thank you.

R. Wolfrum, Chairman:

The next speaker on my list is *Professor Sahrhage.*

D. Sahrhage:

Thank you. Mr. Chairman, I should like to offer a few comments from my experience as the past chairman of the CCAMLR Scientific Committee during the last five meetings. First of all, I should like to join those speakers, including of course, *John Heap*, who stress the usefulness of the independent role of the Scientific Committees. I think that the experience in CCAMLR with the Scientific Committee in this regard has been quite good. So far, we have not had the difficulties which have been outlined by *Ms. Birnie* for the International Whaling Commission. One can, however, observe that as soon as the discussions in the CCAMLR

Scientific Committee were concerned with questions of management advice and options to be proposed to the Commission, national representatives were acting slightly different than during discussions on other matters, in more general scientific fields. But as I said, in general the experience has been quite good. I would encourage that everything be done by members of CCAMLR to keep up the independent role of the Scientific Committee.

A special difficulty is certainly related to the fact that recommendations have to be agreed upon by consensus. Due to these difficulties not infrequently the argument is used in the Commission: "Let us first give these problems to the Scientific Committee," and the scientist must look first into all this, although the Commission could already act, at least to some extent. A second argument is often, "We have too little data, and the scientist must first know 100% what the conditions are." Such arguments seem to provide some kind of excuse for the Commission not to act as speedily as they possibly could.

John Heap has given a very good example about the fish *Notothenia rossii* and I would like to say that the Scientific Committee, in my view, made good progress with the assessment of the status of some of the Antarctic fish stocks. The situation is quite clearly described in the reports of the fish stock assessment working group. There are clear recommendations by the Scientific Committee as to what management measures could be taken. Various options have been offered to the Commission, and it is up to the Commission to act on this.

I fully share the views expressed by *Roger Wilson* about the credibility of CCAMLR and of the Antarctic Treaty System as a whole, which are in danger here if no further progress is made soon. I think there are two main steps which have to be taken in order to achieve further progress. The first is, really, a clear expression from the Commission to the public, and in particular of course to the Scientific Committee, advising them what kind of management strategy they want to adopt. This is decisive for the Scientific Committee, to promote their work so that they could indeed give proper advice and options for further management measures. The management strategy, of course, is very difficult to establish because, in accordance with the Convention, it must consider large parts of this ecosystem, basically from the krill resources, over the fish and squid, to seals and birds and whales. Considering that again there is the need to reach consensus between all members of the Commission, this is a very long way still to go. Following the last four years of development in CCAMLR, I think it is really high time, and it should have started earlier, for the Commission with the help of scientists to discuss in detail what the management goals are and what the management strategy should be.

The second point on how to achieve further progress is the political will, by fishing nations specifically, to implement the management measures particularly required for the fish stocks. These management measures have already been proposed by the Scientific Committee, and I think it was mainly the lack of political will in a few countries to implement them which prevented faster progress in CCAMLR. I think the reason was that some members were counting the few thousand tons of fish which you can catch in the Antarctic, but I feel that the value of these few thousand tons is absolutely nothing compared to the value of keeping up the credibility of CCAMLR and the Antarctic Treaty System if management measures would be introduced speedily.

As regards the krill, the present quantity of krill caught in commercial fisheries is absolutely small compared to the overall amount of krill in the sea. Nevertheless, experience has shown that after a slack period, when only 100,000, or slightly more, tons of krill were landed annually, suddenly there was again an increase to almost 500,000 tons. This shows that the landings of krill during coming years could increase rather quickly. Therefore, krill fishing should continue, but at the same time a management strategy should be formulated for a step-by-step development of krill fisheries.

R. Wolfrum, Chairman:

Thank you, *Mr. Sahrhage*. The next speaker on my list will be *Mr. Muñoz Seca.*

A. Muñoz Seca:

Danke schön, Rudi. Listening to the very interesting lecture by *John Heap* this morning and having a quick look at the provisions of the CCAMLR during coffee break a question has occurred to my mind for which I would like to have some clarification by *John Heap*. Article XIV, paragraph 1 of the CCAMLR Convention sets out that the Scientific Committee is a consultative body to the Commission. Article IX from the same Convention, paragraph 1, sets out the principles to be applied by the Convention, in accordance with Article II. Article IX, I would say, sets out the function of the Commission, particularly taking care of subparagraph (b) of point 1, to compile data on status and changes, *etc.*

Now, since we have a structure by which the Commission receives scientific advice from the Committee but is not necessarily bound by that advice, I wonder what sort of solution we have if the Scientific Committee comes up with some kind of recommendation, or possible solution for a particular problem, and that possible solution or recommendation is challenged by several members of the Commission. What is the Commission supposed to do then? Thank you very much.

R. Wolfrum, Chairman:

Thank you. I have now two more speakers on my list and I would like, with your permission, as we are a little bit behind schedule, to close off the list. *Mr. Giermann.*

G. Giermann:

Thank you, Mr. Chairman. Mr. Chairman, when *John Heap* talked about that relationship between the Antarctic Treaty Members and SCAR, another example came to my mind, which is perhaps not so close. It is the Inter-Governmental Oceanographic Commission of UNESCO and its relationship to the Scientific Committee on Oceanic Research (SCOR) which is its official advisory body. There is a two-way relationship. In one direction the IOC can ask SCOR for advice and then SCOR gives this advice. On the other hand, SCOR has a right to intervene without being asked. This is already very interesting. SCOR can, if it feels that it should give advice, give advice.

But this is not all I wanted to mention. What I wanted to point out is that the IOC, being the inter-governmental body, at the same time has the possibility to select scientists in the private capacity to form small expert groups and to receive advice, besides the advice that it gets from the officially established advisory body, SCOR. I do not know whether this is a formula that might be of interest to the Antarctic Treaty Members, but I just wanted to say that this type of structure evidently worked over the last 20—25 years in a very satisfactory way, and I think I should at least mention that there exists this other possibility: you are not forced to establish an official advisory body, but can also have advice from independent scientists (*e. g.*, on the formulation of a regional programme, through a workshop or so). There are other ways of getting scientific advice. Thank you.

R. Wolfrum, Chairman:

Thank you, *Mr. Giermann. Mr. Behrendt*, please.

J. Behrendt:

Dr. Birnie and *Roger Wilson* both referred to, I believe they meant negative, aspects of the delay in decision-making by the Commission. I think they were refering to CCAMLR. In the event of a minerals regime, this in some cases might not have a negative effect. For example, if there were conflicting views from the Scientific Committee, such as a majority and a minority report, a delay in decision-making would postpone the activity proposed. Now, I agree that once mineral activity is taking place, that a delay could have the negative effects suggested under CCAMLR.

However, in most cases, in particular the preliminary decades of the minerals regime, the more controversy there is within the Scientific Committee, the longer it will take to make a decision — and therefore this will merely result in the delay of the activity, which is not necessarily negative.

R. Wolfrum, Chairman:

Thank you, *John*. Now *John*, it is your turn for winding up.

J. Heap:

All I would like to do is to try to answer the question that *Muñoz Seca* put to me just now about what happens if, in fact, there is a difference of opinion within the Commission about the advice that it has received from the Scientific Committee. Apart from rather limply replying, "Well, that's life," I would suggest that if the Scientific Committee has done its job properly, it either presents us with one piece of advice, which is unanimous, which is well-supported — in which case it is up to those who are objective in the Commission to show that that Scientific Committee is somehow mistaken, or to show that they are objecting on some quite other ground which is not within the limits of the Scientific Committee to consider. The other possibility is that the major thrust of the advice that you are getting is going one way and you have another view, perhaps representing the views of those who are in fact in the end going to object in the Commission. Well, I think it is preferable to have those two sides clearly stated, rather than to have some sort of compromise in-between them. Then, I think that we know more clearly where we are, and we have a possibility of dealing with a situation which is fairly clear. I think that really is the point that I would want to make in reply to you. Thank you.

R. Wolfrum, Chairman:

Thank you, *John*. Thank you very much again for your presentation as well as for your standing in the discussion. I personally may add that I have learned a great deal in this discussion. Two related points, perhaps, deserve emphasizing: one should not blur scientific advice with political decision-making, which means one should not entrust to an institution, the function of which is to give scientific advice, the power to render political decisons. Equally, one should not try to blend the decision-making process tailored for political decisions, with scientific advice. Scientific advice does not and cannot replace a political decision.

The Institutional Development of the Antarctic Treaty System: The Question of a Secretariat

*R. Tucker Scully**

Thank you, *Rudi*. Let me echo the words of *John Heap*, in expressing appreciation to you, to the organizers, to *Professor Delbrück*, and all those who have welcomed us, once again, to Kiel. It's very good to be back.

I see, however, you have placed me, once again, in the unfortunate position of competing with the lunch. I'm not sure whether I should make a dietary sort of presentation to pre-empt lunch or whether to have a fairly brief presentation combined with lunch.

There is in the topic which you have suggested for me some continuity, in the sense that it is an issue which I have dealt with in the past. I will try to build upon that, as well as the experience of other considerations of the institutional aspects of the Antarctic Treaty System. I will also try to address these aspects from the particular perspective of its discussion at Antarctic Treaty Consultative Meetings (ATCMs), including the upcoming considerations at ATCM XIV in Rio de Janeiro.

The question of some form of permanent infrastructure, as it was termed in the Report of ATCM XIII, has emerged from the consideration of the operation of the Antarctic Treaty System.

At ATCM XIII in Brussels in 1985 there was detailed discussion of the question of a permanent infrastructure and related matters, including the possible sharing of costs for Consultative Meetings and the desirability of more frequent ATCMs. In the report of ATCM XIII it was noted that a number of delegations believed there to be a growing need for some kind of permanent infrastructure for the Antarctic Treaty Consultative mechanism, with a number of delegations indicating that such infrastructure might take the form of a secretariat, a small secretariat. There was, in Brussels, a preliminary discussion of some of the functions that such a secretariat might perform, and mention was made of the question of document preparation and follow-up for the Consultative Meetings, as

---

* *R. Tucker Scully*, Director of the Office of Oceans and Polar Affairs, Bureau of Oceans and International Environmental and Scientific Affairs, United States Department of State, Washington, D. C., U.S.A.; the opinions expressed in this volume are the personal views of their authors only.

well as the dissemination of up-to-date information and reports relating to the Antarctic Treaty and the Antarctic Treaty System. The report of ATCM XIII continued by noting, by indicating, that some felt that, over time, a secretariat might have more extensive functions. It was also emphasized that the establishment of such infrastructure should be proportional to real needs and initially would be very modest in scope and cost. Others expressed reservations about the idea of such an infrastructure.

I would like to examine some of the issues that are posed by the possible establishment of permanent infrastructures. It is my view, however, that the question of a secretariat, or of a permanent infrastructure is, itself, an aspect of a somewhat broader issue. That issue can best be described as how, generally, the Consultative mechanism should function: how it can most effectively and efficiently operate to achieve the purposes and principles of the Treaty. This relationship was recognized in Brussels in that the question of infrastructure was closely linked to other organizational aspects. I will start with a review of how organizational issues have been dealt within the Treaty mechanism as it has evolved during the first quarter-century of its operation.

The provisions of the Antarctic Treaty do not address in detail institutions foreseen for the Consultative mechanism. Article IX provides that its Parties should meet within the first two months after the entry into force of the Treaty, and "thereafter at suitable intervals and places, for the purpose of exchanging information, consulting together on matters of common interest pertaining to Antarctica, and formulating and considering, and recommending to their Governments, measures ...." Thus Article IX of the Treaty called for the Consultative Meetings; scheduled the first one and left for the elaboration by the Parties of the specific ways in which those meetings might function.

There are two other kinds of provisions in the Treaty itself which relate to institutional aspects. The first is Article III. 2, which refers to the establishment of cooperative working relationships with the specialized agencies of the United Nations, and other international organizations having a scientific or technical interest in Antarctica — a point to which I will return.

In addition, there are the provisions relating to the exchange of information in Articles III and VII. They call for direct exchange of information regarding plans for scientific programs in Antarctica as well as scientific observations and results from Antarctica. They oblige the Consultative Parties to communicate to each other specific information relating to the conduct of inspections under the Treaty, and to give notification, in advance, of their expeditions to Antarctica, of stations they occupy in Antarctica, and any military personnel or equipment they intend to introduce into Antarctica in support of scientific research or other peaceful purposes. These provisions relating to the exchange of information bear upon infrastructure, upon the institutional aspects of the Treaty. The only other point in the Treaty that might relate to this subject is the fact that there is provision for a depository. The depository function, as it has evolved in the Consultative mechanism, also has a bearing upon the question of infrastructure.

At the first Consultative Meeting (ATCM I) in Canberra, a number of steps were taken which have had an influence on how the secretariat function has been performed within the Consultative mechanism. There was an informal agreement that the hostship of Consultative Meetings would rotate among the Consultative Parties in their alphabetical order in English. Therefore, Recommendation I-14 foresees that the secretariat function would rotate with hostship, and this principle has been pursued since the beginning of the Consultative process. Recommendation I-14 was characterized as "interim" in nature — though one of those interim measures which has lasted for quite some considerable time. In addition to rotation in hostship, it provided that the host government of the First Consultative Meeting undertake the responsibility for circulating to all participating governments the official copy of the Final Report of the Meeting, and of all documents agreed and adopted at the Meeting. Since ATCM I, the host government has had this responsibility of distributing the documents of the Meeting. The host government was also called upon to provide any additional information on the ATCM that might be requested by participating governments. Thus the documentation function has been associated with hostship.

Looking to the arrangement of future Consultative Meetings, it was provided, also in Recommendation I-14, that the host government for the next Consultative Meeting would consult with the Parties to develop a provisional agenda for that Meeting. Further on, Recommendation I-16 called for each Consultative Party to forward, through the diplomatic channels, to the host of the next Meeting proposals and materials that it wished to place before the ATCM, at least one month prior to that meeting, except in cases of urgency. At ATCM I, then, questions of how rotating hostship included aspects relating to the secretariat function were spelled out on what was termed an interim basis. These "interim provisions" have remained the underpinning of the responsibility of the host for each ATCM to take the steps necessary to prepare for that Meeting. This has led, over time, to the process of holding regular preparatory meetings for an ATCM in order to carry this organizational function in a more structured fashion.

The rules of procedure, adopted at ATCM I, touched formally on the secretariat function. The rules provide for the appointment of the secretary of the Meeting on the proposal of the chairman. The secretary is responsible for the provision of secretarial services and for carrying out such other functions as the Meeting directs.

The elaboration of this system in the first two decades of the operation of the Consultative mechanism has primarily centered on questions of Meeting documentation. There was very little discussion of how the overall secretariat function was being performed. At ATCM VII in Wellington, it was agreed that at the conclusion of an ATCM the host government would send a complete set of all documents circulated, as well as the final report, to the host government of the next ATCM. This was an attempt to spell out, in a little bit more detail, the transitional aspect of the rotational system; the new host of each ATCM would have all the material which had derived from the previous Meeting.

In general, discussion of items relating to infrastructure in the period between ATCM I and ATCM XI was primarily of a routine "housekeeping" nature. At ATCM XI, however, the Consultative Parties began to discuss the operation of the Antarctic Treaty System in more detail. The first major product of those discussions emerged at ATCM XII, in Canberra in 1983. Recommendation XII-6 addressed the documentation of Consultative Meetings. It called for the host governments to send copies of the final reports and documents of ATCMs to all Contracting Parties. This element reflects evolution within the Consultative mechanism, specifically, the invitation to Non-consultative Parties (NCPs), to attend ATCMs. Recommendation XII-6 essentially extends the provisions relating to the circulation of documents to the Non-consultative Parties.

Recommendation XII-6 also addresses the relationship between the Antarctic Treaty and other international organizations. It specifies that the final report of ATCMs should be provided to the UN Secretary-General. Further, pursuant to Article III of the Antarctic Treaty, it provides that if, and when, Consultative Parties believe that particular aspects of an ATCM report are of interest to specialized agencies of the UN, or other international organizations having a scientific or technical interest in Antarctica, the host government of the ATCM should draw the attention of that particular aspect of the report to the specialized agency or other organization concerned.

Recommendation XII-6 also dealt with the question of the Antarctic Treaty Handbook. It calls for the host of each ATCM to bring the Handbook up to date as rapidly as possible following the conclusion of the Consultative Meeting, to provide an up-to-date record of the Consultative mechanism.

Recommendation XII-6 also dealt with the availability of documents of the previous Consultative Meetings, and establishes a process of regular review of such documents to determine their public availability. Finally, the Recommendation invited the depository government to investigate the question of the availability of information about the Antarctic Treaty System, with a view to determining its availability and with a view to identifying and cataloguing, as well as identifying sources of, such information. At ATCM XII in Canberra, in 1983, there was, for the first time since the early days of the operation of the system, a specific elaboration of what I would term the secretariat function. This effort concentrated upon information about the Treaty System — how such information would be made publicly available: how such information, when of relevance to other organizations, would be disseminated.

As I mentioned above, at ATCM XIII in Brussels there was also a major emphasis placed upon the organizational aspects of the Consultative mechanism. The agenda item on operation of the Antarctic Treaty System was the center of attention. As a follow-up to Recommendation XII-6, and specifically to the investigation carried out by the United States, as depository government, Recommendation XIII-1 was adopted. It urges further efforts to ensure that the final reports of ATCMs contain as complete and a full description as possible of those Meetings, including the results and debates that took place in relation to the items on the agenda. It reiterates the call for the Antarctic Treaty Handbook to be maintained as a regular compilation of the Recommendations and other actions of the Consultative Parties, or of the Consultative Meetings.

Recommendation XIII-1 provides for making publicly available, to the greatest extent practicable and feasible, information about the Antarctic Treaty System, including the final reports of ATCMs, the Antarctic Treaty Handbook, and the annual exchanges of information under the Antarctic Treaty. Similarly, SCAR was called upon through its national committees to ensure the public availability of reports relating to its activities. Finally, Recommendation XIII-1 calls for the establishment of a national contact point as a source of such publicly-available information, as well as a point of reference about other sources of information on the Antarctic Treaty System, including the nature and location of depositories of data and information about, and bibliographies on, the Antarctic Treaty System. In combination, the Recommendations of ATCM XII and ATCM XIII represent a significant organizational effort to ensure the availability of information to participants within the Antarctic Treaty System, to those who have an express interest in Antarctica, and to those who wish to learn further about Antarctica and how the System operates.

Recommendation XIII-2, also adopted in Brussels, raises another aspect of the subject of infrastructures. It provides for reports about the components of the Antarctic Treaty System at each ATCM. To this end, invitations are extended to the chairman of CCAMLR, the president of SCAR, the chairman of any Special Consultative Meeting taking place pursuant to a Recommendation of a Consultative Meeting, and to the depository government of the Convention for the Conservation of Antarctic Seals, in order to provide reports on the activities of those components at each regular ATCM.

This Recommendation, in one sense, reflects the effort described above to increase the value of the reports of the Consultative Meetings and to ensure greater availability of information. At the same time, it relates to another aspect of the organizational issue that has come up at the Consultative Meetings — that is, the coordination of the components of the System, the opportunity for an overview so that the activities of the components of the Treaty System can be seen in relation to each other and can provide the information base relevant to coordination among these components.

Recommendation XIII-15 also bears upon the organizational aspect of the Consultative mechanism in calling for Non-consultative parties to be invited to all future ATCMs.

To summarize, the Consultative mechanism, to the extent that it has dealt with the secretariat function, has provided that it rotate with hostship. This rotation of the secretariat with hostship extends not only to the particular ATCM, but to the period leading up to the meeting, to the biennium preceding the Meeting itself. For the rest, the primary secretariat functions have been decentralized to the individual governments, to the individual Treaty Parties. One exception which should be noted is that on several occasions the depository government has been called on to undertake functions which could be considered of a secretariat's nature. For example, Recommendation XII-6 called on the depository government to undertake a study of the public availability of documents and information about the Antarctic Treaty System.

I would also note, with respect to the rotation of hostship, that there have been two instances in which the chairmanship has not shifted with hostship due to the abilities of the individual and the importance of the chairmanship role for the issues involved. These are in the Special Consultative Meetings on the Antarctic mineral resources, of which *Chris Beeby*, of New Zealand, has remained the Chairman, in spite of the fact that the hostship of meetings has varied, and the coordination among the UN delegation of Antarctic Treaty Parties in New York, by the Australian permanent UN Representative, *Dick Woolcott*, whom we are honored to have with us here in Kiel.

If one looks at the other components of the Antarctic Treaty System, there are a wide variety of practices with respect to secretariat functions.

The Convention on the Conservation of Antarctic Marine Living Resources (CCAMLR) establishes a secretariat. Article XVII of CCAMLR provides that the Commission shall appoint an Executive Secretary, describes general conditions of appointment, and foresees additional staffing. There is now a functioning CCAMLR secretariat at CCAMLR Headquarters in Hobart, Tasmania.

There is a somewhat different treatment of the secretariat function at this stage of the ongoing negotiations on Antarctic mineral resources. The draft convention, as it stands, would provide that the Commission may, rather than shall, establish a secretariat. The general view in the mineral resource negotiations is that a secretariat will be needed. The timing of its establishment, however, is an issue that could be decided following the entry into force of the Convention, rather than being decided in the Convention itself, as was the case with CCAMLR.

A third model exists in the Convention on the Conservation of Antarctic Seals. This Convention delegates certain functions of a scientific and of a secretariat nature to SCAR. This delegation is made on an interim basis, pending a decision to establish a more formal mechanism, more formal machinery, including a commission, to carry out the Convention's regulatory requirements. Such a decision would be posed in the event that commercial sealing was initiated. The Seals Convention thus offers the example of secretariat functions being performed on an interim basis.

Finally, SCAR itself suggests another variant with respect to secretariat functions. There is an Executive Secretary of SCAR charged with carrying certain functions for the body. The Executive Secretary of SCAR, on an informal basis, is supported by an academic research institution, the Scott Polar Institute in Cambridge. In addressing the question of whether the Parties to the Antarctic Treaty should consider steps to further develop the secretariat function, or, in a broader sense, to look at the organizational functions of the Consultative mechanism, there are a number of possible models. These derive not only from the evolution of the Consultative mechanism itself, they also exist within the components of the Antarctic Treaty System.

With this background in mind, I would like to turn to the question of why these functions, the organizational functions, including secretariat functions, have come to the fore in the past few years at the most recent ATCMs.

There is one fairly obvious reason — the growth in the Consultative mechanism itself. There were twelve original Contracting Parties upon the entry into force of the Treaty in 1961. There are now thirty-five Parties to the Treaty: eighteen Consultative Parties, seventeen Non-consultative parties. Beginning in 1983, at the Canberra Meeting, the Non-consultative parties attend the Consultative Meetings. Consequently, the ATCMs themselves have grown in size, with the attendant increase in the requirements for their coordination and preparation.

Secondly, the Consultative mechanism has evolved into a complex system: the Antarctic Treaty System, which involves a variety of techniques for dealing with issues, such as meetings of experts and special consultative meetings, and includes as well two separate conventions — the Seals Convention and CCAMLR — and looks toward a third Convention to deal with possible mineral resource activities in Antarctica. In the recent emphasis upon the operation of the Antarctic Treaty System, there has been recognition that there is, and will be, a need to coordinate the diverse and evolving components of the System. As noted elsewhere, there is a view that the Consultative mechanism, as the central feature of the System, is the appropriate forum to provide such coordination. The idea of an overview of the System, which is inherent in Recommendation XIII-2, is illustrative of this view.

Third, there are expanding relationships between the Antarctic Treaty System and other international bodies, other international organizations. Such relationships are provided for in Article III of the Treaty and there have been, since the early days of the Treaty System, contacts with WMO and ITU in the fields of meteorology and telecommunications. More recently, CCAMLR has established working relationships with a number of organizations, both intergovernmental and nongovernmental. Most recently, the Consultative mechanism itself has taken the initial steps towards establishing such relationships with other international organizations. At the preparatory meeting for ATCM XIV, the rules of procedure for ATCMs were amended to provide for the attendance of observers from SCAR and CCAMLR, and of experts from other international organizations, and a decision has been taken to invite such observers and experts from five organizations to attend the ATCM XIV, in relation to particular items of its agenda. These include observers from components of the System, SCAR and CCAMLR, and experts from the World Meteorological Organization (a UN specialized agency), the International Union for the Conservation of Nature and Natural Resources (IUCN) and SCAR. The Consultative mechanism, like other components of the System, now involves a growing and more complex set of relationships with other international bodies.

Fourth, I believe that the question of secretariat functions has come up simply because of the nature and complexity of the issues that arise at the ATCMs. We are on the verge of a growth of activities in Antarctica that will require response in the Consultative mechanism, including new forms of regulation and new ways of dealing with activities to ensure that they are compatible. One example is illustrated by Recommendation XIII-5, which raises the question of managed areas in Antarctica, recognition of multiple use issues and the related matter of an integrated Antarctic data base. The Treaty Parties will have to pursue such approaches to ensure that the growth and activities, both in degree and in kind, will not result in the erosion of, or in consequences which are inconsistent with, the principles and purposes of the Treaty.

These four trends, in my view, have been responsible for the emergence of the institutional aspects of the Treaty System, the question of a permanent infrastructure or a secretariat as important topics within the Consultative mechanism.

One can look at these issues of organization from the point-of-view of the ATCMs themselves and of activity occurring between the ATCMs. The planning and conduct of ATCMs is becoming a more demanding task. The size of meetings, the increase in simple numbers of those who attend Meetings, places and ever-increasing burden upon the host government. Related to this point is a political problem in that there are governments which, because of their lack of diplomatic relations with others, are not in a position to host ATCMs. This results in hostship responsibilities falling upon a reduced number of ATCPs. The costs and the difficulty of hostship have increased, while the number of those who, in fact, are in a position to host has to some extent decreased.

There is also recognition that there needs to be increased coordination and continuity between ATCMs, in terms of the ability of the Treaty Parties to ensure that activities in Antarctica, and the questions relating to Antarctica, are handled in a way that will allow the continued implementation of the objectives of the Treaty, and of the Recommendations and actions taken pursuant to it.

There are two aspects to this latter point. First, emphasis has been placed — and rightly so — upon the continuing and growing need to provide accurate information about the Antarctic Treaty and Antarctic Treaty System. This need is continuous, and there is a view that the biennial ATCMs are not a sufficient basis for dealing with this requirement. Second, the growth and nature of activities in Antarctica referred to above may require more continuous attention. For example, such growth will highlight the need to be able to identify problems requiring collective action, and to respond to them on a more "real-time" basis.

These trends have resulted in a convergence of views — by no means unanimous, however — that the time has arrived within the Consultative mechanism to deal with the question of permanent infrastructure. In approaching the issue, it is first important to define the kinds of functions of an institutional character required by the Consultative mechanism and then to look at them in light of whether some more defined mechanism, secretariat or otherwise, would be desirable. Again, I note the distinction between those functions that are related to the ATCMs themselves, and those functions of a more continuous character.

The first function relates to the planning and organization of ATCMs, including the preparation of the agenda, annotation of draft agenda items, and preparation of documentation for the ATCM, as well as the actual conduct of the Meeting.

A second function relates to Meeting follow-ups, including the publication and circulation of the Final Report and other Meeting documentation.

A third function is the compilation and up-dating of the Antarctic Treaty Handbook. It is an extremely valuable document, one which is deserving of widespread dissemination. *John Heap* has done a magnificent job with the Handbook but the demands grow each year. It has been suggested that a small secretariat, or some sort of permanent infrastructure could provide important assistance to host governments of ATCMs in carrying out these functions, which involve Meeting support.

Another matter related to Meeting support that has arisen in consideration of possible infrastructure is the question of cost-sharing. This item has come up in the discussions of the operation of the Antarctic Treaty System in a manner separate from the infrastructure. However, a number of Treaty Parties have indicated that a secretariat, or some equivalent mechanism, would be necessary in order to provide the vehicle for any cost-sharing system. Some mechanism would be needed to prepare budgets to determine how such costs should be shared, and to receive contributions.

Turning to other functions required by the Consultative mechanism, there are those that relate to information both within the Treaty System and about the System. On the first aspect, there is an archival function, the maintenance of documents relating to the Antarctic Treaty and Antarctic Treaty System. To some extent the Depository Government carries out this function. However, I would note again that a number of Treaty Parties do not have diplomatic relations with each other and even communications with the Depository are sometimes difficult. It has been suggested that some sort of infrastructure could provide a mechanism for an information flow among the participants in the System, which would be of benefit particularly as the System continues to grow.

With respect to information about the Treaty System, a number of steps have already been taken in the Recommendations of ATCM XII and ATCM XIII to ensure the availability to all those who are interested in reliable, readily available information on how the Treaty System operates, what is going on within the Treaty System, and on sources of information about scientific research and other activities in Antarctica. Some form of infrastructure could complement these efforts, particularly where centralization of information would be cost-effective.

There may be a function for a permanent infrastructure or secretariat in representing the Antarctic Treaty System itself. There is a growing set of relationships between the Antarctic Treaty and other international organizations. The Treaty Parties have made provision within the Treaty System for other organizations having a scientific and technical interest in Antarctica to be represented by observers, or experts, at meetings of the components of the System. It may well be that the components of the System and the Treaty mechanism itself will, in the future, need to be represented at proceedings of other international bodies to complete the kind of cooperative working relationships foreseen in Article III. 2 of the Treaty. In addition, it seems to me increasingly important that the Treaty Parties monitor and identify activities of other international bodies, matters which are of relevance to the Treaty System. Research on the ozone layer may be a good example, as it involves a growing number of international and national efforts. It is important that the Treaty Parties are aware of what is occurring in areas such as these in order to coordinate their own activities, as well as to ensuring that their activities are complementary to those that are taking place within other international bodies. A permanent infrastructure could assist in this function.

Finally, and this looks more to the future: there may be certain operational questions which could be performed by an infrastructure or secretariat. I would cite as an example the possible establishment and maintenance of an integrated data base for the Antarctic Consultative mechanism, given the kinds of activities that many emerge, and may need regulating in the future. Here, I would distinguish the maintenance of data, and access to data, from the functions that SCAR provides in terms of scientific advice. In conclusion, I would touch upon the question of how to proceed in this question of dealing with an infrastructure or secretariat particularly in light of upcoming considerations at ATCM XIV.

First of all, it would be useful for the Treaty Parties to identify, on an agreed basis, the kinds of functions that need to be performed on a continuing basis to support the activities of the operation of the Consultative mechanisms. Second, it is important for the Parties to assess how such functions are being performed with a view to determining which functions are being performed on a satisfactory basis and which require attention. Third, the Parties should decide upon how best to achieve needed improvements, including any new mechanisms and the procedure for establishing them. In that regard there may be a variety of options, from informal agreement through a Special Consultative Meeting, if it were determined that negotiation of some formal structure is required. Fourth, in this process, I think that it is necessary for the Parties to distinguish and concentrate upon those functions that are most pressing, those that most need to be carried out in the near future, and take steps to assure that they are undertaken in the time frame that will correspond to the needs. On this point, I think there may be merit in looking at interim mechanisms for the performance of such functions pending determination of whether more formal structures may be required.

It is my personal opinion, that in the long run or perhaps even the not-so-long run the Antarctic Treaty Consultative mechanism will need some form of permanent infrastructure, some form of continuing mechanism that will operate to provide the support and service required by the mechanism itself. I think that at ATCM XIV in Brasil, in Rio, the Treaty Parties should launch the process of developing that mechanism. I do not believe that this will necessarily be accomplished in an extremely rapid fashion. However, by approaching the functions that need to be performed, the Parties should be able to agree on those that are most important in the immediate future and take some form of interim steps to ensure that they are fulfilled, until such time as the efforts towards a more permanent or a more formal mechanism come to fruition. My apologies for delaying lunch; I hope this will at least trigger a bit of discussion afterwards. Thank you.

Comment

*Alberto L. Davérède**

The merits of the Antarctic Treaty and the dynamic system it has generated are widely well-known. The Treaty, its related Conventions, the Recommendations adopted during the past 26 years and the practice of those states actively engaged in Antarctica, make up a set of rules and usages which constitute an entire legal regime. The aim of this paper is not to analyze the different components of this scheme, but to stress the mechanics of its operation and the characteristics of its evolution, which have allowed it to become a highly flexible, practical and successful system.

Since the Treaty came into force, the Contracting Parties have developed an efficient decision-making machinery. They have conceived imaginative solutions in anticipation of new situations which might arise and to meet expanding requirements, and they have been able to find a way to merge divergent opinions and to arrive at satisfactory decisions by consensus. In brief, the Contracting Parties have developed a consensual mentality.

This has been possible, first, due to the fluent and direct communication between the Parties, generated at the very beginning of the System by Recommendations I-XIV and I-XVI, which established the mechanism for consultation via diplomatic channels, and second, due to the lack of a central bureaucracy. Throughout the existence of the Treaty and, in particular, during the last Consultative Meetings, the Contracting Parties have agreed on a series of measures tending towards a more efficient operation of the System. They have up-dated the regime both internally, so as to coordinate and harmonize its different components, and externally, in order to promote broader international cooperation and dissemination of its studies and reports on scientific research, as well as of its deliberations and decisions.

This shows both the determination and the capacity of the Consultative Parties to adapt the Treaty System to changing circumstances, and also the possibility of achieving such changes without distorting the essence of the Treaty and the decentralized and informal mechanism which has

* Dr. *Alberto Davérède*, Minister Plenipotentiary, Director-General of Antarctica, Ministry of Foreign Affairs and Worship, Argentina. The opinions expressed in this volume are the personal views of their authors only.

been the key to its success. Regarding the internal operation, an effective link has been built between one Consultative Meeting and another, by assigning tasks to the host countries and the Depositary Government, related to consultations on the provisional agenda, compilation of the documents circulated in the Meetings, printing and distribution of the Final Reports and Recommendations, availability of documentation and information on the status of approval of Recommendations by the Parties. The biennial reports on the activities undertaken within the framework of the Antarctic Treaty System and on other relevant aspects will provide an overall view of the different components of the regime and will foster coordination among them.

As regards dissemination of information, the Consultative Parties have agreed to distribute the Final Report and documents of the Consultative Meetings to the Non-consultative Parties and to send a copy of the Final Report to the Secretary-General of the United Nations, as well as relevant parts of said Report or any information document to those specialized agencies or other international organizations with scientific or technical interest in the field. The contents of the Final Reports have been broadened so as to reflect the general trends of the discussions, as well as the correspondence between the Recommendations or decisions adopted and the steps consequently taken in later Meetings.

An improved and expanded Handbook of the Antarctic Treaty is being prepared and efforts are being made to publish the Handbook in the four official languages of the Treaty. The proposal to draw up a White Book on the results achieved by the Antarctic Treaty is also under study. Subsequent to Recommendation XIII-1, Final Reports and documents of the Consultative Meetings, the Handbook, the national Reports on Antarctic activities, SCAR reports and the location of Antarctic bibliographies and scientific data centers will be made available to every interested person by national contact points.

Even though since the very beginning of the System practical working relations have been developed with United Nations Specialized Agencies (WMO, ITU, FAO, UNEP, and IOC) as well as with organizations outside the United Nations family, such as SCAR, SCOR, SCOPE, ICSU, IUCN and IWC, in recent decisions the Consultative Parties have agreed to formalize these existing links with some of the above-mentioned organizations, inviting them to participate as observers or experts in the discussion of specific items on the Consultative Meetings agendas. The large range of measures described above clearly proves how the System has evolved to ensure a more efficient internal operation and external accommodation, without changing the nature and the spirit of the Antarctic Treaty, in a decentralized but, at the same time, cohesive manner.

Undoubtedly, there is still scope for further evolution, but any future changes should always preserve the essential qualities of the System and should consolidate the unity of the Contracting Parties, at a time when this unity is facing external attacks and pressures meant to erode it.

These convictions are the basis for objecting to the establishment of a permanent infrastructure or, more plainly speaking, of a Secretariat of the Treaty. The functional or administrative reasons put forward to support this infrastructure are not of such a substantial importance *vis-à-vis* the political risks we may be running if that Secretariat is created. For example, the need to maintain central archives of documentation on the Antarctic Treaty System has been supported. The convenience of concentrating the preparation and distribution of the Final Reports of the Consultative Meetings and of centralizing the dissemination of public information on the System has also been stated.

As mentioned above, many of these functions are already performed in an efficient and decentralized manner. The question of the archives, in turn, no longer poses a problem, due to the progress made in the field of data processing. Archives might well be placed under the responsibility of an interested country, university or governmental institute prepared to assume this role, which, if necessary, might also charge for the services required.

The political risks inherent to the establishment of a Permanent Secretariat are, instead, much more relevant. The Antarctic Treaty is founded on a conjunction of national activities and their harmonious relationship, and not on rigid institutions which could upset the delicate balance on which it rests. Present arrangements enable practical cooperation in an atmosphere free of political rhetoric or contention, which often affects many international organizations. This has been possible because of the direct communication between the Parties. The introduction of a new element, namely a Secretariat, would probably jeopardize this dialogue.

The Contracting Parties would be impelled to accept the intervention of an intermediary in their mutual relationships. This situation might in some cases prove useful, but in others might upset this direct communication which has shown to yield such positive results. The special legal and political condition of Antarctica and the territorial element in the Antarctic Treaty, which directly affects the sovereign interests of some states, instil a high sensitivity into most of the topics dealt with regarding the continent. A direct control by the States Parties over the activities undertaken in Antarctica is thus required. In this context, the intervention of a central bureaucracy might lead to misinterpretations which may divide the Parties instead of bringing them closer.

An administrative institution will sooner or later try to be present in all the programs of international cooperation. It will put forward its own initiatives, give its opinions and own interpretations. It has been argued that the Secretariat must be the servant and not the master of the Consultative Parties, and that it is up to them to see that it continues to be such. But those who are familar with international organizations will surely agree that Secretariats generate their own dynamics. They become a separate entity which, at best, operates independently or sometimes, under the control of some Parties. This circumstance becomes of a paramount importance in view of the different groups of Contracting Parties whose interests are carefully balanced in Article IV of the Antarctic Treaty.

In this regard, the intrinsic difficulty of choosing the appropriate person for the role should also be borne in mind. From the viewpoint of the operation of the System, it has already been stated that the lack of bureaucracy has been one of the keys to the effectiveness of the Antarctic Treaty. Besides, many of those who support the establishment of a permanent Secretariat for the Treaty are, at present, leading a campaign against bureaucracy at the United Nations, or are trying to put a stop to the artificial growth of some UN Specialized Agencies. There seems to be an ideological contradiction in this attitude.

They should be asked whether they have weighed the risks we would be running by creating a Secretariat which — small as it may be at the beginning — would surely grow with time, with the corresponding loss of efficiency such growth implies and which a brief look at the history of some international organizations allows us to foresee. Nobody rejects the idea of changes, but what should be carefully analyzed is the actual need of changing a machinery which has proved so efficient and which has so successfully served the purposes of the Treaty.

Establishing a Secretariat would be a first step towards the internationalization of the System. In this sense, the UN *ad hoc* Committee which has been proposed in the General Assembly by the detractors of the Treaty, is not so far from this idea. We should recall that in this regard, all the Contracting Parties have strongly rejected this proposal as an attempt to undermine or replace the existing System. Furthermore, the creation of a Secretariat will not — *per se* — avert external criticism, as has sometimes been maintained by some supporters of this proposal.

Critics of the Antarctic Treaty do not focus on the existence or lack of an infrastructure, but on more fundamental questions such as — just to mention some — the decision-making process, the special role of the Consultative Parties and the beneficiaries of any possible profit deriving from eventual commercial activities. The Secretariat will not only not be able to give responses to these concerns, but it will also necessarily be considered the representative of the Contracting Parties, to which all these matters should be submitted. This circumstance would place the Secretariat in a difficult situation, having to resist pressures that one way or the other, would certainly influence its work.

The delicate position which the Antarctic Treaty is now facing in the international arena compels the Contracting Parties to continue acting in a coordinated and harmonized way, without any intermediary in their relationship with the rest of the world.

In conclusion, the Antarctic Treaty is an evolving and continued experiment which has successfully achieved its purposes. Efforts should be made to enhance the System it originated and the machinery it installed, avoiding the introduction of elements which may weaken or even destroy the bases upon which the Antarctic Treaty was conceived.

General Discussion

R. Wolfrum, Chairman:

May I now open the discussion? *Ian*, you were first.

I. Nicholson:

Thank you, *Rudi*. I would like to congratulate, if I may, *Tucker Scully*, both on his presentation and his tie. I thought that both were outstanding, even compared with some earlier magnificent presentations. I would like also to thank *John Heap* for his very useful paper, and for the way that you summarized it, which brought out the two principal points, both reassuring in regard to the course we are currently on in regard to that area of the minerals convention. The assistance that we received from *John*'s paper, in regard to our work on the minerals convention, will be similar to the assistance we will recieve from *Tucker*'s paper in preparation for ATCM XIV.

There are, to my mind, strong trends which indicate the need for some form of permanent secretariat. It was useful to recall the original framework set by the first Treaty meeting and to see that in the context that *Tucker* presented. It was useful also, to focus on the watershed that ATCM XII represented, in the sense that it brought together, most intensively for the first time, a number of the trends which have continued and developed further since then. I think, in addition to the elements that *Tucker* noted at ATCM XII — the updating of the Treaty Handbook, the call on the depositary to undertake research about the availability and accessibility of information, the wider distribution of the report to the Secretary-General, and possibly to other UN organizations as appropriate — it might also be mentioned that the ATCM XII report, itself, was the first of a new breed of reports. It sought to record more of the discussion, more of the information that was exchanged at that meeting, not only in the form of informal minutes for the use of the Treaty Parties, but also for dissemination more widely to other governments, and to the general public. That trend was taken further in Belgium.

The great value of *Tucker*'s presentation, I think, is to enable us to see these developments and the factors which have led to them, on the one hand, and on the other hand, to provide us with an overview, a system-

The opinions expressed in this volume are the personal views of their authors only.

wide overview, of the impact of these trends. Thus, he made clear the need for a greater effort to achieve an overview of the system, through Antarctic Treaty Consultative Meetings, and to extend and strengthen attempts at coordination and consistency.

I should like to add a note on the political side also, which *Tucker* did not mention, and that is that, at ATCM XII, we were driven by the needs of the Treaty, by the needs of the Treaty Parties themselves, by the trends which he drew our attention to, in particular the first participation of Non-consultative Parties in the meetings. This participation had many aspects. It resulted in an enrichment of the meetings, a broadening of exchanges, and also an increase in numbers adding to administrative burdens mainly, in terms of staging a meeting and distributing papers. These changes were also, in part, driven by increased international interest from outside the Treaty Parties. This was most directly due to the efforts of the Government of Malaysia to draw attention to Antarctica, and to develop a wider international interest in it. The fact that what was commenced at ATCM XII continued in XIII, and is being further developed in ATCM XIV, was largely a result of that Malaysian interest and is a positive development in two senses. First, in the sense of wider international interest, and secondly, in the positive response which has been made to it by the Treaty mechanism and by the Treaty Parties. All this was very well brought together by *Tucker*.

I shall not go through the other elements summarized, but would underline again that the Antarctic Treaty family, the Antarctic Treaty System, is becoming more active, broader, more complex, and therefore requires greater attention in the sense of an overall direction. I do not think we realized at the time quite to clearly how logical all this development was, how well, in fact, we were responding to it, how far-sighted the proposal for a small secretariat is, and the degree to which it will be a major step forward at ATCM XIV. I might repeat a point I have made at other places, at other times, in terms of reassurance to one or two parties which do not share the full enthusiasm of that view, and that is that the secretariat would be small — a secretary, plus an assistant, plus a word processor, plus a filing cabinet, plus a small travel budget — and that it would, at all times, function within the mandate provided by Antarctic Treaty Consultative Meetings, and be at all times responsible to the members of the Treaty, especially the host country for ATCMs.

Thank you again, *Tucker*, for an excellent overview. I wonder whether we had all seen the situation quite as logically as you presented it; your ideas certainly hold together extremely well.

R. Wolfrum, Chairman:

Thank you, *Ian*. The next speaker on my list is *Alberto*.

A. Davérède:

Thank you very much, *Rudi*. I also would like to congratulate *Tucker Scully* for a very comprehensive presentation, that very adequately described the background of this matter. Now, I have myself prepared a short paper on this subject; I think that it will help us in this very late hour, if I just hand it over to you for whatever purpose you find appropriate. That would not excuse me from making a few comments on the presentation which was made by *Tucker*. My paper is somewhat more controversial than his presentation. It is not limited to the presentation of the background, but tries to go deeper, into some political, legal, and practical problems that I foresee on this matter. Some of you, in this room, might know my personal opinion, which excuses me from being too detailed, but what I think on this matter is that the System, as such, has worked very well in the past twenty-six years since the first recommendations on this subject, which were mentioned by *Tucker*. In all these years we have had a system that has worked effectively, a system based on a pragmatic approach, a flexible approach, and the results have been astounding. That has been mentioned once and again by authors, letcturers, diplomats, scientists, and many others. This shows that we have been able to achieve most of the objectives, if not all, that were mentioned in the Antarctic Treaty, and now it seems that we want to change it with the introduction of an organ that is not foreseen in the Antarctic Treaty.

That leads me to the first legal problem. This is not an international organization, and even if it were an international organization, I do not know of any — there might be one or two, I do not know — but I do not know of any that had created organs outside its own constitution, its constitutive act, or whatever you want to name it. So the need might arise to amend the Antarctic Treaty to be able to have a secretariat. Perhaps that would be the proper solution, to convene a conference to revise the Treaty; 1991 would be the proper occasion. I do not think that many would agree that such a possibility would be convenient. I would not favour such a move.

On the other hand, I mentioned practical problems. We are reassured, once and again, that it would be a very simple secretariat. I doubt that a very simple secretariat would be able to perform all the functions that we were just reminded that it should perform. It would be very difficult for one man to carry out what is needed, if something is needed, and we are presented with many, many functions, which, in my view, are already being performed in a decentralized way, and in this way it has functioned well. Now we want to centralize what is decentralized. Moreover, we see that decentralization is giving good results. We are going against the current in this issue.

I also mentioned political problems. The Antarctic Treaty is not an organization, so there is no need for organs. In spite of that, in the system we have organs already which are carrying out many of those functions. *Tucker* mentioned the CCAMLR Commission. In the future minerals convention there will be organs. There is SCAR, which is co-operating with Antarctic Treaty Parties. So we think that all these activities are taking place, very well done, and we do not see a need for really adding another organ. We have heard in the past that secretariats should be simple, and then the situation was different in practice. We know that secretariats tend to increase, enlarge, take more functions, have their own ideas, their own initiatives, and that, within the scope of the Antarctic Treaty and the political realities of the Antarctic Treaty, might create problems. We have a very delicate balance that is reflected in Article IV of the Treaty, and that would make it very difficult to try to reflect the same balance in any organ of the Treaty itself. I think that is as far as I should go. Anyone needing more information will find it in my paper. Thank you, *Rudi*.

R. Wolfrum, Chairman:

Thank you. The paper will be circulated and published in the proceedings. The next speaker on my list will be *Mr. Gerhard Hafner*, please.

G. Hafner:

Thank you very much. I must confess that I am certainly very interested in the paper of *Mr. Davérède*, and I'm very greatful for the presentation of this general topic. Of course I share the view that an increasing number of Parties to the Antarctic Treaty System called for a certain permanent institution, and I am able to say here that another state is already preparing its adherence to the Treaty so that the number will increase to thirty-six in the near future. But despite all this, I want to indicate a certain caveat an this matter of the establishment of a permanent secretariat, since I would be very careful if I had to decide the usefulness of such an establishment, in the light of the usual outcome of similar negotiations and discussions on institutions. Today we are faced with a certain proliferation of international organizations and with the proliferation of the matters imposed on them, which are left for their decision. I could, for instance, envisage such an increase of competences also in the case of a secretariat of the Antarctic Treaty System, and even an automatic process of enlarging its competences. For instance, I could imagine that Consultative Parties would be induced to shift duties, which they have to perform, onto the secretariat. This means that such establishment of a permanent secretariat could entail a complete restructuring of the total Antarctic Treaty System, and since, as you yourself have said, the decentralization, the manifestation of which is in the permanent rotation system, is the basic feature of the entire Antarctic Treaty System, this system could be changed. In my opinion, the Antarctic Treaty System is not fit for such a centralization, and it is not based on such a centralized system. So certainly such a secretariat could facilitate communications among the Parties, but it should be taken care that the pragmatic and flexible approach pursued so far would not be left, and that the competences of such a secretariat would not go beyond those of merely administrative and clearing house functions concerning the exchange of communications, since otherwise a Pandora's box could be opened, and more problems could be raised than solved. Thank you.

R. Wolfrum, Chairman:

Thank you, *Mr. Hafner*. The next speaker will be *John Viall*, please.

J. Viall:

Thank you, *Rudi*. I have merely a question for *Tucker*, and it may possibly go a little bit beyond the scope of the subject that he has so ably introduced. Among those Parties which so far, it seems to me, have supported the idea of the establishment of a secretariat, most, if not all of them, seem to be talking of a sort of travelling secretariat, that is, not a secretariat established at one permanent place, and that follows, no doubt, from the rules of procedure which provide for the rotation of hosting all these Antarctic Treaty Meetings. My question to *Tucker* is, whether he would see any good reason why these rules might not be amended to provide for the location of a permanent secretariat, which, I guess, would also imply doing away with the rotational system of hosting governments, although there are a lot of advantages, perhaps, to that. Thank you.

R. Wolfrum, Chairman:

Thank you. *Tucker?*

T. Scully:

Thank you, *Rudi*. To some extent, I think I would try to answer *John*'s question with a more general remark, rather than trying to get to the specific question as to an amendment of the rules of procedure, or rotation of a secretariat. I would agree with *Herr Hafner*'s remarks that the decentralization of the system, the pragmatic, flexible approach the system has displayed, is a feature which we should not ignore. It is not my intention, in any way, to call this approach into question. The decentralization of the system has allowed the imaginative and flexible resolution of issues. The question of a secretariat — and here I will go back to a point I tried to stress — to me is more a question of function, rather than form. There are, I think, functions that need to be performed on a more permanent basis, in support of the system with its decentralized character. These relate primarily to the question of information, and not only the dissemination of information, but ultimately to the question of developing an information base, a data base, that will be of importance in taking decisions and making judgments that will have to be made in the future. Any mechanisms, any infrastructure, would be designed to serve the decentralized system. Whether that requires an amendment of the rules of procedure or not, I do not know. But, I do not envisage a situation analogous to that in CCAMLR, for example, in which there is a headquarters site at which the meetings take place. If there were to be an infrastructure of some sort, I would see it continue serving the system with its unique features including the rotating hostship practice. The question of a secretariat viewed as a formal structure, it seems to me, is a derivative one. In my view, the Parties should identify the kinds of functions that need to be performed on a continuing basis, and I think that it is possible to identify such functions, and then to determine what kind of mechanism would be necessary for their performance. It could be a secretariat, as I have said, but there are various mechanisms that might be developed, or might be drawn upon to perform such functions on a continuing basis. The need to carry out these functions is something that simply derives from the evolution of the system and the evolution in the nature of activities in Antarctica. We now are, within the system, beginning to address questions of how not to avoid conflict in uses of Antarctica, how to make judgments about the impacts of activities that are going on, that may take place in Antarctica in terms of scientific research and the support activities and others. The basic point would be to start with functions, the kinds of functions that need to be performed, and then to look at how those functions can be best fulfilled. I do not entirely agree with *Alberto*, but I think he raised very good points that have to be taken into account in looking at this issue. There are legal issues that would be involved in establishing anything permanent, but at the same time, I think that the Antarctic Treaty mechanism, as it has operated over the twenty-six years of its existence, has not been succeeded because it has been static. It is decentralized, it has a loose and pragmatic structure, and, I think, no one would wish to change that. But it is operating well because it has been able to anticipate and to come up with creative and effective ways of dealing with new issues, with new activities and new problems. It has been a mechanism whose stock and trade has been a pragmatic and effective problem solving approach. From this perspective I see the need to address certain support functions on a continuing basis as a means of maintaining the character of the system itself.

R. Wolfrum, Chairman:

Thank you very much again, *Tucker*, for your excellent presentation.*

W. Koschorrek:

With regard to the question of a secretariat, no Minister of Finance would be convinced, to allot money when he hears that everything went smoothly and that all tasks could be accomplished. He would have to be persuaded on the basis of arguments which hold that many of the tasks could not be fulfilled and that this was due to the lack of a secretariat. At least in the budgetary process of my country this chain of arguments would be the necessary prerequisite for a public decision — and I am afraid that this proof has not been produced so far.

* Due to the lack of time, the following statement was delivered in writing — *Ed.*

Cooperation in Antarctica in Scientific and Logistic Matters: Status and Means of Improvement

*Patrick Quilty**

In preparing this paper I have made two assumptions, one simple, one complex. Firstly, I have assumed that we are considering international aspects of the topic, and leaving national coordination to national programs. The second, more complex assumption is that there is a desire among governments of nations in the Antarctic Treaty System for there to be improved scientific and logistic cooperation. This is complicated by several factors, the principal being:

— that matters in the Antarctic context are under the auspices of the Antarctic Treaty signed by Claimants and Non-claimant nations, with each camp having its own diverse policies — and different nations will have different approaches to cooperation;

— that 1991 is approaching and initiatives related to this or to other international moves may well affect national policies in either the short or long term.

I. Why is Science so Important?

Science — the pursuit of knowledge — is one of the great cultural activities, along with art, music and sport, that are apparently characteristic of and restricted to humanity. Research for scientific ends is conducted at all times and by all nations for a variety of reasons.

In the Antarctic context, science has a unique role — it is the means by which a nation achieves Consultative Party status within the Antarctic Treaty, which is a hang-over from the success of the International Geophysical Year, being in turn, the progenitor of the Antarctic Treaty.

It has sometimes been said that science is the currency of credibility within the Antarctic Treaty System, because it was the only major area in which agreement could be reached at the time of formulation of the Treaty. I question this view because the key role of science was in place and was strong well before the Treaty was developed and signed.

* *Patrick G. Quilty*, Department of The Arts, Sport, The Environment, Tourism and Territories, Antarctic Division, Kingston, Australia. The opinions expressed in this volume are the personal views of their authors only.

The international aspect of science probably originates from the need for any scientist to be in contact with literature from all nations so that the scientist's view is, by nature, a world view. This is a fine model for other aspects of humanity's future.

I believe there is a need for improved collaboration as science advances from purely local issues to those of world-wide scope such as in Antarctica, the change being caused both by science and diplomacy-generated needs.

The science programs of all nations and scientists depend on availability of logistics support and of integration between these components of a program.

Any nation active in Antarctic science gains or fulfills the following from the conduct of a science program, apart from the value of pure research itself, the science often best done in Antarctica. These are considerably more than could be expected from the conduct of an equivalent program in the home country. These include:

Credibility within the Antarctic Treaty System — Nations achieve or maintain a credible stance in the Treaty System by diplomatic activity coupled with a significant science program.

Credibility of the Antarctic Treaty System within the Broader International Community — It is now incumbent on all Antarctic Treaty Consultative Parties to work together in science (both individually and collectively), to show nations outside the Treaty System that they mean what they say when they refer to the importance of scientific activity. Programs which are dominantly oriented towards evaluation or are only of a token scope may be viewed cynically by other nations.

Evaluation of Resource Potential — There is good reason why a nation interested in Antarctica may wish to orient a part (although not the major part) of its program to resource evaluation. The data form part of a base on which to make judgements on potential land use.

Responsibilities — In this conference, we represent mainly technologically and economically advanced nations. We have an obligation to generate scientific knowledge to be used for the general good of humanity.

Knowledge of the Impact of Antarctica — As a citizen of a southern hemisphere nation (and more particularly, living in Hobart), I am aware of the impact of Antarctic-influenced weather patterns on my home country. The value to those working on proximate landmasses of knowledge of this impact necessitates support for programs studying weather, sea ice, geology of Gondwana nations and so on.

Knowledge to Protect Antarctica — Environmental programs should be strengthened, and designed to ensure that present and future activities in Antarctica can be monitored against a good data base. This should also lead to an understanding of processes and interactions on the continent, and the data base can be useful as an instrument ensuring that Antarctica is protected from disruptive impact and managed appropriately.

Global monitoring — Antarctica is, in many areas, the best locality on earth to monitor the global impacts of humanity's activities. Baseline Air Pollution studies and similar programs take advantage of Antarctica's uniqueness.

Environmental, technological and adaptability data to advance the ability of mankind as a whole to work in extreme environments — Mankind is forever moving into what, at any given time, are extreme environments. Now they are Antarctica, outer space and the deep sea. In the past, it was to new continents, for example, Australia. The results of Antarctic research will aid man's natural aspiration to expand the area of habitation and use.

The capacity to meet obligations assumed under Treaty instruments — Antarctic Treaty nations, through their involvement in the Antarctic Treaty System and through their membership in SCAR, CCAMLR and eventually in a minerals convention, assume responsibility for meeting a variety of obligations and for contributing to international requirements for data and analysis. This requires the existence of a pool of scientists, working in the relevant disciplines, who can be called on to conduct appropriate research programs and provide expert advice. This is an important stimulus to international communication and collaboration.

In addition to those on the above list, many of which can be seen as preplanned results of a program, there are other results which can be termed "cultural." Much is said of the link between science and technology, with science often being seen as the parent of technology. Antarctic science is no different, and we may well see valuable pharmaceuticals and technologies develop as an unpredictable side result of our activities. Serendipitous results of science are rightly part of the lore of science, as history clearly shows. Who is not moved by reading the exploits of *Scott* or *Mawson*? Activities in Antarctica generate adventure and illustrations of great beauty from scenery and wildlife. These inspire the people of our nations, and others, and give life an extra dimension.

II. The Science/Logistics Nexus in Antarctic Affairs

Antarctica has no indigenous population and is the coldest, windiest, most isolated continent on this planet. For that reason, any expedition to Antarctica is very expensive, as it must be self-contained. Each expedition calls for the presence of a group of people with particular personal characteristics and diverse expertise. In the early days of Antarctic exploration, that was even more true, because now there are many nations active in the area; ships, aircraft and land vehicles are better and more available.

Working at my office in Australia as a scientist, I provide my own accommodation, clothing, transport, food and entertainment. Even if I wish to work in the field as a geologist, there are roads, communications links, pleasant climate and little need for a dedicated search and rescue effort to monitor my "expedition." To a very large extent, I can go where I wish and when I wish to. Science is part of a broad array of the community's activity, not its *raison d'être*. In Antarctica, it is very different. For office or field work in science there — which is the reason for the existence in Antarctica of a facility — my government must provide an entire community infrastructure — accommodation, entertainment, office space, food, clothing, transport and support staff.

This logistics facility must be brought in from outside the continent, and is a very expensive operation in terms of both staffing and funding. As time passes and as society's needs for a more complex, expensive infrastructure develop, the Antarctic operation — even at a constant level — requires more funds and people to support it. This pattern of total dependence by science on an imported, expensive logistic support is clearer in Antarctic activity than anywhere else on the face of the earth. It is a key feature of Antarctic activity. This need for cooperation between logistics and science on a national basis must also be extended to international activities.

Because knowledge is universal, because scientists publish in internationally reviewed journals and because the papers have an international audience, scientists have an international perspective and context, often at variance with those of our political confreres, who take a much shorter-term, nationally-bounded view. This will probably always be true, but our view is, I contend, a superior one which will, hopefully, eventually prevail.

The International Geophysical Year of 1957/58 led to the development of the Antarctic Treaty, which refers throughout to the spirit of science mentioned above. That spirit in the Treaty must be fostered, nurtured and protected so it will grow and help the Antarctic Treaty System itself grow as a shining example among international agreements which allows nations to put aside some of their national aspirations for the general good. The next few years are critical for Antarctic affairs and if the system is to survive in its present form, every effort must be made to ensure that the cooperative, communicative spirit of science is not submerged under other issues.

As nations' Antarctic programs come under closer home scrutiny, the chances of greatly increased logistics support becomes less, and thus there is a need to integrate logistics support to achieve advances in science. As technology, especially satellite technology, develops with a global value, it is up to us to use it to achieve results which would cost a great deal more were they achieved any other way. Some areas of science depend on integration of data from many areas; there is a need for the coordination of data-gathering activities of many nations.

This cooperation is not new. International cooperation in logistics, staffing and funding has been fundamental to Antarctic activity throughout the last century. Early expeditions were usually multi-national, even if credited to one flag. The *Borchgrevink* expedition of 1899 — the first to overwinter on the continent — is just one example. Funded as the British Antarctic Expedition of 1898—1900, its staff consisted of three Englishmen, two Finns, and *Borchgrevink* and *Bernacchi* as Australians. The other members of the expedition were Norwegians. Later expeditions were no less international.

There is another dimension to the spirit of total cooperation between nations based on science. It is tragic, but laudable, that some of the best examples of logistic cooperation have come from the medical field. The classic example, to my mind, of such cooperation was the evacuation of an Australian expeditioner in January 1978, by Soviet helicopter from Davis to Mirny, a U.S. Hercules aircraft to McMurdo, and then to Christchurch, New Zealand.

III. Modes of Coordination of Antarctic Science/Logistics

There are several modes in which science and logistics are at present integrated internationally in Antarctica of a large enough dimension to accommodate any improvements which may be suggested later.

SCAR

The longest-serving coordinating body is SCAR (initially the Special, but later, the Scientific Committee on Antarctic Research). This forum, one of the ICSU (International Council of Scientific Unions) family, grew out of CSAGI (Comité Special de l'Année Internationale) and has been, through its Working Groups and Groups of Specialists, the principal means of international coordination of scientific programs until recent times. Examples of such coordinated efforts are the IGY (International Geophysical Year) itself, IAGP (International Antarctic Glaciological Project), BIOMASS (Biological Investigation of Marine Antarctic Systems and Stocks) and IBEA (the International Biomedical Expedition to Antarctica).

The projects or programs are established by scientists, coordinated by scientists and finalized by scientists, all with science as the number-one priority. Logistic support for international collaboration is incorporated into national programs which then are seen, in part, to be in support of international agreements.

SCAR's brief constitution and relaxed working mode have been exceedingly effective with regard to the international freedom and exchange of ideas which are central to the scientific way of doing things. Long may SCAR continue to operate in this mode!

SCAR is a non-government agency, and membership is through a nation's senior academic body. This means that the advice given by SCAR is independent of national policy constraints. SCAR's effectiveness is reflected in several references to science and the spirit of science in the Treaty and to the role of SCAR in Recommendations such as Rec. I-IV, which states:

(1) that the free exchange of information and views among scientists participating in SCAR, and the recommendations concerning scientific programmes and co-operation formulated by this body constitute a most valuable contribution to international scientific co-operation in Antarctica;

(2) that since these activities of SCAR constitute the kind of activity contemplated in Article III of the Treaty, SCAR should be encouraged to continue this advisory work which has so effectively facilitated international co-operation in scientific investigation.

One of SCAR's strengths lies in the presence of a working group in Logistics, in addition to the scientific working groups. This allows scientific and logistics working groups to come together at the same meetings. There is a large overlap in membership, and communication between science and logistics is strong. The generation of ideas and the program coordination conducted by SCAR are very cost-effective. The cost of organizing BIOMASS was minuscule in proportion to the international links that were forged and the results which were generated. I might point out that the fruits of SCAR's work are about to be published in popular book form, and as one who was concerned with the science editing of the book, I can recommend it to you.

Treaty Instruments with a Scientific Component

A new mode of international scientific cooperation and/or coordination has now developed through the Antarctic Treaty System itself. Largely following the initiative of biologists active in SCAR, under the umbrella of the Treaty, the Convention for the Conservation of Antarctic Marine Living Resources (CCAMLR) has developed. The CCAMLR Commission, which services the Convention, has its headquarters in Hobart. It is the only instrument of either SCAR or the Treaty with a permanent infrastructure.

This Convention establishes a Scientific Committee wherein scientists of member nations meet each year to identify scientific matters (including future research programs) to be undertaken in support of CCAMLR's objectives. The recommendations go to the CCAMLR Commission for consideration. Individual nations then conduct appropriate research as part of their own programs.

While it is true that BIOMASS had scientific objectives and CCAMLR's are management-oriented, there is a general feeling that progress was more rapid in BIOMASS than in CCAMLR. The objectives of both required a science data base; BIOMASS seems to have had a more fruitful and a cheaper one. Two types of criticism are levelled at CCAMLR. Conservation groups and nations outside the Treaty System tend to point to CCAMLR as having been developed in secrecy as an exclusive "club." Conservation groups and some members have been critical for a variety of reasons, including the lack of commitment to the provision of information for a data base which is to be used for estimating a reasonable fish and krill catch. Other reasons include the lack of enforceable interim catch limits, as well as the feeling expressed by some nations that fishing should be unrestricted until there is indisputable evidence of overfishing.

Global Programs with Antarctic Components

There is a third mode of development of programs, outside both SCAR and the Treaty, although both the Treaty and SCAR are aware of it. SCAR is kept even more aware of it because of the involvement of scientists in both SCAR and this third mode.

Many programs in science are of global scope and include an Antarctic Component. Such a program is the Ocean Drilling Program, an international venture funded principally by the National Science Foundation (U. S. A.), with financial support and participation of other nations such as Canada, the Federal Republic of Germany, France, Japan, the European Science Foundation and the United Kingdom, some of which are not in any way involved with Antarctic matters.

This program has already drilled in the Weddell Sea and plans to drill in Prydz Bay in early 1988. Its predecessor — the Deep Sea Drilling Project — also drilled in Antarctic waters, the Ross Sea, in 1972/73. Both

DSDP and ODP have been coordinated by scientists following the development by scientists of programs with a detailed and responsible review. Other such programs include various upper atmosphere physics projects, Baseline Air Pollution Stations (BAPS), those under the World Meteorological Organization, seismological and magnetic observatory operations and the World Ocean Circulation Experiment (WOCE).

Small Group Arrangements

There are many cases in which scientists from two or three countries cooperate to conduct a science program of joint interest. The U.S. / N.Z. / Australian program on R.V. *S.P. Lee* off the Wilkes Land Margin was one such program. Others include Belgian, Swedish and Dutch participation in Australian summer programs of biology and geomorphology. These are generated on an *ad hoc* basis at conferences or by national program leaders. Logistics usually are supplied by a single institution which then calls on scientific expertise of other institutions, which happen to be foreign.

Private Expeditions

In recent years there has been a series of private expeditions to Antarctica, some with a science component. Project Blizzard, the Oceanic Research Foundation, Greenpeace, Footsteps of Scott, to name several, have had to organize their own funding and logistics.

Managers of National Antarctic Programs (MNAP)

There has been instituted very recently, a new forum, the MNAP. It has recently had its first meeting to carry out its functions of contact and communication between program managers. It is to be a meeting place for "national officials responsible for planning and conducting that nation's presence in the Antarctic." It will thus be responsive to the nation's own government policy.

IV. Scope for Improvement

The following ideas are presented more as discussion points than firm proposals, and I hope others will arise during discussion. Some have already been raised as ideas during the meeting coordinated by the International Institute for Environment and Development in Racine, Wisconsin, in June 1986.

Exchange of Scientists

The strength of SCAR lies in the exchange of information on a person-to-person basis among friends and colleagues, and through direct correspondence and exchange of publications. This also is a mark of such successful projects as DSDP and ODP. Strengthening the means of communication between scientists is critical to any attempt to improve the system. I would identify an international commitment to exchange of scientists, in the spirit in which I have been supported in coming here, as a valuable move.

Conference on the Future of Antarctic Science

We have been working for many years in a piecemeal fashion and now have a rough, non-integrated data base in many areas of science. It would be a valuable exercise to have a major conference to review the present knowledge, to decide where the major future thrusts of internationally coordinated Antarctic science should be directed and to establish appropriate international project committees to see that such projects are coordinated and brought to fruition.

Such a review should include statements by senior scientists from those nations with an active interest in Antarctic science and from SCAR Working Group chairmen. The meeting should then summarize independent advice on where the major thrusts should be.

Advance Notice of Future Science Programs

Through SCAR and the Antarctic Treaty there are annual exchanges of information. The Antarctic Treaty refers to radio frequencies, expected shipping, aircraft, staff numbers, general scientific programs and so on — what is dominantly the logistics base. The SCAR exchange refers to specific science projects, investigators and publications from the previous year.

Both these sets of documents are highly valuable, but generally are circulated at a time when little use can be made of them in a way which would help international use of another country's logistics. That is, they are information exchange documents rather than documents designed to aid international personnel and logistics cooperation for the purposes of scientific research. However, I would be very reluctant to suggest an earlier exchange because of the rigidity that that would impose on planning and the reduction on the ability of science to change plans quickly.

While the documents outline the season ahead in detail, it would be possible, I believe, for such documents to be modified to include a short statement on plans an extra year or two ahead. This would not be a serious imposition as modern planning must look several years ahead, albeit not in fine detail.

Common Use of Facilities

While Antarctica is a reasonably large continent (13.9×10^6 km^2), the area of outcrop is quite small (estimated at 330 000 km^2 by *Budd*, 1986). This is approximately the same size as Finland.

There is a divergence of opinion on the question or philosophy of occupation. One school believes that a number of widely dispersed facilities (and their impacts) is preferable to a higher concentration in a small area. The converse view is also held. Whatever the philosophy, it is already true that there are areas of Antarctica — particularly King George Island — where many nations have separate facilities in a small area. Such areas are of course also popular with the native inhabitants of Antarctica, as their home.

To reduce the impact of humanity, is it possible that nations could cooperate in using joint facilities on such areas? Use of joint facilities would reduce the array of buildings, the impact on the atmosphere from power generation, waste generation, the area alienated for humanity. It would also reduce duplication of many activities — even scientific ones such as gathering meteorological data. A useful side effect of this "common-use" concept is that nations learning their way, or even just testing the water or ice could be involved actively in a program, rather than acting as a supernumerary.

CATSA

I would like to see reviewed discussion of the concept of *CATSA* (Cooperative Air Transport System Antarctica). As time passes, more nations are using and will establish air transport links to Antarctica and within Antarctica, leading to several advantages:

a) quick access to the continent;

b) scope for science programs which are only possible with air support or more efficiently done with air support;

c) access to the continent by more senior scientists and senior policy makers; and

d) better emergency evacuation procedures, both as part of Antarctic operations and for transpolar commercial aviation.

A full development of CATSA would make it possible to transfer scientists and support staff between the different national facilities within Antarctica perhaps more cheaply and more effectively than elsewhere on earth. It is possible that eventually elements of CATSA could be operated by normal commercial airline operators, thus reducing the capital outlay in national dedicated Antarctic agencies.

Common Publication

One of the reasons for the success of the Deep Sea Drilling Project and Ocean Drilling Program is that participants are involved in a cooperative approach to a particular project, in both field and laboratory phases. After working together to gather data, they disperse to their home nations, have a year to process data or samples and write up results in draft form. At the end of that year, they meet again and eventually produce a volume of scientific results from the program. This volume is one of a continuing series in a common format, which is highly regarded and widely distributed.

It may be that there are areas of Antarctic endeavour in which this approach can be taken. The success of the Antarctic Treaty has been discussed and acknowledged in numerous published works, including those proceeding from the two earlier conferences in the "Antarctic Challenge" series. That success emanates, I believe very strongly, from the spirit of international cooperation and communication that are central to science.

Mixing Specialists from Various Fields of the Antarctic Treaty System

The ideas I have proposed above have a direct relationship with the title of the paper. I would like to raise another point, perhaps less directly related to it.

One of the great aspects of a meeting such as this is that I, as a scientist, can meet and mix with other important elements of the Treaty System — diplomats, ambassadors, international lawyers, institute directors, relevant academics and other scientists — those who see science as so important. Through this, I become much more aware of developing trends within the System, and I believe that knowledge enhances my respect for, and determination to work for, the Treaty System.

It is an aspect peculiar to the Antarctic, because the population involved in Antarctic affairs is not very great, and because there is a human need to be aware of one's role in the scheme of things. Anyone who works in the Antarctic arena is aware of the unusual circumstances and becomes very interested and knowledgeable in many areas outside his own field of specialty. Where else is a geologist also a mechanic, or other scientists also tractor drivers?

Any steps that can cause greater mixing of specialists from different parts of the Antarctic Treaty System will enhance the operation of that System. For this aspect I include SCAR in the Treaty System.

I hope and trust that Antarctic affairs will continue to be conducted and organized in compliance with that spirit.

V. Conclusion

The Antarctic Treaty System and the Scientific Committee on Antarctic Research have served Antarctic science well, and doubtless will continue to do so for some time in the future. There are areas where the cooperation between nations and between science and logistic aspects can be improved. Some changes are easy to implement, some will take considerable time and effort before they can come into force. I have outlined a few ideas and hope these and others will form a basis for discussion.

The most important force in any potential cooperation is that of the goodwill that is now traditional in Antarctic affairs between people representing different nations and political systems.

Acknowledgements

I give a most sincere vote of gratitude to the Federal Ministry of Research and Technology, both for the invitation to speak and the means to make it possible.

LITERATURE:

BENTLEY, C. R. (1984),
International Science Programs in Antarctica, in: *Alexander, L. M.* and *Carter-Hanson, L.* (eds.), Antarctic Politics and Marine Resources: Critical Choices for the 1980s, Proceedings Eighth Annual Conference, Center for Ocean Management Studies, University of Rhode Island, 45—54.

BUDD, W. F. (1984),
Scientific Research in Antarctica and Australia's Effort, in: *Harris, S.* (ed.), Australia's Antarctic policy options, Monograph 11, Centre for Resource and Environmental studies, Australian National University, 217—247.

BUDD, W. F. (1986),
The Antarctic Treaty as a Scientific Research Mechanism (Post IGY) — Contributions of Antarctic Scientific Research, in: Antarctic Treaty System: An Assessment, National Academy Press, Washington, 103—151.

CARO, D. E. (1982),
The Role of Science in Australian Antarctic Policy, in: *Herr R., A., Hall, R.* and *Davis, B. W.*, Issues in Australia's Marine and Antarctic Policies, Public Policy Document, University of Tasmania, 139—150.

DAVIS, B. W. (1986),
Background to the Present Situation, in: *Millar, T. B.* (ed.), Australia, Britain and Antarctica, Australian Studies Centre, University of London, 4—18.

DREWRY, D. J. (1986),
International Scientific Cooperation in Antarctica, in: *Millar, T. B.* (ed.), Australia, Britain and Antarctica, Australian Studies Centre, University of London, 25—36.

EITTREIM, S. L. and HAMPTON, M. A. (1987),
The Antarctic Continental Margin: Geology and Geophysics of Offshore Wilkes Land, Circum-Pacific Council for Energy and Mineral Resources, Earth Science Series, vol. 5 A.

FIFIELD, R. (in press),
International Research in the Antarctic, Butler and Tanner Ltd, for SCAR and the ICSU Press, Oxford University Press, 139 p.

GJELSVIK, T. (1984),
Scientific research and cooperation in Antarctica, in: *Wolfrum, R.* (ed.) Antarctic Challenge, Duncker and Humblot, Berlin, 41—51.

KIMBALL, L. A. (ed.), (1987),
Future Directions for the Management of Antarctic Science, International Institute for Environment and Development, 41 p.

LOVERING, J. F. and PRESCOTT, J. R. V. (1979),
Last of Lands: Antarctica, Melbourne University Press, Melbourne,1—212.

MOSLEY, G. (1986),
Antarctica: Our Last Great Wilderness, Australian Conservation Foundation. Our Last Great Wilderness, Australian Conservation Foundation.

PODKOLINSKI, M. T. and SEMMENS, K. (1979),
Intestinal Haemorrhage in Antarctica, A Multinational Rescue Operation, Medical Journal of Australia, 2:275—277.

RAMAKRISHNA, G. (1986),
A Critique of the Convention on the Conservation of Antarctic Marine Living Resources, in: *Sharma, R. C.* (ed.), Growing Focus on Antarctica, Rajesh Publications, New Delhi, 179—183.

ROOTS, E. F. (1986),
The Role of Science in the Antarctic Treaty System, in: Antarctic Treaty System: An Assessment, National Academy Press, Washington, 169—184.

SHEUMACK, M. D. (1985),
Sovereignty and Minerals in Antarctica, M. Sc. Thesis, Griffith University, Queensland, 168 p.

ZUMBERGE, J. H. (1986),
Research and the Antarctic Treaty System. in: Antarctic Treaty System: An Assessment, National Academy Press, Washington, 153—168.

International Agreements Applicable to Antarctica: A Survey

*Scott A. Hajost**

The purpose of my presentation is to survey international agreements, including those that establish intergovernmental organizations (formed for the most part by treaty), that have some application or relevance to the area of and activities under the Antarctic Treaty and which are not part of the Antarctic Treaty System or ATS. The ATS can most succinctly be described as the Antarctic Treaty and its progeny: the body of recommendations adopted pursuant to Article IX of the Antarctic Treaty, the Convention for the Conservation of Antarctic Seals, the Convention on the Conservation of Antarctic Marine Living Resources (CCAMLR) and the interaction among those components.[1] The Antarctic minerals convention currently under negotiation will be another constituent part of the ATS in the future.

I have focused this survey on international agreements in force of basically a global nature and thus have not included regional organizations and agreements nor non-governmental organizations. I start with the proposition that there are existing global instruments consistent with the ATS that should apply to Antarctica and which it would be useful to identify. In this regard, it has been interesting to confirm, taking into account the ATS, that Antarctica is very much a place subject to the rule of law. I have endeavored to include agreements that might presently have application in Antarctica, not by virtue of State territorial application, but on which Non-claimant and Claimants might agree to be relevant. I should stress that my survey is not intended to be exhaustive, nor have I studied the negotiating history of the agreements to ascertain whether their application to Antarctica was considered. Setting aside an Antarctic specific connection, I have based my conclusions on an exclusively textual analysis. In addition, although in compiling this survey I had to review how an agreement might be applied, I have not gone into the details in this regard (including case

* *Scott A. Hajost*, Attorney Adviser for Ocean, International Environmental and Scientific Affairs, Office of the Legal Adviser, U.S. Department of State. The opinions expressed in this volume are the personal views of their authors only.

[1] The Scientific Committee on Antarctic Research (SCAR), of the International Council of Scientific Union, while not formally linked or derived from the Antarctic Treaty, is often considered as part of ATS.

studies), nor actually tried to assess fully which might be easier or more difficult to apply from a Claimant/Non-claimant perspective. I have taken my task to be a first step: that is, one of identification. Finally I should note that the UN Secretary-General's Study and expanded study on Antarctica provided useful information for this survey.[2]

Before starting, it might be useful to revisit what the Antarctic Treaty itself says about its relationship with other international organizations. Article III, para. 2 of the Treaty provides:

> In implementing this Article [III], every encouragement shall be given to the establishment of cooperative working relations with those specialized agencies of the United Nations and other international organizations having a scientific or technical interest in Antarctica.

This provision is the basis on which the Treaty Parties themselves have collaborated with other relevant organizations over the years. In this regard, Recommendation XII-6 provided that in furtherance of Article III (a) of the Treaty, reports of Consulative meeting be transmitted to the UN Secretary-General and that relevant portions thereof be brought to be attention of concerned specialized agencies and international organizations. Its evolution took its most recent step forward with the decision by the May Rio Preparatory Meeting to the Fourteenth Antarctic Treaty Meeting to invite the World Meteorological Organization (WMO) and the International Union for the Conservation of Nature (IUCN) to designate experts to attend the Fourteenth Antarctic Treaty Consultative Meeting (along with observers from the Scientific Committee on Antarctic Research (SCAR) and the CCAMLR Commission).

The logical starting point for this survey is the Charter of the United Nations.[3] The Preamble to the Antarctic Treaty makes clear the fundamental relationship of the Charter to the Treaty:

> Convinced also that a treaty ensuring the use of Antarctica for peaceful purposes only and the continuance of international harmony in Antarctica will further the purposes and principles embodied in the Charter of the United Nations . . . .[4]

The relationship of the Treaty to the Charter is further emphasized by the obligation of Treaty Parties "... to exert appropriate efforts,

---

[2] Question of Antarctica: Study requested under General Assembly Resolution 38/77 — Report of the Secretary-General A/39/583 and Question of Antarctica: Study requested under General Assembly Resolution 40/156A — Report of the Secretary-General.

[3] UN Charter, 3 Bevans 1153.

[4] UN Charter, Preamble, paragraph 5.

consistent with the Charter of the United Nations, to the end that no one engage in any activity in Antarctica contrary to the principles or purpose of the . . . Treaty."[5]

The purposes of the United Nations, as stated in Article 1 of the Charter, are to maintain international peace and security, to develop friendly relations among nations and to achieve international cooperation in solving international problems. Members are to settle their disputes by peaceful means and refrain from the use or threat of force.[6] It is undisputed that the Antarctic Treaty furthers these purposes and fulfils these obligations. It is also true that the UN has a generalized interest in Antarctica in light of the General Assembly's role in fostering international cooperation in political and other fields, its continuing interest in the peaceful relations of States and because of the UN's relationship with specialized agencies active in Antarctica.[7] Recognition of this interest is reflected in Recommendation XII-6, referred to previously.

For the remainder of the survey, I have grouped agreements generally by subjects. Since the principal purpose of the Antarctic Treaty is arms control, I shall proceed with that category next.

I. Arms Control

The Treaty Banning Nuclear Weapons Tests in the Atmosphere, in Outer Space and Under Water (Test Ban Treaty), provides that each Party to the Treaty undertakes to prohibit any nuclear weapon test explosion or any other nuclear explosion at any place under its control "... in the atmosphere ... or under water, including the high seas ... or any other environment if such explosion causes radioactive debris to be present outside the territorial limit of the State ..." conducting the explosion.[8] The Convention further provides that each Party undertakes to refrain from ". . . causing, encouraging or in any way participating in, the carrying out of any nuclear weapon test explosion or any other unclear explosion, anywhere which would take place ...," *inter alia*, underwater or in the atmosphere, or if it causes radioactive debris outside its territory.[9]

This Convention can be viewed as complementary to the Antarctic Treaty's prohibition in Article V, para. 1, on nuclear explosions in Ant-

[5] Article X, The Antarctic Treaty (entered into force June 23, 1961), UNTS 402 (1961) 71—102.

[6] UN Charter (note 3), Arts. 2, 3, and 4.

[7] *Loc. cit.*, Arts. 11, 13, and 57.

[8] Entered into force Oct. 10, 1963, UNTS 480 (1963) 43, Article I, 1. 1.

[9] *Loc. cit.*, Article I, 2.

arctica, particularly as it relates to any interpretation of Article VI of the Treaty to the effect that the prohibition does not apply to the "high seas" areas of Antarctica south of 60° S. latitude.

The 1971 Treaty prohibiting the emplacement of nuclear and other weapons of mass destruction on the Seabed could also be read as applicable to marine areas in the area of application of the Antarctic Treaty. Pursuant to the "Seabeds" Treaty, Parties undertake not to implant or emplace on the seabed and the ocean floor and in the subsoil thereof, any nuclear weapons or any other types of weapons of mass destruction or means for storing, testing or using such weapons.[10] The Treaty additionally provides for rights of State inspection. As with the Test Ban Treaty, depending on one's reading of Article VI of the Antarctic Treaty, the Antarctic Treaty already addresses the substance of the Seabeds Treaty. The latter is nontheless complementary and the marine areas of Antarctica are part of the ocean floor, seabed, and subsoil.

The 1972 Convention on the Prohibition of the Development, Production and Stockpiling of Bacteriological (Biological) and Toxin Weapons and on their Destruction might also be cited.[11] Specifically, Article IV of the Convention requires that each Party take all necessary measures to prohibit and prevent development, production, stockpiling, acquisition or retention of biological agents, toxins weapons, equipment and means of delivery ". . . under its jurisdiction or under its control *anywhere*" (emphasis added). Anywhere, without more, may be read to include Antarctica and reinforce Article I, para. 1 of the Antarctic Treaty.

Finally, the 1977 ENMOD Convention prohibits Parties from engaging in military or other hostile environmental techniques against any other State Party.[12] Environmental modification techniques refers to any technique ". . . for changing — through the deliberate manipulation of natural processes, dynamics, composition or structure of the earth, including its biota, lithosphere, hydrosphere and atmosphere, . . ."[13] Each Party is to take measures to prohibit and prevent violations of the Convention "... *any where* under its jurisdiction or control" (emphasis added).[14] While it might take a somewhat science-fiction bent (intentional melting

[10] Treaty on the Prohibition of the Emplacement of Nuclear Weapons and Other Weapons of Mass Destruction on the Seabed and the Ocean Floor and in the Subsoil Thereof (entered into force May 18, 1972), in: UNJYB (1970) 121, TIAS 7337, Article 1. These obligations do not apply to a "coastal State" with respect to the seabed within twelve miles of its coast — see Arts I. 1. and 2. and II.

[11] Entered into force March 26, 1975; in UNJYB (1971) 118, TIAS 8062.

[12] Convention on the Prohibition of Military or any other Hostile Use of Environmental Modifications Techniques (entered into force Oct. 5, 1978), UN Doc. A/Res./31/72, in: UNJYB (1976) 125, TIAS 9614, Article I, 1.

[13] *Loc. cit.*, Article II.

[14] *Loc. cit.*, Article IV.

of the ice cap?), the Convention could be read as applicable to environmental modification techniques in Antarctica directed against States outside the Treaty area, or possibly even against their activities in Antarctica.

II. Hijacking, Sabotage and Terrorism

I shall continue by citing some agreements which are also designed to promote peaceful purposes. The 1963 Convention on Offenses and Certain Other Acts Committed on Board Aircraft applies to acts jeopardizing the safety of aircraft or passengers committed on board aircraft (excluding military aircraft) while the aircraft is in flight "... or on the surface of the high seas or of any other area outside the territory of any State."[15]

The State of registration is obligated to establish its jurisdiction over offenses committed on board its aircraft.[16] The Convention contains a number of provisions concerning the authority of the aircraft commander to deal with offenses covered by the Convention, including restraint, disembarking the offender and the taking into custody of offenders. Since these are largely defined in terms of territory of a State, for a Non-claimant there are difficulties in accepting the formal application of the Convention to aircraft that may fly to Antarctica, in that landings are defined in relation to territory. However, there might be no disagreement on the Convention's applicability to a flight over Antarctica from one State to another or from Antarctica. As far as the Non-claimant might be concerned, any offense on the surface of Antarctica and on the marine waters in the area of application of the Treaty might also be covered (its claimed territory and the unclaimed area, for a Claimant).

The 1970 Hijacking Convention provides that it is an offense or any person to seize, or attempt to seize, an aircraft in flight.[17] The Convention applies if the take-off or place of landing is outside the territory of the State of registration.[18] Each Party is to establish its jurisdiction over the offense with respect to its registered aircraft as well as when an aircraft lands in its territory with an alleged offender aboard.[19] It would seem possible that the Convention could be applied to a hijacking in

[15] Convention on Offences and Certain other Acts Committed On Board Aircraft (entered into force Dec. 4, 1969), UNTS 704 (1963) 219, Article 1.

[16] *Loc. cit.*, Article 3.

[17] Convention for the Suppression of Unlawful Seizure of Aircraft (entry into force Oct. 14, 1971), UNTS 860 (1970) 105, Article 1. The Convention does not apply to military aircraft, Art. 3, 2.

[18] *Loc. cit.*, Article 3, 3.

[19] *Loc. cit.*, Article 4, 1.

Antarctica, *e. g.*, if a tourist plane hijacked in or over Antarctica is forced to land in territory outside the area of application of the Antarctic Treaty. It is more difficult in the event that there is a hijacking into Antarctica, because from the Non-claimant perspective, there can be no territory of a Party where the plane would land and the hijacker would be found. The State of registry could still be seen as possibly having an obligation to exercise jurisdiction over the offense. It is interesting to note that unlike the 1963 Convention, no reference is made to areas outside the territory of any State.

The 1971 Convention for the Suppression of Unlawful Acts against the Safety of Civil Aviation, the "Sabotage Convention," is structured similarly to the Hijacking Convention.[20] It applies to intentional acts to damage or destroy aircraft, (other than military aircraft), in service or in flight.[21] Like the Hijacking Convention, the Convention applies, *inter alia,* if the place of take-off or landing is outside the State of registry, theoretically, Antarctica, although it makes no reference to high seas or areas beyond national jurisdiction as does the 1963 Convention.[22] As with the Hijacking Convention, a Party is obligated to establish its jurisdiction over offenses committed against or aboard its registered aircraft.[23] The question of applicability of the Convention basically involves the same analysis as that of the Hijacking Convention, with basically the same conclusion, due to the territorial references.

Lastly, the 1979 International Convention against the Taking of Hostages makes it an offense to kill, injure or to continue to detain a person in order to compel a third party to act or desist from acting.[24] The rest of the Convention, however, speaks in terms of action to be taken by the Party in whose territory the hostages or offenders are located, thus rendering its application problematical if the offense takes place and remains confined to Antarctica. If the hostage-takers and hostages somehow made it to a country outside Antarctica, the Convention's operation might be clearer.[25] A Party is, however, obligated to establish its jurisdiction over the offense committed on board a ship or aircraft of its registry, which could occur while in Antarctic waters.

---

[20] Convention for the Suppression of Unlawful Acts against the Safety of Civil Aviation (entered into force Jan. 26, 1973), in: UNJYB (1971) 143, TIAS 7570.

[21] *Loc. cit.*, Article 1.

[22] *Loc. cit.*, Article 4, 2.

[23] *Loc. cit.*, Article 5, 1 (b).

[24] International Convention Against the Taking of Hostages (entry into force June 4, 1983), UNGA Res. 34/146, GAOR, 34th sess., Supp. 46, 245, in: ILM 28 (1979), 1457.

[25] *Loc. cit.*, Articles 3 and 6.

III. Wildlife Conservation

There are also some wildlife conservation agreements that either apply to or could apply to Antarctic waters.

The 1946 International Convention for the Regulation of Whaling, as amended, which established the International Whaling Commission (IWC) provides the basis for the global management of whaling.[26] The Convention applies to all waters in which whaling is prosecuted, and as such, the IWC has been the responsible body for regulating whaling in Antarctic waters. The last IWC-authorized quota for any whaling in Antarctic waters ended in 1986 in conjunction with the effective date of the overall commercial moratorium. Prior to then, the IWC had regulated whaling in Antarctic waters in some detail, including the establishment of areas. Article VI of CCAMLR expressly provides that it does not derogate from the rights and obligations of Parties under the International Convention for the Regulation of Whaling. The effect of this Article is to recognize that direct regulation of whales will not be undertaken under CCAMLR, though whales are covered by CCAMLR in the application of its conservation standard as part of the Antarctic marine ecosystem. The IWC attended as an observer at the 1980 diplomatic conference adopting CCAMLR and has been an observer at meetings of the CCAMLR Commission.

The 1973 Convention on International Trade in Endangered Species of Wild Fauna and Flora (CITES) is designed to protect wildlife by setting up an international system regulating trade in endangered and threatened species.[27] Specifically, commercial trade in species listed in Appendix I of CITES is prohibited while trade of species listed in Appendix II is to be strictly regulated.[28] Trade is defined as export, re-export, import and introduction from the sea, the latter being "transportation into a State of any specimen of any species which were taken in the marine environment not under the jurisdiction of any State."[29]

CITES lists a number of species found in Antarctic waters. As such, it is relevant to Antarctica in that (at least, from a Non-claimant point of view), it would be applicable to the taking of listed species in Antarctic waters which were to be transported to a State Party. (For a Claimant, at least in the unclaimed areas or waters not subject to a claim south of 60° S. latitude.) In such case, the authorization for introduction of an

[26] International Convention for the Regulation of Whaling (entered into force Nov. 10, 1948), in UNTS 161 (1949) 72; (as amended May 4, 1969) in: UNTS 338 (1957) 366.

[27] International Convention on International Trade in Endangered Species of Wild Fauna and Flora (entered into force July 1, 1975), UNTS 993, 243.

[28] *Loc. cit.,* Articles II, III and IV.

[29] *Loc. cit.,* Articles I, c) and e).

Appendix I specimen could only be given if it would not be detrimental to the survival of the species (the same standard would apply for Annex II) and is not to be used for primarily commercial purposes.[30]

In theory, there could also be a shipment directly from Antarctica to a state outside involving two different states and not be an introduction from the sea. This could possibly be construed as an export and import thereby coming under the export and import requirements, both of which include similar determinations as required for introductions from the sea.[31] Otherwise, any trade in Antarctic species would seem to be similar to trade in species found elsewhere.

The 1979 Convention on the Conservation of Migratory Species of Wild Animals is intended to conserve species that cross one or more "national jurisdictional boundaries."[32] To this end, "Range States" are to conserve habitats and prohibit the taking of migratory species listed on Appendix I to the Convention, and for Appendix II species, conclude agreements for their protection.[33] In this regard, "Range" is defined as all areas of land or water that a migratory species crosses, and a "Range State" is a state that exercises jurisdiction over any part of the range of a migratory species, or the flag vessels of which are engaged, outside national jurisdictional limits, in taking the migratory species in question.[34] In general, Parties are to cooperate, including through a Conference of Parties, in research on migratory species and other forms of protection, as well as list species on the appropriate annex.

As drafted, the Convention's applicability to Antarctica relies on the listing of whales in Annex I which migrate through Antarctic waters. The application of the provisions of the Convention would, however, have to be based on an obligation of a Party exercising jurisdiction over species outside Antarctica with a range extending into Antarctica (since there is no agreed exercise of state jurisdiction over species in Antarctica), or because a Party was taking species outside national jurisdiction in Antarctic waters. Overall, while the Convention might list species which migrate into Antarctic waters and can be stretched to provide a basis for conserving those species therein, it is not particularly well-crafted or designed for this purpose.

I would next like to turn to a number of ocean-related agreements which I shall divide into those relating to the marine environment and those on general maritime matters. I shall address law of the sea separately.

---

[30] *Loc. cit.*, Articles III, 5., and IV, 6.

[31] *Loc. cit.*, Articles III and IV.

[32] Convention on the Conservation of Migratory Species of Wild Animals (entered into force Nov. 1, 1983), in: ILM 19 (1980), 15.

[33] *Loc. cit.*, Article III.

[34] *Loc. cit.*, Article I. f) and h).

IV. Marine Environment

The Protocol of 1978 Relating to the International Convention for the Prevention of Pollution from Ships, 1973 (MARPOL 73/78) establishes the basic international standards for regulating the operational discharges of harmful substances from ships in order to prevent pollution of the marine enviroment.[35] It defines ships as those operating in the marine environment including fixed and floating platforms. As such, waters off Antarctica would as a general matter seem covered.[36]

MARPOL contains two mandatory Annexes: I on Regulations for the Prevention of Pollution by Oil and II on Regulations for the Control of Pollution by Noxious Liquid Substances in Bulk.[37] A question arises in their application, however, in that many are defined in relation to distances from the "nearest land" defined in terms of the baseline from which the breath of the territorial sea in question is measured.[38]

While this provision may give a Claimant no pause in application of the Annexes off Antarctica, a Non-claimant would not recognize there to be territory or a territorial sea in Antarctica. Though this would not render the Annexes inapplicable to Antarctica, one might ask whether the conditions for no discharges within certain distances of the "nearest land" would be applicable off Antarctica and need be respected. I would venture to say that putting substance over form, the overall interest in protection of the marine environments calls for application of the mileage distance off Antarctica, without prejudice as to whether there is a baseline. In this regard, the Antarctic Treaty Consultative Parties have in part already provided an answer. Contamination by oil of the Antarctic marine environment including applicable conventions has been discussed at the Ninth, Tenth and Eleventh Consultative Meetings. At the Eleventh Consultative Meeting, it was concluded that the application of provisions contained in existing international agreements for prevention of pollution at sea were for the time being adequate — a practical and non-prejudical arrangement.[39]

---

[35] Protocol Relating to the 1973 International Convention for the Prevention of Pollution from Ships (MARPOL) (entered into force Oct. 2, 1983), 95th U. S. Congress 1st Sess. Sen. Exec. E and 96th U. S. Congress 1st Sess. Sen. Exec. C, Article 1 (1). MARPOL superceded the International Convention for the Prevention of Pollution of the Sea by Oil, 1954, as amended, for Parties to that Convention, Article 9 (1).

[36] *Loc. cit.*, Article 2 (4). It does not apply to warships or other State vessels solely on government non-commercial service, Article 3 (3).

[37] MARPOL also has three optional Annexes, none of which are in force, on packaged harmful substances, sewage and garbage. The latter, Annex V, is close to entry into force and would address the problem of plastic marine debris.

[38] *Loc. cit.*, Annex I, Regulation 1 (9) and Annex II, Regulation 1 (4).

[39] ATCM 11 Report, Para. 15. See also *W. M. Bush* (ed.), Antarctica and International Law, vols. I—III, London *et al.* 1982, vol. I, 434—450 (438).

It may be noted that Antarctic waters are not considered as a special area requiring special measures for purposes of MARPOL (*e. g.*, more stringent discharge requirements) and such designation by the IMO, in consultation with the Treaty Parties, could be a future consideration. In this regard, the IMO presently is considering the subject of particularly sensitive areas and may have a role in the future with respect to marine specially protected areas identified under the Antarctic Treaty.

MARPOL also contains general provisions on reporting incidents involving a discharge of oil or noxious liquid substance, or harmful packaged materials resulting from damage to the ship or in excess of that authorized.[40] The master of a vessel is to report to the nearest coastal state.[41] Of course, there is no recognized coastal State in Antarctica, and a question could be raised as to whether to simply notify a state closest to the region. Setting aside legal precision, logic would seem to indicate that rather than saying there is no obligation to report, the master should attempt to report, to the nearest Antarctic station and elsewhere.

Overall, it would seem that it is in the interest of the Antarctic Treaty Parties to see the effective application of MARPOL by vessels operating in Antarctic waters as it represents the most important contribution to date in protecting the marine environment from pollution from ships.

The 1972 Convention on the Prevention of Marine Pollution by Dumping of Wastes and other Matter (LDC) establishes the global rules regulating ocean dumping (including ocean incineration). The LDC applies to deliberate dumping by vessels, aircraft platforms or other man-made structures in all marine waters other than international waters of states.[42] The LDC bans the dumping of certain substances and limits the dumping of others, with all allowed dumping to be regulated by a system of permits.[43] Each Party is required to issue permits for waste intended for dumping when loaded in its territory, or loaded by a vessel or aircraft registered in its territory, or flying its flag when the loading occurs in the territory of a non-party.[44] It is also required to apply the measures necessary to implement the LDC to all vessels and aircraft registered in its territory or flying its flag.[45]

---

[40] *Loc. cit.*, (note 35), Article 8, and Protocol I, Article II (1).

[41] *Loc. cit.*, Protocol I, V (1).

[42] Convention on the Prevention of Marine Pollution by Dumping of Wastes and other Matter (entered into force Aug. 30, 1975), UNTS 1046, 120, TIAS 8165. See Article III.

[43] *Loc. cit.*, Articles IV and VI, and Annexes I and II.

[44] *Loc. cit.*, Article VI, 2.

[45] *Loc cit.*, Article VII, 1. Vessels entitled to sovereign immunity are excluded pursuant to Article VII, 4.

It is quite clear that dumping at sea, as defined by the LDC, includes Antarctic waters. It should also be clear that any waste leaving the territory of a Party to the LDC, outside the area of application of the Antarctic Treaty, or for any vessel of a Party to the LDC for dumping in Antarctic waters would be covered by the LDC. What may be questioned is whether the LDC applies to loading in Antarctica for disposal in Antarctic waters or elsewhere.[46] For a Non-claimant, such application would have to flow from the obligation to apply the LDC to its vessels and aircraft. The LDC itself does not address the question as to whether the flag State Party should, or may, also be responsible for issuing a permit if there is no loading state at all, an issue not limited to Antarctica in light of possible at-sea transfers. It would seem to further the purposes of the LDC (and protection of the Antarctic marine environment) if an interpretation were made that the flag state had an obligation to apply the LDC in such a situation.

The 1969 International Convention Relating to Intervention on the High Seas in cases of Oil Pollution Casualties and its 1973 Protocol concerning substances other than oil codify the principle that Parties may take measures on the high seas "... to prevent, mitigate, or eliminate grave and imminent danger to their coastline or related interests from pollution or threat of pollution of the sea by oil (or other substances) following upon a maritime casualty ... which may reasonably be expected to result in major harmful consequences."[47] Related interests for purposes of the Convention and Protocol are defined as directly affected or threatened interests of a coastal state, such as maritime activities including fisheries, tourist attractions and conservation of living marine resources and wildlife.[48] As such, a Non-claimant would not regard the Convention and Protocol *per se* to be applicable in the area of application of the Antarctic Treaty, in that they do not recognize any coastal states therein. An incident arising in that area whose effects were upon a State outside could be cognizable. I would imagine, however, that if there were a serious maritime casualty in the area of

---

[46] The Code of Conduct for Antarctic Expeditions and Station Activities, Annexed to Recomendation VIII—11, provides for disposal at sea for non-combustible solid wastes and ash from wood and paper products, 1. (a) (i) and (iii), see: *Bush* (note 39), 325.

[47] International Convention Relating to Intervention on the High Seas in Cases of Oil Pollution Casualties (entered into force May 6, 1975), in UNJYB (1969) 166, TIAS 8068; Protocol Relating to Intervention on the High Seas in Cases of Pollution by Substances other than Oil (entered into force March 30, 1983), in: UNJYB (1973) 91, TIAS 10561. See Article I. 1. The Convention and Protocol do not apply to warships or other ships owned or operated by a State being used for government, non-commercial service, Article I, 2 — nor do they apply to any device engaged in seabed exploration and exploitation, Article II, 2. (b).

[48] *Loc. cit.*, Article II, 4.

application of the Antarctic Treaty, posing serious threats to the Antarctic environment, a way would be found to take the appropriate action by those most able, without recognition of a coastal state.

The IMO 1969 International Convention on Civil Liability for Oil Pollution Damage (CLC) and 1971 International Convention on the Establishment of an International Fund for Compensation for Oil Pollution Damage (FUND) establish an international system of liability and compensation for oil pollution damage from ships.[49] In that the Conventions apply only to oil pollution damage caused on the territory or territorial sea of a Party, and to measures to prevent such damage, there can be no consensus that they would be applicable to an incident whose impacts were confined solely to the Antarctic coast.[50] As such, the CLC mechanisms for the presentment and adjudication of claims and enforcement of judgments could not work, except possibly between two Claimants. Moreover, even in that case, any attempt to present a claim for compensation to the FUND in the event, for example, it exceeds the limits of the CLC, would not be cognizable by Non-claimant members of the FUND. Thus, the CLC and FUND Conventions only agreed that an application could be to an incident in the area of application of the Antarctic Treaty, whose impact is in a territorial sea and territory outside the area.[51]

V. Maritime

The 1974 International Convention for the Safety of Life at Sea, as modified by its 1978 Protocol (SOLAS) is intended to promote safety of life at sea by ensuring that a ship is fit for the service for which it is intended.[52] Except as otherwise provided, SOLA's Regulations apply only to ships engaged on international voyages.[53] An international voyage is defined as a voyage from a country to which SOLAS applies to a port outside that country or conversely.[54] There could be a question as to whether a station in Antarctica qualifies as a "port," and how

[49] International Convention on Civil Liability for Oil Pollution Damage (entered into force June 19, 1975), UNTS 973, 3; International Convention on the Establishment of an International Fund for Compensation for Oil Pollution Damage (entered into force Oct. 16, 1978), in: UNJYB (1971), 103.

[50] *Loc. cit.*, Articles II and III, 1.

[51] The 1984 Protocols to the CLC and Fund Conventions, which are not in force, would extend their application to the EEZ of a Party, Articles 3 (a) and 4 (a) respectively, IMO Doc. Leg/CONF. 6/66 and IMO Doc. Leg/CONF. 6/67.

[52] Protocol Relating to the 1974 International Convention for the Safety of Life at Sea (entered into force May 1, 1981), TIAS 10009; Convention for the Safety of Life at Sea (entered into force May 25, 1980), TIAS 9700.

[53] *Loc. cit.*, Chapter I, Regulation 1 (a). Except as provided otherwise, the Regulations do not apply to warships nor fishing vessels, Chapter I, Regulation 3 (a) (i) and (iv).

[54] *Loc. cit.*, Capter I, Regulation 2 (d).

SOLAS should be applied to a vessel normally sailing straight from a Party to SOLAS to a destination in Antarctica. However, to the extent that a vessel stops in other ports along the way, SOLAS would be fully applicable.

In general, SOLAS sets forth standards for construction, stability, machines, fire protection, life saving, communications carriage of dangerous goods, surveys and certification of vessels and safety of navigation. In this regard, the Regulations of particular relevance to Antarctic waters are in Chapter V on Safety of Navigation. It applies to all vessels unless otherwise excluded, and this would include fishing vessels.[55] A master of a ship meeting dangerous ice or subfreezing temperatures associated with gale force winds causing severe ice conditions on board is required to communicate such information to ships in the vicinity and to the first point on the coast he can communicate with.[56] Each Party receiving such information is to provide it to other Governments.[57] Chapter V also provides for Parties to encourage the collection of meteorological data at sea in order to aid navigation and to cooperate in issuing weather bulletins by radio.[58] These provisions are particularly important in Antarctic waters.

Finally, the Chapter recognizes the paramount role of the IMO in establishing measures on routing and areas to be avoided, something the Antarctic Treaty Parties may wish to pursue in the future with IMO if shipping increases.[59]

The 1972 Convention on the International Regulations for Preventing Collisions at Sea, or COLREGS is yet another maritime agreement whose applicability would extend to Antarctic waters.[60] The rules apply to all vessels upon the high seas and in all waters connected therewith which are navigable by seagoing vessels.[61] The regulations set forth detailed rules relating to operation of vessels, including safe speeds, rights of way, actions to avoid collisions, lighting, signaling, fishing vessels and provision for traffic separation schemes.[62] Thus, fishing vessels covered by CCAMLR and other logistic support vessels in Antarctica would apply the regulations just as they would elsewhere.

---

[55] *Loc. cit.*, Chapter V, Regulation 1.

[56] *Loc. cit.*, Regulation 2 (a) and 3 (a) and (e).

[57] *Loc. cit.*, Regulation 2 (b).

[58] *Loc. cit.*, Regulation 4.

[59] *Loc. cit.*, Regulation 8. The Chapter also sets up a North Atlantic ice patrol which indicates the negotiators had that part of the world in mind, but Antarctica is not excluded.

[60] Convention on the International Regulations for Preventing Collisions at Sea (entered into force July 15, 1977), TIAS 8587.

[61] *Loc. cit.*, Rule 1 (a).

[62] *Loc. cit.*, see *inter alia*, Article 6.

The 1976 Convention on the International Maritime Satellite Organization (INMARSAT) and its Operating Agreement, is directly relevant to Antarctica.[63] INMARSAT, a commercial body, was set up to make provision for the space segment necessary for improving maritime communications and seeks to serve all areas where there is a need for such communications.[64] The Convention provides that the space segment will be open to ships of all nations without discrimination, to earth stations or structures operating in the marine environment on a case-by-case basis authorized by the Council, and to earth stations on land, located on "land territory" under the jurisdiction of a Party, as authorized by the Council, which must be wholly owned by Parties or entities subject to their jurisdiction.[65] INMARSAT has provided an invaluable service in Antarctica, both on land and at sea, including Antarctic stations, and for which the above language has apparently not posed a problem.

The 1979 International Convention on Maritime Search and Rescue (SAR Convention) is designed to establish an international maritime search and rescue plan and provides a multilateral framework for search and rescue service for world shipping.[66] Many of the Convention's provisions are defined in terms of search and rescue around the coast of States Parties. As such, there would be no consensus application of these provisions in Antarctica. However, a number of provisions are relevant, including the basic operational framework, and could be used by the Antarctic Treaty Parties.[67]

A search and rescue region is defined as an area of defined dimension within which search and rescue services are provided.[68] It is further provided that each search and rescue region shall be established by agreement among the Parties concerned, and that if agreement is not reached by the Parties concerned they shall endeavor to reach agreement on appropriate arrangements for equivalent coordination of search and rescue in the area.[69]

It would seem open to the Antarctic Treaty Consultative Parties, most of whom are Parties to the SAR Convention, including all Claimants, to draw from the SAR Convention in a non-prejudical way and to identi-

[63] Convention on the International Maritime Satellite Organization (entered into force July 16, 1979), TIAS 9605 and its Operating Agreement, TIAS 9605, ILM 15, 233.

[64] *Loc. cit.*, Article 3.

[65] *Loc. cit.*, Article 7.

[66] International Convention on Maritime Search and Rescue (entered into force June 22, 1985), IMCO, London (1979), Sales No. 79.07.E.

[67] See *e. g., loc. cit.*, Annex, 2.1.1.

[68] *Loc. cit.*, Annex 1.3. 1.

[69] *Loc. cit.*, Annex 2.1.4. and 2.1.5.

fy SAR regions, to establish operational modalities following the procedures for search and rescue and coordination contained in the Annex to the Convention and to notify the Secretary General of the IMO.[70]

The 1910 Convention for the Unification of Certain Rules with Respect to Assistance and Salvage at Sea (the Salvage Convention) provides rules on assistance and salvage of seagoing vessels in danger, and services, in whatever waters the services have been rendered.[71] The Convention establishes the basis for remuneration, including apportionment, and excludes recompense from persons who are rescued and sets forth how salvage actions are to be maintained.[72] A key provision is that every master is bound, so far as he can do so without serious danger to his vessel's crew and passengers, to render assistance to anyone found at sea in danger of being lost.[73] In the event of an emergency in Antarctic waters, or a situation in which salvage was required, the Convention would provide a basis for such actions.

The 1884 Convention on the Protection of Submarine Cables might also theoretically apply to Antarctic waters if a cable was laid from Antarctica to a state outside the region.[74] Article 1 of the Convention provides that it shall be applicable outside territorial waters to all legally established submarine cables landed by a Party. The Convention sets forth a number of provisions designed to protect the cables and vessels laying them as well as establishes liability for damage thereto.

In passing, I might also note some International Labour Organisation Conventions that would be applicable to vessels engaged in maritime navigation in Antarctic Waters: No. 53 concerning the Minimum Requirement of Professional Capacity for Masters and Officers on Board Merchant Ships, No. 55 concerning the Liability of the Shipowner in case of Sickness, Injury or Death of Seamen and No. 58 on fixing the Minimum Age for the Admission of Children to Employment at Sea.[75]

VI. Nuclear

In that the Antarctic Treaty addresses things nuclear, other than explosions, and is an issue that has been discussed in Treaty meetings, I have included a number of nuclear agreements.

[70] The Secretary General is the repository of information on SAR Conventions regions and plans and is responsible for transmitting that information to other parties, *loc. cit.*, Annex 2.1.2., 2.1.3. and 2.1.6.

[71] Entered into force March 1, 1913, Bevans 1, 780. The Convention does not apply to warships or to Government ships exclusively on public service, Article 13.

[72] *Loc. cit.*, Articles 2 to 10.

[73] *Loc. cit.*, Article 11.

[74] Convention for the Protection of Submarine Cables (in force May 1, 1888) Bevans 1, 89.

[75] UNTS 15, 35; UNTS 40, 153, 169; UNTS 40, 205. The cited Conventions all exclude warships.

To the extent that nuclear power (other than ships propulsion) or nuclear fuel is used in or nuclear materials stored in Antarctica, the 1963 Vienna Convention on Civil Liability for Nuclear Damage could be applicable.[76] (One would expect IAEA standards would also be applicable.) The Vienna Convention provides for liability of an operator of a nuclear facility without regard to fault, subject to certain defenses and limits, for nuclear damage not linked to territory and establishes rules for financial responsibility and seeking compensation. The "Installation State," with respect to a nuclear installation, is the party in whose territory the installation is situated "or, if it is not situated within the territory of any State the ... Party by which or under the authority of which the nuclear installation is operated."[77] As such, an Installation State may be covered by the Convention without reference to territory. A nuclear installation is defined as a nuclear reactor (other than for propulsion at sea) and any nuclear material storage facility.[78] Nuclear damage and incident are defined in such a way as could cover harm to humans and property in Antarctica.[79]

Jurisdiction over actions are to be brought before the courts of the Installation State where the incident occurred outside the territory of any Contracting Party (*e. g.*, in Antarctica?).[80] While the possible employment of this Convention in Antarctica may seem remote, it would seem that it is something that might be taken into account in the consideration of any use of nuclear power in Antarctica.

To this end, Article 1 of the IABA Notification Convention applies to any accident involving facilities or activities of a Party or natural or juridical person under its jurisdiction or control from which a release of radioactive material occurs or is likely to occur, and which has resulted or may result in an "international transboundary" release that could be of radiological safety significance for another state. The Convention defines facilities and activities as including any nuclear reactor "wherever located," the transport and storage of nuclear fuels or radioactive wastes and the use or storage of radioisotopes for scientific and research purposes.[81] The Convention provides for notification to the IAEA and those states which are or may be physically affected by the accident and for the type of information to be transmitted.[82] The reference to "international transboundary" release and to impacts on other states

---

76 Entered into force Nov. 12, 1977, UNTS 1063, 265.

77 *Loc. cit.*, Article I, d.

78 *Loc. cit.*, Article I, j.

79 *Loc. cit.*, see Article I, k and l.

80 *Loc. cit.*, Article XI, 2.

81 IAEA Conventions on Early Notification of Nuclear Accident and on Assistance in the Case of a Nuclear Accident or Radiological Emergency, ILM 25 (1986), 1369; Article 1, 2.

82 *Loc. cit.*, Articles 2 and 5.

might lead to a conclusion that the Convention would only be applicable to an accident in Antarctica having an effect on a state outside, as the impacts are qualified as territorial. However, as a practical matter, it might be argued that there should be a notification to other states which have stations in Antarctica and which might be affected.

The Assistance Convention provides mechanisms for a state to request assistance from another in the event of a nuclear accident. Direction and control of such assistance, however, is linked to the territory of the requesting and assisting states unless otherwise agreed.[83] If such states were able to agree without prejudice to any question of territorial claims it is conceivable that the Convention could be activated for impacts only in Antarctica, although the way it is drafted in terms of actions internal to a state, might make this an odd reading of the Convention.

VII. Outer Space

Unlikely as it may seem, there are a number of outer space-related agreements that at least in principle, if not normal practice, could be applicable to Antarctica.

The 1968 Agreement on the Rescue of Astronauts, the Return of Astronauts and the Return of Objects Launched into Outer Space requires that each Party which receives information or discovers that astronauts have made an emergency, unintended landing "... in territory under its jurisdiction or *on the high seas or in any other place not under the jurisdiction of any State* ..." immediately notify the launching authority, or if it cannot notify it, publicize the incident and notify the Secretary-General of the United Nations (emphasis added).[84] In addition, Parties in a position to do so are to extend assistance in search and rescue operations to such astronauts.[85] The Agreement requires the safe and prompt return of astronauts found "... on the high seas or in any other place not under the jurisdiction of any State ..." (or landing in territory under the jurisdiction of a Party).[86] Finally, the Agreement provides that a Party receiving information or discovering a space object having returned to earth "... in territory under its jurisdiction or on the high seas or in any other place not under the jurisdiction of any State ..." must notify the launching authority and the Secretary-General of the United Nations and upon request take steps to assist in return of the object.[87]

Although it may be unlikely that an astronaut would make an unintended landing in the area of application of the Antarctic Treaty, if it

[83] *Loc. cit.*, see Article 3.
[84] Entered into force Dec. 3, 1968; UNTS 672, 119; Article 1.
[85] *Loc. cit.*, Article 3.
[86] *Loc. cit.*, Article 5.
[87] *Ibid.*

occurred, the Agreement would be applicable. (Of course, unless the landing was in the unclaimed area or clearly on the marine areas beyond which any Claimant might claim jurisdiction, there could be a dispute over who had the obligation, or who should undertake the obligations under the Agreement.)

In theory, the 1972 Convention on International Liability for Damage Caused by Space Objects could also be applicable to Antarctica.[88] The Convention provides that a launching State is absolutely liable to pay compensation for damage caused by its object "... on the surface of the earth or to aircraft in flight."[89] The surface of the earth is not defined, but there appears to be no reason that it would exclude damage caused by a space object in the area of application of the Antarctic Treaty as well as to aircraft flying there. However, there would be a question of who might present a claim for damage to Antarctica itself, as compared with physical property such as a research station.

The 1976 Convention on the Registration of Objects Launched into Space would also appear to be applicable to Antarctica.[90] A launching state, defined as a state which launches, or procures the launching of a space object, or from whose facility an object is launched, has an obligation to register the object with the Secretary-General of the United Nations. It would seem that a launch of a space object from the area of application of the Antarctic Treaty would be covered by the Convention.[91]

VIII. Law of the Sea

No survey of international agreements would be complete without mentioning the 1982 UN Convention on the Law of the Sea, which although not in force, generally reflects customary international law outside of its deep seabed provisions, and which contains a number of provisions which are applicable to Antarctic waters just as elsewhere.[92] I do not intend to deal with the question of the relevance of the deep seabed mining provisions of the Law of the Sea Convention to Antarctica, a matter I spent some time on last year in a paper I presented at the Law of the Sea Institute. I also will not spend time on the 1958 Geneva Conventions on the High Seas and on the Fishing and Conservation of Living Resources of the High Seas, applicable though they are to the high seas off Antarctica, as they are basically reflected in the

---

[88] Entered into force Sept. 1, 1972; UNTS 961, 187.
[89] *Loc. cit.*, Article II.
[90] Entered into force Sept. 15, 1976; UNTS 1008, 15.
[91] *Loc. cit.*, see Articles I, (a) and (b), II, III and IV.
[92] UN Doc. A/CONF. 62/122, ILM 21, 1261.

Law of the Sea Convention.[93]. Their relevant provisions of course, such as freedom of the high seas, (as referred to in Article VI of the Antarctic Treaty) due regard for others, suppression of piracy, rendering of assistance at sea, prevention of pollution and cooperation on conservation of living resources, are applicable to the high seas off Antarctica.

Part VII of the 1982 Convention, on the high seas, contains many relevant provisions. It confirms the freedom of the high seas, including navigation and overflight (Article 87), that the high seas must be used for peaceful purposes (Article 89), identifies the duties of the flag states (Article 94), contains the obligation of masters to render assistance Article 98), and confirms the duty to repress piracy and sppress traffic in illicit drugs (Article 100 and 107). It provides for the right to fish on the high seas and measures for cooperation in the conservation of such fisheries (Articles 116 to 118) as reflected by CCAMLR.

Part XII sets forth important provisions calling for states to protect the marine environment and threatened ecosystems and habitants (Article 194), to notify others in case of possible damage to the marine environment (Article 191), for monitoring of and assessment of projects potentially affecting the marine environment (Articles 204 and 206) and measures for the prevention of pollution of the marine environment by land-based sources, dumping and from ships (Articles 207 to 211) and liability for damage to the marine environment (Article 235). The Convention also contains in Part XIII a number of provisions on marine scientific research whose application to Antarctic waters depends on one's juridical point-of-view, but the principle of promoting such research is without question.

The Treaty Parties have thus far taken limited steps (setting aside conservation of Antarctic marine resources) with respect to the Antarctic marine environment other than some specially protected areas with a partial marine component and Article VI, para. 3 of the Agreed Measures calling for steps to be taken to alleviate pollution of waters adjacent to the Antarctic coast and ice shelves. Thus, the 1982 Convention and the other IMO agreements I referred to previously provides valuable rules for protection of the Antarctic marine environment. To this end, the CCAMLR Commission at its fifth meeting called upon members to adhere to the LDC and MARPOL in recognition of the role they play in addressing the problem of marine debris that might affect Antarctic waters. (In addition, at their ninth meeting, the LDC Parties called for cooperation with other competent bodies on the problem of marine debris which was extended to include the CCAMLR Commission.)

---

[93] Convention on the High Seas (entered into force Sept. 30, 1962), UNTS 450, 82 and Convention on Fishing and Conservation of the Living Resources of the High Seas (entered into force March 20, 1966), UNTS 559, 285.

IX. Intergovernmental Organizations

I conclude my survey with intergovernmental organizations that have been or that may be in the future concerned with Antarctica. These organizations of course include those that the Antarctic Treaty Parties have already recognized as having an interest in Antarctica and with whom they have already cooperated. I have already made reference to the UN and the IWC.

The Food and Agriculture Organization (FAO), established by its 1945 Constitution, has had an active interest in Antarctic fisheries.[94] A major purpose of the FAO is to improve food production and distribution, thereby improving nutrition.[95] Article I of the FAO Constitution lists as its first function the collection, analysis, interpretation and dissemination of information relating to food and agriculture.[96] Agriculture is defined therein as including "fisheries and marine products."[97] The Constitution charges FAO to promote and recommend international action relating, *inter alia*, to scientific, technological and economic research relating to agriculture, the conservation of natural resources and improvement of agricultural production and the improvement of the processing, marketing and distribution of agricultural products.[98]

The FAO has a long and active role in fisheries development, such as collection of statistics, operating through its regional fisheries commissions and its Fisheries Committee.[99] Taking into account its purpose and functions, it is logical that FAO has taken an interest in Antarctic fisheries matters consistent with its mandate.

While I will not go into the details, this interest led FAO in the 1970's to consider a role in the question of exploitation of the living resources of the Southern Oceans prior to conclusion of CCAMLR. Recognition of FAO's important role in fisheries management led to its invitation to the 1980 diplomatic conference adopting CCAMLR and to a specific reference in the Convention calling for cooperation by the CCAMLR Commission with FAO.[100] FAO has since attended meetings of the Commission as an observer. It has actively collaborated with the Commission on Antarctic fisheries identification, research, and provision of information.

---

[94] The Constitution of the FAO (Bevans 3, 1288, reprinted in: AJIL 40, Supp. 76) has been subject to a number of technical amendments, see TIAS 8982.

[95] *Loc. cit.*, Preamble.

[96] *Loc. cit.*, Paragraph 1.

[97] *Ibid.*

[98] *Loc. cit.*, Article I, 2.

[99] *Loc. cit.*, Articles V and VI, 6. (The waters off Antarctica are in FAO's Yearbook of Fishery Statistics.)

[100] *Loc. cit.*, Article XXIII, 2.

I shall not say a great deal about these two organizations, the World Meteorological Organization (WMO) and the International Telecommunications Union (ITU) as their cooperation with the Antarctic Treaty Parties has been fairly well documented in Treaty reports. The WMO established by the Convention thereon of 1947 (as amended) has as its basic purposes the facilitation of worldwide cooperation in the establishment of networks of stations for making meteorological observations, the promotion of systems for rapid exchange of meteorological information, standardization of meteorological observation and operational hydrography and the furtherance of the application of meteorology for aviation and shipping.[101] As such the WMO has a world-wide mandate which includes Antarctica. Its importance, both for disseminating meteorological information generally and for purposes of contributing to Antarctic telecommunications requirements, were recognized early on by the Antarctic Treaty Parties. There has been a long history of close cooperation between them and the WMO, including its participation in the Antarctic Treaty Meetings of Experts on Antarctic Telecommunications.

The WMO has established an Executive Council Working Group on Antarctic Meteorology and includes Antarctica as a region in its World Weather Watch (WWW). The Working Group has addressed the requirement for collecting meteorology observations in Antarctica, and how they should be reported, which includes cooperation with the ITU. The WMO is involved in basic climate research including Antarctica, and has worked with the International Oceanographic Commission (IOC) on ocean data collection and ocean services in Antarctic waters.

The ITU, established and governed most recently by the 1982 Nairobi Convention, has as its basic purposes the extension of international cooperation in improving telecommunications, improving the efficiency of telecommunication services, the responsibility to allocate the radio frequency spectrum and register assignments to avoid harmful interference and to improve its use, the coordination of efforts to harmonize development of telecommunication facilities and promotion of the adoption of measures for ensuring safety of life through cooperation of telecommunications services.[102]

As such, the ITU and its work is relevant to the operational side of Antarctic telecommunications. It was involved with the Antarctic telecommunication experts meeting that I mentioned previously, and contributes to WMO's Global Telecommunications System component of WWW. Among other things relevant recommendations of the ITUs

[101] Constitution of the WMO (UNTS 77, 143), Article 2.

[102] Entered into force Jan. 1, 1982, 99th U. S. Congress, 1st Sess., Treaty Doc. 99-6.

International Consultative Committee and the International Telegraph and Telephone Consultative Committee, as well as the 1979 Radio Regulations, would be taken into account in Antarctic communication.[103]

The International Oceanographic Commission of UNESCO is another intergovernmental organization concerned with Antarctica. Pursuant to its Statutes, a major purpose of the IOC is to promote scientific investigation in order to learn more about the oceans and their resources.[104] Its functions include the development of programs related to scientific investigation of the ocean and related services and the promotion of the exchange of oceanographic data.[105] In this regard, in 1967 the IOC established the Program Group for the Southern Ocean, designed to develop and coordinate oceanographic research programs in the region and plans for a gradual evolution of a comprehensive study of the region.[106] (I have previously noted its cooperation with WMO.) In addition, the IOC attented the 1980 CCAMLR diplomatic conference and continues to cooperate with the Commission and attend meetings as an observer.

As another speaker is to address air traffic in Antarctica, I shall limit my remarks on the Convention on International Civil Aviation (as amended) which established the International Civil Aviation Organization (ICAO).[107] Recently SCAR and its Logistics Working Group have begun to look into air safety and the role of ICAO standards in cooperation with ICAO. The subject of air safety is on the agenda of the Fourteenth Consultative Meeting.

ICAO is the international body responsible for adopting and recommending international standards and recommended practices and procedures concerning safety and efficiency of air navigation. Such standards and practices, adopted as annexes to the Convention, have been established for such matters as air traffic services and search and rescue.[108] Regional air navigation agreements or plans have been promulgated establishing responsibilities in identified areas for purposes of implementing the standards and procedures such as for search and rescue, air traffic control and meteorological services, including the high seas and areas of undetermined sovereignty.[109] Regional plans have identified flight information and SAR regions that extend into Antarctica. It should be noted that publication of such plans and charts represent no position

[103] See for example, Proposal 5, 2. of the report of the Second Telecommunication Experts Meeting (Buenos Aires, Sept. 1—12, 1969) calling for Treaty Parties to apply the relevant recommendations.

[104] IOC Manual, Article 1.

[105] *Loc. cit.*, Article 2.

[106] IOC Resolution V-5.

[107] Entered into force May 1, 1942; UNTS 161, 229; as amended UNTS 1008, 213.

[108] *Loc. cit.*, see for example Annexes 11 and 12.

[109] *Loc. cit.*, Annex 12.2.1.1.

on the legal status of territory. Overall, to the extent air traffic in Antarctica increases, it seems worthwhile that there be a future examination of the relationship between the Treaty and ICAO as has been initiated, with a view in particular to considering how and by whom services are to be provided.[110]

I might point out that as far back as 1969, the Report of the Second Antarctic Treaty Meeting of Experts on Telecommunications proposed that radio aids to air navigation in Antarctica be provided to compatible standards available from ICAO and that when air navigation standards are required and the ICAO standards are applicable, they be used in Antarctica.[111]

The International Maritime Organization, formed by the 1948 Convention thereon, is the global body concerned with all aspects of shipping.[112] A significant part of the purposes of the IMO is to encourage the general adoption of the highest practicable standards in matters concerning maritime safety, the prevention and control of marine pollution from ships and the consideration of matters concerning effects of shipping on the marine environment as referred to it by organs or specialized agencies of the UN or by other intergovernmental organizations.[113] Under its auspices, numerous agreements and measures have been developed promoting these ends, many of which I have cited.

Thus far, it does not appear that the IMO and the Antarctic Treaty Parties have established a real working relationship. Its purposes and responsibilities are certainly relevant to Antarctic waters and agreements and measures developed under its auspices may be an important contribution to protection of the Antarctic marine environment. It may be likely that the future will see increased cooperation between the Treaties Parties (possibly through a minerals convention) and the IMO, including on matters such as the problem of marine debris.

The World Health Organization, established by its Constitution of 1946, has as its primary objective the attainment by all peoples of the highest possible level of health.[114] Among its functions, the WHO is to promote and conduct research in the field of health, provide information and assistance in the field of health, to develop, establish and promote international standards with respect to food and biological

---

[110] See the 1985 Regional Plan for the Caribbean and South America, ICAO 8733/13.

[111] Proposal 9, reprinted in: *Bush* (note 39), 223—224.

[112] Entered into force March 17, 1958; UNTS 289, 48. It has been amended several times.

[113] *Loc. cit.*, Articles 1 and 3.

[114] Entered into force April 7, 1948; UNTS 14, 185. The Constitution has been amended.

products, promote cooperation among scientific groups, further advancement of health and to advance work to eradicate disease.[115] Thus far, to my knowledge, the WHO has not had an active direct working relationship with the Antarctic Treaty Parties, although its activities may be relevant to protection of both the environment and human health in Antarctica and to scientific research there.

Activities under the auspices of the International Hydrographic Office (IHO) established by the 1967 Convention thereon, are also relevant to Antarctic waters.[116] The IHO is a consultation and purely technical body whose objectives, *inter alia,* are to bring about coordination of the activities of national hydrographic offices, uniformity in nautical charts and the carrying out of hydrographic surveys in order to contribute to safe navigation by improving nautical charts.[117] Under the auspices of the IHO (and the IOC) the Government of Canada has published a bathymetric chart of Antarctica and surrounding waters.[118] I know that my country has had occasion to use this chart for Antarctic Treaty-related purposes and it is a valuable piece of work.

The 1964 Constitution of the Universal Postal Union (UPU) (as amended), which established the international body governing international postal services, provides in Article 3 (b) that the jurisdiction of the UPU includes "post offices established by member countries in territories not included in the Union."[119] While it seems relatively clear that the UPU was never intended to cover Antarctica and outer space, it has been suggested in the past that this provision be interpreted so as to include those areas.[120] Though no such action has been taken to date, it is conceivable that in the future there may be efforts to bring Antarctic post offices under the purview of the UPU. It may be noted that Recommendation I-12 called for cooperation in distributing mail in Antarctica and the Report of the First Consultative Meeting made reference to communicating with the UPU.[121] The issue does not appear to have been pursued seriously since.

Finally, and last but not least, I should also mention the United Nations Environment Program (UNEP), whose mandate is to promote in-

---

[115] *Loc. cit.,* Article 1.

[116] Entered into force Sept. 22, 1970; UNTS 751, 41.

[117] *Loc. cit.,* Article II and Preamble paragraph 1. Pursuant to Articles 1 and 2 of the General Regulations, the IHO has no authority over the hydrographic office of Parties and its activities are not to include matters of international policy.

[118] See IHO General Bathymetric Chart of the Oceans (GEBCO), 5th edition 1980, reprinted 1983.

[119] Entered into force Jan. 1, 1966; UNTS 611, 7.

[120] For example, see Union Comitee 3 (General Doc. 19), 1982.

[121] Paragraph 11 (b), reprinted in: *Bush* (note 39), 127.

ternational cooperation in the environment field, to keep under review the world environment situation and to promote contribution of relevant international scientific communities to assessment of environment knowledge.[122] UNEP, a program of the General Assembly, in the past has expressed an interest in cooperating with the Treaty Parties, has worked on matters relevant to protection of the Antarctic environment and is supporting programs with an Antarctic dimension such as the World Conservation Strategy.

X. Conclusion

In researching this very broad brush survey, I was fascinated by the variety of international agreements outside the ATS that might be applicable to Antarctica in some fashion, many or most of whose negotiators probably never thought about the Antarctic implications. I hope in some small way that I have contributed to the awareness of Antarctica as a place not without law, and stimulated some interest in considering how the agreements I have cited might work in practice in Antarctica.

[122] See GA Res. 2997 XXVII, 1972, para. 2.

Effect of Article VI of the Antarctic Treaty on Scientific Research

*Patricia Birnie**

I. Introduction

1. The Meaning, Value and Relevance of Scientific Research

As one writer has said, scientific research has been established as the "currency" of Antarctic politics;[1] without the spending of that currency, however, progress cannot be made in achieving either the object and purposes of the Antarctic Treaty[2] itself or any of the measures, recommendations, and linked treaties that now compose what is known as the Antarctic Treaty "System." The effect of the relevant provisions of the 1982 United Nations Law of the Sea Convention (UNCLOS)[3] and of the developing customary law of the sea, to the extent that it is incorporating these provisions, could be, if not to stop the cheques, at least severely to curtail this expenditure, given the inter-relationship of Articles VI and IV of the Antarctic Treaty and, in turn, their relation to corresponding rights and duties of states laid down in the UNLOSC within the limits of the maritime zones included in that treaty.

2. Definition of "scientific research"

Before examining the relevant provisions of both the UNLOSC and the Antarctic Treaty, it is necessary to clarify what we mean by the term "scientific research," since neither the UNLOSC nor the various Antarctic Treaties define it, and to add to the confusion the Antarctic Treaty itself uses both the terms "scientific research" and "scientific investigation" apparently inter-changeably.[4] In his report to the General Assembly on the question of Antarctica, the UN Secretary-General assumed long-standing scientific interest in that continent on the premise

* Dr. *Patricia Birnie*, London School of Economics and Political Science, Univ. of London, U. K.

[1] *F. M. Auburn*, Antarctic Law and Politics, London 1982, 93.

[2] The Antarctic Treaty, done at Washington on 1 Dec. 1959, UNTS, vol. 402 (1961), 71.

[3] United Nations Law of the Sea Convention, done at Montego Bay, Dec. 10, 1982, I.L.M. vol. 21 (1982), 1261. UN Doc. A/CONF 62/122 (hereinafter cited as UNLOSC).

[4] *Auburn* (note 1), at 99 takes the view that the two terms may be taken to have the same meaning.

that scientific research could be broadly defined as "the pursuit of the unknown."[5] Dictionaries define each term in terms of the other, *e. g.*, "research" is defined as "a careful search, investigation, systematic investigation towards increasing the sum of knowledge;"[6] "investigation" is "the act of examining, research;"[7] "science" itself is "knowledge; knowledge ascertained by observation and experiment, critically tested, systematised and brought under general principles."[8] To maximise knowledge of the hitherto unknown aspects of Antarctic ecology and resources, and systematically to add to this store requires the maximum freedom of access and operation, particularly in the contexts of the impact of living and non-living resource exploitation.

3. *Scientific Research Requirements under the Antarctic Treaty*

In the Preamble to the Antarctic Treaty the Contracting Governments acknowledge "the substantial contribution to scientific knowledge resulting from international cooperation in scientific investigation in Antarctica" and state their conviction that

> the establishment of a firm foundation for the continuation and development of such cooperation on the basis of freedom of scientific investigation in Antarctica as applied during the International Geophysical Year accords with the interests of science and the progress of all mankind.

Substantive Articles of the Convention effect these aims. Thus, Article II provides:

> Freedom of scientific investigation in Antarctica and cooperation towards that end, as applied during the International Geophysical Year, shall continue, subject to the provisions of the present Treaty.

It will be noted, however, that this Article does not provide for unfettered freedom of scientific investigation but subjects it to other articles of the Treaty; in particular Articles III, IV, VI and IX should be noted in this connection.

Article III (1) states:

> In order to provide international cooperation in scientific investigation in Antarctica, as provided for in Article II of the present

[5] Question of Antarctica: Study requested under General Assembly Resolution 38/77; Report of the Secretary-General, A/39/583 (Part I), 31 October 1984, 79 (hereinafter: Question of Antarctica).

[6] Chambers Twentieth Century Dictionary, Revised Edition 1970, 937.

[7] *Op. cit.*, 559.

[8] *Op. cit.*, 937.

Treaty, the Contracting Parties agree that, to the greatest extent feasible and practicable:

(a) information regarding plans for scientific programs in Antarctica shall be exchanged to permit maximum economy and efficiency of operations;

(b) scientific personnel shall be exchanged in Antarctica between expeditions and stations;

(c) scientific observations and results from Antarctica shall be exchanged and made freely available.

It adds, in a second paragraph that:

2. In implementing this Article, every encouragement shall be given to the establishment of cooperative working relations with those Specialized Agencies of the United Nations and other international organizations having a scientific or technical interest in Antarctica.

It does not, however, name these organizations. It should be noted that both this provision itself and the absence of specifics may be relevant in considering the effect to the application of the UNLOSC to the Antarctic Treaty area.

Article IX (1) requires that the Consultative Parties meet, *inter alia*, to formulate, consider and recommend to their Governments, measures regarding

. . .

b) facilitation of scientific research in Antarctica;

c) facilitation of international scientific cooperation in Antarctica;

. . .

f) preservation and conservation of living resources in Antarctica.

With regard to (f), although it does not make direct reference to scientific research requirements, clearly these are of the essence of such measures.

Finally, in order to participate in the Consultative Meetings, Article IX (2) insists that during the period of participation, the Contracting Party concerned "demonstrates its interest in Antarctica by conducting substantial scientific research activity there, such as the establishment of a scientific station or the despatch of a scientific expedition." Clearly maximum freedom of research and supportive cooperation is essential to the fulfilment of this condition, especially for maintenance of the entitlement of non-Claimant states and those parties that have not yet attained Consultative Status — for reasons that will become apparent on analysis of the UNLOSC provisions' effect on Article VI, in the light of Article IV of the Antarctic Treaty. Before we look at these Articles, however, let us see how vital the role played by scientific research is throughout the burgeoning Antarctic Treaty System.

4. Scientific Research under the Agreed Measures for the Conservation of Antarctic Fauna and Flora[9]

In the Preamble to the Agreed Measures, Governments participating in the Third Consultative Meeting recognized the scientific importance of the study of Antarctic fauna and flora, their adaption to their rigorous environment and their inter-relationship with that environment, and expressed their desire by "further international collaboration within the framework of the Antarctic Treaty to promote and achieve the objectives of protection, scientific study and rational use of these fauna and flora," having regard to conservation principles developed by the Scientific Committee on Antarctica Research (SCAR),[10] a committee of the International Council of Scientific Unions (ICSU). As pointed out elsewhere, "SCAR is a planning committee, not an international organization;"[11] it is not referred to in the Antarctic Treaty itself and does not come within the scope of Article III (2), though it is open to all states actively engaged in Antarctic research, to scientists appointed by ICSU and all the international scientific unions federated to ICSU. All the ATCPs are currently members.

The Agreed Measures treat the Antarctic Treaty Area as a Special Conservation Area and to this end require, *inter alia*, that the governments concerned take appropriate measures to minimize harmful interference with the "normal" living conditions of native mammals, or birds, except under permit, which can be issued to provide, amongst other purposes, specimens for scientific study or scientific information. Areas of outstanding scientific interest that can be designated Specially Protected Areas (SPAs) are listed; governments must specially protect these SPAs to preserve their unique ecological system. So far, none of these are a marine area but there appears to be nothing, except the jurisdictional uncertainty generated in Antarctica by the UNLOSC and practice related to it, to prevent such an extension. Permits (for example, to take plants) can have effect in a SPA only if issued for a compelling scientific reason for activities that will not "jeopardise the natural

---

[9] Recommendation III-VIII, printed in: *W. M. Bush* (ed.), Antarctica and International Law, vols. 1—3, London *et al.* 1982, vol. 1, 146 *et seq.*

[10] For a succinct description of SCAR *see* Antarctica: A Continent in Transition, a collection of documents and Fact Sheets prepared by the International Institute for Environment and Development, Doc. XI, Scientific Committee on Antarctic Research; *see also Auburn* (note 1), 171—183; Question of Antarctica (note 5), 24, para. 76; *Peter Beck*, The International Politics of Antarctica, London 1986, 162—166.

[11] *Auburn* (note 1), 183.

ecological system" in the area. Obviously establishment of all these values requires detailed research and free exchange of information (provided for in Article XII).

5. *Convention for the Conservation of Antarctic Seals*[12]

The Preamble to this Treaty recalls the Agreed Measures, recognizes the need for effective conservation measures for these species, which are regarded as "an important living resource in the marine environment;" they thus, if harvested, should be regulated to maintain the optimum substainable yield. The Contracting Parties recognize that to improve scientific knowledge and put exploitation on a rational basis, "every effort should be made to encourage background and other research" on the seal populations and that SCAR is willing to carry out the required tasks. They express the desire "to promote and achieve . . . scientific study . . . and to maintain a satisfactory balance within the ecological system."

The substantive articles of the treaty permit the adoption of measures for conservation and scientific study, *inter alia*, including prescription of catches, protected and unprotected species, protected areas and other conservation measures requiring detailed scientific information and advice; indeed Article 3 (2) insists that these measures shall be based upon "the best scientific and technical evidence available" and Article 5 provides for exchange of scientific information and advice.

Contracting Parties (the Antarctic Treaty States) participating in the conference, and any states subsequently invited by consensus to accede must affirm the provisions of Article IV of the Antarctic Treaty, which are discussed later in this paper.

6. *Convention for the Conservation of Antarctic Marine Living Resources*[13]

This treaty, above all, requires the conduct of the most extensive and sophisticated scientific research since its objective is conservation of all the marine living resources within both the Antarctic Treaty area *and* the Antarctic Convergence which form part of the Antarctic marine ecosystem (Article 1) on the basis of specific principles including: prevention of decrease in size of harvested populations below the stable recruitment level; maintenance of ecological relationships between

---

[12] Convention on the Conservation of Antarctic Seals (hereinafter: Seals Convention), printed in: *Bush* (note 9), vol. 1, 248 *et seq.*

[13] Convention on the Conservation of Antarctic Marine Living Resources (hereinafter: CCAMLR), printed in: *op. cit.*, 398 *et seq.*; see also: *Rüdiger Wolfrum* (ed.), Antarctic Challenge, Berlin 1984, Annex 229 *et seq.*

harvested, dependent and related populations of these resources and restoration of those that are depleted; and prevention or minimization of changes in the marine ecosystem which are not potentially reversible over twenty to thirty years taking account of various complex scientific factors.

The Contracting Parties, in the Preamble, recognize the importance of safeguarding the environment and protecting the integrity of the ecosystem in "the seas surrounding Antarctica" (which are defined on an ecological basis to include all waters within the Antarctic Convergence) and the need "to increase knowledge of the Antarctic marine ecosystem" in order to base harvesting decisions on sound scientific information. Their belief is that this calls for international cooperation "with due regard to the Antarctic Treaty" and the active involvement of all states engaged in harvesting or research in the area; they also recognize the need to establish suitable machinery for promoting required measures and scientific studies. They therefore establish a Commission with wide powers to facilitate research into the marine ecosystem, collect and analyse data and promulgate a variety of conservation measures on the basis of "the best scientific advice available" (Article IX).

Contracting Parties which are not parties to the Antarctic Treaty acknowledge the special obligations and responsibilities of its parties for protection of the Antarctic environment and all parties also are bound by Articles IV and VI of that Treaty.

7. *Draft on Antarctic Mineral Resources*

It is not possible to say at this stage precisely what terms any eventual convention on mineral resources will contain but on the basis of drafts available to date it seems likely that it too will note, *inter alia*, the scientific and ecological and even possibly the "wilderness" value of Antarctica; that the regime must take full account of environmental protection and independent ecosystems, and that activities be compatible with the scientific investigation permitted under the Antarctic Treaty. To this end, the special responsibility in the area of Parties to the Antarctic Treaty will again have to be recognized by all parties to the new convention, whether or not they are parties to the former, and Article IV will again be incorporated as in the CCAMLR. In fact, prior adherence to the Antarctic Treaty will probably be required as a prerequisite to accession. The Convention will be regarded as an integral part of the Antarctic Treaty System and will provide means for assessing the environmental impact of resource activities, and their compatibility with the Agreed Measures and CCAMLR as well as objectives of the Convention itself. Protection of the ecosystem and respect for scientific values are also likely to be included, with provision made for cooperation with the parties to the related treaties and relevant international organizations and for ecosystem monitoring and the establishment of a Commission, aided by a Scientific, Technical and Environmental Advisory Committee.

Again, considerable scientific knowledge and investigation will be required to provide a basis for decisions on exploitation, but in this case the required research may be difficult to distinguish from the commercial activity at which it is aimed and is likely, as we shall see, to be particularly affected by the relevant provisions of the UNLOSC, if applicable.

Of particular relevance, also, will be the area of application of any Minerals Convention, which is likely to comprehend not only the Antarctic land territory and ice shelves but the seabed and subsoil of adjacent submarine areas, though it is, as yet, unclear how these will be designated — as continental shelves, offshore areas, or both, because of the jurisdictional ambiguities generated in Antarctica by the UNCLOS negotiations.

Scientific research will be indispensable, not only to location of the minerals and identification and evaluation of them but also to assessing the impact of their exploration and exploitation on the marine ecosystem. IUCN, however, has noted in a Resolution on Antarctica "the importance of Antarctica and its continental shelf and seabed for the world as a whole, particularly in maintaining the stability of the global marine environmental atmosphere . . . ."

Having established the nature and importance of scientific research, not only under the Antarctic Treaty itself but to related regimes which are so closely and specifically linked to the original Treaty, let us now look at Articles IV and VI to ascertain why these are so crucial to the System and to evaluate the impact of the developments in the law of the sea deriving from the UNLOSC upon that System.

II. Article VI of the Antarctic Treaty: Its Relation to the Law of the Sea

Article VI, with which this paper is concerned, states:

> The provisions of the present Treaty shall apply to the area south of 60° south latitude, including all the ice shelves, but nothing in the present Treaty shall prejudice or in any way affect the rights, or the exercise of the rights, of any State under international law with regard to the high seas in that area.

The deliberate ambiguities latent in this important Article have often been discussed;[14] they conceal the different views of Parties about the

[14] *See* for example: *Alfred van der Essen*, The Application of the Law of the

area of application, which are closely related to Article IV and its ambiguities concerning recognition and non-recognition of territorial claims in the area, ambiguities which themselves represent the disguising of significant disagreement. The 60° S boundary represented the outer limit of the claims made by 1959. The relationship derives from the fact that under the international law of the sea, whether based on the four 1958 UN Conventions on the Law of the Sea, on the 1982 UNLOSC, or on customary international law, rights to maritime areas are exclusively referred to as pertaining to the coastal state. Coastal states, under the current law of the sea, are *ipso facto* entitled to a belt of territorial sea of up to 12 miles measured from their baselines, which arguably may either be drawn in the case of ice-covered areas from the outer edge of ice-shelves, or from normal baselines following the low-water mark on the landbased shore, or, in certain special circumstances, from straight baselines, taking in fringing islands or drawn across deep coastal indentations and other features.[15] The 1958 Conventions make no specific reference to the use of ice shelves as base points, nor do they refer to the legal status of such shelves as land or sea regimes. Though germane to the application of the new LOS relating to coastal state control of scientific research, these questions are dealt with in *Prof. Mangone*'s paper, and no more will be said about this point here. At the time of drafting of the Antarctic Treaty, the most prevalent limit adopted for the territorial sea was 3 miles, but some of its Parties applied limits up to 12 miles. The 1958 Convention on the High Seas refers to that area as "beyond and adjacent to the territorial sea." The Antarctic Treaty could not, therefore, be specific concerning the location of the high seas if it was to be acceptable to all its Parties. The resultant ambiguity has, however, led some to argue that Article VI implies that *all* the Antarctic surrounding seas are high seas, *i. e.* that no legal territorial sea or continental shelf exists.[16] This conclusion is not, however, sustainable, given the need evidenced in this Article exceptionally to preserve states' international right to freedom of the high seas; this would not be necessary if the Treaty did not apply to the adjacent maritime areas. States can, of course, voluntarily limit their freedoms — as they have done in relation to freedom of sealing in the Seals Convention, and krill and other fishing in the CCAMLR. Correspondingly, coastal states, if it is accepted that these exist in Antarctica, can subject their rights in the territorial sea or other zones to international obligations.

Sea to the Antarctic Continent, in: *Francisco Orrego Vicuña* (ed.), Antarctic Resources Policy, Cambridge, U.K. *et al.* 1983, 231—242; *Auburn* (note 1), 129—138.

[15] UNLOSC, Article 7.

[16] *Robert Guyer*, The Antarctic System, in: RdC vol. 139 (1973), 149—226 (163).

The problems raised by the ambiguity in Article VI are exaggerated by certain provisions of the UNLOSC, which allows not only for a 12 mile limit to the territorial sea, but for the archipelagic states' archipelagic waters and for the new 200-mile Exclusive Economic Zone (EEZ; Article 56) measured from the baselines of the territorial sea (Article 57) and applies the high seas regime only to the parts of the sea that lie beyond these zones. It also provides a more expansive definition of the continental shelf, defining it in terms of 200 miles distance from the baselines and also as including the outer edge of the continental margin, when the shelf is naturally prolonged beyond that distance (Article 76). Although the EEZ was primarily constituted to award to the coastal state sovereign rights over the resources of the sea and seabed (Article 56 (b) (ii)), it also accords to the coastal state:

> (b) jurisdiction as provided in the relevant provisions of this Convention with regard to . . .
>
> (ii) marine scientific research.

The "relevant provisions" referred to in Article 56 are contained in Part XIII on Marine Scientific Research (MSR). Although this Article confirms the right of *all* States to conduct MSR and requires states and unspecified "competent international organizations" to promote and facilitate MSR and to cooperate, it subjects these freedoms, in areas subject to coastal state jurisdiction, to the rights and duties of other states under the Convention, and lays down general principles for the conduct of MSR in all areas. These considerably restrict the former freedoms both in relation to the area in which they are now applicable and in relation to their content.

1. *Territorial Sea (Article 245)*

Coastal states have exclusive rights to regulate MSR; their express consent is required for the conduct of MSR and specific conditions can be imposed upon it, as set out in Article 249.

2. *EEZ and Continental Shelf (Article 247)*

Coastal states do not have exclusive rights, but do have considerable jurisdiction over MSR under the UNLOSC to regulate, to authorize and to control the conduct of MSR in these zones. Their consent is required, though in "normal circumstances" it should be granted for projects by both states or competent international organizations, (we must remember here that SCAR is not an organization) as long as the purposes are peaceful and increase scientific knowledge for the benefit of mankind as a whole — the first objective is already required by the Antarctic Treaty. Coastal states must establish rules or procedures for obtaining consent, to avoid delay, but few have yet done so; the position of the various Treaty Parties in this respect is unknown at the time of writing.

Though "normal circumstances" are not defined, four specific circumstances in which consent can be refused are identified, *viz.* if the project:

(a) is of direct significance for the exploration and exploitation of natural resources; whether living or non-living;

(b) involves drilling into the continental shelf, the use of explosives or the introduction of harmful substances into the marine environment;

(c) involves the construction, operation or use of artificial islands, installations and structures (referred to in other Articles);

(d) contains information communicated pursuant to the researching state's specific obligations under the Convention (Article 248), which is inaccurate, or if the researching state or organization has outstanding obligations from a prior research project.[17]

Given the detailed research requirements on which the Agreed Measures, the Seals Convention, the CCAMLR and the prospective Minerals Convention are premised, it is clear that if coastal states are recognized as such in Antarctica, they could control and restrict research in any EEZ they may declare, and relating to certain designated areas of the natural continental shelf beyond (Art. 246) if such a prolongation exists, since much of such research would be directed at resource exploitation and in the case of the minerals resource exploitation might involve explosives, erection of installations *etc.* Even if they did consent they could impose the numerous conditions listed in Article 249 concerning participation in the project, sharing of data and samples, reporting *etc.*

To resolve the question whether coastal states exist, which might claim EEZ and shelf rights and activate the above provisions if the UNLOSC comes into force for them or becomes part of customary law, we must turn to Article IV of the Antarctic Treaty.

III. Relation of Article VI of the Antarctic Treaty to Article IV

Article IV (1) states that nothing in the present Treaty shall be interpreted as a renunciation by any Contracting Party of previously asserted rights or claims to territorial sovereignty based on its previous activities there, or any basis of claim to territorial sovereignty, or as prejudicing the position of any Contracting Party (*i. e.*, whether with or without Consultative status) as regards its recognition or non-recognition of

[17] Article 246 (5) UNLOSC; consent cannot be refused for projects on the continental shelf beyond 200 n. m. outside areas designated as areas in which offshore activities are taking place [Article 246 (6)].

such rights or claims by any other state. Of the 18 existing Parties, 7 have made such claims. Of these only two, the United Kingdom and Norway, have *not* specifically claimed some formal maritime zone in Antarctica, although states, by virtue of their sovereignty, automatically have territorial seas beyond their land territory and do not need to claim them.[18] As this is also the case in relation to the 200-mile continental shelf,[19] as well as that based on natural prolongation,[20] according to the decisions of the International Court of Justice in the *Malta-Libya Cases*,[21] it would appear that, potentially, Claimant coastal states could exercise the jurisdiction over MSR described earlier, as and when it becomes applicable. It is, however, unclear at present, in the writer's view, whether coastal states need to positively declare EEZs before the rights pertaining to MSR therein apply, or whether, prior to the entry into force of UNLOSC, all the EEZ rights yet exist in customary law, in the context, for example, of the United States' declaration of an EEZ, and the accompanying official statements, which, *prima facie*, excludes such jurisdiction over marine research in the absence of the consent of the researching state to its exercise.[22] The relevant articles of Part V of the UNLOSC, establishing the EEZ jurisdiction, unlike those in Part VI pertaining to the continental shelf, do not expressly state that this jurisdiction automatically applies without need for express proclamation.

The position of the Claimant states in relation to EEZs or EFZs is as follows: the United Kingdom has not applied its 1976 fisheries zone (enacted for its mainland) to its Antarctic Territories and does not claim an EEZ even from its mainland territories. Norway similarly has not applied the 200-mile EEZ it declared for its mainland in 1976 to its Antarctic territory. New Zealand proclaimed a 200-mile EEZ off its mainland in 1977 and this proclamation makes provision for proclamation of an EEZ off Antarctica by regulation at any time but so far New Zealand has not enacted any such regulation. France has enacted a 200-mile

[18] UN Convention on the Territorial Sea 1958, UN Doc. A/CONF. 13/L. 52-L 55, Article 1.

[19] UNLOSC, Article 2.

[20] UNLOSC, Article 77 clearly states that the continental shelf rights (*i. e.* as defining Article 76) do not depend on occupation, effective or national, or any express proclamation. UN Convention on the Continental Shelf 1958, Article 3; UNLOSC Article 76.

[21] *North Sea Continental Shelf Case*, I.C.J. Reports 1969, 2; *Gulf of Maine Case Judgement*, I.C.J. Reports 1984, 246 (360); *Libyan Arab Jamahiriya/Malta Case*, I.C.J. Reports 1985, 13.

[22] CCAMLR deals with the problems thus created by specifically providing in Article XI that its Commission "shall seek to cooperate with Contracting Parties which may exercise jurisdiction in marine areas adjacent to the Convention area in respect of the Conservation of any stock or stocks of associated species which occur both within those areas and the area to which this Convention applies, with a view to harmonizing the conservation measures adopted in respect of such stocks."

zone off mainland France but has not applied it to its Antarctic territory (though it has enacted such zones round Kerguelen and Crozet which intrude into the Antarctic convergence.[23] Australia enacted a 200-mile fishing zone in 1979 that was specifically applied to its Antarctic territory, but on the following day announced that its application to the latter would be suspended. Chile, when declaring its maritime zone in 1947, extended it to all territory over which it had sovereignty; as did Argentina when proclaiming its 200-mile territorial sea in 1966. It is not, therefore, clear whether zones proclaimed with application to the areas south of 60° S after the Antarctic Treaty came into force (and only Chile proclaimed its zone before 1961) are in violation of the second paragraph of Article IV which states:

> No acts or activities taking place while the present treaty is in force shall constitute a basis for asserting, supporting or denying a claim to territorial sovereignty in Antarctica. No new claim, or enlargement of an existing claim, to territorial sovereignty in Antarctica shall be asserted while the present Treaty is in force.

In fact, such maritime claims are not, in current international law, regarded as extensions of sovereignty but of sovereign rights, although the Chilean and Argentinian claims appear to be phrased in terms of sovereignty claims.[24] The position of Antarctic Treaty Parties on the territorial claims differs, as is well known: Claimants mutually recognizing the validity of the claims made, though differing on their areal scope, and non-Claimants disputing the validity of all claims.

Antarctica can be regarded as a coastal state. Some writers argue that the Antarctic continent itself, regardless of questions of state sover-

---

[23] For a discussion of this point and its effects see *Auburn* (note 1), 219. For the Chilean view on the compatibility of EEZs in general and the Chilean zone in particular with the Antarctic Treaty, see *Francisco Orrego Vicuña*, The Application of the Law of the Sea and the Exclusive Economic Zone to the Antarctic Continent, in *Orrego Vicuña* (note 14), 241—251. He takes the view that Article VI does not exclude the possibility of institutions of the law of the sea other than the high seas regime being applied within the Treaty System. Chile's 1940 Presidential Decree establishing its Antarctic territory expressly included the territorial sea and pack ice, thus, in his view, applying the law of the sea, though this did not require specific application; the rights concerned derive in international law from the appurtenance of the land territory. Chile's 1947 proclamation merely applied the further developments of the law of the sea, as asserted by it, to the area.

[24] This problem is discussed by *Edvard Hambro*, Some Notes on the Future of Antarctic Treaty Collaboration, in: AJIL vol. 68 (1974), 217—226 (esp. at 224—225), where such solutions as that devised for Spitzbergen are dismissed and those of condominium or UN Trusteeship discussed in the context of economic exploitation and the need to know which government or authority will have power to grant licences, *inter alia*, for exploratory research. As *Hambro* says, trying to draw a line between pure and applied science in this respect would be completely futile and not warranted by the Antarctic Treaty.

eignty, can attract the rights of a coastal state in the absence of any specific provision to the contrary.[25] The UNCLOS was silent on this question, and advisedly so, as the Antarctic Treaty Consultative Parties did not want such complex issues raised in such a wide multilateral forum.

IV. Articles IV and VI of the Antarctic Treaty and their Relation to Research under the UNLOSC Deep Seabed Regime

It is not proposed to discuss this relationship extensively as the questions have already been aired in the first Antarctic Challenge Symposium.[26] Some writers argue that as Antarctica is not a coastal state, none of the jurisdictional zones applicable under the UNLOSC can be applied there, and the whole area thus will fall within the "*common heritage*" international Area "beyond the limits of national jurisdiction," defined in Article 1 of the UNLOSC and subjected to the regime established in Part XI.[27] MSR in the Area would then be subject to Article 143, which requires that it be carried out for peaceful purposes only and for the benefit of mankind as a whole in accordance with Part XIII. Though Article 56 accords to all states and competent international organizations the right to conduct MSR in the Area, Article 143 allows the Authority also to do so, and to encourage research generally in the Area, co-ordinating, disseminating and analysing the available results. States themselves must, moreover, promote international cooperation in MSR in the Area by, *inter alia*, participating in international programmes and ensuring that programmes are developed through the Sea-Bed Authority or international organization for the benefit of developing and less technologically able states.

All activities in the Area are to be "organized, carried out and controlled by the Authority" (Article 153); Article 1 defines these to include "all activities of exploration for, and exploitation of, the resources of the Area." This should exclude from the Authority's control MSR not directed at exploitation; is it, however, possible to clearly make this distinction?

---

[25] By *Scharnhorst Müller*, The Impact of UNCLOS III on the Antarctic Regime, in: *Wolfrum* (note 13), 169—176. He concentrated primarily on the issue of mineral exploitation. See also: Research, International Law and the Sea in Man's Future, UNESCO 1983 No. 3/4 Impact of Science on Society, *passim* but esp. *M. E. Goncalves*, Science, Technology and the new Convention on the Law of the Sea, 347—355.

[26] *E. E. Hounold*, Thaw in International Law? Rights in Antarctica under the Law of Common Species, in: Yale JIL vol. 87 (1978), 804—59, (844 *et seq.*); *M. C. W. Pinto*, The International Community and Antarctica, in: U. Miami L. Rev. vol. 33 (1978) 475—487 (482), cited by *Müller, op. cit.* (note 25), 170, n. 2; *G. P. Wilson*, Antarctica, the Southern Ocean and the Law of the Sea, in: J. A. G. Journal vol. 30 (1978), 47—85, (73).

[27] Similar concllusions arrived at by *Orrego Vicuña* (note 23), 249—250.

V. Marine Scientific Research in Antarctica: The Way Ahead

It seems likely that the opener provided by the law of the sea for the worms canned in Article VI of the Antarctic Treaty in the context of marine scientific research will reveal complex jurisdictional problems of such political embarrassment to the Antarctic Treaty Parties, and given the provisions of Article IV, danger to the Treaty's future, that they will prefer to avoid them rather than to address them explicitly. To keep the lid on the can the parties will have to continue to work within both the spirit and letter of Antarctic cooperation, as provided in the 1959 Treaty and those linked to it within the so-called Antarctic Treaty "System." The rival views on Claimant coastal states' marine jurisdictional rights will continue to exist and be internally accommodated, as they must be, given that maximisation of research, which is vital to achieving the objectives of the whole System, will be facilitated (at least theoretically) only by reliance on the requirements of co-operation in research, exchange of information and personnel required by each separate treaty and the Agreed Measures.[28] Those with claims will need to continue voluntarily to subject these to the Treaty requirements (and in due course to the requirements of the UNLOSC also, if they become parties to it, and when it enters into force). This does not, in the writer's view, amount to the exercise of a coastal state power, the "collective jurisdiction" suggested by some, equating the ATCPs to a "collective," since the Antarctic Treaty Parties (pace the claims made by some states) have no territorial basis for the exercise of the jurisdiction accorded under the UNLOSC. But it can also be argued that the peculiar situation and status of Antarctica under its Treaty, and the silence of the UNLOSC on the subject, implies that it merits special treatment outside the UNLOSC coastal state or *common heritage* regimes. Its Antarctic Treaty obligations require each party to exercise its powers in a way that achieves an effect similar to "collective" jurisdiction: this would be in accordance with Article 311 of the UNLOSC which provides not only that it prevails over the 1958 Geneva Conventions on the Law of the Sea but that it "shall not alter the rights and obligations of States Parties which arise from other agreements *compatible* with this Convention and which do not affect the enjoyment by other States Parties of their rights or the performance of their obligations under this Convention" (*emphasis added*). The Antarctic Treaty System obligations concerning the conduct of MSR and cooperation in that activity, subject to the requirement that it be undertaken for peaceful purposes only, and recognition that it is in the interest of all mankind that Antarctica shall not become the scene or object of international

[28] See UNESCO's Research, International Law and the Law of the Sea (note 25), *passim*.

discord, would seem to be fully compatible with the UNLOSC objectives and provisions, though more may have to be done to disseminate results more widely, encourage participation of developing states, and to facilitate the transfer of technology and know-how to them as encouraged, though not required, by the UNLOSC.[29]

The possibilities for the better management of Antarctic science in the future were discussed at a recent workshop,[30] which concentrated on examining the value of and means for increased international co-ordination and the implications for decision-making within the Antarctic Treaty System of greater co-ordination and possible shared use of programme and logistic facilities, following the increase in number of ATCPs, all of which are required to actively engage in scientific research, which is becoming increasingly sophisticated, inter-disciplinary and global in nature, and imposing new strains on the Antarctic Treaty System.[31] Few countries could, in fact, achieve unilaterally the demanding levels now required to meet the System's objectives as set out at the beginning of this paper; financial as well as technical burdens are increasing, putting pressure on the more easily accessible coastal sites, especially for new and aspiring entrants, many of whom complain that it is difficult to know what the guidelines are for executing the required scientific research levels.

As far as MSR is concerned, the UNLOSC offers, even to coastal states, an alternative to unilateral approaches and a means of modifying the inhibiting effects of the consent regime in coastal zones, by encouraging research by international organizations and providing that the assent of coastal member-states of an organization undertaking a co-ordinated programme will be presumed. As already pointed out, SCAR cannot properly be regarded as such an organization; perhaps in future more use will have to be made of UNEP, FAO, IMO, WMO, ICAO, ITU, IUCN, and others mentioned in *Mr. Hajost*'s paper. This would simultaneously fulfil the objectives of the UNLOSC whilst at the same time avoiding the difficulties that that treaty and the customs emerging from it create for MSR. But such organizations themselves will, in order not to undermine the beneficial effects of the Antarctic Treaty System's many obligations concerning the conduct of scientific research, need to

---

[29] Future Directions for the Management of Antarctic Science: A Conference convened by the International Institute for Environment and Development, held at the Wingspread Conference Center, the Johnson Foundation, Racine, Wisconsin, June 28—30, 1986: report prepared by *Lee A. Kimball*, January 1987, available from IIED.

[30] See *D. J. Drewry*, International Scientific Coordination in Antarctic, in: *T. B. Miller* (ed.), Australia, Britain and Antarctica, Paper of a Conference held at the Australian Studies Centre, London, U.K., June 4, 1986, 25—36.

[31] A distinction is made between needs for communication, cooperation and coordination by *Drewry*, *op. cit.* (note 30), 27.

co-ordinate their own programmes relating to Antarctica. This would necessitate wider and more active participation as observers at relevant Antarctic Treaty meetings. If this can be done, an external accommodation of the Antarctica System's obligations and objectives, and those of the UNLOSC parties and the community at large concerning the interest of and benefit to mankind as a whole can be brought about. Some clarification is required, however, of the respective roles and actions required of SCAR, individual governments, international organizations and the related Antarctic Treaty forums if Article VI is not to be allowed to undermine the Treaty System in respect of MSR. The case for a Secretariat is also enhanced.[32]

The aim of the 1959 Treaty was to ensure that more, not less, science be carried out in Antarctica.[33] In 1959 it was assumed that freedom of scientific research was one of the unwritten freedoms of the high seas that must be preserved, hence the exception of high seas rights under international law made in Article VI. It will be unfortunate if developments in the law of the sea are allowed to defeat that objective, particularly as the Antarctic is no longer viewed as an exotic region which can be investigated in isolation — the luxury of a few fortunate nations. Recognition of the important and integral role of its environmental systems with those of the remainder of the Earth must be accorded within and outside the Antarctic Treaty System.

---

[32] *Miller* (note 30), Summary and Points of General Consensus, 2—7; see also *Drewry* (note 30), who points to some of the tensions generated by the arrival of the new ATCPs, 32—33, and the need for reconsidering existing organizational structures, 35—36.

[33] That much more needs to be done is confirmed by all Antarctic scientists. See also, *J. P. Croxall*, Antarctic predator-prey interactions, Natural Environment Research Council News Journal, June 1985, 4—6.

Panel Discussion

Participants: Dr. *Orlando R. Rebagliati**
Dr. *Wolfgang E. Burhenne***
Prof. Dr. *Reinhard Müller****
Mr. *Alfonso Muñoz Seca*****

R. Wolfrum, Chairman:

Thank you, *Pat*, for your presentation. I now open the panel discussion.

O. Rebagliati:

Thank you, *Professor Wolfrum*. My colleagues on the panel have suggested that I may begin, so I will benefit from all the omissions I can make, because I will rely on what they are going to say and just confine myself to a few points. If still omissions are made by the panel, the general discussion will certainly cover all queries and comments that we expect.

I would mention some of the points which arose this afternoon, with due regard to what has been already the subject of general discussion this morning after the presentations. It impressed me very positively, *Mr. Quilty*'s presentation in relation to cooperation and coordination — in relation to the Antarctic Treaty functions, and particularly in relation to scientific research, preservation of the environment, and related matters. He fully described all the possibilities already being carried out, either by states themselves or through Antarctic Treaty System components, and/or between Antarctic Treaty components and other organizations which he mentioned in full detail, though not trying to be exhaustive. What he had mentioned, and I want to stress, is the flexibility and the evolving nature of this cooperation, already envisaged, as he put it, in the preamble of the Antarctic Treaty, which was coupled with the concert of the peaceful purposes of the Treaty and the consistency of this Treaty with the principles and purposes of the United Nations Charter.

---

* Dr. *Orlando R. Rebagliati*, Cónsul General de la Argentina, Valparaiso, Chile.

** Dr. *Wolfgang E. Burhenne*, Secretary General (elected), Interparliamentarian Working Group, Bonn.

*** Prof. Dr. *Reinhard Müller*, Martin-Luther-Universität, Halle-Wittenberg.

**** Mr. *Alfonso Muñoz Seca*, Deputy Director of Terrestrial, Maritime and Aerial Cooperation, Ministry of Foreign Affairs, Madrid, Spain.

The opinions expressed in this volume are the personal views of their authors only.

I would like to stress these two points, in particular the principle for the *maintenance of peace and security*, which is fully consistent between the Antarctic Treaty and the UN Charter, and the principle of *international cooperation*, which is also embodied in the Charter. These have been subject to a positive evolution in the Treaty, on both purposes and function, and have shown already concrete results. I agree with him that there is a broad field for further building up this area of cooperation; I would just think that the area of respect of the peaceful uses of Antarctica is almost unquestionable. No country in the world, either a Party to the Antarctic Treaty or non-party, has ever contested this principle, and of course, many countries, including many countries which are not party to the Antarctic Treaty fully subscribe to this, either individually or in United Nations deliberations. That was one of the merits that the Antarctic Treaty was duly paid respect for. I agree with him that the enhancing of international cooperation is an open field, as the Antarctic Treaty is an open Treaty, and other Antarctic Treaty System components are also open. What can be done is for the benefit of all countries, either present Parties to the Antarctic Treaty or potential parties to that Treaty, or even members of other institutions or organizations which can be engaged in a positive manner. But "all together" means that we are, in a way, on the path of a strengthening of the Antarctic Treaty System and making it more and more consistent and compatible with the functioning of other international organizations and with the interests and needs of other countries, even countries which are not, at present, parties to the Treaty.

I see in this a kind of, and I mentioned it in private to him if I may confess, a kind of possible optimism about progressing and achieving concrete results for countries which are not parties to the Treaty at present, and will even not necessarily have to become parties in order to benefit from this cooperation. Relating to *Scott Hajost*'s extensive presentation, it draws to me the particular point that many of you have stressed, that many times drafters of several treaties — of a general nature or a particular nature but mostly multilateral treaties — were not thinking about the territorial applicability of those treaties or, at least, that was not explicitly built in — meaning that they would explicitly apply to Antarctica. Of course, we are aware that some of the multilateral treaties were subject to some reservations or unilateral interpretation by signatories of those treaties, which happen also to be Antarctic Treaty Parties, or within those Antarctic Treaty Parties those named by the qualification of Claimants. Sometimes those countries felt that at least some clarification about their position had to be expressed in connection with the new treaty that was being concluded. Nevertheless, the general picture that I gathered from *Scott Hajost*'s presentation is that a number of fields in international law, particularly very sensitive fields in modern international law, which he also mentioned, were able to be codified and both, Parties to the Antarctic Treaty System and non-parties to the Antarctic Treaty System, were able to agree to legislate on those fields. This included the possibility of applying that legislation to Antarctica — which so far occurs without arousing conflicts between the Antarctic Treaty System as a legal system and those new, or "X" number of new, multilateral treaties, dealing with several aspects of modern international law.

What I would like to summarize is that the Antarctic Treaty and the Antarctic Treaty System, as we assessed it, was not and is not meant to cover all possible legislative aspects relating to Antarctica. It was confined at the very beginning to some specific aspects. It evolved — but it never occured to the drafters, nor to the State Parties, to create a self-sufficient international legal regime dealing with that particular area of the world. It was an *ad hoc* legislation relating to *ad hoc* problems addressing actual potential conflicts or even real conflicts at that time, and successfully functioning so far. It did not imply that international legislation to all aspects, even when concluded with parties not Party to the Antarctic Treaty, was precluded. And, in fact, international practice showed that it was even permitted and welcomed by Antarctic Treaty Parties which participated in that new legislation. That is why I like to stress that the compatibility of the Antarctic Treaty with the rest of international law, either newly drafted or codified, or previous international law, is almost evident; we should not be discouraged in trying to further harmonize present and future international law with international law, old international law, that conformed with the Antarctic Treaty System.

Lastly, I would like to refer to the can of worms without trying to wear some gloves in relation to Article VI which cannot be referred to without Article IV, meaning that they should be read together, of course, in the context of the rest of the provisions of the Antarctic Treaty.

I should mention that at the time of the drafting of the Antarctic Treaty, it was not so broadly shared — the view that the territorial sea or maritime areas were confined to three or twelve miles. Some countries, including Chile and Argentina, had already proclaimed maritime areas subject to their sovereignty or jurisdiction, without excluding the Antarctic territorial claims they had made. When they claimed maritime areas, they meant adjacent to the respective territories, and of course, they did not define the territories, but at that time they already were claiming Antarctic territories. There was a particular situation in 1958, for those countries that did neither ratify nor acceed to the Geneva Conventions, although they had maintained their territorial claims and the maritime claims relating to all territorial claims. Therefore, it is not so clear that at that time maritime jurisdiction was confined to three to twelve miles and all the institutions were clearly developed in general international law. In fact, the continental shelf institutions had evolved quite before the Antarctic Treaty — and not only these two countries were maintaining the continental shelf doctrine, but particularly one country, which is not a Claimant country, as we all know, was the inspiration of the continental shelf doctrine, back in 1945. So the law of the sea prior to the Antarctic Treaty was not so clear-cut in relation to maritime claims and jurisdictions.

The question and the ambiguity is that the maritime claim we are referring to as recognized in international law was not fully recognized by any sufficient number of countries, and that was one of the reasons for the 1973—1982 UN Conference. The reason is that the non-recognition of a state as a coastal state was, and is, the corner-stone of the problem. If we do not recognize the state as a coastal state, the discussion relating to whether the maritime jurisdiction goes up to 3-12-200 miles, plus the continental shelf, is subsidiary to that. Of course, the question of the claims to Antarctic territory was not solved, and therefore the maritime jurisdiction in which these territorial claims originate, for those who are Claimants, cannot be of course accepted by those who are Non-claimants, and that was clearly the picture of Articles IV and VI. So there is not much value in discussing whether, up to which extent, a Claimant (of a coastal state) can exercise those rights. For those states, they would be limiting themselves in exercising those rights, as *Pat Birnie* mentioned, but they would do that because they chose to and they acceded to or ratified both the Antarctic Treaty and/or CCAMLR. Countries which are Non-claimants and do not recognize the claims, will see the source of this not as a certain limitation of a coastal state but just an obligation which arises from the Treaty itself. It is quite a subsidiary issue, this one of the maritime claims; it is totally connected with the recognition or non-recognition of their rights by themselves over the claimed territory.

I do not think that Article VI or present international law as codified by the Convention adopted in 1982, in respect of the economic zone or the continental shelf, gives us substantially a new picture. The picture is almost the same, because, for some states, either Parties to the Antarctic Treaty or non-parties to the Antarctic Treaty, there exist no coastal states in Antarctica: therefore, whatever the law of the sea is at this time or at that time, there are non-coastal states, there is no territorial sea, there is no economic zone, there is no continental shelf and therefore, scientific research is being regulated by other norms of international law. According to the coastal states they will still be coastal states, but they would be limiting themselves in exercising those rights, in particular in asking for consent and filling all the requirements relating to scientific research. They freely accepted those obligations under the Antarctic Treaty or under present international law relating to the law of the sea — either already Parties to the Convention or non-parties — but with national legislation coinciding with that Convention in substance.

Now, what I would like to highlight is a paradox that we might address, which is that if we are trying to see that there are non-coastal states in Antarctica, that means that that area, in relation to being a maritime area adjacent to Antarctica, has to be addressed necessarily with a bifocal approach. For some states whose claims are recognized as such, not the claim itself but the existence of the claim, by Article IV and any article in the mineral regimes, or the similar article in CCALMR — that is a fact which exists, and because of that fact, that area is an *ad hoc* area, with regard to its legal status as a maritime area. That is why that area cannnot be regarded as falling within an area beyond national jurisdiction: as it were, the high seas in the middle of the Pacific Ocean. It is a specific maritime area, which some states consider subject to their sovereignty, although with self-imposed limitations; some other states consider otherwise, but still recognize that some legislation, *ad hoc* legislation, analogous to the Antarctic Treaty, may be drafted, as in the case of the mineral regime.

That is the present situation which we envisage, that following the same pragmatic approach as before in relation to Article VI and IV, or in relation to the scope of the Antarctic Treaty, in relation to scientific research — following that same pattern and that same pragmatic approach, these mineral negotiations are tackling the point of exercising rights over a so-called continental shelf or territorial sea or economic zone. Only that pragmatic approach will allow us to draft in harmony a treaty which again, I am going back to the previous statement, again will be and can be consistent with prior and present international law. But it will also have to meet the present political reality which the Antarctic Treaty System evidences and which we can test everyday, and we can even test going back to 1961. Thank you.

W. Burhenne:

I would like to stress a completely different point which was mentioned many times this morning: the inter-disciplinary cooperation. Scientific knowledge on the one hand and legal drafting and decision-making on the other, are subjects I have to deal with every day, both professionally, as the Secretary General of the Inter-Parliamentary Working Group in Germany, and as a volunteer, as chairman of the IUCN Commission on Environmental Policy, Law and Administration.

Let me start with the second. *Mr. Scully* and *Pat Birnie* already mentioned IUCN today, which is a very specific creature you could say, with a two-chamber system, a governmental chamber and a non-governmental chamber. At the General Assembly we have 127 states represented, but the main point is, we have six commissions: four scientific commissions and two which we call service commissions. One of these is the Commission for Policy, Law and Administration.

We lawyers, I must say, are very happy with all these — nearly 3000 — volunteer scientists and practitioners to back us up. We need this scientific advice every day in all that we are drafting and all that we are proposing. We need it, for example, for drafting national legislation, but especially in international law. I would like to mention the African and the ASEAN Conventions; *Scott* (*Hajost*) mentioned today the difficult formulation brought up by scientists during the diplomatic conference for finalizing CITES concerning the introduction of specimens from the sea. We discussed, I think, for nearly two weeks alongside the general discussion, how we should finally formulate this, since the Law of the Sea Conference was not finished at that time — I am speaking of 1973 — and we had to find a formulation not prejudicial to the Law of the Sea Convention, so we had to reach a middle-of-the-road consensus. The same scientific and legal difficulties we had when we drafted are quite simply also those which you mentioned before, with regard to the Migratory Species Convention.

Actually, we still have a very difficult task following the General Assembly in Madrid three years ago, as we had to draft a Convention on the *in situ* Conservation of Biological Diversity. You can imagine what this means on the legal side. On the one hand, the legal difficulties to draft this, and on the other, the need for the scientific input. As *Mr. Wolfrum* said, we are learning continually. And, I must say, we have no problems with the scientists, but the scientists always want to be convinced that we, the terrible lawyers, are taking their aspects into account. This is quite easy during the time between the General Assemblies with a small Council, but during the General Assembly with hundreds of delegations from governments, agencies and NGOs, then, it looks different. *John Heap* had an experience with this situation at the General Assembly, in Madrid, when last time we had to re-draft the resolution already mentioned before on Antarctic problems and the Antarctic regime. We needed days to find a majority for the resolution we drafted. The problems are similar, for example, for a parliament.

The German Federal Parliament tried to create something like the TAB in the US, the Technological Assessment Board. We could not go about it in the same way, creating our own body in parliament. We went to the German Research Council (the *Deutsche Forschungsgemeinschaft*) and said, "You are getting so much in public funding and help, can you not provide a service for us?" But, in the discussion, the President of the German research organization said, "Rarely, if ever, have we found a consensus on a scientific opinion. If there is no clear scientific opinion, we don't like to take any responsibility." This was the answer we got. Our response was, "We are not looking for scientific advice on a consensus or majority or minority basis. This is not what we want." But, finally, we had no success. Many scientists have been refusing to work closely with politics and now we are in the situation that parliament has to establish its own scientific body, which I think is a mistake. Quite simply, we are now creating a special *enquête* commission for possible climate changes. The Federal Parliament will start the work because the majority is there, immediately after the summer recess.

I would like to state, in general, that mainly for the decision-makers there are not enough alternatives presented. In many cases, the administration is also coming up with only one possibility. There is more need for advice, not for screened scientific advice, but for a broad scale of scientific opinions and a broad scale of possible impacts. I think, on the other hand, that the decision-makers have to decide on the basis of available advice. The decision-makers have to be responsible also, if this has an effect on jobs, on cost, or perhaps on requirements for investment. I think, and I would like to stress what was carefully mentioned this morning, that we should never ask scientific organs to take responsibility for political and legal measures. I would like — perhaps I can express this carefully enough — that there should be no possible effects from social and economic impacts on scientific advice. I hope what I am trying to carefully express with this, is clear enough. There is really a need for a separation of powers, and I think especially where international treaties are concerned we never come through, when the powers are not clearly divided.

I would like to add one aspect. I think that scientific error, or lack of knowledge, or need for more research are to be accepted. Decision-makers can hardly postpone, they have to make decisions already when the scientific research is not yet available. But errors, mistakes of decision-makers are generally not accepted; they are normally connected with consequences. I can say for example, for my own constituency, for both my professional as well as my voluntary activities, that there would not be a readiness to accept bigger mistakes, and at the least I could say that I would not be re-elected. I will never forget to listen to the advice of the scientists. I think we can live in a biosymbiosis without any difficulties if the tasks are properly divided. Thank you.

R. Müller:

I will limit my remarks to some points not only in order to leave time for the discussion, it is also to keep the image. I promised *Mr. Wolfrum*, shortly before the coffee break, I would be brief. I would like to thank, first of all, the speakers of today for their excellent presentations, which deepened my knowledge on important questions of the Antarctic Treaty System.

I would like to come to the contribution of *Mr. Heap*, and especially the question he raised: "How should the main views be represented in the advisory committee of the future mineral regime?" I do share his view that the search for a consensus or the attempt to force a result might lead to a loss of information which is necessary for the decision-making body. But on the other hand, I feel a little bit opposed to my panel colleague. I am of the opinion that some kinds of rules of procedure should be provided for the advisory committee in order to ensure that the clear picture on the main trends would be presented. This means a majority, if there is any, to support the decision-making body in preparing this decision, and so far, the proposed solution in MR/17 Rev. III (Antarctic Mineral Resources), to report on the majority view and all other views expressed, is, in my opinion, a satisfactory solution.

With regard to the question of the secretariat as it was dealt with by *Mr. Scully*, I would like to express that it is extremely useful to have such a comprehensive presentation on the development of this issue, and all the aspects in favour of establishing some kind of a permanent infrastructure. But at the moment, I feel unable to decide for myself whether the Antarctic Treaty System needs such an organ or not. I agree with those who stress the effectiveness of the present system and the necessity to maintain the special role and responsibility of the Consultative Parties. For this reason it should be ensured, if it would be agreed to build up such a permanent body, that its functions are limited to organizational technical aspects, and that the role of the host country is completely maintained. I believe the whole question needs further consideration, taking into account all aspects related to it.

A variety of cooperation — related questions, in the broadest sense, were discussed today including possibilities of improvement. Having in mind *Mr. Hajost*'s very interesting analysis on the relationship of the Antarctic Treaty System and other international instruments, I think it might also be worth examining how, and to what extent, the cooperation obligations contained in the Antarctic Treaty itself may influence these instruments. I will not do it now, but it seems to me that even a general comparison between the Antarctic Treaty System's cooperation norms and similar obligations in general international law, or its special branechs, leads to the conclusion that there is more than the legal basis of Article II of the Antarctic Treaty, which contains the principle of *freedom of scientific investigation*, and details duties of what has to be done in order to implement the clause, "in the interest of science and the progress of all mankind."

Also, the practice of the Member States could serve as a model for other international relations in the field of scientific and technical progress, inasmuch as the Antarctic Treaty, in my view, is able to develop, for example, the 1970 Friendly Relations Declaration. The cooperation rules of the Antarctic Treaty have the substantial advantage that they contain legally binding duties for all Member States, and not only for the benefit of their own, but also for the benefit of interested states — independent of whether they are Parties to the Treaty or not. This level of cooperation is not achieved in any other field of international relations: one can take, for example, the Outer Space Treaty, it is limited almost solely to a cooperation program under the so-called "common benefit cover." One can take legal relations concerning environmental protection or the whole issue of non-navigable uses of international water courses; one will not find the same level of cooperation, and this is, in my view, worthy of being pronounced — without considering once more the most important achievement of the Antarctic Treaty, the complete demilitarization of the whole continent and the duty to use it exclusively for peaceful purposes. Thank you.

A. Muñoz Seca:

I will be very brief so that we can open the floor for discussion. I think, *Rüdiger*, I am especially grateful for your invitation after having listened today to the debate, because I come from a country which has only recently started being interested in Antarctica. It is extremely useful, I think, to realize how many things can be exchanged in an open discussion, as we are having here today, which, with a lack of formality which you yourself indicated this morning, has helped us to air our thoughts much more openly. Therefore, I am going to throw a few thoughts to the audience.

My personal impressions are of the general situation where we now find ourselves, and I do apologize for my lack of experience in Antarctic matters; I am going to say what I am going to say. The first thought is that we are faced with a System established by the Treaty of 1961, which has performed marvellously. It is a masterpiece of equilibrium, of care taken of the different and difficult tasks that the drafters of the Treaty had in front of them, and it has done very well for nearly 30 years of existence. The second thought is that whether we like it or not, the world has moved in the last 28 to 30 years and new elements have come into play, and as several speakers have indicated today, there are many new concepts today that were not "in force," or even considered possible in 1959—1960.

That does not necessarily mean that we have to amend anything, but I think we have to adjust ourselves to the new trends of maritime law. Certainly there are new elements to be considered in terms of jurisdiction, in terms of scientific investigation, *etc.* There is another important element, I think: there is much more world preoccupation with environmental problems. We have to pay a lot of attention to all these questions from those organizations concerned with environmental problems. And, I think, the Antarctic Treaty Parties, whether Consultative Parties or non-Consultative, are very capable of adapting themselves as I just explained: the System itself is extremely open, and seen from the outside, and I can say this particularly as a newcomer, we never had the feeling that it was an exclusive system.

So, I do not think that there should be any difficulty in the coming years to maintain that openness, and possibly to admit new members that would permit a much more worldwide representation. Because the other trend, as I said before, whether we like it or not, is that the world has changed. The world was not, generally speaking, in 1960 what it is now, a brand-new set of countries has emerged, and we have to take it into account also for the future of the regime. Thank you.

General Discussion

R. Wolfrum, Chairman:

Mr. Bølset will start with general discussion. *Mr. Bølset.*

N. Bølset:

Thank you, Mr. Chairman, I shall be very brief. When I asked for the floor before we broke for lunch, it was just to mention that we in Oslo have given the idea of setting up a secretariat in some form or another considerable consideration. We agree with those who have said that the System that we have has up until now worked quite satisfactorily. But we think that the time may have come for the Parties to the Treaty to consider some form of permanent infrastructure. We consider the growing number of Parties to the Antarctic Treaty, we look at the growth of the activities in Antarctica and we are also considering the growing inter-relationship between the Treaty Parties and other international bodies. And this in sum, we believe, should make us consider, whether it would be appropriate that we try to find another instrument, some kind of a secretariat: I think we should move slowly, should be modest, but at least we should launch this idea. Thank you, Mr. Chairman.

R. Wolfrum, Chairman:

Thank you, *Mr. Bølset*. *Mr. Orrego*, please.

F. Orrego Vicuña:

The comments made this morning by *Tucker Scully* prompted an interesting discussion on the question of a secretariat and it is first on this question that I would like to make a short comment. If one compares the Treaty System that was drawn up in 1959 to what the Treaty System is today, one cannot but wonder how much it has changed and, in fact, to what extent the operations today are so much more complex than they were ever before. This means that, in fact, the Treaty System has been evolving towards a kind of international organization *de facto*, lacking, of course, institutions, because no institutions were provided. And we can see from contemporary practice that the Treaty System is, with every passing day, working more like an international organization

---

The opinions expressed in this volume are the personal views of their authors only.

or in a manner comparable to an international organization but, as I mentioned, lacking the necessary institutionalization.

To this end, one could also recognize the argument in favour of a secretariat, not only in terms of the resource regimes, in which each regime has its own secretariat, actually or potentially, but also in terms of the activities of the Consultative Meetings themselves. One can also see, of course, that there is some reluctance to this, often rooted in historical circumstances and claims, but if one is to be in any way consistent with the evolution that the Consultative Parties have imposed or developed within the system, one would also have to recognize the institutional requirements that it has, in turn, demanded. And this is why I think that it is quite an attractive idea to consider.

There is one other situation I would like to mention in this regard. If the Consultative Meetings and Parties are to have an overview role of the system as a whole, in order to coordinate the system and to continue with the trend to control its main development, which is quite apparent from the last Consultative Meetings, it can only be done with the existence of a secretariat or some similar institutional arrangement. As the resource regimes, in particular, will have their own permanent and standing machinery, they cannot be easily overviewed by a meeting that meets every number of years and which is not on a continuing basis. It is also true that the idea of a secretariat is linked to other initiatives within the Treaty System. For example, the many times that references have been made to a scientific research fund, or a scientific research institute or other arrangements of that sort: this would necessarily have to count on some permanent or standing institution, probably of a secretarial nature, if it is going to work at all. The same is true for the handling of information.

So, the approach for a secretariat has two advantages. One is an advantage of the Treaty System as a whole in relation to the international community, in that it would facilitate its operations both internally and externally. The other is an advantage in terms of the role of the Consultative Parties themselves, which certainly could be strengthened through the performance of secretarial functions in order to keep that role active in relation to the system as a whole.

There is also a second point: which is the correct interpretation of Article VI? There are two ways one can read the article. The first is the most common way, to read the article as entirely separating the regime of the high seas from the operation of the Treaty System and virtually construing the article in terms that whatever happens in the high seas, however you define the high seas, it is going to be beyond reach for the Treaty System as such. This has been an interpretation rather favoured by many authors and views, but I think that there is also one other interpretation which makes more sense from the point-of-view of the actual operation of the Treaty, which is to read it in terms that the high seas freedoms are kept with within the Treaty area, but those freedoms are subject to the fundamental provisions of the Treaty as such. In fact, if you read carefully Article VI, you will realize that it starts stating that "the provisions of the present Treaty shall apply to the area south of 60° South Latitude, including ice shelves," *etc.* The record on this particular article is quite clear, this particular aspect having been published and discussed. That record shows that the article at one point had been drafted to say that the area of the high seas south of 60° South Latitude was beyond or excepted from the provisions of the Antarctic Treaty System. And precisely in order to extend the provisions of the Treaty to the whole area, including maritime areas, it was redrafted in the present way. The meaning is that, even if you argue that parts or all of the maritime areas surrounding Antarctica are partly or entirely the high seas, they will be anyhow subject to some of the main provisions, like demilitarization, provisions on prohibition of nuclear explosions of Article V, freedom of scientific research, and others.

The same is true if you regard it from the point-of-view of the application of other maritime areas that could be claimed in Antarctica, in particular the Exclusive Economic Zone. The application of the Exclusive Economic Zone, to the extent that might be feasible, would in any case be subject to the limitations set up by the Treaty. That includes, for example, the limitation on the need to respect the freedom of scientific research, or observing the fisheries arrangement that had been enacted under CCAMLR. So in fact the Exclusive Economic Zone that could be implemented, and for some countries has been implemented in Antarctica, must be in accordance with those restrictions deriving from the 1959 Treaty and not exclusively with the general terms of the Law of the Sea or some other arrangements. Thank you.

R. Wolfrum, Chairman:

Thank you, *Mr. Orrego*. *Mr. Rajan*, please.

H. P. Rajan:

Thank you, *Professor Wolfrum*. This morning I had requested the floor to make a brief comment on the institutional arrangements for the Antarctic Treaty System. However, with your permission, may I also have an opportunity to make a second comment on Article IV and VI of the Antarctic Treaty with reference to *Professor Birnie*'s presentation?

With regard to the institutional mechanisms, *Mr. Scully* had pointed out several existing models on the basis of which we could draw a parallel. But I thought there was a very striking parallel available in an existing institution. The Asian-African Legal Consultative Committee, which has a Secretariat in New Delhi, is a forum, established 30 years ago, which provides a mechanism for consultations between member governments on questions of international law. Originally, the Secretariat was established by seven Governments. The tenure of the Committee was for five years; it had the mandate to prepare briefs and to advise on matters referred by any member state. In addition, it could take up the work of the ILC and the UN and prepare papers for discussion by member governments. All discussions of the Committee take place in the regular annual meetings, held in one of the member states which bears the expenditures. The Committee's role is purely recommendatory; it offers excellent secretarial facilities for transmitting all necessary documents, recommendations, and references to members and other concerned bodies. Its meetings are attended by international organizations and non-member states, its tenure has been periodically increased, and it itself has recently been granted observer status in the UN.

Perhaps a secretariat along these lines would work for the Antarctic Treaty System; the functions would be purely administrative: rendering secretarial assistance, organizing, disseminating information and co-ordinating with other organizations such as SCAR, SCOR, and CCAMLR.

My second comment relates to the interpretation given to Article IV and VI of the Antarctic Treaty, which *Professor Birnie* had said was quite ambiguous and perhaps, as she had said, the ambiguity was deliberate. While elaborating the ambiguity of the Continental Shelf doctrine, she had drawn reference to paragraph 2 of Article IV which states that "no new claim or enlargement of an existing claim to territorial sovereignty in Antarctica shall be asserted while the Treaty is in force." Her arguments tended to extend the interpretation of the *North Sea Continental Shelf Cases* and the continental shelf doctrine as enunciated by those cases to the Antarctic Treaty provisions. I would like to draw attention to Article IV para. 1 (a), which, read with para. 2 of the same article, would mean that no enlargement of territorial sovereignty or previously asserted right is permitted while the Treaty is in force. If we apply the interpretation of the 1969 *North Sea Continental Shelf Cases* to the Antarctic Treaty it would mean that the sovereign right to the continental shelf, which in 1959 was restricted to a 200-mile depth criterion, would now extend to the continental margin under the UNLOSC; in short, while territorial sovereignty cannot be enlarged it would be illogical to assume that the same article permits extension of sovereign right.

In this context, Article VI makes reference only to ice shelf and not continental shelf. I feel that this was deliberately and carefully drafted;

otherwise, the term "continental shelf," which was defined in 1958, would have been used.

I also feel that it is essential to interpret the Treaty in the light of the situation that was prevailing in the years 1957—59 and the background against which Articles IV and VI were formulated. Although the Treaty was drafted through careful confidential consultations amongst the original members, the intentions are quite obvious from the manner in which the arcticles have been placed in the Treaty. The objectives of the Treaty, to promote freedom of scientific investigations in Antarctica (Article II) and ensuring international cooperation towards that end (Article III), introduce Article IV, which suspends the exercise of territorial sovereignty or territorial rights while the Treaty is in force. Having thus drafted Articles II, III and IV the Treaty defines the areas of application in Article VI and carefully uses the word "ice shelf." The term "ice shelf" in Article VI has been used precisely to avoid extension of territorial sovereignty to areas beyond which some of the Contracting Parties have "previously asserted" territorial sovereignty. My submission is that the sequences in which these articles have been drafted are of very great significance considering the nature and the objectives of the Antarctic Treaty.

R. Wolfrum, Chairman:

Thank you, *Mr. Rajan*. The next speaker will be *Mr. Lagoni*.

R. Lagoni:

Thank you. I have a brief remark regarding *Dr. Hajost*'s presentation, which in my mind opened up an important perspective on the international law concerning Antarctica. I must say that I particularly like *Dr. Hajost*'s distinction between Treaty provisions which require territorial jurisdiction — at least a kind of functional jurisdiction with respect to the continental shelf or an exclusive economic zone or a fisheries zone on the one hand, and those Treaty provisions which do not require any of these kinds of jurisdiction on the other hand — but which are applied instead by way of flag state or personal jurisdiction. Distinguishing between these kinds of jurisdiction makes it much easier to resolve the thorny question of the application of the 1982 Law of the Sea Convention to the Antarctic Treaty, once the Convention will enter into force. I agree with him that Part VII of the Convention on the High Seas and certain provisions of Part XII concerning the Protection and Preservation of the Marine Environment will apply within the Antarctic Treaty area. One should also add that Part XV on the Peaceful Settlement of Disputes will apply, whenever and wherever the respective substantial provisions apply. Whether or not Part XI on the Deep Sea-Bed would apply too, was the matter of a scholarly controversy at an earlier Antarctic Challenge Symposium, here at Kiel, and I do not want to return to this issue.

If I understood him correctly, *Dr. Hajost* did not consider his list of intergovernmental organizations and agreements as an exhaustive one, so I may tentatively add some more items which I came across during my own research on this matter: *i. e.*, the four Geneva Red Cross Conventions of 1949, in particular Convention II on Wounded and Shipwrecked and the 1977 Additional Protocols to those Conventions apply to Antarctica, and so do a number of international treaties on the Law of Warfare, in particular several of the 1907 Hague Conventions. It seems to me that it is worthwhile to pursue *Dr. Hajost*'s approach by asking which customary rules of international law do apply in Antarctica. Here again, one will probably find that all rules of customary international law, which are not related to any kind of territorial jurisdiction, or jurisdiction concerning the continental shelf, the exclusive economic zone or the fisheries zone, will apply to Antarctica. Thank you Mr. Chairman.

R. Wolfrum, Chairman:

Thank you, *Mr. Lagoni*. The next speaker on my list will be *Mr. Quilty*.

P. Quilty:

Thank you, Mr. Chairman. Just a brief point, I think. In relation to *Tucker Scully*'s comments this morning, I think he gave a very good review of the reasons why a secretariat would be valuable and he also gave a review of some of the functions of such a secretariat. But he used, as an example of one of the topics that such a secretariat could examine, or supervise the examination of, the ozone-hole or the ozone-layer question. To my mind, it was probably an example of one of the things that such a secretariat should not supervise. I see it as a scientific area, one that I would see as more properly handed over to SCAR for independent advice.

R. Wolfrum, Chairman:

Thank you, *Mr. Quilty*. Next Speaker will be *Mr. Jørgensen-Dahl*.

A. Jørgensen-Dahl:

Thank you very much, Mr. Chairman. We have not yet left the issue of the secretariat. The remarks I would like to make will be addressed to *Tucker Scully*'s paper, but I'm glad that *Mr. Hajost*'s paper came in between, because I think that when you see those two together, you almost inevitably will have to arrive at a particular view of the question of the secretariat. It seems to me that in most of the comments today, it is implied that the Antarctic Treaty System owes its success to its decentralized character. But the question is, do we in fact know this? Is it perhaps because the decentralized character is the Antarctic Treaty System's most salient or obvious feature and that therefore we attribute success to decentralization? Could it not be, for example, that it is the nature of the issues with which the Antarctic Treaty System deals, which can account for the relative success of the System, or perhaps a combination of the two?

When the talk is about the secretariat, some seem to believe that the formation of a secretariat is the thin wedge of an eventually enormous or at least out-sized international bureaucracy! It is as if this is an almost inevitable consequence of the formation of a secretariat. However, is it in fact inevitable that a secretariat will grow into a monster of this kind? The international experience in this field is almost infinitely variable. All manner of international organizations and international institutional structures have come and gone, been formed or been disbanded and have grown in size or retracted in size. Could it be, for example, that the decentralized structure of the Antarctic Treaty System has served well until now but will cease to do so from now on, or will be inappropriate because of, for example, the increasing number of members of the Antarctic Treaty System or states operating within the Antarctic Treaty System?

I recall that *Mr. Nicholson* suggested a secretariat, consisting of a director, an assistant, a word processor and a couple of suitcases. Well, after having heard *Mr. Hajost* and others, it strikes me that *Mr. Nicholson* will have to add a personal computer or two at least, to his ideas of the size of the possible secretariat. Thank you.

Air – Sea – Ice Interactions in the Antarctic Pack Ice Region

*E. Augstein**

I. General Considerations

The thermodynamic and kinematic state of the ocean and the atmosphere is effectively controlled by heat and momentum exchanges across the air-sea interface. In general, the heat flux is directed from the ocean towards the atmosphere in order to compensate for the radiative energy deficit within the air column. In polar regions, particularly during the winter season, the oceanic heat losses to the atmosphere can only be balanced by cooling of the upper part of the water column. When the water temperature drops below the freezing point, sea ice begins to form. The heat released by this process contributes to the energy fluxes from the ocean to the atmosphere.

As soon as an ice layer covers the water surface the air-sea exchange mechanisms are modified. The hydrodynamical roughness of the air-sea interface becomes larger, which increases the momentum transfer from the atmosphere to the ocean. The solid ice layer allows only for heat fluxes by molecular conduction thereby drastically reducing the oceanic heat loss to the atmosphere. The process of sea ice formation itself modifies the ocean surface by separating fresh water and brine. The brine that is rejected from the ice increases the surface layer density and destabilises the water column. This mechanism may create deep oceanic mixing and it can be so intensive as to cause deep or even bottom water formation.

During the melting season in summer, the relatively less dense fresh water accumulates at the sea surface and hampers vertical mixing in the ocean, so that the air-sea interaction may be limited to a rather shallow surface layer. These heuristic considerations demonstrate the effect of the sea ice cycle on air-sea exchange processes. Because of the magnitude of this effect, sea ice development needs to be treated in satisfactory detail in coupled ocean-atmosphere models, especially for long-term variations such as climate changes to be studied.

---

* Prof. Dr. *Ernst Augstein*, Alfred Wegener Institute for Polar and Oceanic Research, Bremerhaven. (This is a summary of an audio-visual presentation — *Ed.*)

II. Antarctic Sea Ice

Antarctic sea ice covers up to 20 million square kilometers at the end of winter; by the end of summer an area of only about 3 million square kilometers remain. This large annual variation means that a vast oceanic area is affected by the above-mentioned consequences of freezing and melting at the sea surface. In order to understand sea ice development sufficiently its whole annual cycle must be carefully investigated. Due to logistic difficulties, past field work in the Antarctic ice belt was nearly exclusively limited to summer expeditions. This gap was filled to a certain extent by the intensive sea ice programme of the Winter Weddell Sea Project 1986 (WWSP) with R. V. "*Polarstern.*" During the two phases of this expedition, lasting from July to December 1986, the entire ice belt was penetrated four times in the longitude range between the Greenwich Meridian and 15° East. Measurements were taken of the ocean, the atmosphere and the sea ice. The comprehensive data set will serve as the basis for process studies and will provide initial and boundary values for numerical model experiments.

The observations showed that the Antarctic pack ice area may be subdivided into four different regions: a) the *marginal ice zone* which extends from the open water to about 200 km into the ice; b) the *inner pack ice regime*, covering the central part of the sea ice region; c) the 100 to 200 km wide *ridging zone* off the coast; and d) a 2 to 15 km coastal strip, the so-called *coastal polynya*, which is free of ice or only sparsely covered with very new ice.

The marginal ice zone on the open water side is characterized by slushy ice. Farther inwards small pancake-like close-packed floes (10—30 cm in diameter) dominate. These parameters tend to join together and to form clusters of three to seven units on the iceward side of the marginal ice zone. These larger floes drift in waters which are still generally perturbed by wind-induced surface waves. At the transition to the inner pack ice the multiple pancakes are frozen together into big plates. But even here the sea swell — generated in the open water — was observed to break the big plates into smaller pieces from time to time. Due to the surface wind stress, the floes may either collide and raft, or they may diverge and create leads which freeze over again in a short period of time. Consequently, new ice is not only created in the edge zone but also in the interior.

Because the coastal barrier obstructs the free drift of the wind-driven sea ice motion, considerable internal ice forces come into play. They lead to intense ridging in a broad band along the coastline. Ridges may have a vertical extent of more than ten meters, and their horizontal spacing may fall below 200 meters. This region, with heavy ice conditions, can hardly be penetrated even by ice-breaking ships.

The navigational conditions are normally much more convenient again in a narrow strip immediately off the coast, which quite often is kept ice-free by strong continental slope winds. Because the continental air is relatively cold, a large amount of heat is transferred from the polynyas into the atmosphere, and the new ice which forms at the sea surface is pushed offshore. This process, which operates nearly throughout the year, makes the coastal polynyas an important ice factory for the Antarctic ocean.

III. Atmospheric Forcing

The atmospheric pressure, wind velocity and temperature fields over the sea ice were measured with the aid of about 20 automatic floating stations deployed on ice floes across the sea ice belt. From these data, it is obvious that the motion of sea ice in the marginal ice zone and the interior pack ice is closely correlated with the surface wind vector. In the ridged coastal zone internal ice stresses gain importance in comparison to the wind and water drags. The air temperature contours and measurements of the turbulent vertical atmospheric heat flux at R. V. "*Polarstern*" suggest that both the cold air flowing off the continent and the warm air originating from the open ocean adjust to the new surface conditions within the first 150 km of the air mass trajectory over sea ice. The sensible and latent heat exchanges between the ice and the atmosphere drop almost to zero farther downstream. Here, the surface radiation budget gains importance, since the heat flux from the ocean to the atmosphere through the ice must be balanced at the upper sea ice boundary through net radiative cooling. Therefore, over ice surfaces radiation forms an essential element of the air-sea-ice heat balance.

IV. Final Remarks

The field observations during the Winter Weddell Sea Project 1986 have already contributed to a better understanding of the sea ice processes in the Antarctic. The complete set of oceanic, atmospheric and sea ice data will favourably support future modelling efforts in this area of research.

General Discussion

G. Hempel, Chairman:

Now, I am sure we have a few minutes to ask questions.

P. Quilty:

The helicopter-mounted ice-thickness measuring system, how does that one operate?

E. Augstein:

That is a radar. It sends radar signals into the ice, and these radar signals are scattered at the ice or at density variations, and by that you find the upper and the lower boundary of the ice. You get stronger signals at these boundaries. And it sends a signal down and measures the back-coming signal, and also the time differences.

G. Hempel, Chairman:

A question from *Alberto:*

A. Davérède:

How can satellites differentiate between the ice that is on the continent and the ice that is on the sea?

E. Augstein:

The satellites have microwave sensors for various frequencies, which they radiate down to the ice, and through a combination of the various channels you can get information on the ice structure, on the snow cover or liquid water on the ice surface, and some other details. Thus, you can find out if you have dry or wet ice, for instance. And you do have the different temperatures. The strongest indicator for land and sea ice is the surface temperature. The surface temperature over the Antarctic continent is about - 20° or less and the surface temperature of the sea ice during most periods is higher than - 10°. So there are several possibilities to distinguish them.

CCAMLR – Its Practical Side: The Polarstern Expedition

*Dietrich Sahrhage**

Your Excellencies, Ladies and Gentlemen — first of all, I would like to mention that on the 24th of September next, the sixth *Polarstern* expedition will leave Bremerhaven to go south. So, I would like to tell you a little bit about the practical side of CCAMLR, after all the arguments which we have exchanged during the two earlier meetings of Antarctic Challenge. Also, much was said yesterday about CCAMLR, and it may be useful for you realize how the practical work at sea is done.

Of course, much of the work at this stage directly concerned with CCAMLR concentrates on krill and also on the stocks of Antarctic fish. What I outline now about the German expedition on board the *Polarstern* is done more-or-less in the same way by our colleagues in other countries — and on each of our expeditions we have a number of colleagues from foreign countries who are fully integrated into the work during the expedition.

The main krill distribution in the Antarctic seems to be in the South Atlantic area, although they are also abundant in the Indian and Pacific Ocean Sectors. The Antarctic krill grows up to six centimeters long, and its life-span is much larger than Antarctic biologists originally thought: up to six, or possibly even seven years. When caught it has a bright red colour, and it smells like a very fresh, very nice crustacean.

Krill fishing for human consumption started in the early 1970s, and after some trial years, there was an increase (in 1979—80) to more than 400,000 tons per year; the highest landing was about 530,000 tons, in 1981—82. Most of this comes from the Atlantic Sector. I might refer you here to the graphs and illustrations in the Proceedings of Antarctic Challenge I, pages 67—88.

More than eighty per cent of the krill is landed by vessels of the Soviet Union, some by Japanese, and the remaining by those of Poland, GDR, and other countries. What was astonishing is that the landings decreased because of difficulties with the marketing and processing of krill, specifically in the Soviet Union. For a few years it remained at lower levels,

* Prof. Dr. *Dietrich Sahrhage*, Leitender Direktor des Instituts für Seefischerei, Bundesforschungsanstalt für Fischerei, Hamburg (This is a summary of an audiovisual presentation — *Ed.*)

until recently in the 1985—86 season it went up again to almost 500,000 tons. This shows that it is very easy to have a large fluctuation in the landings and if the marketing facilities are there, krill catches may easily reach higher levels. Therefore, it is important to collect data on the krill resources so that CCAMLR can ensure that sudden steep increases in krill fishing will not endanger the many other species which live upon krill.

Our main area of investigation is around the Antarctic Peninsula in the South Atlantic Sector, from Elephant Island to Adelaide Island, together with the Bransfield Strait and the South Shetland Islands. In earlier investigations we also visited the South Orkneys and South Georgia. The two most important, and persistant, krill-catching areas are north of South Orkneys, and west of Elephant Island. Out of about 500,000 tons in the 1985—86 season, about 225,000 were caught north of the South Orkneys. This raises some concern about such heavy fishing in such a restricted area, that this catch could have detrimental effects upon the predators of krill, such as penguins and seals. As a long-term program of the Federal Republic of Germany, we are engaged in integrated investigations, specifically around Elephant Island, to see the connection between the oceanographic conditions, the krill distribution and abundance and the fish distribution and abundance, in order to estimate how much krill the fish are consuming. We are not now concerned with South Georgia, because our British colleagues have a very intensive program there.

Turning from krill to the Antarctic fish stocks, there are rather limited areas on the shelf around the Antarctic islands which provide possibilities for bottom trawling for fish. It was discovered that the size of fish stocks was much less than originally thought; the fish grow slowly and cannot be fished very heavily without detrimental effects. We have been, and shall be, concentrating our investigation on the fish stocks around Elephant Island. This is part of the longer-term monitoring of both the krill and the fish resources, which is part of a related program of CCAMLR on an international basis. Altogether there are about 200 fish species south of the Antarctic Convergence. However, only seven are of commercial importance. The most is *Notothenia rossii*, the marbled notothenig, which is an excellent eating fish. When the stocks of this species were reduced due to serious over-exploitation, fishing turned to the Antarctic ice fish (*Champsocephalus gunnari*), and overfishing also of some other species occurred. During the early period of fishing, the *Notothenia rossii* were very large, up to 90 cm. One hardly sees them grow that large anymore.

The latest expedition of the *Polarstern* on CCAMLR matters was in May/June 1986, in early winter. Up to 50 or 52 scientists can be accommodated on board. The bridge is full of electronic equipment, echo sounders, *etc.* The ship is about 11,000 gross tons, with four engines of 5000 horsepower each. The full power of 20,000 hp is used only when we have to break through the ice. There are monitors all over the ship, indicating the position, speed, water temperature, wind direction, *etc.*, at all times as we work. There is a helicopter deck as well as a 12-meter launch, the *Polarfuchs*, which is fully equipped for independent research at sea. It has four berths, satellite navigation, radar, *etc.* The deck aft is very useful for biological and oceanographical work.

The main instrument used in krill research, by many countries, is the Rectangular Midwater Trawl developed in Britain. The upper net has an opening of one square meter, and fine-meshed net for catching small zooplankton and krill larvae; below is an eight-square-meter opening net with a larger mesh size where we catch adult krill. We use this for hauls down to, mostly 140 meters. We can open and close the net at different depths by electronic means, which allows us to calculate the differentiation and the composition of the krill catches at the various water depths. We often put living krill in aquaria, and even take them home to Germany. An important instrument for measuring the horizontal and vertical distribution of krill is, of course, the echo-sounder. Krill rarely go deeper than 140 meters.

The krill research is combined with "stations," as we say, in the field of oceanography. We collect water samples, and electronically measure the water temperature, salinity, and density. Water samples are being used by our colleagues who investigate the phytoplankton, which is food for the krill. With regard to the investigation of Antarctic fish, we use 140-foot bottom trawls of commercial size; the duration of each tow is 30 minutes. Despite her size, the *Polarstern* proved to be an excellent fisheries research vessel. The fish samples are partly worked-up on board, partly deep-frozen and carried to Germany for further investigation in the laboratory. We also find juvenile fish, or larvae which are caught in the krill shoals, which helps us investigate the question of whether krill fishing could have an impact on the recruitment of fish.

With regard to the conditions under which we work, last winter the whole Bransfield Strait was, unexpectedly, completely covered with thick ice due to long periods of easterly winds. Sometimes one can see brown layers in the ice: these are ice algae, which play an important part in the ecosystem and which we collect directly from the ship. We took several days to break through the ice, which was about one meter thick with an additional snow cover, by moving four ship-lengths forward and three back to ram our way through. We had to change our program (one has to be very flexible, particularly in winter-time) and accept that nature is stronger. In winter there are large quantities of krill under the ice or inside the cracks; they feed upon the algae. This has been confirmed in the laboratory here in Bremerhaven. Before these investigations no one knew, really, what the krill do during the wintertime. Last year was the first time we had winter expeditions and the results already had a great impact on our investigations on the krill biology and ecology. They are also important for the management regime by CCAMLR. What is now required, internationally, is a continuation and further development of close cooperation. The university circles need to work together with the governmental research institutes. Yesterday there was a hint, that there might be a separation of basic research from research concerned with the more "economic" aspects. With regard to the oceanographic and biological marine resources field, I would really warn against this. In many cases, we work from the same ship. It is the cheapest means, to combine our research, use the same instruments, fully utilizing all our resources in the most economic way possible. Thank you very much.

General Discussion

R. Wilson:

You mentioned during your presentation that some of your studies on krill were also giving you insights into the recruitment of finfish and the relationship between catches of krill, and whether that was having any effect on finfish recruitment. What have you come up with on that?

D. Sahrhage:

What I was referring to was that krill catches, made also by the commercial krill fishery, include a certain amount of small, young fish, and fish larvae. The proportion of fish and krill was investigated by the biologists in several countries. Our Polish colleagues found a rather high amount of young fish, which raised concern at some earlier meeting of the Scientific Committee of CCAMLR. However, by further investigations in the Federal Republic of Germany and some other countries, it was found that obviously on the average the amount is much, much smaller than originally thought. The findings were discussed in the Scientific Committee of CCAMLR, and their report stated that the by-catches of small fish in the krill fishery were not considered to be a problem at the present time.

Geology and Geophysics of the Weddell Sea

*Dieter Karl Fütterer**

I. Introduction and Physiographic Setting

The Weddell Sea is located between the Antarctic continent and South America. It stretches from approximately 60° to 75° S and from the Greenwich Meridan to 60° W (*Figure 1*). As the most southerly extension of the Atlantic Ocean, the Weddell Sea forms a deep incision into the Antarctic continent. It separates the geologically very old East Antarctic craton in the east — formed mainly by Precambrian to Paleozoic and some early Mesozoic rocks — from the younger Antarctic Peninsula in the west, which is mainly built up by late Mesozoic and Cenozoic rocks. Its southern limit is occupied by the vast ice sheet of the Filchner-Ronne Ice Shelf. To the north, the Weddell Sea is separated from the Scotia Sea by the South Scotia Ridge and the South Shetland Islands.

The southern Weddell Sea deep basin is an abyssal plain (sloping generally towards the north-east), separated from a more northern area of much greater basement relief caused by seamounts and fracture-zone ridges. A unique feature of the Weddell Sea is its pack-ice cover, which shows strong seasonal variations in areal distribution and thickness. West of a line at 30—40° W, a permanent heavy pack-ice cover makes this part of the Weddell Sea nearly inaccessible for research vessels. This, naturally, has a strong influence on the scientific data base and information from that region. Our present knowledge of even the large scale topography of the Weddell Sea deep basin, therefore, is rather inadequate and the reliability of the existing data base is still a severe problem in this remote and hostile region. This is, as an example, documented by the inset "no source data" for the vast shelf of the southern Weddell Sea on the General Bathymetric Chart of the Ocean (*Figure 1*).

Poor data coverage holds true not only for the vast shelf regions of the southern Weddell Sea but generally as well for large areas of the deep basin. Another very impressive example of poorly-known bathymetry came to light during a recent bathymetric survey in the central Weddell Sea during *Polarstern* cruise ANT-IV/3 in austral summer

* Prof. Dr. *Dieter Karl Fütterer*, Alfred Wegener Institute for Polar and Marine Research, Bremerhaven.

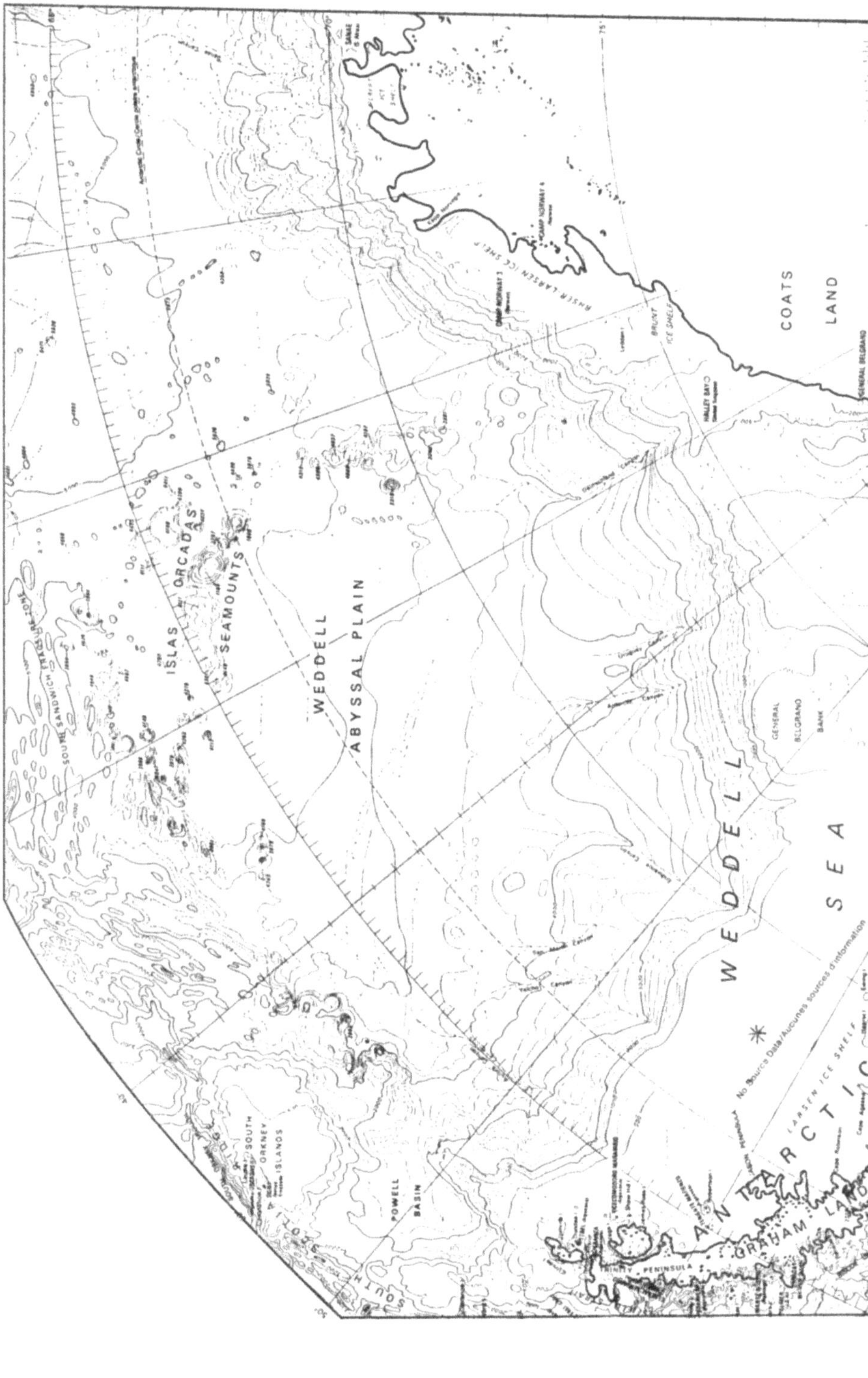

Fig. 1: **Geographic setting and bathymetry of the Weddell Sea. From General Bathymetric Chart of the Ocean (GEBCO) Sheet 5.16, 1981 * No Source Data.**

1985/86. It has been demonstrated that a large chain of seamounts, some 200 km in extension and rising more than 3000 m above the Weddell Abyssal Plain, the so-called Islas Orcadas Seamounts, which is shown or earlier bathymetric maps for the central Weddell Sea (*Figure 1*), does not exist at all, and should be removed from future compilations.

Such aspects have to be kept in mind when discussing the Weddell Sea, its evolution and geological history.

The following presentation outlines briefly the structural and geological evolution of the Weddell Sea embayment. New information from *Polarstern* cruises and from Leg 113 of the international Ocean Drilling Program (ODP) is included.

II. Plate Tectonic Setting

The Weddell Sea region is one of the key areas in the puzzle of plate tectonic reconstruction of the pre-Jurassic super-continent Gondwanaland. The plate tectonic fits between Africa and South America and between Antarctica, Australia, and India have been satisfactorily established, although many details are still waiting to be solved. However, serious problems remain with the plate tectonic fit between South America and Antarctica, that is, the region of the Antarctic Peninsula and the Weddell Sea. An understanding of its tectonic evolution would resolve most of the remaining problems, amongst which the most serious, with respect to deep ocean circulation and southern hemisphere as well as global climatic evolution, is the precise timing of the opening of Drake's Passage (*Barker* and *Burrell*, 1977).

Just to illustrate the key problem in the plate tectonic puzzle: a plate tectonic reconstruction, based on the analysis of marine geophysical data, runs into overlap problems with the Antarctic Peninsula superimposed on the Falkland Plateau (*Figure 2 a*; *Norton* and *Sclater*, 1979).

One of the many different reconstructions (*Harrison et al.*, 1979) based on land geology supports a reconstruction with the Antarctic Peninsula on the Pacific side of southern South America (*Figure 2 b*).

The modern plate tectonic setting of the South Atlantic — Weddell Sea region is indicated in *Figure 3*. It shows the Weddell Sea as part of the large Antarctic Plate bounded to the north by the South America Plate along the American-Antarctic Ridge, some of which has been subducted beneath the Sandwich Microplate. The large transform fault of the South Sandwich Fracture zone separates the Weddell Sea from the Sandwich Microplate and further west from the Scotia Plate. The back-arc spreading center of the Bransfield Strait forms a structurally active boundary at the extreme northwest. The Antarctic Peninsula,

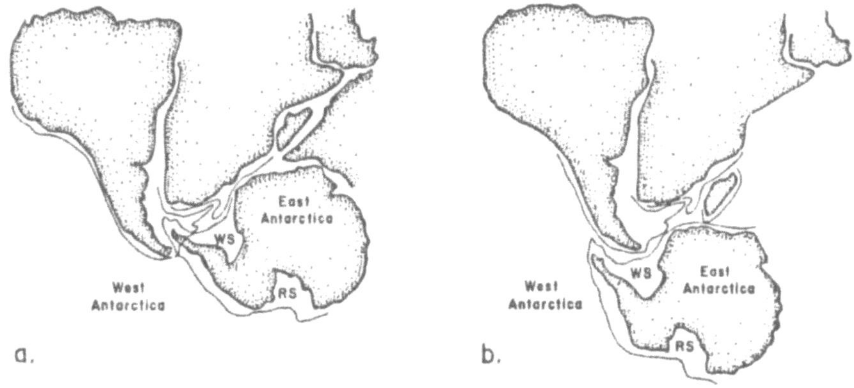

Fig. 2: Different Gondwanaland reconstructions:
a) of *Norton* and *Slater*, 1979, which runs into overlap problems with the Antarctic Peninsula superimposed on the Falkland Plateau.
b) of *Harrison et al.*, 1979, which shows the Antarctic Peninsula lying on the Pacific side of South America.
WS = Weddell Sea, RS = Ross Sea. From *Dalziel* and *Elliot*, 1982.

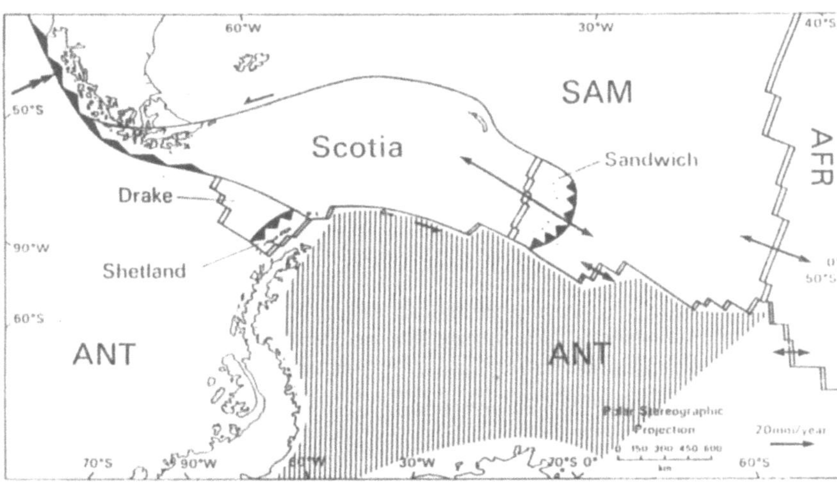

Fig. 3: Modern plate tectonic setting of the South Atlantic — Weddell Sea region. Weddell Sea: hatchured ANT = Antarctic plate; SAM = South America plate; AFR = African plate; double line = mid-oceanic spreading centers; single solid line = fracture zone; jagged line = subduction zone. From Tectonic Map of the Scotia Arc.

western edge of the Weddell Sea, is presently a structurally inactive intra-plate feature of the Antarctic Plate.

The tectonic development of the Weddell Sea is supposed to be closely related to the very early break-up of Gondwanaland in Early to Mid Jurassic times.

III. Age of the Weddell Sea Basin

Geophysical data from the Weddell Sea basin, which could be used to elucidate its presumably very complicated history, are generally scarce. From paleomagnetic data (*LaBrecque* and *Barker*, 1981; *Okuda et al.*, 1983; *Spiess*, 1985), however, we can depict a reasonably reliable scenario. *Figure 4* shows the magnetic anomaly profiles and interpreted magnetic lineation pattern with assigned ages in million years of the Weddell Sea deep basin (*LaBrecque* and *Barker*, 1981). From the strongly east-west lineated magnetic anomaly pattern and other geophysical data we can conclude that the Weddell Sea basin started to form prior to magnetic anomaly M-29, that is, 165 million years ago within the Callovien of the Middle Jurassic. The oldest oceanic crust occurs near the Antarctic continent and basement age becomes progressively younger to the north. The youngest oceanic basement identified in the northern Weddell Sea is of anomaly 6a, which corresponds to a Lower Miocene age of 21 million years.

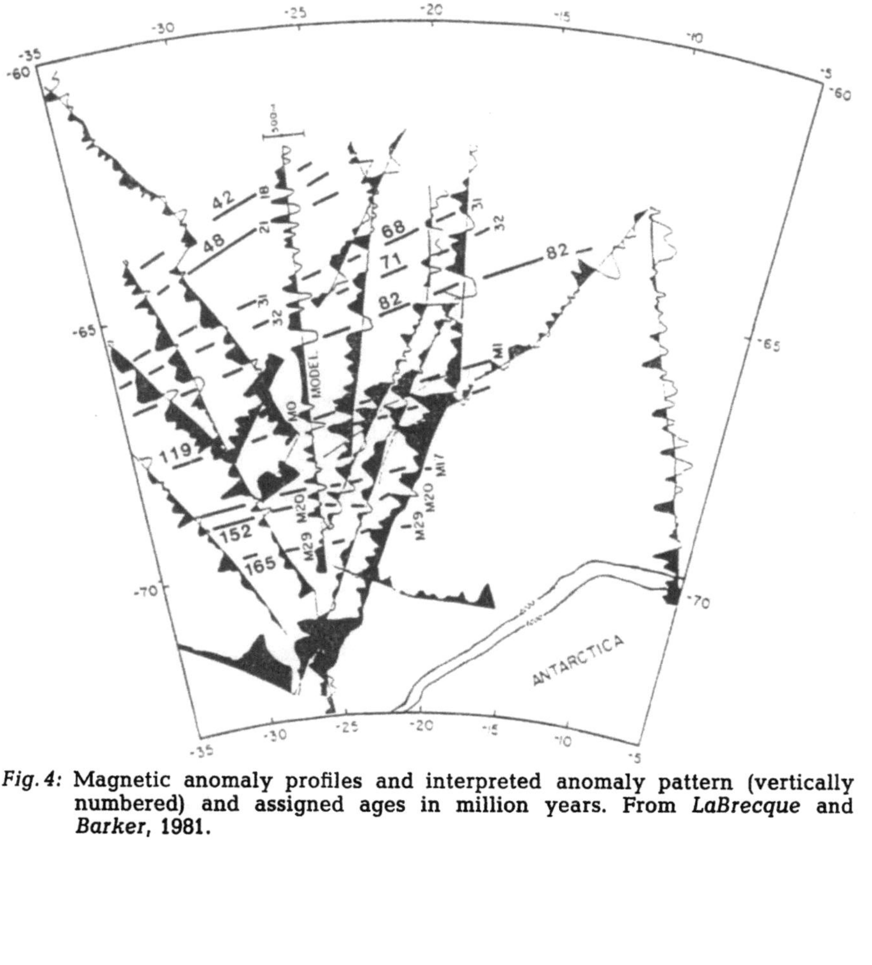

Fig. 4: Magnetic anomaly profiles and interpreted anomaly pattern (vertically numbered) and assigned ages in million years. From *LaBrecque* and *Barker*, 1981.

It is further concluded that the Weddell Sea deep basin was formed at the southern flank of a spreading centre. The northern flank has been subducted beneath the Scotia Sea in the then-active island arc of Jane Bank (Jane Bank is a submarine morphological structure east of South Orkney Islands, see *Figure 1*). The estimated time of collision and subduction of the Weddell Sea spreading centre with Jane Bank island arc is estimated to be 20 million years ago.

Recently published data on poles of rotation and reconstructions of Antarctica and Africa in relation to South America (*Lawver et al.*, 1985) reveal an opening between the tip of the Antarctic Peninsula and South America that began prior to magnetic anomaly 13, that is, 35 million years ago and roughly 10 million years before Drake's Passage opened. The trace of the movement is roughly indicated by the Shackleton Fracture Zone between the tip of South America and Elephant Island in the South Shetlands.

The first indication of a complete closure between South America and the Antarctic Peninsula in the configuration which the two continents now have is at anomaly 28 time, some 64 million years ago.

Because of different geometrical relations and different spreading rates at the Bouvet triple junction — the place where the active margins of the African, South America and Antarctic plates meet — no significant overlap occurs which could not be explained by slight crustal extension due to crustal thinning during early rifting prior to that time.

Prior to anomaly M-0 of the Lower Cretaceous, 119 million years ago, however, we need some major translation or rotation of the Antarctic Peninsula with respect to East Antarctica to overcome an overlap of South America and Antarctica. This would affect very strongly the configuration of the Weddell Sea.

At present, we do not have any data to give a reliable answer. However, one possible reconstruction of Gondwanaland in the Weddell Sea is given by *Dalziel* and *Elliot* (1982). It is based on the assumption that the West Antarctic, including the Weddell Sea region, consists of several discrete or semidiscrete microcontinental blocks, which moved relative to one another and to the East Antarctic craton during the fragmentation of Gondwanaland and the development of the Weddell Sea (*Figure 5*).

IV. Geology of the Weddell Sea Embayment

Some details of the geological and structural framework of the Weddell Sea may represent the first steps towards a better understanding.

To the southeast and east, in Coats Land and western Neuschwabenland, the Weddell Sea is bounded by the East Antarctic craton. The

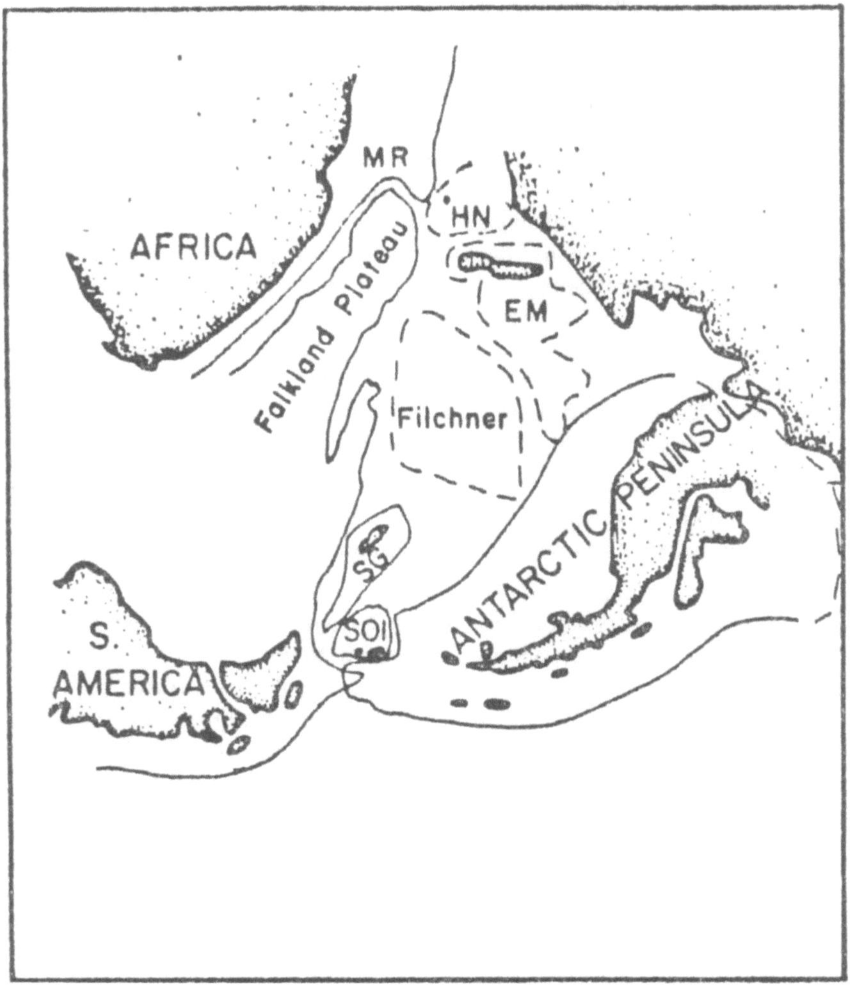

Fig. 5: Possible reconstruction of the Weddell Sea embayment during break-up of Gondwandaland. HN = Haag Nunataks; MR = Mozambique Ridge; EM = Ellsworth Mountains; SG = South Georgia; SO = South Orkney Islands. Modified from *Dalziel* and *Elliot*, 1982.

basement rocks, mainly deformed Precambrian metamorphics outcropping in the Kottas Escarpment, are overlain by a middle Paleozoic to Mesozoic non-marine sedimentary sequence, the Beacon Supergroup (*Barrett et al.*, 1972). These continental sediments contain a rich flora and locally thin coal seams occur in the Kottas Mountains. In the Kraul and Kottas Mountains the Beacon sediments are capped and intruded by Jurassic basalt lavas, sills and dikes respectively. Jurassic igneous rocks are generally widespread for 3500 km along the entire chain of the Transantarctic Mountains and are believed to indicate the initial rifting leading to the break-up and fragmentation of Gondwanaland (*Kyle et al.*, 1983).

Strong down-faulting occured in western Neuschwabenland, most probably caused by Early Jurassic rifting and continental thinning in connection with the initial opening of the Weddell Sea (*Figure 6*). This assumption is supported by basalt geochemistry showing an evolution from continental-rift basalts in the Kirwan Escarpment, which is slightly east of the Kottas Escarpment, to basalts similar to mid-ocean-ridge extrusives in the Kraul Mountains. Potassium-argon dating on the basalts is in the range of 173—162 million years for the Kottas Mountains (*Rex*, 1972) and 173—156 million years for dikes in the Kraul Mountains (*Furnes* and *Mitchell*, 1978); those are all Middle Jurassic ages.

According to the down-faulting — a total vertical displacement of some 5 to 6 km is assumed — the most complete section of rocks is expected to occur off-shore at the continental margin.

The continental margin of the eastern Weddell Sea was explored by multi-channel seismics during several Norwegian and West German expeditions during recent years. According to *Hinz* and *Krause* (1982) the crustal basement is overlain by the Explora Wedge, a thick sequence of seaward-dipping seismic reflectors interpreted to represent a sequence of predominantly volcanic and volcaniclastic rocks. A Middle Jurassic age is assigned for the volcanic wedge in accordance with the age of the on-shore volcanics.

Formation of wedges of seaward-dipping seismic reflectors takes place by extrusion of lavas under sub-aerial or shallow water conditions on continental crust during crustal extension and thinning during early

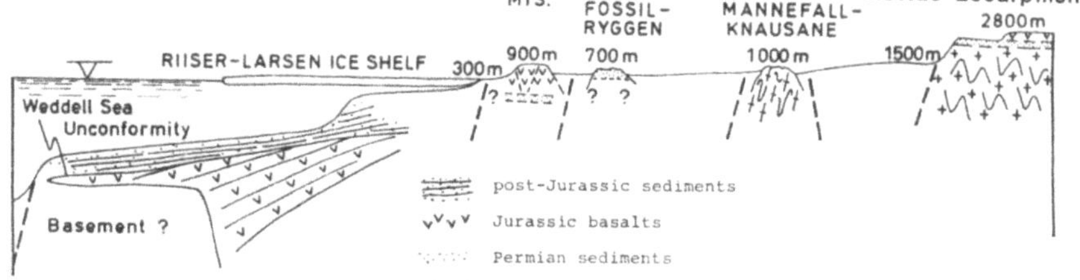

Fig. 6: Schematic geological section from the Kottas Escarpment, East Antarctic craton to the Explora Escarpment in the eastern Weddell Sea.

stages of rifting. Subsequent sagging, under the load of the volcanic build-up and cooling, causes reversal of dip of the volcanic rocks towards the active center (*Hinz*, 1981).

The seismically very distinct upper boundary of the Explora Wedge, the Weddell Sea continental margin unconformity (*Hinz* and *Krause*, 1982), is thought to mark the onset of the typical sea-floor spreading phase.

The predominantly undisturbed Mesozoic to Cenozoic sedimentary unit overlying the Weddell Sea unconformity consists of several seismic sequences which are speculated to be of regional importance for seismic stratigraphy.

Major linear outer basement highs have been found along the lower slope of the southeastern Weddell Sea margin separating it from the Weddell Sea basin (*Figure 7*). The WSW-trending Explora Escarpment, which is morphologically very prominent in the northeast, becomes more subdued towards the SW. A similar WSW-trending, deeply buried basement structure, the Andenes Escarpment [named of the Norwegian Expedition Vessel of the Norwegian Antarctic Research Expedition 1985 (NARE 85)] forms a continuation of the Explora Escarpment at 26° W.

The Andenes and Explora escarpments, consisting of several segments, form a linear basement structure more than 1000 km long. This basement

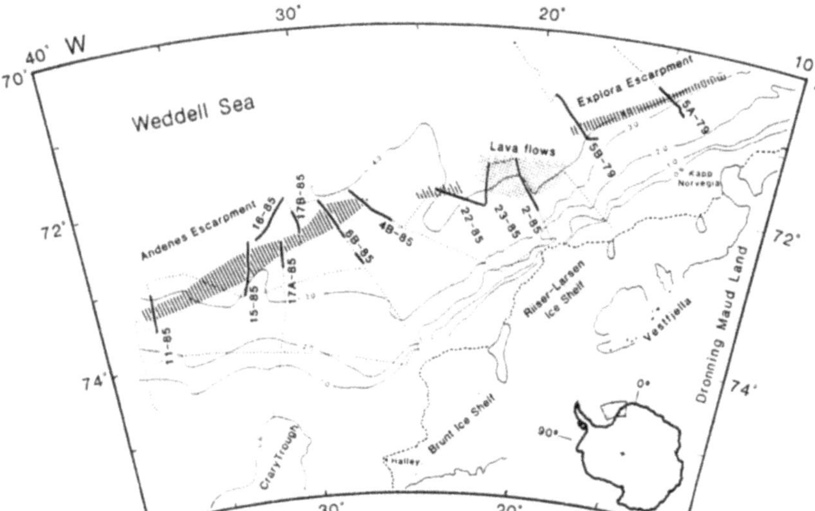

Fig. 7: Morphological escarpments and outer basement higher along the East Antarctic continental margin. From *Kristoffersen* and *Haugland*, 1986.

ridge is interpreted to represent a part of the East Antarctic plate boundary during the early break-up of Gondwanaland (*Kristoffersen* and *Haugland*, 1986).

Seismic data very recently collected by the RV *Polarstern* in the field season 1985/86 during a site survey for the Ocean Drilling Program revealed the presence of some remarkably symmetric basement structures (*Hinz* and *Kristoffersen*, 1987). Between 20° and 40° W an elongated NNE-SSW-trending depression of the basement, structurally similar to oceanic basement, is surrounded by two wedge-shaped basement units. The northern wedge terminates against the Andenes-Explora Escarpment. Its seismic reflection pattern has a southward (landward) dip. The southern wedge, identical with the Explora Wedge, shows a northward (seaward) dipping reflector pattern. This striking structurally symmetrical feature, cut by the Andenes-Explora Escarpment, is interpreted to represent a failed drift basin. Gravity and magnetic data (*Masolov, 1980*) support this interpretation.

This failed drift basin represents a very early stage of Gondwanaland fragmentation which, as documented on-shore, was connected with an enormous volcanic activity of Middle Jurassic age. Classic sea-floor spreading started later when by the formation of the Andenes-Explora Escarpment a new plate boundary was established.

The presence of such a linear plate boundary extending to the vicinity of the Antarctic Peninsula makes a post-rift microplate motion, as suggested in *Figure 5*, rather unlikely for the Weddell Sea embayment.

V. Climatic and Sedimentary Evolution of the Weddell Sea

During Leg 113 of the international Ocean Drilling Program (ODP) the paleoclimatic, paleoglacial and paleoceanographic history and biotic evolution of the Weddell Sea was investigated in nine drill sites (*Figure 8*). These included open-ocean pelagic biogenic sediments on Maud Rise, hemipelagic and terrigeneous sediments on or close to the continental margin of both East and West Antarctica, and a deep-sea hemipelagic sequence in the Weddell abyssal plain (OPD Leg 113 Shipboard Scientific Party, 1987 a and b).

From all sites of Leg 113, it was determined that there was a sequential cooling and glacial development of Antarctica and the surrounding oceans during the Cenozoic. Glacial development began during the Paleogene in East Antarctica. Iceberg-transported coarse drop-stones start to occur in the hemipelagic sequence of Site 693 in the early Oligocene, some 35 million years ago. They document at least a polar ice cap distributing icebergs by glaciers to the open ocean.

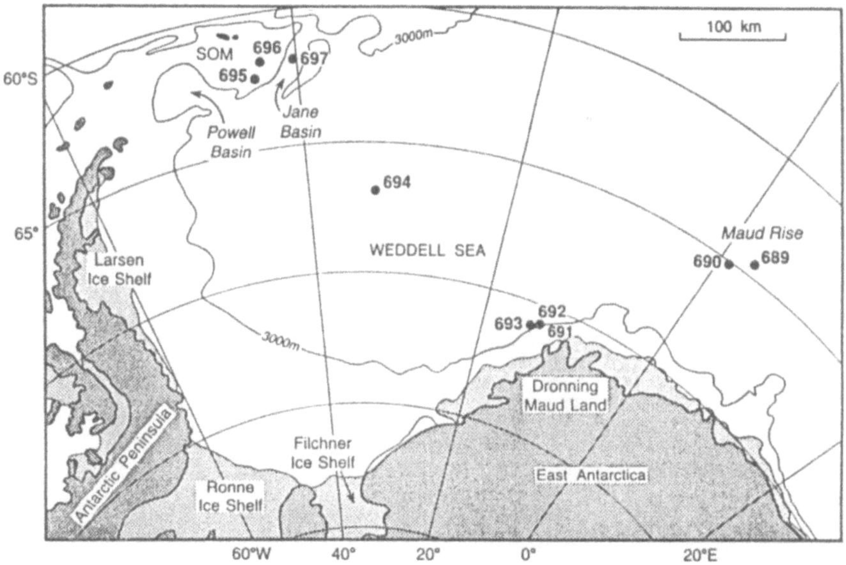

Fig. 8: Location of ODP Leg 113 drill sites in the Weddell Sea. From ODP Leg Shipboard Scientific Party, 1987 b.

The data suggest that the East Antarctic ice sheet, once formed, underwent no significant deglaciation, even during the early Pliocene for which stratigraphically expanded sequences have been recovered. The data also indicate that the West Antarctic ice sheet did not begin to form until the late Miocene, that is, some 12 million years ago.

A more detailed, but short look at Site 693 at the East Antarctic margin gives an outline of the sedimentary evolution. This site is situated on the Explora Wedge mentioned above (*Figure* 9), which probably represents a volcanic sequence formed during the earliest break-up of Gondwanaland. One of the main targets at this site was to drill this seaward dipping reflector sequence in order to directly date the volcanics. That means to drill through the Weddell Sea unconformity which, in terms of seismic stratigraphy, is called simply "U-9" *(Figure 10)*. Unfortunately this attempt failed due to technical problems.

A sedimentary sequence of 400 m of lower Oligocene to Pleistocene diatrom-rich, hemipelagic muds was recovered before drilling into Lower Cretaceous (Albian) diatomites and diatom-rich and organic-rich mudstones and claystones. The organic carbon average, 2.6% in the Albian section, is less than that at Site 692, where average carbon content reached 8.6%. However, despite strong ocidation at Site 693, the Albian mudstones have to be considered as a potential hydrocarbon source rock of considerable thickness.

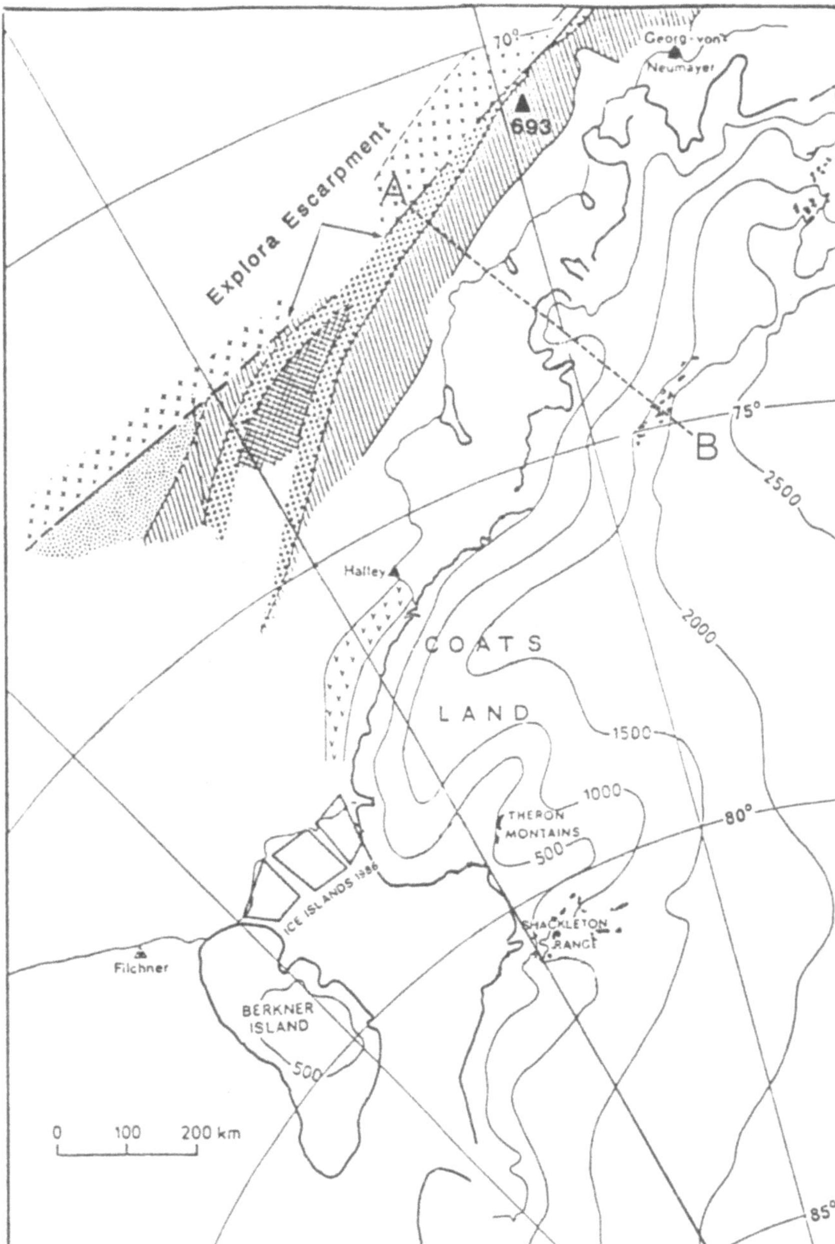

Fig. 9: Geology of the East Antarctic continental margin. Heavy triangle marks location of ODP Site 693 on the Explora Wedge. A - B = Geological section of Figure 6. Modified from *Hinz* and *Kristoffersen*, 1987.

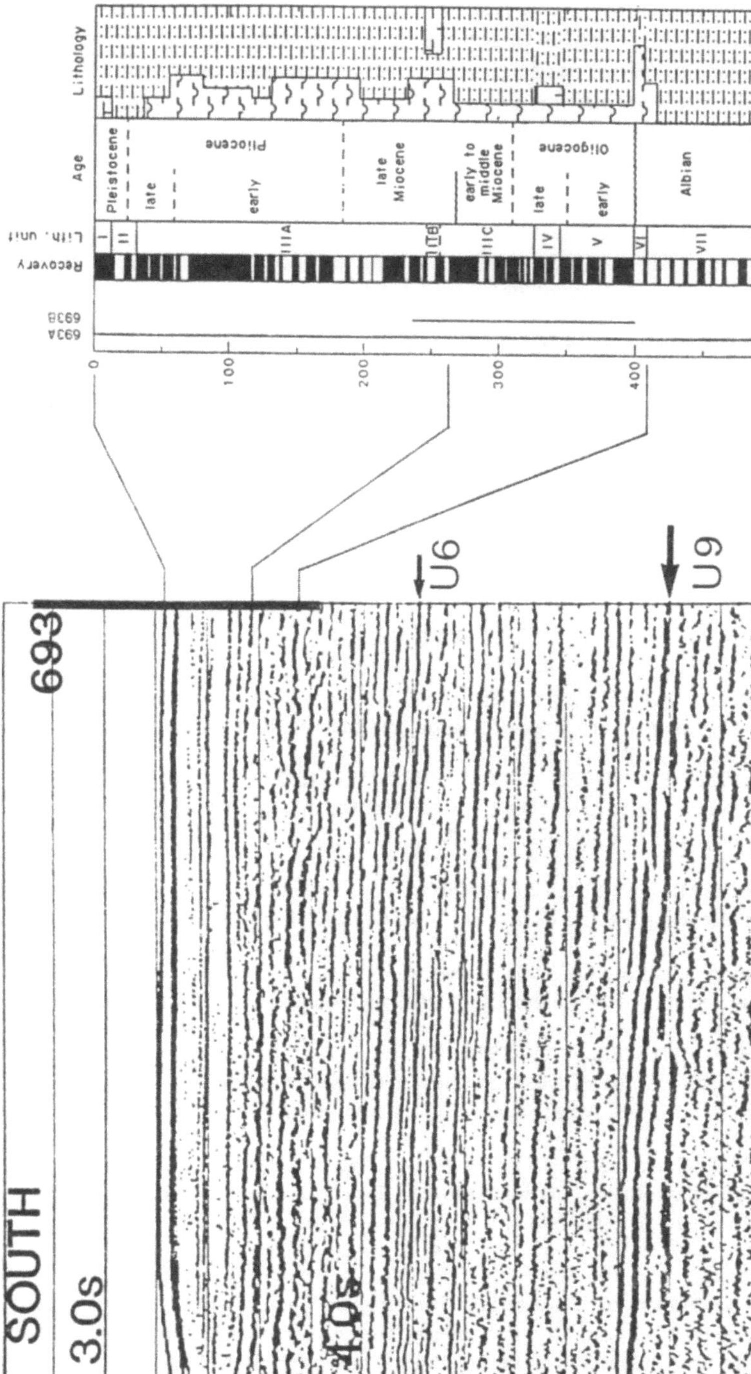

Fig. 10: Representative lithostratigraphy, lithology, age and core recovery at Site 693 combined with seismic reflection profile. U 6 and U 9 mark seismic reflectors / unconformities of regional importance. The latter is correlated with the Middle to Late Jurassic Weddell Sea unconformity (*Hinz* and *Krause*, 1982; *Hinz* and *Kristoffersen*, 1987). Modified from ODP Leg 113 Scientific Shipboard Party, 1987 a.

The mudstone was deposited in anoxic to oxic conditions of poor circulation and it is similar to sediments of the same age recovered from Falkland Plateau (Shipboard Scientific Party *et al.* Leg. 36, 1976). A hiatus of approximately 65 million years separates the Lower Cretaceous mudstones from the lower Oligocene to Pleistocene sedimentary sequence which by varying abundance of ice-rafted debris indicates glacial conditions throughout the Cenozoic sequences recovered. The erosional event that caused the 65-million year hiatus is tentatively placed close to the Eocene/Oligocene boundary, a time of global cooling and generally vigorous circulation of deep and bottom waters.

Drilling Site at 693 and the seismic reflection profiles (*Figure 10*), show that 70—80 % of the sediments of the East Antarctic continental margin of the Weddell Sea are Lower Cretaceous or older.

REFERENCES

BARKER, P. F. / BURRELL, J. (1977),
The Opening of the Drake Passage, in: Marine Geol., 25, 15—34.

BARRETT, P. J. / GRINDLEY, G. W. / WEBB, P. N. (1972),
The Beacon Supergroup in East Antarctica, in: ADIE, R. J. (ed.), Antarctic Geology and Geophysics, 319—332.

BRITISH ANTARCTIC SURVEY (1985),
Tectonic Map of the Scotia Arc, 1:3.000.000, BAS (Misc.) 3.

DALZIEL, J. W. D. / ELLIOT, D. H. (1982),
West Antarctica: Problem Child of Gondwanaland, in: Tectonics, 1, 3—19.

FURNES, H. / MITCHELL, J. C. (1978),
Age relationships of Mesozoic basalt lavas and dikes in Vestfjella, Dronning Maud Land, Antarctica, in: Norsk Polarinstitutt Skrift., 169, 45—68.

HARRISON, C. G. A. / BARRON, E. J. / HAY, W. W. (1979),
Mesozoic evolution of the Antarctic Peninsula and the southern Andes, in: Geology, 7, 374—378.

HINZ, K. (1981),
A Hypothesis of Terrestrial Catastrophes — Wedges of very thick Oceanward Dipping Layers beneath Passive Continental Margins — Their Origin and Paleoenvironmental Significance, in: Geol. Jb., E 22, 3—28.

HINZ, K. / KRAUSE, W. (1982),
The Continental Margin of Queen Maud Land / Antarctica: Seismic sequences, structural elements and geological development, in: Geol. Jb., E 23, 17—41.

HINZ, K. / KRISTOFFERSEN, Y. (1987),
Antarctica: Recent Advances in the Understanding of the Continental Shelf, in: Geol. Jb., E 37, 3—54.

KRISTOFFERSEN, Y. / HAUGLAND, K. (1986),
Geophysical Evidence for the East Antarctic Plate Boundary in the Weddell Sea, in: Nature, 322, 538—541.

KYLE, P. R. / SUTTER, J. F. / McINTOSH, W. C. / CHERRY, E. / NOLTIMIER, H. (1983),
^{40}Ar / ^{39}Ar Age Spectra and Paleomagnetic Measurements of Ferrar Supergroup Samples from the Transantarctic Mountains, Antarctica, in: OLIVER, R. L. / JAMES, P. R. / JAGO, J. B. (eds.), Antarctic Earth Science, 242.

LaBRECQUE, J. L. / BARKER, P. F. (1981),
The Age of the Weddell Basin, in: Nature, 290, 489—492.

LAWVER, L. A. / SCLATER, J. G. / MEINKE, L. (1985),
Mesozoic and Cenozoic Reconstructions of the South Atlantic, in: Tectonophysics, 114, 233—254.

MAŠOLOV, N. N. (1980),
Stroenie magnitoaktivnogo fundamenta jugovostocnoj casti bassejna morja Uedella. Geofiziceskie issledovdnija v Antarktide, in: Naucno Issledovatel'skij Institut Geologii Arktide (NIIGA), 14—28.

NORTON, S. O. / SCLATER, J. G. (1979),
A Model for the Evolution of the Indian Ocean and the Breakup of Gondwanaland, in: Jour. Geophys. Res., 84 (B 12), 6803—6830.

ODP Leg 113 Shipboard Party (1987 a),
Leg 113 Explores Climatic Changes, in: Geotimes, July 1987, 12—15.

ODP Leg 113 Shipboard Party (1987 b),
Glacial History of Antarctica, in: Nature, 328, 115—116.

OKUDA, Y. / YAMAZAKI, T. / SATO, S. / SAKI, T. / OIKAWA, N. (1983),
Framework of the Weddell Basin inferred from the New Geophysical and Geological Data, in: Mem. Nat. Inst. Polar Res., Spec. Issue 28, 93—114.

REX, D. C. (1972),
K-Ar Determinations on Volcanic and Associated Rocks from the Antarctic Peninsula and Dronning Maud Land, in: ADIE, R. J. (ed.): Antarctic Geology and Geophysics, 133—136.

The Shipboard Scientific Party *et* HARRIS, W. / and SLITER, W. V. (1976),
Evolution of the southwestern Ocean Basin: Results of Leg 36, Deep Sea Drilling Project, in: BARKER, P. F. / DALZIEL, I. W. D. *et al.*, Initial Reports of the Deep Sea Drilling Project, Vol. 36, Washington (U.S. Government Printing Office), 993—1014.

SPIESS, V. (1985),
Analyse und Interpretation zwei- und dreidimensionaler mariner magnetischer Anomalien, in: Ber. Inst. Geophys. Ruhr-Univ. Bochum, A 17, 170 pp.

Geophysical and Geological Research in Antarctica Related to the Assessment of Petroleum and Mineral Resources and Potential Environmental Hazards

*John C. Behrendt**

Introduction

There are no known petroleum or mineral resources in Antarctica (*Fig. 1*), and no deposits have been found that would be economically feasible even if they were present in other parts of the world. Antarctic research, carried out primarily since the International Geophysical Year (IGY) 1957/58, has provided a great deal of information on all aspects of Antarctica, not the least of which are results from geologic studies related to mineral resources and the environmental hazards that might impact their future development. During the IGY, geology was the one discipline conspicuously absent from Antarctic research because of possible political difficulties associated with the potential mineral resource aspects. Nonetheless, the geophysical and glaciological over-snow traverses conducted during that time provided a large amount of information on geologic structure. Geologic investigations have been frequently carried out by all of the countries in the Antarctic Treaty since that time. One cannot always clearly separate geologic research into resource assessment efforts and environmental hazards studies because the same type of data may provide evidence for either or for both. In this paper I show examples of the similarities and differences of the two types of studies. One significant difference is that prospecting and development of petroleum or mineral resources depends on geological similarities to other parts of the world where these deposits have been found and economically developed in the past. However, the Antarctic environment is unique and any future mineral resource development will have to deal with its associated hazards as well as any potential adverse impact on the unique *biota* which inhabit it.

Antarctica is large, and potential mineral deposits are small in comparison. As examples, the distance across Antarctica is comparable to that of Anchorage to Miami in the United States, Delhi to the North Pole, or westernmost Australia to easternmost New Zealand. For example,

* Dr. *John C. Behrendt*, United States Geological Survey, Denver, Colorado.

Prudhoe Bay, the only super-giant oil field in the United States, is only 12 km across and large scale mines are only a few kilometers wide at most. Therefore, the difficulty of finding potential economic deposits in Antarctica is apparent. It is very unlikely that any would be identified in the course of normal scientific research, although the understanding of the geologic framework necessary for mineral prospecting could develop from this research.

Antarctica is high; the average elevation in East Antarctica is above 3000m, reaching almost 4000m in places. West Antarctica averages about 1500m elevation. Antarctica is covered by a moving ice sheet, averaging about 3000m thick. Only two percent of the bedrock in Antarctica is exposed. This projects through the ice as occasional small nunataks and other rather large extensive mountain ranges (*Fig. 1*).

Fig. 1: Index map of Antarctica showing major geographic features discussed in text, including the continental margin. Bathymetric contour interval 3000 meters; ice-sheet surface contour interval 1000 meters.

The old oversnow traverse program was carried out between 1956 and 1966. Seismic reflection, seismic refraction and glaciological observations were made and measurements of gravity and magnetic field intensity were taken along very widely spaced lines across the entire ice sheet of Antarctica. When nunataks were encountered, geologic observations were also made. During the last 30 years, geologists from a number of the Antarctic research countries have sampled the extensive Transantarctic Mountain range and other mountain ranges and have visited, at least once, almost all of the widely separated nunataks where rock is exposed in Antarctica. This extremely sparse sampling, done with helicopters, aircraft, and snow mobiles supported by aircraft, still leaves Antarctica several orders of magnitude less studied geologically than any other region of the earth including tropical rain forests in areas of Africa and South America. *Rowley et al.* (1983) discussed the occurrence of various minerals reported as a result of this research and presented maps showing locations. It should be noted that occurrences are not ore deposits. There are no deposits reported in Antarctica that would be considered economic were they located anywhere else in the world.

Modern radar ice-sounding methods can be used to measure the thickness of the Antarctic ice sheet. The technique has been widely used in the last 15 years and has largely supplanted the more costly seismic reflection methods used prior to that time. In combination with the radio echo ice-sounding method, the aeromagnetic techniques provide probably the best quick and simple remote sensing tools with which to study the geology of Antarctica beneath the ice sheet. This method allows the extrapolation of geological knowledge obtained with great difficulty at widely spaced rock outcrops.

Although widely spaced aeromagnetic traverses have been made in Antarctica since the 1950s, the first standard aeromagnetic survey in Antarctica was carried out by the F.R.G.'s *Bundesanstalt für Geowissenschaften und Rohstoffe* (BGR), and the United States Geological Survey (USGS) in North Victoria Land and the Ross Sea in the 1984/85 field season.

Landsat and other high-resolution satellite images are being used extensively in Antarctic research for studying the ice sheet, but they are utilized as well in studying the geology where rock outcrops do occur. Unfortunately, these data do not provide information on the geologic structure beneath the thick ice sheet.

During the past 15 years marine multichannel seismic measurements have been made by researchers in various countries across the continental margins and ocean basins throughout the world. As this technique, which was developed originally for the petroleum industry, has become available to the scientific research community, these data are now being collected in Antarctica as well, starting in 1976. Marine multichannel seismic methods are very much more expensive and difficult to apply in Antarctica than the earlier single channel profiling methods used by research ships. In addition to elaborate computers and airgun systems installed on the ship, a long streamer up to 3km in length and a complex array of airguns is towed behind the ship in ice free areas.

By combining the results of types of research, we have a general idea of the locations of basins containing thick sedimentary rock and of the types of mineral occurrences in the outcropping mountains of Antarctica. *Fig. 2*, from *Behrendt* (1988), illustrates a generalized version of sub-ice topography, major topographic features, and regional sedimentary basins which would be the likely areas to be prospected for petroleum resources under the minerals regime. Because Antarctica is covered by a moving ice sheet about 3km thick, the continental margins would be the likely areas for any future petroleum development. West Antarctica, comprising the margins of the Weddell, Bellinghausen, Amundsen, and Ross Seas, is the most promising area but the Amery ice shelf area (*Fig. 1*) of East Antarctica is also considered likely (*Behrendt*, 1983).

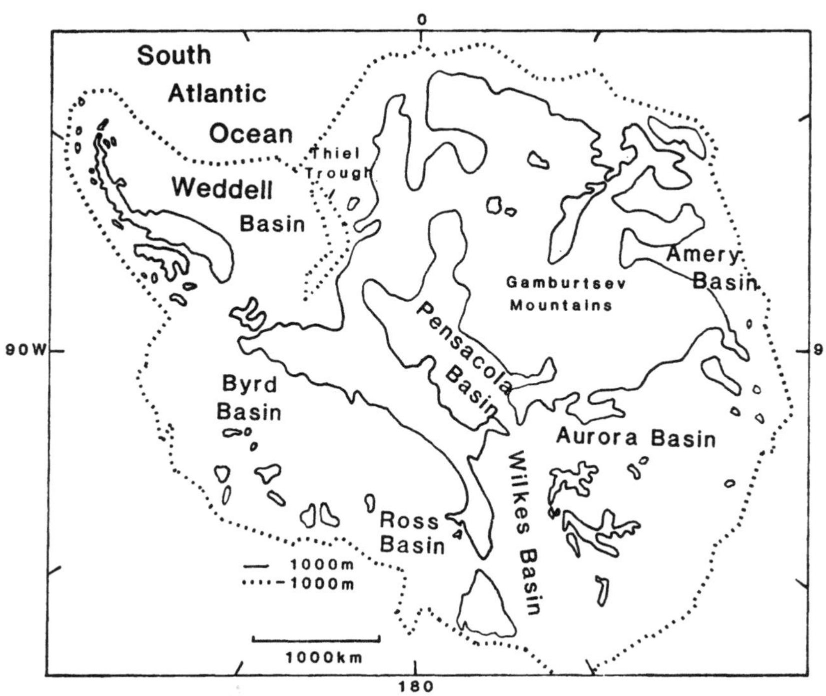

Fig. 2: Generalized bedrock topography of Antarctica and locations of sedimentary basins inferred from geophysical data. Modified from *Webb et al.* (1984).

Examples of Resource Assessment and Environmental Hazards Types of Research

Dufek Intrusion

Several writers (*Elliot*, 1976; *de Wit*, 1985) have used the Dufek intrusion (*Fig. 1*) as an example of a potential mineral resource deposit that might be mined in Antarctica. This geologic structure might be expected to contain platinum group metals (*Ford*, 1983), although, as yet, none has been identified in any quantities that would be remotely suggestive of economic development. The Dufek intrusion lies about 1000 kilometers south of the front of the Filchner Ice Shelf in the northern end of the Pensacola Mountains. It is a large layered gabbroic body, which covers about 50,000 square kilometers, and was first visited by an IGY traverse in 1957. On the basis of a study of the magnetic field and radio echo ice-sounding surveys in the area, probably only about 3 per cent of the Dufek intrusion is exposed in the Forrestal range and the Dufek massif where it was first identified; the remainder lies buried beneath the grounded ice sheet and the Filchner Ice Shelf (*Behrendt et al.*, 1980). The Dufek intrusion is similar to geologic structures in other areas such as the Bushveld complex in South Africa (*Ford*, 1983) where large deposits of economic minerals have been mined. For this reason it has attracted attention in Antarctica.

Although we have known of its existence and its potential mineral value, because of its remoteness, geologists from the U.S., Soviet Union, and Argentina have spent only a few tens of geologist field days studying this feature, during the last 30 years. No drill holes have been put down for research purposes because of the high cost and difficult logistical requirements for such an effort, although geologists have expressed interest in doing this for some time.

Although there may be potential mineral resources in the Dufek intrusion, this most promising area of Antarctica is still so logistically (including energy requirements) expensive a prospect that it would not be economically feasible to consider it for many decades, after similar deposits of minerals have been mined in other parts of the world. To provide an accurate resource assessment would require a systematic detailed aeromagnetic survey as well as other types of geophysical surveys such as gravity and electrical conductivity measurements. Many core holes would need to be drilled and assays made to determine whether or not any economic minerals were present. Probably these would be in a presumed ultramafic layer (most likely to contain economic minerals) at the base of the intrusion (*Ford*, 1983) about 2km below exposed rock at the southeast end of the Dufek Massif.

Assuming such studies were made and indications of an economic deposit were obtained, substantial research would be needed for a transportation route to the front of the Ronne or Filchner Ice Shelf. *De Wit* (1985), proposes transportation of minerals that might be mined and concentrated in the Dufek intrusion to the Ronne Ice front by road. I believe he has underestimated the difficulties of this problem and also that of transporting the concentrated ore through the Weddell Sea, which is the most heavily ice covered area of the oceans surrounding Ant-

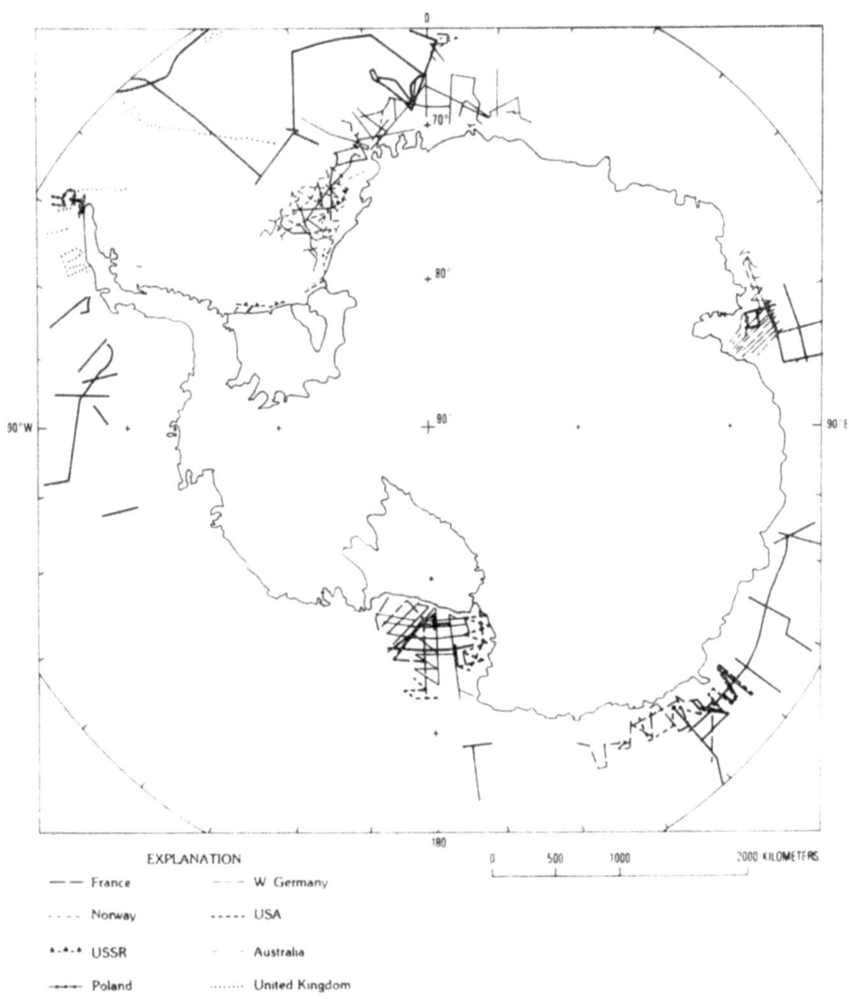

Fig. 3: Map of Antarctica showing locations of marine multichannel reflection (CDP) profiles collected through 1986.

arctica. Any transportation route would cross the moving Antarctic ice sheet including the heavily crevassed Ronne or Filchner Ice Shelf which moves about 2km per year at the ice front. Construction and use of such a route would involve glaciological engineering problems that have not yet been solved in other ice-covered areas of the world. Foı these reasons and more, hard mineral development in Antarctica does not appear feasible in the next few decades, if ever.

Petroleum Resources in the Ross Sea

I will use the Victoria Land basin in the Ross Sea as an example of the type of research that would be needed for petroleum resource assessment, and then indicate the type of environmental hazards that might be encountered in this or other areas of Antarctica.

Fig. 4 shows the extensive multichannel seismic survey in the Ross Sea carried out by the U.S., F.R.G., France, and Japan (*Behrendt*, 1988). As a result of this and earlier single channel work, three basins (*Fig. 5*) have been identified beneath the continental shelf. *Fig. 6*, from *Cooper et al.* (1987), indicates the seismic interpretation of a USGS seismic section across the Victoria Land basin, the westernmost of the three. The age of

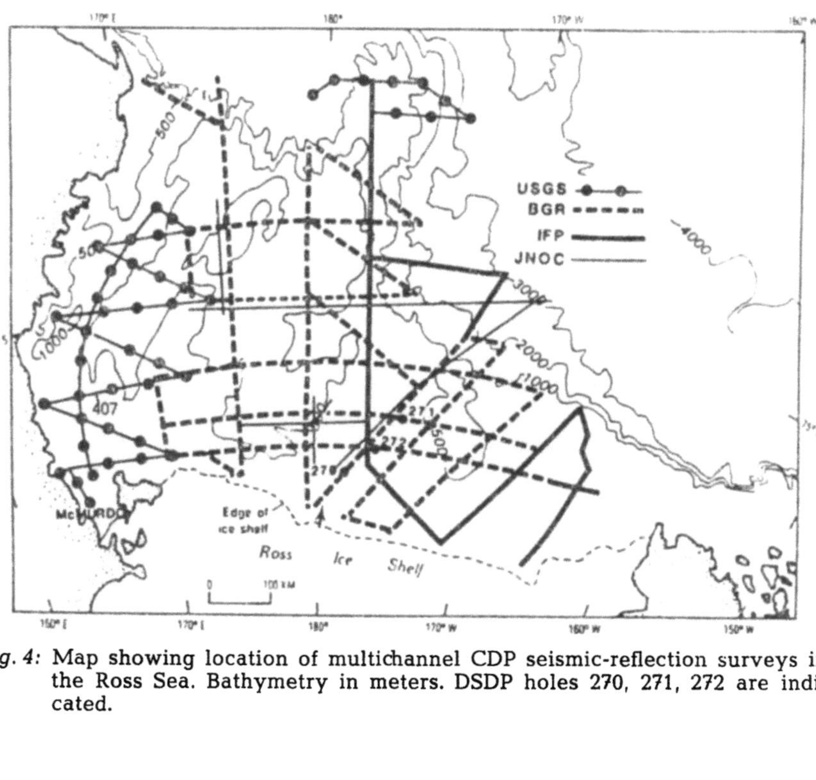

Fig. 4: Map showing location of multichannel CDP seismic-reflection surveys in the Ross Sea. Bathymetry in meters. DSDP holes 270, 271, 272 are indicated.

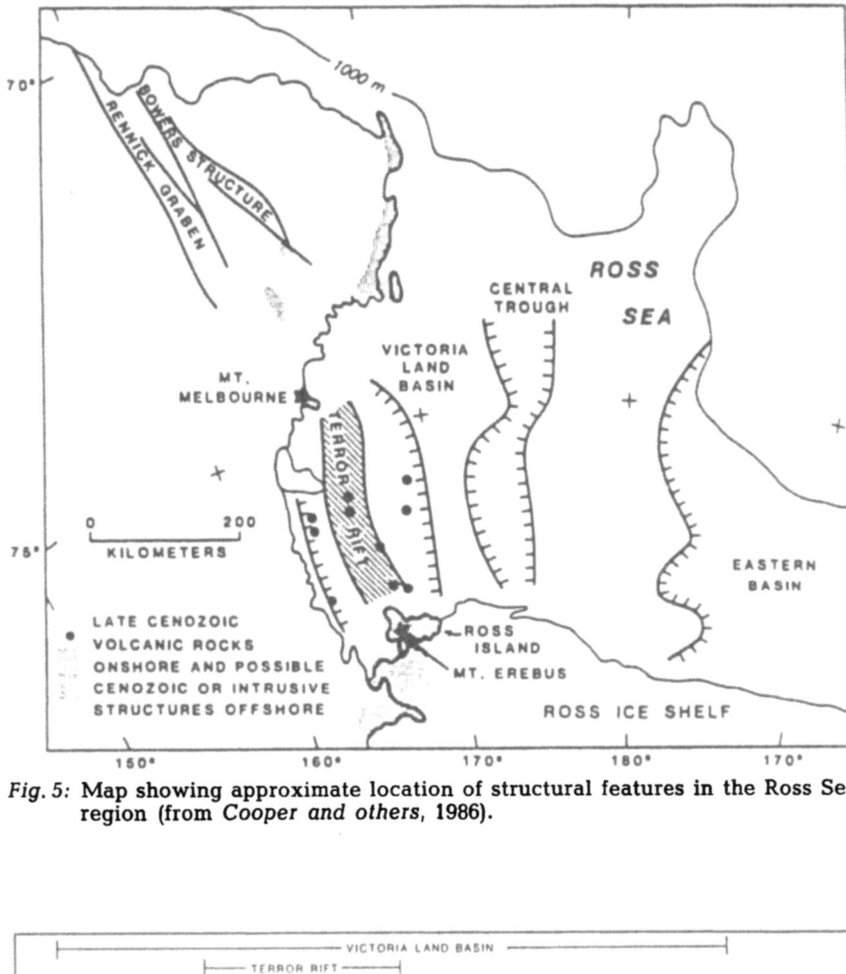

Fig. 5: Map showing approximate location of structural features in the Ross Sea region (from *Cooper and others*, 1986).

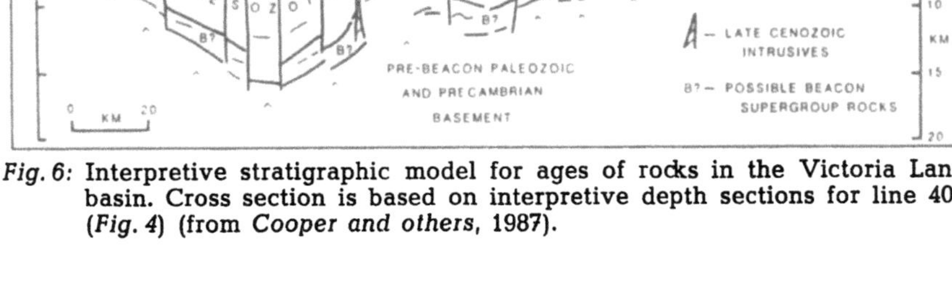

Fig. 6: Interpretive stratigraphic model for ages of rocks in the Victoria Land basin. Cross section is based on interpretive depth sections for line 407 (*Fig. 4*) (from *Cooper and others*, 1987).

the geologic strata shown in *Fig. 6* is extrapolated from the DSDP drill holes (*Fig. 4*) to the east (*Hayes and Frakes*, 1975) and approximately tied by the multichannel seismic data reported by *Hinz and Block*, (1983) and *Cooper et al.* (1987). Future drilling would be needed to provide more information on source rocks, traps, and reservoirs as well as stratigraphic age to make petroleum resource evaluations. These examples illustrate the types of research that can lead to an understanding of the geologic framework of the area relevant to resource assessment. They have not lead to the identification of any specific prospects for an oil exploration. Only detailed surveys and drilling could do that.

Environmental Hazards, Ross Sea

Research ships carrying out multichannel seismic-reflection surveys over the continental margin in Antarctica normally carry out a number of other studies as well, such as high-resolution, seismic-reflection profiling, seismic refraction studies, side-scan sonar, shallow coring (less than 5 m), hydrocarbon analyses, *etc.* The results of the *S. P. Lee* described in the two volumes by *Eittriem and Hampton* (1987) and *Cooper and Davey* (1987) provide a number of examples of this multi-disciplinary approach.

Mt. Melbourne and Mt. Erebus, along the west side of the Ross Sea, are examples of active volcanoes. There are numerous other outcrops of Cenozoic age volcanoes, which erupted during the last 19 million years, extending along the west coast of the Ross Sea (*Fig. 5*). The geophysical surveys of the *S. P. Lee* found examples of penetrative structures as inferred Cenozoic intrusions extending through the sedimentary basins in the Victoria Land Basin (*Fig. 6*). These have short wavelength high-amplitude magnetic anomalies associated with them (*Behrendt et al.*, (1988), and might be evidence of potential volcanic and neotectonic hazards to operations on the sea floor above the Victoria Land basin. Ash layers exposed in the ice front of glacial tongues near Mt. Melbourne indicate recent volcanic eruptions (within the last 50 years as suggested by G. *Werner* and *L. Viereck* (personal communication 1984). Aeromagnetic anomalies (*Behrendt et al.*, 1988) that were observed over Mt. Melbourne and Mt. Erebus show a good correlation between these active volcanoes and the magnetic anomalies and indicate the presence of about 100 inferred volcanic structures in the Victoria Land basin (*Fig. 5*) area. A number of these interpretations were substantiated by the seismic-reflection profiles collected by the *S. P. Lee* in 1984 (*Behrendt et al.*, 1987). Some of the interpreted volcanic features having associated topographic expression on the sea bottom appear younger (*Behrendt et al.*, 1987) than latest glaciation (less than 20,000 years) and further support the idea of active volcanism in this area.

High-resolution (3.5-khz) bathymetric profiles measured along the multichannel seismic lines and other seismic lines showed evidence of fault scarps, in the Victoria Land basin area (*Behrendt*, 1988). This is another example of the type of surveys that are needed to identify hazards associated with active faulting which might displace pipelines or structures placed on the sea bottom.

One of the most significant hazards to petroleum development on the Antarctic continental margin is collision with icebergs. Bergs can damage a drilling rig at the sea surface, or damage supporting structures, pipelines and other seafloor structures when scraping along the sea bottom. High-resolution profiles in the Ross Sea (*Karl et al.*, 1987) suggest iceberg scour has occurred there. Side-scan sonar data collected by the *S. P. Lee* along the Wilkes Land margin (*Barnes*, 1987) showed good examples of iceberg scour even in water depth exceeding 500 meters. *Barnes* (1987), interpreted the data on the Wilkes Land margin as evidence of modern iceberg scour. Previously, the Norwegian Antarctic Research Expedition (*Fossum et al.*, 1982) reported deep water iceberg scour in the Weddell Sea area. Although this scour is possibly a relict from older glaciation, the burden of proof would be on the potential developer to secure enough geophysical data on iceberg scour in a particular area and demonstrate the age of the features before petroleum development on the sea floor in such an area could be considered safe. Remote sensing data from space such as Landsat imagery can reveal iceberg frequency and size which will aid in studying this problem. Radio-echo sounding profiles over floating icebergs in the sea in the area to be considered for petroleum development can be used to measure thickness and consequent likelihood of seafloor scour.

Finally, this non-inclusive list of hazards should include the presence of gas hydrate, which might be expected beneath the 500-meter-deep continental shelf of Antarctica. Gas hydrates are solid, crystalline, ice-like combinations of water and gas (commonly methane) that form within the sediments. The presence of gas hydrate is usually interpreted from bottom simulating reflections (BSR), unrelated to geology, that parallel the sea floor in seismic reflection profiles. The only area of the Antarctic margin where BSR have been observed is off Wilkes Land. *Kvenvolden et al.* (1987) reported several examples and concluded that gas hydrate was present in this area. Although the presence of gas hydrate in a particular area, might at first appear as evidence for a resource there, I believe the environmental hazards associated with it would outweigh the potential resource value. The hydrate may act as a seal, keeping oil or gas from escapting into the ocean. Drilling or development activities could disrupt the seal and release large amounts of hydrocarbons into the marine environment. Therefore, the presence of any BSR in a particular area should be considered as evidence of gas hydrate and be treated with caution. The absence of the BSR in an area would not prove the absence of gas hydrate and drilling would have to proceed cautiously to examining the cores for evidence of gas hydrate. By analyses of the hydrocarbons present, the Deep Sea Drilling Program (DSDP) cores collected in the Ross Sea suggested that gas hydrate could be present there (*Rapp et al.*, 1987).

Summary

In this brief exposition of types of research related to resource assessment and environmental hazards assessment studies in Antarctica I wish to emphasize the following:

1. Antarctica is an immense ice-covered area and potential mineral resource deposits are extremely small in comparison. Finding them will be very difficult, even unlikely. Only very detailed geophysical surveys and geologic mapping will enable such deposits to be located.

2. When deposits have been identified by geophysical and geological surveys and are proposed for exploration and development, careful environmental surveys such as those briefly described in this paper will be necessary before they can be approved.

3. Some of the same types of studies that are commonly used for resource prospecting (*e. g.*, multichannel seismic reflection and aeromagnetic surveys) might also reveal these environmental hazards. In general, however, different types of surveys (*e. g.*, high-resolution seismic profiling, shallow coring, *etc.*) will be needed to study the environmental hazards. Release of these data would not compromise a potential developer's economic advantage over a competitor. In fact, these are the types of surveys that would provide the "sufficiency of information" required under the Antarctic minerals resources regime.

4. Any mineral resources located in Antarctica will be found by applying the knowledge, techniques and experience gained in the other parts of the world where mineral and petroleum development has already occurred and, therefore, would be other examples of general cases, whereas the Antarctic environment must be considered unique. Even though the techniques might be similar to those developed elsewhere, Antarctica will require special research efforts and technology that are not commonly done in other parts of the world.

Acknowledgements

I thank my colleagues in the USGS for valuable consultations resulting from our cooperative research in the past and used here as examples. The National Science Foundation supported the Antarctic fieldwork done by USGS reported in this paper.

REFERENCES

BARNES, P. W. (1987),
Morphologic Studies of the Wilkes Land Continental Shelf, Antarctica; Glacial and Iceberg Effects, in *Eittreim, S. L.*, and *Hampton M. A.*, (eds.), The Antarctic Continental Margin: Geology and Geophysics of offshore Wilkes Land, Earth Science Series, Circum-Pacific Council for Energy and Mineral Resources, Houston, 175—194.

BEHRENDT, J. C. (1983),
Are there petroleum resources in Antarctica?, in *Behrendt, J. C.*, (ed.), Petroleum and Mineral Resources of Antarctica: U.S. Geological Survey Circular 909, 3—24.

BEHRENDT, J. C. (1988),
Scientific Studies Relevant to the Question of Antarctica Petroleum Resources Potential, in *Tingey, R. J.*, (ed.), Geology of Antarctica, Oxford University Press, in press.

BEHRENDT, J. C., DREWY, D. J., JANKOWSKI, E., and GRIM, M. S. (1980),
Aeromagnetic and Radio Echo Ice-sounding Measurements Show Much Greater Area of the Dufek Intrusion, Antarctica: Science, v. 104, 1014—1017.

BEHRENDT, J. C., DUERBAUM, H. J., DAMASKE, D., SALTUS, R., BOSUM, W., and COOPER, A. K. (1988),
Preliminary Interpretation of an Aeromagnetic Survey of the Western Ross Sea Continental Shelf, Antarctica, in Proceedings of 5th SCAR Symposium on Antarctic Earth Science, in press.

BEHRENDT, J. C., COOPER, A. K., and YUAN, A. (1987),
Interpretation of Marine Magnetic Gradiometer and Multichannel Seismic Reflection Observations over the Western Ross Sea Shelf, Antarctica, in *Cooper, A. K.*, and *Davey, F. J.*, (eds.), The Antarctic Continental Margin: Geology and Geophysics of the Western Ross Sea, Earth Science Series of the Circum-Pacific Council for Energy and Resources, Houston, 155—178.

COOPER, A. K., and DAVEY, F. W. (Eds.) (1987),
The Antarctic Continental Margin: Geology and Geophysics of the Western Ross Sea, Earth Science Series of the Circum-Pacific Council for Energy and Resources, Houston, 253 p.

COOPER, A. K., DAVEY, F. W., and BEHRENDT, J. C. (1987),
Seismic Stratigraphy and Structure of the Victoria Land Basin, western Ross Sea, in *Cooper, A. K.*, and *Davey, F. J.*, (eds.), The Antarctic Continental Margin: Geology and Geophysics of the western Ross Sea, Earth Science Series of the Circum-Pacific Council for Energy and Resources, Houston, 27—76.

DE WIT, M. J. (1985),
Minerals and Mining in Antarctica, Science and Technology Economics and Politics: Clarendon Press, Oxford, 127 p.

EITTREIM, S. C., and HAMPTON, M. A. (eds.) (1986),
The Antarctic Continental Margin: Geology and Geophysics of offshore Wilkes Land, Earth Science Series, Circum-Pacific Council for Energy and Mineral Resources, Houston, 221 p.

ELLIOT, D. H. (1976),
A Framework of Assessing Environmental Impacts of Possible Antarctica Mineral Development, Ohio State University Institute of Polar Studies unpublished report, 620 p.

FORD, A. B. (1983),
The Dufek Intrusion of Antarctica and a Survey of Its Minor Metals and Possible Resources, in *Behrendt, J. C.*, (ed.), Petroleum and Mineral Resources of Antarctica: U.S. Geological Survey Circular 909, 51—75.

FOSSUM, B. A., MAISEY, G. H., and TORSEN, H. O. (1982),
Marine Geophysical Research in the Weddell Sea during the Norwegian Antarctic Research Expedition 1976—1977, in *Craddock, C.*, (ed.), Antarctic Geoscience, University of Wisconsin Press, 46, 397—404.

HAYES, D. E., and FRAKES, L. A. (1975),
General Synthesis Deep Sea Drilling Project Leg 28, in Initial Reports of Deep Sea Drilling Project, v. 28, 919—942.

HINZ, K., and BLOCK, M. (1983),
Results of Geophysical Investigations in the Weddell Sea and the Ross Sea, Antarctica, Explorations in New Regions, Eleventh Petroleum Congress, London, p. PD 2 (1), 1—13.

KARL, H. A., REIMNITZ, R., and EDWARDS, B. P. (1987),
Extent and Nature of Ross Sea Unconformity in the western Ross Sea, Antarctica, in *Cooper, A. J.*, and *Davey, F. W.*, (eds.), The Antarctic Continental Margin: Geology and Geophysics of the western Ross Sea, Earth Science Series of the Circum-Pacific Council for Energy and Resources, Houston, 77—93.

KVENVOLDEN, K. A., GOLDEN-BAC, M., and RAPP, J. B. (1987),
Hydrocarbon Geochemistry Offshore from Antarctica: I. Wilkes Land and Continental Margin, in *Eittreim, S. L.*, and *Hampton, M. A.,* (eds.), The Antarctic Continental Margin: Geology and Geophysics of offshore Wilkes Land, Earth Science Series, Circum-Pacific Council for Energy and Mineral Resources, Houston, 205—214.

RAPP, J. B., KVENVOLDEN, K. A., GOLDEN-BAC, M. (1987),
Hydrocarbon Geochemistry of Sediments Offshore from Antarctica, in *Cooper, A. K., Davey, F. W.*, (eds.), The Antarctic Continental Margin: Geology and Geophysics of the western Ross Sea, Earth Science Series of the Circum-Pacific Council for Energy and Resources, Houston, 217—224.

ROWLEY, P. D., WILLIAMS, P. C., and PRIDE, D. E. (1983),
Mineral Occurrences in Antarctica, in *Behrendt, J. C.*, (ed.), Petroleum and Mineral Resources of Antarctica: U.S. Geological Survey Circular 909, 25—49.

WEBB, P. N., HARWOOD, D. M., MCKELVEY, B. C., MERCER, J. H., and STOTT, L. D. (1984),
Cenozoic Marine Sedimentation and Ice volume Variation on the East Antarctic Craton: Geology, v. 12, 287—291.

Geophysical and Geological Data in Antarctica – The Overlap Between Science and Prospection

*Franz Tessensohn**

In recent negotiations on the Antarctic minerals regime, quite extensive discussions have taken place on the geological and geophysical data, on the protection of this data, on the one hand, for the agency that has received them, and for the availability of the data to the scientific community, on the other. I would like to take this opportunity to talk a little bit about this data, mainly using examples that are somewhat in the centre of the discussion at the moment, examples from the Antarctic.

Perhaps I should distinguish geological and geophysical data. Geological data are generally those that are recovered from rock outcrops, by the geologists working there recovering samples, or which are recovered from the bottom of the sea by sampling methods. Geophysical data are usually the indirect information that you get, using sophisticated instruments, such as "X-raying" ice, water, and the sub-surface. One needs a lot of interpretation for the geophysical data, because of the indirect method. Of extreme help in interpretation are drill holes and drill operations, which allow one really to calibrate certain geophysical sections with a means of geological data, so drill data would also be geological data.

To start with some general remarks on marine geo-science in Antarctic waters: it is quite often assumed that these scientific investigations are aimed at detecting large deposits of oil and gas, and the scientific side of these investigations, which are expensive and difficult to carry out, is often underestimated. For example, if you look at the Antarctic continent and its surrounding oceans, you can immediately see the system of mid-oceanic ridges, in the oceanic areas surrounding Antarctica, which surrounds three-quarters of the continent. This system, we now know, is a pattern of ocean growth and new crusts which always develop in the center of the ocean, and, as has been found out by using mainly magnetic methods, they form a symmetry between the continents. The oldest parts of the ocean floor are always closer to the continents. The youngest part is in the center. So, the Antarctic, in this case, and

* Dr. *Franz Tessensohn*, Head of the Antarctic Research Group, Federal Institute for Geoscience and Raw Materials, Hannover. (This is a summary of an audiovisual presentation — *Ed.*)

the oceans around it, are just one piece of evidence in a much larger global pattern. Another important feature here is that of the seven major plates which we have on the globe, only two are at present stationary, because they are surrounded by these mid-oceanic ridges; the other one is Africa. Marine research contributes, in a large respect, to our knowledge of global features, even in these remote areas.

Let me use one other example: the Ross Sea. *Dieter Fütterer* has already given an impression of the research that is carried out in the Weddell Sea area, and the Ross Sea area is almost as interesting scientifically. We have a very pronounced depression, and we do not know what causes this depression, or what causes the up-lift of the flanking Transantarctic Mountains, which are related to this feature, and a lot of research is going on in order to solve this problem. We are trying to find answers as to why we have these two depressions in the Antarctic continent, one from the Weddell Sea, and from the Ross Sea side.

Now, let me take three examples of geological and geophysical data in the Antarctic and let me demonstrate how ambiguous these data are and how differently they can be interpreted from the point-of-view of the scientists, on one hand, and the prospector on the other. I can use the example of the Victoria Basin, that *John (Behrendt)* has already mentioned. Then I will talk about the drill hole, as a second example, in the McMurdo Sound area, and as a third example, I will turn to the Dufek Massif. So, there are two off-shore examples and one on-shore.

The Ross Sea Basins have already been shown, and if we look at the Victoria Land Basin again, at a cross-section of seismic data, we have a similar set of data to that *John* has already shown. Then one can start with interpretations. At the bottom there is a basement in red and a lot of yellow sedimentary strata with some in green in-between. For the layman, it is hard to detect these structures, for the seismic specialists, it is just pure fun.

Normally, the first step when you do an interpretation is to try to work out, statistically, a sequence of the different layers. Then you somehow try to correlate them over different sequences, try to find an internal sequence, internal order, in the sediment of the basin. As you do not know the absolute age of the different strata, you look around to wherever else you can find information. There are other seismic profiles and there is other information available which you can use, and you can work out a certain sequence of probable horizons which you may encounter in your basin.

An important point, certainly, in the sequence of these layers, are the unconformities, which are breaks in sedimentation. One important time-mark that can be derived from the analysis of sediments, is the onset of the circum-Antarctic current, which is a very important time-point — when the Antarctic became isolated from other continents and had a large influence on global weather development, as well as on the history of glaciation. This time-mark can be detected in seismic profiles.

Other important scientific targets are, for example, the break-up of Gondwanaland. Antarctica, although isolated from the other southern continents, was not always so. To figure out the history, to get an idea of age and the movements between the different continents one must use the seismic data. Another important feature of research in relation to the seismic data is volcanism. You can see green areas which are off-shore volcanoes, and in the center of the Victoria Land Basin are two points of volcanic indications. Obviously, the whole system of volcanism has some kind of relation to these basin formations. The active volcanoes are of course related to the huge structures which have formed the basin, which provides ways for the lava to rise to the surface. As a final approach in the interpretation, one starts to develop the history of the basins. The crust is constructed under the basin, and possibly under the mountains in the neighbourhood, and this is an important fact in the interpretation of the development of basins as well as the use of the Transatlantic Mountains.

Now, let us take the view of a prospector, who looked at the seismic data. The first thing of interest to him are the sedimentary areas, for example the lines of equal sediment thickness for the Victoria Land Basin. If it goes from yellow to green, and green are the deepest part, according to this data, you have a thickness of fourteen kilometers (which is quite enormous for a sedimentary basin). The prospector would certainly be happy about such a sedimentary thickness. Then, the prospector's happiness would be dimmed when he looked at a map of seismic lines in the sea area as the spacing there is much too far apart. They are about 100 kilometres apart, which is too far to derive anything of importance for the internal structure of the basin. The prospector would like a line density of, maybe, ten kilometres.

The kind of work that is then done is not "prospecting activity." There are calculations one can do to look for the maturity of the sediments and the possible heat that had been generated in the Basin, which kind of "cooks" the oil out of the organic materials. You need a certain pressure and thickness, and then can calculate this area when you have the right temperature, using general data of the neighbourhood about the heat flow. Then, finally, you would look for traps for oil and gas. These are structures where the rising hydrocarbons, oil and gas, could be trapped under an impermeable layer. An example would be where the upper layers cover the lower layers, and although there are certainly ways for the gas to rise, they may be blocked further up. If it is too close to the surface the upper layer would certainly not seal off the structure.

Now let us come to the example of drilling. In the Ross Sea holes have been drilled in the ice. These can be used to calibrate seismic sections that have been gained in other areas.

If you have drill holes, you try to look for fossils, to date the different horizons. One of the main problems in the Antarctic is that although you have fossils, you cannot really date the sequences, because these are all cold-water forms, and they do not match with the fauna that you find in other areas farther north. Drill holes also provide information, from the scientific side, on the glacial events. If you have a dating of the events you can get information about the onset of glaciation, which is much more precise than anything one can work out from the distribution of moraines on shore.

If you look at the cores of a drill hole from the prospector's point-of-view, what would interest him, in the first place, would be of course the question of reservoir rocks. He would check whether there are suitable rocks in the drill holes, which would take the oil as it migrates up. He would look for source rocks. Returning to *Dieter Fütterer*'s presentation, in the Weddell Sea they have discovered a rock with a high organic contact, which is considered a possible source rock. The prospector would look for other, similar features, and may even get very interesting results. In one of the most recent drill holes, drilled last year, they found lumps of asphalt. Asphalt is a hydro-carbon product. It was at the bottom of the hole, and it was reworked, so it is not something that comes out of the basin underneath. It must have been transported there somehow, but in any case, it is a hydro-carbon product, and as such, is certainly of interest, at least from the point-of-view of the generation of this product.

Now, let us move on to an on-shore area, the Dufek Massif. Most of you have seen the figure before, and have an idea of the size of this huge layered intrusion, almost in the center, and in a very badly accessible area of the Antarctic. These layered massives, or layered intrusions, are of great interest from the scientific point-of-view, because it is thought that they represent fossil magma chambers, and that the heavy crystals in this magma have settled down, and formed certain layers. You can see in photographs the very pronounced layering of this type of igneous rock.

The layered intrusions are one magmatic expression of larger processes which are known over large areas and which, in many cases, have the same age. On a reconstruction of Gondwanaland you can see the reconstruction of the volcanic rock, which have a certain relation to the break-up of Gondwanaland. This is a very important magmatic act, as during this act we had volcanics on the one hand, basalts, and on the other, these layered intrusions. There are basalts in the Transantarctic Mountains, and they are well-known in South Africa and also in South America and Tasmania. Of course, these complexes are compared with other layered intrusions and the famous one is the Bushveld Igneous Complex in South Africa. This is a prospective platinum-bearing intrusion. The only difference, if you compare it to the Dufek Complex, is that it is much greater in age; it is about 1500 million years, whereas the Dufek Complex is something like 150 million years old.

Whether you can see the same kind of magmatic processes in different ages is still an open question. Let me again state the view of a prospector. In this case, the other thing he would do is paperwork — he would compare it to the large amount of information that is published on other igneous intrusions. The Bushveld Complex of South Africa has basalt layers, bowl-shaped, with the lowermost part of the bowl coming out on the outer side. In the lowermost layers are the most heavy minerals, in this case, platinum.

If one compares the internal stratigraphy of the two intrusions, one can see that there are quite a lot of similarities. Both have roof rocks, an upper zone, and in both cases, a central or main zone. Only in the case of the Bushveld Massif do you have a basic concentrated layer. This layer, in the Dufek Massif, is covered at present by some 100 metres of ice; it is not very deep. Drilling to discover prospective layers in the igneous intrusion could definitely be considered as "prospecting." Thank you.

General Discussion

G. Hempel, Chairman:

Thank you very much, indeed, for this presentation, and now I open the floor for discussion. Yes, *Professor Orrego*.

F. Orrego Vicuña:

This is a lawyer's question, to *Professor Tessensohn*. One of the difficulties that there has been in the distinction between scientific activities and prospecting, has been the data necessary to judge whether one activity is one thing or the other. The argument is usually that the activity that qualifies as scientific research will of course be made public and circulate under the Antarctic Treaty. But when it is a question of prospecting, then the situation is that the data that might be available is restricted proprietary data or subject to some form of protection. The question is this: would there be a possibility to have some sort of judgment, for example by a data center or by an independent panel of experts or so, to determine whether the information that has come in, is properly scientific research and that hence it would fall under the rules of the Treaty, or else whether it is data which would qualify as prospecting, subject then the rules applicable to prospecting and the minerals regime. Would that make any sense, from a scientific point-of-view?

F. Tessensohn:

I think, I have tried to demonstrate that in many cases, it is just not possible to make this decision from a scientific point-of-view. It rather has to be made by someone else. If you set up a body you will have endless discussions about it but you will never arrive at a clear-cut boundary. So, I think the distinction at the moment is to make, on the one hand, data available: then, it is science. Otherwise, apply the prospecting rules, then you are prospecting in that case; you have certain rights for later stages which you do not have if you stay with the science. But the data certainly allows both interpretations.

J. Heap:

Can I suggest that there is in fact a perfectly simple test as to whether data collected at the present time, prior to there being a minerals

---

The opinions expressed in this volume are the personal views of their authors only.

regime, is looked upon by a Claimant as being prospecting data or scientific data. One merely has to ask for it. If he will not give it to you, it is proprietary (laughter) — it is prospecting data — and the question would then arise under Recommendation IX-1, paragraph 8, as to whether the policy of voluntary restraint had been abided by. But if he says, "Oh yes, you can have it, but of course, transcription costs are going to be so much a kilometer of seismic track," and if you are then prepared to pay for that information, that seems to me that that is being made available in accordance with Antarctic Treaty practice. Thank you.

J. Behrendt:

There seems to be some question about what is actually going on right now; although most people have published scientific results, there is somewhat of a delay in actually making these results public in the sense of seismic record sections and magnetic tapes. To my knowledge, nobody has actually requested a section and been refused.

J. Heap:

Could I come back on that, ask you, *John Behrendt*, in what way do you indicate, there has been a "delay," if in fact nobody has asked for the information. I mean, how do you suggest there has been a delay?

J. Behrendt:

I assume that was a rhetorical question. In fact, of course, as you phrase it, there is no evidence of a delay. There just have been about twelve years of data collected and, as I said, some of the data have been published in papers and some might argue, that is sufficient. In the case of the data collected by the *S. P. Lee* (the U.S. ship) that I showed examples of, two years later the cruise results were placed in a data center. Copies of seismic-record sections and magnetic tapes of data are available. Requests are coming in, people are obtaining copies of data and the seismic-record sections at full scale are being copied.

O. Rebagliati:

Since I am also not from a natural science field I will make a few remarks relating to this issue from another perspective. First, I think that we always have to address the subjective intention of the activity. In one way or another, research is being carried out for the purpose of finding out about some particular field. If the orientation of the activity is clearly, according to what has been deployed and what has been collected and what has been gathered, addressed to some particular mineral resources, it will be very difficult to say that is purely scientific research. On the other hand, there is the other test that *John Heap* mentioned, and then of course, if it is so, it should be made readily available to any Contracting Party wanting to have that information. But now, is that information or data? Having in mind the new techniques, so sophisticated, that you summarized and described this afternoon, and all this sophisticated equipment — ships, aircraft, satellites — would that data gathered be meaningful to many scientific institutions in all countries, or will it just be a bunch of tapes, recordings and many elements that of course most will not be able to even achieve very, very modest interpretations of?

Then comes the question of good faith, in relation to fulfilling obligations under the Treaty. We are fulfilling obligations under the Treaty, and under the Antarctic Treaty Recommendations, namely, the one *John Heap* mentioned about not engaging in mineral resource activities until a regime has been established, provided this regime is negotiated in good faith. Also, activities being carried out while these negotiations take place should be in good faith, and of course, information requested should be transmitted, not only timely as you mentioned, but in good faith, in the sense that they are meaningful to those who are requesting it. Of course, I am not claiming that countries should embark in covering the cost for this, to process the data they have expensively gathered, with their expertise, and give it to the others free. However, there has to be one way of accomodating this issue in order to on the one hand, allow the widest possible scientific-research activities by all, but on the other hand, to make sure that these activities are carried out legally, and in good faith. Thank you.

J. Behrendt:

Well, first of all, I think there are geophysicists and geologists in all of the countries operating in the Antarctic, all the Consultative Members, certainly, but actually any of the Non-consultative Members have access, within their own countries, in almost all cases, to quite competent geophysicists and geologists, who can interpret these data. If they do not, they could easily obtain this information through consulting geologists or geophysicists. So, I think the fact is that the data tapes or the satellite photographs or the seismic-reflection record sections, that we have shown examples of today, would be readily interpretable by professional geologists and geophysicists in all of the countries represented here or in the Antarctic Treaty.

F. Orrego Vicuña:

Forgive my insolence for intervening in this highly expert debate but when I raised the same question with a geologist from a big oil company, his explanation was that while someone undertaking, prospecting, or whatever kind of geological or geophysical activity, would reply to a request to make that information available in a positive manner, what in fact he would be providing would be something that would be useless from the point-of-view of the expert eye that would need to interpret that. The useful material would come, if at all, years later, in an untimely manner that would be useless. This is why I was developing the thought that if eventually under a regime of some sort the entity that has undertaken the activity in quesiton provides all the information in a manner that is useful for any expert eye, then it would qualify as scientific research without any problem. But if what he provides is incomplete or not sufficiently complete, or information that would take years to obtain in a complete manner, then as long as he has not complied with the availability of information, he would be in fact performing or putting himself in the position of undertaking a prospecting activity, and then he would be treated as such, which eventually would mean that he would have to take care of all the obligations that will be imposed on a prospector.

G. Hempel, Chairman:

I really see the problems of the legal people, but with scientists things are far more difficult and complicated than you think. First of all, someone said, "It's a question of keeping the data, and that is an indication that the country is prospecting ..." — if that is the case, then most of the scientists and most of the countries are just prospectors, because they are slow in publishing. They go to the next expedition before they have published their earlier data. Indeed, it is a crucial problem in all scientific institutes, to get the scientific data out in time. This is just a question of human attitude, typical of the scientists. In most cases, they are looking for new things and they are not really bothering too much about publishing their data.

The next point mentioned was: "If those data are really meaningful, then they are scientific. If they are not meaningful to the colleague, then they are prospecting." That would mean a good number of the data published by scientists are "prospecting" data, and they are not quite meaningful to their colleagues, because they are not done in the excellent way they should be. So it is very hard, really, to identify the dividing line between scientific research and exploration. On the other hand, I run now into certain difficulties with all this prospecting business.

We have heard, during the last three Antarctic Challenge meetings, that it is very difficult to find mineral resources in the Antarctic, and if you find them, then it is very difficult to really explore them in a proper way. And then, it is even more difficult, virtually hopeless, to exploit them. If you want to exploit them on the spot, then it is hopeless to transport them. So, either all our geologists and geophysicists have the incorrect view, or there is very little prospecting at the moment or for the next fifty years in the Antarctic; all the data here, whether they are delivered or not, are scientific by definition because exploration at the moment is nonsense. I wonder whether that is not true.

J. Behrendt:

Well, all of the data on the maps that we showed, suggest that there has been a great deal of activity in the last decade. That is why I made the point in my presentation, that this is going on in all the continental margins in the world, by university and government researchers like the BGR and the USGS, that have access to the Multi-Channel Seismic method, which is really the type of data we are talking about. I think that despite accusations of prospecting, most geologists and geophysicists who want to go to Antarctica would accept that burden just for the opportunity to collect the research data. In fact, I know from personal observation that all scientists, krill biologists or geologists or whatever, are so excited about their own research that they will use any excuse to go and collect data to support it, even if in some cases it gives the appearance of mineral prospecting. I do not think anyone is actually deliberately carrying out prospecting, even though perhaps, in some countries, the funding agencies might be thinking along those lines.

G. Hempel, Chairman:

Funding agencies might believe in direct economic aspects of those studies or be talked into it, even by scientists looking for funds, yes.

I. Nicholson:

Is not the question there more directly what *John Heap* suggested? If the data is sought by someone and it is not given in response to that request by the person asked, then he is entering the area of prospecting because he is failing to make available the data requested. If there is no request, there is no test. If there is a request, the test is whether it is supplied within a reasonable time, and as *John* has said, at a reasonable price. That is, the price of the magnetic tapes and making it available — not the price of collecting it but the price of making it available. Is that not a better way to look at it? If that is so, then there is a test case on at the moment and we will have the result next year.

G. Hempel, Chairman:

I am not quite sure whether it is that easy because scientists rather often sit on their data and do not want to deliver their data for scientific reasons — because they want to clean them up before giving the raw data to their colleagues for further interpretation.

J. Heap:

I personally think that that does not really provide any problem. If I go around to scientists of another nation and say, "You have been doing some multi-channel seismic," and then in the week after he comes back, say, "Please, can I have your data?", he will say, "No, because I have not worked it out." If I go along to him two years after he has come back and say, "Please, can I have your data?", and he says, "Well, I've, you know, the work's sort of going on a bit, but I hope ...," I would say, "O. K., when will it be published?" If he then says, "Well, I hope in about a year's time," I will say, "Alright, I'll be back on your doorstep in a year's time."

G. Hempel, Chairman:

O. K., now, I have at least three speakers marked.

I. Nicholson:

Just to wind up this debate, I do not go as far as *John*. I take the point which *Arthur* actually interjected. Under the Treaty, there is an obligation to make data available. You have a reasonable time to get in front of somebody else, to work it up. But if you do not get on and work it up, you cannot hold it, you would be in breach of your Treaty obligation. It is "bad-luck," scientist: publish, or lose your lead.

J. Heap:

Just to recall what the Treaty says, you've got to make the data available to the greatest extent feasible! (laughter).

G. Hempel, Chairman:

Finn Sollie, please.

F. Sollie:

Well, I think the point here also is, and that was pointed out, *inter alia*, by *Dr. Behrendt* that if you are really looking for something that you hope to be able to develop eventually, you have to do surveys that are much more intense and much more detailed than the type of work that is now being carried out. You do not look for one-hundred kilometer line distances but ten- and possibly five-kilometer lines; the question that could be asked would not merely be to get the data before it is interpreted but you could request, I think, details on what type of research was carried out. And you know that if a series of lines in a given area down to five kilometers were taken, that would indicate rather more intense interest than that of the pure scientist — even if that scientist is trying to have an oil company pay for his scientific research, which means again that there would be some indications of commercial versus pure scientific research. One might imagine that the minerals regime, if and when established, would be able to define pretty well what kind of investigation would be perfectly allowable as science and what kind would qualify for some type of submission to "regime" rules, and "regime" rules, presumably, would be fairly similar to those that you see in most countries with regulation of commercial exploration. Usually a series of explorations would be first carried out, or surveys, and the data would be deposited in a central authority — in the case of nations, it is a state authority — and then be available for purchase, as no one can exploit unless they have a licence or concession. So, it seems to me that we are trying to overdo a question that is a valid question, but which has no practical value before you reach a certain stage in the development.

B. Rolle:

I would just like to remark that I see a strong parallel with, for an example, genetic research, where scientists break the barrier for a future technology and then the technology makes use of the findings, the discoveries, they make today. I would like to appeal to scientists, to feel responsible for things which may follow their research of fifty years or however long: awcknowledge that they prepare the road. And we are aware that this has happened very often before, that then the development could not be stopped by the persons who actually made it start. Thank you.

G. Hempel, Chairman:

Yes, *Herr Tessensohn.*

F. Tessensohn:

This remark is very much on the line that geologists, whatever they do, are in fact the triggering people for any kind of resource evaluation, so from their profession, they are alrady the bad guys.

B. Rolle:

One could add more examples, like the invention of the nuclear bomb; the person who actually had the first ideas about this technique, perhaps never thought it through to the end it was finally used for.

G. Hempel, Chairman:

No one else for the time being? Well, then we come to the last talk on Antarctic resources, on Antarctic Resources and Remote Sensing, by *Professor Joyner,* from the George Washington University. He is not a natural scientist; he is in the Foreign Relations field, and is also Senior Fellow at Woods Hole. *Dr. Joyner,* please.

Antarctic Resources and Remote Sensing by Satellite: The Interplay of Technology, Mission and Law

Christopher C. Joyner[*]

I. Introduction

Remote sensing by satellite is playing an increasing role in contemporary life, contributing significantly to activities ranging from weather forecasting and international communications, to charting surface elevations and mapping coastlines, to measuring pollution output and searching for locations of natural resources. Indeed, satellites are capable of observing vast regions in a very short time, although data acquired from remote sensing coverage must be interpreted in terms of the physical characteristics of that segment of the surface sensed. Given the largely unexplored, environmentally harsh, and desolately estranged nature of the Antarctic, the southern circumpolar area would appear to invite serious consideration as a prime target for remote sensing activities, especially insofar as resource detection, location, and assessment is concerned.

This paper, therefore, has three principal purposes. First, it seeks to examine the remote sensing technology presently available for polar resource detection operations. The view here is towards ascertaining the adequacy of those techniques in the mission programs tentatively scheduled over the next decade. Second, an analysis is performed of the application of current technology to resource evaluation in the Antarctic region. With respect to the continent, the principal resources targeted as candidates for remote sensing are minerals and ice; for the Southern Ocean, attention is focused mainly upon phytoplankton detection (which presumably means krill detection as well) and seabed resources. The third aim of the paper is to address the legal implications of conducting remote sensing operations by satellite over the Antarctic region. During the last two decades, the international law governing satellite remote sensing has undergone marked evolutionary progress. In recent months, the course of that evolution has become crystallized into a number of fundamental principles generally acceptable to the international com-

[*] *Christopher C. Joyner*, Senior Research Fellow, Marine Policy Center, Woods Hole Oceanographic Institution; Associate Professor, The George Washington University. The author would like to express his appreciation to Dr. *Kenneth C. Jezek* for his assistance in the completion of this study.

munity. This treatment seeks to place those quasi-universal legal trends for remote sensing within the more specific context of the Antarctic Treaty System and the national objectives of those States conducting polar sensing activities. In the process, the analysis also strives to derive broad conclusions regarding the permissibility of States to conduct remote sensing operations in the Antarctic region, as well as the responsibilities and obligations attendant to those sensing activities. At the outset, some comment needs to be made about those resources in the Antarctic which appear to hold promise as candidates for satellite remote sensing operations.

II. The Antarctic Resource Base

1. The Continent

Antarctica's natural resource base, both real and imagined, has generated heightened international interest in the area since the early 1970s. With respect to non-living resources on the continent, some sizable mineral deposits have been discovered, consisting notably of iron and low-quality coal. Occurrence of several other metallic elements — including, *inter alia*, gold, cobalt, manganese, zinc, lead, silver, uranium, copper, chromium, nickel, platinum, and tin — have also been found there.[1] Estimations based on the theory of continental drift, when coupled with the Gondwanaland thesis, have led some commentators to speculate that Antarctica potentially could contain these minerals in superabundant quantities.[2]

At present, no known deposits have been discovered of either petroleum or natural gas in or offshore of the continent. Informed geological opinion regarding the prospective existence of recoverable hydrocarbons is guardedly speculative at best, and decidedly uncertain in the main. Given current extraction technology, logistical impediments, exorbitant costs and demand needs, hydrocarbon exploitation in the Antarctic appears to be remotely distant in the future, if it ever comes about at all.[3]

---

1 See generally *John C. Behrendt* (ed.), Petroleum and Mineral Resources of Antarctica, in: U.S. Geological Circular No. 909 (1983); *J. F. Splettstoesser*, Mineral Resources Potential in Antarctica — Review and Predictions, in: *R. L. Oliver, P. R. James*, and *J. B. Jago*, Antarctic Earth Science, Canberra, 1983, 413; *T. Gjelsvik*, The Mineral Resources of Antarctica: Progress in Their Identification, in *Francisco Orrego Vicuña* (ed.), Antarctic Resources Policy: Scientific, Legal, and Political Issues, Cambridge, 1983, 61—76.

2 See, *e. g.*, *Maarten J. De Wit*, Minerals and Mining in Antarctica, Oxford, 1985, 73—81; *N. A. Wright* and *P. L. Williams*, Mineral Resources of Antarctica, U.S. Geological Survey Circular No. 705 (1974).

3 See generally *John C. Behrendt*, Scientific Studies Relevant to the Question of Antarctica's Petroleum Resources Potential, in: *R. J. Tingey* (ed.), Geology

The most plentiful mineral resource on the continent — and indeed, its predominant feature as well — is ice. Antarctica is covered by an ice sheet nearly 14 million square kilometers in area, which contains a volume of water calculated at some 24.5 million cubic kilometers.[4] The Antarctic ice cap comprises 91 percent of the Earth's glacier surface. Clearly, most significant for the future is the realization that Antarctica's ice mantle represents a reservoir of more than 70 percent of the world's fresh water supply.[5] In the impending era of dwindling fresh water availability, Antarctica's ice resources are bound to receive increasing attention and, coincidently, inspire numerous schemes for exploiting that ice to accommodate worldwide fresh water demands.[6]

2. *The Southern Ocean*

The circumpolar southern seas teem with biological bounty. Whales, seals, squid, fish, and birds are found in notable quantities. The living resource presenting the greatest economic potential in the region is krill, a small shrimp-like crustacean comprising more than half of the zooplankton crop found in the Southern Ocean. Krill contain as much as 50 percent protein by weight in processed form, and thus appear to hold lucrative potential as a food source for human consumption.[7]

The distribution of krill is circumpolar, albeit discontinuous. Major concentrations of krill swarms are found in the eddies and gyres of the East Wind Drift, and especially in the Weddell Gyre, just north of the Antarctic Peninsula. Large swarms of krill are also located in the Ross Sea, Amundsen Sea, Bellinghausen Sea, around South Georgia Island, in the Scotia Sea north of the Orkney Islands, around the South Shetland

---

of Antarctica, Oxford, 1987 (in press); compare the conclusions of *V. L. Ivanhov*, The Geological Prerequisites for Petroleum Prediction in Antarctica, International Geological Review, No. 27 (1985), 757—769.

[4] International Union for Conservation of Nature and Natural Resources, International Council of Scientific Unions, and International Committee on Antarctic Research, Conservation in the Antarctic: Report of the Joint IUCN/SCAR Working Group on Long-Term Conservation in the Antarctic, 15 May 1986, 3 (mimeo). In frozen form as ice, this volume of water on the continent swells to some 30 million cubic kilometers. United Nations General Assembly, Question of Antarctica: Study Requested under General Assembly resolution 38/77, Report of the Secretary General, PART TWO: Views of States, Vol. I, UN Doc. A/39/583 (Part II), 1984, 63 (Views of Australia).

[5] International Institute for Environment and Development, Antarctica I: Vital Statistics, in: Antarctica: A Continent in Transition (Information Packet), 1983.

[6] See generally *Peter Schwerdtfeger*, Antarctic Icebergs As Potential Sources of Water and Energy, in: *Rüdiger Wolfrum* (ed.), Antarctic Challenge II: Conflicting Interests, Cooperation, Environmental Protection, Economic Development, Berlin, 1985, 377—390; *A. A. Husseiny* (ed.), Iceberg Utilization, Oxford, 1978.

[7] *Barney Brewster*, Antarctica: Wilderness at Risk, San Francisco, 1980, 68. See also *S. Z. El-Sayed*, Protein of the Last Frontier, in: Oceanus (Spring 1979), 17.

Islands, and west of the South Sandwich Islands. Of important note, it is in these locations where rich patches of phytoplankton production occur that krill populations tend to swarm.[8] Significant, too, is that scientific estimates of krill stocks in the circumpolar seas vary widely — from some 500 million to 5 billion metric tons. A more reasonable range in estimated total krill biomass in the Southern Ocean may be put at between 500 to 750 million metric tons.[9]

Finally, some polymetallic nodules have been discovered in scattered amounts on the circumpolar ocean floor. These nodules, however, which are of low ore density and would be extremely costly to recover given the extraordinarily stormy conditions of the southern seas, appear to be less than commercially attractive.[10]

III. The Technology of Remote Sensing in Antarctica

1. Techniques and Instrumentation

Remote sensing may be generally defined as the collection and interpretation of information about an object without being in physical contact with it.[11] Remote sensing systems operate to detect the intensity of electromagnetic radiation that an object reflects, emits, or scatters at particular wavelength bands. Differences in the intensity of electromagnetic radiation from the terrain are commonly displayed as brightness variations on images. Thus, space-based remote sensing first records reflected and emitted radiation from the Earth's surface in different spectral bands in the visible and infrared wavelengths, which are then relayed to ground stations. Here, imagery from the varied bands is selected and combined so that not only a recognizable depiction of the planet's surface can be rendered, but, through digital image processing, the composition of the Earth's surface, its soil moisture content, and variant stress conditions can also be coherently ascertained.[12] With specific regard to Antarctic waters, remote sensing has furnished a new ability to distinguish sea-ice from open water, to differentiate multi-year

---

[8] See *N. A. Mackintosh*, Distribution of Post-Larval Krill in the Antarctic, in: Discovery Report, Vol. 36 (1973), 157—178; and Central Intelligence Agency, Polar Regions Atlas, Washington, D.C., 1978, 54 (map of krill distribution).

[9] *Richard M. Laws*, The Ecology of the Southern Ocean, in: American Scientist, Vol. 73 (Jan.-Feb. 1985), 32. See also *George A. Knox*, The Living Resources of the Southern Ocean, in: *Vicuña*, note 1, 27—34.

[10] *D. R. Horn, et al.*, Metal Content of Ferromanganese Deposits of the Ocean, cited in: *James Zumberge*, Potential Mineral Resource Availability and Possible Problems in Antarctica, in: *Jonathan I. Charney* (ed.), The New Nationalism and the Use of Common Spaces, Towtowa, 1982, 152.

[11] *Floyd R. Sabins, Jr.* Remote Sensing: Principles and Interpretation, (2nd ed.) New York, 1987, 1.

[12] *Ibid.*

ice from first-year and younger ice, to map sea-ice concentrations, and to designate more clearly seasonal variations of ice types. In fact, satellite remote sensing offers the only practical means today of obtaining synoptic coverage of the polar oceans.[13]

In late 1987, the far side of the moon remains better mapped than much of the Antarctic continent. With regard to the polar regions, valuable but limited data are currently being gathered by three principal types of sensors: visible and infrared scanners; microwave radiometers; and synthetic aperture (or imaging) radar (SAR). More of these instruments will be deployed in space throughout the rest of this century to survey resources and monitor surface feature of, and environmental conditions in, Antarctica.

2. *Visible and Infrared Sensors*

Visible imagers have been carried by Landsat 4 and 5 satellites, NOAA's weather satellites, the French SPOT satellite and, most probably, will be on board Canada's Radarsat scheduled for launch in 1990. These visible sensors are capable of providing fine spatial resolution as they pass over areas of the Antarctic, but have considerable limitations. Information is not obtainable when the region is obscured by cloud cover, nor during the hours of darkness. These conditions impose restraints upon the utility of such systems in the Antarctic, where cloudiness is common and darkness exists for nearly half the year. Moreover, with a maximum spatial resolution of only 30 meters, visible sensors are often unable to distinguish thin sea-ice from open water, which can lead to possible significant error.[14] Landsat data, having a 30 meter resolution capability and covering a swath of some 185 kilometers, are not collected continuously. Visible and infrared weather satellites obtain data continuously, but have a lower resolution — some 1 to 4 kilometers — and a swath width of some 3000 meters. Total coverage, however, is limited to only cloud-free situations, and for visible imagery, sunlit conditions are prerequisite as well.[15]

---

[13] European Space Agency, A Programme for International Polar Oceans Research (PIPOR), Science Working Group Report (ESA-SP-1074), Paris, 1985, 1. (Hereinafter cited as PIPOR Report).

[14] *Norbert Untersteiner, et al.*, Passive Microwave Remote Sensing for Sea Ice Research, in: Report of the NASA Science Working Group for the Special Sensor Microwave Imager (SSM/I) Washington, D.C., 1984, 9. (Hereinafter cited as NASA SSM/I Report).

[15] *R. H. Thomas, et al.*, Satellite Remote Sensing for Ice Sheet Research, NASA Technical Memorandum 86333, 1985, 18. (Hereinafter cited as Satellite Ice Sheet Research).

3. *Microwave Sensors*

Passive microwave radiometers measure the thermal radiation from the Earth's surface, which is expressed as brightness temperature. Spatial resolution is determined by the size of radiometer antennae, the operating frequency, and the orbital height of the sensor. Though its resolution tends to be relatively coarse, about 30 kilometers or more, a major advantage of the microwave sensor is that it permits global viewing of widespread phenomena. As a consequence, microwave remote sensors can supply sufficient data about Antarctica to enable construction of a complete map of the continent on a daily basis.[16] On land, microwave radiometry can assist in determining ice morphology, in indicating the onset of snow melt, and in deducing snow accumulation rates over the ice sheet. In addition, earth-observing satellites carrying microwave sensors have the unique all-weather capability to acquire sea-ice data throughout the year. Passive microwave remote sensing also may be used to distinguish water from ice, and to characterize different kinds of ice. This advantage facilitates routine mapping of Antarctica's sea-ice extent, as well as of its concentration and types.[17]

The first satellite sensor to supply passive microwave data was the Electrically Scanning Microwave Radiometer (ESMR), launched by NASA on board Niumbus 5 in December 1972. ESMR, with a spatial resolution of 30 kilometers and a swath of 1400 kilometers, provided total coverage of both polar regions daily until 1983.[18] In 1978, a Scanning Multichannel Microwave Radiometer (SMMR) was flown aboard both Seasat and Nimbus 7, the latter of which still is operational.[19] Beginning in 1986, a spacecraft in the U.S. Defense Meteorological Satellite Program (DMSP) series was scheduled to carry a Special Sensor Microwave/ Imager (SSM/I), which would collect remote sensing data over a 1300-kilometer swath. The DMSP satellite will fly in a circular, sun-synchronous, near-polar orbit, at an altitude of 843 kilometers. With an orbit period anticipated at 101 minutes, highly redundant coverage of the polar regions will be supplied.[20] Another SSM / I is scheduled to be flown aboard the U.S. Naval Research Oceangraphic Satellite System (N-ROSS) spacecraft in 1989.

4. *Radar Sensors*

Radar altimeters have proven to be valuable tools for glaciological investigations from space. Flown on board two NASA satellites, Geos-3

[16] NASA SSM/I Report, note 14, 9.

[17] See generally *H. Jay Zwally, et al.*, Antarctic Sea Ice, 1973—1976: Satellite Passive-Microwave Observations, Washington, D. C., 1983.

[18] Satellite Ice Sheet Research, note 15, 21.

[19] *Ibid.*; PIPOR Report, note 13, 24.

[20] Satellite Ice Sheet Research, note 15, 21; NASA SSM/I Report, note 14, 40.

(from April 1975 to December 1978) and Seasat (July through October 1978), the data received from these radar altimeters have been used to improve elevation maps depicting surface undulations in northern portions of the Antarctic ice sheet. Further, while radar altimeters heretofore have been relatively little used in the Antarctic, they have nonetheless contributed valuable data for mapping ice sheet margins, the seaward limit of sea-ice, and iceberg occurrences.[21]

Respective to technique, the satellite-stimulated radar beam is designed to produce a broad footprint on the surface, with a radius of around 12 kilometers. Measurements conducted over a decade would furnish clear indications of any significant regional changes in ice topography. However, were the entire Antarctic sheet to be sensed completely, six months of continuous operations, containing some 10 million measured pulse ranges, would be required.[22] As a result, much of Antarctica's surface topography will not be mapped until launches of the European Space Agency's ERS-1 in 1989 and the United States' N-ROSS satellite in 1990. Both these missions are scheduled to carry altimeters that will cover latitude bands between 82° North and 82° South.[23]

Synthetic Aperture Radar (SAR) uses the satellite's motion along well-defined paths to synthesize a larger antenna, which thereby allows for higher resolution of the sensed surface. The advantages of SAR imagery are several. It provides for high resolution coverage, and is able to supply images similar to those seen with a naked eye. This permits data obtained from SAR sensors to be comprehensible to the interested, untrained observer. In addition, SAR is an all-weather mapping instrument; it is weather independent, and therefore is highly desirable in Antarctica's cloud-covered, darkened conditions.[24]

A SAR instrument flew in 1978 on board Seasat, with a spatial resolution of 25 to 40 meters and traversing a swath some 100 kilometers in width. Plans call for SARs to be flown on a number of missions in the coming decade: SAR instrumentation will be carried on board the United States' Shuttle Imaging Radar missions in 1988 and 1989; on the European Space Agency's ERS, scheduled for launch in 1989; on Japan's JER-1, in 1990 and on Canada's Radarsat, also in 1990. Moreover, to underscore the importance of SAR technology for sensing the south polar region, the Federal Republic of Germany has announced that it is considering plans for constructing a mobile facility at the Georg-von-Neumayer Station in Antarctica for receiving ERS-1 SAR data in the 1990s.[25]

---

[21] Satellite Ice Sheet Research, note 15, 14—16.
[22] *Loc. cit.*, 15.
[23] *Loc. cit.*, 16.
[24] *Loc. cit.*, 18—20; PIPOR Report, note 13, 20—23.
[25] Satellite Ice Sheet Research, note 15, 21.

Polar-Orbiting Remote Sensing Satellite Missions, 1985—1995

Country	Mission	Main Sensors	Orbit/Max. Latitude	Operations Dates
Canada	Radarsat	Synthetic-aperture radar Wind scatterometer Visible sensor	1007 km altitude Sun-synchronous 80° latitude	1991—1995
European Space Agency	ERS Series	Synthetic-aperture radar Wind scatterometer Radar altimeter Scanning radiometer Microwave sounder	780 km altitude Sun-synchronous 82° latitude	1989—1994
France	SPOT Series	Radar altimeter Microwave sounder	832 km altitude 82° latitude	1985—1994
Japan	MOS Series	Multispetral Elec. Scanner Radiometer Visible & Thermal Radiometer	909 km altitude Sun-synchronous 82° latitude	1986—1993
Japan	JER-1	Synthetic-aperture radar Visible & near-infrared	570 km altitude Sun-synchronous 82° latitude	1990—1993
United States U.S. Navy NASA NOAA	N-ROSS	Radar altimeter Wind scatterometer Special Sensor Microwave Imager (SSM/I)	830 km altitude Sun-synchronous 82° latitude	1990—1993
NOAA	Weather Satellite Series	Advanced Microwave Sounding Unit High-Resolution Infrared Radiation Sounder	833—870 km Sun-synchronous 98.9° Inclination	1985—1995
EOSAT	Landsat Series	Multispectral Scanner Thematic Mapper	918 km altitude Sun-synchronous 81° latitude	1985—1989
U.S. Navy	DMSP	Special Sensor Microwaver Imager	86° latitude	1986—1994
U.S. Navy	Geosat	Radar Altimeter	72° latitude	1985

Sources: *R. H. Thomas, et al.*, NASA Technical Memorandum 86233, 14;
European Space Agency, PIPOR Working Group Report ESA SP-1074, 19.

IV. Application of Remote Sensing to Antarctica

1. The Continent

a) Prospecting for Minerals

Generally speaking, remote sensing by satellite multispectral scanner has proven to be a valuable tool in geologic mapping of the Earth's surface. Sensing methods used for geological purposes have usually derived observations of geological features using visible and near-infrared spectral instruments. It was, in fact, the launch of Landsat in 1972 which first provided synoptic, global multispectral scanning (MSS) data for geological applications.[26] The MSS images produced by Landsat led to the discovery of numerous, previously unrecognized regional linear features on the Earth's surface. These features, known as lineaments, entailed alignments of various regional morphological structures, such as rivers, escarpments, and mountain ranges, as well as tonal characteristics that in many places represent surface expressions of fracture or fault zones. Lineaments hold special importance in mineral resource surveys, simply because several, albeit not all, ore deposits are localized astride fracture zones.[27] As suggested by this discussion, the concept of plate tectonics is neatly tied into the application of space-based remote sensing mineral detection on the Earth's surface.

With respect to exploitation, remote sensing methods have demonstrated noteworthy promise for both reconnaisance observations and detailed exploration of non-renewable resources in at least four ways:

(1) By facilitating the mapping of regional lineaments along which groups of ore deposits may be located;

(2) By permitting the charting of local fracture patterns that might influence individual ore deposits;

(3) By assisting in the detection of hydrothermally altered rocks that are associated with ore deposits; and

(4) By providing basic geologic data about the region.

Information derived from remote sensing operations consequently can offer much in the way of calculated geological estimates as to what minerals may be located where and in what possible concentrations,

---

[26] See generally the discussion in *Sabins*, note 11, 72—123 (Landsat Images) and *S. C. Freden* and *F. Gordon*, Landsat Satellites, in: *R. N. Colwell* (ed.), Manual of Remote Sensing, (2nd ed.) Falls Church, Va., 1983, 517—570.

[27] See generally *Michael J. Abrams, et. al.*, Geologic Mapping Using Thermal Images, in: Remote Sensing of the Environment, Vol. 16 (1984), 13—33; *Bob Jaques* and *Ramon Lopez*, Looking Down for Money, in: Space Markets, No. 2 (Summer 1986), 73—80.

given the observed geophysical, vegetational and morphological conditions on that part of the Earth's surface.[28]

In the case of the Antarctic continent, however, use of remote sensing data to ascertain the presence of mining districts or mineral provinces is severely constrained. The principal limitation is plainly imposed by the tremendous ice sheet which overlays the continent's geological crust. To the extent that two percent of Antarctica's surface is ice-free, those portions of the continent may be targeted for remote sensing operations with some positive expectation that useful results might be obtained in prospecting for mineral locations. As previously mentioned, many ore deposits are found along regional and localized fracture patterns that were created when ore-forming solutions penetrated the host rocks. To the degree that these lineaments may be detected in ice-free areas (which lie primarily along Antarctica's coast), remote sensing can contribute serviceable data for mineral prospecting on the continent. However, for the remaining 98 percent of Antarctica's surface, which is covered by the massive ice cap, remote sensing operations will have only little relevance for mineral-related prospecting activities. Present remote sensing technology is not capable of penetrating the massive ice sheet, which has an average thickness of 2000 meters and reaches depth levels of 4500 meters at the interior of the continent.[29] Subglacial bedrock mapping, much less the possibility of reliable mineral detection, is not realistically feasible given present satellite remote sensing technology.

In the long term, more detailed knowledge of the surface formations of the ice sheet may make it possible for space-based remote sensing to assist in deducing the general character of bedrock morphology, perhaps even with greater accuracy than is practical today from airborne radio soundings made of the ice depth. Yet, location of subglacial bedrock mineral provinces and determination of their mineral composition lie far beyond the capabilities of contemporary remote sensing systems. For at least the next two decades, moreover, the most effective measurements for ice depth determination in Antarctica still are likely to be derived from aircraft soundings. As one commendator concisely put it, satellite ice soundings for bedrock mapping in Antarctica within the foreseeable future are "not promising."[30] Nevertheless, detection and evaluation of surface undulations will retain value as remote sensing activities, largely because these features are linked to the velocity of

[28] *Sabins*, note 11, 279; Also see *A. F. H. Goetz*, and *L. C. Rowan*, Geologic Remote Sensing, in: Science, Vol. 211 (Feb. 1981), 781—791.

[29] CIA Polar Atlas, note 8, 35; *Behrendt*, note 3, 2 (mimeo).

[30] *Gordon deQ. Robin*, Polar Glaciology, in: NASA, Earth Observing System, Science and Mission Requirements Working Group Report, Technical Memorandum 86129, Vol. I (Appendix), 1984, A 38.

ice sheet movements, to stress gradients in the ice mass, and to variations in basal shear stress.

b) Determining Glaciological Conditions

The predominant roles in which satellite remote sensing activities over Antarctica are presently engaged concerns analysis and assessment of the character of ice, the most pervasive resource on the continent. As a recoverable resource, Antarctic ice thus far has received only scant attention, both in terms of public consideration and the Antarctic Treaty Consultative Parties' policy concerns. The Antarctic ice sheet contains more than 90 percent of the world's ice, and covers and area of 13.9 million square kilometers, larger than that of the United States. If the entire ice cap were to melt, the global sea level would rise by some 70 meters.[31] Intimately related to Antarctica's ice sheet is the continent's surrounding belt of sea-ice, which represents one of the most salient features of the circumpolar region. Antarctic sea-ice expands to a maximum area of approximately 20 million square kilometers in September and recedes to a minimum of 4 million square kilometers in February. Interestingly enough, while the areal extent of winter ice in the Southern Ocean is 50 percent larger than the ice sheet overlaying the continent, the volume of that ice mantle is one thousand times greater than that of the sea-ice.[32] In any event, satellite remote sensing provides broad spatial coverage which is capable of monitoring the immense size of these ice sheets, as well as overcoming the desolate inaccessibility and bleak harshness of the southern polar environment.

Three types of ice sheets characterize the Antarctic continent and have been subjects of remote sensing activities. First, there is the terrestrial ice, which rests on land that is mostly above sea level and would be well above sea level if the ice mantle were removed and isostatic recovery were permitted to occur. Most of the ice in East Antarctica represents the main terrestrial ice sheet on the continent. Second, there is a marine ice-sheet. This ice formation rests on land substantially below sea level, and would remain so depressed even if the ice were to be removed. The West Antarctic ice sheet, and also two major drainage basins in East Antarctica, are ice sheets of the marine variety. Third, there are the ice shelves. These are floating extensions of grounded ice sheets, from which ice flows into the circumpolar seas. The Ross, Filchner and Ronne ice formations are the largest shelf areas, albeit ice shelf structures cover nearly every major embayment along the Antarctic coastline.[33]

---

[31] Satellite Ice Sheet Research, note 15, 1.
[32] Antarctic Sea Ice, 1973—1976, note 17, 1.
[33] Satellite Ice Sheet Research, note 15, 2—8.

The Antarctic ice sheets are in flux and are constantly changing. Snowfall is compacted to form ice, which eventually is transported to the ocean by the outward spreading of the ice sheet. The ice sheet moves into the ice shelves, whereafter substantial portions of the ice mass is lost through the calving of icebergs, or melting at the surface between the ice/ocean interface. Even so, fundamental questions remain unanswered. How great are these changes, and in which ways are they manifested? Do observed changes primarily represent redistribution of mass within the ice sheets, or do they entail exchange of mass with the oceans? What are the rates of ice thickening, or for that matter, of ice thinning? What, in essence, is Antarctica's mass balance? We also do not know how much snow falls on the ice sheet, or how much ice flows into the ocean in the form of icebergs. Moreover, scientists are still not able to calculate with precision the forces that propel ice motion, or to assess the degree to which ice affects the heat transfer between the ocean and the atmosphere — a process that inevitably impacts upon both the ocean environment and world climate conditions.[34]

Remote sensing by satellite, particularly with radar altimeters, has proven to be worthwhile in collecting scientific information relevant to finding answers for these queries. Data received from remote sensing satellites have confirmed that ocean circulation and sea-ice cover around Antarctica exert strong influences on melt rates from beneath the floating ice shelves which, in turn, can determine in large part ice discharge rates from the continent.

In its compressed annual layers of deposited snow, the continent's ice sheet contains within it a unique record of the world's climatic and atmospheric composition over the last several hundred millennia. To get at this information, ice sheet dynamics first must be determined; remote sensing satellite data from visible, infrared, and microwave radiometers, as well as that from SAR instruments, can contribute greatly to these ice sheet investigations. Accurate satellite altimeter measurements of ice sheet topography over prolonged periods may be employed to ascertain whether the continental ice sheets are in fact expanding or contracting. Such a determination would be derived from comparing the rate of composite ice accumulation with the melting and calving rates of ice from the sheet.[35]

As for the ice shelves, existing satellite techniques already have provided valuable data for evaluating ice dynamics, such as information

---

[34] See generally *Robin*, note 30, A 37—A 40.

[35] Satellite Ice Sheet Research, note 15, 14—16. Also see *Kenneth C. Jazek*, SAR Mapping of Antarctica, in: NASA Ocean Processes Program, Annual Report-Fiscal Year 1985, NASA Technical Memorandum 88987, Washington, D. C., 1986, II-28—II-29.

about the driving stress on floating shelf formations, surface strains and snow accumulation, deep bottom water formation and eddy transport. Regional interest areas for these studies have focused primarily on the Weddell and Ross Seas. These achievements notwithstanding, much remains to be learned in general about the critical process of shelf bottom melting and local accretion rates.[36]

Until the use of remote sensing satellite observations, little quantitative information was available about seasonal and interannual changes in sea-ice cover. However, within the last two decades, the data flow has changed appreciatively. Respective to sea-ice — specifically the ice pack interior — remote sensing has provided estimates of the field of ice-motion and surface dynamics, as well as of ice corrugation and concentration. This set of data has contributed substantially to scientific examination of sea-ice rheology.[37]

Sea-ice consists of fractured ice floes. Winds and currents keep the ice mass constantly in motion, causing it to undulate, segregate, and thus expose within its fissures the sea's surface; conversely, the sea's motion can push the ice together with crushing force, compressing it violently into a disjointed solid mass. The capricious situation of sea-ice poses obvious hazards for man-made structures, navigation and shipping in the region, and would undoubtedly impede any offshore resource development — including fishing — in the Antarctic. Such conditions necessitate routine, regular observations and short term forecasts of sea-ice behavior, which are obtainable from space-based remote sensing operations.

The operational application of remote sensing to sea-ice rests on the disparate appearance of open water and ice over the electromagnetic spectrum. That is, the open ocean is nearly black and absorbs most of the incoming solar radiation. In contrast, sea-ice cover shows up as nearly white and reflects practically all of the incoming radiation. Satellite images derived from visible, infrared and microwave sensors are capable of distinguishing these features, and can supply reliable, regionally uniform information on the global distribution of sea-ice and its seasonal variations.[38] The special value here of remote sensing satellite observations is their ability to furnish comprehensive coverage of the ice pack at brief intervals, as short as one day. In terms of ice profiling, however, existing remote sensing techniques are not yet able to determine directly ice thickness distribution. The best, and at present only, viable method of measuring the thickness of the ice pack is by using an upward-

---

[36] Satellite Ice Sheet Research, note 15, 4—7.
[37] See generally Antarctic Sea Ice, 1973—1976, note 17.
[38] NASA SSM/I Report, note 14, 9.

scanning sonar, usually by means of a submarine which serves as a platform underneath the ice floe.[39]

The glaciological community was among the earliest advocates of remote sensing by satellite. Some relevant data have been received from both the Landsat and Nimbus series, as well as from Seasat's short-lived monitoring activities during 1978. Nonetheless, comprehensive data collection on Antarctic ice dynamics has been sorely hindered by low priority assignments for ice sheet information and limited funding to process over-ice data. This point underscores the real need for more extensive international cooperation in the coming decade with regard to improving remote sensing technology and promoting more extensive exchange of data — not only as regards ice behavior in the Antarctic, but in all sensing realms. The 1990s will likely find that utilization of remote sensing has notably increased as a quantitative tool for monitoring sea-ice behavior. Anticipation of a substantial increase in polar-orbiting satellites with remote sensing capability has already prompted formation of a special group — the Committee on Earth Observation Satellites (CEOS) — by several national and international non-governmental entities involved in satellite development and operations. The purpose of CEOS is to serve as an informal forum for coordinating remote sensing satellite missions. Such a joint effort seems essential if the needs and objectives of space agencies and scientific communities are to be adequately served. In particular, CEOS can play a useful role in defining and coordinating several facets of the remote sensing operation, including determination of the orbit configuration to maximize data return, arrangement of a satellite's duty cycle to optimize sensor coverage, placement of ground stations to receive raw data without overlap, and expedition of data processing and cataloging, as well as promoting its exchange and accessibility.[40]

Remote sensing by satellite holds great potential for glaciological applications in Antarctica. It will allow for more accurate assessment of the continent's ice flow patterns and for monitoring the geographical distribution of temperature and accumulation rates which could detect progressive changes in the ice sheet over time. Remote sensing operations also can be used to acquire new data indicating surface elevations, snow accumulation rates, variations in surface temperatures, and calving rates of the Antarctic ice sheet. In sum, remote sensing technology can aid in ascertaining the mass balance of Antarctica's ice sheets, defining individual drainage basins on the continent, and determining those basins

---

[39] *Loc. cit.*, 35—37.

[40] This cooperation essentially underpins the ambitious and multifaceted Earth Observing System planned by NASA over the next decade. See generally Earth Observing System: Science and Mission Requirements, Working Group Report, Vol. I, Technical Memorandum 86129, 1984.

which are most active glaciologically. Such information will be of immense value in more clearly understanding the overall geophysical stability of the continent, the pulsating behavior of its circumpolar ice pack, and perhaps even the prospects for eventually harvesting portions of Antarctica's tremendous ice mass for human consumption and irrigation purposes.[41]

2. *The Southern Ocean*

a) Phytoplankton Determination

Satellite observing systems have progressed sufficiently to facilitate sophisticated, more advanced studies of polar oceanography. In this respect, temporal and spatial variabilities remain constant hallmarks of the circumpolar marine ecosystem. Consequently, mapping the large scale distribution of phytoplankton would entail significant progress towards determining the role of primary production in the Southern Ocean. There is, in short, the relevant need to ascertain the spatial variability of phytoplankton biomass and its productivity over time, in order to gain better understanding and appreciation of the link between biological and physical processes in the southern seas. Remote sensing imagery can be of great assistance in attaining those ambitions.

Images produced by satellite remote sensing can determine sea-surface temperature and phytoplankton chlorophyll pigment concentration. In the open ocean, where nutrient levels and phytoplankton counts are both low, the color of the seawater is deep blue. However, in zones where upwelling occurs and nutrient levels are rich, phytoplankton bloom; the resultant presence of chlorophyll creates a green hue in the water. These transitions in water coloration are distinctly detectable by satellite remote sensing operations.[42]

The Coastal Zone Color Scanner (CZCS), which was launched on board the Nimbus 7 satellite in 1978, was specifically designed to study living marine resources. The CZCS measures the intensity of light reflected from the first few meters of the ocean's surface. The color of seawater is predominantly a function of photosynthetic pigments in the phytoplankton. These microscopic marine plantlife tend to absorb blue and reflect green light. The presence of more plentiful phytoplankton thus creates a green shade on the ocean, which in turn, is detected by the CZCS sensor and figures in calculating the chlorophyll pigment concentration in the region. In effect, then, the CZCS operates to map chlorophyll

[41] See *W. F. Weeks* and *W. J. Campbell*, Icebergs as a Freshwater Resource: An Appraisal, in: Journal of Glaciology, Vol. 12 (1973), 207—233.

[42] *Sabins*, note 11, 323—324.

fluorescence concentrations in the ocean water, from which can be derived measurements of oceanic biomass and circulation patterns.[43]

A forthcoming, improved version of CZCS, the Ocean Color Imager (OCI), will be capable of measuring light reflected from the ocean in a few selected bands. This should permit better assessment of pigment patterns in the upper layers of the ocean, such that more accurate determination might be made of the composite phytoplankton biomass, as well as of its net productivity. If launched into a sun-synchronous orbit, the OCI would be able to supply daily global coverage of its near-surface phytoplankton mapping — a feature highly desirable for marine monitoring, if it can be achieved.[44]

For the Antarctic region, use of these detection processes assumes particular significance with regard to making accurate determination of krill locations. Krill tend to swarm in areas of upwelling where nutrient levels are high and phytoplankton bloom. Phytoplankton serve as the principal food source for krill. The reasonable deduction here is that if areas of dense phytoplankton concentrations can be located, then one is also likely to find in those same areas high populations of zooplankton, many of which undoubtedly will be krill swarms. This information should provide a clearer picture not only of the location of krill swarms, but also a better idea of their composite biomass and productivity trends.[45]

While these color imaging processes have not been applied to the Southern Ocean to the same extent as they have been along coastal regions, their potential utility appears appreciable for determining with greater precision estimates of the net biological productivity in the circumpolar oceans. A follow-on instrument being developed by NASA, the Moderate Resolution Imaging Spectroradiometer (MODIS), will be capable of measuring all of the visible and much of the infrared spectrum in several narrow bands. MODIS thus offers the possibility of identifying dominant phytoplankton groups and perhaps even of distinguishing different materials suspended in the ocean water. With a proposed resolution of 500 meters, MODIS will produce visible data which can be used to characterize the global distribution of phytoplankton biomass as it relates to its temporal and spatial variability. Scheduled for launch in the mid-1900s, MODIS is to be part of the United States' multifaceted research projet, the Earth Observing System.[46]

[43] *W. A. Hovis, et al.*, Nimbus-7 Coastal Zone Color Scanner-system description and initial imagery, in: Science, Vol. 210 (1980), 60—63.

[44] *Mark R. Abbott*, Biological Oceanography, in: Earth Observing System, note 30, A 12, and *Robert G. Kirk*, Ocean Color Instrument, in: NASA Oceanic Processes Program, note 35, II-30—II-31.

[45] NASA, West Coast Upwelling, in Oceanography from Space: A Research Strategy for the Decade 1985—1995, Washington, D. C., 1985 (portfolio packet).

[46] *Ibid.*; *Wayne E. Esaias*, MODIS Instrument Requirements, in: NASA Oceanic Processes Program, note 35, II-30—II-31.

b) Polymetallic Nodule Location

Beneath the stormy, wind-driven waters of the Southern Ocean there have been found scattered deposits of polymetallic nodules on the deep seabed. One would surmise that remote sensing operations from satellites might be ideal for pinpointing the locations of these and other deposits of ocean floor minerals. Unfortunately, because of geophysical conditions, that is not the case.

Remote sensing of the seafloor from satellites is largely precluded by the physical fact that water absorbs or reflects most wavelengths of electromagnetic energy. Only visible wavelengths can penetrate water, and the capability of depth penetration by those wavelengths is strongly affected by the turbidity of the water mass. Increased turbidity creates decreased light transmittance, meaning the lessened possibility for remote sensing image translation. At great depths, such as those earmarking the circumpolar Southern Ocean, inconsequently energy is reflected from the ocean floor; hence, useful image depiction of seabed terrain, never mind that of dispersed deposits of ferromanganese nodules, is largely prevented.[47] As a result, detection of polymetallic nodules on the ocean floor will be relegated for the foreseeable future to shipborne sidescanning sonar techniques, which produce sound waves that are readily transmitted through the water. Satellite instrumentation, however, does not appear very likely to contribute much insofar as sound navigation ranging (sonar) is concerned for mapping the ocean floor, or in aiding in site fixation of mineral deposits under the Southern Ocean. That job seems likely to remain the main function of surface vessels pulling submarine buoy technology equipped with sonar scanners.[48]

Use of remote sensing for gauging Antarctica's natural resource potential is limited, as several desirable applications are presently beyond the scope of technological capability. Space-based remote sensing cannot penetrate the continent's ice sheet to locate deposits of subglacial minerals, if they exist. Determining size and locations of krill swarms in the ocean, and finding ferromanganese deposits on the deep seabed also lie beyond the present competency of remote sensing. Neither resource discovery nor recovery in Antarctica yet has been revolutionized by remote sensing.

V. International Law Governing Remote Sensing over Antarctica

The international law affecting remote sensing is still in a process of gestation. Importantly, remote sensing, either by public or private

[47] *Sabins*, note 11, 326.
[48] *Loc. cit.*, 328—332.

satellite system, is not precluded by any existent treaties or other international legal agreements on outer space. Legal attitudes toward remote sensing have tended to vary according to the nationality of the satellite performing the sensing *vis-à-vis* that of the subjacent state whose territory is being sensed. Significant, too, is that remote sensing by some state of its own territory, or of the high seas, or of the moon or other celestial bodies, has not yet generated any real legal concern. These activities are generally viewed as lawful.[49] Given the emergent law thus far, the legal situation for Antarctica can be regarded in the same vein.

Since 1974, the Legal Sub-Committee of the United Nations Committee on the Peaceful Uses of Outer Space (COPUOS) has considered the question of the legal implications of remote sensing. In those discussions, the critical international law issues pertaining to remote sensing have focused on three broad subject areas which remain, as yet, not fully resolved. These issue areas relate, first, to national sovereignty and consideration of a prior consent regime for remote sensing; second, to state responsibility and liability for damage caused by a remote sensing satellite; and third, to the evolutionary course of legal development affecting remote sensing.[50] Each of these legal considerations holds specific relevance for remote sensing activities over the Antarctic region.

1. *Sovereignty Issues and Remote Sensing*

When remote sensing is applied to the Earth's land surface, differences usually arise over perceptions of its lawfulness. This situation is due in large part to disparate interpretations of national sovereignty by interested states. On the one hand, a space-based legal conceptualization of remote sensing is held by the advanced sensing states.[51] Accordingly, remote sensing represents an exercise of their sovereign rights to explore, exploit, and use space freely. Remote sensing is interpreted to be a peaceful and beneficial use of outer space, beyond the realm where national sovereignty is legally applicable over man's activities. On the other hand, an Earth-based legal conceptualization of remote sensing is

---

[49] *Carl Q. Christol*, The Modern International Law of Outer Space, New York, (1982), 731.

[50] For the early work of the Legal Sub-Committee of COPUOS, and the draft proposals tracing the evolution of a set of legal principles for remote sensing, see UN Doc. A/AC. 105/147, Annex 3, 11 March 1975; UN Doc. A/AC. 105/171, 28 May 1976; UN Doc. A/AC. 105/196, Annex 3, 11 April 1977; UN Doc. A/AC. 105/216. 6 March 1978; UN Doc. A/AC. 105/240, Annex 1, 10 April 1979; UN Doc. A/AC. 105/271, Annex 2, 10 April 1980; and UN Doc. A/AC. 105/288, Annex 1, 20 April 1981. Discussion of the negotiations producing these documents can be found in: *Christol*, note 49, 720—764.

[51] See text *infra* at notes 56—66.

held by other, mostly Third World states.[52] When placed in this context, political sensitivities toward the legal notion of national sovereignty have persuaded these still developing states that a valid legal basis exists for prohibiting remote sensing activities over any state's territory absent appropriate consent.

The questions posed by these opposing schools of thought have salient import for international law, particularly as it might come to affect a remote sensing system overflying Antarctica: would national sovereignty be infringed upon by a sensing state, or its commercialized agents, if remote sensing operations were conducted over and/or data were distributed about another state or territory, without consent or permission from the latter's government? Do states, or territorial sovereigns, possess a legal right to forbid or deny permission for remote sensing operations to pass over their territory? Similarly, do governments of sensed states or territories have legitimate prior rights to receive, appraise, and evaluate either sensed data or analyzed information before it is made available to third states? In short, does remote sensing by some state constitute an unlawful invasion of territorial privacy presumably guaranteed by national sovereignty?

The technologically advanced states consider remote sensing of the Earth in general, inclusive of Antarctica, to be unquestionably lawful under provisions of the Outer Space Treaty, the accepted customary freedom to use outer space for peaceful purposes,[53] as well as under provisions of the Antarctic Treaty. Hence, the view espoused is that unfettered acquisition of data and open dissemination of information are consistent with aspirations for a better world community, one which will benefit from a more open society. An opposing view is generally held by developing states who assert that remote sensing may not be lawful because it could violate basic principles of national territorial sovereignty. That is, national sovereignty conveys an implicit legal right for any state to maintain a closed society, if that particular state so chooses.[54] The argument thus is made that accumulation of primary data through remote sensing, analysis of that data and the subsequent international dissemination of its information perforce would invade the sovereign privacy right of a sensed state, or of a territory, unless permission had been granted *a priori* by the government of the targeted

[52] See text *infra* at notes 67—76.

[53] See generally *R. F. Stowe*, United States Presents Guidelines for Remote Sensing of the Natural Environment From Outer Space, in: U.S. Department of State Bulletin, Vol. 72 (1975), 419.

[54] See generally *M. A. Dauses*, National Sovereignty and Remote Sensing of Earth Resources by Satellite, in: Proceedings of the XVI Colloquium on the Law of Outer Space, (1974), 121, and *S. M. Williams*, Earth-Surveying from Space in the Light of the Principle of Sovereignty, in: *op. cit.*, 164.

polity. The legal cases for these disparate approaches, which could affect the role which sovereignty considerations might play in polar-orbiting remote sensing operations, have been cogently set out in national position papers presented since 1975 to the United Nations Committee on the Peaceful Uses of Outer Space.[55]

a) Freedom to Sense, with Open Dissemination

Led by the United States, many developed states contend that free collection of primary data and analyzed information is lawful and necessary to promote global security and more efficient use of the world's resources.[56] Accordingly, all states have the freedom to acquire data by remote sensing without any necessary legal obligation of securing consent of sensed states beforehand.[57]

In the United States' view, there should be free and unrestricted access to, as well as open dissemination of, remote sensing data concerning Antarctica to all interested parties — irrespective of whether they are states, international organizations, corporations, or individuals.[58] Moreover, all states directly receiving data from remote sensing operations also should make it available to all interested parties.[59] As a consequence, this provision would render open dissemination a requirement for all ground stations receiving Antarctic-related data transmissions from remote sensing satellites.[60]

With regard to data dissemination, the United States supports the position that both primary data (*i. e.*, that transmitted directly from a satellite) and analyzed information (*i. e.*, that end product which results from the interpretative / assessment processes) ought to be made avail-

---

[55] See text *infra* at notes 55—66 and 70—76. In addition to these rather polarized views, the Soviet Union and France submitted a proposal in 1974 which, while accepting the legal propriety and necessity of states to conduct remote sensing operations, nonetheless would have permitted sensed states to retain the legal right to mandate prior consent for any dissemination of sensed data or analyzed information. See Working Paper of France and the USSR on Draft Principles Governing Activities of States in the Field of Remote Sensing on Earth Resources by Means of Space Technology, UN Doc. A/AC. 105/133 (June 1974), Annex IV.

[56] *Christol*, note 49, 733. Also see *M. Leigh*, United States Policy of Collecting and Disseminating Remote Sensing Data, in: *Nicholas Mateesco Matte* and *Hamilton DeSaussure* (eds.), Legal Implications of Remote Sensing from Outer Space, Toronto 1976, 147.

[57] *David A. Greenburg*, Third Party Access to Data Obtained via Remote Sensing: International Legal Theory versus Economic and Political Reality, in: Case Western Reserve Journal of International Law, Vol. 15 (1983), 361, 371 (1983).

[58] Working Paper of the United States, UN Doc. A/AC. 105/C. 2/L. 103, (19 February 1975).

[59] *Ibid.*, Art. V.

[60] *Greenburg*, note 57, 364.

able for distribution to any interested third parties. Even so, an important policy distinction must be drawn between primary data and analyzed information, namely, that analyzed information, which is derived from raw data by some purchaser (or commercial sensor), should remain the property of that analyst or sponsoring agency by virtue of the time, capital, and intellectual investment made in preparing that product.[61] The United States, nonetheless, maintains that sensed data ought to be shared with those states from which it was derived prior to its dissemination to any third parties.[62]

The legal grounds for the United States position rest heavily upon principles contained in the Outer Space Treaty. As specifically provided for in Article 1 "The exploration and use of outer space ... shall be carried out for the benefit and in the interests of all countries, irrespective of their degree of economic or scientific development, and shall be the province of all mankind."[63] Remote sensing of Antarctica, therefore, is considered to be a proper excercise in the legitimate use of outer space.[64] For the United States, the *free-use* principle extends above the vertical limits of territorial sovereignty.[65] That is, remote sensing takes place beyond the reaches of sovereign jurisdiction; hence, the contention that any consent requirement might exist for conducting remote sensing operations over Antarctica is held to be misplaced,[66] irrespective of the condition of sovereignty on the continent.

b) Prior Consent for Remote Sensing and Data Dissemination

Some developing countries argued during the United Nations COPUOS debates that states should retain the legal right of prior consent over

[61] U.S. Working Paper, note 58, Art. V.

[62] *Loc. cit.*, Art. VI.

[63] Treaty on Principles Governing the Activities of States in the Exploration and Use of Outer Space, Including the Moon and Other Celestial Bodies, 18 U.S.T. 2410, T.I.A.S. No. 6347, 610 UNTS 205, done Jan. 27, 1967, Art. I. (Hereinafter cited as Outer Space Treaty).

[64] As provided for in Article III of the Outer Space Treaty, which mandates that "States Party to the Treaty shall carry on activities in the exploration and use of outer space ... in accordance with international law including the Charter of the United Nations, in the interest of maintaining international peace and security and promoting international cooperation and understanding." *Loc. cit.*, Art. III.

[65] *Greenburg*, note 57, 366. The United States has premised its objections to a consent-based remote sensing regime on reasons of pragmatism, as well as principle. A sensed state's veto is deemed an impracticable policy approach because State boundaries can not be discerned by satellites; the purposes and techniques of remote sensing satellites are not state-specific, but rather regional and global in scope; and with respect to dissemination, a restrictive consent regime would undoubtedly redound to exacerbating the political and economic disparities between developed and less developed countries. *Leigh*, note 56, 149. These objections clearly are seen in the case of Antarctica as well.

[66] UN Doc. A/AC. 105/C. 2/SR. 387 (1983), 8—9.

who is given access to data about their resources.[67] These states remain apprehensive that data might be used by some government or corporation, for strategic, political or economic purposes contrary to the sensed state's best national interests,[68] or ostensibly in the case of Antarctica, the best interests of the international community. As a result, these states would like to be able to exercise a legal right to deny the opportunity of remote sensing if such sensing activities were undertaken without their express consent, approval or, at least, prior notification.[69]

The particulars of this legal position were well articulated in a joint proposal introduced by Argentina and Brazil to COPUOS in 1975.[70] Put bluntly, this proposal would have mandated that prior consent of a subjacent state must be secured for both aquisition and dissemination of remote sensing data.[71] The propriety of remote sensing was acknowledged in this proposal, so long as it was conducted on the basis of *sovereign equality of states*. Specifically in this regard, respect was mandated for those legal rights inherent in national sovereignty. Of these, a cardinal right is the exclusive economic right of a state to utilize and distribute its natural resources as it sees fit.[72] Thus, sensing states would have been required to respect the legal principle of permanent sovereignty over natural resources,[73] and concomitantly, to refrain from sensing any national natural resources of a state absent that state's consent.[74]

In cases where a sensing state might have acquired information relating to the resources of another state, the sensing state would not have been permitted to divulge or transmit that information to any third party absent the observed states's consent.[75] This fiat likewise would

---

[67] See generally *Eleonora Ambrosetti*, The Relevance of Remote Sensing to Third World Economic Development: Some Legal and Political Aspects, New York University Journal of International Law and Politics, Vol. 12 (1980), 569, 569—70.

[68] This apprehension was alluded to in the 1983 COPUOS discussions as a major concern. See UN Doc. A/AC. 105/C. 2/SR. 383 (1983), 8.

[69] As recently asserted in COPUOS, less developed countries remain seriously concerned that remote sensing might impair their economic interests and in the process constitute a violation of the national sovereignty. See UN Doc. A/AC. 105/C. 2/SR. 383 (1983), 2 and UN Doc. A/AC. 105/C. 2/SR. 387 (1983), 4. Also see the text *infra* at notes 94—100.

[70] Joint Proposal of Argentina and Brazil on Draft Articles for a Treaty on Remote Sensing of Natural Resources by Means of Technology, UN Doc. A/C. 1/1047 (1974). This proposal originally had as co-sponsors Chile, Mexico and Venezuela, but their support subsequently, shifted. See, *e. g.*, Mexico Working Paper, Doc. WG/RS (1981) / WP. 2., in: UN Doc. A/AC. 105/288 (1981).

[71] Argentina - Brazil Proposal, note 70, Arts. IV, IX and X.

[72] *Ibid.*, Art. IV.

[73] See the discussion in the text *infra* notes 94—100.

[74] Argentina - Brazil Proposal, *loc. cit.*, note 70, Art. V.

[75] *Loc. cit.*, Art. IX.

have been predicated upon the assertion of permanent sovereignty over natural resources.[76]

That these concepts contained in the Argentine-Brazil proposal were taken seriously was clearly evidenced by their inclusion in early drafts of general principles drawn up by the COPUOS. Nevertheless, that they were contentious was equally evinced by their being relegated in the draft to bracketed provisions, a practice used to indicate interpretative disagreement or unresolved points.

2. *International Liability and Remote Sensing*

Remote sensing systems operated by states remain their national responsibility, and those governments will incur international legal liability in the event damages may be caused by their satellites. The government of the launching state is held accountable under both treaty laws and customary practice for obligations and responsibilities associated with remote sensing activities. This would remain true even if that remote sensing program were conducted in the private sector.[77]

That this would be the legal case underscores an ironic dichotomy for the United States and France, the only two governments which presently support privatized sensing programs. Through the commercialization of remote sensing satellites, the United States and French Governments essentially handed over to private firms specific international rights and legal privileges accrued from such space activities. Yet, in spite of doing so, those governments nonetheless remain liable for any injury or damage that might emanate from the exercise of remote sensing rights.[78] To substantiate this point, Article 6 of the Outer Space Treaty provides:

> States Parties to the Treaty shall bear international responsibility for national activities in outer space ... whether such activities are carried on by governmental agencies or by non-governmental entities, and for assuring that national activities are carried out in con-

[76] *Ibid.*; Provision is also made for the sensed state to refrain from soliciting or accepting from third parties — including private entities — any remote sensing information pertaining to a state's natural resources without first securing that state's express consent. *Loc. cit.*, Art. X.

[77] Article 6, Chapter 2, of the U. S. Constitution makes treaties part of the supreme law of the land and, therefore, "U.S. citizens would be bound as a matter of domestic law by the self-executing provisions of space treaties in exercising actions or activities covered thereby, and the authority settled upon by the United States governing any transfer [of remote sensing satellites from the public to the private sector] might expressly provide for actual fulfillment of international requirements." *Zafren*, Part II: The Commercialization of Space Technologies: Some Present and Future Legal Issues, in: Policy and Legal Issues Involved in the Commercialization of Space, Senate Committee on Commerce, Science, and Transportation, 98th Congress, 1st session, (1983), 23.

[78] See generally *Carl Christol*, International Liability for Damage Caused by Space Objects, in: American Journal of International Law, Vol. 74, (1980), 346.

> formity with the provisions set forth in the present Treaty. The activities of non-governmental entities in outer space ... shall require authorization and continuing supervision by the appropriate State Party to the Treaty.[79]

Significantly, no distinction is made between a state's activities in outer space and those of private commercial agents under its legal *aegis*. The state, accordingly, remains responsible for the activities of firms engaged in remote sensing, even if the government had no direct control over those activities.[80] To be sure, the second sentence in Article 6 explicitly makes this point as it requires for space-related activities "authorization and continuing supervision" by the State Party.[81] The state must assume responsibility for all its activities in space, irrespective of whether they are performed by governmental agencies or non-governmental commercial entities.[82]

Commercialization of polar-orbiting satellites by the United States and France — the Landsat and SPOT programs, respectively — fails to relieve those governments of liability should extraterritorial damages or injuries occur, in Antarctica or elsewhere. International liability for any damages caused by space objects or their component parts accrues to the launching state, *i. e.*, the state from whose territory the object was launched.[83] This principle is confirmed in Article 7 of the Outer Space Treaty, which provides that

> Each State Party to the Treaty that launches or procures the launching of an object into outer space, including the Moon and other celestial bodies, and each State party from whose territory or facility an object is launched, is internationally liable for damage to another State Party to the Treaty or to its natural or juridical persons by such object or its component parts on the Earth, in air space or in outer space, including the Moon and other celestial bodies.[84]

The issue of state liability for space-related activities, inclusive of remote sensing operations, was substantially clarified in 1972 by a special liability agreement, the Convention on International Liability for Damage Caused by Space Objects.[85] This multinational accord supplies in

---

[79] Outer Space Treaty, note 63, Art. VI.

[80] *Christol*, note 49, 831—832.

[81] As noted in *Nicholas Mateesco Matte*, Aerospace Law — Telecommunications Satellites, Toronto 1982, 81.

[82] *Ibid.*

[83] This principle is well-founded in the historical development of the law regarding liability for damages caused by space objects. See the discussion in: *Christol*, note 49, 61—70.

[84] Outer Space Treaty, note 63, Art. VII.

[85] Done Mar. 29, 1972, 24 U.S.T. 2389, T.I.A.S. No. 7762 (1973).

considerable detail definitions for allocating responsibility,[86] the extent of accessing liability,[87] the procedure for presenting claims,[88] and the means for determining compensation.[89] Moreover, it highlights an important realization regarding international law and polar-orbiting remote sensing satellite operations: it is the national government which is responsible and perforce liable for any deaths, injuries or property damage done extraterritorially by a remote sensing system owned and operated by a private, non-governmental enterprise. Such treaty-based responsibility for international liability necessarily would compel a state to fashion some regulatory framework for authorizing and supervising private commercial firms involved in remote sensing operations. Similarly, it would appear incumbent upon a state whose private firms were engaged in remote sensing operations to enact legislation designed to insure their compliance with the treaties and principles of extraterrestrial law.[90] Non-governmental entities involved in remote sensing are likewise legally obligated to abide by that state's domestic regulations pursuant to fulfilling the latter's responsibilities under international law.[91] In the final analysis, however, under international law the liability implications of polar-orbiting remote sensing systems are clear: states are internationally responsible for all their national activities in space, and in the event that damage or injury should occur in the Antarctic under a public or privatized remote sensing operation, the launching state would be liable for prompt and adequate compensation.[92]

---

[86] *Loc. cit.*, Art. I.

[87] *Loc. cit.*, Arts. II—VI.

[88] *Loc. cit.*, Arts. VII—XI. Dispute settlement is covered in Arts. XIV—XX.

[89] *Loc. cit.*, Art. XII.

[90] See generally *Christopher C. Joyner* and *Douglas R. Miller*, Selling Satellites: The Commercialization of LANDSAT, in: Harvard International Law Journal, Vol. 26 (Winter 1985), 63—102. Also see generally United States Congress, Office of Technology Assessment, Remote Sensing and the Private Sector: Issues for Discussion — A Technical Memorandum, OTA-ISC-20, 1984.

[91] As one observer wryly noted in the course of debate over the United States Government's decision to transfer operation of the Landsat system to the private sector,

> Internationally, such a transfer would appear to place the United States in a theoretical dichotomy. It will have given certain direct rights and privileges it has enjoyed under international law to the private commercial interests of its citizenry while still being primarily liable for a wide array of adverse effects that might emanate from the exercise of those rights.

Zafren, note 77, 23.

[92] The Liability Convention makes this point unmistakably. The United States is a party to this treaty, and is so obligated. As the preeminently active remote sensing state, not only generally, but also over Antarctica, particular significance is attached to the role which liability is treated legally by the United States Government.

3. Concerns by Lesser Developed Countries over Remote Sensing

By the end of the 1980s, at least six remote sensing systems are expected to be operational.[93] It is not surprising, therefore, that commercialization of the Landsat system by the United States in 1985 aroused concern in the Third World over the internationalization of natural resource data.[94] This apprehension stemmed not only from dissemination of remote sensing data, but also from the developing countries' desire to preserve their national privacy over natural resource wealth, and in the case of Antarctica, presumably to secure greater access to circumpolar resources. Such a legal attitude should neither be surprising nor unexpected, given the historical legacy of colonization and commercial exploitation which these lesser developed countries generally experienced during the past century and a half.[95] Resentment was also felt by newly independent states that they were being compelled to consider the legal parameters of a remote sensing regime grounded in Western-derived interpretations of international law, with a proclivity evidenced towards open dissemination.[96] In short, the aforementioned consent requirement emanated directly as a reaction by developing country governments to their being asked to accept another aspect of international law in which they had scant influence in creating, had little likelihood of participating, but which apparently presented serious impacts upon their national economies and self-esteem.[97]

---

[93] Report of the Second United Nations Conference on the Exploration and Peaceful Uses of Outer Space, UN Doc. A/CONF. 101/10/Corr. 1, (1982), 24. In addition to the United States and the Soviet Union, States expected to possess remote sensing systems technology by 1990 include Brazil, Canada, China, France, Japan, and India, *Ibid.* Of these, the Soviet Union, Brazil China and India have not yet publicly announced explicit plans for conducting remote sensing operations over Antarctica.

[94] *Joyner and Miller*, note 90, 89—95; and *Hamilton DeSaussure*, Remote Sensing by Satellite: What Future for An International Regime?, in: American Journal of International Law, Vol. 71 (1977), 707. See also *Carl Christol*, Remote Sensing and International Law, Annuals of Air & Space Law, Vol. V (1980), 375, 394.

In December 1985, the Landsat system and marketing of its data was turned over to the EOSAT Corporation. In return for a government subsidy of $ 250 million, EOSAT was supposed to build and operate Landsats 6 and 7. However, because it has received only partial payment of the agreed sum, and because of other technical delays and cost overruns, construction of Landsat 6 has been stopped. As a result of these difficulties, coupled with the general malaise affecting the space program in the aftermath of the Challenger disaster in early 1986, the U.S. remote sensing program is experiencing serious disruptive difficulties. See National Research Council Space Applications Board, Remote Sensing of the Earth from Space: A Program in Crisis, Washington, D. C., 1985.

[95] *Ambrosetti*, note 67, 583—84.

[96] Primarily because the United States has been the only state operating a civilian remote sensing system, the U.S. policy of open dissemination has served as the international rule for data dissemination. See *Ambrosetti*, note 67, 583—84.

[97] *Greenburg*, note 57, 380—81.

Developing states have been apprehensive that remote sensing information might be used to the detriment of their national economic self-interest — not only over their sovereign territories, but also over common spaces as well. Remote sensing systems evoke concern over a global data and informational regime that is controlled by wealthy governments or profit-motivated corporations whose economic objectives ostensibly might come at the expense of developmental priorities of developing countries. Relatedly, there is fear that widespread dissemination of remote sensing data could render developing states more vulnerable — and hence susceptible — to foreign exploitation of their natural resources.[98] Similarly, there is concern that the advanced space-faring governments or their commercialized agents might seek to withhold selective resource-related information derived from remote sensing operations over common space areas, such as Antarctica, when it was in their politico-economic interests to do so. Important, too, is the realization that developing countries are heavily reliant upon primary commodities trade, including minerals and hydrocarbons, and therefore are anxious about the economic consequences that an unregulated remote sensing information system might detract from their economic opportunities. There is also anxiety that information about minerals and fossil fuel deposits in the hands of an insensitive government or commercial remote sensing operator could give foreign companies superior bargaining leverage when negotiating concession or exploration contracts within a developing country.[99] As a result, the qualification of prior consent has been regarded by most developing countries as a minimal safeguard against possible market abuse or manipulation by

---

[98] One commentator put it aptly when he observed:

> The primary fear of the lesser-developed nations, virtually all of whom favor restrictions on dissemination, is exploitation. Specifically, they fear large international monopolies acquiring primary data and analyzed information, and using it for purposes of prognosis in different branches of the world economy, thus determining the most profitable fields of capital investment, and dictating their own conditions for natural resource development. While it is argued that since remote sensing encompasses only data gathering and that access to and control of resources can still be restricted by domestic legislation, lesser-developed nations reject this argument because it does not take into account the value of the data and information itself in the hands of sophisticated government and non-government entities in developed countries. Such data and information would put those entities in a much superior bargaining position.

Greenburg, note 67, 379—80.

[99] See generally *DeSaussure*, note 94. A new issue which is likely to breed anxiety among developing countries over the use of space-based remote sensing is the suggestion that these satellites be used as news-gathering instruments for worldwide information purposes, *i. e.*, in the form of a "mediasat." See generally, U.S. Congress, Office of Technology Assessment, Commercial Newsgathering from Space, — A Technical Memorandum, OTA-TM-ISC-40, Washington, D. C., 1987.

sensing states or their commercialized corporate agents.[100] These resource-related concerns have prompted debate in the United Nations, not only in COPUOS over the course of evolution for the law affecting remote sensing operations in outer space, but also in the General Assembly's First Committee regarding the most appropriate status of the regime which should be governing Antarctica. Both these debates have presented certain intriguing legal implications affecting remote sensing operations over Antarctica.

After twelve years of debate in the Outer Space committee over what general legal principles should be applied to remote sensing, on April 1, 1986, a special Working Group of the Legal Sub-Committee of the COPUOS reached consensus agreement on a set of Draft Principles on Remote Sensing.[101] This draft embodied the so-called "Austrian text," which had evolved out of the group's deliberations, and was so designated because the Austrian representative had served as chair for the sessions.[102] The text actually had been submitted in a slightly modified version as an Austrian proposal to the 1985 session of the COPUOS, and was subsequently submitted by the Austrian representative without alterations to the Legal Sub-Committee.[103] Following consensus approval by the Sub-Committee on April 1, 1986, the Draft Principles were then transmitted to the COPUOS. On June 13, 1986, they were approved by the COPUOS, and reported out to the General Assembly for consideration at its 41st Session. Following their consideration in the General Assembly's Special Political Committee, the Draft Principles were formally adopted as General Assembly Resolution 41/65 in late 1986.[104]

---

[100] In a proposal submitted to UNISPACE 82 by Mexico on behalf of the Group of 77 (*i. e.*, the developing countries), this view was reaffirmed. See UN Doc. A/CONF. 101/L. 3 (20 August 1982), reprinted in: UNISPACE '82. Report and Hearing before the House Subcommittee on Space Science and Applications, Committee on Science and Technology, 97th Congress, 2nd Session, 1982, LXXXII.

[101] Report of the Legal Sub-Committee in the Work of Its Twenty-fifth Session, UN Doc. A/AC. 105/370, Annex I (1986).

[102] UN Doc. A/40/20, Annex V (1985). The Legal Subcommittee's working group on remote sensing, which acted under the chairmanship of the Austrian delegate, *Dr. Franz Cede*, worked out the set of draft principles. When no participant chose to assume principal responsibility for the draft, the Chairman did so, hence the designation "Austrian draft." Interestingly enough, *Peter Jankowitsch*, who subsequently served as plenary chairman of COPUOS when the draft principles were endorsed, is also an Austrian. I am indebted to *Dr. Gerhard Hafner* for his clarification of these particular points. For general commentary on these developments, see Draft Principles on remote sensing activities approved by Outer Space Committee, UN Monthly Chronicle, Vol. XXIII (August 1986), 84—86.

[103] UN Doc. A/AC. 105/L. 158 (1985).

[104] UN General Assembly Resolution 41/65 (1986). See UN General Assembly, Official Records: Forty-first Session (Supplement No. 20, UN Doc. A/41/20), Report of the Committee on the Peaceful Uses of Outer Space, Annex II, reprinted as the Draft Principles Relating to Remote Sensing of the Earth from Space, in: International Legal Materials, Vol. XXV, (September 1985), 1334—1336.

Considering past patterns of outer space law, it seems very likely that in due time the Legal Sub-Committee will work on translating these principles into the text of an international convention on remote sensing, which then would be submitted for approval in turn to the COPUOS and, ultimately, to the General Assembly for approval as an international treaty.

The set of fifteen agreed principles holds direct relevance for remote sensing operations over Antarctica. The principles declare that remote sensing should be carried out such that it is for the benefit of and in the interests of all states, "taking into particular consideration the needs of the developing countries."[105] Further, they instruct that remote sensing activities should be conducted in accordance with international law, particularly the principles contained in Article 1 of the Outer Space Treaty, the United Nations Charter, and the relevant instruments of the International Telecommunications Union.[106] Principle IV addresses the sensitive sovereignty issue, albeit in relatively mild fashion. In part, this provision stipulates that remote sensing activities

> shall be conducted on the basis of respect for the principle of full and permanent sovereignty of all States and peoples over their own wealth and natural resources, with due regard to the rights and interests, in accordance with international law, of other States and entities under their jurisdiction. Such activities shall not be conducted in a manner detrimental to the legitimate rights and interests of the sensed State.[107]

Importantly, the agreed principles do not contain any requirement that consent must be secured from a state, either before foreign remote sensing activities are conducted over its territory, or before dissemination is made of information relating to its territory. Moreover, principle IV makes clear that remote sensing should be conducted in accordance with the principle of "freedom of exploration and use of outer space on a basis of equality." Other principles call for the promotion of international cooperation in remote sensing activities, including opportunities for participation in these activities,[108] the operation of data collecting stations,[109] the exchange of technical assistance,[110] the protection of the Earth's environment,[111] and the protection of Mankind from

(Hereinafter cited as Agreed Principles). See also the "Introductory Note" by *Carl Christol, loc. cit.*, 1331—1332.

[105] Agreed Principles, note 104, Principle II.

[106] *Loc. cit.*, Principle III.

[107] *Loc. cit.*, Principle IV.

[108] *Ibid.*

[109] *Loc. cit.*, Principle VI.

[110] *Loc. cit.*, Principle VII.

[111] *Loc. cit.*, Principle X.

natural disasters.[112] The principles also would give sensed states access to primary and processed data collected from their territory "on a non-discriminatory basis and on reasonable cost terms."[113] Principle XIV reaffirms that states conducting remote sensing operations "shall bear international responsibility for their activities and assure that such activities are conducted in accordance with these principles and the norms of international law," irrespective of whether such activities are carried out by governmental or non-governmental entities or through international organizations to which such states are parties.

The 1986 set of agreed principles plainly authorizes states, non-governmental entities, and international organizations to undertake remote sensing activities. In notable contrast to previous draft proposals, the central theme which emerges out of this set of principles is international cooperation to benefit mutual interests, rather than insistence upon national privacy and consent, derived from considerations of national sovereignty. Although the agreed principles are cast in the form of a General Assembly resolution and therefore are not legally binding upon member states, they do represent the culmination of prolonged debate over which direction the international law governing remote sensing is headed.[184] Moreover, while controversy still persists over what sovereignty considerations are due the sensed state,[115] insofar as remote sensing activities over Antarctica are concerned, the agreed principles serve to clarify the lawfulness of those activities, and at the same time, enhance the legal opportunities for further sensing operations. To that extent, they make a major contribution towards facilitating space-based scientific research of the Antarctic region.

4. *Remote Sensing and the Antarctic Regime*

a) The Antarctic Treaty System

There is no question that the conduct of remote sensing operations over Antarctica is lawful and permissible under the Antarctic Treaty System. In fact, it is plainly evident that such investigations are explicitly facilitated, as well as forthrightly encouraged, by the Antarctic Treaty itself. Article II of that agreement simply declares that, "Freedom

---

[112] *Loc. cit.*, Principle XI.

[113] *Loc. cit.*, Principle XII.

[114] For discussion of the place of General Assembly resolutions in international law and their potential to make important legal contributions, see *Christopher C. Joyner*, U.N. General Assembly Resolutions and International Law: Rethinking the Contemporary Dynamics of Norm-Creation, in: California Western International Law Journal, Vol. 11 (Summer 1981), 445—478.

[115] See *Paul Szasz*, Report on the 25th Session of the Legal Sub-Committee of the UN Committee in the Peaceful Uses of Outer Space, 24 March — 11 April 1986, in: Journal of Space Law, Vol. 14 (1986), 48—51.

of scientific investigation in Antarctica and cooperation toward that end, ... shall continue, subject to the provisions of the present Treaty."[116] Correlatedly, Article III provides in full that:

> 1. In order to promote international cooperation in scientific investigation in Antarctica, as provided for in Article II of the present Treaty, the Contracting Parties agree that, to the greatest extent feasible and practicable:
>
> a) information regarding plans for scientific programs in Antarctica shall be exchanged to permit maximum economy and efficiency of operations;
>
> b) scientific personnel shall be exchanged in Antarctica between expeditions and stations;
>
> c) scientific observations and results from Antarctica shall be exchanged and made freely available.
>
> 2. In implementing this Article, every encouragement shall be given to the establishment of cooperative working relations with those Specialized Agencies of the United Nations and other international organizations having a scientific or technical interest in Antarctica.[117]

For those Antarctic Treaty Governments who operate polar-orbiting remote sensing satellites over Antarctica — which today include the United States, France, Japan, and the members of the European Space Agency — the legal rights here are clear: these satellites plainly qualify as instruments of "scientific investigation" as construed within the meaning of Article II; moreover, the Antarctic-related data which these satellites sense and collect fall within the conceptual scope of "scientific observations and results" that are subject to open exchange and free availability (*i. e.*, presumably at reasonable cost) to all interested Treaty Parties. As such, these provisions go far in affirming two fundamental tenets of the United States' legal position towards remote sensing in general, namely: (1) that there should be free use of and unrestricted access to outer space for conducting remote sensing operations; and (2) that in the interest of freedom of scientific research, sensed data should be openly disseminated without discrimination.

In addition to promoting freedom of space-based research and scientific exchange of collected data, the Antarctic Treaty goes further insofar as remote sensing operations are concerned. In Article VII, which relates to on-site inspection provisions, paragraph 4 specifically stipulates that,

---

[116] The Antarctic Treaty, done December 1, 1959, 12 U.S.T. 794, T.I.A.S. No. 4780, 402 UNTS 71, Art. II.

[117] *Loc. cit.*, Art. III.

> Aerial observations may be carried out at any time over any or all areas of Antarctica by any of the Contracting Parties having the right to designate observers.[118]

To be sure, this right of unlimited aerial inspection was principally intended to facilitate effecting paragraph 2 of Article VII, which provides that observers are to be granted "freedom of access at any time to any or all areas of Antarctica." The general purpose here was to ensure that obligations under the Antarctic Treaty were being met, particularly those relating to demilitarization of the continent.[119] Even so, the explicit right of aerial inspection concurrently serves to highlight the attendant right to enjoy freedom of access throughout Antarctica for scientific purposes and investigations, as provided for in Article II. For the United States in particular, the right of aerial observation over Antarctica has been interpreted to be part and parcel of an "open skies" policy, that is, the notion promoted since the Eisenhower Administration that the most proper regime for aerial inspection (*i. e.*, remote sensing) should be based on the free collection and open dissemination of assimilated information.

Not to be overlooked is the character of sovereignty conditions in Antarctica which might have some bearing on the propriety of conducting remote sensing operations over the region. As is well known, seven states — Argentina, Australia, Chile, France, New Zealand, Norway, and the United Kingdom — have made national claims to portions of the continent. No other state in the international community, including any of the other Antarctic Treaty Consultative Parties, recognize the validity of these claims. Obviously, this circumstance presents certain political complications and sovereignty problems for the legal situation in Antarctica.

Respective to remote sensing activities in the foreseeable future, however, the claims to Antarctica appear to present little legal difficulty. Primarily this is due to the mollifying effects of Article IV in the Antarctic Treaty, which stipulates that the Treaty does not recognize, reject, dispute or establish territorial claims to the continent.[120] The question of sovereignty as an attribute of Antarctic territory in effect is "frozen" in limbo — neither explicitly accepted nor rejected by the Parties —

---

[118] *Loc. cit.*, Art. VII, para. 4.

[119] As provided for in Article I,

> (1) Antarctica shall be used for peaceful purposes only. There shall be prohibited, *inter alia*, any measures of a military nature, such as the establishment of military bases and fortifications, the carrying out of military maneuvers, as well as the testing of any types of weapons.

The Antarctic Treaty, note 116, Art. I.

[120] See the discussion in *Peter Beck*, The International Politics of Antarctica, New York, 1986, 115—19.

in order to accommodate all the Parties' legal views, and thus permit the Treaty to function effectively, without internal squabbling over sovereignty rights asserted by some Parties and non-rights acknowledged by others. A second consideration also weighs in with regard to mitigating the possibility that sovereignty concerns might somehow preclude remote sensing activities over Antarctica. That is, sectorization of the Antarctic continent ought not to be legally considered tantamount to the drawing of international boundary lines for designating frontiers. Rather, it is suggested here that Antarctic sector lines should be regarded more aptly as lines of demarcation which are supposed to indicate spheres of influence on the continent, embellished with the legal connotation of sovereign claim.[121] There are no recognized borders in Antarctica over which a remote sensing satellite might pass; stated more precisely, there is no column of sovereign airspace bounded by territorial limits through which satellites would orbit. Thus, for all intents and purposes, the sovereignty issue as it relates to remote sensing over the Antarctic continent today is rendered moot, both by Article IV in the Treaty and by the fact that there exists no recognized borders which that satellite could breach.

b) The *Common Heritage of Mankind* Regime

Since 1983, suggestions have been made in United Nations General Assembly debates that the interests of the international community would be better served were the legal status of Antarctica to be made part of the so-called *common heritage of mankind* (*CHM*).[122] Political impracticalities and legal reservations of this possibility aside,[123] the legal implications of conducting remote sensing operations over Antarctica were the continent to be designated and accepted legally a *common heritage of mankind* regime deserve some treatment. Under such a *CHM* condition, certain fundamental legal principles and guidelines purportedly would govern all activities in the Antarctic region, including the conduct of remote sensing operations. In sum, these principles would entail the following:

---

[121] See *F. M. Auburn*, Antarctic Law and Politics, Bloomington (Indiana), 1982, 23—31.

[122] See Question of Antarctica: Study Requested under General Assembly resolution 38/77, Report of the Secretary-General, PART TWO: Views of States, UN Doc. A/39/583 (Part II), Vol. I, (29 October 1984), 92 (Bangladesh); Vol. II, (2 November 1984), 107—111 (Malaysia); Vol. III, 32—36 (Pakistan); and Vol. III, (9 November 1984), 71—73 (Sri Lanka).

[123] For this author's views on the notion of *common heritage of mankind* in general, see Legal Implications of the Concept of the Common Heritage of Mankind, in: International and Comparative Law Quarterly, Vol. 35 (1986), 190—199; on *CHM* as applied to Antarctica in particular, see Remarks by *Christopher Joyner*, in: American Society of International Law, 1985 Proceedings of the 79th Meeting (1987), 62—67.

1. Antarctica and its resources would be declared the *common heritage of mankind*;

2. Antarctica would not be subject to appropriation by any means by any state or person, and no state would be permitted to claim or exercise sovereignty or sovereign rights over any part of the continent;

3. No state or person, natural or juridical, could claim, exercise, or acquire rights to Antarctica or its resources which would be incompatible with the international regime established;

4. Antarctica would be reserved exclusively for peaceful purposes and all measures of a military nature would be prohibited;

5. Antarctica would be open to use by all states, without discrimination, in accordance with the established international regime;

6. The exploration of Antarctica and the exploitation of its resources would be carried out for the benefit of mankind as a whole, taking into particular account the interests and needs of the developing countries;

7. There would be freedom of scientific investigation in Antarctica and states would be obligated to cooperate in scientific research exclusively for peaceful purposes; and

8. States would be required to take appropriate measures and to cooperate in adopting and implementing international measures for the protection and conservation of the Antarctic environment, its ecosystem, and its natural resources, as well as the prevention of damage to its flora and fauna.[124]

What emerges as especially striking about these fundamental *CHM* principles *vis-à-vis* remote sensing over Antarctica is that they so closely mirror the basic attributes of the legal regime currently in place for governing satellite investigations overflying the continent. Save for the nuances of claimed sovereignty — which present no obstacles for remote sensing activities above the Antarctic today — these guidelines for a *CHM* regime are functionally incorporated into the actual operations of remote sensing satellites, as well as the policies of open access, freedom of scientific investigation, unrestricted data dissemination, and use of the technology for peaceful purposes only. This is neither to dismiss, nor to minimize conflicting sovereignty considerations in Antarctica, because they obviously persist as central contradictions to the legal character of a *CHM* regime. However, the fact remains that the current Antarctic Treaty System, when coupled with the legal essence of the

---

[124] This synthesis of the attributes of a *CHM* regime for Antarctica was extrapolated from the Views of Pakistan in UN Doc. A/39/583, note 122, 35.

"open skies" policy for remote sensing, supplies in substantial part the *CHM* prerequisites for a governing order that operates for the benefit of all mankind. Irrespective of ideological predispositions, this point must not be lost in the final analysis.

VI. Conclusion

Present remote sensing satellite technology contributes much to the amount of available information concerning the geophysical processes and structure of Antarctica, as well as biological conditions in the Southern Ocean. However, certain expectations exceed the current capability of remote sensing to contribute significantly to resource detection, evaluation and assessment on, under or around the continent. For the foreseeable future, remote sensing is not likely to play a critical role in locating mineral resources on the continent, or on the circumpolar seabed. To the degree that phytoplankton blooms can be pinpointed, there is reasonable expectation that remote sensing will aid in the general location of krill swarms and other zooplankton populations. The most salient use of remote sensing, however, is likely to remain in the field of glaciology, particularly in the gathering data regarding ice dynamics on and around the continent.

There is no question that the conduct of remote sensing activities over Antarctica is today permissible and lawful. This is substantiated by the Antarctic Treaty itself, as well as by recent trends in the evolution of outer space law for governing remote sensing. It is, finally, worth observing that the process of remote sensing serves a constructive role in the Antarctic Treaty process. That is, remote sensing contributes importantly to the enhancement of scientific investigation and knowledge about the Antarctic, a cardinal purpose of the Treaty's function. To that end, remote sensing activities yield much for the Treaty's success, and offer prominent opportunities for further cooperation and scientific exchange. In this era of pronounced political competition and all too often strained ideological debate, it would be sound, healthy advice to keep these positive points in mind.

General Discussion

G. Hempel, Chairman:

Dr. Behrendt, please.

J. Behrendt:

You made the remark that technology has a way of creeping up on us, so I thought you might be interested in knowing that the Geosat data recently collected in Antarctica, in waters surrounding Antarctica, complement the Seasat data of some years ago. In fact, by looking at subtle variations in the sea-surface elevation it is possible to determine the topography of the sea bottom, the mid-ocean ridges and the fracture zones. Sea-bed topography can be seen as slight gravitational effects on the sea surfaces, noted in the Geosat data, so in fact, the sea-bed, to a fair amount of detail, can be mapped by satellite, even though electromagnetic radiation cannot penetrate sea water, as you pointed out.

G. Hempel, Chairman:

But to see the nodules on the sea-bed is something different.

O. Rebagliati:

Well, a little comment on the question of the principles that *Dr. Joyner* was kind enough to quote and remind us of, and in fact at this very moment it is a little premature for me to judge that those principles are part of an international law. They are just draft principles adopted by a subsidiary organ of a subsidiary organ of the General Assembly. There is still a long way to go to acquiescence and a treaty regulating the legal aspects of remote sensing by satellite — which regretfully is taking so long, since this activity is being carried out — and so far the general international community has not been able to agree upon such a sensitive issue. Now, the lawfulness or unlawfulness of the remote sensing, when it is addressed to natural resources, of course, poses an analogy in relation to Antarctica. If it depends on the legal conditions in the rest of the world, it is very difficult to say, "Would that law be different in Antarctica?" I would like to conclude by asking, what are the legal requirements for carrying out remote sensing by satellite?

The opinions expressed in this volume are the personal views of their authors only.

Remote sensing by airplanes and by other means, it is subject to regulations which have been already adopted. It could be also lawful in relation to Antarctica. But on top of that, whatever the general legal framework, for remote sensing by satellite is, if the activity is relating to Antarctic mineral resources, of course it should also be governed by the legal framework applicable to mineral resources in Antarctica. So there would be two legal regimes. And of course the assumption is that both regimes, as international law (and as the Antarctic Treaty does) will take due regard of the legal status of Antarctica and in particular those principles embodied in Article IV of the Antarctic Treaty. Thank you.

C. Joyner:

Your points are well taken, and several generalities I made in my presentation are actually addressed in the paper. Your comment about the principles not yet being international law is accurate, they are nothing more than guidelines. They have not yet been converted into a treaty form, which, I understand, may be a future step to be considered by the General Assembly. Were they to be converted into a convention, and were that convention to come into force, then I think there would be more legitimacy in my tagging them "principles of international law." They are, at present, merely guidelines.

But the thing that makes them important in my mind, and this is really the point I was trying to underscore, is that they are consensus guidelines by a legal committee which had not been able to arrive at a consensus for over twelve years. However, that does not mean that because there was consensus, everybody was happy with them. Certainly, they were not.

With respect to the other point concerning sovereignty and mineral resources, I think that too is accurate. Again, the technology has not the law that far that fast yet, but if it comes, the law will have to catch up or else there will be political problems.

G. Hempel, Chairman:

O. K., *Finn Sollie* and that should close this meeting. Please.

F. Sollie:

I think, *Chris*, that you made an excellent presentation, but let us suppose for just a moment that in fifteen years' time, or thirteen, it will be possible to prospect directly from space for mineral resources. In that case, do you think that countries having control, not only of the technology, but also of the space platforms used for that, would accept restrictions on the use of their technology? Do you think it would be possible to inspect the uses of that technology, in other words, to detect what people are doing? And, eventually, is not the real issue that of controlling and regulating the application down here *where we are*, of such technologies? In other words, the regulating agency and the regulating process and rules, and the inspections on whatever you want to introduce under international or any other law, will have to be made for use on the ground, on sea, and on the basis of that we have to establish a system rather on the hope, I would call it, a pie-in-the-sky, that you could control activities up there.

C. Joyner:

My reply will be quick. I think that, to the extent that data is able to be disseminated freely — which is the United States' policy and something that has been advocated freely in terms of cost and access to people (the open-skies policy) — then international law will be served. Under the present system governing the Geosat arrangement, where data may be sold for a profit, the situation is complicated, because you have a corporation, a commercialized venture at stake. That venture is in trouble. And it may fail within the next four or five years if it does not get serious governmental help. I think you are right in terms of governing activities in space. It must be done on the ground and it must be done by responsible governments. But you do have two things here which need to be considered, and I will mention them in conclusion. One: a minerals regime will be coming into force hopefully within two years, or a year perhaps. That will have a significant impact, I would think, upon that data, or at least, governing geological prospecting and defining it. Second, I think those who will be conducting remote sensing operations will undoubtedly be part of that regime. And I think that is an important point.

G. Hempel, Chairman:

I think we have now covered a very interesting field. Imagine now, we have an Antarctic research station, put in outer space by Outer Mongolia, to be inspected by Malaysia. On one hand, this would be really interesting, and on the other hand, prospecting from outer space would not cause as many environmental problems as just drilling dirty holes. So I think just with your lecture you have opened a wide field, not only for legal advisers but also for imagination. Thank you so much.

The Legitimacy of the United Nations' Challenge to the Antarctic Treaty

*Richard Woolcott**

This morning we turn our attention to the United Nations — or, to the more political dimension of the challenge to the Antarctic Treaty.

However, before I start I would like to join others in saying how very grateful I am to *Professor Wolfrum*, of the Institute of International Law at the University of Kiel, and to the Alfred Wegener Institute for Polar and Marine Research, both for the interest they have taken and are taking in Antarctica, and for their invitation to me to participate in this Symposium in this charming city.

Now, I have been asked to speak on "The Legitimacy of the United Nations' Challenge to the Antarctic Treaty." It is said that fools rush in where angels fear to tread. So, having no legal training, I intend to concentrate on the political and the international aspects of this subject rather than on the judicial aspects, which, I am confident, can be dealt with more authoritatively by other participants.

I should add that I am speaking primarily in my personal capacity, rather than as the Australian Permanent Representative at the United Nations, or as the Chairman of the informal New York Group of Parties to the Antarctic Treaty, a position which devolved on to me in 1983. I would, I believe, be more comfortable speaking on the related subject of the "Question of Antarctica at the United Nations," which *Cristian Maquieira* will address later this morning, but I shall do my best with my assigned task.

I think everybody in this room would agree that the competent management and the protection of the vast Antarctic continent, in conditions of cooperation and peace, is a very important international matter now and for the future. As we are approaching the 21st Century, it is timely and appropriate that sympathetic public interest and understanding about the future of this continent should grow. Clearly, the United Nations has a role to play in this.

---

* Ambassador *Richard Woolcott*, Australian Permanent Representative to the United Nations, New York. The opinions expressed in this volume are the personal opinions of their authors only.

I. Background

If I may start on a personal note, I visited Antarctica in 1985. This fulfilled a long-standing ambition because, for Australia and Australians, Antarctica is not some mysterious and distant continent. It lies immediately to the south, off the southern part of Australia. Indeed, the earliest maps of the southern hemisphere often showed a huge mass called *Terra Australia* and in those ancient maps, Australia and Antarctica were, in fact, connected. While they are now separated by sea, they remain connected by proximity, and by a tradition of continuing interest, of exploration and of research.

I have experienced many remote parts of this world, including the vastness of northern Siberia, the empty silence of central Australia, and even that fabled symbol of remoteness, Timbuktu in central West Africa. But none of these experiences — nothing I had ever done — had quite prepared me for the vastness, the emptiness, the total silence, the harshness, the ultimate remoteness — and, indeed, the unsullied beauty — of Antarctica. This experience reinforced for me, in a personal way, the very great importance of the effective management and the protection of this wonderful continent from contention and damage in the future.

My friend and colleague *Cristian Maquieira* will be dealing with the handling of Antarctica in the United Nations in some detail but, by way of background to my own remarks, I should mention, as you all probably know, that the United Nations General Assembly considered the question of Antarctica for the first time in 1983 and then, subsequently, in 1984, 1985 and 1986.[1] At the conclusion of last year's debate, it was agreed to inscribe the item again on the provisional agenda for the Forty-second Session of the United Nations General Assembly, which starts next September. In fact, the debates on Antarctica at the United Nations are already becoming somewhat repetitive. Malaysia and its supporters challenge the Treaty as being exclusive, unfair, self-appointed, secretive and potentially avaricious; also, the racist South Africa is included amongst its members. On the other hand, the Treaty Parties and their supporters respond that the Treaty is a successful, open, flexible, evolving and effective legal Treaty.

In my view, Antarctica now runs the risk of becoming a sterile ritual on the agenda of the United Nations for no particularly good reason, other than that some states want to keep the question before the General Assembly.

---

[1] UN GA Res. 38/77, 15 Dec. 1983, in: GAOR, 38th sess., Plenary, 97th mtg., 69; GA Res. 39/152, 17 Dec. 1984, in: GAOR, 39th sess., Plenary, 102nd mtg., 94; GA Res. 40/156 - ABC, 16 Dec. 1985, in: GAOR, 40th sess., Plenary, 117th mtg., 105—106; GA Res. 41/88, 4 Dec. 1986, UN Press Release GA/7463, 190—192.

In the years before the signature of the Antarctic Treaty in 1959, a number of individuals and organisations, and even some states, made suggestions for some relationship between the United Nations and Antarctica. As long ago as 1956, India, which has of course since joined the Treaty and whose scientists now conduct regular research at Antarctic stations, proposed that the question of Antarctica be included in the agenda of the United Nations General Assembly. In the event, however, that did not happen; and it was not until 1983 that Antarctica became a subject for discussion in the General Assembly, after the Prime Minister of Malaysia, *Dr. Mahathir*, unexpectedly proposed that it should, in his statement to the General Assembly in September 1982.[2]

To some, this might suggest that there has been little interaction between the United Nations system and the Antarctic Treaty System. Some might even see this lack of discussion in the United Nations of Antarctica prior to 1983 as evidence of what has been alleged to be the "secretary" or the "exclusivity" on the part of the Antarctic Treaty Consultative Parties. It would be a mistake to reach such conclusions, as I am sure *Cristian* will point out.

The fact that states have not, until relatively recently, discussed the subject of Antarctica in the General Assembly stems more from an earlier lack of interest among the majority of countries with no actual involvement in the continent. It also suggests that until Malaysia stirred up the issue there was a measure of acquiescence on the part of the world community in the evolving system of management established by the Antarctic Treaty.

II. Relationship with the United Nations Charter

I wish also to touch briefly on the Treaty and its links with the United Nations Charter. It is worth recalling that the framework of cooperation, operating under the Treaty System, has promoted the principles and purposes of the United Nations Charter and that, in appropriate areas, there has been some practical cooperation between the two systems, as previous speakers have noted.

The Charter of the United Nations defines the purposes of that organisation, including the development of friendly relations between nations, the achievement of cooperation between nations in solving international problems, and, most importantly, the maintenance of peace and security.

The Antarctic Treaty has given practical effect to all of these important principles and purposes of the United Nations Charter. In particular, it

[2] Malaysian Statement to the General Assembly, GAOR, 37th sess., vol. 1 Plenary, 10th mtg., 129 (132), paras. 36,37.

has encouraged international cooperation in Antarctica and it has insulated the continent from international conflict and rivalries for more than a quarter of a century. To measure the achievements of the Antarctic Treaty System and to relate them to United Nations principles, we should reflect briefly on the situation in Antarctica before the signature of the Antarctic Treaty in 1959.

Territorial claims, and non-recognition of these claims by other nations active in Antarctica, had led to political tensions. Rivalry amongst certain of the Claimant States had led to incidents and protests. One country took steps to bring its claim before the International Court of Justice and the other countries involved declined to accept the jurisdiction of the Court. In short, a complex and tense international situation had developed, which posed a potential threat to peace in the Antarctic region.

In retrospect, that time — the mid-fifties — would have been a more logical and propitious time for Antarctica to be raised in the General Assembly. But it was not the United Nations, which acted in this situation in the mid-1950s. It was the Antarctic Treaty which came into being and which defused these tensions.

As has been quoted before at this Symposium, the Preamble of the Treaty states that "it is in the interest of all mankind that Antarctica shall continue forever to be used exclusively for peaceful purposes and shall not become the scene or object of international discord." It continues: "a treaty ensuring the use of Antarctica for peaceful purposes only, and the continuance of international harmony in Antarctica, will further the purposes and principles embodied in the Charter of the United Nations."

This is true. And what could be a more forthright commitment to the aim of the United Nations in respect of peace and security? The Treaty also goes beyond this general commitment by including a number of specific provisions designed to ensure that this commitment is upheld.

III. The Present Challenge in the United Nations

In these circumstances, we need to examine why a treaty, which is consistent with the principles of the United Nations Charter, has come under challenge in the United Nations itself.

I said a few minutes ago that I am not a lawyer by training, but I believe this need not preclude me from advancing one or two general (and, to me, common-sense) propositions.

Under Articles 10, 11 and 14 of the United Nations Charter, the General Assembly may discuss any issue. The only limits on this competence relate to issues on which the Security Council may be acting, and to the obvious need for the General Assembly not to act in a manner inconsistent with the Charter itself. There is, therefore, no legal restriction on the General Assembly examining any matter, even a matter like Antarctica, where there are no political tensions and which is regulated by an international treaty to which a considerable number of Member States adhere.

While it follows that any challenge in the General Assembly to an existing treaty system, such as the Antarctic Treaty System, is a legal action in terms of the Charter, there is the related and pertinent question of legitimacy.

There is in my opinion a distinction between legality and legitimacy. Legitimacy, as distinct from legality, involves value judgements and political judgements.

We need to ask ourselves whether the consideration of an issue in the General Assembly, including one like the question of Antarctica, is legitimate — in the sense that is it expedient for the General Assembly to embark on a course which could undermine an effective and successful treaty? Also, we should explore whether it is practical, and whether it contributes — or is likely to contribute — to international peace and security, for the General Assembly to seek to act in this manner?

In the case of the Antarctic Treaty it is, in my view — and in that of several international lawyers with whom I have discussed the matter — neither legitimate nor practical for the General Assembly to try to subsume or replace a substantial, effective and tested treaty with some new, and as yet ill-defined, United Nations machinery.

There is, I think, another aspect of legitimacy which involves a judgement as to whether the criticism of a treaty, by the parties raising the issue in the General Assembly, is justified criticism. In the case of the Antarctic Treaty, the Parties to the Treaty regard much of the criticism of the Antarctic Treaty, so far made in General Assembly debates as unjustified in that it is based on misunderstandings or false premises. *Cristian Maquieira* will, I am sure, deal with this in greater detail in his paper.

I might add that I know of no precedent in the United Nations or, indeed, even going back to the League of Nations, for an established, major international treaty being subsumed in some way or replaced by the League or by the United Nations.

The United Nations' interest in Antarctica and the discussion of Antarctica in the United Nations can be productive. There is already a measure of constructive interaction between the Treaty partners and the United Nations system, which I have noted. As *Ian Nicholson* has also pointed out, it can be argued that the United Nations' scrutiny of the Antarctic Treaty System since 1983 has encouraged the provision of more information on Antarctica to the Secretary General, and has encouraged more openness on the part of the Treaty.

What Treaty Parties oppose is pressure — to some extent, artificially stimulated pressure — in the General Assembly, for some institutionalised United Nations political involvement, at the expense of an existing legal treaty, in an area in which there are currently no threats to the peace or substantial political, economic or social problems.

I would like to turn now to the practical situations which, in my opinion, circumscribe the role the United Nations can expect to play in Antarctica.

IV. Practical Considerations

No country is bound by a General Assembly resolution. Only the Security Council is empowered to make binding decisions. If — in a hypothetical situation — the General Assembly were to establish, by a simple majority, a parallel regime to that of the Antarctic Treaty, it would not result in the disappearance of the Antarctic Treaty. Nor could any such United Nations regime, so established, function effectively. The establishment of a parallel system by the United Nations would, in fact, lead only to acrimony and confusion.

While General Assembly resolutions are not binding, they dc carry a certain moral force, especially when they are adopted by very sustantial majorities. The Law of the Sea Convention, for example, has attracted some 159 signatories although the United States, the Federal Republic of Germany and the United Kingdom have not signed the Convention: the fact that so many states have done so generates pressure on those countries to join because of the near universality of the Convention. But even the Law of the Sea Convention may prove to be ineffective in practice unless it becomes universal. In this context, the resolutions which challenge the Antarctic Treaty System have not attracted support at a level which even approaches that accorded the Law of the Sea Convention.

V. Need for Consensus

Those of us who work in the United Nations know that it is just not realistic for one group of countries to expect to impose its will on another group of countries, through the General Assembly. Initiatives in the United Nations can only succeed if they move forward on the basis of consensus, or with very broadly-based support.

The active pursuit of Global Negotiations, earlier this decade — the concept of dealing with all of the world's economic problems in one package — failed to eventuate, despite very substantial support amongst Member States, mainly because of the opposition of just one of the two Superpowers, although divisions within the Group of 77 also contributed to the failure.

Opposition to the Malaysian initiative on Antarctica in the United Nations is much more broadly-based, compared with the opposition to Global Negotiations. Here, both Superpowers and many other countries, including a growing number within the Non-Aligned Movement, oppose the Malaysian initiative.

In short, I cannot foresee a successful challenge to the Antarctic Treaty being sustained through the United Nations, or the replacement of the Treaty by some United Nations machinery, unless the unity of the Parties to the Treaty ruptured.

VI. Majorities in the General Assembly

To illustrate, I would like to refer to the voting patterns on the resolutions on Antarctica at the last General Assembly.

On December 4th of last year the General Assembly had a roll-call vote on the three Antarctic resolutions before it. Resolution 41/88 A, calling for the United Nations to function as a "central repository" for all information on Antarctica, and for an updated report by the Secretary-General, was adopted with 94 votes in favour, none against and 12 abstentions.[3] Forty-three delegations chose not to participate in the voting.

Resolution 41/88 B, which called for a moratorium on the negotiations to establish a minerals regime, was adopted with a similar pattern: 96-0-12 with 43 delegations not participating in the vote.[4]

Resolution 41/88 C, which called for the exclusion of South Africa from meetings of the Consultative Parties and was regarded by the Treaty Parties as essentially a political issue, rather than a substantive Antarctic issue, was adopted 119-0-8 with 25 delegations not participating.[5]

Given the way the United Nations works as a political forum, and the Treaty Parties' principal objective of defending the Treaty and limiting potential damage to it, the votes on the two substantive resolutions (88 A and 88 B) were regarded by the Treaty Parties as quite

[3] GA Res. 41/88 A (*loc. cit.* note 1).
[4] GA Res. 41/88 B (*loc. cit.* note 1).
[5] GA Res. 41/88 C (*loc. cit.* note 1).

satisfactory. Although, in a formal sense, these two resolutions were adopted, the number of positive votes — in the mid-90s — was not high by United Nations standards. Also, 55 delegations, virtually one-third of the membership, abstained or did not participate in the vote. These countries included all those countries actively engaged in Antarctica. There were also a number of absences at the time of the voting, some of which were deliberate.

The main change in the voting in the General Assembly from the previous year was on the South African resolution (resolution 88 C). On this resolution the number of countries not participating in the vote was reduced, from 37 in the case of the comparable resolution in 1985[6], to 24 in 1986. This resolution is regarded by Parties to the Treaty as essentially a political resolution. It is a reflection of the growing anger and frustration which Member States feel about the continuance of the policy of apartheid and it is intended to increase pressure on South Africa to change its policy. Treaty Parties who voted for this resolution made the point that they were doing so on political grounds and that their vote should not be seen as detracting from the force and value of the Antarctic Treaty.

As recently as July 1st, 1987, last week, Treaty Parties put this view to the Secretary-General of the United Nations, in response to his Note of 10 February seeking information on the action countries had taken in relation to this resolution 41/88 C on South Africa. In this Note, Treaty Parties which had decided to vote for Resolution 88 C stated that their decision — and I quote — "should be seen as being without prejudice to their views on the merits of a consensus approach to Antarctica and on the successful functioning of the Antarctic Treaty." In the same Note, States Parties to the Treaty strongly reaffirmed that "Treaty Parties are united in their determination to safeguard the effective functioning of the Antarctic Treaty System."

These voting figures, except for resolution 88 C, were much the same as last year. The "yes" vote was down two on resolution 88 A and up four on resolution 88 B when compared with 1985.[7]

On issues which are gaining momentum in the General Assembly, votes tend to increase year by year. On issues which are deadlocked, or not progressing, in the General Assembly, votes tend to be static. The debate at the Forty-first Session of the General Assembly was shorter than it was at the Fortieth Session, and less countries spoke in the debate — also suggesting that the number of countries actively seeking

[6] GA Res. 40/156 C, UN Doc. A/40/53 (1985).

[7] *Ibid.*

to advance the issue in the United Nations is not increasing, except perhaps on the essentially political issue of South Africa.

The Treaty Parties therefore had reasons to be well-satisfied with the outcome of the consideration of the issue at the Forty-first General Assembly, although they would have preferred a consensus resolution or no resolution at all.

I do not intend to beg the question of what constitutes a substantial majority in the General Assembly. Issues which are regarded as "Important Questions" under the Charter require a 2/3 majority to be carried.[8] But the increase in membership to 159 and concerns about "automatic majorities" mean that we really need to address the question of what, in 1987, could be fairly regarded to be a substantial majority, which could be said to impose a moral obligation, if not a binding obligation on states. If a very great number of states, for example, 150 out of the present membership of 159, support a resolution, such a degree of support can bring pressures to bear on even the more politically and economically powerful countries.

Realistically, we also need to give weight to the nature, power and influence of countries both supporting or opposing a particular resolution. This is not simply a reflection of the "might is right" syndrome; rather, it is a practical recognition that certain countries, through their size, resources, population and their economic and political strength, will inevitably influence the outcome of any proposed United Nations action. If the Soviet Union and the United States vote against a resolution and, for example, Guinea-Bissau and Solomon Islands vote for the same resolution, their votes in theory carry the same weight. But in practice, the reality is different. All countries in the United Nations have an equal right to be heard and to vote in the General Assembly. However, we cannot realistically expect this to be translated into an equal right to determine action.

The General Assembly is a deliberative body, and, like any parliament, is influenced by political atmosphere. The policy of apartheid causes great anger and frustration amongst countries, and in the efforts to escalate pressure on South Africa to oblige it to change its policies, the reasonable arguments against the expulsion of South Africa tend to be lost in the emotional heat generated by apartheid itself. First, the Treaty has no provision for expulsion. Second, would it not be a mistake to have South Africa released from the obligations, including the obligations not to conduct nuclear tests, imposed on it by the Treaty? Moreover, in terms of proximity, any future government, based on universal franchise

[8] UN Charter Art. 18, para. 2.

and majority rule in South Africa, would in all probability feel a need to be a member of the Treaty if it had not inherited membership from a previous administration.

VII. The UN Does Not Have to Deal with Everything

We should also keep in mind that the United Nations should deal with real international problems. There are no such problems in Antarctica at present. The United Nations, despite its acknowledged competence to deal with virtually any issue, needs to be selective. It is not expected to deal with every issue on earth. There is no reason why legal regimes should not function outside of the United Nations, as indeed they do. The international system foreseen by the United Nations Charter is comprehensive only in the security field. A treaty system can exist separately from and side by side with the United Nations.

In the case of Antarctica, we already have a functioning Treaty with existing links with the United Nations system. The only circumstances in which greatly extended United Nations involvement would be justified would be if serious political or security problems were to erupt in Antarctica, or if a very large majority of Member States, say 150, were to come to believe that the United Nations could establish an equally good or a better regime to manage Antarctica than the one which already exists.

Another point which is sometimes overlooked is that the Antarctic Treaty is, *de facto*, a universal treaty. It is open to all states to become members and it is misleading to suggest, as its critics have done, that it is "closed" or "exclusive." The growing openness and transparency of Consultative Party Meetings, and of the minerals negotiations, have also mitigated the argument about there being two classes of membership.

Since the Malaysian challenge to the Treaty was launched in 1982, six countries have acceded to the Treaty, the most recent being the Republic of Korea, the Democratic Republic of Korea and Greece. Other countries are considering accession, so it would seem that the challenge to the Treaty in the United Nations, including the issue of South African membership, has not prevented the growth and development of the Treaty.

I referred earlier to the united reaction of the Treaty Parties to the Malaysian challenge in the United Nations. Let me give two recent examples. In an important new development in the debate on Antarctica at the Forty-first General Assembly, I addressed the First Committee on the Question of Antarctica on 19 November 1986, not as the Australian

Permanent Representative, but on behalf of States Parties to the Antarctic Treaty.[9] The members of the Treaty did not make 32 statements in the debate. There was just one statement reflecting the agreed view of Parties to the Treaty.

It was not only an honour to have been entrusted to speak on behalf of so many countries representing such a diverse range of international view-points on other issues; it was a clear manifestation of the continuing unity of Parties to the Treaty on the handling of Antarctica in the United Nations and of their determination to defend the Treaty against any challenge to its integrity through the General Assembly.

Because of its clear relevance to our discussion this week I would like to quote the final words of that joint statement of 19 November last:

> [I]f Malaysia and its supporters continue on their present path, the inevitable reaction of many countries — not necessarily only the Treaty Parties — will be to conclude that there is little value in or reason for further institutionalized discussion of Antarctica in the United Nations. We hold the view firmly that the links which have already been established, and are developing further, between the United Nations and the Antarctic Treaty system should be permitted to work unhampered in the interests of all mankind. We sincerely believe that the international community as a whole should recognize that something of international value has been developed in the Antarctic Treaty which has preserved the peace, advanced scientific knowledge, protected the environment and maintained a problem-free management of the Antarctic continent. The goal of the growing number of Treaty Parties is the protection and enhancement of that system and its operation for the universal good. The only useful and practical role for the General Assembly would, we suggest, be to assist, and not to hinder, that process.[10]

It is a matter for regret that, in the United Nations, we have seen appear in some debates ideological and unrealistic attitudes in certain committees. The introduction of emotional rhetoric about the New International Economic Order and residual Colonialism in the debate on Antarctica is unlikely to attract support from moderate countries within the United Nations. We need to guard against such attitudes spreading, further than they already have, in the consideration of the question of Antarctica.

As *Philip Quigg* wrote: "Just as the Antarctic's unique environment

---

[9] Statement of Antarctic Treaty Parties, General Debate on Draft Resolutions on the Question of Antarctica, UN Doc. A/C. 1/41/PV. 51 (1986) 11—21.

[10] *Loc. cit.* p. 21.

must be protected from exploiters, so must its political and economic future be protected from idealogues."[11] The Treaty, he continued, "deserves the opportunity to prove again its adaptability and the capacity of its members for adjustment and compromise, not only among themselves but with the rest of the world."[12]

I can only endorse those sentiments. Diplomacy is the art of the possible, the art of accommodation and compromise. If we are to avoid continuing and fruitless dispute and confrontation, there is a responsibility on the part of all concerned with Antarctica in the United Nations to show realism and flexibility.

Attempts to replace the Antarctic Treaty System, or to set up new institutional arrangements for the management of Antarctic affairs within the United Nations, are proving to be neither practicable nor productive.

On the other hand, Antarctic Treaty Consultative Parties should continue to find ways, through improving the operation of the Treaty System, of overcoming the reasonable concerns of other countries, including the legitimate concerns of Third World countries, related to what might be called "fairness."

Supporters of the United Nations and the multilateral system, like myself, have another general concern. It relates to the United Nations moving into areas in which there are no particular problems and in which it cannot expect, in practical terms, to prove effective.

It is generally accepted that the United Nations as an institution and the multi-lateral system is facing serious criticism. Its credibility has been eroded and its financial situation is serious. The Organisation has embarked on an essential program of administrative and budgetary reform. It should concentrate on the reform program and of course on the serious political problems, with which it deals. It should not, in my opinion, dissipate its energies in areas in which it is not really needed and in which it will risk, through failure to prove effective, a further erosion of its credibility.

VIII. Conclusion

While the United Nations debates the issue, the fact is that the Treaty continues to operate effectively and, indeed, to grow stronger.

I believe the United Nations had really made the main contribution it could be expected to make to Antarctica by the time consensus broke

---

[11] *Philip W. Quigg*, A Pole Apart, New York *et al.* 1983, 218.
[12] *Ibid.*

down in December 1985. Since then we have had what might be called an unproductive stalemate. I believe the prospects for an effective challenge to the Treaty in the United Nations have since receded and that the issue is virtually decided. Except for some continuing monitoring role, on the basis of consensus, I can really see no further role for the General Assembly, unless the proponents of the challenge are willing to sustain a situation in which the divisions and the deadlocks of 1985 and 1986 are to continue to drift on. Such a course will not bring credit to the United Nations or the multilateral system.

So I repeat that, in my view, the challenge to the Antarctic Treaty in the General Assembly cannot succeed, although there is a prospect of strengthening the existing Treaty through the United Nations on the basis of consensus and cooperation. As realists we know that General Assembly resolutions are not binding. They have even less force with countries which did not participate in the voting or which abstained. Moreover, the Treaty Parties constitute a group which is too *large*, too *diverse*, too *representative*, too *politically* and *economically* influential and, most importantly, too *united* on the substantive Antarctic issues, to allow the challenge to the Treaty in the United Nations to lead to its erosion or its replacement.

As I began on a personal note, I would like to end on one.

When I became Australia's Ambassador to the United Nations in 1982 and, then, Chairman of the Informal New York Group of the Antarctic Treaty Consultative Parties, when the issue arose there in 1983, I had only limited experience of the inner workings of the UN system and of those of the Antarctic Treaty System; although I had, of course, been interested in a general way in both matters. In earlier days — in the 1960s and 1970s — I was generally attracted to international approaches to questions, such as that of Antarctica, and to the concept of the *common heritage of mankind.*

But my personal experience in New York, over the last four and a half years, and in Antarctica itself have been educative and have led me to the conclusion that the UN system, to my disappointment, works less effectively than I had hoped while the Antarctic Treaty System works more effectively than I had expected. This background and personal experience has turned me away, both from attempts to apply the *common heritage* principle to Antarctica, and from efforts to have the United Nations assume, from a successful, open and legal Treaty, the management of Antarctica, however well-intentioned these efforts may be.

Safeguarding the Interests of Mankind in the Use of Antarctica

*Abdul Koroma**

Antarctica has been described as the last and fifth largest continent on the earth's surface. Its territorial extent is more than 14 million square kilometres (5.5 sq. miles) and it represents about 10% of the Earth's land surface. It is bigger than China and India combined, or Mexico and the United States put together. Although it is the highest continent on Earth, stripped of its ice layer — nearly three miles thick at some points — much of the continent lies below sea level.[1]

Antarctica can also be described as the "Ice Continent," as it is virtually covered by a thick layer of ice. Mammoth icebergs, some more than 100 miles long, have on a number of occasions been observed drifting away from the continent. More than 90% of the Earth's fresh water, it is estimated, can be found in the form of Antarctic ice. Some modern ships have the capacity to tow these icebergs to the arid regions of the globe for irrigation and agricultural production.

Apart from its huge water potential, the "Southern Continent" is also the last reservoir of resources — both living and non-living. At the core of the living resources of Antarctica is krill — a shrimp-like crustacean said to be rich in protein and which could be of immense benefit to the populations of various Third World countries where famine and drought are endemic. Antarctic krill can be harvested at quantities of up to 70 million tons annually without depleting the species. This amount is equal to the current world total catch of fish.[2] The current annual world catch of krill is about 500,000 tons.[3]

It should be emphasized though, that krill are central to the ecosystem of the continent and their depletion could have an adverse effect on its fish and birds. Because of this dependence of the higher life forms on

---

* Ambassador *Abdul G. Koroma*, Embassy of Sierra Leone, Brussels. The opinions expressed in this volume are the personal views of their authors only.

[1] Encyclopaedia Britannica 5 (1969).

[2] *Finn Sollie*, Trends and Prospects for Regimes for Living and Mineral Resources in the Antarctic, in: *J. K. Gamble, Jr.* (ed.), Law of the Sea: Neglected Issues, Hawaii 1979, 193—209 (200).

[3] *Michael Koch*, The Antarctic Challenge: Conflicting Interests, in: Journal of Maritime Law and Commerce 15 (1984), 117—126 (120).

krill, it has been suggested that in order to maintain the delicate eco-system of the continent, and to prevent over-exploitation, krill should be harvested to not more than four or five million tons per annum.[4]

Antarctica is also known to contain traces of a wide variety of metals and hydrocarbon. Traces of cobalt, copper, chromium, gold, lead, molybdenum, manganese, nickel, silver, tin, titanium, uranium, as well as zinc, have been found in the continent. Geological survey has postulated large quantities of oil and gas.[5]

Given the size of the continent together with its resource potential, a number of countries over the years — basing themselves on the traditional modes of territorial acquisition: discovery, occupation, cession, contiguity, *uti possidetis* and even Papal Bull — have laid claim to 85% of the continent. In several cases the Claimants assert sovereignty over the same territory while in others the claims not only overlap but their boundaries are arbitrarily drawn. Such uncertainties have not only in the past led to territorial disputes but even military confrontations. It is against this backdrop, namely the unique nature of Antarctica with its vast potential in both living and non-living resources, which has made it an attractive prize over which states are prepared to compete, even to the point of military conflict.

On the other hand, it is with a view to preserving the unique nature of the continent and quelling potential discord that various solutions at "internationalizing" the territory has been proposed. Already in 1947 the *New York Times* had advanced that Antarctica be placed under United Nations trusteeship, to be held in trust for the peoples of all the world. In 1948, the United States, with a view to quelling disputes among several Antarctic Claimants, proposed a trusteeship for the continent that would have included itself together with Argentina, Australia, Chile, France, New Zealand, Norway and the United Kingdom.

In 1950 India made two attempts to inscribe "the Question of Antarctica" on the agenda of the General Assembly of the United Nations. In its explanatory memorandum India stated:

> [I]t would be appropriate and timely now for all nations to agree and affirm that the area will be utilized entirely for peaceful purposes and for the welfare of the whole world ... this subject is of great importance to the international community as a whole and not merely for certain countries ... the United Nations should call upon all states to utilize this territory solely for peaceful purposes ... the

---

[4] *Koch* (note 3), 120.

[5] Question of Antarctica: Report of the Secretary-General, UN Doc. 4/39/583 Part I (1984), 91.

> Government of India are of the view that the action proposed can only be taken by the world community as a whole ....[6]

In 1956, the Government of New Zealand proposed to make Antarctica a world territory under the control of the United Nations. Throughout the 1970s various United Nations specialized agencies, UNEP, UNDP and FAO, attempted to interest themselves in the continent, but the Consultative Parties did not allow them to play a role. It can thus be seen that the current effort to "internationalize" Antarctica and apply the *common heritage of mankind* principle to it has a long pedigree.

Evidently, the underlying theme running through all those efforts has been to preserve the unique nature of Antarctica and utilize it exclusively for peaceful purposes, while ensuring that benefits that might accrue from its resources will be used for all mankind. But before considering how best to safeguard the interests of mankind in the continent, it will be worthwhile to examine the regime that presently exists there.

As has already been stated, prior to 1959, Antarctica had become a source of competing territorial claims and even of military confrontation.

In addition to the need to quell the existing territorial disputes and promote scientific research in the continent, there was the feeling, given the then-existing global East-West rivalry between the United States and the Soviet Union, particularly in the military field, that unless action was taken to keep the continent peaceful, Antarctica could become a site for the emplacement of nuclear weapons.

It was with a view to obviating this potential conflict, which at the same time acted as a hindrance to the promotion of scientific research in the continent, and the danger that the continent could become militarized, that the seven Claimant States (Argentina, Australia, Chile, New Zealand, France and the United Kingdom) and five Non-claimant States (Belgium, Japan, South Africa, the Soviet Union and the United States) negotiated and concluded the Antarctic Treaty of 1959 which entered into force in 1961.[7] The Treaty had as its main objectives:

(1) the use of Antarctica exclusively for peaceful purposes;
(2) the freezing of all territorial claims or potential claims;
(3) the facilitation of scientific research;
(4) the promotion of international scientific cooperation.

According to Article VI, the Treaty covers the "area south of 60 degrees latitude including the continental shelves." Thus, virtually the entire continent was placed under the Treaty regime, and even though

[6] UN General Assembly Doc. No. A/3852, 15 July 1958, 2—3.

[7] The Antarctic Treaty, UNTS 402 (1961), 71, reprinted in: *Rüdiger Wolfrum* (ed.), Antarctic Challenge II, Berlin 1986, Annex II, 446 *et seq.*

the Article was said not to prejudice the high seas freedoms, subsequent conduct and activities by the Treaty Parties has encouraged a claim of competence on the oceans south of 60 degrees, in order to foreclose it from regimes such as the 1982 Convention on the Law of the Sea.[8]

The Antarctic Treaty had as one of its objectives the resolution of the territorial conflicts among rival Claimants, which were in danger of escalating if not resolved. Article IV, which is pivotal in this connection, reads as follows:

1. Nothing contained in the present Treaty shall be interpreted as:

   a) a renunciation by any Contracting Party of previously asserted rights of or claims to territorial sovereignty in Antarctica;

   b) a renunciation or diminution by any Contracting Party of any basis of claim to territorial sovereignty in Antarctica which it may have whether as a result of its activities or those of its nationals in Antarctica or otherwise;

   c) prejudicing the position of any Contracting Party as regards its recognition or non-recognition of any other State's right of or claim or basis of claim to territorial sovereignty in Antarctica.

2. No acts or activities taking place while the present Treaty is in force shall constitute a basis for asserting, supporting, or denying a claim to territorial sovereignty in Antarctica nor create any rights of sovereignty in Antarctica. No new claim, or enlargement of an existing claim to territorial sovereignty in Antarctica shall be asserted while the present Treaty is in force.

An analysis of Articles IV and VI leads to an interesting conclusion. In the first place, Article VI assumed jurisdiction over the area in favour of the Treaty Parties, and excluded it from regulation by a possible international regime, as was proposed by various Governments and other bodies. Thus about 10% of the Earth's surface was appropriated by a relatively few number of states to the exclusion of the rest of the international community, notwithstanding the interest of the international community. Second, an analysis of Article IV leads to the inescapable conclusion that the various attempts to claim sovereignty over the continent, the matters of overlapping claims and ill-defined boundaries, were not resolved but merely held in abeyance.

The legal effect of Article IV was to freeze the existing claims on the continent by declaring that they would neither be recognized nor denied, and that neither new claims nor existing claims would be recognized.

---

[8] See *F. M. Auburn*, Antarctic Law and Politics, London, 1982, 134—135; LOS Convention, UN Doc. A/CONF. 62/122; reprinted in: ILM 21, 1261.

This provision, it is submitted, and as subsequent events have shown,[9] did not resolve the issue of sovereignty over the continent, nor did it resolve the matter of territorial claims or ill-defined boundaries. Historically, territorial and boundary disputes have a tendency to lay dormant over a long period only to explode at a time when they are least expected to do so. Judged against this background, and given the significance of Antarctica and the rival claims to appropriate it, the danger of Antarctica posing a future threat to international peace and security has not been eliminated by the Treaty.

Therefore, one significant way of resolving the problem of sovereignty and the issue of competing claims is to "internationalize" the territory and have sovereignty vested in the United Nations. Such a solution will not only meet one of the primary objectives of the Treaty itself — that of maintaining the continent exclusively for peaceful uses — but will also eliminate the urge to claim or appropriate areas of the continent and preclude the possibility of future territorial and boundary disputes while at the same time ensuring that the interest of the present Claimants will be accomodated in an international regime for the continent.

International law should be able to play a significant role in this regard. In fact, all the Claimants of territory in Antarctica have based themselves on one or other of the traditional modes of territorial acquisition, which in a way has itself become a problem in a society that has become very dynamic and even more global in outlook. For while it is true, as *Jennings* has written, that the traditional mission and purpose of international law may be described as "the delimitation of the exercise of sovereign power on a territorial basis,"[10] however, international sovereignty is being increasingly proposed for areas of the globe in which all nations have a common interest, as is the case with Antarctica. This approach has so far been applied with various degrees of success to outer space, the moon and other celestial bodies, as well as to the Area of the sea-bed beyond national jurisdiction.

In fact, both the Outer Space Treaty of 1967[11] and the subsequent 1979 Moon Treaty[12] contain provisions similar to the 1959 Antarctic Treaty.

---

[9] See *B. J. Theutenberg*, The Evolution of the Law of the Sea, Dublin (1984), 72—73, where it is suggested that the explanation of the South Atlantic conflict of 1982 had its roots in Antarctica. Also see *Peter J. Beck*, The International Politics of Antarctica, Croom Helm, London and Sydney, 1986.

[10] *Robert Y. Jennings*, The Acquisition of Territory in International Law, Manchester 1963, 2.

[11] Treaty on the Principles Governing the Activities of States in the Exploration and Use of Outer Space, Including the Moon and Other Celestial Bodies (entry into force Oct. 10, 1967), UNTS 610, 205.

[12] Agreement Concerning the Activities of States on the Moon and Other Celestial Bodies (entry into force July 11, 1984), UN General Assembly Res. 34/68, GAOR 34th Sess., Supp. 46, 77, in: ILM 18, 1434.

The Outer Space Treaty in particular called for non-militarization, freedom of scientific research and the exchange of information and inspection. It also stipulates in its Article I that outer space should be regulated "for the benefit of and in the interests of all countries ... and shall be the province of all mankind." According to Article II, outer space is not subject to national appropriation by claims of sovereignty. The 1979 Moon Treaty also makes similar provisions when it declared that "the moon and its natural resources are the common heritage of mankind" (Article II), and establishes rules for the orderly and safe development of resources and the equitable sharing of benefits. Article 136 of the United Nations Convention on the Law of the Sea declares that "the Area [*i. e.*, the sea-bed and ocean floor beyond the limits of national jurisdiction] and its resources are the commoo heritage of mankind."[13]

What the foregoing regimes have in common is that with respect to outer space, the moon and the sea-bed beyond national jurisdiction all have been placed outside the realm of national claims, and together with their resources are to be used in the interests of mankind as a whole. This is in sharp contrast to the Antarctic Treaty which, though it covers a 'common' space, includes no such provision and hence has not resolved rival territorial claims; the majority of states are excluded from its operation.

Reference has been made to the vast amount of resources, both living and non-living, with which Antarctica is said to be endowed. For understandable reasons, the 1959 Treaty made no provisions regarding their exploration and exploitation. With development in science and technology, the prospect of exploiting those resources no longer seems as impossible as it once did. In 1980 the Treaty Parties negotiated and concluded the Convention on the Conservation of Antarctic Marine Living Resources (CCAMLR)[14] which, although essentially a conservation measure, also regulates their fishing interests. Negotiations are currently underway among the Treaty Parties which will regulate the mining of minerals and hydrocarbons on the continent when the technology will have been developed and it becomes feasible to undertake mining in the continent.

Unfortunately, the three agreements which have already been negotiated by the Antarctic Treaty Parties, namely, the Agreed Measures for the Conservation of Antarctic Fauna and Flora (1962),[15] the Convention for the Conservation of Antarctic Seals (1972),[16] and CCAMLR (1980), while

[13] LOS Convention (note 8).

[14] CCAMLR (entered into force April 7, 1982), TIAS 10240, in: ILM 19, 841.

[15] Agreed Measures, reprinted in: *W. M. Bush* (ed.), Antarctic and International Law, vols. I—III, London *et al.* 1982, vol. I, 146 *et seq.*

[16] Convention for the Conservation of Antarctic Seals (entered into force March 11, 1978), TIAS 8826, in: ILM 11, 251.

detailing conservation measures, have followed the precedent set by the Antarctic Treaty itself to exclude the rest of the international community. A significant departure from this concern for exclusion are the present negotiations dealing with the question of mineral resources in Antarctica, in which the Consultative Parties have indicated that "in dealing with the question of mineral resources in Antarctica, they should not prejudice the interest of all mankind in Antarctica."[17] As the minerals regime negotiations are still going on, it is not yet clear what this objective will include, whether it will involve, for example, revenue-sharing or not. Be that is it may, it would seem that the minerals regime also aims to exclude those who are considered outsiders from 'interfering' in the affairs of the continent.

In spite of the efforts to keep Antarctica as an exclusive preserve of the Treaty Parties, the developing countries, most of whom were either not independent or did not participate in the construction of the Antarctic Treaty, have identified the continent as an area which requires the participation of all countries in its administration and in the management of its resources. The developing countries share the objectives of the Antarctic Treaty: to use it exclusively for peaceful purposes, to promote scientific research and cooperation. On the other hand, developing countries are of the view that the present claims to sovereignty over the territory must give way to an international regime which will accomodate all the competing claims relating to the territory. With regard to the resources of the territory, the developing countries have taken the position that these should not be exploited for the benefit of the Treaty Parties only, but that the principle of the *common heritage of mankind*, which outer space, the moon and the Area of the sea-bed beyond national jurisdiction embrace, should equally apply to the exploitation and distribution of the resources of Antarctica. As noted above, in accordance with Article 136 of the Convention on the Law of the Sea, "the Area [*i. e.*, the sea-bed and ocean floor beyond the limits of national jurisdiction] and its resources are the common heritage of mankind." Article 137 sets out the legal status with respect to the Area and its resources as follows:

1. No State shall claim or exercise sovereignty or sovereign rights over any part of the Area or its resources, nor shall any State or national or juridical person appropriate any part thereof. No claim or exercise of sovereignty or sovereign rights, nor such appropriations shall be recognized.
2. All rights in the resources of the Area are vested in mankind as a whole, on whose behalf the Authority shall act. These resources

[17] Recommendation XI, para. 5 (d), reprinted in: Handbook of Antarctic Treaty Measures (5th ed.), Cambridge 1987, 1612—1613.

are not subject to alienation. The minerals derived from the Area, however, may only be alienated in accordance with this Part and the rules, regulations and procedures of the Authority.

3. No State or person, natural or juridical, shall claim, acquire or exercise rights with respect to the minerals of the Area except in accordance with this Part. Otherwise, no such claim, acquisition or exercise of such rights shall be recognized.

Article 140 stipulates: "Activities in the Area shall ... be carried out for the benefit of mankind as a whole, irrespective of the geographical location of States, whether coastal or land-locked, and taking into particular consideration the interests and needs of developing States ...." The Article then goes on to state that "the Authority shall provide for the equitable sharing of financial and other economic benefits derived from activities in the Area . . . ."

The sea-bed regime therefore represents a paradigm for Antarctica, if agreement could be reached to construct a similar regime. The Antarctic Treaty itself could form a basis for setting up an Antarctic Treaty Authority to which all states could become eligible for membership. This will involve amending the present criteria of accession to the Treaty either as a Consultative or Non-consultative Party. The present criteria to qualify for membership as a Consultative Party is so onerous that most developing countries will not qualify.[18] On the other hand, a renegotiated Antarctic Treaty with the participation of all states should retain the objectives of peaceful use, non-militarization, the promotion and facilitation of scientific research, the conservation of its living resources and the orderly exploitation of its non-living resources, when this becomes feasible.

To internationalize sovereignty over Antarctica will be a departure from the traditional method of determining the extent of national territory. But the nature of Antarctica and the present rivalry over it suggests that international law will have to find new solutions for the problems of 'common space,' which Antarctica is, because of its remoteness and the need for advance technology if it is to be developed. It has been shown that with regard to outer space, the moon and other celestial bodies, and with respect to the sea-bed beyond national jurisdiction, the territorial solution was not considered appropriate and individual state sovereignty was denied. Hence, to safeguard the interest

[18] It is estimated that the Federal Republic of Germany, to become a Consultative member, had to found a programme at a cost of US $ 100 million. Clearly this is a figure that most developing countries will find prohibitive to spend and will therefore not qualify for full membership. See *Christopher Joyner*, Antarctica and the Law of the Sea: Rethinking the Current Legal Dilemmas, San Diego Law Review 18 (1981), 421.

of mankind in the use of Antarctica and develop its resources it will be necessary to adopt an approach similar to what *Richard Falk* has proposed, namely, "the adoption of a series of interlocking social, economic, political, technological and ecological tendencies that would by-pass the territorial state as the main actor."[19]

The establishment of an international regime for Antarctica would seem to be the best way to safeguard the interests of mankind in its use. In the first place, it would mean that no state could claim it or any portion of it, while at the same time access will be guaranteed for the development of its resources for the benefit of all mankind. Instead of the present competing claims, an 'Antarctic Authority' would be charged with overseeing the management of the continent for the benefit of all countries. Furthermore, such an authority will be best placed to conserve and protect the continent from environmental pollution and to ensure that its delicate ecosystem is maintained through appropriate measures. The Authority can also act as a repository of scientific research and investigation as well as a clearing-house for scientific knowledge and information.

Finally, declaring Antarctica to be the *common heritage of mankind* will not only safeguard its present use but will also ensure that it is conveyed to future generations unpolluted and without damage to its environment, which cannot be said for similar areas which have been components of the territories of some states.

In summation:

(i) States in particular and mankind in general have demonstrated a determination to preserve Antarctica. The Antarctic Treaty was primarily designed to quell the territorial disputes which had broken out around the continent and were assuming dangerous dimensions. Although the Treaty has to some extent succeeded in that limited objective, the territorial claims are still outstanding and could flare up when they are least expected to do so. It is therefore propitious to review the Treaty with a view to finding a permanent solution to outstanding problems.

(ii) Antarctica presently generates renewed interest, and is perceived as the last reservoir of natural resources, both living and non-living. With progress in science and technology, it will become possible to develop these resources. It will not only be fair and equitable that the less-endowed members of the international community should be able to participate in the distribution of those resources, but it will add to international stability as well.

---

[19] *Richard Falk*, A Paradigm for International Legal Studies: Prospects and Proposals, Yale Law Journal 84 (1975), 4.

(iii) To achieve the above objectives, it seems most prudent to renegotiate the Antarctic Treaty to ensure participation in the administration of Antarctica by all states. An Antarctic regime could be set up which would guarantee adequate representation for the present Consultative Parties or states that may consider themselves to have acquired rights by dint of their long activities there. The Antarctic Authority will not only be concerned with the short-term development of the continent but will also ensure its long-term use.

The Question of Antarctica at the United Nations: The End of Consensus?

*Cristian Maquieira**

I

For the past four years, the General Assembly of the United Nations has conducted a debate on "The Question of Antarctica," adopted a number of resolutions and requested the Secretariat to produce two studies on Antarctica and related matters. Even though the United Nations had been called upon in the past to consider Antarctica as an item of its Agenda, it is the first time since the Antarctic Treaty came into force that prolonged and in-depth debate occurred, and it is also the first time that the Secretariat has been mandated to produce documentation regarding the issue.

It must be added that while the debate itself has shown a marked difference of focus between the Antarctic Treaty Parties and the Non-Treaty Member States, consensus for the adoption of resolutions was possible in the years 1983 and 1984. These consensus resolutions were, basically, of a procedural nature. Consensus agreement became unattainable when, in 1985 and 1986, the draft resolutions purported to introduce substantive changes in the functioning of the Antarctic Treaty System.

The end of consensus with regard to the Question of Antarctica in the United Nations can be clearly explained in the final outcome by the difference of perception existing between the Treaty and the Non-Treaty Parties regarding the possible role of the Organization in this issue. That difference of perception was apparent at the beginning of the Malaysian initiative and has been present, both in ambigous and clear ways, throughout the consideration of the matter by the General Assembly. That this situation came about may be due, in part, to the dynamics of the General Assembly itself, which has a tendency to politicize issues along well-established lines, particularly "North-South" and "East-West," that may not be necessarily applicable to the issue itself. Antarctica could be an example of this dynamic.

---

* *Cristian Maquieira*, Counsellor of the Permanent Mission of Chile to the United Nations. The opinions expressed in this volume are the personal views of their authors only.

As is well known, the Prime Minister of Malaysia, *Dr. Mahatir Bin Mohamad*, while addressing the General Assembly in September of 1982,[1] stated that the United Nations should turn its attention to Antarctica now that the Third Conference on the Law of the Sea had been concluded. He added that Antarctica, like the seas and the seabed, belonged to the international community and that, while recognizing some merits to the Antarctic Treaty, a new international agreement was required. He also questioned the existing sovereignty claims in Antarctica.[2] A similar tune was struck by the Foreign Minister of Malaysia at the signing ceremony of the Law of the Sea Convention, at Montego Bay, in December of the same year.[3] It has never been clear why Malaysia undertook the task of promoting this initiative at the United Nations. Delegates from that country have repeatedly stated that Malaysia has no direct interest in Antarctica.[4] Nevertheless, Malaysia has placed this issue among those of their highest priority in the United Nations, such as Kampuchea and others.

During the New Delhi summit of the Non-Aligned movement, held in March of 1983, it became clear that Malaysia intended to pursue the issue in a more concrete manner. Notwithstanding reservations from some members of the Non-Aligned movement, the Declaration that emerged from that meeting called upon the United Nations to prepare a comprehensive study on Antarctica. It also requested that the item be inscribed on the Agenda of the 38th Session of the General Assembly.[5]

Placing the issue before the Non-Aligned movement could well have been done in order to rally support for the initiative. At the same time, it enhanced the possibilities of a political treatment of the Question, particularly by the application of analogies to Antarctica which were not obvious then nor demonstrated later in the ensuing debate.

II

The next step following the Declaration by the Non-Aligned movement was inscription of the item. This was done by the representative of Malaysia, supported by Antigua and Barbuda, through a letter sent by them to the Secretary-General, who submitted the request to the General Committee of the General Assembly.[6] In turn, the representative of Australia, on behalf of the Antarctic Treaty System, also sent a letter

[1] UN Doc. A/37/PV. 10 (1982).
[2] UN Doc. A/37/PV. 10 (1982).
[3] United Nations Conference on the Law of the Sea (UNCLOS III) O.R. 118.
[4] UN Doc. A/C. 1/41/PV. 49.
[5] UN Doc. A/38/132 (1983). Sec. III paras. 122—123.
[6] UN Doc. A/646, para. 2.

to the Secretary-General, in which they highlighted the merits and advised against consideration of the item by the United Nations.[7]

In the General Committee, Antigua and Barbuda and Malaysia stated that it was not their intention to undermine the Antarctic Treaty or its accomplishments, but they considered it necessary that the Consultative Parties inform the international community about the region, in order to widen international cooperation in Antarctica. They also emphasized the need to widen participation in the decision-making process of the Antarctic Treaty, and again included the question of claims.[8]

These statements, offered as an explanation to the need for the United Nations to occupy itself with Antarctica, reflected two assumptions on the part of the sponsors of the request. The first one is that information regarding Antarctica was not widely available and therefore there was a need for the United Nations to consider the issue. The second assumption is that irrespective of the existence of the Antarctic Treaty and its provision for participation in it, in the view of the sponsors, there remained a need to increase participation in the decision-making process. To effect these purposes, they considered the General Assembly to be the appropriate forum. The consequence of that was to increase the possibilities of political action by the United Nations on the issue.

As will be seen, the Antarctic Treaty Parties disputed these assumptions, considering them an inaccurate presentation of the Treaty, and rejected any effort to use the United Nations to revise the Treaty. Malaysia and Antigua received the support, in the General Committee, of the Philippines — who became a co-sponsor — Thailand, Pakistan, Bhutan, Sierra Leone, Singapore and others.

The representative of the United Kingdom expressed the position of the Antarctic Treaty Parties in the General Committee. He stated the following:[9]

> The Antarctic Treaty, which is open to all countries of the world and is of unlimited duration, establishes Antarctica as a region of unparalleled international co-operation in the interests of all mankind.
>
> It is based on the Charter of the United Nations, promotes its purposes and principles and confirms Antarctica as a zone of peace.
>
> It excludes Antarctica from the arms race by prohibiting any measures of a military nature such as the establishment of military

[7] *Ibid.*
[8] UN Doc. A/38/47 (1983).
[9] UN Doc. A/38/439 (1983).

> bases and fortifications, the carrying out of military manoeuvres or the testing of any type of weapons, including nuclear weapons.
>
> It encourages and facilitates scientific co-operation and the exchange of scientific information beneficial to all States.
>
> It protects the natural environment for all mankind.
>
> The Treaty establishes a comprehensive system of on-site inspection by observers to promote the objectives and ensure the observance of the Treaty.
>
> The Treaty serves the international community well and has averted international strife and conflict over Antarctica. It removes the potential sovereignty disputes between Treaty Parties.
>
> Revision or replacement of the Treaty, which is now being suggested by Malaysia and Antigua and Barbuda would undermine this system of international law and order in Antarctica with very serious consequences for international peace and co-operation. It is unrealistic to think that, in the present state of world affairs, a new or better legal regime for Antarctica could be agreed upon. The undermining of the Treaty could open the way to an arms race in the region and might lead to new territorial claims. It would not serve the interest of any country, or group of countries, if Antarctica became an area of international conflict and discord.
>
> The Treaty system has proved to be a remarkably successful, practical and dynamic arrangement. Every effort should be made to preserve and maintain it.
>
> It is for these reasons that the Consultative Parties to the Antarctic Treaty have serious reservations about the initiative by the governments of Malaysia and Antigua and Barbuda and about any attempt to revise or replace the present Treaty system.
>
> This initiative inaccurately represents the Antarctic Treaty of 1959. It implies that there is a need for revision or replacement of the Antarctic Treaty system, something which could only be achieved under international law by the Parties to the Treaty.

The statement by the British delegate highlighted the merits and achievements of the Antarctic Treaty as perceived by Antarctic Treaty Parties and questioned the possibility of obtaining a new or better agreement in the current state of world affairs. His declaration clearly implied that the United Nations had a limited role in this matter since any changes to the Treaty could only be carried out, in accordance with established international law, by the Parties themselves.

In light of the above, the Antarctic Treaty Parties that were members of the General Committee announced that they would not participate in the decision to recommend, to the General Assembly, the inscription of the item "Question of Antarctica." The recommendation was adopted without a vote but a clear difference of opinion regarding the substance of the initiative remained. The General Assembly proceeded in the same fashion with the Antarctic Treaty Parties not participating in the decision. The delegate from Chile explained the non-participation of his country by supporting the statement made by the United Kingdom in the General Committee.[10]

The item was inscribed in the Agenda and allocated to the First Committee, which deals with disarmament issues. This allocation was the result of a compromise where the sponsors of the issue desired that the question be dealt with by the plenary of the General Assembly, and thereby giving the impression that the Assembly was awarding the question top political priority. The Parties of the Antarctic Treaty considered that the Sixth Committee, which deals with legal issues, was the appropriate place to engage in a debate relating to the functioning of an international convention, as was the case with the Antarctic Treaty.

The process which led to the inscription of the item in the Agenda of the General Assembly has been outlined in some detail because, in retrospect, it seems that the seeds that brought about the breakdown of consensus were planted during this stage. The political approach, the unclear need to involve the United Nations with a view towards revising what is a well-functioning treaty, and the position, stated from the very beginning, to resist any attempt to undermine the Antarctic Treaty contributed to bringing about the end of consensus.

At the first debate the sponsors of the initiative made a sustained effort to demonstrate that the Question of Antarctica required active involvement on the part of the United Nations because, in their view, a new international agreement was required, due to the perceived shortcomings of the Antarctic Treaty. Thus, the delegate from Malaysia, in his speech before the First Committee during the 38th Session, stated that there were efforts being carried out to ensure a universal participation of the world community contained in the efforts favoring a new international economic order, a new information order and a new humanitarian order. He went on to add that, with regard to what he considered the serious limitations inherent in the Antarctic Treaty, the moment had arrived for the United Nations to take into account these efforts and consider new international modalities to deal with the Question of Antarctica.[11]

---

[10] UN Doc. A/38/PV. 3 (1983).

[11] UN Doc. A/C. 1/38/PV. 42.

The delegate from Sierra Leone said it was timely and proper that the United Nations study the question of establishing an international regime for Antarctica which, after all, should be considered an international territory.[12]

The Permanent Representative from Ghana stated, also at the 38th Session, that he was inclined towards an objective revision of the Antarctic Treaty, under the auspices of the United Nations, which would strengthen the modern concepts that the Treaty barely touches upon.[13]

The delegate from Pakistan, after describing the evolution of the concept of the *common heritage of mankind* in the United Nations' instruments, added that "as a first step in that direction" he supported the proposal for the Secretary-General to carry out a global study on Antarctica.[14] Similar statements were made by the delegations of Indonesia, Yugoslavia, Sri Lanka and others. These statements included commendatory paragraphs on certain aspects of the Antarctic Treaty, but the Treaty was generally perceived, as one delegate (Ghana), put it, as "too restrictive and exclusive to permit wide cooperation and elaboration of necessary policies."[15] Other issues were also raised, such as the participation of South Africa, the Antarctic minerals negotiations and the question of sovereignty claims.

For their part, the Consultative Parties considered that, as has already been stated, the debate was unnecessary because there was no "Antarctic Problem" which required United Nations intervention.[16] The Treaty functioned well and had produced enormous accomplishments in the political, scientific and environmental areas. Nevertheless, the Question was in the General Assembly, so they participated actively in the debate with a view to widening international acceptability of the Treaty as well as to resist any attempt to undermine or revise what they considered to be an extraordinary international instrument.

The Permanent Representative of Australia, speaking on behalf of the Consultative Parties, at the 38th Session, reiterated their position with regards to the merits and accomplishments of the Treaty and the potential dangers of any revision or undermining of the system.[17] The delegate from Chile said that due to the existence of a treaty, a system and a regime which was integrated and open to the United Nations, there was no room for a process of "*lege ferenda*" in the General Assembly.[18] The

[12] UN Doc. A/C. 1/38/PV. 42.
[13] UN Doc. A/C. 1/38/PV. 43.
[14] UN Doc. A/C. 1/38/PV. 44.
[15] UN Doc. A/C. 1/38/PV. 43.
[16] UN Doc. A/C. 1/38/PV. 44 (Statements by the representative of the U. K.).
[17] UN Doc. A/C. 1/38/PV. 42.
[18] UN Doc. A/C. 1/38/PV. 42.

delegate from Norway called the Antarctic Treaty "an example of that rare species, a dynamic international legal instrument."[19]

Other delegates, members of the Antarctic Treaty, also approached the debate from the point-of-view that the accomplishments of the Treaty and its capacity to evolve to accomodate new circumstances should be praised. They contrasted the achievements of the Treaty to the uncertainty entailed in any revision.

In summary, the delegate of Malaysia had called on the United Nations to act as a means to institutionalize change.[20] The Treaty Parties were saying that change was dangerous and unnecessary in this particular case. The first debate showed a sharp difference of views regarding the Question of Antarctica where those who criticized the Treaty did so on the basis of apparent misunderstanding, lack of adequate information regarding the Treaty and suspicion about the Treaty Parties. The defense of the latter was based on the substance of the Treaty, although as the delegate from New Zealand stated, "maybe we have not done what is sufficient to explain and publicize the system of the Antarctic Treaty and the work done by it." He added that it was also fair to recognize that up until then the international community had shown little interest in Antarctica, and indicated his willingness to speak about Antarctica and the Treaty System, be it in the United Nations or anywhere else.[21]

That same year, a resolution was adopted by consensus calling upon the Secretary-General "to prepare a comprehensive, factual and objective study on all aspects of Antarctica, taking fully into account the Antarctic Treaty System and other relevant factors."[22]

Just before the second debate (1984), the Secretary-General produced an exellent document,[23] which was praised by all. It consists of two parts. The first one was the work done by the Secretariat itself on the basis of existing information, and the second part is a compilation of the responses provided by 54 member states, 28 of which were Antarctic Treaty Parties.

The study can be credited with clearing up some of the misconceptions and misunderstandings about the Antarctic Treaty System which were expressed the year before, and confirmed most of the assertions made at that time by the Consultative Parties. It was probably due to the contents of this report, combined with some of the statements made a year

[19] UN Doc. A/C. 1/38/PV. 43.
[20] UN Doc. A/C. 1/38/PV. 42.
[21] UN Doc. A/C. 1/38/PV. 42.
[22] GA Res. 38/77, 15 Dec. 1983, GAOR, 38th sess., Plenary, 97th mtg.
[23] UN Doc. A/39/583.

earlier, that there was an evolution in the debate. While the Antarctic Treaty Parties maintained their approach to the discussion based on the Treaty and its accomplishments, the promoters of the initiative had apparently abandoned their position to replace from scratch the Treaty with an alternative regime. Instead, they concentrated on what they perceived to be the shortcomings of the Treaty and tried to repair them in order to build upon it with the same final objective in mind. At the same time, praise for the Antarctic Treaty System had generally increased.[24]

Thus, the Malaysian delegate, after stating that it was the policy of his Government to proceed on the basis of consensus regarding the Question of Antarctica, proposed during the 39th Session, the establishment of an *ad hoc* committee in the United Nations. This committee would analyze some of the problems and shortcomings of the Treaty, to which he pointed out, and discuss some questions which were not included in the Secretary-General's report.[25] He was supported by Yugoslavia, Sri Lanka, Ghana, and others. The proposal for a committee was offered as a procedural mechanism. The Consultative Parties did not agree to the idea of establishing an *ad hoc* committee because, in their view, it was not a simple procedural proposal but a questioning of the ability of the Treaty System to deal with the issue. Furthermore, it entailed a criticism of the system that was not shared by the Consultative Parties. The Representative of Australia, speaking on behalf of the Treaty Parties, stated that, while they wanted to proceed on the basis of consensus, they were not prepared to accept proposals that would eventually undermine the Treaty System. He called for an end of the consideration of the item.[26]

As had happened the year before, certain aspects of the Antarctic Treaty System were again raised. These aspects were the system of administration of Antarctica with regard to participation, decision-making and publicity, the negotiations for a minerals regime, the question of sovereignty claims and the participation of South Africa.[27]

Intense negotiations were carried out in order to reach a consensus resolution on the basis of the Malaysian proposal which had been rejected by the Antarctic Treaty Parties. At the same time, the report prepared by the Secretariat had only appeared a few days before the beginning of the debate in November of 1984, so it was finally agreed only to thank the Secretary-General for the work done. This would

[24] UN Docs. A/C. 1/39/PV. 50—55.
[25] UN Doc. A/C. 1/39/PV. 50.
[26] UN Doc. A/C. 1/39/PV. 50.
[27] UN Doc. A/C. 1/39/PV. 50.

allow time for all delegations to study the contents of the report before deciding the need for any future action.

One new development that occurred before the debate in 1985 was the declaration by the Heads of State and Governments of the Organization of African Unity (O.A.U.) that Antarctica was the *common heritage of mankind.* The Ministerial meeting of the Non-Aligned movement, held in Luanda, Angola, did not go as far as the O.A.U., but did declare that the General Assembly should remain seized of the Question of Antarctica. It also expressed the hope that the report by the Secretary-General would contribute to a wider debate with a view to adopting adequate measures bearing in mind the interest of the members of the movement.

The debate itself followed the pattern established the year before, where the supporters of the initiative were looking for ways to advance the treatment of the issue in the United Nations. At the same time, they reiterated their criticism of certain aspects of the Treaty, particularly with regard to the question of claims, the minerals regime, participation and decision-making in the Treaty System, and calling for the expulsion of South Africa from the Treaty System. It was interesting to note that an increasing number of statements were directed towards preserving certain aspects of the Antarctic Treaty, such as demilitarization, denuclearization, non-use of force, freedom of scientific research and protection of the environment while, at the same time, the desire to look for different ways, in the United Nations, to deal with the question of mineral resources.[28] Clearly, the main idea of changing the Antarctic Treaty System is maintained with this approach, but with a more modest or limited objective in mind.

The Consultative Parties, while rejecting this approach as inapplicable in Antarctic affairs, continued to put in doubt the convenience of maintaining the issue before the United Nations, particularly in the light of the content of the report prepared by the Secretary-General. The report became the central piece of the debate and was once again widely praised by the majority of delegations. For the Consultative Parties it definitely confirmed their assertions that the Antarctic Treaty was an extraordinary international instrument, which was best left alone.[29]

For the supporters of the initiative the study had increased their knowledge and understanding of Antarctica, but they felt that there were still some areas that required further consideration, particularly

[28] UN Docs. A/C. 1/40/PV. 48—54.
[29] UN Doc. A/39/583.

with regard to the importance of the Law of the Sea Convention in relation to the southern oceans.[30] This was clearly a way of continuing the consideration of the question within the scope of their final objectives. They called for an updating of the report.

The Consultative Parties, whose initial preference was to put an end to the discussion, agreed to the possibility of updating the Secretary General's report in the name of consensus. But they doubted the wisdom of pursuing the effects of the Law of the Sea Convention on the southern oceans in the framework of the General Assembly. In the words of one delegate, ". . . that should be left, for the time being, to the Academic Community."[31]

Furthermore, besides the question of updating the report, during the debate references were made about the availability of information regarding the negotiations for an Antarctic Minerals Regime.[32] The negotiations toward a consensus resolution were very intense during the 40th Session of the General Assembly. Agreement became elusive and, in the final outcome, impossible to obtain. Initially, the issues involved were the nature of the mandate to be given to the Secretary-General for the updating of his report, and the possibility of requesting the Consultative Parties to inform the Secretary-General about the status of Antarctic Minerals negotiations. Finally, there was an additional draft calling upon the Consultative Parties to exclude South Africa from participating in Antarctic meetings.

Intense negotiations were carried out between the Representative of Malaysia, and the Consultative Parties, through the Representative of Australia, who was their spokesman. The informal consultations proved to be unsuccessful and, for the first time since the beginning of the consideration of the item, resolutions were tabled without prior agreement between interested parties.

Malaysia and other co-sponsors presented two drafts to the Committee, one requesting an updating of the report, with the reference to the Law of the Sea Convention in the southern oceans included.[33] The second draft contained the request for information regarding the Minerals Regime.[34] Finally, Mauritius, on behalf of the Group of African States, tabled the resolution requesting the Consultative Parties to exclude South Africa from participating in Antarctic meetings.[35]

---

[30] UN Doc. A/C. 1/40/48.
[31] UN Doc. A/C. 1/40/PV. 49.
[32] See the statement made by the delegate of Pakistan, UN Doc. A/C. 1/40/PV. 50.
[33] UN Doc. A/C. 1/40/L. 82.
[34] UN Doc. A/C. 1/40/L. 83.
[35] UN Doc. A/C. 1/40/L. 85.

In the light of the above, the Delegation of Australia, on behalf of the Consultative Parties, tabled a draft resolution requesting an update of the report by the Secretary-General.[36] *Ambassador Alatas* of Indonesia, Chairman of the First Committee during the 40th Session of the General Assembly, seeing that there were at least two similar draft resolutions, made an appeal to continue negotiations with a view to achieving consensus. Informal consultations were pursued in order to see if, as in past years, there might be only one resolution, agreed on by all sides.

To that end, Malaysia was prepared to withdraw its own resolutions and accept the draft tabled by Australia but it could not convince the African Group to do likewise. It was very difficult for the African Group to withdraw a resolution on South Africa once this text had been circulated. There is a UN political dimension here that goes beyond Antarctic matters. It was also a way of telling the Antarctic Treaty System how to go about its business, and this is the particular reason for the breakdown of consensus. Given this development, the Consultative Parties withdrew their draft and made a statement regretting that the tradition of consensus had been broken in spite of the efforts made by the Consultative Parties.[37]

The resolutions were adopted by a vote.[38] With regard to the updated report and the request for information on the minerals negotiations, the Consultative Parties, with the exception of China, did not participate in the vote due to the fact that consensus had been broken. China abstained and made a statement.[39] China was joined by India in voting in favor of the resolution calling for the exclusion of South Africa from Antarctic meetings. Mauritius did not vote for this resolution.

In 1985, the Secretary-General produced an updated report[40] which was well-received by all concerned, although some Consultative Parties questioned some of the assumptions regarding the chapter on the importance of the Law of the Sea Convention with regard to the Antarctic.[41]

The following year, efforts were made by the Consultative Parties to re-establish a consensus approach, but their overtures in this direction were unsuccessful, due to the fact that there was an unwillingness to bring the situation back to the moment before consensus had broke

[36] UN Doc. A/C. 1/40/L. 84.
[37] UN Doc. A/C. 1/40/PV. 55.
[38] UN Doc. Press Release GA/7095, 180.
[39] UN Doc. A/C. 1/40/PV. 55.
[40] UN Doc. A/41/722.
[41] UN Doc. A/C. 1/41/PV. 50.

down a year earlier. Therefore, a similar scenario occured during the 41st Session of the General Assembly with regard to the adoption of resolutions. There were three drafts, one that establishes the United Nations as a repository of all Antarctic information, with a second calling upon the Consultative Parties to impose a moratorium on the minerals negotiations until all members of the international community can participate in the negotiations. The third one calls upon the Antarctic Treaty Parties to take urgent measures to exclude South Africa from Antarctic meetings. The first two drafts were co-sponsored by Malaysia and others and the third one by members of the African Group. They were adopted by a vote and again the Antarctic Treaty Parties did not participate on those that were on Antarctic issues. Argentina, Brasil, China, India and the Soviet Union voted in favor of the South African Resolution.

With regard to the debate, the only new development was that there was only one statement from Antarctic Treaty Parties, given by *Ambassador Woolcott* on their behalf. This was prompted by the breakdown of consensus the year before and as an indication of their reluctance to continue participation until it was restored. It was also clear indication of the unity of the Antarctic Treaty Parties.

III

The wide exchange of views in relation to Antarctica during the debate showed a marked difference of opinion with regard to a variety of issues relating to the Treaty System. Notwithstanding the impressive record exhibited by the Treaty System, an effort was made to establish a case against it, in order to justify changes to be carried out in the framework of the General Assembly. What were the elements in this case?

First, that there was not sufficient information available with regard to Antarctica. Second, that some aspects of the Treaty System were acceptable while others required modifications. Another criticism was that Non-Treaty Parties had no real access to the System. The distinction between Consultative and Non-consultative Parties was defined as unjust and concentrated decision-making on the former while the latter had to assume all obligations without any rights. The Antarctic Treaty System was unaccountable. There was a serious potential for conflict since the question of claims had been frozen but not resolved.

As has been stated by *Ambassador Woolcott* to the General Assembly, the main arguments for change appear to be that the System is anachronistic and discriminatory, that claims to sovereignty should be put to one side as a form of colonialism, that the System is secretive, that it is exclusive and controlled by developed countries, that it should be replaced by a universal regime and that the benefits derived from the exploitation of Antarctic resources should be shared as the *common heritage of mankind.*

What is the response of the Antarctic Treaty Parties to this set of criticism? With regard to availability of information, the reports prepared by the Secretary-General seemed to put to rest this question. Second, with reference to retaining some aspects of the Treaty while modifying others, the debate demonstrated that this was not possible. The delegate of the United Kingdom explained this by using one of the "retainable" aspects such as demilitarization. He said that "the original parties had sought to demilitarize the Antarctic because they feared the consequences of disagreement on certain issues which they could not resolve and, therefore, they ruled out the use of force. Demilitarization had been a means to an end, not an end in itself."[42] On this same point it has been pointed out that "all activities taking place in Antarctica are closely bound together because of their very nature, and all of them have an effect on the values protected by the Treaty."[43]

One of the initial criticisms was that the Non-Treaty Parties had no real access to the System, that it was "exclusive." These allegations, probably originating in ignorance or misunderstanding, were quickly cleared up in the debate. From 12 original members the Antarctic Treaty System consists today of 35 Consultative and Non-consultative States. Simply put, the System is open to anyone that has a real interest.

Related to the above is the question of distribution of rights and obligations among Consultative and Non-consultative Parties. There is some value to the argument that Non-consultative Parties assume the general obligations imposed by the Treaty while having limited rights. On the other hand, it is clear, as the delegate of Chile said, "that the harshness of the environment and the fragility of the ecosystem require a certain degree of knowledge and expertise" in order to manage the region without risking constant disasters.[44] The expertise approach has been severely criticized.[45] But there seems to be no viable alternative applicable to Antarctica.

Furthermore, it has to be recognized that it is a system proportionate to the degree of interest that a given country is willing to commit to Antarctic affairs, something similar, as one delegate put it, to "an

[42] UN Doc. A/C. 1/40/PV. 53.
[43] UN Doc. A/C. 1/40/PV. 53.
[44] UN Doc. A/C. 1/39/PV. 51.
[45] See *Zain Azrari*, Antarctic Treaty System. An Assessment, Washington, D. C. 1986, 305—313.

Antarctic career,"[46] which ensures proper consultation among those engaging in the same activities, and leads to decisions that do not affect those outside the decision-making process. It has to be recognized that the situation has improved considerably, since the Non-consultative Parties participate as observers in Consultative Meetings and in the mineral negotiations.

Another criticism launched against the Antarctic Treaty is that it is not accountable for its actions. During the debate it was pointed out that it was accountable to the provisions of the Antarctic Treaty. Besides that, this criticism flies in the face of international law, particularly with regard to the concept of *pacta sunt servanda*. Countries not parties to a legally binding treaty cannot question, through the United Nations or by other means, the obligations of those parties to the Treaty.

Another area of severe criticism had to do with participation of South Africa in the Antarctic Treaty System. This is a very sensitive question, particularly in the United Nations, where it is the object of a highly political debate. The essence of the criticism is that due to the System of Apartheid existing in that country it should be excluded from participation, at least, in Antarctic meetings, (possibly expelled from the Antarctic System altogether), as has been done in many international organizations.

Nevertheless, it must be recalled, as it was during the debate,[47] that the Antarctic Treaty is one that essentially imposes obligations. In this sense, it is in the interest of the international community that South Africa be bound to a prohibition on all military activities, nuclear explosions and disposal of nuclear waste. As it is contained in the Treaty, this prohibition is subject to on-site verification. The fact that some Consultative Parties voted in favor of the resolutions adopted with regard to South Africa does not necessarily mean that those countries detract from what is stated above.

On another matter, the knowledge that the Consultative countries were conducting negotiations to approve a regime that will regulate Antarctic mineral resources was the source of much suspicion and criticism, particularly due to the fact that the Treaty is silent when it comes to the question of resources.

This is one of the areas where the Antarctic Treaty System has been subject to considerable misrepresentation. The assumptions underlying this criticism is that there are considerable resources in Antarctica

[46] UN Doc. A/C. 1/39/PV. 51.
[47] UN Doc. A/C. 1/40/PV. 48.

that are secretly being negotiated between the Consultative Parties, to the exclusion of the rest of the world. According to the Consultative Parties, nothing could be further away from the truth.

First, the quantities of available resources mentioned by the delegate of Malaysia during the debate[48] are based on purely speculative calculations that have no backing with hard facts. Also, the economics of Antarctic resources — the minimum market prices needed to make the risks worth taking and the investment profitable — make the exploitation of these resources a highly unlikely operation, not to mention the technological and other problems that remain to be solved.

It is correct that the Treaty is silent on the question of resources but that should not be an impediment for the Parties to fulfil their obligation to preserve Antarctica from becoming the scene or object of international discord as it is stated in Article IX. This is precisely the reason, as was pointed out during the debate,[49] why the Consultative Parties are engaging in this exercise.

If ever there is a possibility of commercial exploitation of Antarctic resources in the absence of a regime the probabilities of bringing about conflict in Antarctica become certain. In that case, the various national positions would tend to prevail over the objectives of the Treaty and there would be a serious possibility of confrontation. It would be tantamount to irresponsible international behavior if the Consultative Parties did not utilize the absence of certain exploitation to arrive at a regime that would govern those eventual commercial activities.

There is also the accusation of secrecy regarding the negotiations: secrecy that makes the exercise all the more suspect. As the Representative of New Zealand pointed out during the debate,[50] it is not a question of secrecy but merely one of privacy, which is common in any international bargaining, particularly when the negotiations have not yet been concluded.

It has been said in the General Assembly that some of the issues in this negotiation, particularly on the relationship of Claimants and Non-claimants with regard to minerals, make any agreement impossible. The answer to that assertion is to be found in the history of the Antarctic Treaty itself, specifically in Article IV, regarding the question of claims. Nothing seemed more difficult, in 1959, than accommodation on this problem, and yet a lasting solution was found. As was stated by the Representative of the United Kingdom ". . . these negotiations, that constitute a demanding and imaginative exercise, may produce new

[48] UN Doc. A/C. 1/38/PV. 42.
[49] UN Doc. A/C. 1/40/PV. 48.
[50] UN Doc. A/C. 1/38/PV. 42.

ideas about the way States can agree among themselves, which is exactly what has happened with the Antarctic Treaty."[51]

Finally, one of the issues relating to Antarctica that was heavily criticized, and less understood, was the question of existing sovereignty claims. This issue lies at the heart of the Antarctic Treaty System. Article IV of the Treaty is probably one of the fundamental provisions of that instrument, and it is the oil that has permitted the wheels of the system to turn in such a remarkable way. As it is well known, there are seven Claimant states[52], three of which have overlapping claims[53]. These claims are based on a variety of instruments recognized by international law which have been exercised by the Claimants for over 75 years. In the period prior to the Antarctic Treaty the contention for sovereignty gave origin to a series of confrontations that negatively affected the possibilities of conducting scientific research activities.[54] This issue was the first one that required solution, during the negotiations of the Treaty, before other aspects could be tackled. That is why Article IV is the central Article of the Treaty.

In essence, this Article says that neither the Treaty itself nor acts or activities taking place during the life of the Treaty shall prejudice the position of countries which claim to exercise sovereignty, countries which do not recognize those claims, or countries which assert a basis of a claim. During the debate at the United Nations[55] it was suggested that the Article had frozen the rights to territorial sovereignty in Antarctica or rendered them ineffective. This is incorrect. The Treaty does not allow during its lifetime — which is indefinite — the claims to be enhanced, but neither have they diminished. What Article IV has done, as was stated by *André Gros*, is suspend the contentious aspect of the question with regard to Antarctica. Also, it has safeguarded all relevant rights, while at the same time laying the groundwork for building an effective mechanism for international cooperation. That is the key to the question, which seems to not have been understood by those in the General Assembly who have criticized it severely. Thus, the claims were rejected on the grounds that they constituted a "vestige of colonialism,"[56] and a source of "future disputes" because the Treaty had postponed the issue, not solved it[57].

---

[51] UN Doc. A/C. 1/40/PV. 53.
[52] Australia, Argentina, Chile, France, New Zealand, Norway, United Kingdom.
[53] Argentina, Chile and United Kingdom.
[54] See *Francisco Orrego-Vicuña*, Antarctic Treaty System. An Assessment, Washington, D. C. 1986, 55—64.
[55] UN Doc. A/C. 1/38/PV. 42.
[56] UN Doc. A/C. 1/39/PV. 54.
[57] UN Doc. A/C. 1/39/PV. 50.

Calls were made to replace the current solutions with the institution of *common heritage of mankind*,[58] by applying the provisions contained in the Law of the Sea Convention. The response of the Consultative Parties, particularly the Claimant states, rejected these assertions on the ground that the claims were based on solid rights accepted by international law,[59] protected by Article IV of the Treaty, and that furthermore they constituted a political reality of the region. Any reopening of this question would bring the situation back to the period prior to the Antarctic Treaty, which has been characterized as one of intense conflict. Those who criticize Article IV as an example of the weakness of the Antarctic Treaty System do not realize that on the contrary, its greatest strength is that it has allowed the System, in the face of irreconcilable differences, to reach incomparable results through international cooperation.

Related to the above are the references made in order to apply to Antarctica the concept of *common heritage of mankind*, as has been done with outer space and the sea-beds beyond national jurisdiction.[60] Some of the Consultative Parties have pointed out that while that concept may be applicable, even welcomed, to the areas mentioned, it cannot be to Antarctica. There are three fundamental differences between Antarctica, outer space and the seabed. There has been secular activity by man in Antarctica, which is not the case with the seabeds and outer space. There is a long-standing and well-functioning international legal regime in Antarctica, and last, but very much not least, there is the question of claims.

Conclusion

It would seem that the Question of Antarctica was introduced in the General Assembly with a view to first exposing what were perceived to be fundamental weaknesses and then repair them through existing United Nations mechanisms and possibly to replace the current Antarctic Treaty System. Altogether this effort was initially meant to include the Antarctic Treaty Parties, in a way similar to the establishment of the wide consensus that led, at its inception, to the Convention of the Law of the Sea and the Outer Space and Moon Treaties.

On the part of the Antarctic Treaty Parties, their reluctance to consider the issue in the United Nations gave way to using the initiative in order to describe in detail what has been achieved by the Treaty,

---

[58] UN Doc. A/37/PV. 18 (1982).

[59] See "Question of Antarctica: Report of the Secretary General," UN Doc. A/39/583 (1984).

[60] UN Doc. A/C. 1/38/PV. 46.

the type of issues it has resolved, and the nature of its contribution with regard to scientific research and protection of the environment, disarmament and peaceful uses.

Consensus broke down because there was a difference of perception as to the role that United Nations should play in this matter. The proponents of the initiative, while recognizing that the Treaty had great significance, still insisted upon their effort to determine, from outside the system, the way it should function in certain areas. This was done without offering clear alternatives and was based more on a political approach than on an adequate evaluation of the merits of the Treaty or of the inherent dangers of their proposals, particularly with regard to preserving Antarctica from becoming the scene or object of international discord, which is a paramount objective.

The general approach of the United Nations to issues is on the basis of a North-South or East-West criteria. This issue falls within neither of these categories and using them can only lead to a difficulty in understanding the intricacies of the System.

As has been pointed out by one distinguished scholar, "the current debate about Antarctica has not been at all futile. It has once again proved the limits of internationalisation and, more importantly, has, as a result greatly strengthened the System itself. It can be confidently said that the importance attached to the System by the Treaty Parties is greater today than at any other time before, not because the existence of an external threat but because the case put against the Treaty System has not proved convincing and hence the positive contribution this System to the regulation of activities in Antarctica has emerged with even greater clarity."[61]

T. S. Eliot once said that you shall investigate, and investigate only to arrive to the point where you started and know it for the first time.

One would hope that this has occurred with those that have proposed the debate of Antarctica in the United Nations.

---

[61] See *Francisco Orrego Vicuña*, The Regulation of Resource-Oriented Activities, in: *Gillian D. Triggs* (ed.), The Antarctic Treaty Regime — Law, Enivronment Resources, Cambridge 1987, 75.

The Issue of Antarctica — A Commentary

*Mohamed Haron**

One of the very real pleasures of the Kiel Symposia series is the opportunity it provides for discussions on Antarctica that are always interesting and very often both thought-provoking and illuminating. Also refreshing is the absence of polemics and the necessity for point-scoring and posturing, in a forum characterised by a spirit of enquiry and scholarly sobriety. The papers presented by *Ambassador Woolcott* and Mr. *Maquieira* certainly deserve greater reflection than has been possible in the time available, and I certainly would not do justice to their efforts by hasty commentary.

The parameters of debate on Antarctica is already fairly well-defined through successive sessions of the United Nations General Assembly (UNGA) since 1983 and through various seminars and symposia, not least Antarctic Challenge I and II. Broadly speaking, three main streams of opinion may be said to have emerged on Antarctica — "institutionalists" who see the entrenchment of the Antarctic Treaty System (ATS) and its further expansion to cover such new areas of Antarctic endeavour as may arise, on the one hand; "universalists" who believe that the ATS should make way for a new international regime in Antarctica, on the other; and "evolutionists," who accept both the reality and utility of the ATS as presently constituted and yet recognize the need for system transformation at some stage, even if they remain uncertain over the extent of such a transformation, somewhere in between. (I should add that the labels I have used may or may not be apt and are resorted to for convenience alone.) The arguments for and against each stream of opinion are equally valid and equally persuasive, depending on the premise that one begins from, and there is perhaps little point in indulging in such advocacy here. It should be sufficient for advocates of the various streams of opinion to merely agree to disagree. Which stream of opinion eventually becomes dominant, depends, it seems to me, on the future record of the Antarctic Treaty System as well as developments within the international system itself.

---

* Mr. *Mohamed Haron*, High Commissioner for Malaysia, Malaysian High Commission, New Delhi. The opinions expressed in this volume are the personal views of their authors only.

I should like instead to use the time available to me, to present the issue of Antarctica in its international perspective. It is not obviously an issue that is going to disappear anytime soon. The probability is that it will gain greater salience as an international issue, as "institutionalists" seek to entrench and expand the ATS (the better to preserve it) and as "universalists" seek at the very minimum to limit its scope (the better to transform it).

The question may well be posed as to why a largely functional treaty arrangement, with very specific, territorial limits and one that is generally conceded to have worked reasonably well for close on three decades, should suddenly come up for scrutiny and resultant criticism? To attribute the situation to the irresponsible activism of one or two unrepresentative countries is perhaps too simple an answer. That they should have struck a responsive enough chord among a motley constituency to have kept the issue of Antarctica alive at the United Nations and other fora for several years now, perhaps point to the existence of deep-seated doubts and uncertainties among many of them concerning the Antarctic Treaty System. It is useful to ponder the possible mainsprings of these doubts and uncertainties.

In the immediate context of Antarctica, doubt and uncertainty may well be traceable to the suspicion, consciously or unconsciously entertained by many, that the high idealism of the Treaty language is merely the cloak for the determined pursuit of national policy objectives, or in other words that the Treaty is not what it is cracked out to be. The steady expansion of the Treaty System, beyond promotion of scientific research to apparent tentative efforts of an economic nature, has served to heighten that suspicion. The Antarctic Treaty in itself is probably not fundamentally unacceptable to the many who recognize its very real contribution to international peace, in holding in abeyance territorial claims that might otherwise be pressed and in the non-militarization and non-nuclearization of Antarctica. They would readily concede that the world is better off with the Treaty than without it, though they may not be inclined to accede to it in its present form. But the apparent use of the Treaty mechanism to attempt to justify the entrenchment of prior rights to economic exploitation, through condominium or other arrangements, has fed the perception, fairly or unfairly, that the Treaty itself may perhaps be inimical to the aspirations of the larger international community for a future equitable order in Antarctica. Erroneously or otherwise, they appear to have entertained the hope that the Treaty represented a sort of half-way house towards an international arrangement on Antarctica, rather than a bastion for keeping alive territoriality claims by Claimant states. This perhaps explains the strong opposition to the Treaty-based minerals negotiations. The fear is that in the rush to conclude a Minerals Regime, the positive contribution of Article IV of the Treaty might be compromised and that in the process, the interests of the developing countries both within and outside of the Treaty System will not receive due consideration. The reach of an Antarctic Minerals Regime is equally a matter of much apprehension. Many Non-Treaty parties grasp the proposition that it may be decades before exploitation of the Antarctic land mass and the ice-shelves become possible, but they are aware that exploitation of the Antarctic Continental Shelf and the deep sea-bed south of 60° latitude is a lot less distant. The possibility that Treaty Parties may decide to extend a Minerals Regime to cover the Continental Shelf and the deep sea-bed in spite of Article IV of the Treaty and the Law of the Sea Convention is a source of acute concern to the international community.

In the larger context, reservations about the legitimacy of the Treaty, spring from what may loosely be termed an anti-colonial mind-set. Rightly or wrongly, the Antarctic Treaty System has tended to be viewed as a historical extension of the colonial order, in the sense that the discovery of Antarctica and the subsequent claims made on its territory all flowed from that historic era of European maritime expansion that saw the creation of global colonial empires. With the rolling back of colonialism and the first stirrings of a universalist global order, emerged the expectation — naive, perhaps — that such territorial claims should also be allowed to lapse. That the ATS was an arrangement principally of the efficacious and of the territorially involved and remained so until very lately, that little or no attempt was made to educate the world as to its purposes and its activities, that it tended to function as if Non-Treaty parties were an irrelevance, all tended to breed a sense of exclusion among members of the international community, the majority of whom secured independence in the decades after the conclusion of the Treaty in 1959. The attitude of mutual disinterest as between Treaty and Non-Treaty parties was not shattered, until interest in the exploitation of marine and sea-bed resources became pronounced consequent upon negotiations toward the Law of the Sea Convention. The apparent potential of Antarctica and the Southern Ocean aroused outside interest, while the unexpected and generally unwelcome attention unsettled Treaty Parties whose efforts to consolidate the System reinforced suspicions of their selfish exclusivity. The loose Non-Treaty constituency of the developing world, conscious of their number and newly assertive, felt they had little choice but to pry open a system they felt had deliberately or otherwise excluded them from Antarctic concerns. That this sentiment did not necessarily accord with objective reality was quite beside the point.

How can the sense of alienation felt by so many developing countries over the issue of Antarctica be addressed? Indeed, should their sense of alienation be addressed at all? These are questions the Treaty Parties have to consider.

It would seem to me that the Treaty Parties should be very clear in their own minds what their true objectives are with regard to the Antarctic Treaty System. Are they fundamentally committed to the letter and spirit of the Treaty, or is the Treaty essentially a "cloaking device" for the pursuit of narrow national goals? If the Treaty is perceived to be a good in itself, that is worthwhile preserving because any alternative would be much worse, then Treaty Parties have the political duty and the moral obligation to patiently persevere in building a majority constituency internationally around the Treaty. As I have observed earlier, the Treaty to a certain extent suffers from a legitimacy problem. The pace of its evolution, especially with respect to its decision-making structure through its nearly three decades of existence, has tended to give the impression that its central purpose is to safeguard the influence of its decision-making parties, rather than to attract the largest possible number of adherents. The seeming ambivalence of many decision-making parties in the matter of advancing the collective Treaty System interest *vis-à-vis* advancing separate national interests, has not escaped the notice of Non-Treaty parties and caused doubts about the long-term survivability of the Treaty System itself. The apparent reluctance of Treaty Parties to engage in an open airing of how the Treaty System functions, its weakness and its strengths, its problems and its potentialities, give the impression that it has deep dark secrets to keep from an unsuspecting world. I have personally thought that I have acquired a much better understanding of the workings of the Treaty and of the issues involved from attending open symposia such as this, than from sitting through interminable political debates on Antarctica. If Treaty proponents were more confident and less apologetic of the moral foundations of the Treaty System and if they were both more clear and open about their purposes, the probability of building a majority constituency would appear far less insurmountable. I recall the Malaysian proposal, still-born, about the desirability of setting up an United Nations *ad-hoc* committee on Antarctica, that could have served precisely the mutually-educating process required as between Treaty and Non-Treaty parties. There is a gap of distrust and ignorance to be bridged, if consensus on the issue of Antarctica is to ever have any hope of emerging.

No area of Treaty System activity has the potential for international divisiveness as the closed negotiations towards an Antarctic Minerals Regime. The logic of conducting those negotiations under the *aegis* of the Antarctic Treaty, if a Minerals Regime were to be at all feasible and if a free-for-all, certain to result in conflict, were to be avoided, is one that deserves careful presentation to the international community. The processes of negotiation and the issues under negotiation equally deserve to be openly presented to the international community through the United Nations, if the community's fears of being given short shrift are to be allayed. The international community needs to be convinced that an Antarctic Minerals Regime is not arrived at, at the expense of the erosion of rights it already enjoys by virtue of relevant provisions under the Law of the Sea Convention. Again, the crying need is for Treaty System proponents not to be diffident about, or to be disinclined to engage in, open discussions with Non-Treaty parties, as if there were indeed something to hide. A prerequisite naturally would be the ability of the Treaty Parties themselves to present a cohesive front on principles that would be acceptable to the international community as a whole.

The "bottom line" concerning the survivability and workability of the Antarctic Treaty System is its ability to acquire legitimacy across a wide spectrum of the international community. In order to acquire that legitimacy, Treaty Parties have to win over enough Non-Treaty parties to claim at the very least a majority constituency within the international community. That exercise is less likely to achieve success by a resort to political browbeating, than by the superior logic of persuasive presentation, genuine commitment to protecting and advancing the interest of the international community even as individual interests are served, a willingness to be open and transparent concerning motives and objectives, and above all, the readiness to persist in dialogue. If Treaty Parties are absolutely convinced that objective reality permits no other course in Antarctica than to maintain and expand the Antarctic Treaty System, and they are morally convinced of the justice of their endeavour, the task then before them should surely be to press the issue before the international community. The international community may well perceive Antarctica from a diametrically opposite premise, but then neither is it immune to the dictates of reality. It has often been stated that both Treaty and Non-Treaty parties subscribe to common objectives on Antarctica, but they disagree on the political structures for realizing those objectives. It seems, to me at least, that political structures have their own logic, that they develop the way they do because of the requirements of sustaining dynamics. Perhaps there should be greater willingness to discuss structures between Treaty and Non-Treaty parties — it would at the very least provide the opportunity for the mutual-education process that would appear to be so necessary.

I have attempted in my remarks to put the issue of Antarctica in its international perspective, I hope intelligibly and dispassionately. It would be a pity if through a failure of communication, we should persist in mutual distrust and suspicion and allow an endeavour that should bind us together, divide us unnecessarily. I have spoken entirely on my own behalf of course, but I reflect nevertheless the commitment of Malaysia to a constructive role in ensuring the interest of all mankind in Antarctica. Malaysia has been guided by the objectives of "accountability," "involvement" and "equity" in its Antarctica exercise. In the real world we understand the reality that these objectives are achieveable, not in absolute, but in relative measure. We feel that it is not only in the collective interest of all mankind, but also in the enlightened self-interest of individual Treaty Parties, that the relative measure be substantial enough for an Antarctic regime to command the broad support of the international community. Malaysia welcomes the progress made in respect of "accountability" and "involvement," inasmuch as the flow of in formation and the involvement of specialized agencies and other international bodies have shown discernible improvement, and would hope that this represents an irreversible improvement. "Equity," perhaps understandably, has been rather more interactable. The sensitivity and wisdom with which this question is approached and handled, will likely determine in the long run whether Antarctic developments promote international harmony or provoke international discord.

Panel Discussion

Participants: *Nils Bølset**
*Vladimir Golitsyn***
*Ian Hendry****
*H. P. Rajan*****
*F. Orrego Vicuña******
*Jost Delbrück*******

J. Delbrück, Chairman:

Ladies and Gentlemen, we decided to follow the issue first by conforming to the list that was read to you, so we will start with *Mr. Bølset.*

N. Bølset:

Thank you, Mr. Chairman. The representatives of the twelve countries that met in Washington in 1959 certainly set themselves ambitious goals. The Preamble of the Antarctic Treaty says that it is in the interest of all mankind that Antarctica shall continue forever to be used exclusively for peaceful purposes and cannot become the scene or object of international discord. This is really something. I wonder how many international treaties, after more than a quarter of a century of existence, can stand examination and declare themselves faithful to their goals. I think the Antarctic Treaty has been a remarkable example of international cooperation and, I dare say, one of the best we have seen. Antarctica is an effective zone of peace, and the principles and purposes of the UN Charter are fulfilled in practice. Now, some of the UN members have questioned the right of self-chosen nations to act as protectors in Antarctica. The exclusivity of the membership has been questioned. I do not think that they actually can be heard on this point.

---

* *Nils Bølset*, Ministry of Foreign Affairs, Oslo, Norway.

** *Vladimir Golitsyn*, Office of Legal Affairs, United Nations Secretariat, New York.

*** *Ian D. Hendry*, Legal Counsellor, Foreign and Commonwealth Office, London, U. K.

**** *H. P. Rajan*, Principal Scientific Officer, Department of Ocean Development, New Delhi.

***** Prof. *Francisco Orrego Vicuña*, School of Law and Institute of International Studies, University of Chile.

****** Prof. Dr. *Jost Delbrück*, LL.M. (Indiana), Director of the Institute of International Law and Rector of the Christian Albrecht University of Kiel.

The opinions expressed in this volume are the personal views of their authors only.

The original twelve countries have, in the meantime, become 35, and more than half of those are Consultative Parties. And I think you would all agree that this Antarctic Treaty family is a diversified one. Here you find developed countries, developing countries, Western countries, Eastern countries, non-aligned countries and so forth. Together they have about two-thirds of the world's total population. And it is not a rich men's club: I suppose that if that were so, the people of many of these countries would be very surprised to learn it.

The comparison of Antarctica with the deep sea-bed and outer space has been made. I think this is a rather misleading comparison. Antarctica is no *terra nova*. Active scientific, commercial, and related activities have taken place in Antarctica over the years. Some countries, including my own, maintain claims to territorial sovereignty. Although these claims are not universally recognized, they, nevertheless, represent constitutional and political realities that cannot be overlooked. With some good will, and I am a man of good will, I hope, I can see some merits in the motives behind those who want a UN involvement in Antarctica. I place much trust in the UN — and indeed, the Norwegian Government does, shifting Norwegian Governments have — but in spite of some sympathy for the idea, from a more, let us say, idealistic point-of-view, I think we should not dare to break up the very fine legal and political balance that exists under the Treaty. Any chance to rebuild this balance, once broken, I think would be very, very difficult to do, if at all possible. So, I think, we should use the instrument we have got. Any member of the UN may join the Antarctic Treaty. And, as I say, the Treaty has worked very well, not only reasonably well, as was mentioned earlier, but, I think, very well. We should bear in mind that the Antarctic Treaty has paved the way for cooperation in various fields, in spite of conflicting territorial claims and despite frequent and often acute bilateral differences between them on other matters. What could demonstrate this more clearly than the recent accession of both North Korea and South Korea to the Treaty?

Indeed, the Antarctic Treaty embodies much of what the United Nations Charter espouses. That is a success not to be destroyed. Thank you, Mr. Chairman.

J. Delbrück, Chairman:

Thank you. So, *Mr. Golitsyn*, will you go on, please.

V. Golitsyn:

The subject of our discussion today is the question of Antarctica — the end of consensus. In approaching this subject, it would be logical of course to look for the reasons that made consensus, which presumably existed, not possible any longer. But, any researcher who would make an attempt to study the situation retrospectively, might be surprised at the very beginning by a difficulty to figure out the essence of consensus on the item when it was first inscribed on the agenda of the United Nations.

As is well known, on 11 August 1983, Malaysia and Antigua and Barbuda submitted a request for the inclusion of a supplementary item on Antarctica in the agenda of the 38th session of the General Assembly. In an explanatory memorandum, they emphasized the considerable environmental, climatic and scientific significance of Antarctica to the world and its economic potential in terms of living and non-living resources. While admitting the progress made within the framework of the Antarctic Treaty in collaborative scientific efforts, they at the same time expressed the view that there was a need to examine the possibility for a more positive and wider international concert through a truly universal framework of international cooperation through the United Nations, to ensure that activities carried out in Antarctica were for the benefit and in the interest of mankind as a whole. In conclusion, they called for a comprehensive study on Antarctica which should take into account all relevant factors, including the Antarctic Treaty — the idea initially approved by the Seventh Summit Conference of the Heads of State or Government of the Non-Aligned Countries.

In explaining further the motivation which guided Malaysia, the Deputy Prime-Minister of Malaysia stated during the general debate of the General Assembly that the Antarctic Treaty of 1959, although open to all members of the United Nations, was restrictive, exclusive in nature and also discriminatory, since only the Consultative Parties could make decisions concerning the continent. In his view, the present arrangement regarding Antarctica had created inequities which could not be allowed to continue. He also stated that it was timely for the international community to be prepared to apply to Antarctica the concept of *common heritage* and common benefit.

From the very beginning the initiative of Malaysia and Antigua and Barbuda met strong resentment from the Parties to the Antarctic Treaty, in particular the Consultative Parties. On 19 September 1983, the Permanent Representative of Australia to the United Nations sent, on behalf of the Consultative Parties, a letter to the Secretary-General of the United Nations arguing that revision or replacement of the Antarctic Treaty which was being suggested by Malaysia and Antigua and Barbuda would undermine the system of international law and order in Antarctica with very serious consequences for international peace and cooperation. The letter characterized the Antarctic Treaty as an open-to-all-countries international instrument promoting purposes and principles of the Charter of the United Nations, as a dynamic arrangement which had averted international strife and conflict over Antarctica. Serious reservations were expressed in it about the aforementioned initiative of Malaysia and Antigua and Barbuda and about any atttempt to revise or replace the Antarctic Treaty and an international system based on it.

Acting as a spokesman for the Antarctic Treaty Consultative Parties, the Australian representative in his statement at the 38th session of the General Assembly pointed out that despite pronouncements to the contrary, the initiative on Antarctica could lead the Assembly down a path which might ultimately imperil the functioning and integrity of the Antarctic Treaty and put at risk the substantial achievements of the Treaty System. While admitting that the present Treaty System might not be perfect, he said it did allow for evolution. At the same time, according to his statement, any attempt to negotiate a new international agreement on Antarctica or to renegotiate parts of the Treaty would be likely to prove counterproductive, introducing uncertainty and possible instability into a region of hitherto unparalleled international harmony.

Because of their opposition to the initiative of Malaysia and Antigua and Barbuda some of the Antarctic Treaty Parties which were members of the General Committee of the General Assembly at the 38th session (Belgium, Czechoslovakia, France, GDR, Japan, Norway, USSR, and the U.S.), indicated that they would not participate in the decision of that Committee on the inclusion in the agenda of an item on Antarctica. The same position was taken by all Consultative Parties when the matter was later addressed by the General Assembly itself.

It is evident from the record cited above that from the very beginning there was no agreement, even with regard to the need for having an item on Antarctica being discussed by the United Nations. Reasoning for it is not disagreement on procedure, but derived from the fact that states concerned have diametrically opposite views of how Antarctica in general should be managed by the international community. It appears that their divergent positions have not become closer since 1983, but on the contrary, that the parties concerned have hardened their approaches, making it more difficult to find areas for compromise. As one delegation stated during the last session of the General Assembly (41st session), if an honourable consensus were unachievable, this delegation would prefer to have its principled approach adhered to and submitted to the vote. "If we had to choose between the maintenance of principles and the pursuit of consensus," pointed out another delegation, "it would only be logical that we decide to maintain the principles."

Let us look now at the main areas of disagreement between the parties.

The initiators of the item on Antarctica and their supporters proceed from the understanding that because Antarctica is of serious interest for the entire international community, ecologically, meteorologically, economically and ultimately, in the all-important area of war and peace, the decisions relating to Antarctica must be regarded either under the auspices of the United Nations or through a decision-making mechanism worked out under the auspices of that universal Organization. The Antarctic Treaty System, in their view, is inadequate for this purpose and has become an anachronism.

The first and the most important drawback of the Antarctic Treaty System cited in this regard is the deficiency in the system of management of Antarctica established by the Treaty. It is argued that the Antarctic Treaty of 1959 was a limited initiative taken at a time when competing claims to areas in Antarctica raised the possibility of tension and crisis in the region. The Antarctic Treaty in its present form, however, is inadequate in the light of existing conditions for the management of the continent in the best interests of mankind. As one delegation put it, the system established by the Antarctic Treaty for administering the continent is unjust and undemocratic, because it envisages two classes of States Parties: the Consultative Parties and the Non-consultative Parties and the right of participation in decision-making is denied to the latter. It is observed that the Non-consultative Parties, although admitted as observers since 1983 to Consultative Meetings — in other words 21 years after the Treaty came into force — and most recently also as observers to the minerals negotiations, still do not have any decision-making power and doubtfully exercise any influence on the deliberations of the Consultative Parties. It is concluded therefore that the main deficiency of the Treaty System derives from the fact that only a limited group of States, on the basis of criteria which they themselves determine, confer on themselves the exclusive right to make decisions affecting all activities in Antarctica without accountability to the international community.

In reply to an argument that acquisition of the Consultative status implies assumption of special responsibilities, Malaysia, Antigua and Barbuda and their supporters note that even if one accepts the notion of special responsibility — which may or may not be justified — there is no denying that it has generally translated into an exclusive right to make decisions on all matters affecting Antarctica, not only on, say, scientific research and environmental protection and questions of peace and security, but also on the possible exploitation of mineral resources of Antarctica and equitable sharing of its benefits. It is emphasized that while the Antarctic Treaty is open for accession to all states, very few developing countries have the means necessary to qualify for Consultative status under the Treaty. Therefore, such accession would be meaningless to them, since they would be locked out permanently from participation in any decision-making on Antarctic matters; in other words, they would be excluded from sharing in the benefits of the patrimony of all mankind which Antarctica, in their view, should be.

In conclusion, it could be said that one of the main concerns of the initiators of the item on Antarctica at the United Nations is that under the present system of the Antarctic Treaty they should be bound by decisions made without their involvement. Therefore they consider this system as unfair and unjust. Consequently, sach a system, in their opinion, cannot validly be defended as committed to the interest of mankind as a whole.

The above-mentioned approach has been very strongly contested during the debates in the United Nations, throughout all these years, by the supporters of the Antarctic Treaty System.

They argue that the Antarctic Treaty System has demonstrated itself as a remarkable achievement in multilateral international cooperation. According to them, the Treaty, which is the basis of the System, has many virtues: it is open to all countries, it is based on the United Nations Charter and promotes its purposes; it establishes Antarctica as a zone of peace; it excludes Antarctica from the arms race; it forbids nuclear weapons and their use in the continent; it has set aside conflicting territorial claims; it encourages scientific cooperation; it protects the fragile natural environment of the Antarctic; and, finally, it guarantees the protection, management and careful monitoring of Antarctic living resources.

The supporters of the Antarctic Treaty System contest the criticism of the Consultative status as being based on a misunderstanding of what is essentially a valid distinction. They argue that any party to a treaty that establishes a scientific programme in Antarctica immediately assumes a range of practical, financial and legal responsibilities relating to its activities and the effective discharge of these responsibilities requires regular consultation and cooperation with the other countries carrying out similar activities. In their view, it makes sense for the countries with these wider responsibilities to play a more active role in running the Treaty System. As one delegation stated, in fact the Antarctic Treaty and its supplementary instruments are no different from other multilateral treaties and in no way contradict either the law of treaties or the United Nations Charter; on the contrary, they give expression to them. Nothing prevents — indeed everything encourages — a group of states with avowed rights, interests and activities in the given area to agree to cooperate there.

It is explained that two categories of participation reflect only degrees of participation, with equal opportunities for all. The participation of states within the System — the Treaty and its complementary instruments — depends on interest and activities. Mere accession confers a number of rights. Carrying on scientific activities allows a state to aspire to a higher level of participation.

It is noted that acceding Parties, for their own good reasons, have presumably wished to limit their commitment to the Antarctic, short of that implied by the Consultative status. Therefore, it is not so much that the Consultative Parties enjoy benefits from their status, as that they share obligations and responsibilities, often at very considerable cost. It is argued that those benefits which flow are essentially benefits of a scientific and technical nature and these benefits have been made available to all states and to the international community as a whole, without discrimination.

There is one argument in the position of the defenders of the Antarctic Treaty System which deserves special attention, because it might be crucial for the understanding of whether the consensus on Antarctica is achievable at the United Nations.

The supporters of the Treaty System have constantly stressed in the course of the debate that everything in the Treaty is strictly balanced. Consequently, a hope, expressed by opponents to the Treaty, that certain elements of the Treaty could be replaced under the United Nations auspices by some other arrangement to meet their concern, in their opinion, is illusory. The condition for the continuing effectiveness of such provisions of the Treaty as demilitarization, freedom of scientific research, on site inspection, *etc.*, according to the statement made by one delegation, is that no one shall attempt to prejudice the delicate balance under which the original disagreement was set aside in the Treaty. Summarizing the results of the debates during the last forty years, one could say that we have here two groups of states with quite opposite views on what should represent a fair international regime for Antarctica.

One group continues claiming, and the recent 41st session of the General Assembly was clear evidence of it, that the present situation in Antarctica is deficient, because of its non-democratic and exclusive character, which requires improvement through the establishment of a new system that would cater to the interest of mankind in its entirety.

Another group considers the present Antarctic Treaty System as a valuable international instrument and sees the role of the United Nations in encouraging greater international participation in this System. Any effort based on the assumption that the Treaty System requires substantial modification or replacement, as well as any attempt to build some sort of a parallel mechanism at the United Nations for dealing with Antarctic issues, for this group, is unacceptable.

The attitude towards the Antarctic Treaty represents only one major aspect of the debate. The other aspect is related to the principles that should govern an international regime for mineral resources in Antarctica and to the problem of choosing a proper forum at which such a regime should be negotiated. On the one hand, the issue of an international regime for the Antarctic mineral resources is closely linked to the destiny of the Antarctic Treaty. On the other hand it is, to a certain extent, separate from it. As is well known, although the Treaty has no provisions on mineral resources, its Article IV on the sovereignty claims in Antarctica would inevitably affect any mineral resource regime to be negotiated.

Opponents to the Antarctic Treaty System emphasize that since the continent of Antarctica must be used and managed for the benefit of and in the interest of everyone, and all nations should participate in the decision-making process affecting it, living and non-living resources of this continent should be considered the *common heritage of mankind.* They draw attention to the fact that the principle of the *common heritage of mankind* was clearly the prime motivating factor in the conclusion in the recent past of such important agreements as the Convention on the Law of the Sea and the Treaty on Principles Governing the Activities of States in the Exploration and Use of Outer Space, including the Moon and other Celestial Bodies. Statements were made that the realization of that principle had been one of the most important developments in contemporary international law which must be sustained. Therefore, any future agreement for the exploration and exploitation of the resources of Antarctica must be based on the principle of the *common heritage of mankind.*

The application of the concept of *common heritage of mankind*, in the view of its advocates, requires a completely different international administrative machinery than the current one posited by the Antarctic Treaty. The United Nations or an institution established by it, according to their position, is better suited than any other international institution to accomplish such a momentous undertaking.

Supporters of the *common heritage of mankind* concept consider that its application will result in the democratization of the existing situation in Antarctica because it will require the abolishment of the exclusive decision-making system there. They also believe that the declaration of Antarctica as a *common heritage of mankind* would resolve the hitherto nagging problem of sovereignty. Without a *common heritage of mankind* principle, territorial claims and counter-claims, in their view, could be frozen in Antarctica in perpetuity. If the United Nations were to administer Antarctica as a *common heritage of mankind*, any claims and counter-claims about sovereignty would automatically be discharged, stated one delegation.

Opponents to the Antarctic Treaty strongly object to the idea that a subscription to the Antarctic Treaty should be a pre-condition of participation in the negotiation on the mineral regime. They argue that, because of the discriminatory decision-making system of the Treaty, a just and reasonable minerals regime may not be negotiated within the framework of the Treaty. Therefore, negotiations of the Treaty Parties on the mineral regime should be suspended. As one delegation put it, the interests of all mankind cannot be preserved in a regime negotiated by a few. Since the exploitation of resources in Antarctica falls within the purview of international concern, it requires the participation of all states in determining the type of regime required to govern the activities related to Antarctic mineral resources, stated another delegation.

The Antarctic Treaty Parties take a quite opposite position on the issue of mineral resources.

They argue that the prerequisites for applying the *common heritage of mankind* concept are an international consensus that designated areas are beyond the limits of national jurisdiction and that they are not governed by an existing legal regime. In their view, while it is true of outer space and true of the deep sea-bed, it is not so in the case of Antarctica. They stress that a legal regime, a multilateral system of international regulation of activity in the form of the Antarctic Treaty System has existed there for a quarter of a century. It is also pointed out that unlike the deep sea-bed, which has never been considered as belonging to anyone, in Antarctica, territorial claims were made by several countries over a large part of this area. Even if those claims are not universally recognized, they constitute an essential element in the continent's legal regime, embodied in the Antarctic Treaty and other related instruments. According to the position stated, any attempt to compare the legal regime of Antarctica to that provided for the deep sea-bed by the Convention on the Law of the Sea would necessarily call into question the compromise achieved in 1959 and thus run the risk of reopening contentious issues of sovereignty, which by their very nature are likely to increase tensions in international relations.

For reasons mentioned above, the Antarctic Treaty Parties argue that it is not only legitimate but almost imperative to use the Antarctic Treaty as a basis for the regulation of possible mineral resource exploration and exploitation. In their view, negotiations among states with a common objective must start from a basis or a principle to which all parties agree and by which they are all bound, and the Antarctic Treaty provides the only cornerstone on which a workable and effective regime can be built.

The Antarctic Treaty Consultative Parties express their conviction that the negotiations on a minerals regime within the Treaty provide the only opportunity to prevent a possible future scramble for resources and to protect the fragile and unspoiled Antarctic environment.

The limited time given for this presentation does not allow for the in-depth description of all the arguments used by the two groups of states in defence of their positions during the four years of discussions at the United Nations. As was said, both sides prefer now to go to a vote rather than sacrifice their principled positions.

The question could be raised, of course, that if the positions of two groups of states are so far apart, why in the course of two consecutive years (1983 and 1984) was the General Assembly able to adopt resolutions on the question of Antarctica by consensus? Without going into details of these resolutions, analyses of the negotiating process which led to them, and of the different interpretations given to them by the parties concerned, the following answer could be given to this question. These resolutions were of a procedural nature. They never touched the matters of substance. Therefore, it could be said that we did not come to an end of consensus on the question of Antarctica at the United Nations. In effect a consensus has never really existed. Is it possible to achieve it in the future? Although chances for consensus look rather slim, one should always be optimistic.

J. Delbrück, Chairman:

Thank you. Now I ask *Mr. Hendry*.

I. Hendry:

I come to this subject as a newcomer, and although I have read about the debate concerning Antarctica in the UN I have not heard it at first hand before, so I have found it very interesting and enlightening to listen to the contributions this morning. It would be presumptuous of me, I think, to try to offer any legal or scientific remarks about what I heard. If I may say so, the presentation by *Ambassador Woolcott* seemed to me to be absolutely convincing as far as the pragmatic international political situation is concerned, and indeed, the international legal position is concerned. As regards *Ambassador Koroma*'s remarks, I would only say that it seems to me not correct to assert that the Antarctic Treaty Parties appropriated to themselves Antarctica with Articles IV and VI.

That was not the purpose at all, as *Mr. Maquieira* explained in the following presentation. It also seems to me unrealistic to draw a comparison between Antarctica and outer space, the moon or the deep sea-bed over which there have been no claims to sovereignty and no purported exercise of sovereignty, whereas in Antarctica there are ancient claims to sovereignty, ancient exercise and actual exercise of sovereignty. It makes one wonder, if the states, from one of which I come, were to be asked to give up those claims for some international regime, whether, for example, the states exercising sovereignty in the Sahara Desert or in the Himalayas or in Kashmir or in other inaccessible or remote places would be prepared to do the same.

Essentially, Mr. Chairman, this seems to me a political question much more than a legal question, and if I were a politician I think I would feel obliged to ask the ordinary person in the street what he would think about the proposition which I have just posed in perhaps a rather stark form. And if I were trying to explain it to him, I think I would say something like this: "Imagine that you live in a village and that far away from this village is a field, and it's difficult to get to that field, and it is expensive to get to that field, and ancestors of yours found that field, or part of it, and some of them died in trying to get there and in trying to work there; now you go and work in that field; and sometimes you go and camp in that field; it's a dangerous and cold place, and some of your friends also go and work there. From time to time you may argue about who owns parts of that field and you certainly believe that you do. And there are some others who are also active in that field, looking after the strange creatures that are there and seeing whether it's a useful place for the whole community. Moreover, those friends of yours get together with you, set aside their arguments about who owns the field and agree to cooperate together, working, and from time to time you all get together, drink together, and agree on how to manage the place. And then all of a sudden, along come some other people from the village and they say: 'Well, we have never actually been there, and we haven't really taken much interest in it, but we hear a whisper that there is something very interesting in that field and what we would like you to do is just to give it up so that we could all have it and share it together.' "

Now if I posed that sort of question in — inevitably — very simplified form to somebody in the United Kingdom and asked, "Do you think you should give up that field", the answer without hesitation would be "No," and with typical understatement it might be, "It does sound a bit of a cheek to me." I think if it were asked in Glasgow, for example, there would be a very much ruder answer, as there would in Sydney. I can imagine there would be an even ruder answer in Nashville,

Tennessee. But I think the same answer would come if it were asked of a villager in the Maldives, or Sierra Leone, or St. Kitts and Nevis, and I think if the programme here allowed us to go to the bars of Kiel, you would certainly get the same answer there. Thank you.

J. Delbrück, Chairman:

Thank you. We now go on with *Dr. Rajan*.

H. P. Rajan:

Thank you, *Professor Delbrück*. In my comment on the competence of the UN to challenge international treaties I would first of all try to reflect on the five major stages of development in international law, witnessed in this present century. The first and the longest stage, spread over fifty years, was confined to the development of the law of peace, to prevent war and international conflicts: hence, codification was directed towards that end only. The second stage, for about a decade or so, witnessed the development of the law of international institutions, but then the 'Sixties also witnessed another important development, namely the emergence of several newly independent nations with their demand to participate in all codification processes and their challenge to the existing traditional international law as being Eurocentric. The third stage witnessed a new era of international law, that is, international trade law, international economic law and the demand for a New International Economic Order. The fourth stage is rather a recent stage, where the demand is for law governing the new natural resources — be that the resources of the sea-bed, Antarctica or even of the moon. Interestingly enough, even as late as 1956 the International Law Commission had expressly stated that the exploitation of sea-bed resources beyond the continental shelf, then defined in terms of the 200 metres depth criteria, was not possible in the foreseeable future. The Antarctic Treaty of 1959 also possibly did not envisage any exploitation of Antarctic resources and that is probably the reason why the Treaty makes no reference to either living or non-living resources, except for a small clause on the conservation of the living resources.

We have now already stepped into the fifth stage of development, where the law has to take into account the highly sophisticated and rapid technological growth and scientific progress: international law of science and technology, if one may term it so, such as governs the geostationary objects, space regime, the new information and satellite communication systems, genetic engineering and more specifically, Antarctic research. Law in these areas is highly dependent on the nations and people who are directly concerned with this research. Law-making processes will be dependent on the imputs derived from these highly technical and scientific subjects — subjects that were unheard of, or even unthought of, during the framing of the UN Charter. The importance of the technical and scientific advice in the law-making process has already been discussed very ably by some of the previous speakers, and therefore I will not go into these details again.

The UN Charter, which was originally signed by 50 states, now represents more than triple that number and is undoubtedly the largest attribute of exercise of sovereignty. As the Under Secretary-General and Legal Counsel of the UN had pointed out, the entry into force of the UN Charter and the establishment of the ILC had settled, on the political plane, by the will of sovereign states, the question of convenience, usefulness and the measure of progressive development of international law and its codification. He went on to say that from that moment the progressive development and codification of international law organized and centralized in the UNO had an official diplomatic and formal character.

Article 13 (1) (a) of the UN Charter confers on the General Assembly the mandate to initiate studies and make recommendations for the purpose of promoting international cooperation in the political field, and encouraging the progressive development of international law and its codification. However, codification of international law is not confined to the work of the UN or the International Law Commission. Codification takes place outside the frame of the United Nations also, and it is in this context that the emphasis has to be on progressive development rather than on the codification of previously established principles. This is exactly where I would like to refer to the fifth stage of development, that I mentioned before, where the law has to take into account the highly complicated technological, scientific and specialized imputs. However, such codification has to be in conformity with certain basic tenets, the principles and purposes of the UN Charter. The UN will have the power to examine this, as the most representative organization of the world community, and, having been expressly entrusted with the task of codification and progressive development of international law has already codified the law relating to codification, that is, the Vienna Convention on the Law of Treaties.

It appears, however, that these aspects have already been taken into account by the Antarctic Treaty itself. The objective of the Treaty is to promote scientific research on the continent, without hindrance, and protect the environment from destruction through waste disposal, dumping, militarization or nuclearization. Although originally drafted by twelve states through confidential consultations, these states took care, in the Preamble, to state that the Treaty was in furtherance of the principles and purposes of the UN Charter; in Art. III (2) they expressly envisage cooperative working relations with the United Nations and with its specialized agencies. More importantly, the Treaty is open for accession to all members of the UN. In other words, to put it simply, the criteria for accession is envisaged as membership in the United Nations, (Article XIII). Furthermore, Article X provides that all Parties undertake to exert appropriate efforts consistent with the UN Charter. From this Article it is clear that the forum for any member of the Antarctic Treaty not satisfied with the functioning of the Treaty is the UN. Thus linkage between the Antarctic Treaty and the UN is very close-knit. The objective of the Treaty cannot be achieved without the imputs derived from the nations and persons who have long experience and direct concern with Antarctic matters. That objective of the Treaty is itself in furtherance of the principles and purposes of the UN. Thank you.

F. Orrego Vicuña:

I would also like to address the problems of legitimacy of the UN to challenge international treaties and derive from this argument some practical implications as to other problems that have been addressed by the speakers this morning. Firstly, there is no doubt that the UN General Assembly has the power under the Charter to discuss and examine any matter, virtually everything which has some bearance on the general powers of the Organization, which is so comprehensive that there is virtually nothing left outside. But it is one thing to recognize the general power of discussion and examination and another thing altogether to recognize a power to review, or enter into a discussion of challenging international agreements in force, particularly if they are to be regarded as valid treaties or agreements under international law.

Certainly, on this point I would not be prepared to recognize any role whatsoever of the UN, nor of its particular bodies. The argument is not new; it was already made in the UN General Assembly debate of 1983 and 1984 by *Mr. John Heap*. But I would say that it goes much further than that. You may recall Article 19 of the Covenant of the League of Nations, and particularly the problems which it gave rise to in practice. This was a problem that was particularly serious for my country, since some treaties to which Chile is a Party were challenged before the League of Nations. The argument, already made at that time, was that even if Article 19 gave some general power to revise international treaties, this did not amount to the possibility of going into such depth as to declare any such treaty void or null, or to undertake any major legal revision.

It was because of that background at the League of Nations that when the UN Charter was drafted changes were made precisely on this point, in order to deprive the new UN Organization from any power of revision or challenge, allowing only a very general examination of conditions related broadly to peace and security. This is not an academic discussion but a very practical one: if one concludes that the UN has the legitimacy to challenge international treaties in force, or valid treaties, then one could follow with the argument that it would be entitled to set up some sort of parallel treaty arrangement, or a treaty arrangement that would replace the one being challenged. But if, on the other hand, you conclude that no such power exists under the UN Charter, as I do, then the idea of the UN being able to develop alternative treaty arrangements would fall rather flatly.

Because of this I think that the approach that some countries have taken that the UN could be a forum entitled to develop parallel treaty arrangements to those under the Antarctic Treaty System, is a question that has to be addressed in this discussion. First, any such arrangement would have to be different from the Antarctic Treaty System, and hence a conflictive arrangement. This would not ensure efficiency, because as we have been commenting on and hearing this morning, the fact that the UN might undertake this task does not ensure that it will be done well, and to the contrary, the Antarctic Treaty record does give such an assurance. But on the other hand, one would have to bear in mind that whatever the alternative regime might introduce, it would certainly be introducing a factor that would amount to unsettling valid international agreements, and this is certainly not a function that one would recognize in the UN Charter or the General Assembly. Because of this argument, I think that the whole approach to this parallel arrangement would be very questionable on legal grounds, not only because of its lack of legitimacy but also because it would have an underlying assumption, with which I am not satisfied, and which is: who gave the title for Antarctica to the United Nations, or for any such matter that would come under the treaty arrangement coming up which would replace, in this example, the Antarctic Treaty System? This, I think, is a problem that one cannot find neither in the Charter nor in the practice under the Charter. So it amounts to a situation where those countries that have been arguing in favour of a parallel treaty arrangement undertaken under the United Nations in fact are putting themselves in a position very similar to that which they themselves criticize where other countries set up their own parallel legal arrangements, in matters such as the seabed, for example. This is, in itself, a contradiction taking place in the UN General Assembly, depending on what subject is being addressed.

Finally, I would like to mention that there is also a question of what is the underlying assumption from the point-of-view of the value to be assigned to any such exercise. Is it a question of representation of humanity and hence a discussion on *common heritage*, distribution of resources and so on, or is it a question of an entirely different historical origin, including questions of sovereignty? I think that in fact we are faced here with two different approaches: historically, Antarctica emerged as a subject, as a region, as an activity, much earlier than any such question of representation of humanity arose, and that explains why it was accompanied by expressions of sovereignty. That being so, it is difficult to transform any such arrangement into some other kind of exercise, which will be related to questions of *common heritage*, of representation, of humanity and the like. But even if one were to accept that the question of representation of humanity was a real value that has to be addressed, or the issue that has to be discussed or answered, I would say that there are two approaches. The first is a quantitative approach, and it involves the question of whether the UN represents humanity in view of the number of countries participating therein. We have heard figures like ninety or so countries voting in favour of a set of resolutions. Numbers of course are not decisive in international law, but even from the point-of-view of numbers, the Antarctic Treaty System appears quite impressive on a global level and particularly outstanding at the regional level. The number of countries participating in the Antarctic Treaty System, looked at either as a global arrangement or a regional arrangement, is quite an important one, very much more so if it is regarded as a regional arrangement.

But that is one part of the answer; the second part is not quantitative but qualitative, and here I borrow an argument from *Quigg*: is it just a question of quantities or a question of quality? And from that point-of-view: what is the position of the Antarctic Treaty System to represent humanity as a whole, if that were the exercise we are engaged in? He mentions a figure that is quite impressive: the Antarctic Treaty System as it is composed today represents 3 billion out of 4 billion inhabitants of the world. From this point-of-view it is also quite interesting to note that legitimacy is not entirely beyond the Antarctic Treaty System, and certainly does not lie outside the Antarctic Treaty System. Because of all these arguments linked to the question of legitimacy, my final suggestion is that the Antarctic Treaty System, in itself, is perfectly viable and legitimate for undertaking the regulation of Antarctica and meeting the needs that have been associated with such development, and that no parallel treaty arrangement could be done unless the Antarctic Treaty Parties themselves would agree to such arrangements which, as we have heard, is certainly not the case.

J. Delbrück, Chairman:

Thank you very much. Though I am afraid that I may repeat some of the arguments that have been raised, I would like to highlight a few aspects of the problem involved here. The first one relates to the competence of the UN to deal with Antarctica. I am fully in agreement with those who maintain that as the UN is an international organization of rather comprehensive competences it is hard to make a case that the General Assembly could not concern itself with the problem of Antarctica in general terms. Article 10, I think, is so broad in scope that it would be hard to make a legal argument that the UN was not legally able to deal with Antarctica. On the other hand, I think it has been ably demonstrated here on the panel, and also during this morning's contributions, that the UN is not empowered — as was the League of Nations according to Article 19 of the Covenant — to deal with specific revisions of treaties that might be considered to endanger international peace and security. There is no clause in the Charter comparable to Article 19 of the League of Nations Covenant, Article 14 of the Charter being much more limited in scope. I think this is a very important distinction, that has to be made, and therefore it becomes more of a political question of how far and in what direction the UN concern in Antarctica should or could lead.

Second, I think that most of the arguments that have been brought forward against the present regime, and for a broader participation of the international community in Antarctica, are based on the principle of *equality of states* and certainly in substance on the principle of *common heritage of mankind*. I will be very short on these two issues. First, as to *common heritage of mankind*: even if we accept that this principle is now part of international law — at least, as we have heard, part of certain treaties, we may not consider this principle to be one of overriding legal validity, that is, *jus cogens*. It is hard to make the case that *common heritage of mankind* has already entered the international body of customary law in such a way that it covers all fields. It is, so far, probably limited to specific sectors of the international law system, but certainly it would be very much harder to prove that *common heritage* has already entered the high realm of *jus cogens*, thus overriding existing legal regimes. That leaves us with the question of whether *common heritage of mankind* should be extended to Antarctica, which could then only be done by treaty agreement. As we have heard, this is — politically — probably not a viable course.

As to the *equality of states* argument, the international practice is rather inconsistent. On the one hand, of course, the *equality of states* is a principle which is formally observed; almost every international organization, except for very few, is based on the *one state — one vote* principle, and all subjects of international law are equal before the law in the sense that each state is entitled, as a subject of international law, to rights and duties under international law as it exists. But on the other hand there is a substantive aspect to it. We are certainly faced with a tremendously heterogeneous body of law where states are quite unequal in terms of the rights and duties they undertake under specific international legal instruments. The criteria by which these different burdens, obligations and rights, are attributed to states are taken from specific abilities, specific geographic situations, specific responsibilities, and the ensuing inequality in rights and duties has never been challenged with a view to the principle of the *equality of states*. Thus, there is no compelling reason to argue that the *equality of states* obliges the international community to enforce the principle of *equality of states* at all times, in all fields of individual life. That would be rather burdensome for some states, I would assume. So, there is very little legal ground to argue that the Antarctic regime is in violation of the principle of *equality of states*. Thus, we are left again with political considerations, whether it is more appropriate to bring Antarctica into the United Nations forum, to be dealt with there, or whether we should stick to the regime as it has developed, and as I believe, has worked well.

There are two further points that I would like to raise in this context. One is, and it has already been mentioned, that the Antarctic regime dates back to a time when considerations of *common heritage of mankind* and other recent developments in the international legal community were not yet thought of. We have, in fact, claims to territory in this area, and therefore we would be very hard put to replace the present regime, neglecting these facts as they have developed. I like to be provocative on this point: if we ask the Claimant states, the Consultative states, not being Claimant states, to give up their present position, where would the incentive for these states to carry on the responsibilities they have undertaken in recent years actually be — as, first of all, the development of Antarctica is costly, it is technologically difficult, to say the least, and it is economically risky. Who else but those, who bear the material interests from history in this area, could be induced to undertake all these burdens if we ask them to give up what has developed so far and, to say it again, has worked well?

Second, the most serious issue in this whole problem is, I think, the reluctance of the Treaty Parties to hand over the Antarctic problems to the UN, which is due to the fact that this Organization has proven to be rather ineffective in the eyes of many Member-States because of an "overpoliticization," as it is called. This has led the organized international community to decide serious issues in a rather inconsistent manner. On the one hand, we are advised that, for instance, sovereign claims, territorial jurisdiction, *etc.*, are more-or-less outdated concepts We should approach things internationally. As an example, the law of the sea is especially pointed out. Well, if you look at the Law of the

Sea Convention, indeed, we find in one part the *common heritage of mankind* accepted, implying thereby an international approach. But on the other hand, in the same Convention we have experienced the expansion of territorial jurisdiction into the sea, in an unprecedented manner. So, there is at least a two-way development in this area, and one may well ask why one should be engaged with one way only, in order to solve a problem which, I think, has been taken care of pretty well in the past.

Furthermore, we are facing a development in the UN whereby even decisions on rather "technical," or on very specific subject matters, are increasingly burdened with general concerns of all UN members or groups of members. Thus, for instance, a specific convention, like the Convention on the Elimination of All Forms of Discrimination against Women, is linked to the solution of the complex problem of disarmament. If the problem of Antarctica becomes thrown into the hands of the UN General Assembly, I am afraid that we may be facing a similar problem of overloading the issues with all the great concerns of the international community — legitimate though they may be, thus impeding the necessary progress on the very urgent and pressing problems which were discussed during this Conference and many times before. This may sound very provocative, but I think I was to state my concerns quite frankly. Thank you. The session is adjourned.

The Legitimacy of Concluding an Antarctic Minerals Resources Regime among the Antarctic Treaty Parties

*Finn Sollie**

I. Introductory Remarks

First of all, let me express some surprise that I am here as a participant at Antarctic Challenge III, and that I shall speak on the legitimacy of concluding an agreement amongst the Parties to the Antarctic Treaty to establish a regime on mineral resources. It was not my intention to attend the Symposium this year and, then, having accepted an invitation to sit on one of the panels, I was cajoled into replacing a speaker who was unexpectedly prevented from coming. This means that I have not had the time to prepare a paper for presentation. Now, that may prove to be an advantage, provided of course, that you are willing to share with me a somewhat philosophical attitude to the problems before us.

As for myself, I have had ample opportunity this last night to be philosophical about the Symposium and about my role in it. As some of you will know, I was left behind in Bremerhaven last night when the bus returned from our visit at the Alfred Wegener Institute. My most practical lesson so far from Antarctic Challenge III, is that if you want to go from Bremerhaven to Kiel after 9 p. m. and you depend on public transportation, the trip will take some thirteen hours. Hours are long at night, when you are quite alone in a deserted station, waiting for some train to come your way. The experience is bound to make you philosophical and I shudder to think what would have happened if I had been left out in the cold after visiting some station in Antarctica. Be that a lesson to those who believe in easy trips and free rides for their Antarctic involvement!

At this stage, as an additional remark to introduce my subject of the legitimacy of the Antarctic minerals regime, I should like to introduce into the record of this meeting the name of a person who deserves to be remembered both for his commitment to legitimacy in international relations and for his role in starting the long and slow process toward establishing a minerals regime for Antarctica. He was *Dr. Edvard Hambro*,

* *Finn Sollie*, Director, The Northern Perspectives Group, Oslo, Norway.

and he chaired the Norwegian delegation to the Seventh Consultative Meeting in Wellington (1972), when the subject "Antarctic Resources — Effects of Mineral Exploration" was included for the first time on the agenda for consultation amongst the parties.

It may seem odd today that Norway, which claims a large territory in Antarctica, should have been so involved at that time in the effort to start open discussions of the problem of mineral exploration in Antarctica, in a forum where states opposing such claims were equal participants. It was the skill and foresight of scientific advisers such as *Dr. Tore Gjelsvik* — another name to remember in this context — that taught those of us who were concerned with Antarctic politics about the need to resolve controversial legal issues if the Antarctic Treaty regime were to continue to function effectively and securely so that Antarctica, as the Treaty preamble states, "shall not become the scene or object of international discord."

Eddi Hambro, master diplomat and legal expert that he was, helped the process by making his own government understand the need for exploratory action, to test the ability of the Antarctic Treaty System to adapt to new requirements. He then moved on, with skill and humour, to convince hesitant colleagues at the Seventh Consultative Meeting that it was necessary to take the important first step by agreeing to "Recommend to their Governments that the subject 'Antarctic Resources — Effects of Mineral Exploration' be carefully studied and included on the Agenda of the Eighth Consultative Meeting" (Recommendation VII-6). Mentioning one should not make us forget that many helped start the process, in long nights of discussion, including *Dr. John Heap* who is present here, and who is still active in the Consultative procedure. He was the master draftsman, who had the main responsibility for finding the right wording for that carefully written first Recommendation — and of many to follow.

Mentioning *Eddi Hambro*, I cannot help but recall his version of the story of the visit to the South Pole by the Heads of Delegation after the Wellington Meeting. They were flown down in a US C-130 for a call at the Scott-Amundsen Base. Some time later, I received a post card sent by *Eddi* from the Pole and telling the whole story in a few laconic words, saying: "Dear Finn — It was a long trip for a lousy lunch. Best wishes, Eddi." In the present context, we might see a comment here on Antarctic resources as well, intended for starry-eyed optimists, who believe in instant riches from sharing a *common heritage* in Antarctica. It is certainly true that after the adaption of the minerals regime we still have a long way to go before actual exploitation of resources can begin, and it is most likely that the reward, as a return on investment, may prove to be a meager meal.

II. Approaches to the Problem

Turning to the subject before us, to the question about the legality of concluding an Antarctic mineral resources regime among the Parties to the Antarctic Treaty, I note that earlier speakers have commented quite extensively and lucidly on the legal basis for such an action within the Treaty System. Others have reminded us that the minerals question will be seen in different light from different directions, depending on the basic attitudes, values and priorities of the observer. This makes my task simpler, by relieving me of the need for developing a new set of references, and it allows me the privilege of commenting on the basis of established categories and known approaches.

First, we have been told, there is the approach of the institutionalists, who base their thinking on the fact that an Antarctic Treaty was established in 1959 and who see authority and justification for a minerals regime in the provisions and procedures of the Treaty. To them, the Treaty is indeed a fundamental law and constitution for Antarctica and, consequently, a minerals regime can only be established within the Treaty System, and must be built as an extension of the treaty structure.

As a second category, we have the universalists, who base their thinking on the concept of universal justice and equality and claim that Antarctica is a *common heritage* that will require a new regime and a system different than the present Treaty to manage Antarctic problems. To them, past history and prior operations do not constitute a rightful basis for territorial claims or for joint agreements and arrangements made by the fortunate few states that could engage in Antarctic activities at an earlier stage. Under this approach, the right of new parties to join the Treaty is not a remedy, for acceding parties have not had an opportunity to define the principles of the Antarctic Treaty and to develop the practices of the Treaty System. They may not be bound by rules they did not make and, since most of them lack resources of their own for full participation in the Treaty System, they cannot be forced to submit to rules and procedures dictated by past practice. Hence, an entirely new system must be established to incorporate the principle of *common right* and *universal justice*.

Finally, we have the more pragmatic approach of the evolutionists, who look for practical solutions to problems that arise in the Antarctic development, including those resulting from pressure to explore and to exploit Antarctic minerals. My remarks here will reflect a pragmatic attitude, but are based also on a fundamental belief in principle. Quite frankly, I see continued operation of the Antarctic Treaty as an essential requisite for maintaining the ideals of peace, law and orderly development in Antarctica.

III. Law and Change

The question before us is whether the Parties to the Antarctic Treaty have a right to set up a mineral resources regime for Antarctica. It seems a simple question, and in principle only two answers are possible: either the Parties do have a right to conclude between themselves an agreement to establish an operating regime, with all the provisions and the apparatus required for effective control and regulation of the exploration and exploitation of mineral resources in Antarctica, or they do not have that right. But is the question really so simple? Can a distinction be made between right and wrong in simple and absolute terms, without any regard for time and circumstance, or should we discriminate between that which is desirable now and that which was possible at an earlier stage, and qualify response and judgment accordingly?

In my opinion, it is important to be aware that the debate over the Antarctic Treaty, about its legality and the right of the Parties to take upon themselves the task of adopting a minerals regime, is not merely or even primarily a question about the Antarctic Treaty. In the final analysis the question is about the essential principles of the international rule of law. It is a complex question involving fundamental attitudes about what you accept and respect, of what you want and what you will stand by. In the end, it is a question about change and development in international law and about revolutionary methods for radical change or stable growth in an orderly system.

IV. Law in the Making

It will come as no surprise to listeners and readers that I am a firm believer in the legal basis and the binding quality of the Antarctic Treaty. On the other hand, I must admit that when we took the first initiative in 1972 to move the Consultative Parties toward a free and open discussion amongst themselves of problems relating to mineral exploration and potential exploitation of mineral resources in the Treaty area, the question of legality, or legitimacy and basis in the Treaty for a future minerals regime, was not foremost in my mind.

At that time, some of the Consultative Parties were politically opposed to discussing the minerals problem, and some argued that the subject should be avoided, because the Treaty did not specifically mention minerals or other "economic" issues as "matters of common interest" for joint consultation. Some even claimed that by deliberately excluding economic matters from the text of the Treaty in 1959, in order to avoid a split on the sovereignty issue, the Signatory Parties had tacitly accepted that resource development would remain a prerogative of sovereignty in Antarctica. Non-claimant states, of course, could not accept this particular argument, and most Claimant states had no difficulty in accepting that the minerals problem was one of the "matters of common interest pertaining to Antarctica" that could be included in the Consultative procedure provided for in the Treaty (Art. IX, para. 1).

I cannot speak for the others who took part in the early discussion of Antarctic minerals, but I doubt that any of them had given very serious thought to the question of the legitimacy of a future minerals regime. I for one, had no sense or feeling of what the end result of the process might be, and I doubt that any one else who moved for careful study of the effects of mineral exploration (Recommendation VII-6) had a clear conception of the form and content of any future decision in the matter. That, indeed, would be a question to consider in the process, a matter for the Parties to decide when they had defined the problem and established a common ground for mutual understanding.

The important thing in 1959 when the Antarctic Treaty was negotiated, and in 1972 when the minerals problem was put on the agenda, was that all states with a proven interest in Antarctica were Parties to the Treaty and that the Treaty did provide a Consultative procedure to recommend "measures in furtherance of the principles and objectives of the Treaty" (Art. IX, para. 1). Thus, if the Parties agreed — and remember that agreement among them must be unanimous — the Consultative process could be used to develop new rules or regulations by any appropriate means chosen by the Parties to elaborate upon the Treaty. The main point was that the measures be "in furtherance of the principles and objectives of the Treaty." The truth of the matter is that by including the Consultative procedure in the Treaty, the Parties had in effect established a law-making procedure for Antarctica, where all Parties with an active interest and not just the original signatories, could participate. If the need be there, new law should appear.

Early opposition amongst the Parties to discussing economic matters disappeared when the need for a minerals regime became apparent to all. The point here is that early opposition to act on minerals — or on any other economic matter — was political rather than legal in nature. All the Parties agree that there is a legal basis for negotiating a minerals regime. The fact negotiations began merely marked the political need to solve the minerals problem.

V. Need as Basis for Action

The essential feeling behind the initiative for, and the negotiation of, the Antarctic minerals regime which is now emerging quite simply was one of need. Negotiation of the regime must be seen as a historical process that started in response to signals that mineral exploration might become feasible in Antarctica and in reaction to dangers that would evolve if the Consultative Parties did not act on the question before it was too late. Such danger signals were not apparent when the Treaty was negotiated in 1958—59, but could be discerned in the early 1970s when consultations on minerals began.

"Too late" in this context would be whenever any entity — be that a Party to the Treaty or another state, or a commercial company operating from any country — saw fit to start exploration with clear commercial intent and in such a manner that it could prove detrimental to the continued functioning of the Treaty System, or to the claimed rights and interests of any state, or to the environment, and thus force states to react against the incursion. It also would be "too late" if any state, or states, began to act legally or politically on the assumption that exploration might be imminent, and began to secure their national interest with policies which other parties would deem to be contrary to the agreed principles and objectives of the Antarctic Treaty, *e. g.*, by legislation to ascertain national control and rights in claimed territory or, conversely, to facilitate exploration in areas claimed by other states.

Such policies would lead automatically to dispute and controversy over sovereignty, and could destroy the still fragile political basis for the Antarctic Treaty that had been found in the agreement to freeze all disputes over sovereignty by means of the special *status quo* clauses on claims in the Treaty's Art. IV. Reopening the sovereignty issue could still destroy the Treaty and erase the results of its operation. Thus, there was a need to act to avoid a development where Antarctica could become the scene or object of international discord.

The fundamental purpose of the Treaty had been defined as making sure that "Antarctica shall continue for ever to be used exclusively for peaceful purposes and shall not become the scene or object of international discord" (Treaty Preamble). As a participant in the events that occurred when Antarctic minerals were put on the agenda for Treaty consultations, and as an observer of the negotiations during the next several years, I can honestly say that preservation of the Treaty was the primary concern of those who initiated the move to deal with the minerals problem in the Consultative process under the Treaty.

Such action had not been necessary before, or even possible. At the time when the Antarctic Treaty was being negotiated, mineral exploration still was quite improbable in Antarctica and, equally important, the attitude of the parties to international cooperation in Antarctica had not yet matured to a point where it was politically possible to broach that sensitive issue, without serious risk of total breakdown in the Treaty System.

In 1958—59, the fundamental need had been to secure continuation of the highly successful scientific cooperation which scientists had organized for themselves in Antarctica during the International Geophysical Year (IGY). In the preceding decade, governments had failed to solve the broad political problems and to agree on the legal status of Antarctica, and the scientists solved their pressing need for freedom of scientific investigation, and international cooperation to that end, by an informal gentlemen's agreement that their research and operations in Antarctica during the IGY should neither interfere with, nor be hindered by, political considerations — including disagreement between states on the status of territorial claims and counterclaims. By means of that simple device, the scientists were able to carry out their programmes for research in Antarctic during the IGY as if political disagreements and legal disputes did not exist.

While the scientists' agreement, as "gentlemen," proved sufficient to allow full freedom for research and optimum international cooperation during the IGY, it could not provide a permanent basis for free scientific inquiry in any and all parts of Antarctica without political hindrance and without long-term political effects. After all, territorial claims in many cases, including that of Norway, had been supported by reference to discovery, exploration and mapping of the area. Permanent freedom of scientific investigation and arrangements for international cooperation in Antarctic science could only be provided by governments with sufficient interest in Antarctica to become involved.

The Washington Conference and the Antarctic Treaty came as a well-considered response to needs that were clearly identified at that time, and the Treaty went as far as it was necessary to go at that time. This is exacly what is happening now, with regard to mineral resources. This is indeed a key point in the functioning of the Treaty System: it operates on the basis of joint understanding of needs as they arise and must be understood and judged in the context of the situation at that time in history.

VI. From Science to Resources

As long as scientific research — some would say basic science — was the predominant activity in Antarctica, the Treaty System could operate quite effectively without concern for commercial activities. Traditional commercial operations at sea could continue under standard rules of international law (navigation and fishing beyond territorial waters) or under established international regulations (whaling), but when new regulations were required within the Treaty area, the Consultative Parties were forced to act on the basis of need and of common interest. This occurred in the case of sealing, where a separate convention was negotiated for the conservation of Antarctic seals, and in the case of other marine living resources, where another separate convention for conservation of rescources was adopted.

Mineral resources are a different matter altogether, in that they can only be exploited in the fixed locations were they are found. Historically, such fixed locations are found on land and, as we know, land is subject to occupation by states, and establishment of territorial sovereignty and national jurisdiction. With modern technology offshore mineral resources as well may be exploited, and international law has solved the legal problem of *in situ* control in areas beyond traditional territorial sovereignty, by giving coastal states exclusive national jurisdiction with regard to resources on the continental shelf beyond their territorial waters. I shall not go into any detail, but it is worth remembering that the Continental Shelf Convention had been completed (1958) when the Antarctic Treaty was negotiated (1959) and, we might add, that the Antarctic Treaty had long been in force when the new Law of the Sea Convention, with its international deep sea-bed regime, based on the *common heritage principle*, was adopted (1982).

The point to be made here is that commercial exploration and exploitation of mineral resources in Antarctica, on land and on the continental shelf, will come as a result of prior scientific exploration that has been carried out first by individual states (in some cases with the result that those states claimed territorial rights), and then under agreed principles written into the Antarctic Treaty. At the outset it was felt that scientific investigation in Antarctica was primarily, if not exclusively, a matter of pure science. However, there is no simple or easy distinction between basic research and research for purposes of commercial exploration. By 1970 it appeared that economic and technical progress had reached a point where industrialists looked to even the most inhospitable and distant parts of the world for resources, and that scientific exploration had reached a point where Antarctica might attract commercial interests.

With hindsight, it is easy to see that belief in the mineral resource potential has been a major motivating force behind the growing interest in Antarctica in recent years. We can also see that research has become much more resource-oriented than before. It is true that part of the reason for this is that scientists often cleverly use the commercial temptation inherent in the idea of resources to attract funds for their research, but it is also true that governments and support agencies have an eye for resource potentials, and are willing and sometimes eager to secure access to potential benefits. It is also true that in the last few years a large number of states have acceded to the Antarctic Treaty and that many have qualified for the status of Consultative Party by conducting substantial activity. There is hardly any doubt that belief in the economic potential is a prime motive for this sudden urge to join a Treaty System that used to be regarded as an exclusive little club, although it has always been open to new members. It is interesting also to note that the argument for converting Antarctica into a *common heritage*, to be administered by the United Nations, is based on the premise that Antarctic resources are there to be exploited.

VII. Attitudes

In view of these developments, it seems odd — and feels a bit nostalgic — to remember that the Consultative Parties were hesitant in 1972 to begin discussion of the minerals problem. To help start the process, a private meeting was organized in Oslo by an organization which I happened to direct at that time (The Fridtjof Nansen Foundation). The meeting had separate working groups for economic and technical questions and for political and legal issues, and they began the study of the subject of Antarctic resources "in all its aspects in relation to the Treaty" which the next Consultative Meeting called for (Oslo 1975, Recommendation VIII-14). Since then, the discussion has continued within the Treaty System in a slow but deliberate move to reach common agreement on a minerals regime.

Of course the Parties look after their own interests in these consultations, but they work also to develop an effective minerals regime that will serve the joint interest of all Parties to the Tretay. The Treaty is the common denominator for all Parties alike, Signatories as well as Acceding Parties, and the unifying force between them is an obligation — and a desire — to preserve and promote the principles and objectives of the Treaty. While hesitant at first, the Parties now are determined to establish a minerals regime and to complete the job as part of the operation of the Treaty System.

Opposition to negotiating a minerals regime within the Treaty System comes from different quarters: on the one hand, those who claim Antarctica as the *common heritage of mankind* and, on the other hand, the idealistic environmentalists, who want to protect Antarctica as a nature reserve. The two groups appear to join forces and even coalesce in their opposition to the Treaty, but their approaches to the minerals problem are different and their goals are opposite. The fundamental purpose of the *common heritage* group is to get a share of benefits from expected resources and imagined riches in Antarctica, and the basic idea of the environmentalists is to avoid detection of those resources and to prevent their development. If harmony under the Treaty is not preserved, conflict will arise between its opponents.

VIII. Legality

To return now to the legality question: why is it that the Parties to the Antarctic Treaty can claim a right to negotiate, between themselves and with no outside participation, a special regime for minerals in Antarctica? And why will I, a declared pragmatist and in some respects an idealist, support their claim in the face of collective opposition from universalists who speak partly on behalf of an otherwise silent majority of states, and partly on behalf of the globe's most vulnerable environment? All the relevant points have been made by other speakers and are discussed at length in various papers, at this Symposium and elsewhere, but some points bear repeating in the present context.

First of all, and quite obviously, there is the fact of the existence of the Antarctic Treaty. It is a valid international treaty that has been in force for more than twenty-five years. It was negotiated in orderly fashion and agreed to by sovereign states and duly ratified and registered. As such, it cannot be merely brushed aside, but there are procedures for amending it, as well as a Consultative procedure that can be used as a type of international legislative process to adopt supplementary provisions. Most important of all, the Treaty works, and there is no doubt that it has provided a high degree of international law and order coupled with an unusual degree of freedom and equality in access, in all relevant operations and activities and, of course, in the opportunity to join the Treaty. In fact, the Treaty is widely hailed as a model of international cooperation.

IX. Representation

Moreover, while it is true that the Treaty was negotiated by a relatively small number of states, it is equally true that all states that had an active interest in Antarctica at that time took part in the negotiations. They presented a unique cross-section of states, from the great powers of the time to the very small, from opposite alliances and from the neutral group, from the quite rich to the quite poor. It was a motley group of states, but they all carried with them solid knowledge and experience from Antarctic operations and the highest degree of competence in Antarctic affairs. If there is such a thing as the right constituency for representation in international politics, the Treaty Signatories were it.

It is still claimed by some that the Antarctic Treaty is exclusive and that participation is reserved for the fortunate rich and developed countries. This was not true when the Treaty was negotiated and it is not true today. Accession to the Treaty is open to all states, and any state that is willing to pay the price of necessary expertise, by "conducting substantial research activity there" (Article IX, 2) is entitled to full participation (and not only observer status) in Consultative Meetings and in decisions about Antarctica's future.

The demonstrated interest requirement is sometimes attacked as a particularly insidious feature of the Treaty and a clever trick to maintain exclusivity in all essential aspects of cooperation. In fact, qualifications of many sorts are standard practice in many international organizations, and universality is not the rule even in universal organizations. The UN Security Council certainly has limited membership, partly on an arbitrary principle of status (for permanent members) and partly on the mixed basis of regional and political representation. Membership in the Council of the International Sea-Bed Authority, which is to be set up under the new Law of the Sea Convention as an executive body with wide discretionary powers in the management of our *common heritage* of deep sea-bed resources, is also similarly restricted, with a mix of regional and economic and other status qualifications for election to the steering body. Such practices are neither illegal nor immoral, but are often quite necessary to establish working systems and operational compromises.

X. Competence

The Antarctic Treaty is not unique in restricting participation in an international decision-making process, but it is unique in requiring a proof of interest and, through it, an earned degree of acquired experience and competence — the only condition for participation with full rights. As a pragmatist, I may be partial to systems that are designed to work with optimum efficiency between diverse and contradictory interests, but I do think that competence is as good a criterion as most of the other standards that are used regularly to define rights to participate in the management of international affairs. And I am firmly convinced that competence will continue to be a valid requirement for sensible decisions for and about Antarctica.

Comment: The Legitimacy of Negotiating an Antarctic Mineral Resources Convention among the Antarctic Treaty Parties

*Song Li**

Since 1981, negotiations aiming at the conclusion of an Antarctic Mineral Resources Regime, in the framework of the Antarctic Treaty, have been underway. After being included in the agenda of the General Assembly, some countries proposed that the Antarctic mineral resources issue should be discussed in the framework of the UN,[1] thus raising the problem of the legitimacy of concluding an Antarctic Mineral Resources Regime among the Treaty Parties.[2] For these purposes, the following problems are worthy of note.

I. Legal Bases of the Antarctic Treaty Parties to Negotiate an Antarctic Mineral Resources Regime

Many scholars have researched the models which the Antarctic mineral resources regime should take. Two of these are the "national solution" and the "condominium."[3] The national approach would grant sovereignty to those individual nations claiming rights to Antarctic sectors based on historical reasons. Thus, each Claimant state could more-or-less independently establish a regime governing the utilization of the mineral resources within its sector. This model bases the negotiation of the mineral resources on Antarctic territorial claims.

According to general principles of international law, national sovereignty has, so far as its economic aspect is concerned, been expressed in particular in the permanent sovereignty of a state over its natural resources. Nevertheless, it is contentious whether the claims to Ant-

---

* Ms. *Song Li*, Deputy Division Chief, Department of Treaty and Law, Ministry of Foreign Affairs, Beijing. The opinions expressed in this volume are the personal views of their authors only.

1 "Question of Antarctica", Study requested under GA Res. 38/77, Report of the Secretary-General, UN Doc. A/39/583, Part I, para. 273, 64.

2 *Op. cit.*, para. 151, 36.

3 *Rüdiger Wolfrum*, The Use of Antarctic Non-Living Resources: The Search for a Trustee?, in: *R. Wolfrum* (ed.), Antarctic Challenge, Berlin 1984, 143—163 (143—144).

arctic territory constitute sovereign rights. As indicated correctly in the report of the UN Secretary-General, "the major political difficulty faced from the very beginning by the claimant States was that other States, in particular those active in the area, refused to recognize those claims."[4] Nationals of some Claimant states even expressed the view that the claims previously put forward by the seven Claimant countries could hardly be used as a basis for asserting rights.[5]

Differences on the issue of sovereignty have not disappeared with the signing of the Antarctic Treaty.[6] So, the contentious sovereign claims could hardly be used as a legal basis for negotiating the mineral resources regime without giving rise to dispute. One might think that the Antarctic Treaty does not prohibit the territorial claims. Article IV of the Treaty stipulates: "Nothing contained in the present Treaty shall be interpreted as . . . prejudicing the position of any Contracting Party as regards its recognition or non-recognition of any other State's right of or claim or basis of claim to territorial sovereignty in Antarctica." The Treaty permits both Claimant states to maintain their position of sovereign claims, and Non-claimant states to deny the sovereign claims to Antarctica. This is the compromise between the two groups of State Parties holding different positions.

This very compromise provides the State Parties to the Treaty the opportunity to cooperate on the contentious continent. To base the negotiation of the mineral resources regime of a contentious continent only on the position of one group of Parties will no doubt prejudice the balance established by the Treaty and the Treaty itself. Moreover, if the negotiations among the State Parties of the Treaty were to be based on the sovereign rights claimed by some State Parties, is it not tantamount to saying that only those which have claims are entitled to negotiate the mineral resources regime? If so, with 15 % of the Antarctic continent still left unclaimed, should we negotiate after states have claimed sovereignty to this unclaimed sector? If the newly-asserted claims did overlap the old ones, should we negotiate the mineral resources after the ownership has been resolved? The force of the Treaty will be no doubt challenged. Antarctica will go back to the situation of contradiction and disputes existing before the conclusion of the Treaty. Then, the interests of all mankind, mentioned both in the Antarctic Treaty and the draft of the mineral resources convention, would be defeated. For that reason, the claims to Antarctica could

---

[4] "Question of Antarctica" (note 1), para. 25, 16.

[5] *Evan Luard*, Who Owns the Antarctic?, in: Foreign Affairs 62 (1984), 1175—1193 (1187).

[6] "Question of Antarctica" (note 1), para. 57, 20.

not be made the legal bases of the negotiation on the Antarctic mineral resources regime.

The condominium model also poses problems. The Consultative Parties would make a statement to the effect that they would, as a collective cooperative body, assert sovereignty over the region and that they would negotiate the mineral resources regime by virtue of their collective sovereignty. In the view of some states, this tentative idea is feasible. However, it is difficult to realize in the short term, because to acknowledge condominium is tantamount to denying the existing claims. So, it will produce the same legal effect as the acknowledgement of the sovereign right of some states, and that is contrary to the provisions of Article IV of the Antarctic Treaty, *i. e.*, neither recognition nor non-recognition of the claims to Antarctica. Condominium may be one of the tentative choices of determining the legal status of Antarctica. Nevertheless, it can not be regarded as constituting a legal basis of negotiating the Antarctic mineral resources regime.

Then, what can be the legal bases of the mineral resources negotiation? The Antarctic Treaty provides the best choice. The practice since the signature of the Treaty of 1959 shows that the purposes and principles of the Treaty are good. They facilitate the use of Antarctica for peaceful purposes, prohibit military activities including the prohibition of any nuclear explosions in Antarctica, freeze the claims to Antarctica, prevent Antarctica from becoming the scene of international discord, promote freedom of scientific investigation in Antarctica and international cooperation in scientific research and protection of its natural environment. When the UN International Law Commission was drafting the Convention of the Law of Treaties of 1969, *Sir Waldock*, Special Rapporteur, said: "Reference has already been made in paragraph 8 above to the Antarctic Treaty as an example of a treaty providing at once for demilitarization and for freedom of [the] user .... Although the parties evidently contemplated that States desiring to use Antarctica for scientific purposes would normally accede to the Treaty, their intention to create an objective legal régime for Antarctica seems clear, both from the Preamble to the Treaty and from the objective formulation of the basic principles of the régime in Articles 1 and 2."[7] The fact that *Waldock* considers the Antarctic Treaty as a treaty providing for an objective regime makes it clear that the purposes and principles of the Antarctic Treaty conform to the common interest of mankind. While some jurists do not share his notion of treaties providing for objective regimes, they do not deny that the provisions of demilitarization and

[7] Third Report on the Law of Treaties, by *Sir Humphrey Waldock*, Special Rapporteur, Yearbook of the International Law Commission 1964, vol. II, para. 11, 30.

freedom of use in the Antarctic Treaty have binding force for a third party, only that the basis of the obligation is international custom.

Could the Antarctic Treaty be the basis of negotiating the Antarctic mineral resources regime, although it does not determine the legal status of Antarctica?

Admittedly, the Treaty has not solved the question of ownership of Antarctica, and has not determined the legal status of Antarctica. But, in spite of that, the Treaty has established a legal regime to govern the peaceful use of the continent. The kernel of the regime is to freeze the territorial claims in the interest of mankind, to protect the Antarctic environment and to use Antarctica peacefully. Having undertaken a series of obligations as provided in the Treaty, the Treaty Parties should observe the Treaty provisions in their Antarctic activities. This provides some kind of legal assurance for negotiating and concluding a mineral resources regime which would be conducive to maintaining peace in Antarctica without prejudicing the Antarctic ecosystem.

The Antarctic Treaty does not deal with mineral resources, so could it be the basis for negotiating a mineral resources regime?

The fact that the Treaty does not deal with the mineral resources issue is not due to lack of any foresight.[8] In 1959, no urgent need was felt for negotiations on the mineral resource issue. Therefore, it was considered preferable to avoid them, for fear that disagreement on the sovereignty problem might halt the conclusion of the Treaty.[9]

In the late 'Sixties, as a result of the scarity of global resources, coupled with technological advancements in resource exploration and exploitation, private firms brought up once more the mineral resources issue.[10] Considering that the balance established by the Antarctic Treaty and the implementation of some of its principles, such as freedom of scientific research and protection of the environment, were threatened by possible unilateral commercial development of Antarctic mineral resources by some States[11], the ATCPs decided to convene a special meeting to negotiate the mineral resources issue. This makes it clear that it is not the ATCPs who brought up the mineral resource issue, only that they thought that the mineral issue raised by private firms might hinder the implementation of the Treaty's purposes and principles. The Treaty does not mention mineral resources, and the actual negotiation among the ATCPs on this issue is in fact an enlargement of the scope of the

[8] "Question of Antarctica" (note 1), para. 289, 66.
[9] *Op. cit.*, para. 290, 66.
[10] *Op. cit.*, para. 290, 67.
[11] *Op. cit.*, para. 289, 66.

application of the Treaty, that is, an amendment of the scope of application of the Treaty. Such an amendment is to make the operation of the Antarctic Treaty remain unaffected by the changed situation, so it is beneficial for the maintenance of the Treaty's purposes and principles.

The Antarctic Treaty is a treaty providing for an objective regime, the subject matter of which is Antarctica, instead of a contract treaty dealing with one or two issues concerning Antarctica. That is why the scope of the function of the Consultative Meetings provided for in Article IX is very broad. For example, para. 1 stipulates: "Representatives of the Contracting Parties . . . shall meet . . . for the purpose of exchanging information, consulting together on matters of common interest pertaining to Antarctica . . . ." The mineral resource issue is not isolated; it involves most of the Treaty's provisions, *e. g.*, demilitarization, peaceful uses, protection of Antarctic marine living resources, freezing the territorial claims to Antarctica, *etc.* The Antarctic issue should be approached as a whole. In spite of the fact that the Treaty does not have concrete provisions on the mineral resource issue, owing to the nature of the Treaty, its scope of application, the relationship between the scope of application and the mineral resource issue, and the mineral resource issue not excluded by the Treaty, the Antarctic Treaty can serve as a basis for negotiating the mineral resource regime among the Treaty Parties.

II. Origin of the Question of Legitimacy

The foregoing clearly shows that the objectives and principles of the Antarctic Treaty are consistent with the common interest of mankind, and the negotiation by the Contracting Parties on an Antarctic mineral resources regime on the basis of the Treaty is not violative of any general rules of international law. But why should the question of legitimacy of negotiation by the Contracting Parties on an Antarctic mineral resources regime be raised?

1. Influence of the Third UN Conference on the Law of the Sea and the UN Convention on the Law of the Sea

In the 1960's, not only was it possible to develop mineral resources on the wide continental shelf, it was also technically possible and economically attractive on the deep sea-bed beyond. Under such circumstances, in 1967, *Alvi Pardo*, permanent representative of Malta to the United Nations, put forward the concept of the *common heritage of mankind* and suggested that an international regulatory authority be established to ensure the implementation of this principle. The legal principle of the *common heritage of mankind* is a great inspiration to those initiating the discussion of the Antarctic question in the UN context.[12] The question of mineral resources was raised just after the adoption of the 1970 Declaration of Principles Governing the Sea-Bed and the Ocean Floor and the Subsoil Thereof, Beyond the Limits of National Jurisdiction[13], and consequently aroused public interest among the international community from the outset. At the close of the negotiation on the Convention on the Law of the Sea and after the signing of the Convention, the interest of the international community in the Antarctic question rose to its highest. During the negotiations on the Convention on the Law of the Sea, many delegates referred to the Antarctic question on a number of occasions. In 1975, in a speech before the General Assembly, *Shirley Amerasinghe*, who was then the President of the UN Conference on the Law of the Sea, stated:

> There are still areas of this planet where opportunities remain for constructive and peaceful co-operation on part of the international community for the common good of all rather than for the benefit of a few. Such an area is the Antarctic continent ....[14]

Later on, the question was asked whether any group of countries could confer upon itself the moral or legal right to self-elected determination or management of Antarctica.[15]

The 1982 Convention on the Law of the Sea has made great improvements and developments in comparison with the four Conventions on the law of the sea of 1958, the most conspicuous of which is the question of the international sea-bed. The Convention provides that the sea-bed and its subsoil, as well as the resources thereof, are the *common heritage of mankind* and that in order to give effect to that principle, an international sea-bed authority should be established, which is entitled, on behalf of mankind, to arrange, undertake and control exploration and development activities in the "Area." Unlike the principle of *freedom of the seas* in traditional international law, the international sea-bed regulatory regime advocated by *Alvi Pardo* primarily aims at ensuring common benefit in real terms, in addition to communion in principle. Second, such a new theory is supposed to prevent the deep sea-bed from being used for the armament race, ensure that the sea-bed be used for peaceful purposes, and establish an international sea-bed regulatory regime to prevent the Area from possible domination by or division among big ocean powers. Moreover, the establishment of the inter-

[12] *Op. cit.*, para. 276, 64.
[13] *Ibid.*
[14] *Op. cit.*, para. 277, 64.
[15] *Op. cit.*, para. 151, 37.

national sea-bed regime made it an international duty of states to strengthen international co-operation in sea-bed development.

It is obvious that the sea-bed regime to be established by the 1982 Convention on the Law of the Sea, based on the principle of *common heritage of mankind*, would safeguard the interests of all members of the international community, including both the developing and developed countries. Compared with the 1982 Convention, the draft convention on the Antarctic mineral resources, which only emphasizes the freedom of use and development by Contracting Parties and encourages international participation in Antarctic mineral resources activities without making it an international obligation of the Parties, is influenced to a greater extent by traditional international law. The method of distribution of profit from mineral resources activities, which has not been covered by the draft convention, is likely to be different from that provided in the 1982 LOS Convention. In such a situation, it is understandable that some countries, especially developing countries, contend that the principle of *common heritage of mankind* should be applied in the proposed Antarctic mineral resources regime.

2. *Inadequacies of the Antarctic Treaty System*

It is true that the Antarctic Treaty System (ATS) has made great contributions to the protection of the Antarctic environment and the facilitation of cooperation in respect of scientific investigations in Antarctica. At the same time, however, it should not be denied that there existed obvious inadequacies in the System. First, some provisions of the Antarctic Treaty have not been fully implemented. The Treaty is declared to be an open treaty, but only five countries acceded to it during the first ten years after its entry into force. This is partly due to the unavailability of information on Antarctic activities undertaken by Antarctic Treaty Parties. On the other hand, the ATCPs' reaction to external initiatives, *e. g.*, those made by international organizations in the UN system, had generally been negative and at times even hostile.[16] All this could not but reduce the open nature of the Treaty.

Second, the Treaty was not adapted to the new, changed conditions. For example, the negotiation on the Antarctic mineral resources used to be of a closed nature. It was closed both to countries outside the Antarctic Treaty and to those Antarctic Treaty Parties which are not ATCPs. Recently, the ATCPs have taken some measures to improve the operation of the Treaty, but these measures are not sufficient to clear up the distrust expressed by the Non-parties with respect to the Antarctic Treaty System. The Non-parties doubt whether the ATCPs could work

[16] *Wolfrum* (note 3), 160.

out, on the basis of the objectives and principles of the Antarctic Treaty, a legal regime regulating Antarctic mineral resources activities and acceptable to the majority of the international community. They are concerned that the future mineral resources convention would be favorable only to the few.

Inspired by the Third UN Conference on the Law of the Sea, which has successfully translated the theory of *common heritage of mankind* into the reality of a legal regime, and with distrust of the operation of the Antarctic Treaty System, some countries raised the question of legitimacy of negotiation by the Antarctic Treaty Parties on an Antarctic mineral resources convention.

III. How to Evaluate the Situation Faced by the Antarctic Treaty System

The situation faced by the Treaty System is very rare at least, if not unprecedented. The method of evaluating it will directly affect the solution.

1. The Right of Outsider States to Criticize the Treaty

As stated above, it is legitimate for the Antarctic Treaty Parties to negotiate the Antarctic mineral resources convention. However, is it tantamount to saying that the Treaty is perfect, that outsider states could not criticize the Treaty and that the Treaty Parties may refuse any comment from outside? To answer these questions, we must see whether outsider States have the right to criticize the Treaty.

First, eventual Antarctic mineral resource activities might produce adverse effects to the Antarctic environment, which might also adversely affect other parts of the world. An outsider state, as a member of the international community, may criticize the Treaty on the basis that the Antarctic mineral resources activities to be conducted by the Treaty Parties might produce indirect effects to the environment of the country outside the Treaty. Second, the legal instruments of the Treaty System are open: the third party may, as a potential State Party, make comments on or even criticize the Treaty. Third, as mentioned above, the Antarctic Treaty, as a treaty providing for an objective regime, has some binding force on the third party, *e. g.*, the third party has the obligation not to violate such provisions as prohibition of military activities, or protection of the Antarctic environment. On this basis, the third party may criticize the Treaty. As to the Antarctic Treaty itself, it is a successful treaty; nevertheless, there are still some defects and shortcomings. So it is even in the interest of the Treaty Parties that they should allow outsider states to criticize the Treaty, so as to strengthen and improve the Antarctic Treaty System.

2. *How to Evaluate the Situation*

Among the comments on the legitimacy of the Antarctic Treaty Parties to decide Antarctic affairs, perhaps the most representative one is whether any group of countries should confer upon itself the moral or legal right to self-elected determination or management of Antarctica.[17] The consequent conclusion is that from the point-of-view of the New International Economic Order, the principle of the *common heritage of mankind* should be applied to the region. Should a global regime for Antarctica based on the principle of the *common heritage of mankind* be established?[18]

We should believe that the "motivating impulse of the above-mentioned States is constructive, not destructive."[19] Their main purpose is to make the Treaty System more open and the Antarctic mineral resources convention secure optimum benefits for mankind as a whole and, in particular, for the developing countries.[20] The signing of the Convention on the Law of the Sea in 1982, makes them think that the best way to realize this purpose lies in the application of the principle of the *common heritage of mankind*. But, Antarctica is different from the deep sea-bed, which had been a legal vacuum; it already had an integrate legal system. The members of the international community have different evaluations with regard to the Treaty System, nevertheless, no one has until now denied that the Treaty is successful in promoting the purposes and principles of the Charter of the UN; ensuring that Antarctica be used for peaceful purposes only, keeping it free from militarization of any kind, including the presence of weapons; protecting the Antarctic environment and promoting international cooperation on scientific research in Antarctica. The problem is how to deal with the defects of the Antarctic Treaty. There have emerged three approaches in this respect:

a) The Antarctic Treaty is considered to be a successful example of international cooperation. The experience of more than 20 years has illustrated its merits and efficiency. So the Treaty Parties could, disregarding any opinion of other countries, continue to stick to the purposes and principles and the consistent practice, on the basis of which they could negotiate an Antarctic mineral resources convention.

b) In spite of the merits of the Antarctic Treaty in some aspects, "only mankind can look after its own interest, perhaps in a forum or

---

[17] "Question of Antarctica" (note 1), para. 151, 36.

[18] *Op. cit.*, para. 157, 37.

[19] *Mohamed Haron*, Antarctica and the United Nations — The Next Step?, in: *R. Wolfrum* (ed.), Antarctic Challenge II, Berlin 1986, 321—332 (321).

[20] "Question of Antarctica" (note 1), para. 278, 64.

through representatives that it designates."[21] The UN is the most universal representative of mankind as a whole, so the Antarctic mineral resource issue is better discussed "in a global international forum, preferably established by the UN."[22]

c) The purposes and principles of the Antarctic Treaty are good, but at the same time, there exist some defects in it. The Treaty Parties should progressively eliminate any flaws in the Treaty, change and adjust the existing System from within, not from outside.[23] However, the Treaty Parties should take into account the reasonable demands of all the parties concerned when negotiating the Antarctic mineral resources convention. We can not take sides with respect to the above-mentioned approaches before the following problems have been appropriately dealt with.

a) The Antarctic Treaty Parties should continue to be bound by the provisions of the Treaty, *inter alia*, to freeze any territorial claims to Antarctica, maintain a demilitarized zone of Antarctica and protect the natural environment thereof; otherwise, the peace of Antarctica, and even that of the world, would be threatened.

b) When a treaty negotiated and concluded in accordance with rules of international law has some defects, which does not constitute a violation of the UN Charter or *jus cogens*, could that treaty be replaced disregarding the objection of the State Parties thereto?

c) When the State Parties to a treaty are negotiating within the treaty context for a matter of international interest, could they totally disregard in terms of legal criteria such reasonable claims which have no binding force as those which may be raised by outsider States, or should they take into account these claims in light of the principles of justice and fairness?

These questions may have different answers. All that I want to do here is to raise them, not to answer them. But I do believe that the raising of these questions would be helpful in bridging different points-of-view, or at least in moving a step towards this direction, with a hope that a consensus could be reached on the Antarctic question in the not-too-distant future.

---

[21] *Haron* (note 19), 323.
[22] "Question of Antarctica" (note 1), para. 273, 64.
[23] *Op. cit.*, para. 159, 98.

Lessons to be Learned from the Mineral Resources Negotiations

Arthur D. Watts[*]

I think I could start by saying a couple of preliminary points, the first of which is that looking at the title that you have given me, "Lessons from Mineral Negotiations," I have an uneasy feeling that I am here a year too soon (which is not a hint for Antarctic Challenge IV, that will come later). My second preliminary comment is that there is one very clear lesson of the minerals negotiations that I can identify straight away: coffee breaks always overrun their alotted time but the lesson of Antarctic Challenge III is that they need not. However that may be, you will all realize that if present arrangements go according to plan, it is likely that by this time next year a Convention on Antarctic mineral resource activities will have been adopted, at a final session of the 4th Antarctic Treaty Special Consultative Meeting, to be held in Wellington, New Zealand, in the first half of 1988. Once a Convention has been adopted, and is available in final form for all to look at, the task of analysing its provisions can begin and it will be possible to draw conclusions as to its significance and the lessons which may be drawn from its negotiation.

That process is, however, one upon which we cannot yet embark. To try would be premature: we do not yet have a Convention. However, we do already have a negotiating process. This has been unfolding for the last five years, over ten rounds of negotiations, since they began in June 1982. Accordingly, while we cannot yet look at a Convention, we can look at that negotiating process. Doing so will, I suggest, enable us to discern a number of elements which will have had a real influence, sometimes considerable, on the final shape which the Convention will take.

I should like to stand back from the negotiations a little, as if I were an outsider to them, and adopt an inductive approach:[1] that is, I should like to look at the facts of various aspects of the negotiating process,

[*] *Arthur D. Watts*, Deputy Legal Adviser, Foreign and Commonwealth Office, London; Leader of the UK Delegation, Antarctic minerals negotiations. The opinions expressed in this volume are the personal views of their authors only.

[1] See generally *Georg Schwarzenberger*, The Inductive Approach to International Law, London, Dobbs Ferry, N. Y. 1965, Chapt. 1.

in order to see what underlying principles those facts seem to reflect. I should add that although, for convenience, I will refer to "principles," I will do so subject to two important qualifications.

My first is that my concern is with the negotiations for an Antarctic minerals regime, and I have not concerned myself with any other negotiations. Accordingly, the "principles" to which I will draw attention should not be taken to reflect possible principles of international negotiations in general, but to relate solely to the present Antarctic minerals negotiations.

The second qualification I must make is that these "principles" should not be taken as principles in a strict, normative or academic sense. As much as anything, I use the term "principle" simply as a convenient label to describe, for the present limited purposes, the various elements which I will be noting.

I. Nomadic Negotiation

Perhaps I can make the point clearer by moving straightaway to the first of these so-called "principles." I should like to look at the geographical facts of these negotiations. The first and second rounds were held in New Zealand, in June 1982 and January 1983; the third round was held in the Federal Republic of Germany, in July 1983; the negotiations then moved to the United States for the 4th round, in January 1984, followed by the 5th round in Japan in May 1984; the 6th round was held in Brazil in February and March 1985, and the 7th round in France in September and October 1985; the 8th round was held in Australia in April 1986, and in November of that year the 9th round took place, once again, in Japan; and the negotiations have most recently been held, for the 10th round, in Uruguay. Those were the main negotiating rounds. To them must be added certain informal discussions involving varying numbers of delegations, in varying compositions, in equally varied locations.

The outside observer, looking at that pattern of negotiations, might be tempted to conclude simply that the negotiators must be mad. If our observer were a cynic, he might conclude that they are just addicted to foreign travel. An alternative, at least for the non-cynical observer, might be to conclude that the negotiators were driven by a principle, namely the "principle of nomadic negotiation." The root cause of these homeless wanderings, however, is in reality to be found in the Antarctic Treaty System.

The minerals negotiations have in form constituted the 4th special Antarctic Treaty Consultative Meeting. As such they are held, therefore, within the Antarctic Treaty framework, and are subject to the same sort of procedural and structural advantages and disadvantages, as they are an integral part of the present Antarctic Treaty System. One of the notable features of that System is the very fact that it is a "System," and not the Antarctic Treaty "Organisation." There is no such Organisation, with a permanent organisational infrastructure; there is no annual budget; there is no permanent secretariat; nor is there a headquarters.[2] The regular Antarctic Treaty Consultative Meetings are, in accordance with Article IX of the Antarctic Treaty, held "at suitable intervals and places": in practice this has meant, hitherto, a pattern of meetings every other year, held in the territories of various Consultative Parties to the Antarctic Treaty, selected on the basis of an alphabetical rotation.

There is, however, no such regular pattern for Special Antarctic Treaty Consultative Meetings. They have to be arranged on an *ad hoc* basis. Although to the outsider this might not seem a significant matter, in practice it is. Those who are concerned with the organisation of international meetings, which in the case of the minerals negotiations now involve more than 30 States, will readily appreciate that it is not at all easy to arrange for substantial conference facilities at short notice, or to obtain from prospective host governments authority to meet the expenses which will probably have been unforeseen when budgets were being prepared at the beginning of the financial year. It is, indeed, a tribute to the spirit of cooperation shown by all governments involved in these negotiations that it has been possible to arrange a regular schedule of meetings for the minerals negotiations over the last 5 years. There have sometimes been some cliff-hanging uncertainties as to where and when — and indeed, sometimes whether — the next meeting would be held, but in the end arrangements have always been made.

While that explains why the negotiations have been nomadic, the question remains whether it has mattered to the course of the negotiations. I should like to note one or two respects in which the negotiations have been affected by the constant changes of venue.

First, the arrangements whereby meeting places have been decided have largely dictated the pace at which the negotiations have been conducted. While in many respects holding meetings at the rate of two a year has been about right from the purely bureaucratic point of view of the need for delegations to consider their positions after each round of negotiations, and to seek new instructions for the next round, more frequent meetings would in any event have been very difficult to arrange — even though I think it is fair to say that had the negotiators

[2] These matters are discussed in the paper presented by *Tucker Scully*, *supra*, p. 42.

been masters of their negotiating pattern, on one or two occasions at least the gaps between successive rounds of negotiations would have been shorter than in fact they were.

Two other consequences of these nomadic negotiations are, while real, perhaps more in the realm of social psychology than anything else. It is a fact, which should not be disregarded or treated too lightly, that the process of travelling half-way round the world (as at any one round of negotiations at least half the delegations will have had to do) in order to meet in surroundings that are new and unfamiliar, effective negotiating time is reduced by the inevitable settling-down process. If, as happened with many rounds of negotiations for the Law of the Sea Convention, a session is to lalst for 6 or 8 weeks, the few days taken in settling down need not matter greatly. Where, however, sessions last only 2 weeks — which has been normal for the minerals negotiations — the setting-down period, even if short, has a disproportionate effect on the progress that can be expected to be made at the meeting.

A somewhat similar, and perhaps even more nebulous, factor is the effect upon negotiations of the practical and physical arrangements made for them. This is one of those matters which it is very difficult to assess in advance or in the abstract. As much as anything it is a matter of personal chemistry. It is very much affected by the kind of negotiations which are taking place. Put very starkly, if negotiations are to take the form of long speeches in which delegates speak for the record, and instead of speaking to each other speak at, or often past, each other, a large and formal conference room will be suitable; if on the other hand some hard negotiating is in prospect, smaller and less formal surroundings for meetings are likely to serve the purpose better. During the minerals negotiations a wide variety of accommodation has been generously made available by host governments. One can, of course, learn to live with, and to make the best of, whatever accomodation is available for a meeting: one quickly learns, for example, that meetings seem to go better in certain rooms rather than others, and one can therefore structure the meeting so that more use is made of the one kind of room rather than of the other. However, with a nomadic negotiation such as the minerals negotiations, it has never been possible to make the fullest use of this process of acclimatisation: too much time has been spent on the early part of the learning curve.

II. Continuous Chairmanship

It may therefore be a little surprising, given the disadvantages of nomadic negotiations, that any substantial progress has been possible. However, the discontinuity implicit in the negotiating process has to a large extent been counter-balanced by the continuity of chairmanship. This "principle of continuous chairmanship" is the second principle to which I should like to draw attention.

At the beginning, the question of chairmanship was settled in the traditional way. Since the first round of negotiations was held in Wellington, New Zealand, the proposal that the leader of the New Zeland delegation, *Mr. Chris Beeby*, should be elected Chairman was accepted by acclamation. When it transpired that the second round of negotiations was also to be held in Wellington, it was, of course, natural that *Mr. Beeby* should again assume the burdens of chairmanship. The next round of negotiations, however, was held in the Federal Republic of Germany, in Bonn. There was accordingly a question whether, in accordance with the traditional practice, the chairmanship should be held by the Federal Republic of Germany, or whether *Mr. Beeby* should continue in that role. In the event it was decided that the leader of the Federal Republic's delegation, *Dr. Ernst Jung*, should be the Chairman of the meeting, but that for most of the time of the meeting its main work would be conducted in a plenary working group, the Chairman of which would be *Mr. Beeby*. The next round of negotiations, in Washington, was formally a continuation of the Bonn working group meeting, so it was again appropriate that *Mr. Beeby* should be in the chair.

By this time — and indeed, even much earlier — *Mr. Beeby*'s conduct of the negotiations and his grasp of, and contributions to, the deliberations was such as to have earned him universal respect and admiration. It was generally acknowledged that a successful conclusion for the negotiations very much depended upon his guidance as Chairman. At subsequent rounds of negotiation the various host countries proved generous in their readiness to allow the chairmanship of the negotiations to continue in *Mr. Beeby*'s hands.

It is difficult to over-estimate the contribution made to the deliberations by the fact of having had throughout the same Chairman. In all the different meeting places, and through all the different procedures under which the negotiations have been conducted, the unifying influence of a single Chairman has ensured a cohesion to the negotiations which they would not otherwise have had.

III. Informal Consultation

In practice, the way in which the negotiations have been conducted has depended probably more than usual on the role of the Chairman, and made continuity in that role essential.

It is sometimes the case that a Chairman assumes an almost entirely formal role. He calls upon the speakers, he ensures that the debate is conducted in an orderly manner, he arranges the timetable of meetings, and on certain occasions, for example at Government receptions, he may be regarded as the spokesman for the meeting as a whole. In the minerals negotiations, however, in addition to that formal role, much of the substantive discussion during the ten rounds of negotiations has taken place in informal groups operating under the active guidance of the Chairman. So much has this been the case that I think it merits separate identification as the "principle of informal consultation."

I should emphasize that this is very different from the normal kind of informal discussion which takes place between delegations during any international negotiation. There have, of course, been such consultations throughout the minerals negotiations. But in addition there have during the various negotiating rounds been special informal meetings, convened by the Chairman, in which he has gathered together groups of representatives — not always including all of them, and doing his best to vary the composition of these informal groups so that all delegations would have an opportunity to participate at one time or another. These meetings have been marked by their atmosphere of informality,[3] which has encouraged delegations to indulge (at least to a limited extent) in what passes in the diplomatic world for free-speaking, and thinking aloud — a process encouraged by the Chairman, and which has proved a fruitful way of bringing nearer to resolution some of the more intractable problems.

IV. Personal Proposals

The Chairman's role, however, went beyond arranging and guiding such informal meetings. He has, on a personal basis, made a substantive contribution to the development of the minerals negotiations — so much so that it deserves separate mention, as the "principle of personal proposals."

The Chairman's first major contribution of this kind came as long ago as the beginning of 1983, and has fundamentally influenced the course of the negotiations since then. During the first two rounds of negotiations at Wellington in 1982 and 1983 delegations set out their basic positions. Trough many lengthy and sometimes difficult meetings delegations continued, by and large, to maintain their original views. They could have gone on doing so for many more rounds of negotiations.

At that stage there was not the slightest hope of delegations being able, between themselves, to come up with any kind of common text for a possible minerals regime, even on an *ad referendum* basis. However,

---

[3] As to certain linguistic considerations, see below, p. 328.

some text which would bring the delegations a little closer together, and which could be the focus for further discussion, was essential if the negotiations were to make progress. It was against this background that *Mr. Beeby*, as Chairman, filled the gap by circulating, at the very end of the second round of negotiations, some personal proposals for a minerals regime. As one of the conference documents, it was given a reference, MR 17: it has been more colloquially referred to as "Beeby I."

It may seem at first sight that there is nothing particularly significant in the Chairman producing personal proposals of this kind; and indeed, it is not an unusual way of proceeding in international negotiations. However, two particular advantages of this procedure in the minerals negotiations should be noted. The first relates to the question of timing. The Beeby I text appeared at a relatively early stage in the negotiations. While parts of that text could be said to be based on ideas discussed in the two rounds of negotiations which preceded their appearance, I do not think it could be said that, as a whole, they reflected a structure, let alone detail, which had already been demonstrated in the negotiations to represent a common view among the negotiating delegations. The text was in many ways an exercise in creative diplomacy, putting into a single coherent structure a range of ideas which had a greater or lesser degree of appeal for the various delegations, but at least could be seen by all of them as representing some sort of middle ground, in the sense that for each delegation there were probably as many suggestions which they did not like as there were suggestions which were more acceptable to them. It is a measure of the soundness of the Chairman's original ideas that the basic structure he proposed at that early stage has survived recognizably over the subsequent years of negotiation.

The other element worth noting briefly is that in a negotiation touching on sensitive political and legal issues, it is easier for many delegations to take home with them at the end of a round of negotiations a text which they can truthfully say was presented to them by someone else (in this case, the Chairman) rather than one to which they could in some way be said to have given their consent. While all delegations might have to acknowledge that the Chairman's text was likely to represent the basis for further negotiation, no delegation needed to feel committed to it.

As a way of advancing negotiations this "personal proposal" procedure has much to commend it. So much is this so that "Beeby I" has over the years been followed by three further revisions,[4] each of them still made

[4] These have been circulated under cover of the Chairman's personal reports April 1984 (MR 17 Rev. I; 'Beeby II'), 19 September 1986 (MR 17 Rev. II; 'Beeby III') and 2 April 1987 (MR 17 Rev. III; 'Beeby IV').

available on the basis that they were personal proposals presented by the Chairman in the belief that, from what he knew of the way discussions had gone, they would represent a steadily increasing degree of common ground and would advance the course of the negotiations. They have formed the basis and focus for the successive rounds of negotiations.

V. Consensus

The value of such an approach has been all the greater because the minerals negotiations are taking place within the framework of a "principle of consensus," which is the next influential element which I should like to note. A moment's thought will show how important the voting rules in a negotiation can be. The minerals negotiations, taking place as they are within the framework of the Antarctic Treaty, have been governed by the same principle of consensus as that which applies to Antarctic Treaty Consultative Meetings.[5] While the technical meaning of "consensus" can be the subject of considerable discussion, in practice, in the minerals negotiations (and more generally in the Antarctic Treaty System) it means that a proposal which is unacceptable to one delegation cannot go ahead. For effective practical purposes it gives every delegation a veto power.

This would seem to make it easy for any delegation to prevent progress except on its own terms; and since many delegations in the minerals negotiations have fundamentally differing conceptions of what is acceptable to them, one may again experience some surprise that any progress has been made. A large part of the answer lies, I suggest, in the proposition that power carries with it responsibility; and in the further proposition that all delegations in these negotiations seem to want them to succeed. In those circumstances the ability of any delegation to frustrate progress in order to insist on its wishes being met is in the last resort dependent on its willingness to bring about the collapse of the negotiations. That would be a serious responsibility for any delegation to assume, and, bearing in mind wider considerations affecting the future of Antarctica, it is probably not an outcome which it is in the broad national interest of any delegation to encourage or bring about.

---

[5] See Rule 23 of the Rules of Procedure of Consultative Meetings as regards the approval of recommendations at Consultative Meetings. The Approval of the final report of a Consultative Meeting, and all matters of procedure, require only a majority decision: Rules 24 and 20. Measures recommended to Governments by Consultative Meetings become effective only when approved by all Consultative Parties entitled to attend the Meeting in question: Antarctic Treaty, Aritcle IX 4.

The tension within delegations between their wish to see the negotiations make progress and their wish not to prejudice their national positions has led, in these negotiations as in many others, to a variety of procedural devices whereby informal and unattributable ideas could be floated. The device of the "non-paper" has frequently been resorted to; so too have papers been presented to the Chairman, for him to circulate unattributably as a possible aid to discussion.

There is one further point about the principple of consensus which will have a very considerable bearing on the future, not just the content, of the minerals regime. Although the operation of a consensus rule can sometimes make it very difficult to reach agreement, it does have the compensating value that those agreements that are reached by consensus are more likely to be maintained in the future. If the aim of the Antarctic minerals negotiations is to elaborate a regime which will in practice effectively govern the exploration for and development of mineral resources over many decades to come, that aim would be less likely to be achieved by a text which was voted through by some majority notwithstanding the serious objections of a significant number of other delegations with a major practical interest in its subject matter.

VI. Privacy

Another important element in these negotiations which is bound to strike — and has indeed already struck — an outside observer is that they would seem to represent a "principle of privacy." In practice, and apart occasionally from a formal ceremonial opening session, the negotiations have been conducted in private; that is, they have been conducted in the presence only of those delegations entitled to participate, namely the Consultative Parties and the Non-consultative Parties to the Antarctic Treaty.

Over the last five years much has been written about the minerals negotiations, and considerable public attention has been paid to them. More nonsense has probably been uttered about the privacy of these negotiations than about any other aspect. Broadly speaking, the view which has been propagated is that these are "secret" negotiations, conducted "behind closed doors"; and these complaints are presented as if those characteristics were in some way exceptional, and certainly pernicious.

I could not disagree more fundamentally with that view. There is nothing secret about the negotiations: the time and place at which each negotiating round has been held has been public knowledge. It is true that the negotiations themselves have been held in private:[6] this is wholly normal in international relations. The curiosity felt by outsiders who would like to be on the inside, listening to what goes on, is of course understandable: it is a feeling many people share in relation to many bodies to which they do not have a right of access. But that natural curiosity is no reason whatever to accept that the curious have a *right* of participation. Privacy in international negotiations is usual, and the Antarctic minerals negotiations are no exception to the general practice.

Nor, I firmly believe, is the principle of privacy pernicious, whether applied to international negotiations generally, or to the minerals negotiations in particular. The belief that public negotiation of sensitive issues is desirable or attainable is unrealistic: the thought that the *real* minerals negotiations would in substance take place in an open forum is of a naivety which borders on the irresponsible. The only practical result of opening the doors of the minerals negotiations to all interested states, and others, would be to drive the real negotiations into the corridors and into other meetings of a restricted and private character, leaving the "open" meetings for little more than the delivery of prepared speeches which would mostly either reiterate familiar national positions or announce developments which had in substance been negotiated elsewhere.

VII. Linguistic Restraint

There is one more significant element in the way in which these negotiations have been conducted which deserves comment. The official languages of the Antarctic Treaty are English, French, Spanish and Russian..[7] At regular Consultative Meetings these are the languages used. The outside observer at the minerals negotiations could not fail to be struck by the limited extent to which those four languages have been used in that context. Most of the negotiating rounds have been conducted only in English,[8] and even where interpretation facilities have been available for plenary meetings, they have not always been available or made use of for all working groups. It is in this sense that one might characterise the negotiations as having been conducted in accordance with the "principle of linguistic restraint."

[6] Nevertheless, a considerable amount about the course of the negotiations, including the successive versions of the 'Beeby' text, has, informally and unofficially, become public.

[7] Those are the languages in which authentic texts of the Antarctic Treaty have been prepared (Article XIV), and which are the official languages of Consultative Meetings (Rule 21 of the Rules of Procedure).

[8] Interpretation facilities have been provided for the meetings in Wellington (1982), Bonn (1983), Paris (1985) and Montevideo (1986).

The reason for this restraint is not difficult to discern. As explained earlier, the negotiations have had to be held in those cities where a host government has been willing to offer the necessary facilities. Facilities cost money, and in most cases host governments have felt able only to offer to arrange a meeting on the understanding that it would not be necessary to provide interpretation facilities. The generosity of successive host governments in being willing to undertake, even on that basis, the considerable burdens of hosting a meeting has been matched by the willingness of those delegations whose first language is not English to agree to meetings being held on an English-only basis.

The consequence of this has been considerable for the progress of the negotiations, particularly in the encouragement it has given to the principle of informality which has governed so much of the work. Once you set up microphones, and require speakers always to bear in mind the needs of interpreters, the negotiating atmosphere inevitably becomes stilted. To the extent that that can be avoided by the use of a common language, the negotiating process is improved. However, particularly in specialist areas, the need for delegations to express themselves, and to hear others, in their own languages must not be forgotten if, at the end of the day, all delegations are to feel sufficiently satisfied that they have had a fair opportunity to have their views heard and understood.

VIII. Constructive Ignorance

All that I have said so far has been concerned with the procedures of the minerals negotiations, and I have not concerned myself with their substance, it being perhaps premature at this stage to do so. I would, however, in conclusion briefly mention three principles which might strike an outside observer and which do touch on matters of substance.

The first reflects the fact that these negotiations for a minerals convention are taking place when nobody knows where any minerals are, or even whether there are any in commercial quantities. In a very real sense we do not know what we are talking about. To be negotiating in such circumstances might be said to represent the "principle of constructive ignorance."

The "ignorance" part of the principle is clear enough. But it is also "constructive" ignorance. This audience is well aware of the inherent complexities of the minerals negotiations; I would just mention in particular the differing views as to territorial sovereignty, and the uncertainties as to which countries' operators might have a practical interest in engaging in Antarctic mineral activities. If the minerals negotiations were to await firm knowledge about the existence of substantial mineral resources, or even their actual discovery, the negotiators would be faced with the task of trying to negotiate in circumstances in which several states, through their territorial claims or the involvement of their operators, had immediate practical interests to promote and protect. It is proving difficult enough to negotiate a minerals regime where the essential facts are largely hypothetical; but it would, I think, be virtually impossible if there were several states with interests which had become vested rather than being merely contingent. The result would then be likely to be no minerals regime — but not necessarily no minerals activity. If such activity were to go ahead, it would do so in circumstances of considerable dispute and tension, and without any of the safeguards which the minerals regime would have provided. The "principle of constructive ignorance" might thus equally be referred to as the "principle of prudent forethought."

IX. Procrastination: Present Principle

The other two principles touching upon the substantive provisions of a mineral convention call for even briefer mention. They are linked, and I would refer to them as the "principle of procrastination" and the "principle of present principle."

The first takes account of the realities with which we are dealing — principal among which is the ignorance to which I have just referred. In effect, therefore, the negotiations have proceeded on the basis that it would be unwise to attempt to do today what could with advantage be left until tomorrow — or even the day after.

Just to leave a blank, however, would not serve our successors well. It is to help them that we are finding it useful, even at the present stage, to establish certain principles. It is with the aid of these present principles that the gaps left by our procrastination may be filled in due course, should it be necessary to do so.

X. Conclusion

I have attempted in this paper to identify some of the elements of the negotiating process which have had some influence on the course of the minerals negotiations. At this point, however, I remind myself that the title of this paper refers to the "lessons" of the Antarctic minerals negotiations and there must be a question whether the various elements which I have mentioned can properly be regarded as involving "lessons."

If by that word is meant experiences which commend themselves as models to be followed in other contexts, then I do not think that all the elements to which I have drawn attention do constitute lessons, although some may do, at least to some extent. "Lessons" may, however, refer to experiences from which something can be learned. In this sense, I would hope that most, if not all, of the elements I have mentioned can be regarded as lessons. At the very least, I hope that they may provide a better understanding of some of the practical, diplomatic factors at play in the minerals negotiations, whose contribution to the end result is otherwise easily overlooked.

Non-Consultative Parties: The Peruvian Approach to the Antarctic Treaty System and to Antarctic Mineral Resources

Nicolás Roncagliolo[*]

First of all, I would like to express my appreciation and gratitude to *Professor Rüdiger Wolfrum*, Director of The Institute of International Law at Kiel, and to the Alfred Wegener Institute for Polar and Marine Research for inviting me to participate in "Antarctic Challenge III."

I. Peru's Approach to the Antarctic Treaty System

One legal precedent, important to Peru, is the Declaration of Constituent Assembly from May 3rd 1979. The Declaration, though not part of the Peruvian Constitution, has constitutional hierarchy and has been written in an ample but flexible manner in order to facilitate an adequate interpretation given the dynamics of the politics of this matter.[1]

Peruvian accession to the Treaty in 1981 was preceded by a careful examination of every aspect comprising the complex Antarctic problem, which has grown in importance at both the national and international level in recent years. The Peruvian Ministry of Foreign Affairs published an official Declaration on this subject (April 11th 1981), explaining the reasons behind the move by the Government to gain access to the Treaty, considered to be the only juridical instrument to regulate the Antarctic activities of the Parties. This regulation serves the whole international community, by establishing principles and rules, such as the utilization of the region for peaceful purposes only, the prohibition of all nuclear activity and the freedom of scientific research and international cooperation in order to fulfill the objectives of the Treaty.

The Peruvian Foreign Office Release of June 23rd 1986, marking the five years since the signing of the Treaty, stressed the important fact that Peru was making efforts to secure the status of a Consultative Party. On August 11th 1983, the National Commission for Antarctic Issues

---

[*] *Nicolás Roncagliolo Higueros*, Counsellor, Embassy of Peru, Bonn. The opinions expressed in this volume are the personal views of their authors only.

[1] *Jorge Chávez Soto*, El Tratado Antártico: Anotaciones sobre una política nacional, Revista Peruana de Derecho Internacional 94, Dic. 86, 33.

was created. Its main functions were to study the political, legal, scientific, technical and other matters relating to the Antarctic region; to advise the Peruvian Government in the formulation and execution of Antarctic politics; to expand the National Antarctic Plan and to recommend to the Government the means for the financial support of these activities.

Because of the great interest in Antarctic matters by officials and in academic circles, the Government considered it necessary to explain the Peruvian Antarctic Policy. At that time, articles on Antarctic matters also appeared in several Peruvian publications. Therefore, the Ministry of Foreign Affairs put out a press release on October 22nd 1986. This stated that the Peruvian Antarctic Policy was based on the concepts and guidelines of the Declaration of the Constituent Assembly and the Official Declaration of April 11th 1981, when Peru acceded to the Treaty. Faithful to the traditional Peruvian position of observance of its international agreements, the press release mentioned that the Government was conducting its policies in accordance with the rights and duties in the Antarctic Treaty. The official document also explained the scope of Article IV of the 1959 Treaty, regarding the "freeze" of sovereignty claims in the Antarctic and the prohibition against asserting new claims in the Antarctic while the Treaty was in force. In addition, it stated that the Government considered obtaining Consultative status to be a vital aspect of its Antarctic Policy.

The National Commission on Antarctic Issues has completed a project on Antarctic Policy which considers the activities of Peru in the Antarctic Continent and the budget required to carry on scientific research. Despite this important commitment, we realize that, in the current circumstances, it is not easy for a developing country to produce the large sums of money needed to finance the launching of Antarctic expeditions according to the requirements of Consultative Parties. Hence the financial and economic constraints on a developing country's budget are taken into account in relation to evaluating the status of Consultative Party.

II. Peruvian Interests in the Antarctic

In the permanent process of accommodation between the members of the Antarctic System, we must speak of the interests of these countries. We hear about the interests of mankind, the interests of Consultative countries, the interests of the Non-consultative countries, and so forth. *Roland Rich* states that "the process of accommodation requires the identification of these interests and an examination of the 'mix of benefits' involved in Antarctica. It also requires the assigning of a certain weight to each interest in order to attempt to balance it with comparable benefit."[2] Before we start to deal with the interests of the Non-consultative countries, we are going to describe the particular interests of Peru in the Antarctic.

1. Peruvian Presence and Real Participation in the Antarctic Treaty System

In order to fulfill this commitment, Peru must have access to the level of Consultative Party. This is the only way in which to have important participation in the Treaty System and to influence its future evolution according to its principles. Consequently, Peru has to accomplish its Antarctic project in order to fulfill the scientific research required of Consultative Parties. Also, Peru has to consider its accession to the Convention of Antarctic Marine Living Resources (CCAMLR) and its participation in the Scientific Committee on Antarctic Research (SCAR).[3]

I would bring to your attention the interpretation made by *Mr. R. Tucker Scully* of Article IX of the Antarctic Treaty and, in particular, the requirements for Consultative Status:

> We ought to be looking at the interpretation of Articlel IX as a whole. What should be the basis for making such determination is, in my view, a long-term commitment to research in Antarctica. In some instances, a long-term commitment to research in Antarctica would be less served by the establishment of a station than by pursuing other paths.[4]

2. The Preservation of International Peace and Security

Peru would ratify its support of the principle that the Antarctic region must remain as a region of peace. This means avoiding the return to an era of political dispute over territorial claims. It is necessary to emphasize that the "freeze" on sovereignty claims established by Article IV of the Treaty liberated the Antarctic continent from the tensions that occur in other parts of the globe.

3. Protection of National Economy

One must take into account that, traditionally, Peru is a producer and exporter of minerals and, as such, has a particular interest that the future does not affect those countries already producing them. More

---

[2] *Roland Rich*, A Mineral Regime for Antarctica, British Institute of International and Cooperative Law 31, London 1982, 711.

[3] *Chávez* (note 1), 39—40.

[4] *R. Tucker Scully*, Institutionalisation of the Antarctic Treaty Regime, in: (*Rüdiger Wolfrum*, Ed.), Antarctic Challenge II, Berlin 1985, 294.

than fifty per cent of Peruvian export revenue comes from the mineral sector. The appearance on the international market of large quantities of Antarctic minerals would create serious economic problems for countries like Peru, which have a high dependence on the sale of these products. Peru is aware that commercial exploitation of mineral resources from Antarctica is still a long way of, but that in the "more" foreseeable future, there are possibilities for exploitation of oil and gas. We realize also that because of the attendant difficulties of Antarctica, offshore drilling installations are economically unattractive at the present time. Under new conditions, however, offshore activities would be the first development. In this event, much more attention would need to be given to the potential hazards to the marine environment in order to prevent serious consequences to the marine ecosystem.[5]

4. The Preservation of the Ecosystem and the Antarctic Environment

We fully understand the tremendous importance of keeping the Antarctic environment free of contamination, in order to preserve the particular ecosystem existent in that area. It is also necessary to emphasize the geographical position of Peru and the Peruvian coast in relation to Antarctica and the influence of this region on the weather, ecology and marine biology in Peru. The geographical linkage of Peru with the Antarctic continent is evident through the South Pacific basin. It is impossible at the present time to predict to what extent contamination from any commercial oil operation would negatively affect Peru and its neighbouring countries, but we know that the effect is potentially serious for those countries linked geographically to the region. Furthermore, the Peruvian Sea is considered to be one of the richest seas in plankton in the world, and it is strongly influenced by the Humboldt current which originates in the Antarctic. Consequently, Peru has to be one of the strongest defenders of the Antarctic ecology.

III. Evolution of the Antarctic System

One important aspect of the Antarctic Treaty is its constant evolution, giving flexible and pragmatic answers to specific problems in the region. This means that, aside from the Treaty of 1959, the Consultative Parties have been created as international instruments, independent but connected with the Treaty. We refer here to the CCAMLR and the Convention on the Conservation of Antarctic Seals. All these constituent parts, along with the Recommendations of Consultative Meetings, form what we call the Antarctic Treaty System. The mineral regime to be

[5] *John C. Behrendt*, Environmental Effects of Development of Antarctic Petroleum and Mineral Resources, *loc. cit.* (note 4), 42.

negotiated at the Special Meetings will be regarded as an integral part of the system.

With the mineral regime, the Consultative Parties seek to anticipate the situations which might arise on the commencement of commercial exploration and exploitation of those resources already mentioned. Otherwise, the lack of initiative regarding the Antarctic minerals may be regarded as an inefficacy of the system and would point to the need for replacement with another mechanism.[6] Also, some Consultative Parties consider that the lack of any Conventions could precipitate disputes over claims for mineral exploration and exploitation rights. Generally speaking, in these meetings, only the Consultative Parties, those with important financial and technological resources, participate in the decision-making process of the system. The Non-consultative parties who have arrived late in the mineral negotiation participate in the process only as observers — without veto rights, which have particular importance in the consensus system adopted by the Antarctic Treaty System. We need to think about this in a little more depth; not with the intention of disrupting the Antarctic System process, but in order to give it strength and international acknowledgement, assimilating certain concepts or ideas from the international community and the Third World.

The Antarctic System has been extending some openness to Non-consultative parties, allowing them to participate as observers since the XIIth Consultative Meeting in Canberra and the Special Consultative Meeting on mineral resources held in Tokyo in 1984. We cannot ignore the influence in this change of criticism from non-aligned countries.[7]

---

[6] *Finn Sollie*, Problemas jurisdiccionales en relación con los recursos minerales antárticos, in: La Antártida y sus Recursos, Edit. Universitaria, Chile, 308—309; see also *Francisco Orrego Vicuña*, La definición de un régimen para los recursos mineros antárticos, *loc. cit.*, 270.

[7] *Gonzalo Fernández Puyó*, El Sistema Antártico en el Tratado de Washington de 1959 y en el Informe de las Naciones Unidas, in: Revista Peruana de Derecho Internacional, 84, Dic 86, 56. On this matter, *Fred Parkinson* says: "Meanwhile pressures among the developing countries and, in particular, those in the Caribbean continued to build up, as the Group of Non-Aligned countries discussed the matter in March 1983 at their New Delhi meeting, the Organisation of Eastern Caribbean States in May 1983 and the Caribbean Community (CARICOM) in June 1983. The representatives of Antigua and Barbudos, and Malaysia, backed by those from Algeria, Pakistan and Singapore, successfully requested the Secretary General of the United Nations to place the item 'Question of Antarctica' on the agenda of the General Assembly, where it was allocated to the First Committee. It was only under the weight of those growing pressures that the exclusive club considered it wiser to make some concessions by (i) allowing non-consultative 'acceding' parties (the pejorative 'acceding' is now standard vocabulary) to attend their negotiations on the mineral regime as observers as from May 1984, and (ii) to recognise the need for greater publicity of their meetings." *Fred Parkinson*, Latin America and the Antarctic: an Exclusive Club, Journal of Latin America Studies 17, Great Britain, 444—445.

Nevertheless, the Consultative Parties have assumed a special responsibility, allowing them to play a key role in the development of the system. Under these circumstances, we cannot but be reminded of the interests and expectations of the Non-consultative countries, given that they have accepted the duties and restrictions of the Treaty but are not yet receiving the rights. Furthermore, they do not participate in the decision-making process and consequently there is no appropriate correlation between rights and duties.[8]

We consider, therefore, that the present Antarctic Mineral Negotiations offer a good opportunity to carry on with the process of openness and flexibility of the system to allow incorporation into the regime of the important interests of the Non-consultative parties and the wider international community (external accommodation), presenting a more attractive face to a third party. Under these circumstances, the Antarctic System would obtain wider support from those countries still not members of the Treaty.[9]

Here, I would like to refer to *Mr. Peter Brückner* in Antarctic Challenge II:

> The Regime will probably be a framework without many substantial provisions. It is important for the Non-consultative Parties to be as much involved as possible in the work of the future Regime or of the organs of the Regime. Various models have been considered, from full participation in some organs, to observer status or no seat in other organs. However, the choice is not necessarily between full membership, non-membership or observer role. You might also meet Non-consultative Parties wishes if you try to take care of Consultative Parties', including Claimants, particular interests through the decision making machinery. A weighted voting system has been recognised even within the LOS Convention, *i. e.* the Council of the International Seabed Authority.[10]

---

[8] "La segunda medida que se propone consiste en diferenciar el status de los países miembros del tratado que no son Parte Consultiva, del que se aplica a terceros países en general. Hasta ahora la situación de unos y otros ha sido virtualmente idéntica, con la excepción que sobre los países miembros del Tratado recaen importantes obligaciones y ningún privilegio o derecho. Ello se traduce obviamente en un desincentivo para adherir al Tratado, lo que por cierto no favorece el fortalecimiento del Sistema Antártico. El régimen que se negocia actualmente podría brindar una oportunidad adecuada en este sentido. Cabe pensar, por ejemblo que esta categoría de países pueda obtener un acceso más expeditivo a las operaciones que regula el régimen, que pueda abrirse en su beneficio la participación institucional, en un grado mayor, o incluso podría facilitarse su vinculación con determinados procedimientos para la adopción de decisiones, mecanismos de joint ventures u otras modalidades del régimen en cuestión." *Orrego Vicuña*, (note 6), 282—283.

[9] *H. P. Rajan*, India's Approach to the Antarctic Treaty System as a New Consultative Party, *loc. cit.* (note 4), 318—319.

[10] Comments of Mr. *Peter Brückner*, Panel Discussion, *loc. cit.* (note 4), 352.

IV. Non-Consultative Parties: Peru's Approach to the Antarctic Mineral Regime

Taking into account the interests of Peru and other Non-consultative Parties in having a more dynamic and effective role in Antarctic mining negotiations, we are going to present some proposals in this area.

As we have already expressed, there is a close relationship between the Humboldt current, weather on the Peruvian coast, and fishing resources and the Antarctic ecosystem. This gives us a clear idea of the particular interest of Peru in the negotiation of a new regime in order to establish sufficient safeguards against drastic environmental effects caused by exploration and exploitation of the aforementioned resources. Hence, we consider that unlimited liability must be established against any party causing damage to the Antarctic ecosystem. Furthermore, we feel that it should be extended to the sponsoring state and that, in the first instance, authorization to start any commercial operation should be given only when there is no question over the hazards to the environment. For this reason, we consider it important to reinforce the role and competence of the Advisory Committee.[11] This organ should be in the position to give recommendations which would become binding.

We have to emphasize here that preserving the environment and developing the scientific research in Antarctica should prevail over every other interest. This should be a permanent concern of all the State-Parties, and also of those who are not yet members.[12]

---

[11] Institutions contemplated in the draft Convention on the Antarctic Mineral Resources (Chairman's informal personal report: MR/17 REV III):
a) Commission: considered the most important organ of the Convention. Its main functions are to identify (or not to identify) an area for possible exploration and development, to facilitate the information necessary to assess the possible environmental impact of Antarctic mineral resources activities and to adopt the budget for the Institution of this Convention, as well as that of others. The membership is comprised of Consultative Parties and all other Parties to this Convention who have lodged applications for an exploration permit following certain requirements. The status of observer shall be open to any Party of the Convention.
b) Advisory Committee: shall be open to all Parties of the Convention. The main functions shall be to give technical and scientific advice to the Commission and the Regulatory Committees. The idea is to give the Commission, (the most important organ) sufficient information for the decision-making process.
c) Special Meeting of State Parties: shall have the function of identifying an area for possible exploration and development. Membership of this organ shall be open to all Parties to the Convention.
d) Regulatory Committee: the draft Convention establishes that, for each area identified by the Commission pursuant to Article 39, there shall be a separate Regulatory Committee. The most relevant functions of each Regulatory Committee shall be to identify specific blocks within its area of competence, to establish fees to be submitted with any application in respect of such blocks, to approve Management Schemes and to issue exploration permits in accordance with Article 46.

[12] *Chávez* (note 1), 42.

The negotiators of the new regime should promote and protect the presence of developing countries in the mining activities, giving them adequate participation in mining enterprises by allowing them to establish "joint ventures" in order to reduce the financial and technological gap with industrialized countries.[13] For this reason, we propose to sponsor the role of the Advisory Committee, in recommending and managing the financial, research and cooperation resources in favour of developing countries.

One important part of the mineral regime negotiation process is in the so-called "external accommodation" (acceptance of the Convention by the rest of the international community who do not participate in it)[14] within which it should reinforce the role and contribution of the "Special Meeting" that, along with the Advisory Committee, is the only mechanism of the draft mineral Convention that allows for the presence of all the Parties of the Treaty. Consequently, we should seek to obtain an adequate balance between the Special Meetings and the Commission, the most important organ of the Convention.

A mineral regime which anticipates a substantial contribution to the international market in the future cannot avoid looking at its subsequent effect, particularly in relation to the traditional mining activities in other continents. This must be done to avoid unbalancing the international mineral markets, and to keep the process fair — both to the producers and to the consumers.

It is of particular concern to producers that the draft Convention did not consider a mechanism to protect their legitimate economic interests — all the more serious for developing countries. Although there is not yet an inventory of Antarctic mineral resources, it would be advisable to include at least the elements of such a protection mechanism to provide for the interests of the traditional mineral producers. Hence, we have to mention that, in the tenth session of the Special Consultative Meetings on Antarctic Mineral Resources in Montevideo, the Peruvian delegation presented a proposal to include, in the section "Objectives of the Convention," elements of the aforementioned principle.

Finally, we would like to suggest that Non-consultative countries must coordinate their viewpoints before the next Special Session on Mineral Resources by holding a number of meetings, in order to allow them better powers of negotiation.

---

[13] *Carlos Moneta*, La Antártida y el Atlántico Sur en el Sistema Internacional: Alternativas de Conflicto y vías de Cooperación, in: Revista de Estudios Internacionales 7, No. 3, Madrid, 851; see also *Orrego Vicuñna* (note 6), 279.

[14] *María Teresa Infante*, Los Recursos Minerales Antárticos y su Régimen, Política Antártica de Chile, Estudios Internacionales, Chile 1984, 229.

Panel Discussion

Participants: *Jorge Berguño**
*Alberto Davérède***
*Vladimir Golitsyn****
*Scott Hajost*****
*Abdul G. Koroma******
*Rüdiger Wolfrum*******

R. Wolfrum, Chairman:

Thank you very much indeed. I believe that you have made quite clear what your expectations and interests in the mineral resources negotiations are. Now I would like to call upon the members of this panel to take their seats: *Ambassador Jorge Berguño, Dr. Alberto Davérède, Vladimir Golitsyn, Scott Hajost, Ambassador Koroma,* and myself. The first speaker will be *Alberto.*

A. Davérède:

We have heard a lot about expectations this afternoon and morning. There are expectations from Non-consultative Parties, that we just heard about from *Mr. Roncagliolo.* They want to have a larger participation in decision-making, especially in the minerals resources regime. There are expectations from other members of the United Nations. I would also refrain from saying from the international community, because I would still consider ourselves to be a part of the international community. Other members of the United Nations also want to participate in decisions of the Anatarctic Treaty System, to be able to share possible resources in Antarctica. There are expectations from NGOs, they want to be better informed, they want to

---

* Ambassador *Jorge Berguño*, Ambassador of Chile to Australia.

** Dr. *Alberto L. Davérède*, Minister Plenipotentiary, Director-General of Antarctica, Ministry of Foreign Affairs and Worship, Argentina.

*** *Vladimir Golitsyn*, Legal Officer, Office of Legal Affairs, United Nations Secretariat, New York.

**** *Scott Hajost*, Attorney Adviser for Oceans, International Environmental and Scientific Affairs, Office of the Legal Adviser, United States Department of State, Washington D. C.

***** Ambassador *Abdul G. Koroma*, Embassy of Sierra Leone, Brussels, Belgium.

****** Prof. Dr. *Rüdiger Wolfrum*, Director of the Institute of International Law at the Christian Albrecht University of Kiel.

The opinions expressed in this volume are the personal views of their authors only.

have some more influence in the decisions taken by states. There are expectations, of course from the international organizations who want to be closer to the Antarctic Treaty Parties. There are also expectations from the public, in general. *Arthur Watts* told us that they complain about us being too private in our discussions, and even from inside the Antarctic Treaty there are expectations: because some people want to have their initiatives passed — they have been very persistent for the last twenty-seven years, without any success, but they still insist, so they are expectant. All this would seem to bring apparently an unbearable pressure on us; it would seem to be impossible to accommodate all these expectations and to give satisfaction to all of them. In spite of that, I see that there is a possibility of doing our best, because when we heard people, lectures from different backgrounds, and the media, explain to us the basis for their expectations, in spite of these different backgrounds and media they belong to, they have many things in common. They all have recognized, for example, or many of them have, that the Antarctic Treaty has been successful. They have shared the objectives of the Antarctic Treaty, some of them recognize that it had brought peace to a conflicting area of the world, that it had succeeded in demilitarizing it, or nonmilitarizing it, that it had brought international cooperation in science into a reality. Even a moment ago, in *Mr. Roncagliolo*'s presentation, we recognize that it could have been written by a Claimant developing country with territory close to Antarctica.

From this, I think we can extract some lessons. The first lesson, as *Arthur* would say, is that the Antarctic Treaty somehow had interpreted and even anticipated many of these expectations. For example, the Treaty is open to anyone under certain conditions, of course, which in the case of Non-consultative Parties are not very difficult to reach. It is open to all states, but it went further, because it also brought as I have said before, peace to a region of the world that was presenting some difficult situations. And how were these two main goals attained? They were attained through two main means. One was the famous Article IV, which I do not need to explain to you, and the second was the functional approach. This functional approach has allowed both Claimants and Non-claimants to adhere to the Treaty, and on the other hand, Article IV recognized the special political and legal nature and condition of Antarctica. The functional approach ensured that there was a genuine interest, a concern and a compromise with the continent, and the Treaty was based on that concern; that is why, in my opinion, it is extremely important to maintain these two main elements of the Treaty. The accommodation, the political accommodation, and the functional approach — any satisfaction that would be looked for to try to accommodate the external or internal expectations has to preserve these two main aspects, which are also main goals of the Antarctic Treaty, because if they are not respected, if the political situation of Antarctica is not taken into account, then any of these accommodations might threaten to disturb the system and to go back to conflict and controversy. So, somehow, this accommodation is conditioned; it cannot be freely made, it cannot be hastily made, but it can be made. Thank you very much.

A. Koroma:

Thank you, Mr. Chairman. Mr. Chairman, we have indeed been listening to some very interesting contributions this afternoon. I am not sure I should be taking part in this panel: the main reason being that I have only heard all the contributors for the first time this afternoon, and I am not sure I am doing justice to the efforts the contributors have made if I attempt to comment on their presentations off-the-cuff. Be that as it may, since you have invited me, in the interest of advancing the course of our work here, I will attempt to state my position.

Mr. Chairman, it was recalled this morning that a symposium like this created an opportunity for learning and for the further exchange of views, perhaps much more so than in other forums where you have State-Parties negotiating. And one of the criticisms made of the United Nations is that most of the time delegates or delegations speak at each other and not to each other. Regretfully, some of the contributions here, during the course of the day, were just of that nature; I know we did not have time to list carefully the points that were made, but we nevertheless came to our predetermined positions and so we tried to justify them.

On the other hand, some issues were raised, some of the important issues, for example by *Professor Orrego Vicuña*, who raised a question about the competence of the United Nations to engage in the question of Antarctica. Others have raised the issue whether the Antarctic Treaty is valid, *erga omnes*: is it an objective regime? I think the distinguished lady from China, *Ms. Song Li*, commented upon this, and as we know, eminent legal scholars, without any ideological positions, not third world scholars, have raised the question about the universal nature of the Antarctic Treaty. These are all valid questions; as the learned professor here this morning tried to demonstrate — do all rules of international law have to become *jus cogens* before they are binding? That, again, is a valid question: are all norms not in principle binding? Do they have to become *jus cogens* before they are binding? I think these are some of the issues that one would like to pursue in proceedings like this one.

Again, the United Nations has the reputation for name-calling. I served at the United Nations for almost eight years. And if you look at my statements, at no time did I use that word which is so current, or at one time was so current in the vocabulary of the United Nations: "imperialism." So to talk about, to qualify or categorize, the suggestion or proposal that a *common heritage of mankind* should apply to Antarctica as a "new imperialism" and then to further qualify that as "a measure of frankness," I think is pushing an "accommodation" too far. In my presentation this morning, I also stated that a country like the United States in the past has called for the internationalization of Antarctica and said that it should be put on a form of trusteeship. New Zealand has also in the past called for the internationalization of Antarctica, stating that the UN should be involved in that — and this from a Claimant State. And also, to some measure the Soviet Union in the past has called for increased activity by the international community in Antarctica. I think these, in a way, have a semblance of what perhaps, as I said this morning, was a call for the introduction of internationalization of Antarctica. It has a long pedigree, and to qualify it as "the new imperialism," as I said, would be stretching "comprehension" a little bit too far.

Now, with reference to the Antarctic Treaty itself, some jurists have called it an attempt to create a universal regime — but they went on to say that it cannot be imposed on a third party. It is a basic principle of international law, for a treaty to become binding on a third party you need the consent of the third party. So it cannot be said that because it was constructed by a group of states that it is binding on all states. These matters as I say, are points for argument. On the other hand, it can be argued that it is an objective regime, therefore it is an exception to Article 14 para. 2 of the Vienna Convention on the Law of Treaties. Moreover, it does not follow that because if we attempt to re-negotiate the Antarctic Treaty, that is an act of destruction; we re-negotiated the 1982 Convention on the Law of the Sea while the four 1958 Conventions were still in force. So, Mr. Chairman, as I said before, although I am not sure that I should be taking part in this Panel, I thought that I should try to put a little more weight on the legal questions.

V. Golitsyn:

At our present discussions a lot of references were made to the mineral resources regime for Antarctica, but no one discussed the substance of this regime being negotiated by the Consultative Parties. We have heard that lessons should be learned from the mineral resources negotiations on the assumption that if anything should eventuate from these negotiations, it would be an excellent achievement. *Arthur Watts* said that the lessons are experiences from which we can learn. Thus, if we speak about lessons, that means that we speak about experience that can be used in order to prevent mistakes which might lead to some negative changes. If we look now at the negotiations on the mineral resources regime, in my view the following conclusion can be drawn. As we are all aware, in all of the debates at the General Assembly, the Antarctic Treaty Parties, in particular the Consultative Parties, once and again stressed that the key point, the indispensable tool, or the most important provision of the Antarctic Treaty, is Article IV. It was said that it establishes a balance of interests which should be preserved in any future negotiations. If we look at the Living Resources Convention or the Seals Convention, we can find that, yes, the balance of interests is being preserved.

This assumption of the Consultative Parties is being challenged at the United Nations. Some other countries consider Article IV as the wrong tool for the Antarctic regime. In their view, the international regime in Antarctica should be based on other principles.

However, if we proceed on the assumption that the statements about the validity of Article IV and its importance are correct, then what lessons can be learned from the draft texts of the mineral resources regime prepared by *Chris Beeby*? The answer to which I came after a thorough analysis of these texts is that they ruin the balance established in Article IV of the Antarctic Treaty. They deviate from Article IV, and thus actually made this article as though non-existent. Of course, they contain reference to Article IV, but in other provisions of the draft regime, which are very important for its implementation, there is quite clearly deviation from what was established as a balance of interests in Article IV of the Antarctic Treaty. This is not an opinion of mine alone. At the seminar held in April, in Charlottesville, Virgina, a number of speakers came to the same conclusion. Among them are *Ambassador Takeo Iguchi*, from Japan, and *Professor Oxman*. If this conclusion is correct and the balance of Article IV is ruined by the draft regime, then the lesson to be learned from the mineral resource negotiations up to now is that the role of negotiations is destructive rather than constructive for the future of the Antarctic Treaty System. Without Article IV, there would have been no tool that saved in the past the Antarctic Treaty Parties, according to their own statements. And without it, there seems to be no tool that can save them in the future. Let me once again repeat that the logic of these considerations is based on the assumption which is being put forward by the Antarctic Treaty Parties, namely that Article IV is an indispensable tool for the Treaty System. Other countries, as I have already mentioned, have a different approach and hold the view that an international regime in Antarctica should be based on different principles. Thank you.

J. Berguño:

Thank you, Mr. Chairman. *Finn Sollie* has already told us that the Antarctic Treaty had responded to a need, to a specific need, and he has also expressed the opinion that the Antarctic Treaty was an objective regime. In fact, I think also that the Antarctic Treaty was based on actual state practice, and this is important to recall. It is important to recall that in fact in the Peninsula, where there are overlapping claims, and it has been contended here that the fact that overlapping claims exist is an element still of intensified conflict. In fact, what it did was to orientate the activity of those states which have these overlapping claims into constructive formulations. In 1947, we disposed of the issue of scientific research as being something that would not affect claims, sovereignty, or rights in any way, and which should not be hampered, therefore, by any state activities, but rather fostered and advanced; in 1950, we came to an agreement which would limit our naval activity in the area.

These were antecedents of the Antarctic Treaty which coalesced together with the gentleman's agreement, implemented afterwards in the International Geophysical Year, and gave rise to a substantive instrument, an instrument which already reflected that active practice. It has been recorded here, that there were some incidences of conflict: one state did call upon the International Court of Justice, and two states refused to accept jurisdiction in that case. But it was not said that after all the realization arose in the subsequent correspondence that the pertinent forum for the solution of that dispute was an international conference. Even that particular state which had requested the Court to act in that instance came to accept the idea of an international conference as an appropriate and normal forum to resolve this question.

Now, the internationalist approach to this matter, to which *Ambassador Koroma* has referred: he mentioned, as an example, the Indian Proposal which was put to the United Nations in 1956. It is good to recall that that particular proposal was accompanied by very thorough and clear explanatory memoranda, and that those memoranda addressed not only the safeguarding of the demilitarization, de-nuclearization, scientific research provisions, but also the fundamental principle now embodied in Article IV, of the safeguarding of claims. So it is good to focus on what an internationalist or a nationalist perspective could contribute to the Treaty, but within a context, I would say, of historic antecedence. If we are speaking of history it is good, here in Kiel, to recall another aspect, and this I can say with pride, because it is a recollection of what my country was proposing in 1948, which is very well known, and in 1950, which is less known, when a draft treaty was proposed to the United States. The precedent, the foundation for that proposal was taken from an agreement in 1908, by the countries of the Baltic, to preserve the *status quo* and peace in the Baltic: Sweden, Russia, Germany, and Denmark, and also from the preliminary work to the Svalbard Treaty. This is, we might say, the Baltic origin of the Antarctic Treaty.

So it was not done just on the impulse of the moment, it was done on a thoughtful and very well-founded basis. May I add only to this the fact that looking now at the Antarctic Treaty, with regard to a minerals regime, I find that the point is well taken that Article IV is not to be construed as the foundation for title, title to resources, but must be regarded from this point-of-view: it is the interests of Claimant states to agree with those states which have been active in the area. So in this sense certain states are to be seen as allies of Claimant states. Then, it is in the interests of Non-claimant states to foster across-the-board relationships with Non-consultative Parties, and with countries outside the spectrum of the Antarctic Treaty. It is in the interest of developing states, both Claimants and Non-claimants, within the Antarctic Treaty System, to keep very much in line with the demands of developing countries outside the area. So in general, these elements which do exist, because we have to look at the Treaty as a political entity, call for moderation and for restraint, and in general, I hope, for solutions which will be in the interests of the international community.

Now, speaking for my country, I would say that in the future minerals regime, very careful consideration needs to be devoted to externalities that would produce, as a by-product of the development of the mineral resources of Antarctica, environmental degradation and eco-system damage in any way. Since the early 1980s, environmental protection has become one of the values most commonly expressed; we are now in the late 1980s, and this concern has developed three components; an aesthetic, a scientific, and a political element. There is a political element even in the preservation of the environment. It is in the interest of peace, it is in the interest of mankind; and when one says that some countries have promoted a world park, or have gone for internationalization, they have been looking at something which is entirely different from resource apportionment or benefits. Concern for the environment is a value which all Consultative countries share with others concerned, is implicit in the Antarctic Treaty: it was not until the Sixth Consultative Meeting that it erupted, but from then it has grown in concern. Let me say at least this, which goes very much in line with what *Nicolás Roncagliolo* said here: in particular, the SCAR report has listed many possibilities of occurrences which would damage the environment in an irreversible way. Most of these are particularly sensitive for the countries of the southern hemisphere and for those which are close to the Antarctic. One of these is the impact on the earth's climate, as fossil fuel burning in Antarctica would add to the carbon-dioxide burden of the atmosphere. Sulphur-dioxide generated both by burning fossil fuels, and by the roasting of ores would add to the particular load in the stratosphere. Perhaps most importantly, the albedo of the Antarctic ice sheet could be reduced, either from dust precipitation on the surface, or from an increased quantity of dark aerosols; but now we are all very much concerned, I think, by the question of the erosion of the ozone layer. I think again, that although it is a great concern for everyone, it affects more directly the countries of the southern hemisphere. A lot of research has to be put into this. I can only say, as a last word, that for us conditions of acceptability of this agreement are very close to what *Vladimir Golitsyn* has said, and related to Article IV; but our perspective, of course, tends to differ, and I can see, from the interventions made in the seminar at Charlottesville, Virginia, he has mentioned, that these were made from another view of Article IV, than the one that we believe in. Thank you.

S. Hajost:

Thank you, *Rudi*. At the outset, I would like to say, I think that *Arthur Watts* deserves a lot of credit for conveying an excellent flavor and description of the style of the Antarctic minerals negotiations. I can say as a U.S. State Department representative, having participated in a great number of multilateral negotiations over the past six years, I have found the mineral negotiations to be probably the most creative and dynamic of the negotiations I have been involved in, and I think *Arthur* portrayed very well what they have been like, so far. I would like to focus my comments in these few minutes today on the legitimacy of concluding an Antarctic mineral resources regime among the Antarctic Treaty Parties.

I note the previous speakers, *Finn Sollie*'s, and *Song Li*'s, references to the fact that there already is an existing legal regime in the area of application of the Antarctic Treaty; I think that we cannot escape the fact that there is a very extensive and dynamic legal regime that exists in Antarctica. In this regard, I would note that for over twenty years, the Antarctic Treaty Parties have had the responsibility for managing the natural resources of Antarctica, and they have done a really effective job of that so far. It dates back to the Agreed Measures.

I would say that there is no existing rule of international law, no agreements, and no principles of international law which purport to remove the competence of the Antarctic Treaty Parties to manage Antarctic minerals and to conclude an Antarctic minerals regime. I take into account the Law of the Sea Convention and the concept of the *common heritage of mankind*. Regardless of your views on their legal quality — neither of these, I think, do anything to remove the competence of the Antarctic Treaty Parties to regulate and manage the living and non-living resources of Antarctica. The Antarctic Treaty Parties, and more specifically the Consultative Parties, have a long history of activities in Antarctica. They have taken on significant responsibilities, including responsibilities for the protection of the environment. They are the ones most likely to engage in mineral activities, and most likely to do the scientific research there. They will most likely be the ones that can protect the environment in Antarctica. As such, I think it is quite evident that the Antarctic Treaty Parties provide the best forum for the management and establishment of a regime to regulate possible Antarctic mineral resource activities. They stand the best chance of protecting the environment and indeed maintaining the peace in Antarctica. I think it is quite clear over the twenty-six years of the Antarctic Treaty, that these parties have indeed earned the right and the responsibility to manage these activities. I think they are filling a void that would exist had they not stepped in, and just to reiterate, we are not writing on a blank slate in Antarctica.

I think it should also be stressed, and it has been stated by previous speakers, that the Antarctic Treaty is really an open system: it is open to those who wish to accede, and we have had accessions, and we will probably continue to have accessions. I think in response to some of the comments by *Mr. Roncagliolo*, I would note that under the Antarctic Treaty, there has not been a really formalized decision-making system, and there have not been formalized votes. In this regard, I think that it can be quite truly stated, that the NCPs have been able to influence matters in the Antarctic Treaty Consultative Meetings, and indeed in the Antarctic minerals negotiations. Their views have been taken into account, they have been able to attend meetings. They have been able to play a role, and they will have a role to play in the development of the future Minerals Convention, and in activities under the Minerals Convention. I would like to conclude with a sort of a question, which is at the same time a comment: we have heard numerous comments about the interests of the international community, and I have always been a little curious as to exactly what that means, the interests of the international community. I think that the Antarctic Treaty Parties are part of that international community and they have an interest as well. We seem to set up a distinction at times, between the "international community" and the Antarctic Treaty Parties, and I am not certain whether that is a valid distinction. Thank you.

R. Wolfrum, Chairman:

Thank you, *Scott*. I, too, would like to address the question of the legitimacy of the Antarctic Consultative Parties to negotiate, and even conclude, as we all expect, a treaty on Antarctic mineral resources. As you have pointed out, as well as *Professor Orrego Vicuña* and *Professor Delbrück*, I cannot accept the existence of a legal bar, which foreloses such negotiations or concluding such a treaty. Such a bar does neither flow from the United Nations Charter, nor, as I see it, from the Law of the Sea Convention. It cannot be derived, and I would like to emphasize this point, from the *common heritage* principle. I agree that the *common heritage* principle, as enshrined in the Law of the Sea Convention, in the Moon Treaty, or in other treaties, is, as far as these treaties are concerned, a valid legal principle, and as such, applicable to those who have become parties to those treaties. However, the *common heritage* principle has an impact which goes beyond the treaties I have mentioned so far. To that extent I would like to endorse the view as expressed by *Mr. Koroma* and objected to by *Scott*. The *common heritage* principle influences the administration of all areas beyond national jurisdiction. As such I do believe it puts upon those negotiating the Antarctic mineral resources regime an obligation to live up to that principle. One might argue, however, that this principle has no defined content. That is not true; this principle has a content, as it refers to distributive justice or to the equitable distribution of resources. However, this does not mean that the solutions to be derived from the *common heritage* principle are always the ones of the Law of the Sea Convention, or of the Outer Space Treaty. The *common heritage* principle can be put into practice by totally different means.

The United Nations, and this I would like to emphasize, has no monopoly to apply the *common heritage* principle or to put it into reality. Even a single state, or a group of states, could transform this principle into reality, for example, by providing for an intensified kind of cooperation. Thus, the *common heritage* principle can be pursued by a group of states, such as the Antarctic Consultative Parties. Whether the Antarctic Treaty Consultative Parties have lived up to this principle is to be judged by the international community, of which the Antarctic Treaty Consultative Parties are definitely a part. They have a primary interest in this area, and in its administration. We should not focus upon the development of resources, but take into account, too, the protection of the environment, demilitarization and the cooperation concerning scientific research. By this I do not intend to deny that the international community which is not as directly involved in activities in Antarctica, has no valid interest in this area. We all know about the consequences of an environmental damage to the Antarctic, the results it would have on the global environment. I would like to conclude that the Antarctic Treaty Consultative Parties have to pursue permanently the acceptability of the Antarctic Treaty as well as of the other agreements relating to Antarctica. In this respect the policy of the Antarctic Treaty Consultative Parties has been quite successful, as can be seen from the latest ratifications and signatures of the Antarctic Treaty. If they pursue this route they will be successful, if they, however, are not willing to open themselves, then perhaps this system will not survive very long. Thank you.

General Discussion

R. Wolfrum, Chairman:

May I now open the discussion? *Mr. Khan*, please.

R. Khan:

Thank you, Mr. Chairman. I believe I would be justified if I exceed your limit of four minutes, in view of the fact that I have come from a very long distance, and I have not spoken for these last three days. However, if you think that that time constraint should be maintained, I do not mind briefing my comments.

Now, I am greatly impressed by the presentations here, and there is a lot with which I agree. So let me accentuate the positive, and try to tell you what I agree with first, before I can offer my criticism. The first observation made here, that the Antarctic Treaty System has been a fairly successful system, I fully agree with. There is no dispute about that, and I also agree with your last statement, that the United Nations, alone, is not the depository of wisdom; other agencies may try to apply the *common heritage* principle, to two different types of systems, and areas. I also agree, that the Consultative Parties have a right and a responsibility to probably discuss and design a new regime of the mineral resources. What, however, I would like to disagree with are the two observations made this morning by *Ambassador Woolcott*, about the competence of the United Nations to handle this question, especially his observation that the United Nations General Assembly does not have any such competence in view of Articles X to XIV of the Charter which limits its jurisdiction to discussion and deliberation, and not to action, implying thereby that if action is necessary it has to be referred to the Security Council. Now, this might sound a little academic but I am afraid that *Ambassador Woolcott* has ignored a few trivial things that have happened in the last several decades of the United Nations, such as the termination of the mandate of South-West Africa, and the establishment of peace-keeping forces in the Gaza and Congo, and several other things. The General Assembly was, under the Uniting for Peace Resolution, considered to be competent to take certain types of action on a hortatory basis, squarely within the phraseology of Article

---

The opinions expressed in this volume are the personal views of their authors only.

XIV, which authorizes it to suggest solutions for the peaceful adjustment of situations.

The second, more disturbing comment of *Ambassador Woolcott*, with which I would like to take issue, and which is my last observation, relates to the restrictions placed on membership of the United Nations General Assembly, to the effect that the equal rights of the members of the United Nations only means the right to be heard and not to make decisions or to determine the future of Antarctica. This is a routine argument advanced by several western countries, which are generally concerned about the expanding role of the United Nations and, to a certain extent, the disturbing role of the General Assembly in certain matters. But I think this is an extreme point of view, and it flies directly in the face of the principle of *sovereign equality of states*, which has been enshrined in the United Nations Charter, and which to my mind, is *jus cogens*. As this would be an interpretation which contradicts the *sovereign equality* principle, it is an untenable interpretation. Thank you very much.

R. Wolfrum, Chairman:

Thank you, *Mr. Khan*. The next speaker is *Mr. Jim Barnes*.

J. Barnes:

Thank you, Mr. Chairman. Basically, I have two questions. The first is for the Non-claimants on our panel up there, and the question is, "Given the underlying logic of your country's juridical views about Antarctica, and territorial sovereignty there, aren't the waters around the continent therefore high seas, and in that context, is there not some legitimate role for the UNLOSC and eventually the International Sea-Bed Authority?" I ask this question in this context regarding legitimacy; I do not deny that there is a right to negotiate this regime, but it seems like there may be some right for other people to be involved in the negotiation regarding the area of the Treaty, and so forth.

My second question has to do with *Mr. Golitsyn*'s point, which I think is very interesting. Looking at the draft Article 5 (1), which is a direct pick-up of language from Article IV of CCAMLR, it seems to me that, if I recall the negotiating history of CCAMLR properly, those words about the exercise of coastal state jurisdiction are the classic "bifocal" words, and they require a further bifocal basis, that there be some territory within the area of CCAMLR as to which there is no dispute over sovereignty, in particular some islands, and that let both Claimants and Non-claimants have this dual view of reality. In the minerals context, the way the area of the Treaty is defined so far, there does not appear to be any such territory. I would like to hear some comments on that question; there seemed to be several affirmative nods around. Thank you.

R. Wolfrum, Chairman:

Thank you, *Jim*. Let me answer your first question. According to my view the offshore areas of Antarctica are neither part of the high seas nor of the international deep sea-bed. The applicability of the continental shelf regime does not require a coastal state. The next speaker on my list is *Mr. Hafner*.

G. Hafner:

Thank you, Mr. Chairman. On the one hand, I admit that I am very impressed by the contributions of today. On the other hand, I have to say that I am to a certain extent lost, and feeling that I am in a dark room without a light. Nevertheless, I want first to make one remark concerning particularly the difference between the Antarctic Treaty and a possible minerals regime treaty. The Antarctic Treaty lives, to a great extent, from the fact that it is a so-called objective regime; this has consequences for its negotiations, its application and its effect on third states. However, in my view, any mineral resource regime cannot claim to be called an objective regime, with all the consequences concerning its negotiation, and concerning its possible effect on third states.

This leads me to the next problem. I have mentioned that I am somewhat lost. It was said by *Mr. Watts* that privacy is a usual bargaining method in international relations. I must say I doubt this, and the best example is, that I do not know about what we are speaking here, since I have no text of the draft treaty on the mineral resources regime at my disposal.

Finally, I have still a question, in particular to *Mr. Sollie*, by whose contribution I was also very much impressed. I have the impression that the Consultative Parties, in negotiating the mineral resources regime, are pursuing a policy in line with the concept which was developed by Canada in the 'Seventies, which was called the "agent theory" or "custodianship theory." Is any reference made to this theory in the negotiations on the mineral resources regime? Thank you.

R. Wolfrum, Chairman:

I see *Mr. Sollie* shakes his head, does this satisfy you? Not yet? *Finn*, I shall just give you the floor, and then you will be followed by *Arthur*.

F. Sollie:

I do not think that I am the right person to answer this last question about our using Canadian ideas. I think I tried to make a fairly strong case for the fact that there was a legal basis, and that the Antarctic Treaty System works pragmatically and flexibly, trying to solve problems on the basis on which they have been established. Whether one, in some aspects of this process, will see something similar to custodianship ideas, or any other ideas that may have been promoted in other fora, is more incidental, or coincidental, than an active effort to copy someone else's ideas, I think.

R. Wolfrum, Chairman:

Thank you. *Arthur*, please.

A. Watts:

Thank you very much, *Rudi*. I would like to offer one or two comments on the sovereignty question, because I am very glad that *Mr. Koroma* raised it during his contribution this morning. As he rightly pointed out, it is essential to a whole range of Antarctic problems. What I would like to do is to respond, necessarily briefly in view of your time limit, to one or two of the specific points which have been made, and I hope I will do so in an appropriately academic manner.

The first point is that somehow, Article IV of the Antarctic Treaty is seen as representing an appropriation of Antarctica by the negotiating states. I can, I think, just about see how some people, looking at the Antarctic Treaty, could take that view of the Treaty as a whole. On the other hand, I note that it is a view which seems necessarily to imply that there was nothing there before. But that is the real issue, because at least seven states believed, before the Antarctic Treaty, that they had sovereignty over large parts of Antarctica; and, indeed, those seven states were more than half of those negotiating the Antarctic Treaty. Now, while I do not expect the Non-claimant states, or states which do not recognize sovereignty, suddenly to become converted to the Claimant cause and to recognize sovereignty, I think they have to recognize at least the fact claims exist, and the fact that the states concerned did actually exercise, for a number of years, a large number of years, the rights of sovereignty, and, to a considerable extent, still do.

The second comment relates to a proposition which I think was advanced to show that Article IV of the Antarctic Treaty was not, perhaps, as great an achievement as it might have been thought, because, it was said, the Falklands war showed that Article IV had not worked. Now, whatever conclusions might be drawn from the Falklands hostilities, that, it seems to me, could not be one of them. Article IV does not apply to the area of the Falkland Islands, and so far as I can try to think of any analogy, the legal basis for the rival claims to the Falkland Islands are not even the same as the legal basis for the rival claims in Antarctica. But more than that, I would almost turn the argument on its head: in fact, I think the exact opposite is the case. The Falklands hostilities did not demonstrate that Article IV was weak; it demonstrated just how strong it was. During those hostilities, there were no hostilities south of sixty degrees South, and that, if one thinks in geopolitical and strategic terms, was remarkable — and I do not believe that it had nothing at all to do with the Antarctic Treaty and Article IV. But on a point which arises here, *Ambassador Komora* was absolutely right, Article IV did not solve the sovereignty problem. What it did was to put aside the dispute, the manifestation of the dispute. We have lived for a quarter of a century without the tensions which would otherwise arise in a disputed area of sovereignty. That is a record of which many other parts of the world would be very proud.

I may come now to the third point, which is the *common heritage of mankind*. I think, I heard the comment that there was no inherent problem in applying this concept to Antarctica, and the moon and the sea-bed were quoted as examples. I think if one is going to take that view, one has to ask oneself a question which has been mentioned several times here, whether the existence of some kind of ordered regime (whether it is a regime valid *erga omnes* or not is another matter), but whether the existence of some kind of ordered regime for Antarctica is relevant, and, further, whether the existence of claims to sovereignty is relevant. Because both of those two factors distinguish Antarctica from the moon and outer space and the sea-bed.

Fourthly, and perhaps lastly, to pick up on the thought that was expressed that one should resolve the sovereignty problems by vesting the Antarctic in the UN — I think one had better ask oneself what that actually means: and what it means is that the states who assert sovereignty have got to give that sovereignty up, in favour of the United Nations. Now, as an aside, a very interesting legal problem which arises is whether the United Nations has the power to receive that kind of authority. But my main concern is with the relevance of that proposal to the settlement of international disputes in general. Is it a general solution to international sovereignty disputes? In other words, should Gibraltar be given to the United Nations? Should Burkina Faso and Mali have given to the United Nations that bit of disputed territory which was recently subject to a decision of the International Court? Should China and India, who have disputed territories, do the same? Should China and the Soviet Union? Should disputed areas in general be given to the United Nations as a way of solving the dispute? I think the answer is "no," but then the alternative is, is this a solution which is specific to Antarctica? And if that is the answer, then I ask myself, "Why?" Those advancing that solution have to say why, and I think the only answer that was expressed today was that it is a remote open space, like the moon and the sea-bed — *Finn Sollie* drew attention to Siberia, I mentioned the Gobi Desert, and central Australia; and how about the Sahara, where Chad already has a territorial dispute with a neighboring country? I mean, what is the distinguishing characteristic of Antarctica? It seems to be the view (we are back to where I started) that somehow you can ignore the claims to sovereignty. I think that anyone who is proposing solutions to the Antarctic problems, and there are very serious problems, must face up to the sovereignty problem in a realistic way. The Antarctic Treaty does so, I think that CCAMLR does so, and in the minerals negotiations, despite what *Vladimir Golitsyn* has said, I think we are trying to do so. But there will be, there can be, no solution, whether in the minerals negotiations, in the UN, or in seminars, just by ignoring sovereignty and the sovereignty claims as an inconvenient and troublesome concept that can just be forgotten about and swept aside. Over many centuries, it is an observable historical fact that states do not readily give away their sovereignty, and there is absolutely no reason to believe that states with sovereignty in Antarctica are likely to differ in this respect from the behaviour of other states elsewhere.

That was all I was going to say by way of comment. But can I answer three questions that have been asked? In one word each.

First of all, *Jim Barnes*, who asked about the bifocal reference to coastal state areas; and to him I would simply say that the area to which the minerals regime would apply is still very much a matter under negotiation, and therefore the comment he made, while justified on one set of assumptions, may not be justified by the time we get to the end of our negotiations. We must wait and see. Second, there was the comment about privacy being normal in international organizations. Well, I think we can all have differing views about that. My view, and certainly my experience, is that real negotiation, as opposed to posturing, takes place in private. Thirdly, there was the question about the Canadian theory of custodianship. I think my comment on that is that it is not something that I am aware has actively affected the course of the minerals negotiations. It may well be one which commentators, when we have finished our work, will imply to us. Thank you.

R. Wolfrum, Chairman:

Thank you *Arthur*. *Cristian*, I believe it is your turn now.

C. Maquieira:

Thank you, Rudi. Since I have spoken in the morning I will be telegraphic with my comments. The first one is that this debate has been going on all day on the legitimacy of the Antarctic Treaty Parties to engage in a minerals negotiation. I would turn the argument around, in the sense that questioning the legitimacy would imply that the Antarctic Treaty Parties have made an active usurpation in order to carry this out, and I do not think that that is the case.

With regard to the question of *common heritage*, I think that two things have to be said. As it is reflected in the Law of the Sea Convention, it is a principle which has an emphasis on exploitation. The proof of that is for one to look carefully at the environmental protection provisions regarding the effect of sea-bed mining on the environment, which are very general and imprecise and probably useless — I am sure there are people here who are much more expert on this who would demonstrate that.

The other question, with regard to *common heritage* and besides the arguments of claims, is that if you go back to the 1977 Law of the Sea negotiation, and you are in the summer of 1977 and you are meeting in New York, you had, at that time, many scenarios as to what would happen with the Convention, but the one scenario you did not have at that time was that you would have four major industrial and technological powers, non-parties to the Treaty, who are capable of exploiting the sea-beds and not members, and you did not have the scenario that you would be organizing an institution for four mine sites. So, I am in favor of the *common heritage of mankind* in the sea-bed, but I have to look back and observe that ten years ago we had many things in mind, but the two which I have just mentioned, we did not, and that is a current reality which may not change in the short to medium term. So, if you combine the exploitation emphasis of *common heritage*, plus the use of what can be probably called "wrong assumptions," it must be recalled that in 1977 we were being told that by 1988, that means next year, there would be sea-bed mining. Now we are talking into the early to middle twenty-first century, but nevertheless, we have machinery in place, under the assumption that it was going to take place next year. And if you add that to the fact that in Antarctica the criteria for approaching the minerals negotiation is basically a protection from environmental impact, which is not the case in sea-beds, you may find that, besides the question of claims, and besides the question of a regime, that from the point-of-view of approach to Antarctica, and from the point-of-view of the effects of a particular assumption regarding *common heritage of mankind*, there may be basic and fundamental differences. I have some other comments on privacy, but I think they were covered by *Arthur Watts*. Thank you.

R. Wolfrum, Chairman:

Thank you. The next speaker will be *Mr. Koch.*

J. Koch:

Thank you, Mr. Chairman. The presentation made by *Arthur* gave a good picture of the negotiations on the mineral resources regime. I was very much intrigued by the term "Creative Diplomacy," and perhaps this term should be evaluated a little bit more in a further seminar to see which are the limits, and which are the advantages, and disadvantages of such a method. But having listened to other interventions today, I have the impression that the subject of *Arthur*'s presentation was perhaps not the right one; perhaps we should have had a presentation on lessons to be learned from the Law of the Sea Conference, because there are tendencies to bring into the negotiations on the mineral resources regime questions which have been dealt with unsuccessfully in the Law of the Sea Conference, and which prompted some countries not to sign the Convention and to stay outside. It would be a disaster if the same happened again in the negotiations on an Antarctic mineral resources regime and if under the heading of the *Principle of the Common Heritage of Mankind* subjects would be introduced in those negotiations that led to the opposition of major states to Part XI of the Law of the Sea Convention. Therefore I want to caution against such a development, because it would create major difficulties. The principle of *common heritage of mankind* is not well defined, and I think it creates more problems than it solves because the interests of mankind consist of the sum of the interests of all its members. By referring to the interests of mankind the interests of its members do not disappear. They will be pursued further on and the necessity remains to find a reconciliation between the differing interests. By asking for the application of the principle of *common heritage of mankind* one does not solve these problems; they have to be properly addressed and a fair balance must be found. Part XI of the Law of the Sea Convention is far from accommodating the differing interests. Thank you, Mr. Chairman.

R. Wolfrum, Chairman:

Thank you, *Joachim*. I have now four more speakers on my list, the next one will be *Roger*.

R. Wilson:

I would like to preface my comments by saying that for the organization which I represent, Greenpeace International, the question of which body administers the Antarctic is not, from an environmental perspective, especially relevant. What matters is how it is administrated, and whether the form of administration has sufficient international acceptability to ensure continued peace, security, and environmental protection.

I would like to look in the context of today's discussion at some of the ideas which have been floating around about the minerals regime, and I would like to start from the point where the Antarctic Treaty Consultative Parties say that their negotiations will not prejudice the interests of all mankind in Antarctica. They claim this to be one of the fundamental bases of their negotiations, but what I see to be more apparent is that each country, as might well be expected in any international negotiation, is primarily looking after its own self-interest, and I would observe that it is very difficult for countries to reconcile their self-interests with the interests of others. Non-Treaty states, I think, have had their interests hardly considered in such negotiations and I would say that it is perhaps somewhat arrogant of the Treaty Consultative Parties, to take the attitude that they are able to determine, themselves, the best interests of mankind as a whole. Even some of the Non-consultative Parties find that the consultation that they have received in the process of these negotiations is rather limited; I think that the representative of Peru, who spoke earlier on, acknowledged that the real power lay with the Consultative Parties in the minerals regime and, in fact, in the Treaty as a whole.

I think that there needs to be some kind of rapprochement; both the Antarctic Treaty System and its critics seem to have locked themselves into positions from which retreat is very difficult. There needs to be some kind of forum, some kind of debate in which a real interchange of ideas is possible, free of any prejudice as to what the eventual outcome might be. Last year, I think there was a significant movement during the United Nations debate, with many of the developing countries, which had been highly critical of the Antarctic Treaty System, suggesting that the Antarctic Treaty might indeed form a basis for future development of an administration for the Antarctic. It appears, as an observer of the whole process, that the Antarctic Treaty Consultative Parties have yet to match this kind of concession, if you like.

I close by re-emphasizing that my organization's concerns are the maintenance of peace and environmental protection, and that we have no vested interest in one system or the other; however, I would observe that if international discord does exist, as it certainly does on this issue, then it should be faced squarely, with genuine attempts to try and meet the interests of all those concerned. Thank you.

R. Wolfrum, Chairman:

Thank you, *Roger*. I would like to object to what you have just said. I do not think it wise to foreclose off-hand that the Antarctic Treaty Consultative Parties cannot or will not work in the interest of a broader community. May I just draw your attention to a small, but very significant provision in the German Constitution, Article 14, according to which an individual may use his or her property only in the best interests of the community as a whole. The same system, I do believe, could apply to Antarctica.

The next speaker on my list will be *Finn Sollie*, followed by Mr. *Messer*.

F. Sollie:

Well, Mr. Chairman, if I may, I was a bit puzzled about the logic in this last intervention. First, it is irrelevant, in a sense, to Greenpeace, which organization handles Antarctica. Second, the Consultative Parties may be assumed to think only of their own interests, therefore, another forum is needed, in which I suppose, the Consultative Parties will have an equal right to be present. So, that organization, too, would have a group of self-serving states according to the Greenpeace definition.

My experience with what happens in the Treaty System is rather the contrary. Seldom does one meet so many people representing so many states, which are so aware of the broader interests, and the Treaty itself is the best example you can have of that, I think. Now, I can understand that people may feel a bit insulted if they take words and names as characterizations of their inner quality and character; I stick to my guns where the new imperialists are concerned, and I would maintain that there is a danger in allowing certain expressions to blind one's vision. "There is a need to get the discussion back on track," it was said. Yes, a track was provided in the very conclusion of my relatively long statement. Namely, a double track, and this does not allude to NATO's double-track policies, but it rather alludes to international double-track thinking.

I said first as my conclusion, yes, the legitimacy of the Antarctic Treaty is established and must be recognized as being there. I said the Antarctic Treaty States will have to accept that there is a wider international community interest, and act on that basis, and I think that is the track upon which solutions will have to be pursued at all; it is the only way to do it.

Now, in conclusion, just one word about the *common heritage* idea. I think it is extremely unfortunate that this is used as a flag, waved at all times against anyone who has an interest of a different kind from the flag-wearer. That is, by using the phrase *common heritage*, you merely introduce a principle of ethical norms, values, ideas about equity, justice, and all these things. There is no legal function in that, beyond that which can be pursued if the principle is applied in a decision which is legally binding. I think it is important to be aware that "common heritage" becomes *common heritage* if it is enacted in a given context, and only then. Apart from that, it is a good idea, and I am all for good ideas, in the context of a legal structure. There is another side to the question of *common heritage*, and that is this: development has a cost, and if you want to have a heritage, you have to pay the heritage dues, and that, in Antarctica, can be extremely costly. Long before any benefits accrue from the heritage, the costs have to be paid, and that is one question which we have not had in this debate at all, but it should be considered.

R. Wolfrum, Chairman:

Thank you, *Finn*. The next speaker will be *Mr. Messer*.

K. Messer:

Thank you. I would like to add just a short comment on Article IV, because it has been mentioned so often today, and lately this afternoon in connection with the *Beeby* draft. It has been said that if the negotiations on minerals did not follow Article IV, then this might be destructive for the whole Antarctic System. One could ask oneself what is Article IV really about? Does it contain a solution for our negotiations, which we only have to apply? If we really look at this Article IV, we see that it protects both sides, it protects the Claimants and it protects the Non-claimants. That is to say, it protects those who claim to have more rights than others, and it protects those who claim that nobody has more rights. Well, the question really arises, is this not logically impossible? What is it? What is that magical formula which apparently does not contain anything in substance, and yet has made sure that we have done so well for a quarter of a century? I think if we look at what this Article IV really gives to both sides, it is not so much a right, but an obligation, and I think that obligation means moderation. If we apply Article IV in this sense, I think it is indeed necessary not to divert from this road, and to apply it in these negotiations. I think that this is a very important aim, and as I am optimistic, I think we will achieve it. Thank you.

R. Wolfrum, Chairman:

The next speaker is *Ian Nicholson*.

I. Nicholson:

We have had a rich harvest of points during the course of today, and I would like, if I may, to comment on just a couple of them.

First, to say how much I enjoyed the presentations of *Mr. Haron* and *Mr. Koroma.* I hope they do not take me amiss if I say that they presented a seductive idealism of internationalism, but the realities — legal, political, and practical — have been underlined by the panel, and by *Finn Sollie.* In the 'Fifties we, perhaps, and the chance of many different solutions — trusteeship, condominium, some sort of UN role, a world territory — but we chose the treaty course, and it has worked extremely well. In regard to Article IV, a number of important basic comments, I believe, are required in the light of comments earlier during the day, but to a substantial degree, *Arthur Watts* has said what I would have said. Article IV is not a panacea, and not a solution. It is a means ot achieving shared objectives, and it will be reflected in the minerals convention, as throughout the Antarctic Treaty System. It does have a basic element of moderation, as *Kurt Messer* said, moderation on all three sides.

Another important aspect, which seems to have become to my mind unduly blurred, relates to the Law of the Sea. It seems to be assumed that in some way the Law of the Sea Convention automatically applies to Antarctica. I thought that *Scott Hajost* even slipped into that point-of-view in his very useful compendium of treaties possibly applying to Antarctica. The fact is that the Law of the Sea Convention does not, cannot apply to Antartica. During the course of the negotiations, it was considered whether it would or should. It was decided by the negotiators not to enter that area. Obviously the Law of the Sea Convention included many elements of international law before it was concluded and is giving rise to further elements subsequently. How it will be adapted, to be, in some of these aspects, applicable to Antarctica is certainly far from clear.

There was some emphasis also on the review of the Antarctic Treaty, as if a review might answer, to a considerable extent, many of the problems we have been discussing today. I would just ask, how would a review help? Are those countries with sovereignty in Antarctica ready to give it up? Are those directly engaged in activities prepared to hand over management of them to an inexperienced and untried international body? Without answers to questions like these, I wonder where review might lead us. As *Ms. Song Li* said, the Treaty is sound; we must continue to improve it, a course we are firmly engaged upon.

Arthur Watts, if I might add to his very useful review of the negotiating process which I recognized very clearly from his comments, omitted one principle he might allow me to mention — the principle of the lead country or person. It came about that, in order to advance particular areas of the draft during the negotiations, it has been useful to draw on the resources of a particular delegation or a particular person. I think of *John Heap* on the environment, Australia in regard to prospecting, the excellent work being done by yourself, *Professor Wolfrum*, on legal issues and that of *Rolf Andersen* on exploration and development, and so on. This is another principle which *Arthur* might add to his valuable list.

I have two more points; I shall deal with them only by saying that *Mr. Khan*'s comments on *Mr. Woolcott*'s speech are, I believe, a misunderstanding of what he said, and your comments on *common heritage*, I believe I will be able to return to tomorrow.

R. Wolfrum, Chairman:

Thank you. The last speaker on my list is *John Heap.*

J. Heap:

Mr. Chairman, thank you very much. I have a slight problem with my neighbour to my left, but I hope he will allow me to be heard.

R. Wolfrum, Chairman:

You normally handle him quite well.

J. Heap:

Mr. Chairman, I would just like to take this opportunity to talk about two things. One relates to the implication which seems to have run through the interventions of some people here today, that somehow it is the Claimants and their claim to territorial sovereignty which seem to threaten the peace of Antarctica, and the other is to talk about what also seems to be a common thread, and that is that what the law of the sea did was to establish the *common heritage of mankind.* I think it did something else as well, to which I would like to refer.

I start from the proposition that the Treaty requires that any question relating to sovereignty, whether it is an assertion of sovereignty or its non-recognition, shall be dealt with without recourse to the use of force. This is a provision of the Treaty which we all know. A second thing that I want to say is that where there is no ownership of resources, and where these resources are accessible to all states, experience shows that the normal reaction has been a race to get in first, and to plunder those resources. It was indeed, I think, a reaction against this experience which resulted, within the framework of the Law of the Sea Convention, in the assertion of sovereign rights over forty percent of the world's ocean space. That is to say, within forty percent of the world's ocean space in which had previously existed the freedoms of the seas, those freedoms were denied in favour of regulation by individual states. This is looked upon, I think worldwide, as a valuable contribution to the proper and improved regulation of the utilization of resources which had not previously been subject to any form of ownership.

I see in this context the notion of the *common heritage of mankind* itself as somehow almost running against the tide of history. Common ownership of resources has been generally seen, I think, as one which does not work. Instead, the investment of resources in individual ownership is seen as providing for more adequate regulation, even though I admit that such regulation is often in the interest of the owner. In this context, I see the maintenance of the assertions of territorial sovereignty in the Antarctic against non-recognition of such assertions as offering a means of finding solutions to Antarctic resources use, in which the relative strengths and weaknesses of individual ownership and common ownership can be debated. It is implicit that the outcome of such a debate in respect to any resource, would neither be the same as it would have been if assertions to territorial sovereignty were universally recognized, nor would it be the same as it would have been if assertions to territorial sovereignty had never been made.

I therefore see assertions of territorial sovereignty, far from being a threat to the peace, as rather allowing for a creative dynamic tension between the Claimants and Non-claimants, within a context, which because of the Treaty, prohibits the use of force for the resolution of such differences. Thank you.

R. Wolfrum, Chairman:

Thank you, *John*. *Ambassador Koroma*, please.

A. Koroma:

I think it is necessary to state that I did emphasize the positive aspects of the Antarctic Treaty this morning. Unfortunately *common heritage* has been identified and isolated, and I just want to say that some, of course, at least accept that the Antarctic Treaty has certain positive and salient aspects. Secondly, I would like to remind the meeting that in the Middle East neighboring states have agreed on a joint exploration of oil fields which happen to be in areas of dispute. So I think the proposal to apply the *common heritage principle* to Antarctica should not be seen as an attempt to appropriate it by the international community; actually, the intent is positive. It is looking for a positive solution. I would like the meeting to bear that in mind. Thank you.

R. Wolfrum, Chairman:

Thank you, *Mr. Koroma*, for a very appropriate closing remark.*

K. Sander:

In response to *Finn Sollie*'s statement yesterday, on the openness of the Antarctic Treaty System, where he stated that access to the group that makes the decisions is open to all who are willing to pay the price: not all countries are able to pay this price, but they can still have an honest, positive interest in taking part in the scientific activities and the decision-making procedure. These countries will not be able to obtain the experience required for getting Consultative Status unless these criteria are changed, modified or amended — so that this experience from participation in joint projects, or perhaps experience and knowledge from Arctic matters, could be the ticket to open the door. On the other hand, this could be a part of the solution of the problem with the over-concentration of stations in the easily accessible areas.

* Due to the lack of time, the following statement was in writing — *Ed.*

Comment

*Bo Johnson Theutenberg**

Thank you, Mr. Chairman. Since I am participating in this Seminar, and I am glad to do that, I thought that I might as well say something with regard to Swedish activities in polar research, especially with regard to Antarctica.

Sweden has long been engaged in polar research — we had the two *Nordenskjolds*, one in the Arctic, the Northeast Passage, and on Antarctica, *Otto Nordenskjold*. Sweden was on Antarctica in 1901, with the *Otto Nordenskjold* expedition. Another expedition took place in 1949—52, together with Norway and Great Britain, the traditional partners of Sweden in polar science activities. However, Sweden did not become an original signatory to the Antarctic Treaty, because of the very fact that during the IGY in 1957 Sweden was not present in Antarctica. Only those nations which were active in Antarctica in 1957 were invited to the Washington Conference in 1959, which came to adopt the Antarctic Treaty. This Treaty later became one of the most successful treaties, one of the few that actually has worked in accordance with its wording. The coming into being of the Antarctic Treaty in 1959, then, meant actually the termination of Swedish activities in Antarctica, but not in polar science in general. So that is how the Antarctic Treaty worked, in relation to my country. But since much has happened in world politics and international law in thirty years, especially with regard to the polar areas, both the Arctic and the Antarctic, Sweden decided, following the reactivation of polar scientific activities during the 'Thirties and the 'Eighties, to accede to the Antarctic Treaty, which it did in 1984 as a Non-consultative member.

This act of Sweden should be seen as a strong support for the Antarctic Treaty System, which actually, to my mind, is the only way of preserving peace and good order in the Antarctic and in the southern ocean region, as things now stand. I think that one must realize the crucial political importance claimed by Article IV of the Treaty. Realistically speaking, nothing can substitute the political and the legal balance which is being upheld by Article IV. So the Treaty is a corner-

* Mr. *Bo Johnson Theutenberg*, Legal Adviser, Ministry of Foreign Affairs, Stockholm, Sweden. The opinions expressed in this volume are the personal views of their authors only.

stone, from the political and legal point-of-view. The balance implicit in that Article also must be upheld in the mineral resources regime negotiations.

One should take some important factors into consideration when talking about Article IV. I think I would, but perhaps more in my capacity as a professor of International Law, re-direct many interested parties to enter into deeper analysis of the state of the prevailing principles of international law relevant to titles, to land areas. So when talking about the claims, that is, potential sovereignty (I refer here to what *Ambassador Berguño* and *Arthur Watts* were saying yesterday), I think one must take into consideration, for instance, the principles that were set down by the very important judgment in 1933 called the *Eastern Greenland Case*. That was by the Permanent Court of International Justice, and was relevant to claims of sovereignty over desert polar areas. The question was how much *animus occupandi* a state must display in relation to a desert polar area in order to be recognized as the holder of sovereignty — or, as the Court put down, the intention and will to act as a sovereign and some actual exercise or display of such authority.

I believe that many of the claims, perhaps not the entire sectors, but many of the claims, should be seen in these perspectives. There are many more interesting cases to mention here, the *Clipperton Island Case* (1932), the *Caravan Island Case* (1885), the *Island of Palmas Case* (1928), and also the *Western Sahara Case* (1975) — all are of relevance here. A judge of the International Court of Justice would never be able to overlook these principles, especially in relation to the fact that many of the claims were made very long ago, predating the coming into being of the Treaty. Even if the society of states has grown considerably, and new ideas have been introduced in relation to Antarctica (for instance, that it should be the *common heritage of mankind*), we cannot realistically ignore existing principles of international law — in this case, the principles of legal title to land areas — and introduce something else, perhaps now, of a political kind. The International Court would not accept an argumentation of this kind, and it is with those perspectives in mind, I believe, that Article IV plays such an overwhelmingly crucial role. Only if the Claimants freely would give up their claims, then new legal and political factors substituting Article IV could perhaps be introduced into Antarctic affairs. But reality is as it is; the claims are there, and that is why we must have an Article IV and why the Antarctic Treaty plays such a vital role in world politics. But what the future development, or the *opinio juris*, and customary law, would lead up to, is not quite clear now. Perhaps it will lead into the realm of the *common heritage*, but that is not the case now.

Having said this, it must also, however, be emphasized that my country has the fullest understanding of many of those views being expressed by third parties, that is to say, many of the developing countries, and expressed in the United Nations. There is much in those arguments; I will not go into detail. We must thank Malaysia for having made the provisions of the Antarctic Treaty System as well-known as they are today.

This increased knowledge of the Antarctic Treaty System has, however, led to a remarkable increase in international support for the Antarctic Treaty, a fact that governments all over the world certainly take note of. There are new Consultative Parties — China, India, Brazil, Uruguay — and the circle of the NCPs is increasing. The Swedish Government has clarified its position in 1984, when entering the Antarctic Treaty System, on the grounds of the Swedish historical role in Antarctica and its forthcoming Antarctic scientific program. Now, that decision is to support the Treaty, because in spite of all arguments heard, we cannot see any other realistic alternatives. But our view is also that the Treaty System should be open-minded to the arguments of nations outside the Treaty, to enable itself to work out mechanisms of information and possible cooperation with other nations.

Plans have been going on for some years, to establish a Swedish scientific base in the Norwegian Dronning Maud Land area, and next year these activities will increase, and continue for many more years to come. The Swedish Antarctic Program should be seen as only one part of our polar activities; the other part is in the Arctic, together with other Nordic countries and other Arctic nations. This means that the Swedish support of the Treaty will increase. The notification in accordance with Article IX of the Treaty, that is, a request to become a Consultative Party, will be made in the near future.

Mr. Chairman, before concluding, I would also like to mention that Sweden has the view that, for the future, we must discuss more in terms of scientific and logistic cooperation in Antarctica, and I am here referring back to what was said the other day. Some states have the experience, and the economic possibility, to establish themselves as Consultative States. It costs a lot of money. As it is now, we are more-or-less forcing states to flex their "multi-national muscles" in order to become a Consultative State. With this procedure we are in fact adding to the environmental problems of Antarctica and to the proliferation of stations in Antarctica. We know very well the prerequisites for becoming a Consultative State, but I believe that, for the sake of us all and for the sake of Antarctica itself, we must at some point start discussing more in terms of scientific and logistic cooperation in Antarctica. There are such ideas, as you know, within the framework of the European Science Foundation, enabling some European countries to cooperate on the Antarctic issue, and thereby perhaps, in the future, qualify themselves for becoming Consultative Parties. But this concept of scientific and logistic cooperation could certainly be applied also in broader ways in the future.

Science, then, goes together with environmental protection of Antarctica, and this has been a most important factor for Sweden — and continously, we have been advocating a strong environmental protection regime for Antarctica, especially during the mineral resources regime negotiations. We have said that it is important to have a broad independent input of scientific and environmental knowledge. It is important, and natural, I think, for an organization like IUCN, and I am also here referring back, to what *Dr. Burhenne* has previously said, to be given a role in relation to Antarctica, in general and also in an advisory committee of the mineral resources regime. Thank you very much.

The Legal Status of Ice in International Law

*Gerard J. Mangone**

International law has been widely applied to land, sea, air, and outer space, but the status of ice has been largely speculative. Simply regarded as frozen water, ice has been assimilated with the prescriptions for boundary limits and jurisdiction to land, where it is ice-covered, or to the sea, where it has been congealed. In the 1982 Law of the Sea Convention, not yet in force but the broadest consensus of states about international law for marine features, the word "ice" only appears in one of 306 articles, as an adjective, simply permitting states to adopt non-discriminatory laws and regulations to prevent pollution from vessels in "ice-covered areas."[1]

The first serious consideration of the legal status of ice in international law was precipitated by the discovery of the North Pole at the beginning of the twentieth century. It was then generally held that since the north polar region was covered by water, beyond the territorial sea of any state, its status was similar to the high seas, open to the use of all states, not able to be occupied or possessed. Note was taken that the north polar sea was frozen, often solid for long periods of time, but always moving, albeit slowly.

With regard to the south polar region, early legal speculation about the status of ice had to consider a vast area of land, rather than high seas, covered by ice that protrudes in shelves over the marginal waters of a continent, and that is also surrounded by frozen seas. Until the 1930s there was no good map of Antarctica and until the 1950s knowledge about the geography, climate, atmosphere, and other physical conditions of this white wilderness was rather superficial. Without any international agreement on Antarctica until the Antarctic Treaty of 1959 and without any customary law or judicial guidance about the status

---

* Dr. *Gerard J. Mangone*, H. Rodney Sharp Professor of International Law and Organization, Director, Center for the Study of Marine Policy at the University of Delaware, U.S.A.

[1] Article 234: "Coastal States have the right to adopt and enforce non-discriminatory laws and regulations for the prevention, reduction and control of marine pollution from vessels in ice-covered areas within the limits of the exclusive economic zone . . . ." United Nations Convention on the Law of the Sea, done at Montego Bay, Dec. 10, 1982, UN Doc. A/CONF. 62/122 (hereinafter: LOSC).

of ice, scholars tended to discount any special legal status for the frozen sea and were doubtful about the place of shelf ice.

Exploration, research, and the potential for the exploitation of resources in the polar regions have advanced rapidly over the last twenty-five years. An American submarine has sailed under the North Pole and a Soviet vessel has sailed directly to the North Pole. Research stations have proliferated on the ice of the north polar region. During the summer, some four thousand people from thirteen states may be working in Antarctica. Fishing in polar waters has become more feasible and minerals may be available in both the north and south polar regions, whether covered by ice or by the sea.

More pertinent to a consideration of the legal status of ice is the universal extension of jurisdiction by coastal states over the submerged lands and sea contiguous to their coasts. The extension of state jurisdiction over areas that have not been effectively occupied and over which few, if any, displays of sovereignty or administrative acts have been witnessed, according to the traditional tenets of international law, may admit a new legal status for ice.

I. Physical Aspects of Ice for Legal Consideration

About ten percent of the earth's surface is perennially covered by ice, 90 % of which is in Antarctica, and 6 % in Greenland. There are six types of ice that may involve international legal considerations: (1) pack ice or free-floating frozen seawater; (2) fast ice or frozen seawater attached to shores; (3) shelf ice or frozen freshwater; (4) icebergs or free-floating shelf ice; (5) interstitial ice or permafrost; (6) and pingo ice.

1. Pack Ice

Great packs of frozen seawater surround both the North Pole and the continent of Antarctica. Because of the different configuration of the land masses and the variations in climatic conditions, there is considerable difference between the packs of ice in the northern and southern regions. Around Antarctica the packs of ice will range from 2.6 million square kilometers in the summer to 18.8 million square kilometers in the winter, whereas the Arctic pack of ice ranges from 5.2 million square kilometers in the summer to about 11.7 million square kilometers in the winter. The Arctic pack ice is more stable and thicker than Antarctic ice. More new ice is formed each year around Antarctica, which tends to be lighter and thinner than old ice, and there are more winds. Around Antarctica the pack ice can move at speeds as fast as two to two and one-half kilometers an hour. Although thinner ice, with movement, makes the opening of channels of navigation easier, it also presents a hazard by quickly closing up gaps and holding anchored ships steadfast. The north polar ice pack slowly follows a giant clockwise eddy, covering even in the summer an area almost the size of Europe with a thickness of three to six meters of frozen seawater. Emplacements of research stations are more feasible on Arctic pack ice than the pack ice surrounding Antarctica.[2]

2. *Fast Ice*

Along the coasts of Arctic lands, sea water freezes, particularly in rugged shores of rocks, inlets, and bays. Always subject to variations in climate, such ice may or may not melt during the warm months. It is observable that fast ice attached to shores in some areas is virtually permanent and has been used regularly for transportation, for hunting, and even for habitation by indigenous people.

While the edges of fast ice may not be as sharply delineated as land, due to fluctuations of temperature, nevertheless there are good indications of the minimum recess of the ice edge over time and certainty that in some places in the fast ice remains fast perennially.

3. *Shelf Ice*

Both the land masses of Greenland and Antarctica lie under enormous ice sheets, Greenland about 80 % and Antarctica about 98 %. These ice sheets or glaciers are formed by snow and other precipitation, which are frozen, compacted, and re-crystallized into ice under the weight of successive layers. The enormous weight of the ice sheets, gravity, climate, and underlying terrain make the ice sheets spread out and down from centers of accumulation.

Greenland has an area of 1,834,000 square kilometers, about twice the size of Nigeria or Pakistan. In Greenland the ice sheets average about 1,500 meters thick and the glaciers flow from a mountainous basin through a number of outlets into fjords and where their tongues break off they float out to sea as icebergs. There is little shelf ice in Greenland.

Antarctica is the coldest and driest of all the continents on earth. It is about 14,000,000 square kilometers or about one and one-half times the size of the United States. Except for some small marginal and peninsular areas, Antarctica is completely covered by ice sheets with an average thickness of some 2,000 meters. Ice shelves surround about

---

[2] I have drawn my data on pack ice and shelf ice from a number of encyclopedias, including the New Encyclopedia Britannica, 15th edition, Chicago 1987 and the Encyclopedia of Physical Science and Technology, *Robert A. Meyers* (ed.), Academic Press, Orlando 1987. Also useful was U. S. Central Intelligence Agency, Polar Regions Atlas, U. S. Government Printing Office, Washington 1978.

half the coast of Antarctica and make up about 10 percent of its vast area. The shelves are thick masses of ice that protrude beyond the low water mark of the continent out to sea. They are either grounded on the sea bottom or extend further out and float upon the sea itself.

The largest Antarctic ice shelf at the Ross Sea is about the size of France; other large shelves are the Filchner Shelf at the Weddell Sea, the Shackleton Shelf on the Indian Ocean coast, and the Larsen Shelf on the Antarctic Peninsula. The shelf at the Ross Sea may be as thick as 1,000 meters at its grounding line (where it begins to float) to 250 meters thick at its outer edge facing the sea with a cliff that may be 30 meters high. Moreover, shelf ice lies aground to at least 200 meters below sea-level along 60 % or more of the seaward boundary. The scientific view is that in contrast to the growth and disappearance of vast ice sheets in the northern hemisphere during the Pleistocene period (1.7 million to 10,000 years ago), the ice sheet of Antarctica seems to have undergone relatively small changes in size.[3]

4. *Icebergs*

The tongues of ice that break off from the glaciers of Greenland and float out to sea, creating hazards for navigation in the North Atlantic Ocean, are different from the shelf icebergs that crack off from the Antarctic sheets. In the north polar region the many icebergs tend to be about 180 meters long and 45 meters wide, shaped like a mountain (*berg*) with a crest standing some 5 or 10 meters above the water — while about six-sevenths of the mass lies below the water. During World War II a rare giant of an iceberg about 1,350 meters long, 1,110 meters wide, and 18 meters above the sea was observed in the North Atlantic Ocean. Very few of these icebergs are tabular in form.

In the southern polar region, the ice shelf that breaks off from the land-fast ice sheet and floats away, by contrast with the Greenland bergs, is mammoth in size and generally tabular in form. Antarctic icebergs may be up to 60 to 100 kilometers in length, stand about 70 meters above the water and could provide very secure platforms for human activities. Moreover, these huge chunks of frozen freshwater could be a resource of great value to parched areas of the world.

5. *Interstitial Ice*

In regions where temperatures below 0° centigrade persist for two or more years, such as the Arctic and sub-Arctic areas, the rocks and soil

[3] See *D. J. Drewry* and *G. de Q. Robin*, Form and Flow of the Antarctic Ice Sheet During the Last Million Years in: The Climate Record in Polar Ice Sheets, Cambridge University Press 1983.

particles may be consolidated by interstitial ice. Such formations are usually referred to as permafrost. Very large areas, mainland and islands, perhaps some 25 percent of the terrestrial land surface, are underlain by interstitial ice. With temperature changes, particularly in the sub-Arctic, such ice is not completely stable and may raise questions about the definition of the surface area as "land," especially in a legal definition of an island as "a naturally formed area of land, surrounded by water, which is above water at high tide."

6. *Pingo Ice*

In 1969 the American ice-strengthened tanker *Manhattan* made an experimental passage through the Northwest Passage from Baffin Bay to the Beaufort Sea and returned, accompanied throughout by the Canadian icebreaker *John A. MacDonald.* During that voyage the radar brought to the navigator's attention conical shapes sticking up from the sea bottom that clearly posed a hazard to navigation. These cones consisted of very old ice that over a long time had become coated with frozen muck and they were dubbed "pingo" ice.

7. *State Sovereignty Over Territory*

It was *Emer de Vattel's* opinion in the eighteenth century that the law of nations "will only recognize the ownership and sovereignty of a Nation over unoccupied lands when the Nation is in actual occupation of them, when it forms a settlement, or makes some actual use of them."[4] In the nineteenth century, the General Act Respecting the Congo, signed by 14 nations on 24 February 1884, gave substance to this opinion by requiring any party that took a new possession in Africa to ensure that it had sufficient authority to maintain its acquired rights.

In the twentieth century, the prime illustration of the conditions for the recognition of the sovereignty of state over territory was the arbitration between the United States and the Netherlands over the Island of Palmas in 1928. There the arbitrator held that "an inchoate title of discovery must be completed within a reasonable period by the effective occupation of the region claimed to be discovered" and "a continuous and peaceful display of the functions of state within a given region is a constituent element of sovereignty." But the arbitrator also noted that such manifestations of state sovereignty may be different in different areas, depending upon accessibility, and where there are no conventional boundary lines, the actual and continous peaceful display of state functions would be a sound criterion for territorial sovereignty.[5]

---

[4] *Emer de Vattel*, Le Droit des gens, Chapter XVIII, Section 207.

[5] Arbitral Award, *The Island of Palmas* (or Miangas) *Case* (1928), in: RIAA II 829—871, 846, 840; see also AJIL, 22 (1928), 867—912, 884, 876.

Three years after the *Island of Palmas Arbitration*, the King of Italy made an arbitral award of Clipperton Island, a remote, uninhabited island in the Pacific Ocean, to France against the claim of Mexico. A French expedition had visited the island in 1858 and given notice of its claim to a consul in the Hawaiian Islands. But no further display of sovereignty occurred until 1897 when a French naval ship found three Americans on the island and demanded an explanation from the United States. Shortly thereafter Mexican marines landed on the island and hoisted their flag over it. The arbitrator held that since the island was completely uninhabited, the first moment that the occupying state made its appearance and took possession must be considered as a complete occupation. Even if France did not exercise its power in a positive manner, it did not forfeit its right and had never shown any intention of abandoning the island.[6]

Five years after the *Island of Palmas Arbitration*, the Permanent Court of International Justice was called upon by Norway and Denmark to determine whether Denmark's claim to territorial sovereignty over all the vast ice-covered area of Greenland should be recognized under international law. In its opinion the court said that in reviewing the records of decision in cases on territorial sovereignty it was clear that "in many cases the tribunal has been satisfied with very little in the way of the actual exercise of sovereign rights," providing another state could not show a superior claim. And "this is particularly true in the case of claims to sovereignty over areas of thinly populated or unsettled countries."[7]

In the 1950s, moreover, questions arose about the claim of coastal states to exclusive resource rights on and in the submerged continental shelves adjacent to their coasts. A claim to its continental shelf resources was unilaterally initiated by the United States in 1945 and was followed by similar claims thereafter by several states. Obviously "discovery" as a basis for the claim was not relevant, and neither occupation nor displays of sovereignty had been demonstrated in submerged lands beyond the territorial sea. The only possible legal justification was contiguity, a principle that had been largely dismissed in previous territorial disputes and is still denied in arguments over dry land areas.

After the *Island of Palmas*, the *Clipperton Island*, and the *Eastern Greenland* cases, followed by claims to invisible shelf resources, it was apparent that actual settlement or exploitation was not required as a

[6] See the *Clipperton Island Arbitration* (1931), in: RIAA II, 1105—1111; AJIL 26 (1932) 390—394, 394.

[7] *Legal Status of Eastern Greenland Case*, Judgment, 5 April 1933, P.C.I.J. Ser. A/B (1933) No. 53, 22—75, 46; World Court Reports, *Manley O. Hudson* (ed.), Vol. III, 148—251.

basis for effective occupation. As *Humphrey Waldock* put it, "what is required is effective display of state activity in such a manner as the circumstances of the territory demand." On the same question, moreover, *Hersch Lauterpacht* wrote that effectiveness is not a magic formula; it depends upon the situation and circumstances. Indeed, in some circumstances, such as submerged lands, contiguity may be an essential element and may be the only element of substance in an otherwise abstract occupation.[8]

II. Jurisdiction Over Ice

The legal status of ice under international law is unsatisfactory. Earlier opinions that ice is nothing more than frozen water and that its appearance beyond territorial waters makes it part of the high seas, which cannot be appropriated by any state, are no longer sufficient. The acknowledged right of states to extend their jurisdiction out to 200 miles from baselines on their coasts for virtually all activities except marine transportation and even as far as 350 miles on the sea-floor, far from any proof of discovery, occupation, or exploitation ought to dismiss the shibboleth that ice is nothing more than frozen water and that it cannot be appropriated. Indeed, as modern technology increasingly demonstrates, it is a resource, with form, quality, and possibilities of utilization quite different from water.

1. Pack Ice

The vast masses of pack ice floating on the Arctic seas in the north polar region have never been claimed by any state. When the American *Matthew Peary* returned from his expedition to the North Pole and telegraphed *President William Howard Taft* in 1909, "I have the honor to place the North Pole at your disposal," the United States made no claim, regarding the area as a part of the high seas.

Senator Poirier of Canada in 1907, noting the advances in Arctir exploration, urged his colleagues in the Senate to resolve that the time had come to make a formal declaration of possession of the lands and islands north of Canada and extending to the North Pole. He did not mention ice. Although this initiative of a claim to sectors of the northern polar region was not adopted, by 1925 Canada had passed legislation requiring permission to enter the Canadian Arctic, which, according to the Minister of Interior at the time, included areas right up to the North

[8] *Humphrey Waldock*, The Legal Basis of Claims to the Continental Shelf, The Grotius Society. Transactions for the Year 1950 (1951), 115, cited in: *Marjorie M. Whiteman*, Digest of International Law, Vol. 2, 1052, and *Hersch Lauterpacht*, Sovereignty Over Seabed Areas, in: BYIL XXVII (1950), 376—433, 418.

Pole. In 1956 the Canadian Minister of Northern Affairs and Natural Resources stated in the House of Commons, "... we have never subscribed to the sector theory in application to ice. We are content that our sovereignty exists over all the Arctic islands."[9]

The Tsarist Russian government and the succeeding Soviet government were aggressive in claims to polar territories from 1916 to 1926, particularly against any other state's effort to assert discovery or occupation of Arctic islands. A decree of 1926 asserted that "all lands and islands located in the Arctic to the North, between the coast line of the U.S.S.R. and the North Pole, both already discovered and those which may be discovered in the future" were territories of the Soviet Union, unless they were recognized as the territory of another state at the time of the decree. In the same years, a Soviet scholar of international law, *Eugene A. Korovin*, believed that Soviet sovereignty also extended to the ice floes, internal lakes, and straits in the north polar region. This view was adopted and expanded by *W. Lakhtine* in 1930, who gave his opinion that "Floating ice should be assimilated legally to open polar seas, while ice formations that are more or less immobile should enjoy a legal status equivalent to polar territories ...."[10]

While it is true that all the pack ice around the North Pole is moving and that due to seasonal change there is expansion and contraction, freezing and melting, nevertheless the pack ice is different from water. Scientists believe that there has been an uninterrupted existence of this sea ice for three million years. Very large areas are quite solid, even though some 10 % of the area north of 75 degrees may be unevenly liquid, and the ice drifts quite slowly. Ice floes have been used by the Americans and by the Soviets to build research stations, with communication facilities, and human habitation.

It is not unlikely that further technological changes, concerns over national security, resource demands, and environmental considerations will place a higher value on pack ice as a base for operations. Such a development must open the issues of legal responsibility and legal liability in the areas where mighty ice packs are located.

The legal status of the northern polar region is already in flux. A substantial part of the Arctic Ocean has already been encompassed by the exclusive economic zones of the Soviet Union, the United States, Canada, Denmark (Greenland) and Norway. If the 1982 Law of the Sea Convention should come into force, however, some of the seabed under-

---

[9] Quoted from *Marjorie M. Whiteman*, Digest of International Law, Vol. 2, 1268.

[10] *W. Lakhtine*, Rights Over the Arctic, in: AJIL 24 (1930), 703—717, also, *T. A. Taracouzio*, The Soviet Union and International Law, New York 1935, 56 and *Kazimierz Grzybowski*, Soviet Public International Law, Leyden 1970, 190.

lying the polar ice of the Arctic Ocean could be an international area. Moreover, about one-third of the Arctic Ocean is underlain by continental shelf, which is quite irregular and is very likely to raise delimitation problems both in the length of extension under the ocean and in the delimitation between adjacent states in the northern cone. There are some great depths in the Arctic Ocean, with one sounding reaching 5,502 meters, but on average the sea is comparatively shallow. Off the coasts of Alaska and Greenland, the continental shelf may extend from 60 to 120 miles under the polar sea, but off the coast of Siberia, it may extend as much as 300 to 1,100 miles under the polar sea.

To argue for national sovereignty over all ice-covered areas in the northern polar regions would raise grave objections from the Soviet Union and NATO powers. Indeed, submerged transit of vessels under ice in the northern polar region may be just as vital to international security and trade in the future as transit through archipelagoes and straits used for international navigation. The 1982 Law of the Sea Convention has demonstrated, however, that it is possible in international law to extend state jurisdiction over an exclusive economic zone and a continental shelf for some purposes and not others; it is possible to close up the territorial seas of coastal states in some straits, but restrict their jurisdiction with respect to transit passage of vessels and airplanes. Any approaches to a new legal status for pack ice should have these achievements in mind.

Consideration should be given by the states adjoining the northern polar ice and by other interested states to a multilateral convention that would reserve the use of the pack ice for peaceful purposes, allowing non-discriminatory access to such ice for all states, with no legal effect upon the status of the seas or the seabed beyond national jurisdiction, whether covered by ice or not.

2. *Fast Ice*

The legal situation with regard to fast ice is somewhat easier to analyze and open to clearer prescriptions. Essentially that ice is attached to land over which sovereignty is not ambiguous. As early as 1911 an Imperial Russian decree attempted to set limits for commercial fishing by using an ice-edge off its coasts as a baseline. Up to 1970 the statements of Canada on the legal status of fast ice were, to say the least, ambiguous and often contradictory. Then, in a case (*R. v. Tootalik*) where a female polar bear was shot on fast ice several miles from the land's edge, the court held that jurisdiction was conferred by the Northwest Territories Act over that area even though the territorial sea of Canada was only three miles.

International law has addressed the problem of unstable coasts and permitted the drawing of straight baselines in areas where fringing reef or alluvial deltas call for special treatment. Fast ice would seem analagous to this situation and require appropriate legal treatment.

3. *Shelf Ice*

A legal analysis of shelf ice calls for very different deliberations from an analysis of pack ice. Millions of square kilometers of shelf ice in Antarctica are either grounded on the seabed or overhang the sea. This shelf ice is an integral part of the vast ice sheet covering the land mass of the continent. While it is true that there is a slow movement of much of these mighty layers of ice outward from the land core, with subsequent breaking off or calving of giant icebergs, it is equally true that there is a permanent fringe of ice beyond the low-water mark of the continental shore.

In fixing baselines from which territorial seas, contiguous zones, and exclusive economic zones are measured, the 1982 Law of the Sea Convention has already recognized unstable coastlines and provided measures for demarcation.[11] Although Antarctica was deliberately excluded from any deliberations of the Third UN Law of the Sea Conference, the fixing of baselines for the measurement of marine zones may have to be considered.

The 1959 Antarctic Treaty, the Conservation of the Antarctic Marine Living Resources, and the proposed convention on Antarctic Mineral Resources have pointedly suspended the issue of claims to state sovereignty on the continent and, therefore, contiguous seas. The agreements have focused the application of their provisions to the area southward from the 60 degree latitude or the approximate Antarctic convergence line of the seas.[12] Thus any consideration of baselines from which national marine zones might be measured has been held in abeyance. But it is noteworthy that the Antarctic Treaty, with its provisions on demilitarization, scientific research and exchange, and

---

[11] Article 7, para 2, of the LOSC provides ... "Where because of the presence of a delta and other natural conditions the coastline is highly unstable, the appropriate points may be selected along the furthest seaward extent of the low-water line and, notwithstanding subsequent regression . . . shall remain effective until changed by the coastal State in accordance with this Convention." LOSC, *Loc. cit.* (note 1).

[12] The Antarctic Treaty, done at Washington on 1 Dec. 1959, UNTS vol. 402 (1961), p. 71, reprinted in: *Rüdiger Wolfrum* (ed.), Antarctic Challenge, Berlin 1984, Annex 229 *et seq.* The Convention on Antarctic Living Marine Resources, U.S. Department of State, T.I.A.S. 1040, in *Rüdiger Wolfrum* (ed.), Antarctic Challenge, Berlin 1984, Annex 229 *et seq.* Copies of the negotiating text for the Antarctic Mineral Resources Convention (MR/Rev. II) were available from Greenpeace, Washington, D.C. in 1987.

environmental protection, specifically mentions their application to ice shelves, wherever they may be located within the Treaty area.

The claims of the seven states to sovereignty over sectors of the Antarctic continent, particularly the claims of Argentina, Chile, New Zealand, and Australia, are not likely to be abated in the coming years. Negotiations over a mineral resources convention have demonstrated the paradox of attempting to license, by collegial decision, an entrepreneur for exploration and exploitation of a fixed area while recognizing the special interests of Claimant states in that area. Moreover, with respect to the division between the end of the continental shelf under national jurisdiction and the beginning of the international area under the jurisdiction of the International Sea-Bed Authority, as described in the 1982 Law of the Sea Convention, the Antarctic Consultative Parties have opposed any notion that Antarctica does not have a legal continental shelf simply because no territorial claims to the continent have yet been recognized.[13]

A suggestion that ice shelves could become the baselines from which the territorial sea would be measured was made as early as 1926. The Committee on British Policy in the Antarctic felt that normally the three mile limit of territorial sea should be measured from the coastline of firm land, but "that an exception might be made in the case of ice barriers, which are to all intents and purposes a permanent extension of the land proper."[14] Considering the enormous difficulty, moreover, of defining the land edge of large portions of Antarctica that lie buried under thousands of meters of ice, the choice of a permanent shelf-ice edge, with defined surface coordinates, as the coastal baseline makes better legal sense both in fixing responsibility for activities on the ice shelf and providing a visible demarcation of the territorial sea, the contiguous zone, and the exclusive economic zone. In no way should such a change in the legal status of shelf ice affect the measurement of the continental shelf beyond the exclusive economic zone as indicated by the 1982 Law of the Sea Convention.

---

[13] See *M. J. Peterson*, Antarctic Implications of the New Law of the Sea, in: Ocean Development and International Law 16 (1986), 137—181 (167); *Roland Rich*, A Minerals Regime for Antarctica, in: International and Comparative Law Quarterly, 31 (1982), 709—725 (717—718). Negotiations on the minerals resources convention continued from 27 October to 12 November 1986 in Tokyo and in Montevideo from 11 to 20 May 1987.

[14] Quoted from *J. R. V. Prescott*, "Boundaries in Antarctica" from Chapter 3 of a monograph published by the Australian National University, Center for Resource and Environmental Studies, *Stuart Harris* (ed.), Canberra 1984. Professor *Prescott* deals first with the boundary claims made by seven states, noting that Chile in 1940 declared that its Antarctic Territory encompassed "all lands, islets, reefs of rock, glaciers (pack-ice) already known or to be discovered, and their respective territorial waters . . ." He also advances a good argument that an exclusive economic zone ought to include fishing areas, that is, not just the sea covered by an ice shelf.

4. Icebergs

For centuries icebergs have been regarded as a hazard to navigation: great chunks of glaciers that broke loose from an ice shelf, floating dangerously upon the seas until melted by warm temperatures. The story of the sinking of the *Titanic* in 1912 brought world attention to icebergs and led to new international agreements to reduce the perils of the sea. But advances in science and technology in recent years have demonstrated that icebergs can be used for research stations and possibly as a resource for fresh water. In the future the availability of very large, fairly flat expanses of ice that can be mounted and perhaps moved across the sea by people may suggest other uses for these solid frozen masses that are created freely by nature.

In the north polar regions, ice islands (tabular icebergs) have mainly been formed from the shelf ice in an area about 100 km long off the northern Ellesmere Island of Canada. One ice island was occupied by Canada from 1952 to 1954; another from April 1955 to September 1955. The Soviet Union maintained a north polar station from 1956 to 1959 aboard an ice island with no fracture or danger to the installation. In 1961 the United States established a research station on an ice island measuring more than five kilometers by three kilometers with a thickness averaging about 15 meters.[15]

The Canadians more recently have demonstrated the use of an ice island as a semi-permanent floating research station, utilizing a huge chunk of ice, thousands of years old, which moved 300 miles in 1986 along the coast from the Ellesmere Island towards the Queen Elizabeth Islands and is expected to travel to the Beaufort Sea, Alaska, the Soviet continental shelf, around the North Pole and down the coast of Greenland over the next twenty years. A team of 25 scientists have been placed aboard this billion-ton iceberg seven months a year, where they live in 12 pre-fabricated buildings. Political and legal implications are evident: "What better way for Canada to express its interest in sovereignty in the Arctic Ocean than to have a group of peaceful scientists out on the ice," said the director of the Polar Continental Shelf Project.[16]

One instance of the issue of jurisdiction over an ice island came in 1972. A man was killed on an ice island that was occupied by Americans, but located 200 miles north of Canada in an area often suggested but never officially claimed as the Canadian sector. A U.S. Federal court in Virginia took jurisdiction over the defendant after he was arrested and

[15] Data taken from the McGraw-Hill Encyclopedia of Science and Technology, New York 1987, 6th edition, Vol. 9.

[16] Canadian Embassy, Canada Today, Vol. 18 (1987), 14.

flown to that state on the basis of his nationality as an American.[17] It is noteworthy that the Canadian government reserved its position on the question of jurisdiction over the alleged offense, but said it "would not object to having the drifting ice formation in question treated like a ship for the purposes of the particular legal proceedings."[18]

The large, generally tabular icebergs of Antarctica could provide even better platforms for human research and communications, with landing fields, laboratories, and living quarters. It is not inconceivable that direction could be given to these enormous, but relatively light and frictionless, masses of ice so that there would be an enduring, guided, and cost-free base for any state to appropriate under the present legal *lacunae* in the southern polar region.

More vivid in popular imagination have been various proposals to use the icebergs of Antarctica for fresh water. The great ice sheets of the continent contain at least 65 percent of all the fresh water on the planet. Aridity deprives large areas of the earth from agriculture and economic development, while an increasing human population demands more and more fresh water. Considering that only about two percent of all the precipitation that falls on the earth is available in both surface and ground water that is fresh and that this scant amount must supply all the human, agricultural, and industrial activities of the world, the quest for additional fresh water is hardly quixotic.

Schemes to tow Antarctic icebergs northward and tap their water have run aground of engineering and economic difficulties. But it is certainly not impossible to "mine" a giant iceberg, process its tons of water, and transport the elixir of life to the right place at the right price. The cost of transport plus conversion to water plus distribution must not exceed the cost of fresh water from other sources.[19] Technological change will undoubtedly lead to sound economics. It may be forgotten that during the nineteenth century, ice from New England in the United States was transported across the seas to India for several purposes, including its chilling of scotch whiskey and water.

The negotiating text of the Antarctic Mineral Resources Convention that has been under discussion by the special meetings of the Consult-

---

[17] *United Sates v. Escamilla* (1972) 467 F. 2d 341.

[18] *F. M. Auburn*, International Law and Sea Ice: Jurisdiction in the Arctic Ocean, in International & Comparative Law Quarterly, 22 (1973), 552—557 (555).

[19] See on this subject *Peter Schwendtiger*, Antarctic Icebergs as Potential Sources of Water and Energy, in: Antarctic Challenge II, *Rüdiger Wolfrum* (ed.), Berlin 1986, 377; also *Paul-Emile Victor*, Will Deserts Drink Icebergs?, in: UNESCO Courier, May-June 1986 and *C. Epperson*, International Legal Issues Regarding Towing of Icebergs, in: 1978 Law of the Sea Institute Proceedings, *J. K. Gamble, Jr.* (ed.), Honolulu 1979, 209—239.

ative Parties of the Antarctic Treaty does not deal with ice shelves or icebergs. "Mineral Resources" are defined as all non-living natural non-renewable resources, including but not limited to, fossil fuels, metallic, and non-metallic minerals. Ice may be considered a renewable resource, although, in fact, if one iceberg should be mined, it would be rapidly depleted and in itself not renewed.

The occupation of ice islands presages legal issues of jurisdiction and liability that will eventually require international agreements beyond the context of the 1982 Law of the Sea Convention. It is clear that any presumption of value for icebergs as a military or economic resource, as with minerals, has not been addressed yet by the states of the world; but it is also clear that any dismissal of icebergs as simply "frozen water" will not be satisfactory under international law in the future.

5. *Interstitial Ice*

The legal problem with interstitial ice arises out of the definition of an island in the 1982 Law of the Sea Convention. Article 121 prescribes that "An island is a naturally formed area of land surrounded by water, which is above water at high tide." This definition is identical to the description of an island in Article 10 of the 1958 Geneva Convention on the Territorial Sea and the Contiguous Zone, but it departs from the proposal of the French delegation to Subcommittee 2 of the 1930 Hague Conference for the Codification of International Law in 1930, which had suggested the phrase, "which is permanently above high-water mark." There is a difference in the Hague formulation of "permanently" in defining an island. Ice can make that difference.

Every island has its own territorial sea and contiguous zone, according to the 1982 Convention, and some, which can sustain human life or economic life of their own, may have an exclusive economic zone and a continental shelf. Where an island adjacent to a coastal state has a territorial sea that touches the territorial sea of that coastal state, its extent of territorial sea and contiguous zone becomes the boundary of the coastal state; and, if entitled to an exclusive economic zone or continental shelf, such an island would extent the baseline seaward for the measurement of these marine zones by the coastal state.

Furthermore, the recognition of the status of an island may be critical to the measurement of bays that can be enclosed by coastal states, making the waters therein internal waters and providing a baseline for the measurement of all its marine zone across the mouth of the bay. By definition of the 1982 Convention, a bay must have a mouth no wider than 24 miles and must enclose an area no wider than a semi-circle measured from a line connecting its headlands. However, where the presence of an island or islands offers more than one mouth to the bay, "the semi-circle shall be drawn on a line as long as the sum total of the lengths of the line across the different mouths."[20] Finally, islands may be used for the points of straight baselines that enclose internal waters and serve as the mark from which coastal marine zones are measured seaward.

In sum, the recognition of a physical feature as an "island" in international law can have major consequences in boundary demarcation and involve the allocation of valuable resources. Islands must be "naturally formed" areas of "land." Dredge spoils in the Mississippi delta of the United States, which over time cannot be distinguished from natural accretion, have been held to be islands. What about formations of gravel, clay, and sand deposited by drillers for oil in the Arctic when such formations are held together naturally and permanently by interstitial ice? Are they "islands"? They will certainly accrete, erode, changing their elevation up or down over time, and behave like "islands."

An island also "must be above water at high tide." How far above? one meter? one centimeter? and for how long? permanently? on average? a few days? The United States and Alaska were in expensive litigation in 1987 to determine if Dinkum Sands, a tiny formation in the Beaufort Sea, was an island.[21] If it was an island, the Alaskan marine boundary would enclose very valuable oil resources. The Federal government, noting that Dinkum Sands is barely above the surface of the sea, has contended that a substantial portion of the feature is made up of interstitial ice, not land, and therefore the elevation is false and that the feature is truly submerged land.

6. *Pingo Ice*

Only a few words need to be said about pingo ice. These fingers of ice, covered by silt and mud, constitute a hazard to navigation. In areas of the territorial sea, a coastal state has a responsibility for identifying these features and notifying mariners in a reasonable way of their perils during an innocent passage. With regard to the Northwest Passage through Canada, it may be argued whether it is a strait used for international navigation or archipelagic waters or internal waters, but Canada has strongly affirmed its policy to exercise full sovereignty in and over the waters of the Arctic archipelago; sovereignty has both

---

[20] Article 10, para. 3, LOSC (note 1).

[21] For details, see *John Briscoe*, The Use of Islands in International Maritime Boundary Delimitation, an excellent analysis of the issue in several adjudications, paper presented to Symposium on Rights to Oceanic Resources: Deciding and Drawing Maritime Boundaries, Dean Rusk Center For International and Comparative Law, University of Georgia, 2 May 1987.

privileges and responsibilities, including the safety of navigation through hazardous waters with pingo ice.

III. Conclusion

The subject of the legal status of ice under international law is not new, but its consideration has been brought forward because of potential technological developments and the emphasis on marine boundaries and marine resources in the 1982 Law of the Sea Convention. Scholars like *Belch, Rolland, Lindley, Korovin,* and *Lakhtine* discussed the legal status of ice before 1930.[22] In more recent years, the Canadian *Donat Pharand* in 1973 dealt extensively with the legal status of ice shelves and ice islands in the Arctic and in 1984 another Canadian, *Susan B. Boyd,* analyzed the legal status of Arctic sea-ice.[23]

Officially the Second Committee of the 1930 Hague Conference on the Codification of International Law reported that the provisions of a convention on the law of the sea "would not prejudge the questions which arise in regard to coasts which are ordinarily or perpetually ice-bound."[24] However, the 1958 and the 1982 Conventions took no position on the legal status of ice, simply recognizing an extended jurisdiction by states over waters in ice-covered areas to protect the sea from pollution.

What recommendations about the legal status of ice ought to be seriously considered by states and enunciated in an international convention? First, it is axiomatic that all the energy of centuries from *Hugo Grotius* onward to recognize "high seas" that could not be placed under the sovereignty of any state was primarily aimed at freedom for

---

[22] "Balch and a number of other writers take the further point that some polar regions are not land at all but frozen sea. Balch himself rejected the idea that the North Polar ice, which is in slow but continual motion, can be occupied but did not rule out the possibility of immobile ice being made the subject of an effective occupation. J. B. Scott, Oppenheim, and Clute are more sweeping and discount any possibility of frozen ice being occupied outside territorial waters, apparently regarding it merely as high seas in solid form. This was also the view of the United States Government when it declined to endorse Admiral Peary's 'annexation' of the North Pole for the United States. But other writers, such as Rolland, Waultrim, Lindley, Lakhtine, and Smedal, take the view that frozen sea is capable of occupation, though some limit themselves to immobile ice." Quoted in: *Marjorie M. Whiteman,* Digest of International Law, Vol. 2 (Washington 1963), 1266, from *Humphrey Waldock,* Disputed Sovereignty in the Falkland Islands Dependencies, in: BYIL XXV (1948), 311—353 (317, 318), [footnotes deleted -*Ed.*].

[23] *Donat Pharand,* Law of the Sea of the Arctic, Ottawa 1973, and *Susan B. Boyd,* The Legal Status of Arctic Sea Ice, in: Canadian Yearbook of International Law (1984), 98—152.

[24] Acts of the Conference for the Codification of International Law, Vol. III, League of Nations Doc. C. 351 (b) M. 145 (b) 1930, XVI (1930), 217.

navigation and secondarily for fisheries. Where ice is packed so tightly and permanently or fixed against the shore of a state, it seems contrary to sense to assimilate it to the legal concept of high seas or for that matter territorial seas. There can be no passage — innocent or otherwise — by vessels. Fishing through the pack ice is improbable and the fast ice would lie within the new 200-mile exclusive economic zone that has been universally recognized during the past twenty years. On balance, it seems that international law should recognize the option of a coastal state to use the edge of fast ice to draw baselines from which the territorial sea and other marine zones seaward are measured.

Pack ice presents a somewhat different problem. While some of it is virtually permanent, with perhaps 10 % in the most northern region as open channels of sea, it does move. Yet there is always pack ice in each sector of the northernmost polar regions that face the Soviet Union, Alaska, Canada, Greenland, and Norway. Absolute jurisdiction over these ice-covered areas on the sector or extended contiguity theory would go too far in depriving access to other states for research, navigation, or mineral exploitation. But a convention could provide some jurisdiction over the ice itself in the these areas, guaranteeing disarmament with freedom of access on equal terms to all states to the ice, to the sea below, and the sky above, while fixing some responsibility for activities on the ice on the adjacent state. Not all pack ice would be encompassed, only the most permanent areas.

The same prescription for measuring the baselines from fast ice should be recognized and applied by international law to shelf ice for the same reasons advanced above. Again shelf ice that is indistinguishable in its solid characteristic from land should not be treated as water under international law. Where shelves break off and remain as icebergs within an exclusive economic zone, they are a resource and should be regarded as a responsibility of the adjacent state. In the northern polar region there would be no problem. For the Antarctic region, if the Consultative Parties believe they can formulate a regime for mineral resources while sovereign claims are suspended, they can certainly formulate a regime for icebergs. Again all the requirements for demilitarization and protection of the environment can be maintained while navigation and fishing rights continue to be regulated by international law. Where ice islands are utilized, it would be appropriate to treat them as ships — registered under a flag, with national law applicable to the activities aboard the vessel that is floating on the sea, carrying both people and cargo.

It should be stipulated in any convention that the straight baselines measured from fast ice or shelf ice would have to be approved by an international boundary commission.

Approval of the delineation of the fast ice or shelf ice boundaries would face fewer difficulties than the delineation of the continental shelf limits under the 1982 Law of the Sea Convention.

Finally, with regard to interstitial ice, the lack of any qualifying word about an island, "which is above water at high tide" is an error in the 1982 Law of the Sea Convention. The word "permanently" would be one improvement and some significant measurement of height above sea level could be another. Of course, there would be judicial interpretation of these words and measurements too — that is the nature of law. But it would give the judges something more to work with than a muddy bar lapped by shallow waves in a vast, open sea.

Ice on this planet at the end of the twentieth century must be regarded as much more than frozen water. For legal order, for security, liability, and equity, international law should reflect the new status of ice.

Comment:
The Legal Consequences of Antarctic Stations

Sudhir Chopra[*]

I. The Consequences of Polar Stations under the Present Treaty System

The current state practice in Antarctica, at least during the life of the Treaty, indicates the absence of territorial jurisdiction in Antarctica. Antarctic stations and expeditions have been operating without previous permission or subsequent approval by the Claimant states; Claimant states have not protested against foreign stations in their claimed Antarctic sectors. This attitude constitutes acquiescence in the activities of foreign stations and expeditions in Antarctic sectors.

In conformity with Article II of the Treaty, the United States established the Amundsen-Scott Station on and around the South Pole, thus touching an area claimed by six Claimant states, and the unclaimed sector. None of the six Claimant states involved here have ever protested against the location of the American station. The United States has exercised exclusive jurisdiction over its station. This has led to an established state practice where territorial sovereignty is absent and where every state is entitled to exercise its sole jurisdiction over its Antarctic stations. This absence of territorial sovereignty has led to the application of the concept of flag state jurisdiction over the Antarctic stations.

Perhaps a conflict exists between the concept of territorial sovereignty and flag state jurisdiction, arising from the establishment of Antarctic stations. To the extent that the Antarctic continent has the nature of *terra firma*, the establishment of stations in Antarctica may enable the flag state to exercise some kind of "effective control" over a certain area around its stations. This effective control may include a security zone around the polar stations, thus satisfying the requirement of establishing "effective control" over a specified area. Whether or not such an effective control will make any difference, in my opinion is clear from the language of Article IV paragraph 2 of the Antarctic Treaty which clarifies that no acts or activities taking place while the

* Mr. *Sudhir K. Chopra*, LL.M., Antarctica Interest Group, Washington, D.C.

Treaty is in force shall constitute a basis for asserting, supporting, or denying a claim to territorial sovereignty. In the absence of the Treaty, such a control would constitute a basis for establishing "effective control," but I do not see an extended effective control around a station, during the life of the Treaty, which could be used to assert anything but flag state jurisdiction.

Moreover, although the limited degree of control over Antarctic stations at least secures the jurisdiction of flag states, it does not satisfy the requirement of territorial acquisition. Consequently, the operation and establishment of a station in Antarctica cannot result in the acquisition of territorial sovereignty over an Antarctic sector.

The territorial extent of security zones around Antarctic stations is primarily determined by conflicting interests. The freedom of Antarctica requires the limitation of such security zones to a distance necessary for the protection of the flag jurisdiction. Furthermore, the interests of other states in free zones of Antarctica limits the authority of the flag state over such security zones to the period of the actual operation of the Antarctic station.

The system of personal jurisdiction in Antarctica is based on the flag state jurisdiction over Antarctic stations. Exclusive jurisdiction of a flag state over individuals at its stations is in conformity with the doctrine of flag state jurisdiction. However, designated observers and exchange personnels are exceptions to this rule of jurisdiction over individuals.

The authority of states over their Antarctic stations is indicated by their obligation of notification. Article VII paragraph 5 of the Treaty requires that each Contracting Party inform the other Contracting Parties and give them advance notice of all stations in Antarctica occupied by its nationals. This obligation of notice of Antarctic stations establishes an international regime and negates territorial jurisdiction in Antarctica. However, there is an exception: Claimant states are not required to give notice of stations as long as their stations are located in their claimed sectors. Every other state is required to give notice of its station in any area of Antarctica. Since these stations are established and governed by a governmental agency of their state of origin, they carry with them the law and jurisdiction of their state.

Authority of flag state jurisdiction extends also to airfields built in Antarctica. However, there is evidence of the international character of the continent. Article VII provides for designated observers, with access to all areas of Antarctica, and advance notice to the other Contracting parties of expeditions organized to or in Antarctica. The Third Consultative Meeting in 1964 adopted Recommendation III-1, which provides for the exchange of information on facilities for the landing of aircraft in Antarctica. The requirement of notification indicates the authority of states over their airfields while preserving the international character of the Treaty regime.

Both the flag state jurisdiction and international character of the area under Treaty is again suggested by Recommendation III-2, which requires notification through diplomatic channels before the end of November of each year of all unoccupied building huts or caches (referred to as refuges) of a flag state in the Treaty area. It also requires that these refuges be maintained by flag states and kept in a condition suitable for use in emergencies.

Through Recommendation IV-27 the Treaty System requires the government of a country in which a tourist or other non-scientific expedition is being organized to furnish a notice of expedition to other governments whose station the expedition plans to visit. The other governments, having received notice, shall inform the former of the conditions for the grant of permission for tourist groups to visit their station. This Recommendation makes it clear that while organizing states shall have jurisdiction over its nationals, they will be subject to flag state jurisdiction when visiting the station of another state. Recommendation VI-7 clarifies that visitors or tourists shall comply with the conditions or restrictions imposed by the Commander of the station.

It is clear from the examples discussed that legal consequences of Antarctic stations under the Treaty System are minimal. In effect, the Treaty, along with the Recommendations, confirms the flag state jurisdiction over stations, and in the process develops an international regime which is contrary to the exercise of exclusive jurisdictional control.

II. The Legal Consequences of Antarctic Stations in the Absence of the Treaty

I am in no way suggesting or predicting that I foresee an end to the successful era of peaceful cooperation and scientific investigations made possible by the Antarctic Treaty. On the contrary, I would like to see not only the growth of the Treaty System, but also a new and indefinite lease for this wonderful system. But, in order to keep the Antarctic Treaty alive and intact, it is my personal opinion that, from time to time, we need to keep ourselves reminded of the possible dangers and likely discord which may arise if the Treaty System collapses. It is just in the spirit of a healthy dose that I attempt to make this analysis predicting the inevitable if the Treaty fails to survive the test of the coming years.

Irrespective of the legal status of Antarctic stations during the life of the Antarctic Treaty, the situation will drastically change once there is a complete vacuum in the area. The disappearance of Article IV will bring back the claims as well as the right to make claims. This situation, however, will be a little different than in 1959 when Antarctic Treaty was negotiated. This time we will be faced with many more Antarctic stations, and perhaps more stations of a permanent nature than we had before IGY. To the discomfort of Claimant states as well as the states with interest and who have reserved the right to make claims, it will be nearly impossible to remove the well-built foreign stations from their claimed sectors or the areas where they would like to revive claims or make new claims.

Today we find that both American and Soviet stations are spread all over the Antarctic continent. With the addition of new states to the Treaty we have added new stations, spread all over seven sectors. The worst scenario appears to be in the Antarctic Peninsula and Ross Sea areas, which have the maximum concentration of stations. While the Ross Sea area has a large number of Non-claimant foreign stations, the Antarctic Peninsula is full of the Antarctic stations of three Claimants in the disputed territory. I wish I could ignore the political realities of the world outside the Antarctic Treaty area, but perhaps it will not be wise to do so, for once the Treaty's demise becomes certain the outside interests and well-known differences between the Treaty Parties will surface again. Notably the British, the Argentine and Chilean dispute and the East/West and North/South differences will be at hand to turn the polar continent into a hot-bed of international discord.

While it is possible to predict the new political alliances and new rivals in the event of the collapse of the Treaty System, it is perhaps much more difficult to work out the legal consequences of the Antarctic stations. Conversion of Antarctic stations into some kind of military bases might appear to be a logical step — perhaps military personnel, hitherto used for logistic support by some states, will take over from scientists to protect national interests. It is hard to imagine the consequences of such developments.

We might see the revival of claims and an effort to clear the claimed sectors from foreign stations. For Claimant states, first of all, legal pundits will be faced with the age-old problem of perfecting claims, and in the process use their respective "Antarctic stations" as a means to establish "effective control," because Antarctic stations are the only means of proving that Claimants do exercise effective control. If the area chosen is the unclaimed sector the task will be relatively easy. However, there is every possibility that a declaration of claim from either of the two states who have reserved the right to make claims, or from both, will further complicate the situation: it is unlikely that either of them will go for the unclaimed sector only, when their polar stations are spread all over the continent — consequently creating a new scenario with more overlapping conflicting claims. What role the polar stations will play in the new scenario will very much depend on the new areas of conflicting claims. However, one thing is clear: existing polar stations will play a pivotal role in asserting claims and further perfecting these claims.

Of all the states involved in Antarctica, perhaps the most difficult situation will be that of the states without claims or basis of claim. This group of states is involved in Antarctica only on the basis of an interest in scientific research. They have their Antarctic stations, which they may not like to leave behind.

To clarify this, it may be useful to examine the legal status of the polar stations, using some rather rusty concepts of Roman law. One must examine the legal status of Antarctica, because the legal status of Antarctic stations will depend on their location, and on the legal status of that particular location in Antarctica. There are numerous writings which either support or negate the application of the concepts *terra nullius* or *res communis*. More recently, *Ambassador Pinto* suggested that Antarctica may be treated as *res publica* (I support his suggestion, with some reservations). And there are some, who perhaps rightly so, suggest that Antarctica is to be treated as *sui generis*. While these concepts were extensively debated for more than 300 years to determine the legal status of the oceans, such a debate never matured for Antarctica — as the Antarctic Treaty changed the situation in 1959.

A common approach is to presume that Antarctica is *terra nullius*, since Antarctica was imagined to be a land mass and later found to be a frozen continent. Obviously, in the early days of the history of claims it appeared to be frozen land mass; there were no means of determining which part was frozen land and which was frozen ocean. A large part of Antarctica is above the sea level, and can easily be identified as land. However, a significant portion of the Antarctic continent is well below the sea level. These areas are more like frozen sea than frozen land.

According to the Polar Regions Atlas, approximately one-third of the subglacial land support lies below the sea level. Extending to depths of as much as 2500 meters below the sea level, the ice sheet welds the continent together, for if the ice were removed from West Antarctica, only a small part of the continent — located largely in the Western hemisphere — would appear, as an archipelago of scattered mountainous islands. Considering these factors and the possible "green-house effect," I will be very hesitant in treating the areas below the sea level as *terra firma*, because these areas are not precisely land, and if not today, some time in future this *terra firma* may even turn into ocean.

In my opinion, Antarctic stations located in the areas where the land is well below the sea level can claim flag state jurisdiction, nothing more, nothing less. These stations are located, not on land, but on frozen sea or ice. And in the absence of Antarctic Treaty, under customary international law these stations may continue to exist as if they were a floating vessel.

Problems will arise with the Claimant state involved in the area in question. In such a situation, a Claimant state will attempt to insist that the area is *terra nullius*, in order to assert its claim. It will become necessary to prove that the disputed area is *terra firma* and could be treated as *terra nullius*. The contrary argument by the foreign states attempting to refute the Claimant state's position will have to prove not only that part of the area (if it is so) is akin to frozen sea, but also that the rest could not be placed under the category *nullius* for a sovereign claim.

This situation may lead to an interesting conflict between common law and civil law countries. Since the legal status of the polar stations themselves will depend on the definition of property in the above-mentioned systems, and then must be followed by theories of acquisition, it is important to examine the position which some of the states in this conflict may take. Under common law the crown has the ultimate reversion, and sovereignty and property are indistinguishable. Roman law, by contrast, maintained a distinction between sovereignty and property. Based on this, *Grotius* made a distinction between *dominium* and *imperium*, on the ground that it was possible to acquire sovereignty over something which could not be owned.

Let us examine this distinction and ascertain its relevance in the context of Antarctic stations. *Dominium* under Roman law referred to absolute ownership of the property by a person, subject only to the power of state. *Imperium* meant supreme power or absolute dominion over a large area, such as regulatory powers and control. The distinction between these two concepts is that *dominium* referred to individual ownership, wheras *imperium* refers to the ownership by a state in which the state can regulate and control a large area.

Does this mean that to claim sovereignty under *imperium* a state is free from the requirement of proving that it can occupy the area, that it controls the area and that it can regulate the area? No — a state has to prove that it can occupy, control, and regulate the larger area to which it intends to claim sovereignty.

Grotius himself stated that to make a claim of *imperium* or *dominium* one must prove that the area does fall under the category of *terra nullius.* While I dispute the well-established claim of many states that Antarctica can indeed be considered *terra nullius,* on the basis of the very nature of the Antarctic continent (which precludes effective and sustained occupation, control and regulation of a large area), I am willing to concede that in some parts of Antarctica it may be possible to exercise a lesser degree of occupation, control and regulation, which in effect may lead to the establishment of a claim for *dominium* rather than *imperium* over Antarctic stations. That is, it appears that while it is difficult to satisfy the requirements for a sovereignty claim, it might be possible to establish a claim of *dominium* over Antarctic stations based on their location, *i. e.*, if they are on the land part of the continent, and on the basis of continuous occupation, control, and regulation.

This claim of control of stations based on the theory of *dominium* can cause a great deal of problems, for both Claimants and potential Claimants, because of the many foreign stations of Non-claimants all in the claimed sectors and unclaimed sector. This problem will be much more serious in the disputed area of the Antarctic Peninsula, and it will have yet another dimension in the Ross Shelf area, where Antarctic stations may end up with mere flag state jurisdiction.

It is indeed possible to envisage an absolutely chaotic situation, where every state with an Antarctic station will be attempting to establish some kind of legal authority — if not absolute sovereignty, at least a deluded form of control such as *dominium,* or even less control, such as flag state jurisdiction over its stations. While the Claimants will be busily asserting that Antarctica is *terra firma* and had been, at least, *terra nullius,* Non-claimants will refute these grounds continuously. Politically, it can be dangerous. Legally, this situation will then have to be dealt with as *sui generis,* for I see no concrete way to resolve this confusion.

To conclude, if at some point the Treaty fails, the Antarctic stations which currently are the symbol and basis for scientific investigation and peaceful cooperation may suddenly turn into military bases.

It is, therefore, necessary that we preserve this Antarctic Treaty, even at the cost of making some changes in the Treaty System. Thank you.

Air Traffic in Antarctica – The Need for a Legal Regime

*Francisco Orrego Vicuña**

I. The Growing Importance of Antarctic Aviation

The use of Antarctic airspace can already be characterized as an old activity in the area, which has been associated with many events related to the period of discovery and geographical exploration. Perhaps the first such use was the one made by the German expedition of *Professor Erich von Drygalski* in 1901—1903 who surveyed the coast from a balloon after his ship — the *Gauss* — was imprisoned by the ice.[1] The first aircraft flight in Antarctica was made on 16 November 1928 by the Australian *Sir Hubert Wilkins*,[2] and history was made of course on 20 November 1929 when *Byrd* overflew the South Pole.[3] At that point the Antarctic continent was opened to modern aviation.

Geographical exploration led to the assertion of national claims over the Antarctic. In this connection again aviation played a major role. *Byrd*'s second Antarctic expedition of 1933—1935 vastly expanded the area surveyed from airplanes, as did *Ellsworth* immediately after; claims were made by the latter for the United States over large areas so explored.[4] On 25 January 1930 *Sir Douglas Mawson* had also made a proclamation from the air claiming Antarctica territories in the name of the British King.[5] The *Schwabenland* expedition of 1938 alsc made claims for Germany using two "flying boats."[6]

It is interesting to note that since the Norwegian expedition of 1926—1937, every major expedition to the Antarctic has carried or used

---

* Dr. *Francisco Orrego Vicuña*, Professor of International Law at the School of Law of the University of Chile and of the Institute of International Studies, Chile.

1 *Deborah Shapley*, The Seventh Continent: Antarctica in a Resource Age, Washington, D. C. (1985), 75.

2 *Op. cit.*, 33.

3 *Op. cit.*, 34.

4 *Op. cit.*, 38—42.

5 *W. M. Bush*, Antarctica and International Law, Vols. I-III, London, *et al.* (1982), II, 120.

6 *Shapley* (note 1), 75. See also generally, *Clyde Eagleton*, International Law and Aerial Discovery at the South Pole, Air Law Review, 1, No. 1 (Jan. 1930), 127.

airplanes for their operations.[7] Another historical highlight in this development was *Admiral Dufek*'s first aircraft landing at the South Pole on 31 October 1956.[8]

The early stage of discovery and exploration gave place in turn to rivalry and potential conflict and to a successful undertaking of international cooperation under the International Geophysical Year and the 1959 Antarctic Treaty. Under these arrangements aviation has been greatly developed in Antarctica both as an essential means of logistic support and as a tool for carrying out major programs of scientific research in the area.

To the extent that Antarctic cooperation has evolved towards the organization of resource management in the Antarctic, again aviation has been called upon to perform new major functions. Some of the regimes that have been concluded in relation to resources, or that are presently being considered, have had to take into account the new issues arising from this growing use of aviation in Antarctica. It can only be expected that this process will continue to develop at a rapid pace.

In this context of rapid development and growing use tragic accidents have unfortunately taken place. From the crash of the patrol plane George-1 during Operation Highjump of 1946—1947[9] to the dramatic Air New Zealand accident at Mount Erebus in 1979,[10] various other accidents have occurred from time to time. New needs for Antarctic aviation have emerged from these unhappy events.

1. *Main Uses of Antarctic Airspace*

Today, Antarctic airspace is used for three principal purposes: a) trans-Antarctic flights of an inter-continental nature; b) access to Antarctica from neighbouring continents; and c) intra-Antarctic flights.

a. Trans-Antarctic Flights

Flights linking the Southern cone of South America with New Zealand, and occasionally with Australia, have been undertaken either on com-

---

[7] American Geographical Society: Antarctic Map Folio Series, Folio 19, "History of Antarctic Exploration and Scientific Investigation," Plate 7, 1975.

[8] *Loc. cit.*, Plate 11.

[9] Shapley (note 1), 51.

[10] See Recommendation XI-3 on „Air Disaster on Mount Erebus" adopted by the Eleventh Consultative Meeting, 23 June—7 July 1981, *Bush* I (note 5), 448. See also the speech by the Hon. *Peter Mahon:* "The Antarctica air disaster — the role of the black box," Law Institute Journal, 56, No. 12 (December 1982), 1069—1071.

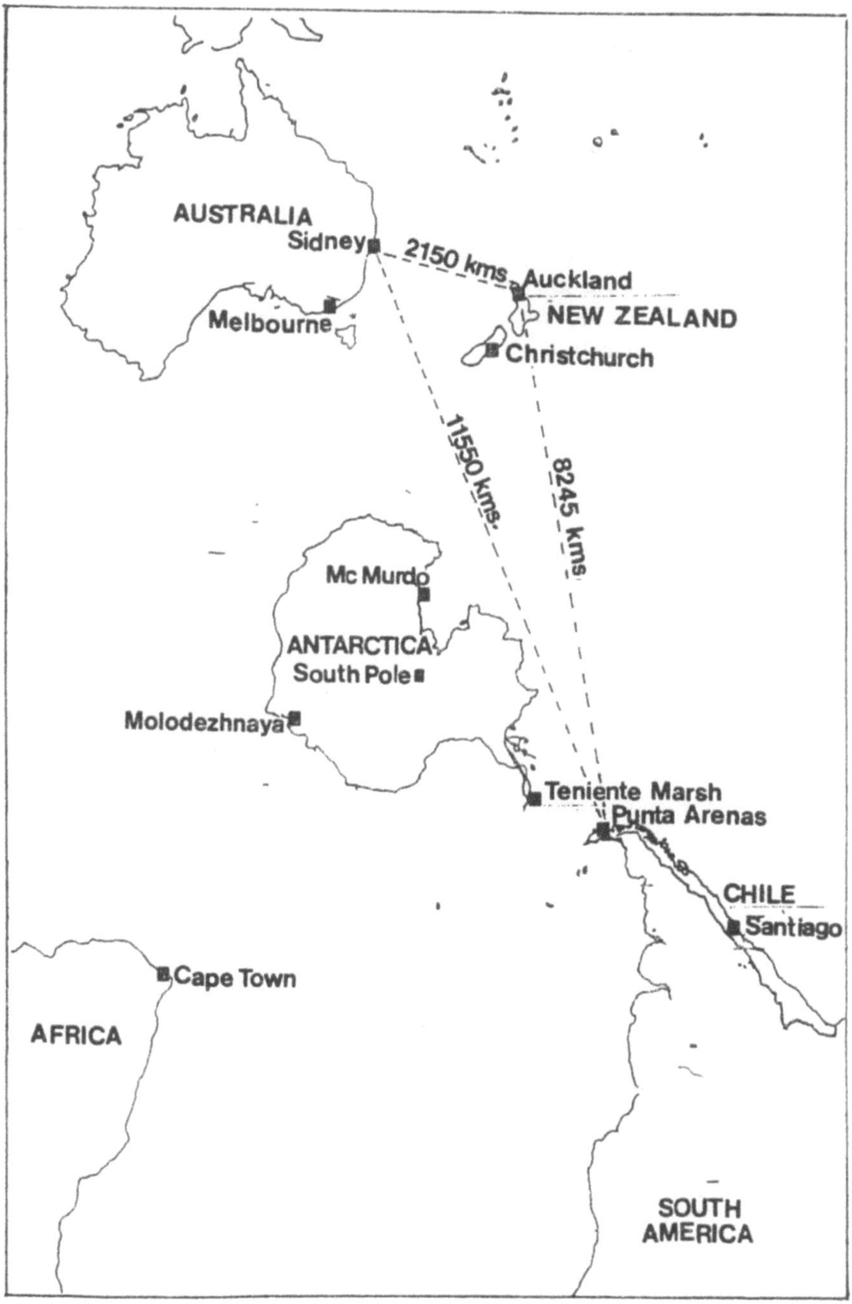

Fig. 1: Trans-Antarctic inter-continental routes[11]

[11] Adapted from *Alaimo, loc. cit.*, 93.

mercial or experimental grounds. *Aerolíneas Argentinas* has a scheduled weekly passenger service linking Buenos Aires — Rio Gallegos — Auckland, while *LAN-Chile* has flown experimentally the route Santiago — Punta Arenas — Auckland; *Air New Zealand* has also used the latter route for cargo transportation.[12]

The main advantage of this route is that it is about 20 % shorter than the conventional route linking Santiago to Auckland via Easter Island and Papeete, with the correspondingly reduced flying time and fuel consumption. The route does not normally pass over the Antarctic continent but over the adjacent maritime areas. This route and distances can be seen in Figure 1.

b. Access to Antarctica

Airborne access to Antarctica is done through three main entry points. McMurdo station is the entry point for flights originating in Christchurch, New Zealand, a route which is intensely used by both the United States and New Zealand Antarctic programs.[13] Molodezhnaya is the main Antarctic facility for the USSR, linking Moscow with this continent via

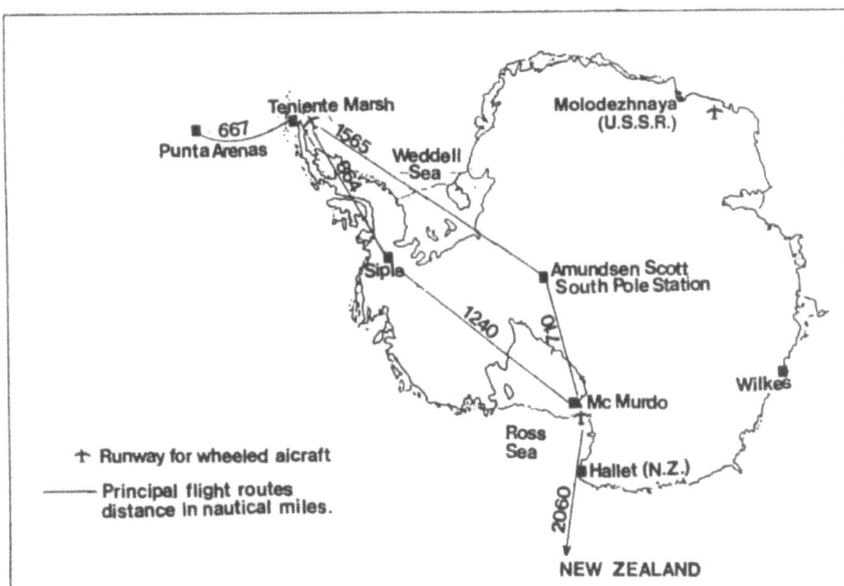

Fig. 2: Main points of air access to Antarctica[14]

[12] See generally *D. Salvador Alaimo*, „Gopolítica de los vuelos transpolares", Revista Escuela de Defensa Nacional, Buenos Aires (mayo 1982), No. 29, 85—102.
[13] *Shapley* (note 1), 198.
[14] Adapted from *Shapley* (note 1), 199.

Odessa, Aden and Maputo.[15] The third main entry point is Antarctic Station Teniente Marsh of the Chilean Air Force in King George Island, providing a link between the Antarctic peninsula and Punta Arenas;[16] occasionally flights have also linked this station with Port Stanley, Falkland Islands. The Argentine station Marambio also serves the area of the Antarctic peninsula from Río Gallegos or Ushuia in the south of Argentina.

It is interesting to note that some of these facilities provide in fact a multinational service for access to Antarctica. As mentioned above, McMurdo serves both the United States and New Zealand on a regular basis. Station Tentiente Marsh serves not only the Chilean facilities in the area but also those of Brazil, China, Poland, Uruguay, the Federal Republic of Germany, the United Kingdom and occasionally the USSR.

All of the above-mentioned facilities have runways for wheeled aircraft, air navigation services, meteorological stations and other services, being opened the year round. Other Antarctic stations provide similar

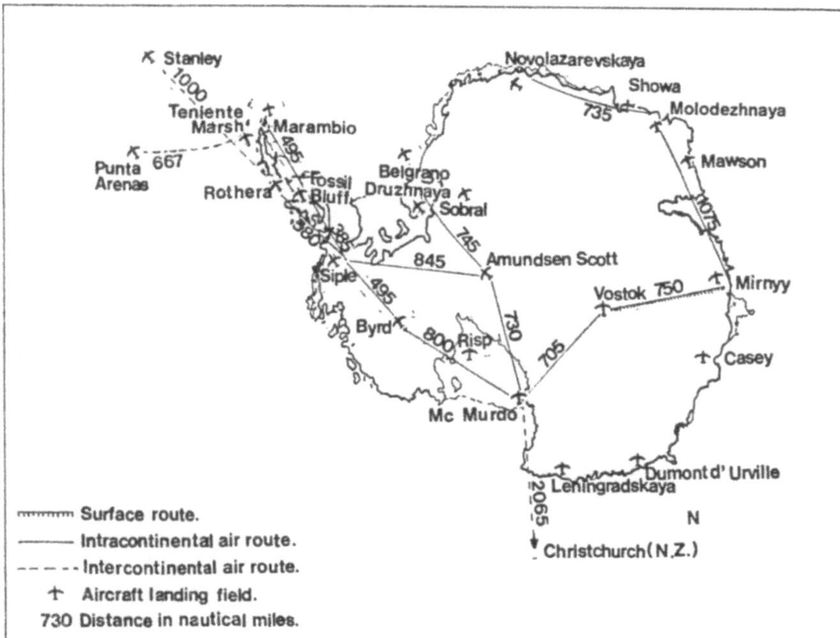

Fig. 3: General Distribution of air facilities in Antarctica[17]

[15] *Alaimo* (note 11), 98.

[16] See generally *R. K. Headland* and *P. L. Keage*, Activities on the King George Island Group, South Shetland Islands, Antarctica, Polar Record, 22, No. 140 (1985), 475—484.

[17] Adapted from C.I.A., Polar Regions Atlas (1978), 49.

services although they have not yet become main entry points to the continent because of their locations; this is the case of Rothera (United Kingdom) or Point Geologie (France) among others. In addition there are many landing icefields throughout Antarctica.

Fig. 4: Access route to Antarctica by the aircraft of the FRG Antarctic Programme[18]

[18] Adapted from Antarctic, Dornier 128 and 228, Dornier GmbH, FRG (February 1984).

The three main entry points are located in a position which constitutes a triangle covering the whole of the continent (*fig.* 2). If all of the principal facilities in Antarctica are taken into account, it will be seen that the continent is virtually surrounded by them (*fig.* 3).

It is also interesting to graph an example of a route followed for air access to Antarctica. The preceding illustration (*fig.* 4) shows the route used by the aircraft of the Antarctic research programme of the Federal Republic of Germany linking Oberpfaffenhofen (FRG) with von Neumayer Antarctic station via Punta Arenas — Marsh.

c. Intra-Antarctic Flights

Flights linking points in the Antarctic continent are a very common occurrence today. In fact most of the research programmes are using aircraft for field work, aerial surveys and other needs. Some other flights of this kind are made on experimental grounds, particularly in order to reach the South Pole from peripheral stations using small aircraft;[19] historically, the first efforts to undertake a trans-Antarctic flight linking East and West Antarctica were closely related to experimentation and exploration.

The following graphic shows routes linking various points in Antarctica and their respective distances (*fig.* 5).

II. Legal Issues Prior to the 1959 Antarctic Treaty

The discussion of aerial navigation in Antarctica did not arise frequently during the period prior to the 1959 Antarctic Treaty, in part because it was so closely related to discovery and exploration that it did not have a profile of its own, and in part because it was subsumed within the context of the more general issue of claims to sovereignty and the policy of non-recognition of claims. The latter issue had of course very strong implications as regards the sovereignty over Antarctic airspace, and the whole argument about claims could be applied to air rights, but this was more of a theoretical question than a practical one, as we shall examine further below.

There were, however, two instances in which aerial navigation and rights were negotiated and formally discussed at the diplomatic or administrative level, providing important evidence about the issues related to such matters.

---

[19] See for example, "Histórico vuelo de la Fuerza Aérea de Chile al Polo Sur," Boletín Antártico Chileno 4, No. 2 (julio-diciembre 1984), 43—44.

MAIN AIR ROUTES IN ANTARCTICA

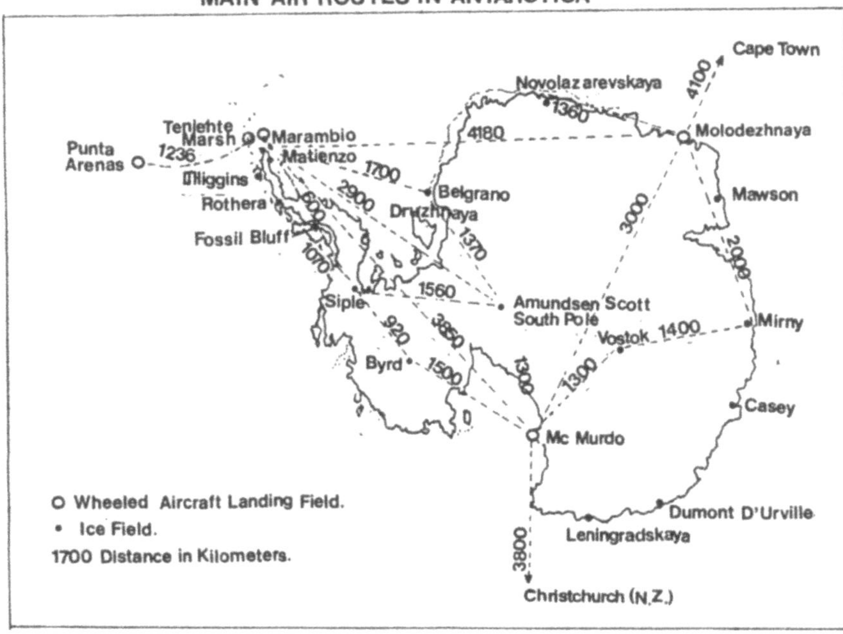

Fig. 5: Main intra-Antarctic flying routes and distances[20]

1. *The Commonwealth-French Negotiation of Air Rights*

The first such instance was the negotiation carried out between the Governments of Britain, Australia and New Zealand, on the one hand, and the French Government, on the other hand, about the limits of *Terre-Adélie*. Although this was a long negotiation, the issue of air rights arose at the end of the process. In a dispatch from the British Foreign Office to the Ambassador in Paris, dated 16 September 1937, the issue was put in the following terms:

> It is ... desired that an arrangement should, if possible, be made whereby a free right of passage by air across the French sector between the Australian territories on either side should be recognised by the French Government. Such a right, indeed, exists under article 2 of the Air Navigation Convention of 1919, but it is desired that it should be reaffirmed specifically in this connexion in case that convention should be denounced.[21]

The French reply to this note, while agreeing to the proposal, introduced quite naturally the condition of reciprocity, in the following terms:

---

[20] Adapted from *Alaimo* (note 11), 101.

[21] Dispatch from the British Foreign Office to the Ambassador in Paris, 16 September 1937, *Bush* II (note 5), 508, n. 5.

> *Le Ministère des Affaires étrangères a l'honneur de faire savoir à l'Ambassade de Grande-Bretagne qu'il ne voit aucun inconvénient à consentir cette autorisation, étant entendu que, réciproquement, les avions français pourront librement survoler les territoires antarctiques de souveraineté britannique.*[22]

However simple the terms of this exchange were, a first important legal issue was brought to the fore, namely that of the extent of air rights in Antarctica. It will be noticed that the above-mentioned British note made an express reference to the "free right of passage by air" as recognized by Article 2 of the Air Navigation Convention of 1919, which meant a restricted right not covering regular services. The French reply was apparently conceived in broader terms and no specific reference was made to that Article of the 1919 Convention. Did it intend to cover regular services as well? The situation did not pass unnoticed to the British negotiators:

> The question accordingly arises whether, assuming that no objection is seen in principle to the grant of reciprocal rights to France in this matter, it should be made clear in the reply to the French Government that the arrangement is intended to apply only to individual flights or whether the position should be allowed to remain ambiguous.[23]

On the ground that the question was largely academic and that in any event the French Government would have to arrange for landing rights in the British territories, the ambiguous construction of the exchange was suggested.[24] Constructive ambiguity does not seem to be an exclusive feature of the Antarctic Treaty. Both the Australian and New Zealand Governments concurred on the advantages of an ambiguous interpretation.[25] As a result of this negotiation, the first agreement relating to aerial navigation in Antarctica was concluded among the governments concerned by exchange of notes of 25 October 1938, in the following terms:

> In their memorandum (Direction Politique) of the 5th March last, the Ministry for Foreign Affairs were so good as to inform His Majesty's Embassy that the *Government of the Republic were prepared to recognise the free right of passage of British Commonwealth aircraft over Adélie Land on the understanding that reciprocal rights would be accorded to French aircraft over British Commonwealth territories in the Antarctic.*

---

[22] Memorandum by the French Foreign Ministry to the British Embassy in Paris, 5 March 1938, *Bush* II, *supra*, 504.

[23] Note from the Dominions Secretary to the Governor-General of New Zealand, 29 April 1938, *Bush* II, *supra*, 506—507.

[24] *Loc. cit.*, 507.

[25] See the references to the Australian and New Zealand replies, *Ibid., in fine*.

2. *I have the honour to state that His Majesty's Governments in the United Kingdom, the Commonwealth of Australia, and New Zealand accept an arrangement on the above-mentioned basis* [emphasis added].[26]

The extent of the air rights granted remained ambiguous. But this was not the only legal issue associated with this negotiation. The question of reciprocity was also considered, since from the point of view of size *Terre-Adélie* is much smaller than the gigantic Australian, British and New Zealand claimed territories, a situation which could have played against France; however, from the point-of-view of the very important geographical location of the French claim, situated between the Australian claimed territories, the situation played to its advantage, and finally led to the acceptance of full reciprocity as requested by France.[27] Another interesting legal issue is that the first British dispatch cited above implies that the 1919 Air Navigation Convention was applicable to aerial navigation and rights in Antarctica,[28] an issue which could today have a bearing on the Chicago Convention of 7 December 1944.

2. *The Underlying Issue of Territorial Claims*

The most important legal issue deriving from the Commonwealth-French negotiation was not so much related to air rights *per se* as to the underlying question of territorial claims, their recognition and non-recognition. As to the problem of recognition, *Bush* has rightly commented that "whatever other effect the ... exchange of notes has, it stands as a public mutual recognition of the French, Australian, British and New Zealand claims."[29] Although such recognition did not result only from the agreement on air navigation, but from the process of adjustment of claims as a whole, the fact is that such agreement came to corroborate quite explicitly the effect of mutual recognition among the countries concerned. This effect has of course a close relationship to the present situation under Article IV of the Antarctic Treaty.

Beyond the implications for the States-Parties to the exchange of notes, the agreement also prompted the question of non-recognition of claims. The United States Government delivered letters to the French and

---

[26] Exchange of notes between His Majesty's Governments in the United Kingdom, Australia and New Zealand, and the French Government, on air rights in Antarctica, 25. October 1938, *Bush* II, at 508. See also *E. H. Wall*, The polar regions and international law, The International Law Quarterly 1 (1947), 54—58 (58).

[27] *Loc. cit.* (note 23), 507.

[28] *Loc. cit.* (note 2).

[29] *Bush* II, (note 5), 509.

British Governments reacting to the said agreement,[30] which meant "to reserve its rights or those of its citizens as regards the question of aerial navigation in the Antarctic as well as the questions of territorial sovereignty raised implicitly on this occasion."[31] The ensuing debate with France dealt only with the question of discovery, validity of claims and related aspects, and not with air rights.[32] The issue of non-recognition would become the other major element dealt with under Article IV of the Antarctic Treaty.

3. *Argentine-Chilean Discussion on Air Transit*

Another instance in which air transit was discussed prior to the 1959 Antarctic Treaty was that of the agreements reached by the provincial authorities of both Argentina and Chile in the southern area in 1959.[33] Although these agreements were related basically to the exchange and cooperation among the southern provinces, the fact that both Antarctic territories were attached to those authorities made the eventual application of these understandings to Antarctica feasible.[34]

Insofar as air traffic was concerned, it was provided that inter-zonal traffic related to sports or assistance could be authorized by a special Commission or other bodies to be set up for this purpose. While the substantive aspects of the agreement were not of great interest, they evidenced a concern which would prove to be relevant for later developments, namely the need to ensure a degree of coordination among air services in neighbouring areas to Antarctica and to organize forms of cooperation in relation to the access to Antarctica. These aspects will be examined further below.

III. Air Traffic under the Antarctic Treaty

Neither the 1959 Antarctic Treaty nor the developments that have taken place under its framework have addressed the issue of air traffic in a straightforward manner, since this problem has always been related to other questions of substance and probably could have meant an additional complicating factor of the negotiations. In any event, the issue of air traffic has been quite at hand in the development of this System,

[30] Note from the American Embassy in Paris to the French Foreign Ministry, dated 7 January 1939, and similar note to the British Government; references in *Bush* II, *supra*, *513* n. 1.

[31] As referred to in the reply by the French Foreign Minister to the American Ambassador, 21 February 1939, *Bush* II, *supra*, 512.

[32] For the pertinent diplomatic material see *Bush* II, *supra*, 513—516.

[33] Agreement between the southern provincial authorities of Argentina and Chile, 11 May 1959, *Bush* II (note 5), 39—40.

[34] *Bush* II, *supra*, 40.

partly because of the kind of historical input that has been mentioned and partly because of the growing importance of air transportation and research in the area.

1. The 1959 Antarctic Treaty

Two interrelated provisions of the Antarctic Treaty deal directly with questions relevant to air traffic. Article VII (3) provides for the inspection of, *inter alia*, "aircraft at points of discharging or embarking cargoes or personnel in Antarctica." This includes, of course, both public and private aircraft, whether they are civilian or military. Apparently no aircraft has so far been subject to inspection; an inspection could eventually have implications in relation to the information about equipment or technologies used by modern aircraft.

The second provision is that of Article VII (4), which provides that "aerial observation may be carried out at any time over any or all areas of Antarctica by any of the Contracting Parties having the right to designate observers." This particular provision gives effect to the "open skies" policy for inspection that had been advocated by *President Eisenhower*, but it has, in addition, a broader implication: any aircraft of a Consultative Party claiming that it is carrying out a mission of observation could avail itself of the open skies provision and therefore automatically acquire the right of overflying and landing in any part on the continent. For this purpose it does not need to provide any justification or explanation. If this is so, sovereignty over the airspace of claimed territories becomes in fact meaningless or only marginally relevant.

If the provisions dealing directly with air navigation are few, those which indirectly refer to the matter are many indeed and most important. Firstly there are the provisions related to the general principles on which the Antarctic Treaty is founded, such as the use for peaceful purposes, the prohibition of military measures and testing of weapons or the prohibition of nuclear explosions, among others of this kind. All such questions have of course a meaningful implication for air traffic and the use made of aircraft in the Antarctic Treaty area,[35] some of which we shall examine further below in relation to the maritime dimension of the Antarctic Treaty System.

The policy of freedom of scientific research embodied in the Treaty is also a fundamental principle closely related to air navigation, including such questions as the exchange of information and personnel, the use

---

[35] See the comments on Article VII (4) of the Antarctic Treaty in *Bush* I (note 5), 73.

of military personnel or equipment for research, advance notice of expeditions and military personnel and equipment introduced into Antarctica and other related matters. It appears that some flexibility has been introduced in the implementation of some of these provisions as regards air navigation, for it does not seem, for example, that every flight into Antarctica should be regarded as an "expedition" and therefore subject to the requirement of advance notice.

The area of application of the Antarctic Treaty, as established in Article VI, has also an important bearing upon air traffic, particularly in respect of the safeguard of high seas rights under international law, which includes of course the right to overfly, and the status of ice shelves. As to the latter it is interesting to note that Japan made a declaration on the extent of Article VI so that it would cover all areas more or less permanently covered by ice "including the airspace above."[36] This statement was of course related to the status of ice shelves.

2. *Article IV and the Question of Claims*

The paramount question dealt with under the Antarctic Treaty is that of territorial claims and the issue of recognition and non-recognition. As was clearly evidenced by the historical record, this question has a direct relationship with the airspace and air rights. Although it appears that no claim has expressly referred to the airspace, the fact is that sovereignty over the land triggers the corresponding rights over the airspace without the need of an express proclamation. Furthermore, some countries have applied their legislation on air transit and related matters to their claimed Antarctic territories, either expressly, like Australia,[37] or through a general extension of their national legal system, as Chile has done.[38]

It follows that Article IV of the Antarctic Treaty applies *mutatis mutandis* to air traffic in Antarctica, together with its very intricate problems of interpretation and implementation. It also follows that the mutual recognition of claims entails a recognition of air rights. This can happen either by entering into air agreements such as the one

[36] Statement by Japan on Article VI of the Antarctic Treaty, *Bush* I, *supra*, 40.

[37] Proclamation by the Governor of Australia fixing the date of commencement of application of the Air Navigation Act 1920—1950, to Antarctica, 11 April 1956, *Bush* II (note 5), 188. See also *Gillian Triggs*, International Law and Australian Sovereignty in Antarctica (1986), 245, 251.

[38] Chile, Decree No. 298 enacting a Statute for the Chilean Antarctic Territory, 17 July 1956, Article 16; it should be noted that under Article 13 of this Statute all breaches of air navigation in Antarctica shall come under the jurisdiction of the Aviation court with the participation of the Legal Advisor of the IV Air Zone at Punta Arenas; *Bush* II, (note 5), 407—413.

commented on between Britain, Australia and New Zealand and France, or by effect of a general recognition of territorial claims. Recognitions of the latter kind have intervened between Australia, New Zealand and the United Kingdom; Argentina and Chile; Norway, the United Kingdom and Australia; Norway and New Zealand, and other instances.[39] Non-recognition is also safeguarded under Article IV, either if it refers directly to air rights, such as the United States policy already discussed, or generally to territorial claims.

However, the important question that needs to be put is not so much which are the theoretical legal implications of claims and of Article IV itself, but rather whether the Antarctic airspace is in fact subject to sovereignty or it follows the "open skies" policy examined in relation to inspection. The practical operation of the Treaty provides strong evidence as to the latter approach, whichever might be the legal standing of the Parties, which will be in any event safeguarded by Article IV.

Indeed, national legislation has not normally been applied to Antarctica insofar as air traffic is concerned except in relation to aircraft of the nationality of the state, and in the cases in which it has been declared applicable it has not been enforced with regard to other countries. Still more important is the fact that it would appear that no permission to overfly Antarctic territory has ever been requested or required.[40] The practical needs of the Antarctic air traffic have led to a situation which evidently transcends the theoretical legal framework of Article IV.

The liberal operation of Antarctic air traffic is a feature that can be observed not only in the relationship between Claimants and Non-claimants, but also in that between competing Claimants, as is the case in the Antarctic peninsula area. Article IV has also provided the necessary safeguards in the latter situation. An interesting case in point has been the transfer by Great Britain to Chile of an abandoned Antarctic station at Adelaide Island, which was possible to arrange by means of a reciprocal safeguarding of rights under Article IV;[41] the importance of this station lies in the existence of a nearby landing ice field which is presently being developed by the Chilean Air Force as a part of the Antarctic station Teniente Carvajal, and which provides an essential

---

[39] See the state of recognitions in *Bush* I, *supra*, 58—59.

[40] When the United States decided to establish its Air Base at McMurdo it was specifically discussed whether notice should be given to New Zealand; it was decided not to issue any formal notification and to do this on informal basis through the New Zealand Forces Attaché in Washington; for the pertinent diplomatic material see *M. Whiteman*, Digest of International Law, Washington D. C. 1963, Vol. 2, 1244—1245.

[41] The transfer of Adelaide Station from Britain to Chile was arranged by exchange of notes effective on 5 October 1984.

facility for the flights towards the Ellsworth Mountains area and the South Pole. No transfer of this kind could have taken place if it would have resulted in a diminution of any claim to territory or airspace. Article IV thus acquires a new and important dimension.

IV. Developments under the Antarctic Treaty System

The developments that have taken place under the Antarctic Treaty System with regard to air traffic have not followed an orderly pattern and are rather of a piecemeal nature. A first source of developments has been the obligation to proceed to an annual exchange of information, which includes many questions dealing with air traffic and facilities.[42] The exchange of information on logistic problems, for example, includes items such as the design of airstrips, performance of aircraft transportation and safety measures.[43]

The most important source of developments, however, has been the norm-creating function of Consultative Parties. In this context commercial flights in Antarctica[44] have been to some extent regulated in the sense that commercial aircraft operators are to be notified if the level of tourist flights "exceeds existing capabilities for air traffic control, communications and search and rescue in the Antarctic," or may interfere with normal operational flights in support of expeditions and scientific research, or even exceeds the capacity to respond adequately to an unplanned emergency landing.[45]

The concern of the Antarctic Treaty System with emergencies also became quite evident with the Mount Erebus air disaster. In addition to the adoption of Recommendation XI-3, the Eleventh Consultative Meeting discussed whether Areas of Special Tourist Interest[46] should be designated and also considered the possibility of adopting a common response to inquiries about the request for assistance of tourism and non-governmental expeditions.[47]

The launching of scientific research rockets in Antarctica is also regulated under Recommendation VI-12, which among other elements considered the possible damage to aircraft in the Antarctic Treaty area

---

[42] For a list of the matters subject to exchange of information see generally *Bush I* (note 5), 74.

[43] See Recommendation I-VII, *Bush* I, *supra* 124; and Recommendation IV-25, *Bush* I, *supra*, 193.

[44] The first tourist flight over Antarctica was done by LAN-Chile in December 1956, departing from Punta Arenas, *Bush* I (note 5), 92.

[45] Recommendation X-8, *Bush* I (note 5), 382—384.

[46] For this concept see Recommendation VIII-9, *Bush* I, *supra*, 322—323.

[47] See the Final Act of the Eleventh Consultative Meeting, para. 16, *Bush* I, *supra*, 438—439.

and in adjacent areas. This development is not only interesting because of regulating the use of the Antarctic airspace insofar as rockets are concerned, but also because it involves a recognition that the effect of some such uses might extend beyond the Treaty area into "adjacent areas."

Other aspects of the development of the Treaty System through the norm-creating function of Consultative Parties have an indirect bearing upon air traffic, as is the case of postal services and telecommunications.[48]

Antarctic air operations in a more technical sense have also been a subject of concern and action under the Treaty System. With occasion of the Seventh Consultative Meeting, the United States made a proposal for a "non-commercial international air transportation system for the Antarctic Treaty Area," with the aim of facilitating scientific research, access to Antarctica and transportation.[49] The proposal included both the improvement of existing facilities and the development of new airfields, as well as the mutual support for the scheduling of aircraft operations.[50] Under this concept, which came to be known as the "Airbus" system,[51] traffic acceding to Antarctica would be concentrated in several Antarctic inter-continental terminals from which it would be distributed to other air facilities in the continent using smaller aircraft. McMurdo, Molodezhnaya and Marambio were at the time considered as inter-continental terminals, but new facilities have been developed since, such as Teniente Marsh.

This proposal led to the adoption of Recommendations VII-8,[52] VIII-7[53] and IX-4.[54] Recommendation VIII-7 recognized "that access to Antarctica by long-range aircraft combined with intra-continental feeder routes by small aircraft would facilitate new levels of co-operation and flexibility in research" and recommended identifying ways in which such co-operative air transport system might be developed. SCAR organized, under the Working Group on Logistics, a Sub-Committee on Co-operative Air Transport System for Antarctica (CATSA), through which further consideration was given to this proposal.[55]

---

[48] See generally *Bush* I, *supra* 91—92.

[49] Report of the Seventh Consultative Meeting, *Bush* I (note 5), para. 22.

[50] *Loc. cit.*, para. 23.

[51] *Philip M. Smith* and *John B. Dana* Airbus: an international air transportation system for Antarctica, Antarctic Journal of the United States, VIII (1973), 16—19.

[52] Recommendation VII-8, *Bush* I (note 5), at 277.

[53] Recommendation VIII-7, *Bush* I, *supra*, 321.

[54] Recommendation IX-4, *Bush* I, *supra*, 352.

[55] See the Report of the XIV SCAR Meeting, SCAR Bulletin No. 56, Polar Record 18 (1977), 547.

Differing national interests, however, made progress difficult in the consideration of this new approach and no specific results came out from it. In any event this was a first effort to coordinate some important issues relating both to the access to Antarctica and to the organization of the intra-Antarctic air system.

1. Air Issues Relating to Resource Regimes

The approach to air issues under the various resource regimes of the Antarctic Treaty System has also been rather an indirect one. The Agreed Measures for the Conservation of Antarctic Fauna and Flora[56] refer to air operations in several articles: Article V provides that the Measures shall not apply in cases of extreme emergency including, among other situations, the safety of aircraft, while Article VII includes among harmful interference "flying helicopters or other aircraft in a manner which would unnecessarily disturb bird and seal concentrations, or landing close to such concentrations . . . ." Some decisions on Sites of Special Scientific Interest approved in the context of these Measures have further refined the reference to helicopters and low-flying aircraft.[57] The Measures also refer to the safeguarding of high seas rights under international law.

It is interesting to note that under the national implementing legislation of some countries it is an offence to act in violation of the Agreed Measures, which eventually could cover aircraft operations in breach of the above-mentioned provisions.[58]

The Convention on the Conservation of Antarctic Marine Living Resources, by its very nature, does not deal with issues relating to airspace, although by means of cross-references to the Antarctic Treaty and the Agreed Measures there can be an indirect connection with such issues. Also, the development of an inspection system under CCAMLR could lead to the use of aircraft or other relationships. Similar to this is the case of the Draft Convention on Mineral Resources, the connection of which with air issues is rather indirect; only the draft article on inspection rights, which follows the Antarctic Treaty arrangements in this regard, refers to aircraft supporting mineral resource activities as subject to inspection at points of discharging or embarking cargoes or personnel in Antarctica.[59] Such inspections should be undertaken not

---

[56] *Bush* I (note 5), 146—169.

[57] SSSI, No. 1, *Bush* I, *supra*, 303—305, para. vi; SSSI, No. 7, *Bush I*, *loc. cit.*, 314—316, para. vi.

[58] *Francisco Orrego Vicuña*, Antarctic Mineral Exploitation: The emerging legal framework, Cambridge University Press 1987, chapter III.

[59] Draft Convention on the Regime for Antarctic Mineral Resources, Rev. II, Article 13.

only at points on the continent but also at other points where activities are developed, like the adjacent maritime areas.[60]

The most important developments relating to resource regimes and air rights have taken place in another context within the Treaty System, namely the extension of this System to the maritime areas of Antarctica. With regard to the high seas there is first the question of the meaning and extent of the safeguard of rights under Article VI of the Antarctic Treaty. As *Van der Essen* has pointed out after examining the legislative history of the Article, its meaning is not to exclude the high seas from the application of the Antarctic Treaty, but on the contrary to apply the basic principles of the Treaty to the whole area south of 60° South Latitude while safeguarding the freedoms of the sea.[61] *Van der Essen* concludes in this regard:

> The only effects of the current text, therefore, are to ban air and naval manoeuvres and weapons testing (stated in Article I), peaceful nuclear tests and the disposal of radioactive wastes (prohibited in Article V) in the Treaty zone, as well as to uphold the freedoms of fishing, navigation and over-flight in marine spaces.[62]

It follows quite clearly that the high seas rights in the Treaty area are subject to the restrictions derived from the Treaty itself, some of which have a very important influence on air traffic and military uses of the airspace.

A second question is that the extent of the high seas in the Treaty area is subject to the safeguard of claims under Article IV, that is, it cannot prejudge or affect the maritime claims related to territorial claims, such as the territorial sea, the continental shelf or the Exclusive Economic Zone, while at the same time the non-recognition is safeguarded.[63] To the extent that these maritime areas are claimed, the corresponding air rights will be claimed as well under international law. This is particularly relevant for the territorial sea, since in the Exclusive Economic Zone the coastal state jurisdiction over air traffic is very limited.[64] However, just as in the case of territorial claims, air rights over maritime areas in Antarctica have been neither claimed nor enforced with regard to other states or their nationals, for which reason there is again in fact a policy of open skies.

---

[60] *Orrego* (note 58), chapter VIII.

[61] *A. Van der Essen*, The application of the Law of the Sea to the Antarctic continent, in: *Francisco Orrego Vicuña* (ed.), Antarctic Resources Policy, Cambridge 1983, 231—242 (233).

[62] *Op. cit.*, 233—234.

[63] *Orrego* (note 58), chapter IV.

[64] See generally, *Francisco Orrego Vicuña:* „La Zone Economique Exclusive: régime et nature juridique dans le droit international," RdC 199 (1986),vol. IV, 9—170.

V. The Need for a Joint Legal Regime

Both the historical evolution and the present legal arrangements that have been discussed evidence a fragmentary approach in dealing with few issues of air traffic and rights, many times in an uncertain and non-conclusive manner. Many other issues, perhaps the most significant, have been left untouched because of the fear of arising national rivalries and competition. The result of this situation is that there is no clear authority governing air traffic in Antarctica, since neither the territorial approach nor that based on nationality are *per se* sufficient to provide a stable legal basis to this end. National influences are paramount at present, having of course a greater weight on those countries making a more intense use of the Antarctic airspace.

The Antarctic Treaty System has been clearly evolving towards the development of forms of joint jurisdiction and responsibility in order to surpass the differences between Claimants, Non-claimants and other competing interests. This is particularly so in the context of the resource regimes and the maritime extension of the System. Not only has this approach proven to be adequate in terms of governing the issues of substance in each matter, but also in terms of clarifying the area of application of the System as a whole, including the unclaimed areas of Antarctica. Could not this same approach be followed in relation to air traffic without prejudicing the legal policy of Consultative Parties? This suggestion will be explored next in relation to the main uses of the Antarctic airspace that have been described above.

1. A Joint Regime Governing Trans-continental Flights over Antarctica

Although, as has been explained, trans-continental flights do not normally overfly the Antarctic continent but only the adjacent maritime areas, the fact is that these operations could greatly benefit from the establishment of a joint regime for air traffic under the Treaty System. It should be kept in mind that such operations are under the obligation to comply with the rules of the Antarctic Treaty applicable to the area south of 60° South Latitude, including the high seas in the terms explained. This is certainly so for aircraft of the Treaty Parties and also for those of third states to the extent that the Treaty has established an objective regime.[65] It follows that there is *ab initio* a close connection with the Treaty System.

[65] *Patricia Birnie*, The Antarctic Regime and third States, in: *Rüdiger Wolfrum* (ed.), Antarctic Challenge II, Kiel 1986, 239—262; *Bruno Simma*, The Antarctic Treaty as a Treaty providing for an Objective Régime, Cornell International Law Journal, 19, No. 2 (1986), 189—209.

It might be conceivable that a joint or coordinated regime could be provided for under the International Civil Aviation Organization, of which all the Consultative Parties are members. This possibility has been raised,[66] but it is unlikely that ICAO will intervene in such a field in view of the legal and political difficulties inherent in the Antarctic Treaty System.[67] The same can be said of the World Meteorological Organization and other relevant agencies. The establishment of a joint regime is therefore basically a responsibility of the Consultative Parties.

This is not to say that ICAO is irrelevant in the context of the Antarctic air traffic, since all the Consultative Parties apply to their operations in the area the "Standards" and "Recommended practices" approved by ICAO, including the organization of aeronautical information.[68] These linkages can of course be developed in various matters and ways.

The most important benefit for trans-continental flights deriving from a common regime is related to the operation of Flight Information Regions (FIR) established under ICAO, including the corresponding Air Transit Services and Search and Rescue. FIRs have been established in Antarctica for Argentina, Chile, Australia and New Zealand, in some cases covering the airspace as far as the South Pole.[69] The Chilean Easter Island FIR, for example, extends southwards to the South Pole within the limits of meridians 90° W and 120° W, providing air traffic services to the "navigation routes Santiago, Chile — Auckland, New Zealand and Punta Arenas, Chile — Auckland, New Zealand and to any other traffic that might be operating south of 40° S in the airspace in question."[70] Integrated operations of this kind among Consultative Parties could result in greater efficiency and improved services and safety.

Bilateral agreements have occasionally intervened in matters related to landing rights and other aspects of trans-national flights over Antarctica. Argentina and New Zealand have negotiated one such agreement, signed on 11 June 1981.[71]

---

[66] *Stephen J. Lovergan*: The legal status of the Antarctic airspace, Institute of Air and Space Law, McGill University, Thesis, January 1972.

[67] *Javier Lopetegui*: "Navegación aérea antártica", 1986, unpublished.

[68] Statement by the Chilean National Committee of SCAR on "Importance of Aviation in Antarctica", XVIII SCAR Meeting, 1984.

[69] *Ibid.*

[70] See ICAO, ASIA/PAC/2-WP/168, 22 January 1983, providing for the extension of FIR's/UIR's in the South Pacific, para. 2. 1. 3.

[71] *María Delia Bueno*: „Valoració jurídico-política de los vuelos transpolares argentinos", Buenos Aires, undated, 38.

2. *A Joint Regime for the Access to Antarctica and Intra-Continental Air Traffic*

The problems related to the access of air traffic to Antarctica from neighbouring continents are still more acute if approached under the traditional schemes of national or flag jurisdiction. This is partly so because of the issues appertaining to Antarctic matters in a strict sense, but also because such traffic will require the cooperation of the countries in the immediate vicinity of Antarctica, from which access flights will normally originate.

The first aspect to be considered is the necessary cooperation among the countries directly concerned. Various forms of cooperation have been undertaken in this regard. A bilateral agreement between the United States and New Zealand has dealt with some jurisdictional and administrative questions posed by the establishment of American Antarctic operational headquarters in New Zealand, and the transit of American personnel, ships and aircraft bound for or coming from Antarctica. The standard requirements in relation to arrival and departure of aircraft, immigration and other aspects, are waived by New Zealand; import and export of goods for Antarctic operations are exempt from taxes and custom duties, salaries are tax-exempt in New Zealand and other jurisdictional matters are settled in this agreement.[72] In a more limited way, Chile has established a regime in bond for the supply of Antarctic stations and other operations.[73]

Other forms of cooperation have also been agreed upon between neighbouring countries in order to facilitate their respective Antarctic operations. Early agreements between southern provincial authorities of Argentina and Chile were already noted. During the Beagle Channel negotiations in 1978 an agreement was reached in order to develop a coordinated system of transportation, postal services, medical assistance and tourism in relation to Antarctica, but it was not implemented thereafter.[74]

A serious problem affecting air traffic access to Antarctica is the lack of a well-defined aeronautical authority in charge of safety, air navigation assistance and eventually search and rescue. The result of this situation is unnecessary risk. As far as the access to the Antarctic peninsula area

[72] New Zealand—United States: Agreement with memorandum of understandings concerning U. S. operations in Antarctica, 24 December 1958, U. S. Treaties, Vol. 9, 1958, 1502—1509; extended indefinitely on October 18, 1960, U.S. Treaties, Vol. 11, 1960, Part 2, 2205—2207.

[73] Chile, Law No. 17.170, 8 August 1969, and Decree No. 1731, 31 July 1970. See generally *Orrego* (note 58), Chapter III.

[74] Agreements of the Commission on Negotiations between Argentina and Chile, 2 November 1978, unpublished.

is concerned, the aeronautical authorities of Argentina, Chile and the United Kingdom control the flights originating in their respective neighbouring territories without any coordination whatsoever. The respective routes dangerously cross each other at various points. Chilean aeronautical authorities have tried to establish Airway W-100 in order to control air traffic acceeding to Teniente March, but this has met with the opposition of rival Claimants in the area. It has been explained that

> a solution could be sought by agreement between the three countries but it should be kept in mind that there is an increasing number of flights by aircraft of other Antarctic Treaty parties in the area. For example, Soviet and German aircraft are presently operating in the area. This problem concerns therefore not only Chile, Argentina and the United Kingdom but all Antarctic Treaty parties as well, which means that the solution has to be found under the Treaty.[75]

Because of this very complex situation, Pope John Paul II proposed on the occasion of his mediation in the Beagle Channel dispute between Chile and Argentina "that a system of terminal air control managed by both parties, should be established on Isla Nueva, in order to regulate air traffic to and from the Antarctic."[76] In the context of subsequent negotiations this suggestion was abandoned in view of its possible implication for Chilean sovereignty over an island disputed by Argentina.

A joint regime under the Antarctic Treaty System also provides an adequate framework for solving these difficulties, while at the same time safeguarding the legal policy of all parties concerned. Here again ICAO could provide important assistance to the Treaty System. There should be no operational problems as to the implementation of this assistance since the air control at Tentiente Marsh is done not by the Air Force personnel but by officials of the Chilean civil aeronautics agency.

A problem of a more political kind is that related to a possible guaranteed access to Antarctica for the aircraft of Consultative Parties. Could it be possible to think in terms of a joint guarantee provided by all Consultative Parties under an air traffic regime in order to ensure unimpeded access to Antarctica, at any rate, in time of peace? The question is not academic since this access could be affected by difficulties in the diplomatic or other relations between Consultative Parties, local or general conflicts and other situations. Although the Falkland Islands conflict did not extend into Antarctica as such, the access to the continent

[75] *Lopetegui* (note 67), 13.

[76] Proposal of the mediator dated 12 December 1980 para. 4 B) b), I.L.M., 24 (1985), 7—10, (9).

could have been affected via Port Stanley or Río Gallegos. It is also necessary to note that the 1947 Inter-American Treaty of Reciprocal Assistance extends as far as the South Pole, covering situations of armed attack or other forms of aggression, eventually prompting measures which could result in the restriction of air traffic in the routes of access to Antarctica. Could the access to Antarctica be thought of in a manner comparable to the access to and transit through straits used for international navigation?

Most of the problems explained above are also applicable to the situation of intra-Antarctic air traffic. It will be remembered, for example, that the Airbus proposal failed mainly because of the national rivalries and differing interests relating to air traffic in general and tc such a proposal in particular. A joint regime in the field of air traffic might also provide the right kind of answers to the problems arising from this other use of airspace in Antarctica.

One problem that needs to be noted in particular is the distinction between public and private aircraft in Antarctica. Public aircraft, belonging to the state, its agencies, armed forces and other services, have of course a privileged treatment in air law that has equally extended to the Antarctic operations of such aircraft. In Chile, for example, such aircraft do not pay landing fees or other similar charges, neither at Punta Arenas nor at the Antarctic station Teniente Marsh. From this point-of-view, the countries managing landing and air facilities in Antarctica and main points of access render a free service to the international community and to Antarctic Treaty Consultative Parties or other Treaty Parties.

Private aircraft have been making an increasing use of these facilities. A private airline based in Punta Arenas flies regularly to Marsh providing services to tourists and other users. A major Chilean commercial airline has a combined service with Air Force flights into Antarctica for tourism and similar purposes. So far, it appears that private aircraft have not been charged for using Antarctic facilities. However, this situation could change to the extent that private flights increase. Also, could it not be thought that public aircraft should also pay for the services provider in Antarctica? These questions would be difficult to settle under the present arrangements, but here again an Antarctic joint regime of the air could develop a policy on the matter. The question of private operations in Antarctica has itself been raised from time to time, and although it is quite clear that they are not very welcome to governments[77] it is also evident that they cannot be prohibited;[78] in any event,

[77] Private expeditions to Antarctica have occasionally met with difficulties arising from government policies. For the problems of a 1976 Itaian expedition in Argentina see *Silvio Zavatti*: "La spedizione antarctica italiana e il diritto internazionale", II Polo 32, No. 2, Giugno (1976), 44—46. A recent British-

air operations could certainly be regulated under a joint regime, as has already been done to a minor extent.

The establishment of an air navigation system adapted to Antarctica and the preparation of an Antarctica Aviation Manual have also been suggested in the context of the development of a coordinated air traffic arrangement in the area.[79]

3. *The Lessons from Beattie et al.*

The lack of a well-defined air authority in Antarctica is not an academic question but one with very strong legal implications. This has become very evident in the case *Beattie v. United States*, in which British and New Zealand residents or citizens appointed as administrators of the estates of individuals killed in the Air New Zealand crash in Mount Erebus, Antarctica, on 28th November 1979, brought action before the U.S. District Court for the District of Columbia, alleging that negligence of U.S. Navy personnel at McMurdo Station air traffic control facilities caused the accident.[80] A basic issue in the case was the determination whether Antarctica is or is not a "foreign country" in terms of the Federal Tort Claims Act. If it was held to be a foreign country the claims would not be cognizable under the Act, for claims arising in a foreign country are exempted from its coverage; otherwise the United State courts would have jurisdiction on the matter.

The question was discussed of course in the light of that particular Act and of various other provisions of the American legislation referring to foreign countries,[81] leading the court to the conclusion that "Antarctica is not a foreign country; it is not a country at all; and it is not under the domination of any other foreign nation or country .... It is also true, on the other hand, that Antarctica is not part of the United

---

Norwegian expedition had difficulties in securing American logistic support for not meeting the criteria laid down in the U.S. Antarctic programme.

[78] The view has been expressed that private ventures, expeditions and aircraft flights in Antarctica cannot be prohibited under the Antarctic Treaty; see "U.S. and private ventures", Antarctic 6, No. 4, December (1971), 119.

[79] Statement (note 68).

[80] *Martin John Beattie et al., v. United States of America*, U.S. District Court, District of Columbia, June 25, 1984, 592 F. Supp. 780 (1984).

[81] See particularly the Tariff Act of 1930, 19 U.S. Code, Sec. 1336 (h) (3), and Sec. 1338 (i); Interstate Transportation of Wagering Paraphernalia Act, 18 U.S. Code, Sec. 1953 (d); and State Conducted Lotteries Act, 18 U.S. Code, Sec. 1307 (c). In all these laws "the term 'foreign countries' means any empire, country, dominion, colony, or protectorate, or any subdivision or subdivisions thereof (other than the United States and its possessions)". In the Foreign Bank Participation in Domestic Market Act, 12 U.S. Code, Sec. 3101 (8) "'foreign country' means any country other than the United States, and includes any colony, dependency, or possession of any such country".

States."[82] The U.S. Court of Appeals confirmed the conclusion of the lower court,[83] allowing the proceedings to move forward on the merits of the claim.

Beyond the issues appertaining to domestic law, these decisions have important implications in terms of international law and the Antarctic Treaty System. The American courts have had to discuss the international legal status of the Antarctic continent, following closely the position of the United States Government on the matter, although occasionally reaching rather far-fetched conclusions, such as that "to the extent that there is any assertion of governmental authority in Antarctica, it appears to be predominantly that of the United States."[84] However, it is also interesting to note that the dissenting opinion of *Judge Scalia* during the appeals proceedings emphasizes the fact of the existence of sovereign claims and foreign jurisdiction in Antarctica, so as to justify the point that Antarctica should be regarded as a foreign country for the purpose of the Federal Tort Claims Act. In this context, the meaning of Article IV of the Antarctic Treaty had also been discussed, for while for the majority of the court the signatory nations agreed "not to exercise sovereignty in Antarctica,"[85] for the dissenting judge that article "merely provides that the treaty does not *prejudice* any nation's claims or basis for a claim to Antarctica."[86]

More important still are the implications of the case in another respect. The District Court made the argument that since there is "neither foreign sovereignty nor foreign law in Antarctica, the responsible parties could not be reached under the laws of any other nation," thus justifying the jurisdiction of the U.S. Courts for determining the liability and damages.[87] Similarly, the Court of Appeals reasoned that "among the two 'forums' with the greatest interest in the outcome of this litigation — Antarctica and the United States — only one has any civil law to apply. And, in fact, Antarctica has no 'forum' either; fundamentally, because Antarctica is not a 'country,' foreign or otherwise."[88] But what about the potential jurisdiction of a Claimant country like New Zealand, in whose claimed territory the air traffic control facilities are located and the accident took place and whose airliner was involved, killing many of its citizens? Under the New Zealand legislation there is ground for the exercise of jurisdiction by this country, as there also is under the bilateral agree-

---

[82] *Beattie v. United States* (note 80), 781, 782.

[83] *Beattie v. United States*, U. S. Court of Appeals for the District of Columbia, 331 December 1984, 756 F. 2d. 91 (1984).

[84] *Beattie* (note 80), at 783.

[85] *Beattie* (note 83), 93.

[86] *Loc. cit.*, dissenting opinion of *Judge Scalia*, 106; emphasis in original.

[87] *Beattie* (note 80), 784, footnote 23.

[88] *Beattie* (note 83), 105.

ments with the United States,[89] particularly if the latter are regarded as applicable to Antarctica, as is the view of the dissenting appellate judge.[90]

While the existence of concurrent jurisdiction arising from different legal approaches to the status of Antarctica is perfectly natural, the reasoning of the Court does in fact deny this possibility, by arguing that the choice is between the American jurisdiction or nothing at all, thus entirely disregarding the role of other bases of jurisdiction in the matter. Perhaps more appropriately, *Judge Scalia* remarked on this point: "If 'foreign country' is given its usual meaning, there will always be 'civil tort law to apply' just as there will always be a district court with venue."[91] It is possible to make the argument that the jurisdiction of the American courts can be established in this case by construing that Antarctica is not a foreign country in terms of the Federal Tort Claims Act, yet without disqualifying other views on the matter, for which purpose Article IV of the Treaty provides a very sound and effective legal foundation.

Whichever might be the outcome of this case in the American courts in relation to the legal status of Antarctica and domestic law issues, one important lesson remains: the need to have an Antarctic regime of the air has become a paramount consideration, which will be every passing day the more pressing as Antarctic traffic develops.

4. *Antarctic: A New Joint Regime*

A distinguished expert on Antarctic air traffic and facilities has suggested the establishment of a system similar to *Eurocontrol*, which organizes the system of European airways from the point-of-view of air safety, without any implications as to sovereignty. It has been explained in the following terms:

> Similarly, the Antarctic Treaty countries could establish a joint aeronautical authority and a system of navigational aids and meteorology which would increase safety of air traffic in Antarctica, one of the world's most difficult areas for flying. This authority would allocate areas of responsibility to the various countries having facilities and equipment or which voluntarily would so undertake. Once an agreement is reached ICAO would participate in order to provide advice and technical assistance and publish documents for the information of all countries.[92]

[89] See *supra* note 72 and associated text.

[90] *Beattie* (note 83), dissenting opinion of *Judge Scalia*, 107.

[91] *Loc. cit.*, 111.

[92] *Javier Lopetegui Torres*: "Infraestructura antártica y política de acceso al continente", in *Francisco Orrego Vicuña et al.* (eds.): Política Antártica de Chile, 1985, 161—177, at 175.

A joint regime of this kind could draw on the experience that has been explained in this article and approach in a cooperative manner the many problems that are present in the field and which can no longer be altogether ignored. An essential feature of the regime would be of course the safeguarding of rights under Article IV of the Antarctic Treaty. Reciprocity would be ensured by means of the participation of all Consultative Parties on equal terms, irrespectively of the actual use made of Antarctic airspace. Consultative Parties would thus exercise a joint jurisdiction over Antarctic airspace, as has been done in other fields, without affecting the rights safeguarded and including situations such as the unclaimed areas of Antarctica. Joint jurisdiction could eventually be linked to joint responsibility.[93] *Antarctair* is the name we suggest for this new development under the Treaty System.

Brownlie has commented that "aircraft have not fitted very readily into the jurisdictional rules of either domestic or international law."[94] *Antarctair* could represent an effort to fit Antarctic air traffic into the legal and political realities of the continent, transforming a *de facto* policy of unorganized open skies into a *de jure* regime governed by well-defined rules and authority. The Antarctic Treaty System can only gain from this development.

[93] *Ian Brownlie*, System of the Law of Nations, State responsibility, Part I, 1983, at 192.

[94] *Ian Brownlie*, Principles of Public International Law, 1979, at 319.

Comment: Air Traffic in Antarctica

*Roberto Puceiro Ripoll**

According to the dictionary, to make some comments is to "give opinion about something," in this case, about the subject we are analyzing through *Dr. Orrego*'s exposition. Fortunately this Symposium is more generous than the dictionary itself, and gives me even more possibilities.

As you will realize, it is rather difficult to meet the requirement of commenting upon *Dr. Orrego*'s high-level speech. However, even recognizing it, some words come to my mind that encourages me to a considerable extent.

In *Novalis*' land, I can remember now his words: "All method is rhythm ... every man has his peculiar rhythm" so, I shall try to reach my method and my rhythm in this difficult and foggy subject we are examining, emphasizing and deepening some special points in order to get some final reflections and conclusions.

The issue of air traffic in Antarctica has never been a simple one and as it is increasing very rapidly, its complexity is proportionally growing. In fact, at least three major aspects can be easily identified in order to attempt a serious analysis: first, the importance of air traffic in Antarctica; second, the legal regime of overflight in the Antarctic area; and third, the regime of air traffic services in the Antarctic zone.

I. The Importance of Air Traffic in Antarctica

First, we should try to get acquainted with the present and future importance of this air traffic. As a result, we shall probably come to a better understanding of it and also the eventual consequences to be dealt with.

The air traffic in the Antarctic area may be affected by two different elements: the general international air traffic and the inherent Antarctic air traffic, that is to say, the air traffic required by Antarctic activities.

* Dr. *Roberto Puceiro Ripoll*, Legal Adviser, Uruguayan Antarctic Institute, Montevideo, Uruguay. The opinions expressed in this volume are the personal views of their authors only.

If we analyze the information published by the International Civil Aviation Organization in the past years, we can state that the air traffic, especially passenger air traffic, increases annually in a significant way; that the regional air traffic continues increasing, and that there is a remarkable movement towards the opening of new routes and services and towards the use of greater range aircraft. Nowadays, air traffic is chiefly oriented through, from and to the northern hemisphere, where there is a dense net of routes, while in the southern hemisphere we find only a few ones. Sometimes, even if we want to travel from the south to the south we must fly south-north-south.

With a new scope of aeronautic relations and the appearance of new realities, we can foresee a considerable change in communications in the next years, especially among Africa, America, Asia and Oceania, developing new routes particularly through the Antarctic area. And in this situation the Antarctic Continent will no longer be an isolated land, but will turn into a friendly bridge joining distant continents. We shall therefore fly along the meridians instead of along the parallels, and this is not merely a poetic image, but actually a means of shortening distances, saving costs and time, and bringing about more comfort and celerity. In this context new and more adequate routes could replace the traditional ones.

Transantarctic flights started to develop in the 'Sixties, the first flight taking place in October 1963, by and Hercules C 130 of the United States of America Navy, taking off from Africa, overflying the South Pole, landing at McMurdo Station and having New Zealand as its final destination, thus providing an aerial bridge joining three continents and demonstrating the viability of this kind of flight. The Antarctic overflights kept on developing in a continuous but infrequent way, and presently we have the weekly flight of Aerolíneas Argentinas Company, with a Boeing 747, following the route Buenos Aires, Río Gallegos, Auckland, in about thirteen hours.

It has been said that transport is civilization, because transport is communication. *John Cooper* said some years ago that aerial power is the more dynamic one in the life of nations. Man has created and developed it, but now we must understand it, and precisely, the fundamental objective of aerial power is to provide transportation. In the context of all these ideas it is not very difficult to imagine that airspace in the Antarctic area will be soon covered by many commercial routes, changing this passive airspace into a very active and competitive one. Clearly and distinctly a question comes to our minds, what is its legal regime?

We must also think about the importance of air traffic in Antarctica applied specifically to Antarctic activities. At present, many scientific stations, spread all over the Continent, establish their communications through airspace, and it can be foreseen that in the coming years this traffic will increase according to more common terrestrial facilities and sophisticated equipment in the aerial vehicles. Likewise, increasing mineral and tourism activities will require more frequent use of aerial vehicles in order to facilitate the operations.

We must undoubtedly consider the advantages of air travel over terrestrial means of transport. Aeroplanes and helicopters can reach inaccesible regions better, faster and more safely over long distances, thus permitting scientific and logistic personnel to remain longer, if so desired, tending to facilitate international cooperation in scientific research, data exchange and other activities.

In this way, in the framework of the Antarctic Treaty System, we find some Recommendations emanating from the Consultative Meetings emphasizing the need for cooperation in air transport. Recommendation VII-8 establishes the principle of using common transport facilities by air for scientists and other personnel proceeding with their equipment to and from Antarctic stations, and encourages bilateral or multilateral consultations between Contracting Parties to establish arrangements in this regard.

Recommendation VIII-7 requires states to identify the ways in which a cooperative air transport system might benefit them. Recommendation IX-4 recognizes that the most effective use of aviation assets will be achieved through coordinated air support projects with major additional construction or investment, and recommends to the Governments to request SCAR to continue the work of the Sub-Committee on Co-operative Air Transport System for Antarctica.

In the preparatory meeting, May 1987, an agreement was reached to include Air Safety in Antarctica as an Agenda item for the Fourteenth Antarctic Treaty Consultative Meeting. We perceive the importance of airspace in the region. And once again we ask, what is its juridical regulation? It is time to stop repeating this question and try to have some answers, nevertheless, this does not mean reaching a definitive conclusion.

II. The Legal Regime of Overflight in the Antarctic Area

The problem of the legal regime of airspace in the Antarctic area is closely related to some other Antarctic questions that have not been solved yet, and that have no specific regulation. Every effort should be made to try to find a solution within the Antarctic Treaty System, bearing also in mind, that State Parties of the regime have not up to this moment assumed on the subject an open and explicit position.

As we know, the Antarctic area is located south of 60° South Latitude according to Article VI of the Antarctic Treaty. That covers the Continent itself and the maritime areas. Here we must separate the analysis by considering two major elements: 1) legal regime of the Antarctic Continent's airspace; and 2) legal regime of the marine areas.

For the first one we can theoretically state at least three possibilities:

a) Overflight over the Continent is completely free, there is no international specific legal regime, and presently no sovereignty claims; we must apply the rules governing areas not submitted to national sovereignty, high seas being the main example. This interpretation cannot be admitted, since though in Antarctica national sovereignty claims have been put on ice by Article IV of the Antarctic Treaty, we have an specific and effective system ruling the area, and therefore, creating a legal regime for it.

b) Airspace over the Continent is submitted to the sovereignty of those states that claim it. This theory has presently no support according to the text of the above-mentioned Article IV of the Antarctic Treaty.

c) The regime of air navigation over the Antarctic continent must be solved within the unique framework of the Antarctic Treaty System, which as we all know, has precise rules, but also undetermined questions.

In this situation we must come to these conclusions:

i) Airspace over the Antarctic Continent is submitted to the same principles which are valid for the Continent itself: peaceful uses, prohibition of military activities; freedom of scientific investigation and cooperation towards that end; prohibition of nuclear explosions and disposal of radioactive waste material.

ii) There is freedom of overflight in the airspace over the continent for the purposes of Antarctic Treaty. This interpretation flows naturally from extending to the superadjacent space the same freedom of movement as that existing for the continent. This principle emerges from the tacit approval of State Parties, through many Recommendations and especially Article VII paragraph 4 of the Antarctic Treaty. In addition, it has been a general and accepted practice among the Parties in the Continent, and for that reason became a customary rule of theirs. However, at this point we face the problem of determining which is the legal regime applicable to those flights with purposes other than Ant-

arctic ones, this is to say, tourism or private flights.
In this case an interpretation by analogy cannot be applied, since we do not have a definite and neat practice between the State Parties.

Notwithstanding, some practice "*in statu nascendi*" can be noticed, admitting freedom of this kind of overflight at least for the Consultative Parties. For example, we know of no protest or objections for the Argentinian commercial flights or for some unscheduled commercial or private flights of other Consultative Parties. On the other side, we do not envisage clearly the position of the State Parties in connection with same kind of operations by non-signatory states.

Let us now take into consideration the legal regime for the airspace over the maritime areas. Theoretically, at least, a greater complexity can be foreseen, since this aspect is very much related to the maritime areas regime. As we know, within both the Antarctic System and as between the Antarctic Treaty Parties we do not have a clear picture of the applicability of the Law of the Sea to Antarctica. In the first instance, two opposite positions are apparent. On the one hand are states supporting the belief that the Antarctic continent is a land mass which has the right to the naturally adjacent areas, the territorial sea and the exclusive economic zone, that international customary law could attribute to coastal states. To the contrary, other states consider that all marine areas around the Continent are part of the high seas. At present we envisage some approach between the two positions: the existence of "adjacent offshore areas" is now the object of a faint admission.

Since the legal regime of the airspace could be subject to the maritime areas' juridical regime, as we do not have a definite solution for it evidently we are in front of an indeterminate regime.

Nevertheless, if we examine the state pactice, we come to the conclusion that airflight over the maritime Antarctic areas is ruled by the same regime as the continent itself, and thus we have a global regime for the airspace of the Antarctic area.

When considering the Antarctic airspace regime some reflections are possible. The regime is not specifically ruled, it is only partially developed by state practice, and it presents some juridical vacuums. As aerial activities in Antarctica become of greater importance and develop, further States Parties will be urged to regulate and control them more precisely, by implementing new measures such as reciprocal information among the State Parties and even effective control and administration of those activities.

If, according to Article VII of the Antarctic Treaty, any contracting Party can, unilaterally, verify the activities carried out by other states in Antarctica, the Parties together have also the right, under Article IX of the Treaty, of controlling the aerial activities in Antarctica as well as to verify that they are developed according to the principles ruling the zone.

Moreover, the Consultative Parties have the right to rule and administrate aerial activities, when they deem it necessary, especially those operations which are not directly executed for Antarctic purposes, or by non-Parties, as commercial or private flights. An objective appreciation of the present situation will lead us to the conclusion that it is a very delicate matter, the analysis of which shows at the very beginning that a quick agreement, although desirable, is far from easy. Perhaps the solution can be found by referring to *Daedalus*' advice to *Icarus*: "Not too high, not too low," in other words, an adequate and suitable control, administration included.

III. The Regime of Air Traffic Services in the Antarctic Zone

Let us finally talk about air traffic services. They are in general terms, regulated by Annex 11 to the Convention on International Civil Aviation, and those services pertain to the establishment of airspace units and services necessary to promote the safe, orderly and expeditious flow of air traffic.

In this connection a distinction should be stated between air traffic control services, flight information services, and alerting services.

Air traffic control services are provided for preventing collisions, and expediting and maintaining an orderly flow of air traffic. Flight information services are provided for the purpose of giving advice and information useful for the safe and efficient conduct of flights. Alerting services are provided for the notification of appropriate organizations regarding aircraft in need of air search and rescue, and assist such organizations as required.

There are also rules regulating air traffic services requirements for communication and information. Flight information services and alerting services are provided within an airspace of defined dimension, called flight information region, which is subdivided into two regions: the flight information region (FIR) located between 200m and 6500m approximately, and the upper information region (UIR) from 6500m on up without limit.

For accomplishing these services, and according to Annex 11, states determine, for the territories over which they have jurisdiction, those portions of the airspace and aerodromes where air traffic services will be provided.

Annex 11 also establishes that "those portions of the airspace over the high seas or in airspace of undetermined sovereignty where air traffic services will be provided shall be determined on the basis of regional air navigation agreements," which are to be approved by the Council of the International Civil Aviation Organization normally on the advice of regional air Navigation Meetings. Once it has been determined that air traffic services will be provided, the states concerned must designate the authority responsible for providing such services.

Moreover, delimitation of airspace, wherein air traffic services are to be provided, should be related to the nature of the route structure and the need for efficient services rather than to national boundaries. And now, what happens in Antarctica? Are those services rendered in accordance with named rules? Who provides those services?

In Antarctica we do not have a general regional air navigation agreement. However, it is quite evident that some states provide air traffic services in some regions, for their own aircraft and foreign ones. In this situation we notice that:

a) air traffic services can be unnecessarily duplicated and overlap, and that could probably cause interference among them;

b) there are some regions where there is a complete lack of said services.

If we admit that air traffic will increase in the near future in Antarctica, that we must have safe, orderly and expeditious flow of air traffic, if we further consider that air traffic services can be also a way of controlling aerial activities over Antarctica, then we must come to the conclusion that it is necessary to have air traffic services regulated by a special regional agreement. To that end, negotiations among Consultative Parties are essential and should determine the responsibility for setting up and providing air traffic services. This suggests to us two considerations:

1. Agreement must arise from the Antarctic Treaty System and then be submitted to the International Civil Aviation Organization.

2. Air traffic services may be collectively performed by the Consultative Parties according to an specific agreement or they may be assigned to some states, for example those neighbour ones, in order to facilitate the services themselves as well as providing the frame for cooperation principles.

We must remember at this instance, that as Annex 11 establishes, "if one State delegates to another State the responsibility for the provision of air traffic services over its territory, it does so without derogation of its national sovereignty." This means that to delegate this responsibility does not imply any kind of renouncement.

We understand, therefore, that the problem of the provision of air traffic services in Antarctica must be treated according to the new realities of the area, and the Antarctic Treaty System is the natural and adequate forum to discuss, negotiate and solve the issue. Problems arise from transition. Air traffic in Antarctica opens now new challenges to the System.

General Discussion

J. Delbrück, Chairman:

We now come to the general discussion. I have already two speakers listed, one is *Mr. Sollie* and the other one is *Mr. Hempel.*

F. Sollie:

Mr. Chairman, I want to thank the organizers for giving us speakers with such fascinating presentations, as we heard today. I think this has been both intriguing and interesting. I do not have much to say by way of comment but I would like to put a question to *Professor Mangone* in connection with a question of "territorial" rights over floating ice. Now obviously, this is a question which is of primary importance at this time in the north, where modern technology is opening the polar sea for navigation. That is, we are living in a time when polar ice packs in the north are no longer an impermeable barrier to navigation. The north is becoming a piece of water in the true sense of the word. Another matter, of course, is that in the East Arctic, that is, that part of the Arctic which lies within the Soviet sector, ice very seldom will be more than three years of age, because there is a constant rotation of the ice and the *Fram* drift, I think back in the 1890s, would indicate that the average age of ice is 3 years before it drifts out through the front strait. For these reasons, one may question, from a political and practical point-of-view, the wisdom of extending territorial or state rights over ice — even if you limit it to the ice proper and not to the water below or the air space above, as some legal philosophers, I would call them, have indicated.

But I have another problem here and that is this: if you extend rights to ice which is floating, I suppose that those rights will also entail certain obligations. In other words, would a world community have a right to expect a state with rights on ice, to secure that ice, to prevent it from causing hazards to those who use the seas? And above all, would that obligation extend to a duty for the coastal state with jurisdiction to prevent its ice from polluting the free waters beyond? After all, that is a type of pollution, too.

The opinions expressed in this volume are the personal views of their authors only.

And then I have one comment on a matter that has been brought up two or three times, the possibility of the melting of the ice in the south polar region, and we had a fascinating presentation also on the legal aspects of that, because if ice melted you would not have a continent but you would have sea and some islands popping up. I would merely say that if you remove 3000—4000 meters of ice on land, then the land below will pop up, literally speaking. It would take a little more than a moment, of course, but nevertheless, the land will rise. So you would be back to the original situation, with a continent. Therefore I think it is better to think in terms of the practical realities as they are today.

J. Delbrück, Chairman:

Thank you. The next speaker is *Mr. Hempel.*

G. Hempel:

I would like to continue what *Dr. Sollie* said. I think the statement that the idea of major parts of Antarctica being frozen seas is not correct from the oceanographic point of view. It is freshwater ice which flows from the continent, and a major part of this ice, even in the areas which are below sea level, is anchored on the continent. So this ice really stays on the continent even if the continent, the hardrock, is 1000 meters below the ice, below sea level. In fact the case would be rather doubtful whether that is really, then, frozen seas. From the oceanographic point-of-view it is not, from the geographical point-of-view I think it is also not.

The sea level has only a theoretical value in this context: much of Holland is below the sea level and it is a continent, and *Finn Sollie* just said, as soon as you remove the ice from the continent it will "pop up." It will take a couple of thousand years or so (it took just as long for Schleswig-Holstein to become a continent again after the ice-age and now we are happy that this is a continent). But as soon as you remove the ice again, the sea level will change considerably and much of this area and much of other coastal areas will be below the sea level and so, I think, all this is very hypothetical. But this, I think, has a strong implication on future policy. If the lawyers, the legal people, say that stations on the ice sheets, on the ice shelves, do not have the same legal status as stations on hard rock, there will be then a tendency by a good number of countries to build their stations on the few places which are on hard rock, which would cause a considerable environmental problem as those places are rather few. And from the environmentalist point-of-view we should rather have the stations on the ice shelves, and not, for legal reasons, just to safeguard our legal rights, put them on the few spots without ice.

J. Delbrück, Chairman:

Thank you. The next speaker is *Jim Barnes.*

J. Barnes:

Thank you. My question goes to what obligations the governments have that are carrying out quasi-governmental authority, so to speak, in Antarctica. What obligations do they have for providing accurate and timely information to pilots, in the case of the airspace, both of nations and in cases of private expeditions — the same kind of information they normally provide according to legal structures and various national laws? A similar case can be made, or question raised, about the obligations regarding ice and weather data for ships, as well. And there are many practical examples of this coming up all the time, so it is a matter of some timely importance. Thank you.

J. Delbrück, Chairman:

Thank you. I think that I will collect the questions raised and will then ask the addressees of those questions to answer later on. *Mr. Hajost.*

S. Hajost:

Thank you. I have a comment and a question in response to *Professor Orrego*'s very interesting presentation. And I thought I might just elaborate a little bit on the *Beattie* case that he mentioned. It is one that I think does not turn so much on sovereignty; it involved the issue of jurisdiction of U.S. courts in the first instance. The question is, whether or not, as he mentioned, the Federal Torts Claims Act could apply in this particular case. The Government's view was that the Federal Torts Claims Act should not apply to accidents occuring in Antarctica, and that Antarctica should be assimilated to a foreign country for purposes of the Act, without any prejudice to our position on the legal status of Antarctica. The Act does not allow for claims to be made which have arisen in a foreign country, and it was argued that in enacting the law, Antarctica was not intended to be covered, that is, no place outside the U.S. was to be covered. The Court found that the Act is applicable to Antarctica consistent with the U.S. position on Antarctica and we are now proceeding on the case on the merits, that is, whether there was negligence.

I do have a question for *Professor Orrego*: it has been mentioned that pursuant to ICAO there has been identification of flight information regions, and search-and-rescue regions that extend into Antarctica. In particular, I believe, there is a Caribbean and South American regional plan that does identify flight information regions extending into Antarctica. I wonder if he might comment as to whether he believes there has been, in the ICAO process, adequate coordination with the Antarctic Treaty Parties, to ensure that there will be provision of the services that are necessary in such regions. Thank you.

J. Delbrück, Chairman:

Thank you. The next speaker is *Arthur Watts.*

A. Watts:

Thank you. I have got two questions, or two comments, but the first of them has largely been overtaken by what *Dr. Sollie* and *Professor Hempel* have already said. It did seem to me that it was an oversimplification to pretend that the ice had been taken off Antarctica, and then look at the resulting land surface as it is now. It seems to me that the underlying land would almost certainly change. And I would be surprised, although the geologists would know better, if anyone could accurately predict what the consequences would be if you took the ice away — given the way in which the land would rise, and the ice itself (or the water contained in it) would have to go somewhere.

This makes me, therefore, sympathize more with the approach that *Professor Mangone* was adopting, which was that you should look at Antarctica as it really is at the moment, against the background of navigational ideas which were at the foundation of current law of the sea, and by implication, territorial law. And I therefore find myself in sympathy with his view that one should treat ice-shelves as if they were land, in effect, and therefore that the ice fronts should be the baseline or coastline of Antarctica. But this however, gives rise to a point, which I should like to put to *Professor Mangone:* I would be very interested in his view of the status of the waters underneath the overhanging ice-shelf. They would be to the landward side of the baseline and might therefore be thought to be appropriately dealt with as national waters — but there may of course be alternative views, particularly if you think of the very large ice-shelves, where the waters underneath the shelves could in fact be very extensive. Given the possible uses of underwater transport for example, and certainly exploration possibilities, *etc.*, it would be of interest to know what the status of those waters is. Thank you.

J. Delbrück, Chairman:

Thank you. *Professor Friedmann*, please.

I. Friedmann:

Several questions have been asked about the obligations to provide services or search-and-rescue operations for private or commercial flights, and I would like to turn around this question on the basis of a personal experience. At the time of the Erebus disaster our group was transported by helicopters from McMurdo Station to the continent. The next hour, literally, all helicopter flights for science were cancelled in order to recover the dead of the Erebus disaster. Our group was left without supplies for two weeks, and all further scientific projects had been cancelled because of this operation. The same thing applied also to the New Zealand search-and-rescue climbing team: everybody was collecting the dead of the Erebus disaster to be transported back for burial.

A similar occurrence happened last year when one of the private expeditions got into trouble, and again the United States had to provide help for these operations. Private expeditions know that there is a safety net they can rely upon. The question is, to what extent can this safety net be saturated by, I would say, sometimes irresponsible planning?

J. Delbrück, Chairman:

So your question would be, who is liable for that, the consequences of such irresponsible planning? OK. Thank you. The next speaker is *Mr. Harders.*

E. Harders:

I would like to direct my question to *Professor Mangone* who gave, in my opinion, a fascinating and convincing presentation. As you made reference to the Arctic Ocean and finally recommended conventional means in order to have territorial sovereignty extended to shelf ice, is there uniform state practice in the Arctic Ocean relating to shelf ice, taking it into account on the application of baselines? Thank you.

J. Delbrück, Chairman:

Thank you. So right now we are at the end of the list of questions — no, I am sorry. *Ambassador Berguño*, please.

J. Berguño:

Thank you. I wanted to say that, with regard to *Professor Mangone*'s paper, *Arthur Watts* has already asked the more pertinent questions and I share very much his own approach. I would only want to say on that respect that the Chilean claim is one that includes pack ice within the sector claimed by Chile. On the question of bases and what inference can be drawn on where they are placed or not, I think it is not a conducive approach to focus on the legal foundation for establishing bases, which is only to be found in the Antarctic Treaty itself. What is, in fact, conducive, is to look at the established uses the bases have had, and to derive from there the consequences, which are not necessarily, let us say, as critical as *Mr. Chopra*'s paper would have implied, but are rather, I think, the expression of the establishment of another Antarctic use. We have to approach, I think, the question of airspace in the same manner. If we do so I would think that the very able paper by *Professor Orrego* and the comments that *Roberto Puceiro* made thereafter nevertheless do not take fully into account what, I would say, is a basic Claimant position.

The basic Claimant position is that under Article IV the rights of Claimants must be safeguarded, must be taken into account. Of course there is nothing that could, let us say, except airspace from a claim, and therefore we have to face the actual question of the use of airspace, not just in terms of what the actual practice or exercise of jurisdiction has been. And there has been jurisdiction; in our case we have established and have the accepted FIR sector, and we try to apply it. But naturally the way that use is approached will differ — if we are trying to establish a very cooperative project like the American Airbus or afterwards CATSA were designed, mostly for intra-Antarctic traffic and to be used particularly for scientific purposes, that is, the logistic help for scientific cooperation in the Antarctic — we focus on the broader and very ambitious concept of having the whole of Antarctica regulated in a regional agreement. If the approach is that of the first, the developments which were pointed to by *Puceiro* in the recommendations themselves show that although there was a difficulty this was a promising approach. If we look at the more broad picture — and the growth of air-traffic in Antarctica, as *Professor Orrego* has indicated, may push us in that direction — the difficulties will be greater, because essentially, we would think that a parallel exercise to that, let us say of the minerals regime, would be required to safeguard the position of the Claimant countries. Thank you.

J. Delbrück, Chairman:

Thank you. The next speaker is Mr. *Muñoz Seca.*

A. Muñoz Seca:

Thank you very much. I think it is relevant to point out, concerning the question of legal status of packs of ice, that in the Arctic Region we had difficulty with the Canadian decision to draw their baselines not from the mainland itself, but from the moving ice in the Arctic. Therefore it is, I think, important to notice that the Community countries made a common *démarche* towards the Government of Ottawa, protesting against the drawing of lines too far up, that is, taking into account the movable packs of ice and not the mainland of Canada itself. That, of course, has been refused by the Canadian authorities, but since several speakers have brought up the topic I thought it was interesting to interject it in the debate. Thank you.

J. Delbrück, Chairman:

Thank you. *Mr. Hafner.*

G. Hafner:

Thank you very much. I want to put a short question to *Professor Mangone*, which relates to the status of ice in international law. If we have to look to the scope of application of the law of the sea, we find that the law of the sea applies to the sea and the sea is defined for instance, by *Oppenheim / Lauterpacht*, going back so far as I remember to *Grotius*, as a coherent body of *salt water*. I emphasize "salt water." Now, I learnt the day before yesterday and today by your explanation that the ice in the polar regions could originate from different sources. It could originate from fresh water as well as from salt water. Could now this definition of the law of the sea be used as defining whether the particular piece of ice relates more to the territorial side or the sea side of international law? Thank you very much.

J. Delbrück, Chairman:

Thank you, now I would like to call upon *Professor Mangone* for his comment on the questions posed to him.

G. Mangone:

I want to express my appreciation for your questions because they do indicate interest, and they do indicate conflict, and that, in a sense, is a source of progress. Let me try to answer them one by one.

The first question is about ice, pack ice, and I think there has been some misunderstanding here. The delimitation of "fast-ice," which is frozen sea-water, is relatively simple in terms of drawing boundaries where fast-ice, attached to the land, is permanent or semi-permanent. The "floating ice" varies considerably and there are a few more problems with it, which have been referred to: namely, whether the ice is two years old or three years old. My approach on the whole matter, whether the Arctic or Antarctica, is that the time is coming when we must fix responsibility for areas of the earth on some agency, whether it is national or international. Nature abhors a vacuum; something will rush in to fill it and it may not be what is most desirable for the community. I am not as disturbed by the sector-theory as some people are. There are reminiscences of European colonialism of the nineteenth century, in which there was exploitation of very rich economic resources and the abuse of peoples. That is not the situation in the polar regions. In the polar regions we are faced with legal lapses, where there is an opportunity to think creatively. That is what our conference and discussion has been about. Whatever regime we may be referring to, whether it be for fish, for minerals, or air transit, we are seeking legal process. When I regard the vast floating mass of polar ice — frozen sea-water, pack ice, I do see a large area of the earth for which there is no responsibility. The sector theory, which has its difficulties obviously, at least presents an opportunity to examine where responsibilities may lie. And I have, at least, tentatively suggested that there could be a regime with international guarantees for access to those areas, for demilitarization of those areas, and for free navigation, free fishing, and free exploitation of the continental shelf, while at the same time, maintaining responsibility and liabilities in the north polar region. To some extent, that is a similar issue for Antarctica as well. The second speaker instructed me that the Antarctic shelf was not frozen sea ice, I do not think I ever said anything of the kind.

G. Hempel:

I agree with you.

G. Mangone:

It is formed by precipitation and then by transformation into ice. Now to Mr. *Watts*'s question, which I really deeply appreciate because he has gone far in analyzing the legal status of the ice shelves, let me state what is known scientifically at the present time: the shelf-ice, which I indicated occupies about half of the Antarctic coast, is also grounded to a depth of at least 200 meters along 60 percent of this boundary. So there, I think, you would have no problem whatsover in saying that the shelf ice itself is still on land, although it is below sea-level. The question Mr. *Watts* raises is, what about the underlying water where the shelf-ice protrudes further out to sea? It is an excellent question, and I have thought about it. It could be that you would draw the baseline at the point where the grounding line ends. That would leave some areas of shelf that would hang over, hypothetical territorial waters. But I cannot accept that; for a good reason: navigation in that area would have to be under the shelf; innocent passage would be impossible under those circumstances. I then must come down on the side that this area would be internal waters.

E. Harders:

My question was whether there is anything like a uniform state practice for taking the shelf-ice into account on the positioning of the base lines?

G. Mangone:

Well, this turns again to the question that was raised about Canada and its recent drawing of baselines. This has caused a bit of consternation in the United States, especially since the article in the Law of the Sea Convention about ice-covered areas was placed there by an understanding, a gentleman's agreement between the United States and Canada, that this would take care of the situation. Instead, Canada has gone ahead, unilaterally, and drawn these baselines. I have just come from Montreal and I have been trying to get more accurate data as to where these baselines are. You seem to allege that they have been drawn at the edge of the fast-ice, is that correct? You said, "floating-ice"; I do not think you meant that, but fast-ice. So indeed, one could say that Canada has made a *démarche*, in the sense of having actually done this already. I would have to verify it, but the people I tried to reach in Ottawa were not reachable.

With regard to the Chilean claim to Antarctica, the government included all the ice of every kind in their sector. My prescription was to put the claim only on the shelf-ice that protrudes from the land and possibly the icebergs that calve from the shelf-ice up to a hypothetical exclusive economic zone. That would be a little different from the Chilean claim and, I think, would have a sounder legal basis.

There was another question about sea-ice water and salt water definitions. The fact is that sea water congeals, it begins to lose its salinity. Indeed, after a year or two, you can melt sea ice and drink it. So the distinction between what is fresh and what is salt is quite variable.

J. Delbrück, Chairman:

If you would stay for a moment, *Finn Sollie* has a second question.

G. Mangone:

Yes, certainly.

F. Sollie:

Well, Mr. Chairman, it is not so much a question as it is a comment in connection with the sector principle, as applied to ice. Of course, the situation we have in the north is entirely different from the south, and we have to face up to the fact that things are happening, in the north. As I said, one of the things that is happening is that modern technology is making it possible now to navigate, and in that connection we run into rather significant questions, both legally, politically, and not the least, militarily, in the north. You could say, in a sense unfortunately, the ice-covered waters, or the drift-ice-covered waters problem was not discussed at the Law of the Sea Conference, and there were some of us who deplored that, and had hoped that time could be taken to discuss the problem to some extent. Some countries were in favour, but most were against it primarily because of the question of time. And the result is, as you have referred to, that one little paragraph, which really does not say a thing. In the north you also have the fact, if you look at that excellent little map of the Arctic, that in a good portion of the season the ice is not only not "fast-ice," but it is not even loosely attached to land, particularly in the eastern part of the Arctic, because the off-land winds are the currents which give you a passage. The passage varies from month to month and from year to year, but it nevertheless is there. Now, the increasing activities in the Arctic, both civilian and military, makes it incumbent upon the international community, and particularly, the regional states obviously, to establish some type of understanding on the uses of the Arctic. First of all, you indicated the possibility of demilitarization. Now, that definitely is out of the question. This is, in military terms, the most important water body, bordering the most important bases in the world. So there will be no military restrictions. We can be quite sure of that.

G. Mangone:

May I interrupt? I said on the ice itself; I was speaking of a special regime for the ice, with freedom of the seas, freedom of access to them.

F. Sollie:

But the point here is that we have increasingly, because of technological progress and the type of uses that have become current, to regard the North Polar Basin, with water and ice, actually as a high seas area, with economic zone borders and all that, we have to look very hard at some of the Canadian and Soviet practices, with long baselines, the Russian interpretation of "internal waters," the Russian interpretation of "historical bays" *etc.*, in view of the future navigational problems that will occur. And for that reason, I think, the position my country is taking, for instance, I think, is that this is water, period. It happens to be ice-covered for a good portion of the year.

G. Mangone:

I think it is more difficult, and I certainly made that modest proposal with regard to the pack ice as such. But you do have a solidity there, and you will have operations on the surface of the ice. I am not surprised at the ingenuity of an international community that can live with the Antarctic Treaty of 1959 or that can invent things like an "exclusive economic zone," in which resources are appropriated but navigation is maintained free or that can create an "International Area," which can be high seas and at the same time allocate resources of the sea-bed to both an "Enterprise" and to states. I think you have a surface portion of the Earth which is, can I make a pun here, drifting to some extent. A regime for the north polar region is more difficult. I am more certain about the "shelf-ice" and the "fast-ice."

J. Delbrück, Chairman:

Thank you very much. I now come to *Professor Orrego*, who will kindly answer the questions posed, and then we will head for a finish, I guess.

F. Orrego Vicuña:

I may group the questions in two or three main points that have been raised. The first is the one related to information, particularly with regard to private flights or expeditions. Here we have a practical situation, where countries managing particular landing or aircraft facilities in Antarctica like McMurdo, or Molodezhnaya, or Marsh, will provide information according to their own national practices about the conditions in the area. Of these the meterological conditions are normally reported on a regular basis because, for that matter, Antarctica is linked through satellite arrangements, so everyone has an advance warning, insofar as it is possible, of what is coming up in terms of weather. As for the rest of the conditions it depends very much on the practice and the national approach of those countries managing those particular facilities.

Precisely because that is not yet coordinated, there have been two kinds of reactions by the Consultative Meetings. The first, which I mentioned in passing, is the fact that conventional aircraft operators are to be notified, that is informed, when there are certain conditions which are adverse for their own flights. This has been mentioned, for example, when those flights exceed existing capabilities for air-traffic control, communications, search-and-rescue, when those flights interfere with normal operational flights in support of expeditions or scientific research, or when those flights exceed the capacity to respond adequately to an unplanned emergency landing. This amounts to a setting-up of priorities, that is, when a given facility is confronted with the need to support its own expedition and scientific research, normal emergency procedures, or normal capabilities of air control, it will attend to that in the first place, and everything else in the second place or afterwards. You may find this policy in Recommendation X-8, which is the one that deals with this particular sort of priority base.

But there is also a second kind of reaction which is interesting, that was to a certain extent related to the Mount Erebus air disaster. The Eleventh Consultative Meeting discussed the idea of establishing areas of special tourist interest, and those would involve the possibility of adopting a common response to enquiries about the requests for assistance of tourism and non-governmental expeditions; that is, in that particular Eleventh Consultative Meeting action, there was the idea of a common response to enquiries about what can be done in terms of tourism or non-governmental expeditions.

This is as far as the Treaty System has gone in terms of provision of information. But of course the question is that normally private expeditions will be requested to undertake their activities with the consent of, or in coordination with, states managing facilities in Antarctica, precisely in order to avoid overlappings, or incurring a situation in which those activities will not be able to be handled adequately at the same time. So there is an encouragement by the Treaty System as a whole, to the effect that private expeditions, or non-governmental expeditions, might be made in a coordinated way so as to ensure that things can be done adequately.

Secondly, there was a reference to flight information agreements and whether the ICAO general area for South America and the Caribbean was to some extent coordinated with the Antarctic Treaty Parties. As far as I know, this has not been coordinated, but I hesitate a bit in giving this reply because I have not looked into that particular point; ICAO has entrusted some responsibilities in terms of transcontinental flights. For example, Chile was assigned, as a consequence of the Easter Island flight information region, the area southwards to the South Pole within the limits of meridians 90° West and 120° West in order to regulate air traffic, provide air traffic services to the route between Santiago, or Punta Arenas, and Auckland, to the extent that there might be traffic operating south of 40° South latitude. That was a particular occasion on which ICAO did this in agreement with one specific Consultative Party, but I am not aware of any sort of more general coordination.

I do know that there have been discussions with the ICAO officials in order to regulate or coordinate this matter, but ICAO, as far as I understand, is rather reluctant to get involved in Antarctic affairs, as long as the Antarctic Parties have not settled their own arrangements in a manner that will allow for a technical intervention by ICAO. That is, ICAO would not like to get involved in jurisdictional discussions.

Finally, there is the question of *Beattie et al.*, which is one of the most interesting cases relating to Antarctica that has come up. The whole discussion of this case was related to the Federal Tort Claims Act, but in doing so the judge did discuss some particular features of the Antarctic Treaty System, among them Article IV of the Antarctic Treaty and its meaning, prompting a very interesting legal discussion. From the point-of-view that interests us here, the problem was that the Court developed the reasoning that the choice was between an American jurisdiction to rule on the case, or no jurisdiction at all, taking the side of the American non-recognition policy. But in fact I think there is another view which the Court did not take clearly into account, although some dissenting opinions did, which is that in this particular case New Zealand had some jurisdictional basis that could have been invoked. First of all, the events took place in the New Zealand claimed area. Second, it was a New Zealand aircraft, and third, most of the passengers that were killed were of New Zealand nationality, so there could have been a concurrent jurisdiction of some sort, which the U.S. District Court for the District of Columbia did not admit.

The problem, in my view, is not whether there was an American jurisdiction or nothing at all, but whether the American jurisdiction was concurrent with some other form of jurisdiction, which in fact does exist in Antarctica. And my argument is that, to the extent that the Treaty Parties might be able to develop some form of joint legal regime in this field, the situation would become much more clear, because it would not be a case of concurrent jurisdiction between America or any other country, but within a legal system on its own, dealing with the problem of Antarctic air traffic and responsibilities. I think that this case, although discussed in the context of the domestic policy, really touched upon some of the issues which have to be settled in any Antarctic discussion if we wish to have an orderly air traffic regime in the area.

J. Delbrück, Chairman:

Thank you all. Well, I think we are now ready to adjourn for lunch.

Micro-organisms in the Antarctic Desert: A Model for Possible Life on Early Mars

*E. Imre Friedmann**

Thank you for the introduction, and it is my special pleasure to be able to talk to the participants of this Symposium. As you know, most of the Antarctic continent is covered by ice and snow, and not everybody knows that other landscapes exist in Antarctica, although *Dr. Behrendt*, the day before yesterday, showed some other types. How do deserts come into existence in Antarctica? Although the Antarctic continent is covered by ice, the Transantarctic Mountains stopped the flow of ice, and created an actual desert area in South Victoria Land as the ice dried up. This desert area is about 5,000 km^2 in extension and is the largest desert in Antarctica. We call it Ross Desert.

The landscape is wild, and the climate of this place characterized by violent winds, low temperatures, and extreme aridity. Granite blocks have been excavated by wind action and they look like sculptures of *Henry Moore*. But what they show is that the winds are really violent and for human existence, the greatest problem to cope with.

Now, imagine we are in one of the dry valleys, and we see here an object before us. It is a carcass of a seal, several of which are present in the dry valleys. How did they get there? Well, some seals were simply disoriented at the ocean and they walked up the valleys toward the desert. They died, according to the carbon dating, some hundreds or even thousands of years ago: the oldest of the seal carcasses is 4,000 years old. When you look at the seal it is not decomposed; it is there as it died, hundreds of years ago. The tissue is oxidized a little but the fur is still intact. This shows us that under these conditions there is no appreciable bacterial decomposition. This is absolutely unique in the world. Anywhere else, you throw away a banana skin, for instance, it will decompose and disappear within days, or maybe weeks. But here, after geologic time has passed, it still will be there.

This shows that there are no micro-organisms and no bacterial decomposition on the surface. But, it also shows something about the

---

* Prof. Dr. *E. Imre Friedmann*, Director, Polar Desert Research Center, Florida State Univesity, and Prof. Dr. *Roseli Ocampo-Friedmann*, Florida A & M University. (This is a summary of an audio-visual presentation — Ed.)

fragility of the Antarctic ecosystem. What does it mean to talk about fragility of the Antarctic ecosystem? *Every* single piece of organic matter will stay where you leave it. Nature does not have the elasticity to absorb it, which illustrates the problem of Antarctic operations.

For the biologist, what is most astonishing about this desert is that it is absolutely dead. There are no animals, no sign of living organisms at all — at least on the surface. But if we get nearer to one of the rocks, and we hit the surface with a geology pick, what we see is that under the surface there is a coloured zone. When we investigate this coloured zone a little closer, what we see are different colours — parallel zones: a black, a white and a green zone. We now look in the microscope at the black and white zone. Under the microscope two different organisms are visible, green cells, which are green algae, and around them, white filaments which are fungi. We know from biology that this is an association of two different organisms into a structure — which is called a lichen. The black and white zones are composed of this lichen. These organisms can be cultured in the laboratory separately. We did this, separated the fungi, and grew them under simulated Antarctic conditions in the laboratory, and then separated the green photosynthetic organism, the algae, and grew them again separately, under Antarctic conditions.

A lichen outside of Antarctica has its own shape and form on the surface of the rock. But in Antarctica, the same lichen will go inside the rock. With a scanning electro-microscopic picture, one can see single sand grains, and between the sand grains, filaments of fungi and the cells of algae. This means that these lichens do not have their own shape and form, but in order to get into the safe protected depths of the rock they gave up their own shape and are growing now in the available spaces between crystals of the rocks. This is an absolutely unusual situation.

Next, we look at the green zone, which are organisms living in the shadow of the lichen. Here green photosynthetic algae are again visible. There are quite a few of them, and we grow them also in the laboratory. There also exist bacteria which can photosynthesize, and a number of other bacteria. Sometimes one will see single bacteria, with high magnification, sitting on the surface of a single sand crystal inside the sandstone.

Next we investigated the chemical effect that organisms exert on the rock itself. First of all, the core of the rocks is brown; why is it brown? This is because the rock crystals are coated by iron compounds. Where the organisms are, the iron is being leached out. They solubilize, they leach out iron from the rocks. Then, the organisms dissolve the substance which cements together the rock crystals, so that the rock crust will peel off from above the head of the organisms. These organisms are now exposed to the murderous climate of the Antarctic desert and they die unless they can grow deeper into safe depths, which they do. At the same time, a new rock crust is being formed. This, of course, takes many thousands of years to be completed. The result is this peeling-off crust on the surface of the rock in different colours, which results from the different grades of leaching of the rock. This type of weathering, a mosaic weathering pattern, is a sign of microbial colonization. So, if we see that type of pattern on the surface of the rock, we know that organisms are there. These organisms, layer-by-layer, slice off the rock.

What are the conditions under which these organisms can survive in the rocks? Why are they inside? There are several problems which these organisms have to solve. First, water, also temperature (it is very cold), and light. They need light inside in order to photosynthesize.

First, water: snow is very rare in the Antarctic desert, but sometimes it does fall. When snow falls it does not usually melt. Either it is blown away by wind or it sublimates into the extremely dry atmosphere. Sometimes after such a snowfall, the sun comes out and warms up the rock surfaces. The result is that the snow melts and the rocks, which are porous, soak up the water like a sponge. In the low temperatures they retain that water for several weeks. So, water is really not the main limiting factor of these organisms.

What is much more important for them, is temperature. We try to measure the different physical parameters inside the rock, trying to determine the microbial climate, the climate for micro-organisms in the millimeter range. We place a number of different sensors in the rock connected to an automatic recording station. An electronic package processes the information, powered by solar cells. An antenna sends signals to a polar orbit satellite. The polar orbit satellite passes over the place about every 200 minutes and receives the data. The data are beamed back to the French space centre in Toulouse, and from there we get, once a month, a big computer tape with all the data.

What did we learn about the microbial climate inside the rock? On a nice sunny day in Antarctica, the air temperature is between -17° C to -6° C. The temperature of the rock in southern exposure is about the same as the air. However, if we look at the rock temperature in northern exposure, then it is 0°. You see that in the afternoon the temperature in the rock rises to around +7° C. Why only in the northern exposure and not in the southern exposure? This is because we are in the southern hemisphere and the sunny side is the northern side and the shady side is the southern side. So, the environment of these organisms will only warm up when the sun is shining on the rocks. We look at this rock and we see on one side the mosaic pattern of microbial colonization, and on the other side not. That side is eroded by wind. This is the southern side and cold winds from the South Pole are cooling and eroding this side of the rock.

We measure wind, snow, humidity inside the rock and in the air, and rock temperatures. In January 1985, every day, there was metabolic activity. While there is continous light during the Antarctic summer, at night the light intensity is lower, because the sun angle is much lower. In the middle of the Antarctic winter in July, there is absolutely no light. There are violent winds, so violent that once our whole weather station was blown away by the wind. But the winds are also high in the summer.

The main problem, for human existence, is not the absolute temperature but the air temperature plus the wind.

Light conditions inside the rock are complicated and we cannot quite measure them in the millimeter range. We constructed a computer model, and this model shows the light intensity every day at different levels. The lichens get some light, but not much, only about 1 per cent of the light on the surface. Those which are living very deep down get much less, maybe 1 per cent of 1 per cent of light. So, they are living in near darkness.

What would be the optimum temperature for these organisms? The optimum is 8 to 12° C. That is what they would like to have. Instead, they get much less. For 50 hours per year, the temperature is between 0 and 5° C, and nothing above 5° C. Between -10 and 0 there are about 700 hours. Between 0 and -10, life processes are absolutely minimal, this is the lower limit. So, in fact, these organisms only have very few hours in a year where they can function, and even then they do not function within their optimal range as most other organisms on Earth. They are really living at the brink of existence. Consider again for a moment what is happening. These organisms are closed in under a crust, formed by geological processes, which take thousands of years. They do not have much room to grow, they are closed in and they metabolize very little, only for a few hours a year. Mostly, they are in a freeze-dried state and inactive.

The age of these organisms is very high and they are closed in by a crust, a geological structure. We know that they are many thousands of years old, probably the oldest living organisms on earth. This result is unpublished and I cannot quite give you very accurate numbers. As mentioned, these organisms are living literally at the brink of existence. If conditions turn just a little bit to the worse, they will die and disappear. We can see this from the differences in colours and the signs of a past colonization, a fossil colonization which lived and died geological times ago. Because of environmental changes, the organisms died, they left behind the mosaic pattern on the surface which has been recolonized here when the conditions got better again. Glacial geologists who dated some of these rocks on the basis of other data say that the age of these formations is between 70,000 and 3-4 million years, meaning that the organisms were there for about the last 3 or 4 million years. During glaciations, ice-ages, they came and died out or became pushed out from here. The rocks were recolonized again, and the age of the entire system is several million years.

It can happen that the organisms die, disappear and the whole rock becomes silicified, meaning that silica fills the pore spaces between the rock. That makes it impossible for the rock to be recolonized, but sometimes the organisms leave behind a trace fossil. A trace fossil is like a dinosaur footprint. Dinosaurs no longer exist, but we can deduce from their footprints that they were here. It is the same situation. The organisms no longer exist but the leaching pattern is here. And we can deduce from the presence of the leaching pattern, which cannot be explained by chemical or physical phenomena, that organisms must have been here thousands or millions of years ago.

Now, let us think a bit about Mars. This slide shows the surface of Mars. As we know, today there is no life on Mars, but there is evidence that this may not always have been the case. We know that Mars and the entire solar system were formed about five billion years ago. The conditions of formation of Earth and Mars were very similar, and it is a fair assumption that on early Mars there was water and atmosphere. In fact, there is geological evidence of the presence of past water on the surface of Mars. If that was so, it is safe to hypothesize that primitive life may have arisen on Mars at the same time as it did on Earth. About 3 or 4 billion years ago, Mars lost its water, lost its atmosphere and cooled down. Earth and Mars went different ways. When Mars cooled down, it probably went through a stage similar to the Antarctic desert today. It became a cold desert — extremely cold and extremely dry. But on the way, Martian micro-organisms may have gone through a process of evolution and they may have withdrawn into the last available niches of life inside rocks. If this is so, it is also a good possibility that they left behind some traces like the present organisms in Antarctica. What we are proposing is the following — that while it is extremely unlikely that life forms are existing today on Mars, it is a legitimate goal of research to look for possible traces of past life on Mars. And these possible traces may be the changes in rocks caused by micro-organisms. Any changes in rocks that cannot be explained by physical or chemical gradients or processes have probably been caused by micro-organisms. This is as far as we can go at this point.

NASA is considering all this as one of the possible goals of Martian exploration, which will probably take place early in the next century. Then we will find out whether we were right or not. Thanks are due to all who cooperated in this complex project, some also from Kiel: Prof. *Peter Hirsch* and Prof. *Kappen*, and others from all over the world. Thank you.

General Discussion

L. Kappen, Chairman:

Thank you very much, *Professor Friedmann*, for your beautiful excursion, taking us around into the area where we work and all those of us who have been down South like to remember. We really feel at home when we see these slides. I think your field of jurisdiction is a little bit exotic, I therefore want to give you five minutes so some questions can be raised. Please, *Dr. Quilty*.

P. Quilty:

Thank you, *Ludger*. On the question of doing this in Antarctica, I can understand why you do it there to some extent, but how different would the results be if you did the same sort of work in, say, the very hot regions of central Australia which, I imagine, would also have some similarities with what you would see at some times on Mars.

I. Friedmann:

This is correct. We have very similar formations also occurring in all hot deserts on the Earth. Antarctica is somewhat different, of course, but similarities exist.

J. Barnes:

Are there any activities that you see proposed or planned by human beings that might threaten the ability to carry out this kind of research in the area where you are doing it?

I. Friedmann:

Well, it is obvious. Due to the absence of bacterial decomposition and because of the extreme time frame that is necessary to repair any damage, we realize that every single minute we spend in Antarctica, we also damage the environment. Of course, we try to minimize this destruction, but we cannot help the fact that by our research activity, we are destroying things. We break up a piece of rock and we know, it will take maybe half a million years to be reconstituted. This is the great danger of tourism or even innocent sight-seeing in this environment. You cannot avoid damage.

The opinions expressed in this volume are the personal views of their authors only.

L. Kappen, Chairman:

Dr. Behrendt.

J. Behrendt:

I would be interested in knowing if there are any organisms of this type or any other type in the snow. I know for example that on the summit of Mount Melbourne some biologists found some plants living in the warmth of the active volcano there. There is some slight evidence of life which maybe you know more about. But what about in the ice-sheet itself? I think we have always just assumed that there is no living material there, but is, in fact, this the case?

I. Friedmann:

Snow micro-organisms are well-known also from Antarctica. I don't think that anybody looked for them in the middle of the ice-sheet during traverses. Probably the organisms are there. The big difference, biologically, between the two types is that snow micro-organisms appear as temporary phenomena while endolithic organisms are permanent colonizers, for geological times.

L. Kappen, Chairman:

Well, the last question will be from *Professor Boczek.*

B. Boczek:

Are there any organisms that might have survived during millions of years during the Gondwana Time?

I. Friedmann:

Very probably not. This has been asked before and we are working on this problem at present. In order to explain the presence of these organisms in the Antarctic today, it is not necessary to assume that they survived from the times before the glaciation because these kinds of micro-organisms are travelling freely through the atmosphere. Even if we could show that there are some organisms surviving from earlier times, this would not rule out the possibility that others, or even most of them, arrived later through the winds.

L. Kappen, Chairman:

Thank you very much for your interest, maybe we have time to ask another question. Well, there is *Mr. Rajan.*

H. Rajan:

Thank you very much, *Prof. Friedmann.* Is it true that pathogenic bacteria have been reported in some lakes in Antarctica? What could be the cause of that, and is it possible that the world will face some new diseases because of the pathogenic bacteria?

I. Friedmann:

One half to the information is correct, the other half is not. In the Antarctic lakes there are micro-organisms, including bacteria, but these are not pathogenic. But let me say something about the danger of pathogenic bacteria coming from strange and distant environments, even from outer space, because this has been asked many times. The probability of this becoming a danger is practically zero. All micro-organisms, especially pathogens, are highly adapted to a particular situation, such as to a host. Organisms living in extreme environments are adapted to these highly unusual environments and cannot live in others. We have great difficulties in keeping these creatures alive in the laboratory, or transporting them from Antarctica without damage. My wife, *Dr. Roseli Friedmann*, who is engaged in this work, can tell you that it is extremely difficult to keep them alive. So there is no real danger that they all go wild and explode in growth, invading the Earth. For this, probability is practically zero.

L. Kappen, Chairman:

Well, another question? So, I see there is no question at all at the moment, so now, after we have really enjoyed the beauties of the vivid Antarctic, I would say, we come to another section of our Symposium, and, taking it as a meal, I would say the dessert. I hope that it will not have a bad aftertaste after having had these beauties! I hope it would be a hopeful perspective for the future, which we have to discuss, even waste disposal and other things which are not so enjoyable. First, however, we consider tourism and, perhaps, its effects as well. We will listen now to the paper given by *Professor Boczek* about the legal status of visitors and non-governmental expeditions in Antarctica.

The Legal Status of Visitors, Including Tourists, and Non-Governmental Expeditions in Antarctica

Boleslaw Adam Boczek[*]

Table of Contents

I. Introduction

Following the early sightings of the Antarctic continent in the 1820s,[1] the exploitation of the Southern Ocean's living resources by sealing and whaling expeditions, and then the exploration of Antarctica's coastline with subsequent penetration of the interior, became — apart from related political considerations — the main motivation for Man's presence on the frozen continent. Today, as a result of the Antarctic Treaty,[2] Antarctica is a focus of unprecedented peaceful international cooperation, with

* *Boleslaw Adam Boczek*, Professor of International Law and Political Science, Kent State University, Ohio.

[1] *F. M. Auburn*, Antarctic Law and Politics, Bloomington, Indiana 1982, 2.

[2] The Antarctic Treaty, opened for signature Dec. 1, 1959 (entered into force June 23, 1961), in UNTS 402 (1961) 71—102.

scientists and their supporting personnel of national government-sponsored expeditions still remaining the typical representatives of mankind in the Antarctic region. However, over the past three decades or so, novel categories of visitors have, in increasing numbers, appeared in the Antarctic wilderness: tourists arriving there on commercially run tours, non-governmental expeditions undertaken by "adventurous individuals,"[3] for such purposes as mountaineering, occasionally groups of scientists on private expeditions, all kinds of VIPs and semi-official visitors, film makers, and, of course, the ubiquitous representatives of news media. Because of the specific international arrangements prevailing south of 60° South Latitude, the status of all these categories of persons remains rather uncertain and complex, to say the least.

This study purports to examine the legal status of tourists and "non-governmental expeditions" against the background of the Antarctic Treaty System and international law in general, but taking also account of national legislation of the states concerned. The inquiry appears the more needed as the numbers of the visitors in question are likely to grow in the foreseeable future, whereas their legal status within the framework of the Antarctic Treaty System has not yet been systematically and comprehensively approached by the Consultative Parties, and regulations pertaining to tourists and non-governmental expeditions are scattered in numerous Recommendations of these Parties over the period of the past two decades — apart from the fact that the concepts involved, and especially that of the "non-governmental expedition," have never been defined. The matter has also been neglected in the legal commentaries on Antarctica.[4]

This paper will first outline the development of tourism in Antarctica and review the activities of non-governmental expeditions. Subsequently it will make an attempt to cut through the thicket of terminological confusion surrounding the problem of visitors to Antarctica who are neither official observers nor members of expeditions sponsored by the Consultative Parties. Inherent in the subject matter of this study are two fundamental legal problems that simply cannot be sidestepped: the right of the Consultative Parties to regulate the behavior of third parties and their nationals, and the related and seemingly intractable question of jurisdiction. These two problems will have to be dealt with briefly

[3] Recommendation X-8 (1979). See note 36 *infra.*

[4] Tourists and non-governmental expeditions are examined by *Ian E. Nicholson,* Antarctic Tourism — The Need for a Legal Regime, in: *Rüdiger Wolfrum* (ed.), Antarctic Challenge II, Berlin 1986, 191—203. A section is devoted to tourism in *Auburn* (note 1) 277—283. But there, tourism is discussed in the chapter on environmental problems, with scanty references to tourism and non-governmental expeditions in other chapters of this basic study of Antarctica's law and politics.

without entering into their complexities, but with constant reference to the focus of the study. The paper then proceeds to outline the framework of the Antarctic System's laws and regulations pertaining to tourism and non-governmental expeditions, both those of general application and those specifically directed at tourists and such expeditions. Following this comprehensive review of the sources of the law of Antarctic visitors the paper will deal with the major substantive issues of the subject: access to Antarctica and the scientific stations; monitoring the presence of tourists and other non-governmental expeditions, including the related duty to exchange information; environmental regulations; and the safety and emergency assistance aspects of tourists and non-governmental expeditions in the Antarctic Treaty area. The conclusions will sum up and briefly assess the current situation concerning the legal status of visitors and non-governmental expeditions, offering some policy suggestions on this emerging concern of the Antarctic Consultative Parties.

II. Tourism and Non-Governmental Expeditions in Antarctica

1. Tourism

Precise data on the development of Antarctic tourism are difficult to obtain and the existing information is rather incomplete and sometimes contradictory.[5] It is, however, clear that the bulk of Antarctic tourists arrive in cruise ships, almost all of which visit the Antarctic Peninsula, the most easily accessible part of the continent.[6] Apart from some Chilean tourist activity already in 1956[7] and four Argentinian and Chilean cruises in 1958 and 1959 which brought a total of 538 tourists to the Peninsula,[8] the history of Antarctic tours started in 1966 with a cruise by Lindblad Travel, an American company then incorporated in New York and today in Connecticut. Following seven cruises (two of which visited the Ross Sea) in chartered Argentinian, Chilean and Danish vessels in the years 1966—69, the following year the company intro-

[5] Items on Antarctic tourism are carried by Antarctica, Antarctic, and Antarctic Journal of the United States. The subject of tourism in Antarctica was the dissertation topic of *Rosamunde J. Reich* for the Diploma in Polar Studies, Scott Polar Research Institute, Cambridge. See also *Rosamunde J. Reich*, The Development of Antarctic Tourism, in: Polar Record 20 (1980), 203—214; *Rosamunde J. Codling [Reich]*, Sea-Borne Tourism in the Antarctic: An Evaluation, in: Polar Record 21 (1982), 3—9. See also a paper for internal use of N.S.F. — Division of Polar Programs: *Patricia J. Scharlin*, Antarctic Tourism — Trends and Impact, [mimeo.] Feb. 1979.

[6] Recommendation X-8 (1979), Statement of Accepted Principles and the Relevant Provisions of the Antarctic Treaty, 10.

[7] United Nations General Assembly 39th Session, Question of Antarctica: Study Requested under General Assembly Resolution 38/77, Report of the Secretary-General. UN Doc. A/39/583, Pt. II, view of Chile, 39.

[8] *Reich* (note 5) 207 (Table 1).

duced regular cruises on its *Lindblad Explorer*, which was registered first in Norway, then flew the Panamanian flag of convenience, and after a brief period of Singapore registry, registered in Sweden. The tours visited primarily the Antarctic Peninsula, averaging five trips a year during the austral summer, with the capacity of about 90 passengers per trip. At the same time in the years 1968—71 Argentina ran some 20 cruises in two much larger liners carrying 394 and 390 tourists respectively. Tourist voyages were also organized in the 1970s by a Spanish company, which used two large 800-passenger ships, and by an Italian line sending a ship of approximately 700-berth capacity. In the austral summer of 1974 - 75 some 3,700 tourists visited Antarctica on all these cruises.[9]

Whereas until 1977—78 the *Lindblad Explorer* was the main Antarctic tourist vessel, in that season another cruise ship, the 193-berth *World Discoverer*, began voyages to the Peninsula. It was operated first by a German travel agency (Neckermann), and then by Society Expeditions, an American corporation of Seattle, Washington. These two cruise ships were the mainstay of tourist trips to Antarctica in the 1980s. In 1987 the veteran *Lindblad Explorer* was acquired by Society Expeditions and after extensive reconstruction began a new cruising schedule under the name of the *Society Explorer*.[10] Currently the company runs two cruise ships: the *Society Explorer*, registered in the Bahamas, an "open registry" country, with 100-passenger capacity; and the 140-berth *World Discoverer*, of Liberian registry, with West German officers and an Indonesian crew. For the 1987—88 season Society Expeditions has scheduled 14 trips to the Peninsula with visits to U.S., U.K., Chilean, Argentine, Polish and Soviet stations, and penguin and other fauna colonies. In addition, the *World Discoverer* is used for a 36-day Antarctica circumnavigation voyage, from Tierra del Fuego around Antarctica to New Zealand — with visits at Antarctic Peninsula, Cape Royds and Cape Evans, McMurdo Sound and Scott Bases, Cape Hallet and Cape Adare.[11] Lindblad Travel continues its tours to the Peninsula aboard the *Illiria*, a Greek registry ship, built in 1962 in Italy but refurbished in 1982 and 1985 in Greece, and carrying 140 tourists. Four cruises are planned for the 1987—88 season.[12]

Generally speaking, as noted by the Consultative Parties, the late 1960s and the '70s registered a steady increase in the number of tourists visiting Antarctica.[13] An estimated total of 16,640 cruise-carried passen-

[9] *Op. cit.* 209 (Fig. 3).
[10] Lindblad Explorer under New Flag, in: Antarctic (1984), 224—226.
[11] Society Expeditions — Project Antarctica 1987 & 1988 (Promotion brochure); Antarctica Circumnavigation (Promotion brochure).
[12] Lindblad Travel's — Antarctica 1987/88 (Promotion brochure).
[13] Recommendation VI-7 (1970); X-8 (1979).

gers (approximately 950 tourists a year) took part in the 80 trips conducted in the period 1958—1980. Some 148 landings were made at various points, primarily at scientific stations.[14] By the end of the '70s tourist interest in visiting Antarctica appeared to be leveling off, but seems to be rising again in the mid-'80s. Assuming full booking of the three major cruise vessels, the number of tourists can be estimated as follows: the *Illiria* - 560 (four cruises at 140 passengers); the *World Discoverer*-1,120 (eight cruises at 140 passengers); the *Society Explorer* - 600 (six cruises at 100 passengers); and the Antarctic circumnavigation voyage - 140 passengers. The total of 2,420 must be augmented by some tourists arriving with Chilean and Argentine tours.

The 1970s witnessed the emergence of a new type of Antarctic tourism: visits by air. Although the first tourist flight to Antarctica took place in 1956 when a Chilean DD-6 flew to the Peninsula,[15] for over twenty years thereafter only some 235 people landed in Antarctica for tourist purposes, all at McMurdo. Then, in 1976—77 QANTAS and Air New Zealand initiated special one-day trips from Australia and New Zealand respectively, with tourist overflights in Antarctica. The planes did not land, spending about one hour and 45 minutes over the continent.[16] Some 11,000 passengers are estimated to have taken part in such overflights between 1977 and 1980.[17] Following the crash of the Air New Zealand DC 10 aircraft on the slopes of Mount Erebus, Ross Island, in November 1979 with the loss of all 257 crew and passengers[18] only two flights were made in this series. While flights of this kind are likely to be resumed sooner or later, there appear to be no plans for this mode of Antarctic tourism at this time. On the other hand, tourism by air began to develop in the Antarctic Peninsula area, where hotel accomodations were built by Chile, with tourists arriving by air from the mainland and landing at the Teniente Marsh station.[19] It is not excluded

---

[14] *Reich* (note 5) 206—208; *Codling* (note 5). This is an excellent assessment of a typical Antarctic cruise. For a list of the most frequented landings see: Sites Most Frequently Visited by *Lindblad Explorer* and *World Discoverer*, in: *Scharlin* (note 5) Annex 2.

[15] *Reich* (note 5) 209.

[16] *Scharlin* (note 5) 10.

[17] See the chronological list of tourist flights, 1956—80, in: *Reich* (note 5) 211 (Table 2).

[18] Recommendation XI-3 (1981). This Recommendation declared the site of the disaster a tomb and area to be left in peace, like a historical monument. On the investigation into the disaster see *Auburn*, The Royal Commission on the Mount Erebus Air Disaster, Polar Record 21 (1983), 359—368.

[19] See: Chilean Tourist Flights, in: Antarctic (1984), 273; United Nations (note 7); *Nicholson* (note 4), 193, citing *R. K. Headland / P. L. Keage*, Activities on the King George Island Group, South Shetland Islands, Antarctica, in: Polar Record 22 (1985), 475—484 (481—482). See also: Chilean Families Begin Colony in Antarctica, New York Times, Dec. 4, 1984, p. 3. The air strip at Teniente

that if adequate landing strips are constructed, other countries will undertake Antarctic air tourism activities.[20]

The harsh environment, lack of accomodations and other facilities present — quite apart from the high cost of an Antarctic trip — major problems impeding growth of tourism in the southern continent. In absolute terms tourism is a negligible activity, but since most tourism has tended to concentrate in the more easily accessible Antarctic Peninsula and its offshore islands,[21] there exists the potential of harmful interference with the Antarctic environment. This is quite apart from the interference with the work of the stations and safety problems in the harsh Antarctic climate, raised both for the tourists themselves and the stations that must provide them emergency assistance. The Consultative Parties, while recognizing that tourism in Antarctica is a "natural development,"[22] have adopted a series of measures to regulate the tourist activities in Antarctica, as discussed in other sections of this study.

2. *Non-Governmental Expeditions since 1961*

Antarctica has always fascinated explorers and other visitors in search of thrill and adventure in its frozen wilderness. The number of these types of visitors as well as individuals taking part in private expeditions with scientific purposes (but not counting official visitors) is not precisely known. It can be estimated at not more than a few hundred since the Antarctic Treaty entered into effect in 1961. Experience has demonstrated that the major problem that such expeditions have raised is regarding the safety of their members and requests for emergency assistance. Mountaineering expeditions have visited Antarctica since the famous *Clinch* expedition in 1966—67, which conquered the major

---

Marsh is 1,200 m. long. Britannica Book of the Year 1982, 179. In addition, the Chilean Air Force has built several small air strips along that Antarctic Peninsula. *Loc. cit.* 1984, 171.

[20] Although work on the year-round air strip at Dumont d'Urville was temporarily suspended, some preliminary earthworks were continued in 1985—86 as part of the plan to connect several small islands in order to establish an 1,100 m. all-weather runway. Britannica Book of the Year 1987, 569. The Soviet Union constructed a compacted snow runway at Vostock and opened air links between Moscow and Vostok and Maputo and that station in 1980 and 1982 respectively. *Boleslaw A. Boczek*, The Soviet Union and the Antarctic Regime, in: AJIL 78 (1984) 834—858 (845). In February 1986 a wide-body IL-76 cargo plane was flown directly to Molodezhnaya, landing on an improved snow and ice air strip. An alternative air strip was also established at Novolazarevskaya. Britannica Book of the Year 1987, 569. The United Kingdom conducted surveys in 1984—85 to determine the feasibility of constructing a hard runway at Rothera. *Loc. cit.* 1985, 601.

[21] See Sites Most Frequently Visited (note 14). See also Recommendation X-8 — Statement (note 6) (10).

[22] Recommendation VII-4 (1972).

Antarctic peaks, including Mt. Erebus. Other adventurers of this kind include *Halfpenny* (1969), *Sir Edmund Hillary* (1968) and various teams of climbers, from France, Italy, Switzerland, Austria, New Zealand, and South Korea.[23]

A different type of expedition is associated with adventurous individuals embarking upon extraordinary feats of courage and endurance. Perhaps the best-known example is the British three-man Transglobe Expedition of 1980 which, as part of its world tour, successfully completed in 66 days 1,800 miles (2,900 km) of trek, from the winter camp on Ryvingen Mountain to Scott Base via the South Pole.[24] Another, less successful, exploit of the Footsteps of Scott Expedition during the 1985—86 season, in which three men walked to the South Pole from Ross Island, is known mainly because of the sinking of its supply ship, the *Southern Quest* in McMurdo Sound in January 1986.[25]

Some private expeditions have had scientific or other scholarly objectives. *Cousteau*'s *Calypso* voyage around the Peninsula has been best publicized, but there have been numerous other expeditions. A private Italian expedition carried out research and climbed mountains in 1976 in the desire to persuade the Italian government to accede to the Antarctic Treaty.[26] Among the more recent examples are: the Australian Project Blizzard (1984—85, 1985—86) which studied the historical relics of the 1911—14 *Mawson* expedition;[27] a small Australian expedition aboard the *Riquita*, which in 1986 carried out a useful scientific program in the Southern Ocean;[28] and the 23-member Norwegian-British geological expedition to retrace *Amundsen*'s route from the Bay of Whales to the South Pole and back, in the summer of 1986—87.[29] A number of private yachts have also cruised along the Antarctic Peninsula, and isolated independent flights to Antarctica have equally been reported.[30]

---

[23] See *Scharlin* (note 5) 12—13; *Reich* (note 5) 212. For more recent expeditions see for example, Antarctic (1985) 352—353 (an eight-man climbing expedition from France, Italy and Switzerland); Second Austrian Attempt to Climb Mount Minto, in: Antarctic (1986) 109—110.

[24] See *Sir Ranulph Fiennes*, Polar Aspects of the Transglobe Expedition, in: Polar Record 22 (1984) 51—56; O. *Shephard*, Transglobe Expedition, in: Polar Record 20 (1981) 572—575.

[25] See British Pole Expedition at Cape Evans, in: Antarctic (1985) 365—371. On the rescue see *Southern Quest* Rescue, in: Antarctic Journal of the United States 21 (No. 1, March 1986) 15—16.

[26] *Auburn* (note 1) 116.

[27] Project Blizzard Completes Second Season, in: Antarctic (1986) 34—37.

[28] *Riquita*'s Voyage — Private Expedition in Ross Sea, in: Antarctic (1986) 102—105.

[29] Expedition to South Pole Postponed, in: Antarctic (1985) 409; 90° Degrees South — Team Will Sledge Back to Bay of Whales, in: Antarctic (1986) 106—109.

[30] *Scharlin* (note 5) 11, 14.

A unique experiment by a non-governmental expedition to Antarctica was sponsored by Greenpeace, a non-governmental environmental organization which, using its flag ship the *Greenpeace*, an ocean-going tug, made an unsuccessful attempt to reach Ross Island with materials for building a station and supplies for a four-man wintering party.[31]

Finally, if one is to follow strictly the terminology of the Consultative Parties which refers to visitors "not sponsored by the Consultative Parties"[32] then any expedition sponsored by a state that is not such a Party should be considered a "non-governmental expedition." Naturally, there have been a number of such expeditions.

III. Terminological and Conceptual Problems

The Antarctic Treaty does not make any reference to tourists or non-governmental organizations, but as part of the duty to exchange information between the Treaty Parties it does refer to "all expeditions to and within Antarctica, on the part of [a Contracting Party's] ships or nationals, and all expeditions to Antarctica organized in or proceeding from its territory,"[33] a concept wide enough to encompass also non-governmental expeditions. In addition, for purposes of jurisdiction, the Treaty makes a basic distinction between two categories of persons.[34] The first category includes (1) observers designated by the Consultative Parties to carry out inspections provided for by the Treaty (who under Article VII 1. must be nationals of the Contracting Parties that designate them); (2) scientific personnel exchanged between expeditions and stations; and (3) members of the staffs accompanying any such persons. While they are in Antarctica for the purpose of exercising their functions, all these — as they are sometimes collectively referred to — "privileged" persons[35] are subject only to the jurisdiction of the Contracting Party of which they are nationals. The other category includes "all other persons in Antarctica" (referred to by some commentators as "non-privileged" persons). Visiting members of the families of persons in the first category, tourists, non-governmental expeditions and their members, media representatives, and VIP visitors (even though some of them may be "sponsored" by a Consultative Party) are among such "other persons" under the Treaty. Since the Treaty speaks of the jurisdiction of "the Contracting Party" of which persons in Category I are nationals,

[31] Britannica Book of the Year 1987, 569.
[32] Recommendation VII-4 (1972).
[33] Art. VII (5) (a).
[34] Art. VIII.
[35] See *R. B. Bilder*, Control of Criminal Conduct in Antarctica, in: Virginia Law Review 52 (1986) 231—285.

the question arises of jurisdiction over scientists from non-signatory states, invited to take part in the scientific work of a Contracting Party's station. Are they "privileged" persons or are they to be treated like tourists for purposes of jurisdiction?

So far, Recommendations adopted by the Consultative Parties in furtherance of the principles and objectives of the Antarctic Treaty[36] have not developed a consistent terminology that would clearly differentiate various conceptual categories of visitors in Antarctica, but in general, "tourists and non-governmental expeditions" emerged as a group of major concern at the Consultative Meetings. Already at the first Meeting in 1961 reference was made, within the context of exchange of information on expeditions, to "expeditions to Antarctica not organized by the Party but organized in, or proceeding from the Party's territory."[37] This formulation, taken from the Treaty, was subsequently expanded by inclusion of expeditions "calling at" a Consultative Party's territory.[38] Other pertinent Recommendations usually refer to "Tourists and Non-Governmental Expeditions," but the terminology is not used consistently. The Statement of Accepted Principles and the Relevant Provisions of the Antarctic Treaty, adopted in 1979 for the guidance of those who visit the Antarctic,[39] distinguishes persons sponsored by governments from those not so sponsored. The latter category is of interest for the present study, and the term itself is used in Recommendation VIII-9 which, within this category, differentiates "tourists" from "other persons." What the term "sponsored" means is not explained anywhere. It certainly refers to members of national expeditions and stations, but it also includes official visitors, VIPs and the like. Whether independent expeditions organized by state institutions (for example universities) are so sponsored is not clear. The quality of being sponsored must probably depend on the determination of the Party's authority, competent in Antarctic matters. There are other Recommendations which refer collectively either to "non-scientific expeditions," a concept including tourist and other expeditions[40] (even though such "other expeditions" need not necessarily be organized by "adventurous

[36] Antarctic Treaty Art. IX. Recommendations of the 1st to 11th Meetings are reprinted and amply commented upon in *W. M. Bush*, Antarctica and International Law: A Collection of Inter-State and National Documents, New York 1982 (vol. 1). The texts of the Recommendations of the 12th Meeting can be found, for example in Antarctic Journal of the United States 19 (March 1984) 4—7; and those of the 13th Meeting in *loc. cit.* 21 (March 1986) 4—8; or in: Polar Record 23 (1986) 221—252.

[37] Recommendation I—VI (1961) (10).

[38] Recommendation VI-7 (1970) (2).

[39] Recommendation X-8 (1979), (adopting Annex to Recommendation VIII-9 (1975)).

[40] Recommendation IV-27 (1966).

individuals"[41] and may be scientifically oriented[42]) or to "visitors" or "visitors not sponsored by Consultative Parties."[43] One recommendation assumes a difference between "all visitors who are not sponsored by Consultative Parties" and "tourists." This unfortunate language would suggest that tourists were so sponsored.[44] Eventually, but without any rigorous analysis of the terms used, "tourists" (or "tourism") and "non-governmental expeditions" became standard terms on the agendas and in the reports and recommendations of the Consultative Parties on "effects of tourists and non-governmental expeditions to the Antarctic Treaty area."[45]

As far as the concept of tourism is concerned, some ten years ago Argentina submitted a draft in which the "tourist" was defined as "any person or member of tourist expeditions whether travelling as crew-member, journalist, scientist, technician, guide, etc."[46] However, the eventually adopted "Statement"[47] intended primarily for tourists and non-governmental expeditions does not define tourism for purposes of the Antarctic Treaty System. As a generic term, tourism denotes private individuals travelling without remuneration individually or in a group for pleasure, recreation or personal curiosity rather than for exclusively scientific or other professional purposes. Whereas tourism in Antarctica is typically this kind of activity, there are also some other types of individuals that come within the scope of the concept of tourism that can be inferred from the various Recommendations of the Consultative Parties. Tourists include here commercial tour operators accompanying the tour, guides, and ships' crews bringing tourists to the Antarctic Treaty area. Other visitors, such as photographers, film makers and news media representatives visiting Antarctica for commercial purposes are subject to the same rules as "tourists," in the common sense of the word. Off-duty tourist activities of members of national expeditions and stations must also be included in this category. Official visitors invited by a Consultative Party, such as parliamentarians, governmental officials, or participants in meetings like the *Beardmore* Workshop in 1985, are

---

[41] A term used in Recommendation X-8 (1979).

[42] For example in February 1986 a modest but useful scientific program was carried out in the Southern Ocean by a five-man Australian expedition on the yacht *Riquita*. See *Riquita*'s Voyage (note 28).

[43] Recommendations VI-7 (1970); VII-4 (1972); VIII-9 (1975).

[44] Recommendation VII-4 (1972), (4).

[45] Recommendation VI-7 (1970); VII-4 (1972); VIII-9 (1975); X-8 (1979). See also agenda items in the Reports of the 11th (1 *Bush*, note 36, 238—239); 12th [Antarctic Journal of the United States 19 (March 1984) 3]; and 13th Meeting [*loc. cit.* 21 (March 1986) 2].

[46] Rules of Conduct for Tourists, para. 1-A, Draft for Annex A of Recommendation VIII-9, submitted at the 9th Meeting by the delegation of Argentina, 19 Sep. 1977, ANT/IX/24, in: *Scharlin* (note 5) Annex 11 (b).

[47] See Statement (note 6).

not tourists in the strict sense of the term since they are sponsored by a Consultative Party or Parties. However, from the international legal point of view their status does not differ from that of the tourists. They are not among the categories of persons included, for purposes of jurisdiction,[48] within the scope of Article VIII 1., and they are expected to observe the same environmental rules as non-sponsored visitors. The "Tourists and Non-Governmental Expeditions" Recommendation of the Eighth Consultative Meeting (1975) explicitly applies to "all those who enter the Antarctic Treaty area, both those sponsored by Governments and those not so sponsored."[49]

The Consultative Parties usually distinguish tourists from non-governmental expeditions,[50] but the dividing line is not clear. Both are occasionally termed "expeditions" and, in general, are simply "visitors," although the term "non-governmental expedition" seems to denote Antarctic travel undertaken by "adventurous individuals"[51] for purposes of exploration or as remarkable feats of courage. But according to the terminology of the Recommendations it must also include any scientific expedition that is not sponsored by a Consultative Party, that is, is not part of a national Antarctic program. It is not entirely clear whether an expedition sponsored by a state that is not a signatory of the Antarctic Treaty is, for purposes of the Antarctic System, a governmental or non-governmental expedition. In general, the rather untidy and confusing way in which the concepts of "non-governmental expeditions" and "visitors" are used in the regulations of the Antarctic System suggests the need for clarifying and sharpening these concepts as well as harmonizing the relevant provisions in a consistent and comprehensive codification.

IV. Two Preliminary Issues: Third Parties and Jurisdiction

The above-noted lack of conceptual rigor in regulations pertaining to Antarctic visitors is one reason why the analysis of the topic under discussion is a difficult task for a legal scholar. There are, however, other reasons of a more profound nature. First, any attempt to analyze the legal status of whatever category of person or activity in Antarctica immediately stumbles upon the fundamental issue of the relationship of

[48] A separate question is whether diplomats enjoy immunity in the Antarctic Treaty area.

[49] Recommendation VIII-9 (1975), (1). As demonstrated by the experience with Cape Royds Adélie penguin colony, these kinds of "sponsored visitors" can also harmfully interfere with conservation measures. See *Auburn* (note 1) 185—186.

[50] But tourist trips to Antarctica are occasionally also called "expeditions." See, for example, Recommendation VII-9 (1975).

[51] *Ibid.*

the Antarctic Treaty regime to third states: that is, the whole question of whether or not this regime can, under international law, be enforced as an "objective regime" against third parties, *erga omnes*. And the other problem is that the discussion of the legal status of visitors and non-governmental expeditions is inseparable from the issue of jurisdiction in Antarctica, which is itself in turn intimately tied to the sensitive issue of sovereignty. The jurisdictional tangle of all kinds of legal permutations in the Antarctic situation is already notorious,[52] but its uncertainties can be particularly vexing with regard to visitors and non-governmental expeditions.

The Antarctic Treaty regime does possess rules and regulations relevant to the focus of this study and even directly addresses itself to its substance. However, it would be an easy way out of the morass simply to limit oneself to discussing these provisions, and sidestep the above-mentioned preliminary but fundamental and inter-connected issues of third parties and jurisdiction in Antarctica. Failure to do so would distort the picture of the legal status of visitors and non-governmental expeditions to Antarctica.

1. Third Parties

The Consultative Parties have always acted in a way implying that they possess exclusive competence in Antarctic matters, acting, as it were, in the interests of all mankind.[53] This is not the place to get involved in the debate concerning the question whether the Antarctic Treaty System is an objective regime, as claimed by some.[54] The present analysis follows the view of the majority of commentators that the rules of the Antarctic Treaty System cannot be enforced against third parties since a well established principle of international law holds that a treaty does not create obligations (or rights for that matter) for any

[52] No wonder then, that when at one time the Commander of the U.S. base at McMurdo was asked what kept him awake at night he replied: the uncertainty of legal jurisdiction. *Philip W. Quigg*, A Pole Apart: The Emerging Issue of Antarctica, New York 1983, 151—152, quoting *Charles Neider*, Edge of the World: Ross Island, Antarctica, New York 1974, 77.

[53] There are numerous references to this in Recommendations. See, for example: Recommendations VIII-8 (1975), Preamble; VIII-13 (1975), (1) (a): VIII-14 (1975), Preamble; XI-1 (1981), (5) (d).

[54] See, for example, *R. Dupuy*, Le Traité sur l'Antarctique, AFDI 6 (1960) 111, 121—122; *G. Tunkin*, Kurs mezhdunarodnovo prava, Moscow 1963, (vol. 3) 402; *Eckart Klein*, Statusverträge im Völkerrecht: Rechtsfragen territorialer Sonderregime (1980) 21; *Alfred Van der Essen*, The Application of the Law of the Sea to the Antarctic Continent, in: *F. Orrego Vicuña* (ed.), Antarctica Resources Policy: Scientific, Legal and Political Issues, (1983) 231, 241; *R. G. Guyer*, The Antarctic System, in: RdC 139 (1973) 153, 223—226. For a comprehensive and cogent criticism of this point of view see *Bruno Simma*, The Antarctic Treaty as a Treaty Providing for an "Objective Regime," Cornell Int'l Law J. 19 (1986) 189.

third party without that party's consent.[55] The matter is relevant here since in their concern about activities in the Antarctic Treaty area of states that are not Contracting Parties to the Treaty — and even treaty Parties that are not Consultative Paries — the latter have been particularly preoccupied with the possibility of such "non-sponsored" expeditions not complying with the Antarctic rules and regulations.[56] Article X of the Treaty stating (but not in clearly mandatory "shall" terms) that "[e]ach of the Consultative Parties undertakes to exert appropriate efforts, consistent with the Charter of the United Nations, to the end that no one engages in any activity in Antarctica contrary to the principles or purposes of the . . . Treaty"[57] has been interpreted to include tourists and other visitors and non-governmental expeditions of whatever origin, but is of particular relevance to non-Treaty states and their nationals since under international law the Parties would be required to do so in any case.[58] It must be added that essentially the same formulation, specifically addressed to tourists and other visitors, can be found in Recommendations on the effects of tourists and non-governmental expeditions.[59]

It is arguable that the very existence of Article X and analogous provisions in Recommendations testifies to the Antarctic Treaty Parties' admission of legal incompetence to regulate the conduct of third parties and their nationals in the Antarctic Treaty area[60] (unless the required conduct is governed by binding treaties or general international law). The matter has been discussed by the Consultative Parties (especially

---

[55] This principle is codified in Article 34 of the Vienna Convention on the Law of the Treaties, opened for signature 23 May 1969 (in force 27 January 1980), reprinted in: ILM 9 (1969) 679. For the application of this rule to Antarctica see, among others, *J. Hanessian*, The Antarctic Treaty, Int'l & Comp. Law & 9 (1960) 436, 470; *M. Mouton*, The International Regime of the Polar Regions, RdC 107 (1962) 174, 257—259; *Auburn* (note 1) 117 *et seq.*; *Rüdiger Wolfrum*, Die Internationalisierung staatsfreier Räume (1983) 96; *R. Lagoni*, Die Vereinten Nationen und die Antarktis, in: Europa-Archiv 39 (1984) 473, 479—480. See also views of states on Antarctica in: United Nations (note 7): vol. 1: Bangladesh 92; Bolivia 102; vol. 2: Brazil 3—12 (Has Brazil changed its view since it became a Consultative Party?); Egypt 46; Mexico 112; vol. 3: Pakistan 35. For a compromise view see *Patricia Birnie*, The Antarctic Regime and Third States, in *Wolfrum* (ed.) (note 4) 239—262.

[56] See Recommendation VIII-8 (1975); Report of the 7th Meeting (1972), paras. 15—17, in 1 *Bush* (note 36) 262, 266; Report of the 9th Meeting (1977), *loc. cit.* 341—342; Report of the 10th Meeting (1979), para. 15, *loc. cit.* 359, 363. See also *Auburn* (note 1) 59, 116, 128 (relating Argentina's concern about Brazilian plans for a non-governmental expedition in Antarctica).

[57] This was recalled in Recommendation VIII-8, Preamble.

[58] In *Wolfrum*'s view they are the object of this provision. See *Wolfrum*, Means of Ensuring Compliance with an Antarctic Mineral Regime, in: *Wolfrum* (ed.) (note 4) 177—190, 177 n. 3. See also 1 *Bush* (note 36) 99.

[59] See, for example, Recommendations VI-7 (1970) (1); Compare VII-4 (1972) (4).

[60] See 1 *Bush* (note 36) 100; *Auburn* (note 1) 129; *Simma* (note 54) 199 n. 54.

widely at the 9th Meeting in 1977), but the Parties could only agree that widened adherence to the principles and purposes of the Antarctic Treaty, including increased accession to the Treaty itself, was a desirable objective.[61] There was also realization of the matter being closely related to the issue of sovereignty, and any attempt at laying down mandatory rules on third parties' activities would open a Pandora's box with incalculable consequences for the Treaty System. It has been suggested[62] that "appropriate efforts" under Article X could involve refusal of logistic support and assistance; but how can "efforts," a concept denoting positive action and not abstention, be something negative, a failure to act? In addition, it must not be overlooked that the Consultative Parties are estopped from denying expeditions of third parties and their nationals entry to the Antarctic under the very treaty in which they guarantee freedom of scientific investigation in Antarctica and cooperation to this end.[63] The conclusion must be drawn that expeditions of third parties are not subject to the provisions of the Antarctic Treaty.

The same is true of the other instruments of the regime: the Convention on the Conservation of Antarctic Marine Living Resources[64] and — of particular interest to the legal status of visitors and non-governmental expeditions — the Recommendations adopted by the Consultative Parties under Article IX of the Antarctic Treaty. Among them, Recommendation III-VIII, which includes the "Agreed Measures for the Conservation of Antarctic Fauna and Flora," has a provision analogous to Article X of the Treaty.[65] Recommendations legally bind only those states, including Consultative Parties, that have approved or otherwise definitively accepted them according to their respective constitutional rules.[66] Theoretically even a non-Treaty state could become a party to a Recommendation. A Recommendation does not automatically bind a new Consultative Party or an existing or new Contracting Party of the Antarctic Treaty. The latter two categories of states were only "invited" and then "urged" by the Consultative Parties to approve or accept the Recommendations already approved by the Consultative Parties as a part of the overall structure of cooperation established by the Treaty.[67] All this means that any Recommendation pertaining or

[61] Report of the 7th Meeting (1972) paras. 15—17, in 1 *Bush* (note 36) 262, 266; Report of the 9th Meeting (1977), para. 14, *loc. cit.* 341—342; Report of the 10th Meeting (1979) para. 15, in *loc. cit.* 359, 363.

[62] *Christopher Beeby*, The Antarctic Treaty (1977) 17, cited in *Auburn* (note 1) 129.

[63] Antarctic Treaty Art. II.

[64] Art. XXII.

[65] Agreed Measures for the Conservation of Antarctic Fauna and Flora, Art. X, Annex to Recommendation III-VIII (1964).

[66] For the Consultative Parties see, Agreed Measures Art. XII.

[67] Recommendations III-VII (1964); VIII-8 (1975).

relevant to visitors and non-governmental expeditions binds a country only if and to the extent that it has been approved by that country.

The Consultative Parties, either collectively or individually, have not interfered with expeditions from third countries. They have even assisted in scientific efforts of states acceding to the Treaty or aspiring to Consultative status.[68] Should the Consultative Parties insist on compliance with expeditions from third countries, any action to this effect would be very difficult in view of the specific nature of the Antarctic environment. On the other hand, no serious cases of non-compliance by visitors and expeditions from third countries have been recorded. The next section of this paper will focus on the problem of jurisdiction, which is closely related to the issue of visitors and non-governmental expeditions from third countries.

2. *Jurisdiction*

a. In General

As an emanation of sovereignty, jurisdiction, in the sense of a state's power over persons, property or events,[69] is a routine institution through which governmental organs exercise authority over individuals and other persons. The problem of jurisdiction in Antarctica is notoriously difficult and complex. The main reason for this is the fact that jurisdiction is intimately related to sovereignty, the most sensitive issue in Antarctica, left unsolved and in abeyance under Article IV of the Antarctic Treaty. Therefore jurisdiction had to be allocated in a way that would not be prejudicial to the rights of Claimant and Non-claimant states alike.

Fortunately, though difficult, the problem has not been an urgent or pressing one since only the status of members of national expeditions of the Treaty Parties needed to be regulated; the scale of activities of other persons, though becoming of increasing concern to the Consultative Parties, has remained relatively low. As already mentioned,[70] the *nationality principle* has been adopted as the basis for jurisdiction (ostensibly both civil and criminal, and including jurisdiction to legislate, enforce law and to try in national courts) only over exchange scientists and official observers and only with respect to all acts or omissions occurring while such individuals are present in Antarctica for the

---

[68] *Auburn* (note 1) 115—116. Participation of scientists from Non-consultative and even non-Treaty countries has not been uncommon.

[69] See *Michael Akehurst*, Jurisdiction in International Law, in: British Yearbook of Int'l Law 46 (1972—73) 145.

[70] See sect. III.

purpose of exercising their functions.[71] On the other hand, because of the well-known deep division among the Antarctic powers at the Washington Conference,[72] the Antarctic Treaty contains no provisions on jurisdiction over "other persons" (the category that includes tourists and other visitors and members of non-governmental expeditions), except that it guarantees no prejudice to the respective positions of the Contracting Parties related to jurisdiction over such "other persons."[73] Any dispute arising with regard to the exercise of jurisdiction in Antarctica must be immediately settled by consultation with a view to reaching a mutually acceptable solution.[74] It is not clear whether an invited scientist from a non-Treaty state is subject only to the jurisdiction of his country since Article VIII speaks of scientists being subject to the jurisdiction of the *Contracting* Party of which they are nationals. Strictly speaking, literal interpretation suggests that such non-Treaty scientists should be treated as "other persons" unless — like member of crews or armed forces — they were to be treated as nationals.

Although questions related to the exercise of jurisdiction in Antarctica are among those appropriate for discussion by the periodic meetings of the Consultative Parties,[75] the Parties have until now essentially ignored them. Thus there exists no Recommendation on jurisdiction over "other persons," including visitors and members of non-governmental expeditions. The matter remains unresolved, but it cannot continue so for the indefinite future, considering the likelihood of increasing numbers of visitors in the Antarctic Treaty area.[76]

What then are, under international law, the jurisdictional rules governing tourists, other visitors and non-governmental expeditions in Antarctica? Strictly speaking, at least in theory, the situation is clear. To be consistent with the legal premise (upheld by scholars and by some Non-claimant states) that Antarctica is an area under no state's sovereignty and thereby is "a place outside the jurisdiction of any

---

[71] Antarctic Treaty Art. VIII (1). Compare CCAMLR Art. XXIV (2) (c).

[72] Naturally enough Non-claimant states supported the *nationality principle* with regard to all nationals. The United Kingdom and Norway also favored this position. 1 *Bush* (note 36) 75. On the other hand, France, Chile and Argentina opposed this point of view and, concerned that the *nationality principle* might impair their respective claims, insisted upon the right to exercise full territorial jurisdiction over their claimed territories (subject, of course to the exceptions under Art. VIII). See statements of representatvies in 1 *Bush* (note 36) 35—36.

[73] Antarctic Treaty Art. VIII (2).

[74] *Ibid.*

[75] Antarctic Treaty Art. IX (1) (e).

[76] It might be added that the possibility of mineral exploitation activities raised similar jurisdictional problems which are reported to have already been discussed by the Consultative Parties. *Nicholson* (note 4) 202.

State,"[77] the whole Antarctic Treaty area, including all the surrounding waters, must be treated as high seas, as if there existed no Antarctic continent at all. Since the law of the flag prevails on the high seas, the same should apply to ships in all the Antarctic waters. Furthermore, by analogy to the jurisdiction over ships on the high seas which is based on nationality (not the "floating territory" doctrine) the *nationality principle* should govern jurisdiction over individuals on land. As suggested below,[78] one could construct the concept of nationality of stations, operating for purposes of jurisdiction like nationality of ships on the high seas.

Unfortunately, the Antarctic Treaty, while sidestepping the issue of sovereignty, expressly does not prejudice the respective positions of the signatories which relate to jurisdiction over "other persons,"[79] provided, of course, that the exercise of jurisdiction does not conflict with any rule of international law. In civil cases international law does not (apart from jurisdictional immunities such as those granted diplomats) seem to place any restrictions upon the exercise of jurisdiction.[80] For purposes of criminal jurisdiction, international law has developed certain principles on bases of jurisdiction, each of which requires the existence of some linkage or contact between the state asserting jurisdiction and the event occasioning it. These well known principles are: the *principle of territoriality*; the *principle of nationality*; the *protective principle*; the *universality principle*; and the *passive nationality principle*.[81]

The *protective principle*, which allows a state to exercise jurisdiction outside of its territory in the defense of vital state interests, is of negligible importance in Antarctica. The *universality principle*, under which any state may exercise jurisdiction with respect to universally condemned crimes, such as piracy or war crimes, could theoretically be applied to Antarctica, not so much against war criminals (Antarctica is not a hospitable shelter for such individuals!) but as an application of the definition of piracy on the high seas to "piracy" in a place outside the jurisdiction of any state. In this way, in the interests of law

[77] United Nations Convention on the Law of the Sea, 1982 Art. 101 (a) (ii) (definition of piracy).

[78] See sec. IV 2 e *infra*.

[79] Art. VIII.

[80] *Akehurst* (note 69) 170—172.

[81] A comprehensive discussion of criminal jurisdiction is found in Harvard Research in International Law, Jurisdiction with Respect to Crime, in: AJIL Supp. 29 (1935) 435; The Restatement (Second) of the Foreign Relations Law of the United States (1965). For the application of the Problem to Antarctica see *Bilder* (note 35); *Clare Cosslett*, United States Criminal Jurisdiction in Antarctica: How Old Is the Ice?, in: Brooklyn J. Int'l L. 9 (1983) 67—89; *Elizabeth K. Hook*, Criminal Jurisdiction in Antarctica, in U. of Miami L. Rev. 33 (1978) 489—514; *E. W. Johnson*, Quick, Before It Melts: Toward a Resolution of the Jurisdictional Morass in Antarctica, in: Cornell Int'l L. J. 10 (1976) 173—198.

enforcement in the vast expanses of the Antarctic continent, any state could enforce law against individuals charged with "any illegal acts of violence or detention, or any acts of depredation, committed for private ends."[82] The *passive nationality* (or *personality*) *principle* allows a state to exercise jurisdiction with respect to conduct which adversely affects the person or property of its citizens, even if committed by a foreign national outside of its territory. This basis of jurisdiction is not favored by a majority of states and commentators, but may be applied in a residual manner if the state of concurrent jurisdiction fails to take action.[83]

The *territoriality principle*, under which a state has the right to assert legislative and enforcement jurisdiction with regard to all persons, property and events in its territory, is the prevailing and universally recognized principle in today's international law. Under the *nationality principle* a state may claim jurisdiction over its nationals regardless of wherever they may be, including outside its territory. These two principles are the main bases for jurisdiction over visitors and non-governmental expeditions in Antarctica, as examined in the following sections.[84]

b. Territorial Jurisdiction

The *territoriality principle* is conceptually easy and welcome to Claimant states in their respective "sectors." Without entering into details,[85] it can be summed up that they assert such jurisdiction over all visitors in the claimed territory, either by enacting specific legislation concerning criminal conduct in Antarctica or — like France and Argentina — treat their respective territories as part of the homeland. There are, however, variations in the application of the *principle of territoriality*. Thus, while Australia's Antarctic Treaty Act of 1960 does not, as a general rule, assert jurisdiction over foreign nationals in the Australian territories, legislation on specific issues does so, as exemplified by the Antarctic Treaty Environmental Protection Act of 1980. On the other hand, New Zealand does not assert jurisdiction over non-nationals even for environmental purposes. The same is true of the United Kingdom.[86] In general, the Claimant states are also cautious in applying their

---

[82] United Nations Convention on the Law of the Sea, 1982, Art. 101 (a).

[83] See *Akehurst* (note 69).

[84] See b. and c. *infra*.

[85] For a detailed treatment and references to national legislation see *Bilder* (note 35) 260—263; 1 *Bush* (note 36) 76; *Cosslett* (note 81) 76—77; *Hook* (note 81) 494; *Johnson* (note 81) 186—187. For Australia see *Gillian D. Triggs*, International Law and Australian Sovereignty in Antarctica, Sydney 1986, 253—257.

[86] *Triggs* (note 85) 256.

enforcement jurisdiction to waters that would normally be territorial sea (and/or the Exclusive Economic Zone).[87]

It must be borne in mind that while it is easy to promulgate the law as applicable in Antarctica, the enforcement of the law may prove infeasible under the stressful conditions of the Antarctic environment, the long distances involved, the lack of appropriate enforcement mechanisms, detention facilities, transportation and the like. Hence, apart from refusal to recognize the territorial jurisdiction of a Claimant state on grounds of non-recognition of the claim,[88] doubts can be cast on the legality of such jurisdictional assertion on the basis of the argument that it fails to meet the international law requirement of effectiveness.

c. Nationality Principle

Although the *nationality principle* is recognized universally as a basis for jurisdiction, some states apply it extensively to offenses committed by their nationals anywhere in the world while others — like the United Kingdom and the United States — assert jurisdiction on the basis of nationality only in the case of very serious crimes. In Antarctica all Non-claimants necessarily apply the *nationality principle*. The United States did not enact legislation to this effect until 1984 when the U.S. Special Maritime Jurisdiction was extended to include "any place outside the jurisdiction of any nation" which purports to encompass the whole Antarctic Treaty area. Only very serious crimes are included (arson, assault, carnal knowledge, larceny, maiming, malicious mischief, murder, rape, receiving stolen property, and robbery). It is interesting that in application of the *passive personality principle* also crimes against U.S. nationals committed by foreign nationals are declared subject to this kind of jurisdiction,[89] presumably only as residual jurisdiction.

Also, some Claimant states, such as New Zealand and the United Kingdom, in general purport to regulate the conduct of their nationals throughout Antarctica.[90] The assertion of the *principle of nationality* in Antarctica may conflict with claims asserted on grounds of *territoriality*, especially by Argentina and Chile in whose claims the bulk of tourist activity is taking place. In such cases the Treaty provides for consultation with a view to reaching a mutually acceptable solution.[91]

---

[87] *Auburn* (note 1) 279.

[88] Australia, France, New Zealand, Norway, and the United Kingdom seem to recognize each other's claims. 1 *Bush* (note 36) 58—59.

[89] U. S. Code, Title 18, Ch. 1, § 7, as amended Oct. 12, 1984, Pub. L. 98—473, title II, § 1210, 98 Stat. 2164.

[90] For reference to national legislation see *Bilder* (note 35) 261; 1 *Bush* (note 36) 76—77.

[91] Antarctic Treaty Art. VIII (2).

As a basis for jurisdiction, nationality may be vested also in legal entities, such as corporations, as well as in ships. The state of incorporation provides the primary test for the nationality of a corporation. In this context, and especially in cases involving liability for accidents during Antarctic tours, the law of the state of incorporation would be appropriate. In view of the international nature of the Antarctic tourist industry, jurisdictional conflicts are possible on grounds of some contact or association with another state.

One method whereby some Antarctic Treaty states have been able to widen their respective jurisdiction over tourist and non-governmental expeditions is by asserting jurisdiction over such expeditions as are in some way associated with the state, such as looking at where the expedition was organized (New Zealand, United Kingdom), or what territory it was proceeding from (United Kingdom). Australia claims jurisdiction over expeditions organized by an Australian corporation or association, citizen, resident, or a person domiciled in Australia.[92] By asserting its jurisdiction over such expedtions the state concerned can extend it over those expedition members who are not its nationals regardless of their consent.[93] As discussed later,[94] asserting jurisdiction in such cases to a large extent reflects the Treaty and Recommendations on the duty to report all expeditions to Antarctica organized in, calling at, or proceeding from a Party's territory.

d. Nationality: Ships

The bulk of tourists travel to Antarctica on cruise ships, such operations being of a very international nature in terms of ship's registry, nationality of crews and of passengers. As noted,[95] currently two cruise ships are registered under the flags of convenience of Liberia and the Bahamas, and one is flying the Greek flag. While the latter has now become a party to the Antarctic Treaty, the Liberian or Bahamian interest in Antarctic expeditions must be doubted.

Since the Antarctic waters from the very coastlines must be considered high seas and have no territorial sea or other maritime zones,[96] tourist ships, like other vessels, and all persons on board remain under

---

[92] 1 *Bush* (note 36) 80.
[93] *Ibid.*
[94] See sec. VI 1, *infra.*
[95] See sec. II 1, *infra.*
[96] However, France extended its territorial sea around Adélie Land to 12 miles. Arrêté No. 5 of 13 January 1972, in: 2 *Bush* (note 36) 279. Argentina claims a 200 mile territorial sea does not interfere with navigation of foreign vessels. Law 17, 094-M-24 of 29 December 1966, Arts. 1 and 3, as translated in Law of the Sea Bulletin, No. 2 (March 1985) 3. The establishment of the EEZ is not relevant for purposes of this discussion.

the jurisdiction of the flag state. Aircraft anywhere in the Antarctic Treaty area are also subject to the exclusive jurisdiction of the state of registry. The rule pertaining to jurisdiction over ships is implied in the Agreed Measures which provide, *inter alia*, that each Party whose expeditions use ships of nationality other than the Party's "shall as far as feasible, arrange with the owners of such ships that the crews of these ships observe [the] Agreed Measures."[97] The Australian implementing legislation extends also to vessels (and aircraft) "in Australian control," which seems to include chartered vessels under a foreign flag.[98] So far no major problems seem to have arisen concerning tourist vessels in Antarctic waters and Claimant states do not interfere with their navigation.[99]

The primary jurisdiction of the flag state does not exclude concurrent jurisdiction by another state, such as the state of the owners' nationality or — under the circumstances — the nationality of a passenger, if such other state's jurisdiction appears to be more appropriate in a concrete case. Jurisdictional conflicts of this kind are common in international shipping and their examination is a separate topic. But it must be remembered that the complexities of the international nature of Antarctic tourist cruises can produce such conflicts.

e. "Constructive" Nationality of Stations

On the premise that Antarctica is an area under no state's jurisdiction, one can argue that, like ships (or aircraft) on the high seas, stations and any one within them, including visitors, are subject to the jurisdiction of the "flag state," that is, the state maintaining the station. It can also be argued[100] that in the Antarctic environment a station, like a ship on the high seas, finds itself in a vast, desolate area under no state's jurisdiction and that in such circumstances it is reasonable to vest in the station's commander — like in a ship's captain — the right to control the conduct of all persons, and apply to them the legislative and enforcement jurisdiction of the state which maintains the station. The Consultative Parties have implied in their Recommendations regulating the conduct of tourist and non-governmental expeditions that, in a certain sense, visitors irrespective of their nationality are under the disciplinary authority of the station commander and that they must comply with any conditions or restrictions of their movements which he may stipulate,

---

[97] Agreed Measures Art. XI.

[98] Australia: Antarctic Treaty (Environment Protection) Act 1980, sects. 4 (1) (b) and 3 (1), in 2 *Bush* (note 36) 212, 226. See also *Triggs* (note 85) 257.

[99] *Auburn* (note 1) 278, 279.

[100] See *Bilder* (note 35) 275—276.

for their safety or to safeguard scientific programs being undertaken at or near the station.[101]

National regulations governing the conduct of tourists and other visitors follow the Consultative Parties' Recommendations.[102]

As far as the United States is concerned, an interesting innovation was proposed in a bill purporting to amend the U.S. criminal procedure to the effect that the President may appoint any member of a U.S. Antarctic expedition to function as police in apprehending suspected offenders, restraining them, search and seize any stolen property, and in general perform any function necessary to enforce U.S. laws in Antarctica.[103]

V. The Sources of the Antarctic Regime Rules on Visitors and Non-Governmental Expeditions: An Overall Review

Subject to what has been said about the relationship of the Antarctic System to third parties, and jurisdictional complexities, Antarctic visitors and non-governmental expeditions are governed by a substantial, though scattered, body of rules and regulations adopted within the framework of the Antarctic regime and, in general, implemented by municipal laws and regulations of the Consultative Parties (and possibly other Contracting Parties). In terms of their origin, the legal obligations of the Parties with regard to visitors and non-governmental expeditions are based on 1) the Antarctic Treaty itself (and any other relevant international agreement such as the Seals Convention, CCAMLR, and any of the general conservationist and environmental treaties); and 2) Recommendations of the Consultative Parties adopted under Article IX of the Antarctic Treaty. In terms of their specificity and focus, the rules governing the conduct of visitors and non-governmental expeditions are 1) either rules applying not to just such visitors and expeditions but

---

[101] Statement (note 6) in 1 *Bush* 382, 384. Compare Recommendations VI-7 (1970); IV-7 (1966); VII-4 (1972); VIII-9 (1975). See also the Report of the Working Group on Legal and Political Questions, para. 8 (c), in: The Report of a Meeting of Experts organized by the Fridtjof Nansen Foundation, 30 May—10 June 1973, in 1 *Bush* (note 36) 283, 284. This report, prepared for purposes of a minerals regime, envisages jurisdiction of leaders of mineral exploration expeditions based on the "origin of operations" and designed to regulate the discipline of the members of the expedition.

[102] See, for example, Conditions Applicable at United States Stations in Antarctica to be Visited by Tourists (no date), in *Scharlin* (note 5) Annex 1 (h). New Zealand Policy Statement Regarding Tourists and Private Antarctic Expeditions, in: *loc. cit.* Annex 12; Argentina: Conditions Concerning Visits to the Argentine Sector of Antarctica, ANT/33/13 June 1975, cited in *Auburn* (note 1) 279, n. 91. See also generally *Scharlin* (note 5) 31—32.

[103] H. R. Rep. 6148, 95th Cong., 1st Sess. (1977), to amend Chapter 203 of Title 18 of the U. S. Code, cited in *Cosslett* (note 81) 80—81 n. 65. This amendment has apparently not been adopted.

generally to all persons in the Antarctic Treaty area, or 2) rules specifically directed at visitors (tourists) and such expeditions.

The Antarctic Treaty does not deal explicitly with tourism or non-governmental expeditions, but, for purposes of information exchange, refers to expeditions of Contracting Parties, a concept that encompasses private expeditions as well, as discussed below.[104] It is obvious that the Treaty provisions bind the Parties with regard to all persons. The very Preamble of the Treaty and Article I, by recognizing the use of Antarctica exclusively for peaceful purposes, implicitly guarantee freedom of tourism, a peaceful pursuit *par excellence*. Freedom of scientific investigation,[105] implying freedom of movement throughout the Antarctic, applies not only to official national expeditions but also non-governmental expeditions of explorers and scientists. On the other hand, the Antarctic Treaty Parties are under an obligation to ensure that visitors and members of non-governmental expeditions of their respective nationality do not contravene the prohibitions of the Treaty: its peaceful purposes[106] and anti-nuclear[107] clauses. In general, each Party undertakes to exert appropriate efforts that "no one" engages in any activity in Antarctica contrary to the principles or purposes of the Treaty.[108] Although this provision is of particular relevance to third parties,[109] "no one" can be widely construed to include any visitor.

The major instrument through which the Consultative Parties further the principles and objectives of the Antarctic Treaty are the Recommendations under Article IX. Any Party (theoretically any other state) that has approved a Recommendation is legally obliged to ensure that visitors of its nationality comply with its provisions. Article IX of the Treaty does not specifically mention tourists or other visitors among the matters with regard to which the Consultative Parties are to make Recommendations. The matter of "preservation and conservation of living resources in Antarctica"[110] (which can be interpreted extensively as granting the Consultative Parties competence to deal with the protection and preservation of the Antarctic environment in general)[111] is clearly relevant to the conduct of visitors and non-governmental expeditions. A large number of Recommendations has been adopted pertaining to human

[104] See sec. VI 1, *infra*.

[105] Antarctic Treaty Art. II.

[106] *Loc. cit.* Art. I.

[107] *Loc. cit.* Art. V.

[108] *Loc. cit.* Art. X.

[109] See sec. IV 1, *supra*.

[110] Antarctic Treaty Art. IX (1) (f.).

[111] *Boleslaw A. Boczek*, The Protection of the Antarctic Ecosystem: A Study in International Environmental Law, in: Ocean Dev. and Int'l Law 13 (1983) 347—425 (366—367).

interference with the Antarctic environment in general[112] and dealing in particular with the conservation of the Antarctic fauna and flora,[113] all being subjects of interest to the topic of this study. Related to this category are Recommendations enjoining governments to adopt adequate measures to protect historical monuments from damage and destruction.[114] Another category of Recommendations of general interest, but adopted primarily with tourists and non-governmental expeditions in mind, deals with the problem of hazards to man in the harsh Antarctic environment and the related problem of emergency assistance, as described below.[115] Finally, the Recommendations implementing the Treaty duty of exchange of information[116] apply not only to officially sponsored expeditions but any other, including private, expeditions to and in Antarctica. This question warrants a more detailed examination.[117]

The Consultative Parties have adopted a series of Recommendations pertaining specifically to tourists and non-governmental expeditions as a special focus of their regulatory activity, starting in 1966 when they recognized that "the effect of tourist activities may prejudice the conduct of scientific research, conservation of fauna and flora and the operation of Antarctic stations."[118] Following that, Recommendations (usually entitled "Effects of tourists and non-governmental expeditions") were adopted at the 6th,[119] 7th,[120] 8th,[121] and 10th[122] Meetings. The Recommendation of 1975 is especially interesting since in it the Consultative Parties recognized that "tourism is a natural development [in Antarctica] and that it requires regulation." The subject matter of annexes on the "Statement of Accepted Practices and the Relevant Provisions of the Antarctic Treaty" (Annex A) and "Areas of Special Tourist Interest" (Annex B) was deferred for consideration until the 10th Meeting in 1979 when the "Statement" (Annex A) was finally adopted, but no tourist areas were disignated. At the 11th Meeting (1981) discussion indicated

---

[112] *Op. cit.* 368—370.

[113] Recommendation III-VIII (1964), Annex: Agreed Measures, is the major act. See generally *Boczek* (note 111) 370—372.

[114] Recommendations I-IX (1961) (1); V-4 (1968); VI-14 (1970); VII-9 (1972); XI-3 (1981);XII-7 (1983); XIII-16 (1985). Recommendation VI-7 (1970) (2) (c), which specifically deals with tourists and non-governmental expeditions, calls upon the Parties to inform organizers of tours and expeditions that visitors must respect designated historical monuments.

[115] See sect. VII *infra.* Of interest are also Recommendations on telecommunications: I-VI (1961); III-V (1964); XII-2 (1983); landing facilities: for example III-I (1961); and unoccupied refuges: III-II (1964).

[116] Antarctic Treaty Art. VII (5) (a).

[117] See sect. VI 1, *infra.*

[118] Recommendation IV-27 (1966).

[119] Recommendations VI-7 (170); VI-11 (1970) (new islands).

[120] Recommendation VII-4 (1972).

[121] Recommendation VIII-9 (1975).

[122] Recommendation X-8 (1979).

a "measure of doubt" whether it would be prudent to proceed further with the designation of such areas.[123] Tourism and non-governmental expeditions were also discussed at the 12th Meeting (1983) particularly because of an increasing number of requests for assistance by such visitors, but no recommendation ensued.[124] At the 13th Meeting (1985) "Effects of tourism and non-governmental expeditions" was one of the items covered by Working Group 2. No specific action was taken, but the Working Group called for a review at the 14th Meeting in Brazil (1987) of the need to combine and, where appropriate, update existing Recommendations relating to tourism.[125]

VI. Access to the Treaty Area and the Stations; Monitoring the Presence of Visitors (Information Exchange)

1. Access to Antarctica; Information Exchange

The Antarctic Treaty System has no rules preventing the entry of tourists or any other visitors in the Treaty area. "The United States does not control access to Antarctica by either U. S. citizens or foreign nationals," states the official U. S. policy statement.[126] Similar policy is followed by the other countries concerned. On the other hand, if reasonable doubt existed that a prospective visitor might "engage in any activity in Antarctica contrary to the principles or purposes of the . . . Treaty"[127] it would be a duty of the government to prevent departure of such visitor for the Treaty area.

In order to ensure the observance of the provisions of the Treaty, it has proved necessary to keep account of and monitor the presence in Antarctica of visitors other than the officially sponsored governmental expeditions. Therefore, in pursuance of the Treaty provision on the duty to give advance notice of all expeditions to and within Antarctica, on the part of any Party's ships or nationals, and all expeditions to Antarctica organized in or proceeding from its territory,[128] the Consultative Parties have, since their first meeting in 1961, been concerned about the "need to maintain an awareness of the activities of tourists in the Antarctic Treaty area."[129] The Treaty provision has been followed by a number

[123] Final Report of the 11th Antarctic Treaty Consultative Meeting, 23 June—7 July 1981, Agenda Item 12 (para. 16) in: 1 *Bush* (note 36) 435, 439.

[124] Eight Recommendations Approved at Twelfth Consultative Meeting, in: Antarctic Journal of the United States 19 (No. 1, March 1984) 1, 3.

[125] Antarctic Treaty Nations Meet in Belgium; Adopt 16 Recommendations, in: Antarctic Journal of the United States 21 (No. 1, March 1986) 1—2, 3—4.

[126] Policy Statement on the Role of the United States in Tourist Expeditions to Antarctica (APG-67-2), in: *Scharlin* (note 5), Annex 1 (a).

[127] Antarctic Treaty Art. X.

[128] *Loc. cit.* Art. VII (5) (a).

[129] Recommendation XIII-3 (1985).

of Recommendations, either specifically concerned with tourists and non-governmental expeditions[130] or spelling out the procedures governing the exchange of information about such visitors between the Consultative Parties.[131]

While it is a clear obligation of all the Treaty Parties to give advance notice of expeditions according to Article VII 5., it appears that the procedures spelled out in Recommendations are legally binding only those Parties that have approved the relevant Recommendation. They can, in any case, be observed as guidelines.

The governments have, in general, two obligations: 1) to report prospective tourist and non-governmental expeditions to all Parties; and 2) to transmit the reports of tour organizers to the next Consultative Parties' Meeting. Each government must give advance notice, not only of all tourist and other non-governmental expeditions that are organized in its territory, but also those proceeding from or even calling at it.[132] In the interpretation of Claimant countries the phrase "calling at" (added in 1975) would mean that they should give notice of expeditions calling at their Antarctic claims.[133] The reporting duty is weakened by the phrase "in so far as is possible,"[134] certainly in recognition of the fact that it is not always possible to obtain advance knowledge of expeditions, especially those calling at the territory of the state concerned.

The information should be exchanged through diplomatic channels as early in each year as possible, and in any case before the end of November each year,[135] presumably on the assumption that the information should be available before the commencement of the Antarctic summer season. In practice, not all the Parties have been scrupulous in providing the required information, and failed to submit the details specified in Recommendations.[136] The governments' duty presupposes enactment of municipal legislation requiring all private expeditions to notify the government of the intended voyage. In the United States, U.S. nationals and any foreign persons that organize, within the United States, any expedition which will proceed to Antarctica from the United States are required to file an advance notification of any expedition to and within Antarctica.[137]

---

130 Recommendations IV-27 (1966); VI-7 (1970); VIII-9 (1975); X-8 (1979).

131 Recommendations I-III (1961); VIII-6 (1975); XIII-3 (1985).

132 The need to report expeditions "calling at" the territory of a Party was added in 1975: Recommendation VIII-6, Annex: Standard Format for the Annual Exchange of Information, para. IX.

133 See 1 *Bush* (note 36) 239.

134 Recommendation VI-7 (1970) (3).

135 Recommendation I-VI (1961).

136 *Nicholson* (note 4) 196.

137 Pub. Law 95—541, Oct. 28, 1978. The Department of State issued implementing Regulations.

The other duty of the Parties concerns reports of tour organizers. In particular, the Parties must require the tour organizers who receive permission for their tourist groups to visit a station, to report their activities in Antarctica. The matters to be reported include: name and nationality of ship, name of captain, itinerary, number of tourists, and places and dates of landings, with the number of persons landed on each occasion. The reports must be submitted by the end of the Antarctic season to the Consultative Parties whose stations the tourist group visited. The Parties who receive such reports must in turn transmit them to the next Consultative Meeting.[138] The governments concerned appear to have neglected this duty;[139] for example at the 9th Meeting (1979) only the United States transmitted a report on Lindblad tours.[140]

2. *Visits to Stations*

Although entry to the Antarctic Treaty area is, in principle, free to visitors, their access to scientific stations maintained by the Parties is subject to the permission of the Party concerned. As noted before, during their visit all persons, irrespective of their nationality, are placed under the authority of the station commander.[141] The main reason for these restrictions is concern that frequent visits to stations or undue dependence on their facilities can prejudice the scientific work of the stations.[142] The governments of the Parties in which a tourist or non-governmental expedition is being organized have a number of obligations with respect to visits to stations. First, the concerned government must furnish notice of an expedition "as soon as possible" through diplomatic channels to any other government whose station the expedition plans to visit.[143] The government in charge of the station should provide on request information "as promptly as possible" regarding the conditions upon which it would grant permission to visit its stations. According to one Recommendation the government is obligated to withhold such permission unless the tour or expedition organizers give reasonable assurance of compliance with the rules and regulations of the Antarctic Treaty System.[144] But there seems to be some inconsistency in the language of the relevant Recommendations, since one ("Statement of

---

[138] Recommendation VIII-9 (1975) and Annex C.

[139] *Nicholson* (note 4) 196.

[140] *Scharlin* (note 5) 29.

[141] Recommendations IV-27 (1970); VI-7 (1970); X-8 (1979), Statement (note 6). These Antarctic System rules are implemented in more detail in national legislations. See, for example, United States, Conditions (note 102); New Zealand Policy Statement (note 102); Argentina, Conditions (note 102).

[142] Recommendation X-8 (1979), Statement (note 6) (10).

[143] Recommendation IV-27 (1966). Tour organizers are required to do likewise, Recommendation X-8 (1979), Statement (note 6) (10).

[144] Recommendation IV-27 (1966) (2) (3).

Accepted Principles") states that the government maintaining the station *may* lay down conditions for granting permission, including *inter alia* such assurance.[145] Other conditions that may be laid down refer to the need to make final arrangements to visit a station between 24 and 72 hours in advance of the expected time of arrival, and to comply with any conditions or restrictions on the visitors' movements which the station commander may stipulate for their safety or to safeguard the station's scientific programs. Visitors must not enter Specially Protected Areas (SPAs) and must respect designated historical monuments.[146] The government in whose territory the expedition proposing to visit a station was organized (or from whose territory it was proceeding or at whose territory it was calling) should inform the expedition organizers of all these requirements.[147] A detailed report on Antarctic activities must be submitted by such organizers to the governments whose stations the expedition has visited.[148] Governments are obliged to "request" all organizers of tourist groups that, except in an emergency, they visit only those stations for which permission has been sought and granted according to the above-mentioned rules.[149]

In connection with the problem of visits to stations the Consultative Parties have, since 1972, considered a possibility of designating an adequate number of areas of interest to which tourists could be encouraged to go as a means of diverting them from stations, Specially Protected Areas and Sites of Special Scientific Interest.[150] However, although an annex was reserved for this purpose in 1975,[151] no such areas were designated. No action was taken to list or define them at the 9th Meeting[152] or the 10th Meeting. At the 11th Meeting in 1981 the discussion in Plenary indicated "a measure of doubt" as to whether it would be prudent to designate such areas. It was only agreed that there should be further study of the problem.[153] But no real progress was achieved on this emerging management issue at the 12th (1983) and 13th (1985) Meetings. The Consultative Parties are still undecided whether confining tourists to such areas is the right course to follow.

---

145 Recommendation X-8 (1979) (10) (i).

146 *Ibid.* i, iii, iv, v.

147 Recommendation VI-7 (1970) (1). An additional condition that may be laid down concerns securing in advance adequate telecommunications, procedures and systems with the office administering the stations to be visited. Recommendation X-8 (1979)), Statement (note 6) (10) (ii).

148 Recommendation VIII-9 (1975), Annex C.

149 Recommendation VIII-9 (1975) (2) (a).

150 Recommendation VII-4 (1972) (3).

151 Recommendation VIII-9 (1975), Annex B.

152 Report of the 9th Meeting, 19 Sept. — 7 Oct. 1977, para. 4, in: 1 *Bush* (note 36) 340.

153 Report of the 11th Meeting, 23 June — 7 July 1981, para. 12, in: 1 *Bush* 434, 439.

The whole question is also related to the regulation of visitors' conduct in the interests of the conservation of the Antarctic fauna and flora and the protection of the Antarctic environment in general, as examined below.

VII. Environmental Regulations

There exists no systematic environmental impact assessment of tourists and other visitors in Antarctica, but it is reasonable to assume that in terms of the Antarctic continent as a whole such impact has been negligible and less pronounced than that produced by activities of the stations. However, since tourist visits are usually localized, as the tours tend to revisit known and more easily accessible sites such as stations and concentrations of fauna, the activities of tourists and other visitors have the potential of harmful interference with the vulnerable Antarctic environment.[154]

Tourists and other visitors are, of course, subject to all those environmental rules and regulations of the Antarctic system that are addressed to all persons and are designed to minimize harmful human interference in Antarctica. There is no need to deal with them here[155] but mention should be made of the Agreed Measures, the key legal arrangement for the conservation of the Antarctic fauna and flora.[156] However, other regulations such as those on exchange of information and access to stations are also environmentally motivated.

Beginning with the 4th Meeting (1966), the Consultative Parties addressed themselves specifically to regulate the conduct of tourists and other visitors. Of particular concern to the Consultative Parties has been protection from visitors of the Specially Protected Areas.[157] Therefore in 1970 a rule was adopted barring tourists and other visitors from entering such areas,[158] a restraint that is rather difficult to enforce against large groups of tourists.[159] Another injunction addressed to tourists concerns preventing them from landing on new islands.[160] Tour operators are encouraged to use guides with experience of Antarctic

[154] See generally *Auburn* (note 1) Ch. 9; *Boczek* (note 111) 361; and *W. S. Benninghoff / W. N. Bonner*, Man's Impact on the Antarctic Environment: A Procedure for Evaluating Impacts from Scientific and Logistic Activities, Cambridge 1985, 51—52.

[155] See a comprehensive analysis in *Boczek* (note 111) 367—381; and Specially Protected Areas as an Instrument for the Conservation of the Antarctic Nature. in: *Wolfrum* (ed.) (note 4) 65—101 (73—79).

[156] Recommendation III-VII (1964), Annex.

[157] See a detailed analysis of SPAs in *Boczek* (note 155) in: *Wolfrum* (ed.) (note 4).

[158] Recommendation VI-7 (1970) (1) (c).

[159] *Auburn* (note 1) 279.

[160] Recommendation VI-11 (1970).

conditions who are aware of the considerations underlying measures to protect the Antarctic environment,[161] and a special "Statement" and "Guidelines" have been prepared for the use of visitors copies of which must be provided by Consultative Parties to visitors in the Antarctic.[162] But, as noted, no Areas of Special Tourist Interest have as yet been designated.[163] In general, the Consultative Parties have recommended that the governments "use their best efforts to ensure" that all the provisions relating to the conservation of the fauna and flora are applied to all visitors who are not sponsored by the Consultative Parties as well as to tourists. This statement contradicts another that applies such provisions to all visitors, sponsored and not sponsored.[164]

While individual Consultative Parties are legally obligated to ensure compliance with the environmental rules by visitors who are their nationals, phrases such as "should use their best endeavors"; "use their best efforts to ensure"; "to the extent practicable encourage"[165] imply that in relation to visitors who are not nationals the Recommendations are only hortatory, "soft" law.

On the national level, some Consultative Parties apply their environmental legislation that gives effect to the Recommendations, not only to their nationals wherever they may be in Antarctica but also to non-nationals. For example, such Claimant states as Australia and France assert territorial jurisdiction in enforcing their legislation implementing the Antarctic System's conservation measures.[166] The U. S. legislation in implementation of the Agreed Measures applies also to non-nationals violating its rules.[167]

VIII. Assistance to Non-Governmental Expeditions

One major implication of the growth in the number of visitors, and in particular non-governmental expeditions, in Antarctica has been the rising potential for accidents in the hazardous and unpredictable Antarctic environment, as demonstrated by the experiences of both sponsored and unsponsored expeditions. As far as tourism is concerned, there have been several incidents involving cruise ships, beginning with the stranding of a party of tourists in the early days of the Lindblad tours in

[161] Recommendation X-8 (1979) (III-Tour Guides).

[162] Statement (note 6); Recommendation X-8 (1979), Guidelines for Visitors to the Antarctic.

[163] See sect. VI 2, *supra*.

[164] Recommendation VIII-9 (1975) (1).

[165] See, for example, Recommendations VI-7 (1970); VII-4 (1972); X-8 (1979), (III-Tour Guides).

[166] See *Triggs* (note 85) 256—257.

[167] Public Law 95—451, Sec. 45, 92 Stat. 2049.

1967,[168] but owing to emergency assistance from national programs there have been so far no fatalities on such cruises. However, the tragic crash on the slopes of Mt. Erebus in 1979 dramatized the dangers inherent in Antarctic tourist activities. As far as non-governmental expeditions are concerned, the sinking of the *Southern Quest* in 1986 with the successful rescue of all 21 survivors by helicopters of the U.S. Antarctic Program is only one late example, showing that in case of emergency such expeditions must ultimately call upon the help of national programs operating in Antarctica.[169]

The Consultative Parties have been concerned that inadequately prepared non-governmental expeditions are likely to get in trouble in Antarctica, consequently needing national programs to respond to requests for emergency assistance, which results not only in financial loss to such programs but also disrupts the research schedule, apart from jeopardizing the lives of sponsored participants.[170] At the 12th Meeting (1983) the matter was considered to be so serious that the problem of tourists and non-governmental expeditions was discussed particularly because private expeditions and resultant requests for assistance had increased.[171]

The legal dimension of assistance to non-governmental expeditions entails primarily the issue of responsibility for the activities of such expeditions, as well as compliance with the regulations of the Antarctic Treaty System. As demonstrated by the litigation that resulted from the Mt. Erebus disaster, liability for injury and death and material and financial loss may be another problem.

In examining the national and Antarctic Treaty System's policies concerning assistance and support of non-governmental expeditions it is useful to bear in mind the distinction between three types of assistance, namely: 1) support of an expedition in its planning stage, 2) necessary assistance at the operational stage in Antarctica (supplying fuel, transportation and the like), and 3) emergency assistance in case of imminent danger to life and property.[172]

The Consultative Parties have consistently reaffirmed their humanitarian and international legal obligation to render all assistance feasible in the event of an emergency request for help. Already in 1961 a

---

[168] For a list of accidents involving tourists ships see *Reich* (note 5) 208. See also *Auburn* (note 1) 278—279.

[169] See *Southern Quest* Rescue (note 25).

[170] In Recommendation X-8 (1979) the Consultative Parties recognized that in considering responses to requests for help from non-governmental expeditions, an important concern was the possibility that such expeditions might, in case of emergency, involve national programs in financial or material loss.

[171] Report of the 12th Meeting, in: Antarctic Journal of the United States 19 (No. 1, March 1984) 3.

[172] *Nicholson* (note 4) 199.

Recommendation was adopted to this effect.[173] Consequently the Agreed Measures exempt the Parties from the obligation to observe conservation rules in cases of extreme emergency involving possible loss of human life or involving the safety of ships or aircraft.[174] The traditional principle of rendering assistance in the event of emergency was reaffirmed in 1979 at the 10th Meeting[175] and in the discussion of the matter at the 12th Meeting in 1983.[176]

In more concrete terms, the "Statement of Accepted Principles" recalled that there was in the Antarctic a number of unoccupied huts and refuges which might be used in an emergency. In such cases the authorities that maintain the hut or refuge should be informed of what use has been made of it.[177] The Consultative Parties have also paid much attention to rescue procedures. Just prior to the Mt. Erebus crash, SCAR drew the attention of the Consultative Parties to the fact that a tourist aircraft was unable to land in Antarctica and would require extensive facilities for search and rescue in case of an accident. A suggestion was also made that tourist flights should be regarded "self-supporting expeditions."[178] At the next Meeting the Consultative Parties noted that commercial overflights in Antarctica were operating in a particularly hazardous environment where aircraft operation systems normally available elsewhere in the world were at a minimum, and where emergencies could arise which were beyond the capacity of permanent Antarctic expeditions to respond to adequately.[179] It was therefore recommended that the governments notify commercial aircraft that the current level of tourist overflight activity exceeded capabilities for air traffic control, communications and search and rescue in the Antarctic, might interfere with normal operational flights in support of expeditions engaged in ongoing programs, and exceeded the capacity of their Antarctic operations to respond adequately to an unplanned emergency landing.[180]

---

[173] Recommendation I-X (1961).

[174] Agreed Measures Art. V.

[175] Recommendation X-8 (1979).

[176] Report of the 12th Meeting, para. 28.

[177] Recommendation X-8 (1979), Statement (note 6) (9). Under Recommendation III-II (1964) lists of unoccupied refuges (buildings, huts or caches) maintained by the Consultative Parties in a condition suitable for use in emergency should be exchanged before the end of November each year. Refuges should have emergency supplies which to the greatest extent possible should be replenished. See also Standard Format for the Annual Exchange of Information, (X), Annex to Recommendation VIII-6 (1975).

[178] *Auburn* 281, referring to SCAR Circular of 3 July 1978.

[179] Recommendation X-8 (1979), Preamble.

[180] *Loc. cit.* (IV-Commercial Overflights in Antarctica). Search and rescue procedures and radio operating standards are spelled out in the Proposals of the Second Antarctic Treaty Meeting on Telecommunications, 1—12 Sept. 1969, Proposal 8, in 1 *Bush* (note 36) 210, 223.

On the other, hand the Consultative Parties have not yet adopted a common response to inquiries when a Party was approached with a request for assistance of the first or second type. At the 11th Meeting (1981) the value of such a common response was recognized but no specific action was taken.[181] The Consultative Parties are likely to adopt a policy that follows the individual governments' approach, namely that they expect non-governmental expeditions to be self-sufficient and that they are unable to offer such expeditions support or assistance in the planning or operational stages. That such would be the direction of the Consultative Parties' policy had been hinted at the 10th Meeting (1979) which recommended to the Parties that they urge non-governmenal expeditions to carry adequate insurance coverage against the risks of their incurring financial charges or material losses in the Antarctic.[182] At the 12th Meeting (1983) suggestions were heard for publicizing the view that private expeditions should be self-sufficient and should adequately insure or underwrite costs for emergency or other assistance.[183]

The Consultative Parties' approach at the Meetings, in general, reflects the position of the individual governments on the issue of assistance to to private expedition[184] emergency assistance is provided, but the government reserves the right to require reimbursement for services rendered beyond a humanitarian assistance and rescue situation.[185] As far as assistance in the planning and operational stages is concerned, governments expect private expeditions to be self-sufficient; hence as a general rule no assistance is granted. A major consideration here is not just financial cost but the fact that such support and assistance cannot be provided without prejudice to national scientific programs in Antarctica.[186] A non-governmental expedition that despite warning about potential problems undertakes a trip to Antarctica, does so at its own risk. The government cannot legally prevent it from departing for

---

181 Agenda Item 12 of of the 11th Meeting (1981), in: 1 *Bush* (note 36) 438, 439.

182 Recommendation X-8 (1979) (II-Non-Governmental Expeditions).

183 Report of the 12th Meeting, reported in: Eight Recommendations Approved at Twelfth Consultative Meeting, in: Antarctic Journal of the United States 19 (No. 1, March 1984) 1, 3.

184 For the United States see Policy Statement (note 126); and United States Policy Statement with Regard to Support of Foreign Government, Commercial, and Private Aviation in Antarctica (APG-68-3), in: *Scharlin* (note 5), Annex 1 (b).

185 For example in the case of the *Southern Quest* the U.S. Government chose to bill the expedition only for the cost of flying survivors from McMurdo to New Zealand and not for the cost of the humanitarian rescue in Antarctica. Emergency Assistance in Antarctica, in: Antarctic Journal of the United States 21 (No. 1, March 1986) 9, 10, 15.

186 See *R. Tucker Scully*, Comments: Panel Discussion, in *Wolfrum* (ed.) (note 4) 209. In the United States self-sufficiency, feasibility and safety of private expeditions are determined by Commander, U.S. Naval Support Force, Antarctica, in coordination with the Special Assistant for Antarctic Affairs. See Policy Statement (note 126).

Antarctica, but it is under no legal obligation to provide support.[187] Support and assistance is exceptionally provided if the activities of the expedition, normally scientific, clearly further national Antarctic policy or generally national interest of the government concerned.[188]

In sum, unless a government has agreed to do so, the Consultative Parties do not assume any responsibility for accidents or injury sustained by visitors and non-governmental expeditions in Antarctica. A government would, however, incur responsibility to the extent that it had failed to provide humanitarian assistance to visitors in distress in a situation where assistance was reasonably possible under the particular emergency circumstances. Beyond these general principles, the Consultative Parties still have to develop a common legal framework that would provide a comprehensive solution to the question of assistance to visitors and non-governmental expeditions.

IX. Conclusions

This examination of the legal status of visitors, primarily tourists, and non-governmental expeditions in the Antarctic Treaty area has revealed that there exists no coherent set of rules governing this question. The Consultative Parties have dealt with it in a rather disjointed fashion by adopting Recommendations on — in what has become their standard terminology — tourists and non-governmental expeditions. Potential environmental impact of such visitors and interference with national scientific programs in the stations, and the possibility that they would tax resources of and disrupt national programs, are the underlying reasons for the regulations adopted by the Consultative Parties. Beyond the specifically "tourists and non-governmental expeditions"-oriented regulations, the legal status of such visitors under the Antarctic Treaty regime must be reconstructed from certain provisions of the Treaty and Recommendations addressed to all persons in Antarctica.

One problem in the analysis of the legal status of visitors and non-governmental expeditions in Antarctica is the fact that there exists no

---

[187] There are numerous examples of U.S., New Zealand, U.K., Australian, and Norwegian governments, among others, refusing support to private expeditions. See, for example, Expedition to South Pole Postponed, in: Antarctic (1985) 409; Second Austrian Attempt to Climb Mount Minto, in: Antarctic (1986) 109—110. The leaders of the "Footsteps of Scott" expedition had been informed by the U.S. and New Zealand governments of the policy on non-governmental expeditions three years before they left for Antarctica anyway, informing the two governments that they would not need any assistance. The events, including the sinking of the *Southern Quest*, proved that they were certainly not self-sufficient. See Emergency Assistance in Antarctica (note 185).

[188] For example, "Project Blizzard" was partially funded by the Australian Government. See Project Blizzard Completes Second Season, in: Antarctic (1986) 34—37.

consistent terminology pertaining to various categories of visitors that are not sponsored by the Consultative Parties. Therefore, there is need to define, sharpen and harmonize the relevant concepts and use them in a consistent way, perhaps in one Recommendation like the Agreed Measures.

Any analysis of the legal status of the persons in question must necessarily touch upon the issues of third parties and jurisdiction. It must be concluded that any relevant rule of the Antarctic System binds only those states that have approved the act recommended; only such states are legally obligated to ensure that their nationals visiting Antarctica comply with the rules involved. Otherwise the language of the Consultative Parties is only hortatory and urging states (presumably even those among them that have not yet approved the Recommendation in question) to ensure compliance by their nationals. The distinction between various possible categories of "parties" is not entirely clear, however. As far as jurisdiction is concerned, visitors and members of non-governmental expeditions are among the "other persons" whose jurisdictional status has not as yet been resolved by the Consultative Parties. The conclusion reached here is that adoption of the *nationality principle* is the only reasonable way out of the jurisdictional tangle in Antarctica.

Although at this time there is not as yet any urgent need to embark upon negotiations on a convention on tourists and other visitors and non-governmental expeditions (that would parallel a minerals regime), it would still be useful to improve the existing situation by integrating all the rules and regulations in one act.

There are also some substantive problems on which action seems advisable both in terms of enacting new rules and strengthening enforcement of the existing ones. The Treaty provisions on the exchange of information need to be better implemented and enforced.[189] Since tourists normally arrive in cruise ships, some rules on vessel construction (for safety reasons) and size (not to strain stations' facilities) might prove useful. The matter of Areas of Special Tourist Interest should finally be resolved within the framework of an overall system of managing the Antarctic environment. The issue of support and assistance to non-governmental expeditions has recently emerged as perhaps the most important one insofar as the topic of this paper is concerned. The modalities of a common response, the value of which was recognized at the 11th Meeting (1981), must be elaborated. The possibility of requiring proof

[189] If a permanent Secretariat is established, it could keep a centralized system of all visitors to Antarctica. It has also been suggested that a system of registration or licensing of commercial tour companies could be adopted. See *Nicholson* (note 4) 197.

of insurance in return for planning support, and even a license fee, might be considered.[190] In the matter of jurisdiction no serious problems have emerged with regard to visitors, but the problem will have to be tackled sooner or later. The solution should strike a balance between, on the one hand, the common interests of all the Contracting Parties and especially those which consider Antarctica a territory under no state's jurisdiction, and the Claimant states on the other. It should be based on the principle of the offender's *nationality*, and on a residual basis (if the state of nationality has failed to act), the *passive nationality* principle. In those cases where neither state asserts jurisdiction, the *universality principle* would have to be resorted to. To overcome the objections of the Claimant states it should be made clear that waiver to exercise territorial jurisdiction need not be construed as renunciation of a claim to sovereignty. In this sense the solution would fit within the purview of Article IV 2. of the Antarctic Treaty: accepting the *nationality* principle would not constitute a base for denying a claim to territorial sovereignty in Antarctica.

Finally there remains the politically difficult issue of the validity of the Antarctic regime's rules toward third parties. Fortunately, within the context of visitors and non-governmental expeditions the problem is not pressing. Ideally, expansion of membership would be the best solution, but this is a more general issue whose outcome will depend on the ability of the Antarctic Treaty regime to adapt to pressures of and changes in the international political system.

---

[190] See *Nicholson* (note 4) 200.

Waste Management in Antarctica

*James N. Barnes**, *Peter J. Lipperman***, *Kelly Rigg****

Table of Contents

I. Introduction

Waste management policies and procedures vary widely among those states active in the Antarctic. Even within individual national Antarctic programs, waste management activities are far from uniform. Some of the guidelines and rules promulgated by individual states to govern their national activities overlap, and sometimes conflict with, regional

* *James N. Barnes*, Senior Staff Attorney, Environmental Policy Institute; Executive Director, The Antarctica Project; Counsel, ASOC.
** *Peter J. Lipperman*, B. S., M. A., J. D. candidate of New York University School of Law; Antarctica Project.
*** *Kelly Rigg*, International Antarctic Campaign Coordinator, Greenpeace International.

guidelines adopted under the auspices of the Antarctic Treaty[1] by the Antarctic Treaty Consultative Parties (ATCPs).[2] To date, the most coherent expression of a waste management policy by the ATCPs is found in the Code of Conduct for Antarctic Stations and Expeditions, although it is far from comprehensive and contains no performance criteria.[3]

Thirty years of increasing human activity in the Antarctic have exerted cumulative pressures on local ecosystems, particularly around major bases and facilities, with waste disposal being the major problem. These pressures are likely to increase, given the recent expansion in the number of states pursuing Antarctic programs, increased exploitation of marine living resources, and potential commencement of minerals exploration and exploitation in the Antarctic after a minerals convention is adopted and enters into force.

Some ATCPs have promulgated regulations that closely mirror the Code of Conduct, reflecting the values and priorities embodied in the fifteen-year old guidelines contained in the Code of Conduct. Other ATCPs have begun to move forward with new policies and waste management procedures that reflect a heightened awareness of the environmental impacts of national activities in Antarctica. Most ATCPs appear to be interested in considering modifications of existing practices to better protect the environment. Numerous studies are either underway or have been proposed in various countries.

The ATCPs, recognizing the importance of waste management issues in the Antarctic, have instructed the Scientific Committee on Antarctic Research (SCAR) to undertake a review of the current guidelines contained in the Code of Conduct.[4] The draft SCAR report is to be discussed

[1] The Antarctic Treaty, Dec. 1, 1959, 12 U.S.T. 794, T.I.A.S. No. 4780, 402 UNTS 71.

[2] The twelve original Contracting Parties to the Antarctic Treaty (Argentina, Australia, Belgium, Chile, France, Japan, New Zealand, Norway, South Africa, the Soviet Union, the United Kingdom, and the United States) designate representatives to meet biennially to consult on matters of common interest, and consider and recommend to their Governments measures in furtherance of the principle and objectives of the Antarctic Treaty. Antarctic Treaty, note 1 at Article IX, para. 1. States which have subsequently adhered to the Antarctic Treaty and conduct "substantial" scientific research in the Antarctic are entitled to send representatives to these biennial consultative meetings, Article IX, para. 2. The group of states participating in these meetings are known collectively as the Antarctic Treaty Consultative Parties (ATCPs).

[3] Code of Conduct for Antarctic Expeditions and Station Activities, Recommendation VIII-11, Antarctic Treaty, Report of the Eighth Consultative Meeting (Oslo: June 1975), Reprinted in Appendix I of this paper. (Hereinafter cited as the Code of Conduct).

[4] Man's Impact on the Antarctic Environment: Code of Conduct for Antarctic Expeditions and Station Activities: Waste Disposal, Recommendation XIII-4, Antarctic Treaty, Final Report of the Thirteenth Antarctic Treaty Consultative Meeting (Brussels: Oct. 1985).

at the Fourteenth Antarctic Treaty Consultative Meeting (ATCM) this October.[5]

This paper first examines the current legal framework governing waste management in the Antarctic, with a special focus on the rules and regulations governing U.S. activities in the region. Next, the waste management practices of states active in the Antarctic are surveyed in the context of this legal framework in order to establish the relationship between waste management policy and practice. Again, the policy-practice relationship of the U.S. is emphasized. It should be noted that the information publicly available regarding practices of states varies widely, and the survey on which this paper is based is far from complete. Finally, based on the available information, a model program is put forward, which draws upon current policies and practices in order to suggest interim and longer-term measures to improve Antarctic waste management, including institutional changes to ensure the long-term protection of the Antarctic environment against degradation caused by the disposal of waste materials in the region. This model program is comprised of thirteen recommendations, and should be seen as the first iteration in an evolving series of improvements.

Although this paper focuses more attention on the U.S. program, particularly at McMurdo, than it does on other countries or facilities, this reflects the greater availability of information available to the authors in Washington about that facility. There have been significant problems identified with McMurdo, partly because it is such a large station, and to that extent it serves as a test case of how policies and practices can be improved. The U.S. National Science Foundation has indicated an evolving awareness of the need to improve the situation at McMurdo as well as other U. S. bases.

II. Legal Framework

1. Global

International concern for the environment of the earth's non-sovereign regions[6] has led to the conclusion of various multilateral conventions,

[5] The SCAR Panel of Experts on Waste Disposal was formed in response to Recommendation XIII-4, and expects to issue an Interim Report in July 1987, Letter dated June 1, 1987, from *J. E. Bleasel*, Chairman of the SCAR Panel of Experts on Waste Disposal.

[6] Seven states have made claims of sovereignty over portions of the Antarctic continent: Argentina, Australia, Chile, France, New Zealand, Norway, and the United Kingdom. These claims are not recognized by any other members of the international community. The seven Claimant states are all original Contracting Parties to the Antarctic Treaty. The Antarctic Treaty reconciled the positions of these Claimant states with those of the Non-claimant Contracting Parties through an ingenious compromise that effectively puts the "claims issue" on hold for the duration of the Treaty. See Antarctic Treaty, note 1, Article IV.

some of which have bearing for the Antarctic Treaty Area.[7] In particular, several international conventions address issues of marine pollution and the dumping of waste material at sea that are relevant to the legal framework for Antarctic waste management. This relevance arises from provisions in the Antarctic Treaty that reserve high seas rights within the Treaty area, and can be read to imply that high seas responsibilities also exist in these waters.[8]

The ATCPs have not, however, taken steps to specifically apply, implement or modify these international conventions in the Antarctic Treaty context.

a) The Convention on the Prevention of Marine Pollution by Dumping of Wastes and Other Matter (London Dumping Convention)[9]

This Convention obligates the Contracting Parties "to take all practicable steps to prevent the pollution of the sea by the dumping of waste and other matter that is liable to create hazards to human health, to harm living resources and marine life, to damage amenities or to interfere with other legitimate uses of the sea."[10] To accomplish this, the Convention prohibits or restricts certain listed substances from being dumped into "all marine waters other than the internal waters of states."[11]

b) The International Convention for the Prevention of Pollution from Ships (MARPOL Convention)[12]

This Convention seeks "the complete elimination of intentional pollution of the marine environment by oil and other harmful substances and the minimization of accidental discharge of such substances."[13]

c) The UN Convention on the Law of the Sea (LOS Convention)[14]

While not yet in force, this Convention contains several provisions related to marine pollution and waste disposal. Specifically, signatories

[7] The Antarctic Treaty Area includes all waters and land masses south of 60 Degrees South Latitude. Antarctic Treaty, note 1, Art. VI.

[8] *Ibid.*

[9] The Convention on the Prevention of Marine Pollution by Dumping of Wastes and Other Matter, done Dec. 29, 1972, 26 U.S.T. 2403, T.I.A.S. No. 8165. (Hereinafter cited as the London Dumping Convention).

[10] London Dumping Convention, Art. I.

[11] London Dumping Convention, Art. III, Annexes I and II.

[12] The International Convention for the Prevention of Pollution from ships, done Nov. 2, 1973, reprinted in International Legal Materials 12 (1973), 1319. (Hereinafter cited as the MARPOL Convention).

[13] MARPOL Convention, 1319—20.

[14] The United Nations Convention on the Law of the Sea, UN Doc. A/CONF/62/122 (1982), reprinted in International Legal Materials 21 (1982), 1261. (Hereinafter cited as LOSC).

are obligated to adopt rules, laws and regulations to prevent, reduce, and control pollution of the marine environment from land-based sources,[15] dumping,[16] and vessel sources.[17] These provisions are meant to reinforce the commitments made by states under other international legal regimes, as well as to underscore the universal responsibility of all states to preserve and protect the marine environment.

2. *The Antarctic Treaty System*[18]

The Antarctic Treaty provides the basic legal foundation for the international management of Antarctica. The Treaty addresses issues of state sovereignty, demilitarization, and scientific cooperation in the Antarctic, but makes only limited reference to general environmental concerns and specific waste management policy for the region. The Treaty directs the Consultative Parties to meet periodically to discuss and propose measures for the ". . . preservation and conservation of living resources in Antarctica."[19] In addition, the Treaty prohibits nuclear explosions and the disposal of radioactive waste material in Antarctica.[20]

a) The Consultative Process and the Code of Conduct

The ATCPs have utilized the Consultative Meeting process of the Treaty to address environmental and waste management issues. The Agreed Measures for the Conservation of Antarctic Fauna and Flora[21] established the Treaty area as a "Special Conservation Area."[22] Furthermore, the Agreed Measures call on each participating government to "take all reasonable steps towards the alleviation of pollution of the waters adjacent to the coast and ice shelves."[23]

---

[15] LOSC, Art. 207.

[16] LOSC, Art. 210.

[17] LOSC, Art. 211.

[18] The Antarctic Treaty System is comprised of the interconnected politico-legal arrangements that have arisen out of the operations of the Antarctic Treaty, including related conventions, agreed measures, and recommendations from consultative meetings. For an overview of how the System operates, see *Colson*, 'The Antarctic Treaty System, in: Law and Policy in International Business, vol. 12 (1980), 870.

[19] Antarctic Treaty, note 1, Article IX, para. 1, sect. (f).

[20] Antarctic Treaty, Article V, para. 1.

[21] The Agreed Measures for the Conservation of Antarctic Fauna and Flora, Antarctic Treaty, Recommendation III-8, 17 U.S.T. 991, T.I.A.S. No. 6058, reprinted in: *W. M. Bush*, Antarctica and International Law, vols. I-III, London *et al.* 1982, vol. I, 146 *et seq.* (Hereinafter cited as the Agreed Measures).

[22] Agreed Measures, Preamble.

[23] Agreed Measures, Article VII (3).

Beginning at the Sixth Consultative Meeting, the ATCPs have made the topic of "Man's Impact on the Antarctic Environment" a more-or-less regular agenda item at the biennial ATCMs, from which an evolving series of Recommendations has emerged. Recommendation VI-4 recognized the "increasingly urgent need to protect the environment from human interference"[24] and declared that "the Consultative Parties should assume responsibility for the protection of the environment and the wise use of the Treaty area."[25] At that time, the ATCPs recommended that their respective governments "take interim measures to reduce known causes of harmful environmental interference."[26]

In Recommendation VIII-11, the ATCPs established the Code of Conduct for Antarctic Stations and Expeditions, which specifically addressed waste management issues.[27] However, in keeping with the relatively loose, non-compulsory nature of the Consultative process, the ATCPs are bound to follow the Code of Conduct only to "the greatest extent feasible."[28] The Code of Conduct represents the first attempt at establishing a comprehensive scheme for Antarctic waste management.

Antarctic Treaty Recommendations are neither self-executing nor legally enforceable, but are adopted by consensus at the Consultative Meetings, thus creating a degree of mutual obligation among the ATCPs to abide by the rules or guidelines contained in them. It is up to any individual state to interpret the Recommendations, to determine what they restrict, prohibit or require in practice, and then to develop implementing regulations and practices.

Since the Code was agreed on, the U.S., New Zealand, Australia and other Member States have had many discussions about better waste disposal practices, some of which have been implemented, but these discussions have not resulted in formal government proposals for modification on the Code. After a decade of operation, however, the ATCPs have recognized the need to revise and update the Code of Conduct in light of the "increasing level and degree of complexity of Antarctic operations" and the likelihood of a "wider range of potentially environmentally damaging substances" being introduced into the Antarctic.[29] The ATCPs have further recognized that advances in technology and logistical capabilities have increased "the feasibility of on-site treat-

[24] Man's Impact on the Antarctic Environment, Recommendation VI-4, para. 3, Antarctic Treaty, Report of the Sixth Consultative Meeting (Tokyo: Oct. 1970).

[25] *Loc. cit*, para. 4.

[26] *Loc. cit*, para. 3.

[27] See note 3. See Appendix I.

[28] See note 24, para. 1.

[29] Man's Impact on the Antarctic Environment: Code of Conduct for Antarctic Expeditions and Station Activities, Antarctic Treaty, Recommendation XII-4, para. 1, Report of the Twelfth Consultative Meeting (Canberra: Sept. 1983).

ment of human and other waste, and the removal of solid waste, residues and noxious substances from the Treaty area."[30] In this manner, the ATCPs have focused upon on-site treatment and retrogradation as two possible cornerstones of future Antarctic waste management policy.

In Recommendation XIII-4,[31] the ATCPs noted the need to reduce to "the minimum level practicable" the spread of all potential contaminants introduced into the Antarctic Treaty Area by man"[32] and called upon SCAR for "scientific advice regarding waste disposal procedures and standards that it is desirable to achieve at coastal and inland stations and field camps."[33]

b) The Antarctic Seals Convention

The ATCPs first went outside the Consultative process to deal with Antarctic issues when they completed the negotiation of the Convention for the Conservation of Antarctic Seals in 1972.[34] The Convention was designed to limit the vulnerability of Antarctic seals to commercial exploitation through over-harvesting, but is also dedicated to the maintenance of "a satisfactory balance within the ecological system" of the region.[35] The regulation of waste management and disposal, while not specifically addressed in the Seals Convention, can be inferred as a concern of the Contracting Parties.

c) The Convention on the Conservation of Antarctic Marine Living Resources (CCAMLR)[36]

The ATCPs next went outside the Consultative process in establishing a regime for the management of the marine living resources of the Antarctic region — the CCAMLR, signed in 1981. The CCAMLR covers ocean spaces not included within the Antarctic Treaty area, establishing a management regime for the regulation of living resource exploitation in the region. The ATCPs took steps to tie the CCAMLR to the Antarctic Treaty, making it an integral part of the Antarctic Treaty System.[37] The recognition of the need to protect "the integrity of the ecosystem of the

---

[30] *Loc. cit*, para. 2.
[31] See note 4.
[32] Note 29, Preamble.
[33] *Loc. cit*, para. 1.
[34] Convention for the Conservation of Antarctic Seals, done June 1, 1972, 29 U.S.T. 441, T.I.A.S. No. 8826, reprinted in *Bush* (note 21), 248 *et seq.* (Hereinafter cited as the Seals Convention).
[35] Seals Convention.
[36] Convention on the Conservation of Antarctic Marine Living Resources, done May 20, 1980, reprinted in: International Legal Materials vol. 19 (1980), 837. (Hereinafter cited as the CCAMLR).
[37] CCAMLR, Articles III-V.

seas surrounding Antarctica," which forms the basis of the CCAMLR,[38] can be viewed as a further step in the evolution of principles for protecting the environment embodied in the Consultative process outlined above.

This view is bolstered by references in the CCAMLR to the "prime responsibilities of the Antarctic Treaty Consultative Parties for the protection and preservation of the Antarctic environment" and the responsibility of CCAMLR parties to heed "such other measures as have been recommended by the ATCPs in fulfillment of their responsibility for the protection of the Antarctic environment from all forms of harmful human interference."[39]

The CCAMLR is principally intended to manage the harvesting of Antarctic marine living resources, and addresses the issue of waste disposal only indirectly. The Convention outlines the principles that should guide "any harvesting and associated activities" in the area to which the Convention applies.[40] The phrase "associated activities" may be interpreted as applying to marine pollution-producing activities engaged in by harvesting vessels, such as deballasting, dumping, and discharging of toxic substances into the Southern Ocean.[41] The purpose of the CCAMLR, namely, to protect the integrity of the ecosystem of Antarctic waters, can be construed as being furthered by agreement on sound waste management policies for the Southern Ocean. The CCAMLR member governments have begun to consider the question of plastic debris at the annual Meetings. As the fishing industry grows, questions of waste disposal practices at sea will be of increasing importance.

d) The Minerals Negotiations

Since 1977, the ATCPs have carried out talks and conducted negotiations aimed at establishing a regime for the management of Antarctic mineral resources.[42] While no exploitation of such resources has taken place to date, or is expected to in the near future, the ATCPs have recognized that if minerals development does take place, important environmental concerns will be raised. Protection of the Antarctic environment has been an important issue in the negotiations for the establishment of a minerals convention.[43]

---

[38] CCAMLR, Preamble.

[39] CCAMLR, Article V, para. 2.

[40] CCAMLR, Article II.

[41] *Joyner*, The Southern Ocean and Marine Pollution: Problems and Prospects, Case Western Reserve Journal of Intenational Law, vol. 17 (1985), 165, 183.

[42] For a recent history of the minerals negotiations, see ECO, vols. 27, 33, 39, 41 (Friends of the Earth-International) and the series of Briefings on the status of the minerals negotiation produced jointly by The Antarctica Project and Greenpeace International (hereinafter cited as Antarctic Minerals Briefing).

[43] See, in general, Antarctic Minerals Briefing No. 12 (March 24, 1987), note 42.

Obviously, all minerals activities — prospecting, exploration and exploitation — will generate waste materials, as will associated logistic facilities and operations. The management and disposal of such materials is not yet directly covered in the draft minerals convention. However, the future minerals regime probably will include the environmental principle that minerals activities be permitted only if they have a limited impact upon the Antarctic environment. The definition of "minerals activities" will be sufficiently broad to require that the minerals regime regulate waste disposal procedures when approving any minerals development in the Antarctic.[44]

In conclusion, the legal structure supporting the ATCP's ability to promulgate waste management policies in the Antarctic is both broad and, with the exception of the Code of Conduct, noticeably vague. The Antarctic Treaty, through the Consultative process it created, has provided a foundation for waste management regulation in the region. By integrating the Seals Convention and the CCAMLR with the Antarctic Treaty and its Consultative process to form a Treaty System, the ATCPs have established a wide basis upon which to regulate the disposal of waste material on land and at sea in the Antarctic region.

The ATCPs have used the Consultative process to enact a Code of Conduct that addresses waste disposal issues, although it is not legally binding and is, therefore, unenforceable. More binding arrangements, such as an Agreed Measure, have not been considered, nor has consideration been given to to applying other international conventions to the region. Consideration of the draft SCAR report at the Fourteenth Consultative Meeting could lead to significant improvements.

3. *U.S. Waste Management Policy*

United States policy-making for Antarctic affairs is formally vested in the Antarctic Policy Group (APG), an inter-agency committee composed of representatives from the Department of State, the Department of Defense (DOD), and the National Science Foundation (NSF). Other Federal agencies participate on an *ad hoc* basis.[45] The State Department, in addition to chairing the APG, acts as the lead agency during negotiations related to Antarctic affairs (*e. g.*, Seals Convention, CCAMLR, minerals negotiations).

The United States Antarctic Program (USAP), operated by the National Science Foundation (NSF), consists of scientific and logistical activities. The NSF directly administers the U.S. Antarctic Research Program (USARP), which covers most of the scientific activity conducted or

[44] *Ibid.*
[45] Office of the White House Press Secretary, Press Release, May 1, 1965.

supported by the U.S. in the region.[46] The U.S. Navy, through Operation Deepfreeze, provides ground, sea, and air support to the USARP on contract,[47] as does the U. S. Coast Guard, which operates two icebreakers serving McMurdo and Palmer Stations as well as providing seaborne research platforms for the USARP. The NSF employs a civilian contractor (ITT/ANS) for additional logistical support at McMurdo Base and at the Palmer, South Pole and Siple stations. The National Oceanic and Atmospheric Administration (NOAA) also operates ships in the Antarctic for research purposes in connection with the CCAMLR.

USAP activities are not presently governed by any single, comprehensive set of guidelines for the management and disposal of waste material generated by the program. The U.S. government, as a State Party to the Antarctic Treaty, the Seals Convention, and the CCAMLR, is bound to obey the provisions of these international legal instruments and the U.S. laws promulgated to give them domestic effect. Furthermore, as an ATCP, the U.S. has adopted Recommendations formulated through the Consultative process that deal with waste management issues. Last, several pieces of U.S. legislation mandate waste management rules and regulations, which may have policy implications for the USAP and its participating Federal agencies.

a) U.S. Policies Based on the Antarctic Treaty System

i) The Antarctic Conservation Act

In 1978, the U.S. Congress passed the Antarctic Conservation Act in order to implement the Agreed Measures for the Conservation of Antarctic Fauna and Flora.[48] The purpose of the Act is to provide for the conservation and protection of the fauna and flora of Antarctica and its dependent ecosystems. The Act is relevant to waste management policy

[46] Other U.S. Federal government agencies, such as the U.S. Geological Survey (USGS) of the Department of the Interior and the National Oceanic and Atmospheric Administration (NOAA), a part of the Department of Commerce, have, from time to time, operated in the Antarctic region.

[47] The Naval Support Force Antarctica (NSFA) provides seaborne supply and on-site maintenance and logistical support. The Naval Air Squadron provides airborne supply and operates Williams Airfield at McMurdo, which serves as the transportation hub of the USAP. In addition, the Navy operates transit facilities at Christchurch, New Zealand, which serves as the primary staging point for USAP materials entering or leaving Antarctica.

[48] Antarctic Conservation Act, 16 USC 2401 *et seq.* The question is raised as to why the U.S. waited fifteen years to enact domestic legislation implementing the provisions of the Agreed Measures. One observer has stated that:

> When the Antarctic Conservation legislation was presented to the US Congress in July 1977, one may assume that its introduction was due to the desire of the United States to press for safeguards for the ecosystem in the Living Resources regime to be discussed at the September 1977 Consultative Meeting. Nine Consultative Parties . . . had approved the Agreed Measures but the United States had not, and had it not moved in that direction, it

because it prohibits, with some exceptions, the discharge or disposal of any pollutant within Antarctica by U.S. citizens.[49]

The director of the NSF is required by the Act to: (i) designate as a pollutant any substance which is liable, if introduced into Antarctica, "to create hazards to human health, to harm living resources or marine life, to damage amenities, or to interfere with other legitimate uses of Antarctica" and (ii) specify those actions which must be taken in order to prevent or control the discharge or other disposal of pollutants in Antarctica.[50]

Pursuant to the provisions of the Antarctic Conservation Act, the NSF issued regulations to conserve and protect animals and plants native to Antarctica.[51] The NSF, however, did not include in these regulations measures to restrict the discharge and disposal of pollutants in Antarctica, indicating that such measures would be forthcoming at a later date.[52] To date, the NSF has neither defined any substances to be pollutants within the meaning of the Act, nor has it promulgated any regulations covering the disposal of pollutants in the Antarctic Treaty area. In June 1983, moreover, the NSF claimed that formal regulations governing waste disposal in Antarctic were "neither necessary nor appropriate" at the time, because "major activities in Antarctica other than scientific research are unlikely for the next several years."[53]

ii) The Antarctic Marine Living Resources Act

The U.S. enacted the Antarctic Marine Living Resources Convention Act (1984)[54] in order to provide the legislative authority necessary to implement the CCAMLR. CCAMLR is principally intended to regulate the harvesting of Antarctic marine living resources; the U. S. implementing legislation does not touch directly upon waste disposal issues. The U.S. Act does make it illegal for any U.S. citizen to engage in harvesting or other associated activities in violation of the provisions of CCAMLR.[55] The use of the term "associated activities" may be interpreted to

---

would hardly have been safe from criticism in taking a strong stand on krill. See *F. M. Auburn*, Antarctic Law and Politics, London *et al.* 1982, 273.

By ATCM 13 in 1985, all twelve of the original ATCPs had approved the Agreed Measures and enacted domestic legislation giving them effect. Of the ATCPs that have acceded to the Antarctic Treaty, only Poland has approved the Agreed Measures.

[49] Antarctic Conservation Act, 16 USC 2403.

[50] Antarctic Conservation Act, 16 USC 2405.

[51] 45 CFR 670 (1979).

[52] 44 Fed. Reg. 32699.

[53] USAP Program Directive No. 84—1, reprinted in Antarctic Journal, vol. 18 (1983), 8.

[54] Antarctic Marine Living Resources Convention Act (1984), 16 USC 2431.

[55] *Loc. cit.*, 16 USC 2435.

encompass activities of harvesting vessels that produce marine pollution, such as deballasting, dumping, and discharging of toxic substances in Antarctic waters.[56] Therefore, the U. S. Act provides a basis for regulating or even prohibiting ocean waste disposal by U. S. vessels operating under the CCAMLR, either for fishing or scientific research.

The Act directs the Secretary of Commerce to promulgate such regulations as are necessary to implement the provisions of the Act.[57] The U.S. and its nationals do not engage in any harvesting under the CCAMLR at the present time, and the Secretary has not promulgated any waste disposal regulations.[58] But vessels carrying out scientific research to help implement CCAMLR (for example, those operated by NOAA) and logistics vessels for the U.S. Antarctic Program could be subject to regulation.

iii) Implementation of the Code of Conduct

The NSF issued an internal administrative directive following the U.S. approval of the Code of Conduct contained in Recommendation VIII-11, which sets out recommended procedures for waste disposal.[59] The NSF directive differs in some important respects from the Code of Conduct adopted by the ATCPs and approved by the U. S. For example, the Code of Conduct states that: "All plastics and rubber products should be removed from the Antarctic Treaty Area."[60] The NSF directive, in contrast, stipulates that such action need only be taken "where feasible," and allows for the disposal of plastics in landfills as an alternative.[61]

The U.S. implementation of the Code of Conduct, as reflected in the NSF directive, also contrasts with the policies of some ATCPs, which have incorporated the Code verbatim into their waste management regulations, and with countries that have gone further than the Code, such as West Germany and Australia. Germany removes from Antarctica all non-burnable waste except for carcasses of imported test animals, and Australia has developed a model retrogradation program. Of course, as noted above, each country has wide scope in interpreting and implementing recommendations such as the Code, so it is not legally wrong for the U.S. and other governments to take such positions.

---

[56] *Joyner*, note 40, 183.

[57] See note 44, 16 USC 2436.

[58] It is not clear what regulations, if any, have been promulgated to cover the activities of U.S. research vessels operating under the directed research program established by the Act, including a Polish vessel that is part of a U.S. and Polish joint venture. 16 USC 2441.

[59] See note 53.

[60] Code of Conduct, (1) (a) (iii), note 3.

[61] See note 53.

b) Domestic Policies

i) The National Environmental Policy Act (NEPA)

The U.S. enacted the National Environmental Policy Act (NEPA), in part, "to promote efforts which will prevent or eliminate damage to the environment and biosphere."[62] NEPA directs that, to the fullest extent possible, all agencies of the Federal Government shall include an environmental impact statement (EIS) with all proposals for major Federal actions that could significantly affect environmental quality.[63] It was not made clear, in either the statute itself or the legislative history of NEPA, whether the Act applied to actions of Federal agencies outside the U.S.[64] The State Department, however, accepted that NEPA obliged the U.S. Government to prepare impact statements for Antarctic activities, and this decision has been adhered to by the NSF.[65] The State Department issued EIS's for the Seals Convention,[66] the CCAMLR[67] and the proposed Minerals Regime.[68] The NSF issued a Programmatic EIS for the entire USAP[69], and a regular EIS for the Ocean Drilling Program.[70] EIS's were also prepared by the U.S. Geological Survey (USGS) for the Ross Ice Shelf Project[71] and the Dry Valleys Drilling Project (DVDP)[72].

---

[62] 42 USC 4371 *et seq.*

[63] Public Law 91-90, Sect. 102 (c) (i).

[64] See *Natural Resources Defense Council v. Nuclear Reg. Com'n* [647 F. 2 d 1345, 1365 (1981)]. NSF issued regulations implementing NEPA that did not, originally, distinguish its Antarctic activities from domestic ones. See 45 CFR 640.

[65] See statements made by State Department spokespersons during the Congressional hearings on the seals Convention in Fish and Wildlife Legislation, Part 4, Hearings, Subcommittee on Fisheries and Wildlife Conservation, Committee on Merchant Marine Fisheries, H. Rep., 92nd Cong., 2nd Sess. (1972), 21.

[66] Department of State, Environmental Impact Statement on the Convention for the Conservation of Antarctic Seals (1974).

[67] Department of State, Final Environmental Impact Statement for a Possible Regime for the Conservation of Antarctic Living Marine Resources (1978).

[68] Department of State, Final Environmental Impact Statement on the Negotiation of an International Regime for Antarctic Mineral Resources (1982).

[69] National Science Foundation, United States Antarctic Program Final Environmental Impact Statement (1980).

[70] National Science Foundation, Draft Environmental Impact Statement for the Ocean Drilling Program (June 1985). This EIS is relevant to Antarctic affairs because the Weddell Sea was chosen as one of the drilling sites. A "Dear Colleague" letter circulated with the Draft EIS cites "compliance with the National Environmental Policy Act" as the statutory authority mandating the preparation of the statement. See letter dated June 21, 1985, from *Adair F. Montgomery*, Chairman of the Committee on Environmental Matters, National Science Foundation, on file.

[71] U. S. Geological Survey, Ross Ice Shelf Project Environmental Impact Statement.

[72] U. S. Geological Survey, Dry Valleys Drilling Project Environmental Impact Statement.

For the most part, the various EIS's performed under the NEPA for U.S. activities in Antarctica do not dwell upon waste disposal issues. The Programmatic EIS prepared by the NSF, however, addresses a number of waste management policy issues. First, the EIS commits the NSF to study alternative solid waste disposal methods and the future installation of waste management technologies such as compactors, baling machines, and incinerators. Second, the EIS includes plans to study alternative sanitary waste disposal methods at McMurdo and Palmer Stations, and to evaluate the impact of sewage on the marine ecosystems in which it is disposed. Depending upon the results of these studies, the NSF indicated in the EIS that it would act to mitigate these impacts through the installation of sewage grinding technology and the relocation of the sewage outfall at McMurdo to deeper water. The NSF also indicated that it might award research grants to assess the impacts of current waste disposal procedures on the Antarctic environment.[73]

In reply to the 1980 NSF Programmatic EIS, the Department of Health, Education and Welfare (HEW) commented that the disposal of untreated wastes in Antarctica appeared to conflict with the intention and spirit of U.S. requirements for pollution control standards.[74] The NSF responded to HEW by pointing out that pollution standards were those of general applicability in the host country or its jurisdiction, and in Antarctica, these standards were contained in Recommendation VIII-11.[75]

ii) Executive Order 12114

In 1979, the President issued Executive Order 12114, "Environmental Effects Abroad of Major Federal Actions"[76] in order to further the purpose of NEPA and the Marine Protection Research and Sanctuaries Act.[77] The Executive Order directly applies to "[m]ajor Federal actions significantly affecting the environment of the global commons outside the jurisdiction of any nation (*e. g.*, the oceans or Antarctica)."[78] The NSF and other Federal agencies operating in Antarctica would appear to be required by the Order to prepare an EIS for "major" actions undertaken in the region.[79] The use of the term "global commons," however,

[73] For a preliminary analysis of NEPA and its applicability to NSF activities in the Antarctic, see letter dated June 3, 1987, from *Bruce Mannheim* of the Environmental Defense Fund to *Erich Bloch*, Director of the National Science Foundation, on file.

[74] See note 69.

[75] For the NSF response, see note 69. *Auburn* has commented that the NSF response implied that, with the exception of NEPA, general U.S. environmental laws do not apply to NSF Antarctic activities. See *Auburn*, note 48, 285.

[76] 44 Fed. Reg. 957.

[77] Marine Protection Research and Sanctuaries Act, 16 USC 1431.

[78] See note 76, para. 2—3.

[79] *Ibid.*, para. 2—4.

is seen by some U.S. officials as not being fully consistent with the position taken by the U.S. on the status of Antarctica and the high seas in international law, thus raisinq questions about the intent and reach of the Executive Order.[80]

The Executive Order has never been cited by a federal agency in an environmental impact statement prepared for an Antarctic activity, in spite of the fact that it purports to represent "the United States government's exclusive and complete determination of the procedures and other actions to be taken by federal agencies to further the purpose of the National Environmental Policy Act with respect to the environments outside the United States, its territories and possessions."[81] The EIS process established by the Executive Order, being "exclusive and complete," was intended to preempt NEPA. It follows that if Executive Order 12114 covers U.S. activities in Antarctica, then the strict EIS procedures mandated by NEPA no longer apply.[82]

Although the Department of Defense has issued regulations implementing Executive Order 12114, neither the NSF nor the State Department have done so.[83] Current NSF NEPA-implementing regulations define the types of NSF activities requiring an environmental assessment: (a) Any project supporting construction, other than interior remodeling; (b) Cases where field work affecting the natural environment will be conducted; and (c) Any project that will involve drilling of the earth, excavation, explosives . . . or other techniques that may alter a local environment.[84] The NSF supports or carries out all of these activities in Antarctica. As mentioned above, the NSF issued a programmatic EIS for the USAP in 1980, lending credence to the view that the entire program is a "major federal action" within the meaning of either Executive Order 12114 or NEPA.[85] That EIS did not mention the Executive Order as its legal basis. The NSF has embarked on a general clean-up of U.S. bases since the 1980 programmatic EIS, which it views

---

[80] Statement of U.S. position with regard to the status of Antarctica and the high seas in international law.

[81] See note 76, para. 1—1.

[82] See, in general, *Almond*, The Extraterritorial Reach of United States Regulatory Authority Over the Environmental Impacts of Its Activities, Albany Law Review, vol. 44 (1980), 739.

[83] The NSF intends to promulgate regulations implementing E. O. 12114 at a "later date." 45 Fed. Reg. 40. State Department regulations implementing NEPA also withhold E. O. 12114 regulations for a later date. 22 CFR 161.3. In contrast, see Department of Defense implementing regulations at 32 CFR 197. In addition to the DOD, the following U.S. federal government agencies have promulgated E. O. 12114 regulations: Dept. of Agriculture (2 CFR 3100), Export-Import Bank (12 CFR 409), NASA (14 CFR 1216.321), Food and Drug Admin. (21 CFR 25.50), and EPA (40 CFR 6).

[84] 45 CFR 640.3.

[85] See note 69.

as being within the ambit of that EIS and, therefore, has not prepared a site-specific EIS for any particular base.

iii) The Ocean Dumping Act

Executive Order 12114 was meant to further the purposes of the Marine Protection, Research, and Sanctuaries Act[86] as well as those of the NEPA. Among the regulations established pursuant to this Act are those covering the dumping of waste at sea. These regulations, commonly referred to as the "Ocean Dumping Act" (ODA), prohibit any vessel or aircraft registered in the U.S. or flying the U.S. flag, as well as all U.S. government agencies, from transporting from "any location any material for the purpose of dumping it into ocean waters."[87]

In seeking to comply with this regulation, the NSF applied to the EPA in July 1981 for a permit to "transport solid wastes from Antarctica for disposal at sea."[88] The EPA never acted on this application by the NSF, but did grant temporary authorization for deep water disposal of waste materials under the conditions that:

1. Disposal must take place at least 50 miles from land or in 100 fathoms of water.
2. The waste should sink permanently and rapidly,
3. No radioisotopes shall be disposed of at sea.[89]

The compliance record of the NSF, the Navy and other federal agencies operating in the Antarctic with this "temporary" authorization is unclear, and may not be well documented.[90] Neither NSF nor EPA personnel have explained why the 1981 permit application has never been either granted or denied.

III. The Waste Management Process

A survey of state practice in the Antarctic regarding waste management procedures was carried out by ASOC and some of its members in 1986 and 1987. Many countries responded with only minimal information. The survey reveals four distinct stages utilized in varying combinations by different countries.

---

[86] See note 77.

[87] 33 USC 1411.

[88] See, letter dated July 9, 1981, from National Science Foundation Counsel *John Slaughter* to *Anne Gorsuch*, Administrator of the Environmental Protection Agency, on file.

[89] See *Waldrip*, The McMurdo Station Sanitary Landfill Evaluation and Recommendations Report, (March 1984). (Hereinafter cited as the *Waldrip* Report).

[90] See discussion on page 17 and footnotes 123 and 124.

(1) regulation and limitation of materials being exported to the Antarctic,
(2) storage and disposal of waste through dumping on land or at sea,
(3) burning of waste, and
(4) the return of waste to the country of origin (retrograding).

The following section begins to examine the degree to which each of these processes is utilized by Antarctic Treaty Members, based on the ASOC member surveys, but because of the rather scanty database available, it must be seen as preliminary. In particular, statistics about quantities of various types of materials and substances and how they are screened and disposed of seem to be unavailable. In addition, it would be desirable to know much more about the impacts such processes have on the Antarctic environment, and the costs and benefits associated with including such processes in a comprehensive Antarctic waste management regime, but it has proven impossible to do this in a comprehensive fashion. It is to be hoped that the SCAR committee on waste disposal will be able to obtain more information on these points.

1. The Regulation of Imported Materials

The first stage in the Antarctic waste management process involves the exclusion or decreased importation of non-desirable materials from the Treaty Area, either because they are inherently dangerous to the environment, or because their future disposal entails environmental or financial costs that could be avoided through non-importation. The Antarctic Treaty expressly prohibits the disposal of radioactive wastes in the Treaty Area,[91] but otherwise is silent as to what materials may be introduced into the Antarctic region and the methods of their disposal. The Code of Conduct recommends that: "Every effort should be made to reduce the plastic packaging of products imported into the Antarctic Treaty Area."[92] In addition, the Code of Conduct states: "If possible the use of leaded fuels or fuels containing ethylene bromide and ethylene chloride should be avoided."[93]

a) General Practice

Australia, which is in the midst of a rebuilding program for its Antarctic Stations, has indicated the intention to adopt a program of controls over the materials being sent to the Antarctic in order to

---

[91] Antarctic Treaty, note 1, Article V. After shutting down its nuclear reactor at McMurdo, the U.S. voluntarily removed tons of contaminated topsoil from Antarctica, to avoid difficulties regarding that prohibition.

[92] Code of Conduct, note 3, para. 1, sect. (e).

[93] *Loc. cit.*, 1 (f).

reduce the waste being generated by the Australian Antarctic Program.[94]

The official Expedition Handbook published by the Alfred Wegener Institute, which runs West Germany's Antarctic program, recommends that the importation of plastics, pesticides and chloride hydrogens into the Antarctic Treaty Area be avoided and/or reduced as far as possible.[95]

The New Zealand Antarctic Division has, in the past, engaged in a degree of pre-screening by giving preference to commodities packed in recyclable containers, while discriminating against undesirable packaging materials and containers, thus minimizing the build-up of unwanted materials at Scott Base.[96]

b) U. S. Practice

Currently, there is no single, comprehensive policy on the part of the USAP for the screening of Antarctic-bound materials, although there are a number of informal directives and contractual terms between the NSF and its contractors — the Navy, Coast Guard and ITT/ANS. The NSF conducts "broad supervision" over its contractors where materials importation is concerned, but that supervision has not extended to establishing firm criteria, incentives, and mandatory regulations for limiting undesirable products.[97]

The NSF has recognized the impact that the importation of large quantities of logistical support material may have on the Antarctic environment. In the programmatic EIS prepared in 1980, the NSF concluded that the "addition of foreign materials to a pristine environment" was a significant environmental impact of the USAP.[98] Each year, in fact, more than 2000 tons of cargo and food, as well as 5 million gallons of petroleum products, are shipped to Antarctica in support of the USARP.[99] Statistics do not appear to be available on how much material, by category, is disposed of in various ways or retrograded.

As previously discussed, the Antarctic Conservation Act requires the Director of the NSF to promulgate regulations that "designate as a

[94] Letter dated April 4, 1986 from *J. E. Bleasel*, Director, Department of Science and Technology, Antarctic Division, on file. (Hereinafter cited as the *Bleasel* letter).

[95] Official Antarctic Expedition Handbook 85, Alfred Wegener Institute, Bremerhaven, FRG.

[96] *Monteath*, Waste Not Left Behind at Scott Base, Antarctic (NZ) (Sept. 1977), 101.

[97] Interview with *Gerald Schatz*, Department of Polar Programs, National Science Foundation (June 1987) on file. (Hereinafter cited as the *Schatz* interview). The assistance of *Mr. Schatz* and other NSF officials is gratefully acknowledged.

[98] See note 69.

[99] See *Mannheim* letter, note 73.

pollutant any substance which the Director finds liable, if the substance is introduced into Antarctica, to create hazards to human health, to harm living resources or marine life, to damage amenities, or to interfere with other legitimate uses of Antarctica."[100] Logic dictates that such items designated by the Director of the NSF under the provisions of this Act would be excluded from Antarctica or strictly regulated. To date, however, the NSF has not identified any substances to be 'pollutants' within the meaning of the Act. Section 6 (a) of the Antarctic Conservation Act provides that the NSF Director "shall prescribe such regulations as are necessary and appropriate ...." NSF takes the position that further requirements for regulation are predicated on the Director's judgment of the environmental effects of possible pollutants, and has indicated that it has no plans to take action at this time.

According to current U.S. policy directives to contractors and scientists, laboratory chemicals that are reactive are neutralized prior to disposal, and all radioactive research materials are stored in containers and returned to the U.S. for disposal. Recently some plastics have begun to be stored, pending a revised official policy on disposal. For example, plastics from Palmer station are required to be segregated and stored for the time being.[101]

2. *Regional Disposal — Dumping*

The disposal of waste on the Antarctic continent and in the sourrounding seas is now practiced by most all the nations operating in the region. Three methods are primarily used: (1) collection of solid waste in dump sites on the continent, (2) dumping of solid waste in the waters of the region, and (3) piping of sewage either into the ice shelf or into the surrounding waters.

a) Solid Waste Dumps

According to the Code of Conduct, "waste should not be buried," except at inland stations or camps in certain situations.[102] The actual practice of the various ATCPs differs widely. Some states utilize land-based dump sites, while others use a variety of other methods for the disposal of their solid wastes.

i) General Practice

Several ATCPs have indicated that their Antarctic programs do not make use of solid waste dump sites in the Antarctic. These states are:

---

[100] 16 USC 2405 (6).
[101] *Fowler* interviews (August and September, 1987).
[102] Code of Conduct, note 3, para. 1 (c).

Argentina, China, the Federal Republic of Germany, and Uruguay.[103]

In addition, Australia, which has in the past utilized land-based dump sites at its Antarctic stations, has closed these dumps in connection with a rebuilding program that includes a new waste management system. The waste materials currently stored in these dumps, consisting mainly of non-combustible and partially burnt material as well as incinerator residue, is being returned to Australia during the course of the next several years.[104] In the future, all non-burnable waste will be returned to Australia for disposal, along with all incinerator residue.[105]

The South African Antarctic program buries solid human waste, kitchen slop, residue from combusted waste and compacted cans, bottles and plastics in the ice shelf near SANAE Station and at the Serie Marais field site.[106]

The Dumont D'Urville French base conveys kitchen refuse and solid waste to the edge of a cliff by monorail, which is automatically dumped down the cliff face into the ocean.[107]

During the mid-1970's, New Zealand operated an extensive retrogradation program and made little use of the Winter Quarters Bay dump operated by the U. S. near Scott Base. Since the early 1980s, however, the New Zealand retrogradation program has fallen off, and increasing use has been made of the Fortress Rock dump site operated by the U. S. for McMurdo Station.

ii) U. S. Practice

The USAP, through the NSF contractor ITT/ANS, operates a large solid waste dump site at Fortress Rock to service McMurdo Station. It also has been used by the New Zealand Scott Base.

---

[103] Argentina adheres to the Code of Conduct's provisions regarding the burial of waste on land in the Antarctic. See letter dated July 24, 1986, from *Orlando R. Rebagliati*, Director General de Antartida, Ministerio de Relaciones Exteriores y Culto, on file, (hereinafter cited as *Rebagliati* letter). China exports all of its unburnable trash from the Great Wall Station. See 1985 United States Antarctic Observer Team Report, 14 (hereinafter cited as the 1985 US Inspection Report). The Federal Republic of Germany adheres to the Code of Conduct with regards to the burial of solid waste on land in the Antarctic. See letter dated Sept. 11, 1986, from *Prof. Dr. G. Hempel*, Director, Alfred-Wegener-Institut für Polar- und Meeresforschung, FRG, on file, (hereinafter cited as *Hempel* letter). Uruguay retrogrades all of its non-burnable trash. See letter dated June 17, 1986, from *Col. Recardo Galarza*, President of the Uruguayan Antarctic Institute, Uruguay, on file, (hereinafter cited as *Galarza* letter).

[104] Telex from *Lyn Goldsworthy*, ECOFUND-Australia and Secretariat for ASOC, June 1987, on file, (hereinafter cited as the *Goldsworthy* telex). *Bleasel* letter, note 80.

[105] See note 104.

[106] Letter dated August 20, 1986 from the Director General, Dept. of Foreign Affairs, Republic of South Africa, on file.

[107] Report of the 1985/86 Australian Observer Team, Visit to the French Station of Dumont D'Urville, 3 January 1986, 5.

In the U. S., solid waste disposal is subject to general guidelines promulgated by the EPA pursuant to the Solid Waste Disposal Act.[108] The formal guidelines established by the NSF to govern solid waste disposal in Antarctica, however, were meant to implement the Antarctic Code of Conduct, and in no way approximate the scope and detail of the Solid Waste Disposal Act.[109]

The Fortress Rock dump site is far from meeting the commonly recognized standards for an EPA-approved sanitary landfill. The EPA defines sanitary landfilling as:

> [A] method of disposing of solid waste on land without creating nuisances or hazards to public health or safety, by utilizing the principles of engineering to confine the refuse to the smallest practical area, to reduce it to the smallest practical volume and to cover it with a layer of earth at the conclusion of each day's operation or at such more frequent intervals as may be necessary.[110]

At Fortress Rock a number of practices engaged in are outside the EPA guidelines, but nevertheless are allowed by the NSF's interpretation of the Code of Conduct. Open burning is used in order to reduce the large volume of combustible waste materials generated by McMurdo Station, a procedure which, by definition, would be prohibited at a sanitary landfill. Because of the periodic burning of the dump and the limited availability of heavy tracked equipment, regular compacting of the solid waste at Fortress Rock does not occur. In addition, the standard landfilling practice of covering over the solid waste with earth is made difficult in the Antarctic due to the scarcity of cover materials and the difficulty in storing them for future use.[111] Last, the establishment of a vegetative cover for the completed landfill, required by the EPA, is problematic in the polar climate of Antarctica, and is specifically prohibited in the Antarctic Conservation Act.[112]

In sum, the waste management operation at Fortress Rock more closely resembles the traditional "open dump" than a sanitary landfill. An open dump is defined by the EPA as a

> land site at which solid waste is disposed of in a manner, generally involving burning, which does not protect the environment and is exposed to the elements, vectors, and scavengers.[113]

---

[108] See note 82.

[109] Solid Waste Disposal Act.

[110] See Questions for the Record from the Senate Appropriatoins Subcommittee — U. S. Antarctic Program, 1987.

[111] 40 CFR 25.7 *et seq.*

[112] See, in general, *Waldrip* Report note 89.

[113] Antarctic Conservation Act, note 48, Section 4 a (1.c).

Clearly, if environmental protection is a primary goal of the U.S. waste management program in the Antarctic, then the operation of an open dump at Fortress Rock, as opposed to a modified sanitary landfill, would appear to be counterproductive. The argument is made, however, that operation of a sanitary landfill in the Antarctic by standard EPA-approved procedures is neither practical nor economically feasible.

Deviations from the EPA guidelines are said by NSF spokespersons to be justified by the fact that overall waste disposal procedures developed for domestic landfills are not suited to the Antarctic environment. For instance, EPA regulations requiring daily soil cover and the planting of vegetative cover over the completed landfill are neither necessary nor possible in the Antarctic, where scavenging animals are said not to be a problem, waste dispersal by wind is said to be at a minimum, and available vegetation extremely fragile. These reasons, added to the harsh operating conditions and difficult logistic problems of the Antarctic, are put forward in order to support the continued operation of an open dump at Fortress Rock, as opposed to a sanitary landfill.[114] These statements ignore the reality that scavenging birds are numerous, the wind scatters materials from the dumps quite widely, and open burning causes air pollution. Depending on what substances are being burnt, there can be quite harmful impacts on the environment.

In the opinion of the NSF, the McMurdo landfill is operated "in accordance with environmentally acceptable procedures."[115] Furthermore, the NSF contractor believes that the USAP "is in full compliance with the Code of Conduct . . . and is in concurrence with the spirit of generally sound environmental practices."[116] Because the interpretation and implementation of the Code is basically up to each member state, it is true that the U.S. and other programs comply with it. Whether current practices concur with sound practice is more doubtful, and indeed, the fact that the U.S. and other countries are taking steps to clean up old dump sites and adopt new policies and procedures belies the statement. In order to deal more effectively with the solid waste generated at McMurdo, the long-range plan drawn up by Holmes and Narver, Inc. called for the installation of compacting and baling equipment to reduce storage volume, as a first step.[117] A compactor was tried at McMurdo in the early 1980s, but the technology is said to have been inadequate.

At Palmer Station, hazardous materials such as batteries and tires are segregated and retrograded via McMurdo, plastics are segregated and

---

[114] See note 111.
[115] *Waldrip* Report, note 89, 42—3. *Schatz* interview, note 97.
[116] See note 110.
[117] Holmes and Narver, Inc., Long Range Development Plan, vol. 2, McMurdo Station, USARP/NSF, Antarctica (April 20, 1979) at section 6. 4. 1. 4. (Hereinafter cited as Holmes and Narver).

are being stored pending a new policy, the remaining solid waste is compacted into bales, which are then taken by ship north of 60 degrees South latitude and dumped into the ocean. At Siple and South Pole stations all waste except hazardous substances are buried in the ice. Field camps in the Dry Valleys retrograde all waste. Camps in the snow-fields or glacial areas follow different practices depending on their size. Large camps generally bury their waste in snow pits. Smaller field parties will retrograde solid waste but dispose of liquid waste in snow pits.[118]

b) Ocean Dumping of Solid Waste

The Code of Conduct allows for non-combustible materials, with the exception of batteries and other toxic materials, to be disposed of in Antarctic waters.[119] Batteries, along with harmful lubricating oils, plastic and rubber products, and waste containing isotopes are to be removed from the area. Logically, that means they should not be disposed of in the waters of the Antarctic Treaty Area.[120]

Thirteen ATCPs are, moreover, parties to the London Dumping Convention, which provides a much more detailed listing of materials proscribed from ocean disposal.[121] Fifteen ATCPs are signatories to the LOS Convention, which contains restrictions on ocean dumping that, like the entire convention, were formulated as part on an overall consensus among virtually all existing states.[122] The LOS Convention has yet to receive the necessary number of ratifications to enter, with its dumping provisions, into force. The Declaration of Principles Governing the Sea-bed and the Ocean Floor and the Subsoil Thereof, Resolution 2749 of the UN General Assembly passed December 17, 1970, may also have relevance for the Antarctic.

The Agreed Measures, the Seals Convention, and the CCAMLR all exhibit a concern for the marine environment of the Antarctic, but do not, as previously discussed, specifically address waste disposal issues. Likewise, MARPOL restrictions on harmful discharges from shipping provide less protection for Antarctic waters because so few of the ATCPs have become parties to that Treaty.[123] Nonetheless, MARPOL provides a good framework for regulation of vessels in the Antarctic by those states that are parties, and other states could be encouraged to join.

[118] *Fowler* interviews, note 101.
[119] Holmes and Narver, note 117.
[120] Code of Conduct, (1) (a) (i), note 3.
[121] *Ibid.*
[122] See in general MARPOL, note 11. Refer to Table I.
[123] Refer to Table II.

i) General Practice

Solid waste at Chile's Marsh / Frei Station is placed in metal drums and dropped from C-130's, while at Poland's Arctowski Station, all non-sewage, burnable waste is incinerated and the ashes are stowed in 55 gallon drums to be dumped at sea.[124] Non-burnable waste generated at the UK's Farraday Station is disposed of primarily through dumping at sea.[125] According to informal conserversations with numerous individuals, most ATCPs dump some quantities of solid waste at sea within the Antarctic Treaty area, in a variety of ways.

ii) U. S. Practice

Until 1977, nearly all solid waste generated at McMurdo Station was staged by the U.S. on sea ice in Winter Quarters Bay. Around this time, however, after successive years when the ice did not move out to sea, the waste began to accumulate closer and closer to shore. These changes in ice conditions left the waste material dumped onto the ice in the Bay "permanently grounded."[126] In December 1983, an attempt to sink the grounded waste material through the use of explosives failed.[127] After 1977, the USAP began to dispose of solid waste at the Fortress Rock land dump site, but continued to ocean dump items such as heavy machinery and waste metals. Theoretically, all heavy equipment dumped into the ocean is supposed to have been emptied of all oil, lubricants, batteries and tires.

Inorganic litter on the bottom of McMurdo Sound, dating from the inception of the program up to about 1984, consists of fuel lines, barrels, clothing, tractors, tires, thousands of beer cans, and many other types of trash. The most detrimental effect of this inorganic litter is the covering of the ocean bottom, which tends to kill the sponges and other benthic life. The introduction of plastic litter is of especial concern, since it will not biodegrade and will kill all organisms beneath it. In addition, an old petroleum spill has been reported to be generally intact on the bottom. According to *Paul Dayton*'s 1983 letter to *Dick Williams* of NSF:

> In 1974 we found WQB (Winter Quarters Bay) to be essentially dead, the sediment so full of DFA (diesel fuel additive) it almost appeared combustible! Clearly there was a massive spill of some sort and I doubt if that amount of DFA will be broken down in the

---

[124] 1985 US Inspection Report, note 103, 19.
[125] See note 103, 6.
[126] See note 115.
[127] See *Waldrip* Report, note 89.

near future. There is a sill which much reduces currents in WQB, and it is probably fair to say that the benthos is biologically dead already.

The source of this fuel oil spill has never been determined, although some NSF personnel believe it could have resulted from the practice of dousing the items to be disposed of with fuel oil and burning them.

Some of the scrap metal from Palmer Station is deposited in the deep ocean, but statistics on the quantities and types are not available. As mentioned above, compacted solid waste from Palmer is dumped in the ocean south of 60 degrees South Latitude.

As discussed earlier, the NSF applied to the EPA for an ocean dumping permit in 1981, but it has never been acted upon. NSF has indicated that it was advised informally by EPA that practices consistent with the terms of the application would be acceptable pending further EPA action. NSF recently directed its civilian contractor and the Navy to cease dumping of inorganic waste materials into McMurdo Bay. This decision has not been formalized in a directive, nor is the scope and date of implementation known. It is reflected in correspondence with the Environmental Defense Fund (EDF) and a newspaper article. In a letter dated June 22, 1987 to *Bruce Mannheim* (EDF), *Erich Bloch* (NSF Director) stated:

> The National Science Foundation has told its contractor, ITT Antarctic Services, and the U.S. Naval Force Antarctica that this practice is to be discontinued. Scrap that would otherwise have been deposited on the ice is to be returned to the United States.

In addition, *Alfred Fowler*, Deputy Director of Polar Programs at NSF is quoted in the Washington Times (August 25, 1987, page D 4) as saying that NSF ordered this type of ocean dumping halted in mid-1986. Efforts to obtain a copy of a formal order or directive have been unsuccessful. The new policy apparently applies only to McMurdo.

c) Sewage Disposal on Land and Sea

The Code of Conduct recommends that human waste, garbage, and laundry effluents, "where possible," be macerated and flushed into the sea.[128] In addition, the Code states that large quantities of photographic liquids should be treated for the recovery of silver, with the residue being flushed into the sea, but provides no definition of "large" or standards for waste.[129]

---

[128] Code of Conduct, (1) (b) (i), note 3.

[129] *Loc. cit.* (1) (b) (ii).

i) General Practice

Waste water and sewage at Argentina's General Belgrano II Station,[130] West Germany's Georg von Neumayer Station[131] and South Africa's SANAE III Station[132] is piped or pumped off the site and into the continental ice-cover.

Sewage at Argentina's Jubany Station, Chile's Marsh / Frei Station, China's Great Wall Station,[133] the U.K.'s Farraday Station,[134] and the USSR's Molodezhnaya[135] and Bellingshausen[136] stations is either piped or dumped, untreated, directly into nearby Antarctic waters. However, the U.K. planned to install a sewage maceration plant at Farraday Station during the 1985—86 austral summer.[137] At the Dumont D'Urville French base, waste chemicals from the laboratories and photography darkroom are passed by overhead pipe, to fall eventually into the sea on the northern side of the island. Untreated sewage is released into the sea nearby.[138]

The Australian rebuilding program includes the construction of a biological sewage treatment plant at Casey Station, which is expected to be completed in 1988.[139] This would be in contrast with Davis Station, where sewage is burned in oil-fired processors.[140] However, even when installed, the sewage treatment plant at Casey will still outfall into the sea.[141] Furthermore, it is unclear what the effluent will be like, or whether Australia intends to monitor it. Poland's Arctowski Station uses a five-stage sewage filtering system and monitors the effluent as it enters Admiralty Bay.

The impact of direct sewage disposal into Antarctic waters, as well as the need for additional, regular monitoring programs, is evidenced by scientific studies undertaken in the Antarctic. For example, benthic organisms near Syowa Station are polluted considerably by PCB and slightly by DDT from station activities, although the PCB and DDT levels in the fish analyzed are low compared with those in other oceans. The scientists who conducted the research at Syowa recommended that, in

---

[130] 1985 US Inspection Report, note 103, 43.
[131] 1983 United States Observer Team Report, 37. (Hereinafter cited as the 1983 US Inspection Report).
[132] *Loc. cit.*, 34.
[133] 1985 US Inspection Report, note 103, 14.
[134] *Loc. cit.*, 6.
[135] 1983 US Inspection Report, note 131, 24.
[136] 1985 US Inspection Report, note 103, 13.
[137] *Loc. cit.*, 6
[138] See note 107.
[139] *Goldsworthy* telex, note 104. 1983 US Inspection Report, note 131, 10—12.
[140] 1983 US Inspection Report, note 131, 18.
[141] *Goldsworthy* telex, note 104.

order to prevent pollution from station activity, stricter waste disposal procedures be applied.[142]

ii) U.S. Practice

A piped sewage collection system, which flushes waste to the sea, was constructed at the McMurdo Station in the mid 1970s. Originally, some 30 buildings were served by the system, with the remainder either having no toilet facilities or using 55-gallon 'U-barrels' to collect sewage. The sewage system has been expanded since then and will soon serve all of the living quarters at the Station. Presently, all sewage is collected and piped, untreated, by a gravity system to an outfall located at the eastern side of Winter Quarters Bay. A new, consolidated sewage outfall is to be relocated to deeper water.[143]

The organic enrichment resulting from sewage and local sinking of garbage has the possibility of shifting the ecological balance of the benthic community with long-range consequences that could be devastating.[144]

According to the long-range plan for McMurdo, the liquid waste management system is scheduled to be overhauled and completed at a cost of US $ 390,000. When completed, the plan envisions a number of integrated steps that should reduce the impact of sewage disposal on the waters surrounding McMurdo Station. First, all facilities occupied on a daily basis will be connected to the sewage system, thus eliminating the use of 55-gallon drums for the collection and disposal of liquid waste. Second, disposal units are to be installed in the kitchen and dining areas to eliminate solid matter at the source. In addition, a maceration plant is being installed in order to process solid waste materials flushed into the sewage system, and thus aid the dispersion of the effluent, minimizing benthic settlement after outfall into the ocean. Brine from the water plant is also to be used to thin the sewage outflow and thus facilitate its dispersal into the ocean.[145] Third, non-human waste, such as chemical and oil wastes, currently are separated or neutralized at their source, and are not disposed of in the sanitary waste system. Last, while the Raytheon Water Quality study report recommended against chlorination of the sewage effluent, which is not currently being monitored, the NSF has requested that ITT/ANS include a

---

[142] *Hidaka, Hideo* and *Tatsukawa, Ryo.* Environmental pollution of Chlorinated Hydrocarbons around Syowa Station, Antarctic Record, vol. 80, (Tokyo 1983), 14.

[143] *Dayton, Paul K.* and *Robilliard, Gordon A.*, Implications of Pollution to the McMurdo Sound Benthos, Antarctic Journal, vol. 53 (May-June 1971).

[144] See, in general, Holmes and Narver, note 117. Also, *Schatz* interview, note 97.

[145] See note 144.

conceptual design of a primary treatment plant in the Fiscal Year 1988 Program Plan.[146]

Liquid waste from Palmer Station is discharged into the sea. At Siple and South Pole Stations, all liquid wastes, unless hazardous, are buried in the ice, leading some observers to reflect that the bases may be sinking into the ice as a result. All liquid wastes at field camps other than in the Dry Valleys are buried in snow pits.[147]

3. *Burning and Incineration (of Waste)*

Many ATCPs either burn waste material utilizing uncontrolled processes (*i. e.*, open air combustion), or have installed incinerators at their bases to dispose of combustible wastes. The Code of Conduct recommends the incineration of wood, wood products, paper, and animal carcasses.[148] In addition, the Code suggests that when incinerators are used, the effluents be monitored.[149]

a) General Practice

It appears that virtually every station burns plastics and/or uses plastic garbage bags for trash dumped at sea, contrary to recommendations in the existing Code of Conduct. Combustible waste at Argentina's Jubany Station, China's Great Wall Station,[150] Japan's Syowa Station[151] and South Africa's SANAE III Station is collected and burned.[152] The Dumont D'Urville French base burns combustible wastes in the open, and also uses incinerators.[153] There is little available information about the definition of "combustible" used at these bases, or the quantities disposed of. Burnable trash at Farraday Station (UK)[154] and the Soviet Union's Bellingshausen Station[155] is incinerated, but there are no statistics available about the composition of this trash.

New Zealand replaced the Harco Industrial Incinerator at Scott Base, which utilized an "uncontrolled" incineration process, with a new Warren Controlled Air Incinerator during the 1986/87 summer season.[156]

[146] See note 110.
[147] *Fowler* interviews, note 101.
[148] Code of Conduct, (1) (a) (iii).
[149] *Loc. cit.* (1) (g).
[150] 1985 US Inspection Report, note 103, 14.
[151] 1983 US Inspection Report, note 131, 28.
[152] *Loc. cit.*, 131, 34.
[153] See note 107.
[154] 1985 US Inspection Report, note 103, 6.
[155] See note 103, 13.
[156] Letter dated June 24, 1987, from *D. E. Geddes*, Operations Controller, Antarctic Division, Department of Scientific and Industrial Research, New Zealand, on file. (Hereinafter cited as *Geddes* letter.) See also *E. P. Le Lievre*, Environmental Implications of the Human Presence in the Antarctic, Masters Thesis, University of Canterbury (1986).

The Harco incinerator, installed during the 1972—73 season, is used to dispose of all of Scott Base's burnable waste, using diesel fuel and waste oils as fuel.[157] In contrast, the Warren incinerator uses an air-starving process that gasifies the volatile part of the waste, and then completely burns this gas in the secondary combustion stage. This method of incineration, more commonly referred to as waste distillation or pyrolysis (the burning of materials in the absence of oxygen), is meant to reduce stack emissions, and thus, it is hoped, to reduce environmental pollution.[158]

The rebuilding program for the Casey, Davis and Mawson Stations operated by the Australian Antarctic Division includes the installation of a new waste management system. Like New Zealand, Australia has installed two-stage, high-temperature Warren incinerators at each of these stations. The new incinerators burn organic matter, paper and wood products and most plastics.[159] Non-PVC plastics are being burnt, while any doubtful plastics and other non-burnable wastes are supposed to be returned to Australia,[160] as are incinerator residues.[161]

Four key points are raised by the intended introduction of pyrolysis technology into the Antarctic at the present time. First, just as with more traditional forms of incineration, there is a great potential for incomplete burning, chemical reformation, and toxic air emissions. Addition of air at a later stage in the process may alter the relative proportions of the chemicals formed, but does not guarantee that they will be of lower toxicity. This is of particular concern given that New Zealand and Australia intend to burn some plastics in their new incinerators. Second, pyrolysis, like any other burn technology, will leave behind a residue that is undeniably more toxic than source waste.[162] Ash from high temperature hazardous waste incineration, for example, is treated as hazardous waste itself, and is appropriately disposed of in landfills at hazardous waste sites. The ash is produced as the result of incomplete combustion. Ideally, solid waste should be incinerated to a fully oxidized state in order to eliminate potentially hazardous residues.[163]

---

[157] See note 96.

[158] See note 156, 114.

[159] *Bleasel* letter, supra note 94. See also letter dated April 30, 1985 from The East Melbourne Laboratories Proprietary Limited to Mr. *S. Lewandowski* regarding its "Appraisal of Atmospheric Pollutants — Garbage Incinerators — Mawson, Casey and Davis Bases, Antarctica", on file.

[160] *Goldsworthy* telex, note 104.

[161] *Bleasel* letter, note 94.

[162] Telex dated April 28, 1987, from *Shelly Stuart* of Greenpeace — Seattle, on file, (hereinafter cited as *Stuart* Telex).

[163] Interview with Dr. *William Linak*, Combustion Research/Hazardous Waste Laboratory, EPA Office of Research and Development. (Hereinafter cited as *Linak* interview).

The management and disposal of the residue from pyrolysis incineration is an important environmental concern.

Third, the technology incorporated by the Warren incinerator has been used only on a "pilot project" basis, and has not been rigorously tested.[164] Pyrolysis was experimented with in the U.S. in the mid-1970s, but is not in use today in the U.S.[165] Thus, a rather slim database appears to exist on which to support claims that the technology is either environmentally benign and/or superior to current methods of waste incineration practiced in the Antarctic.

Fourth, it is unclear how burnable plastics will, in practice, be segregated from PVC and other harmful plastics, which raises the possibility that practices may differ from policies.

Regarding the Code of Conduct's recommendation that all burning of wastes be monitored scientifically, there is insufficient data on the level of compliance by particular countries on which to base any firm conclusion, but this does appear to be an area that deserves particular attention.

b) U.S. Practice

The NSF contracted a study on the installation of incinerators at McMurdo. Although the study recommended the use of incinerators in tandem with compactors and balers, the NSF apparently has decided not to act on these findings for the time being, partly for technological reasons. NSF personnel have expressed skepticism about the efficacy of the incinerators now being installed by the Australians and New Zealanders.[166]

There is no active program in the USAP to monitor air emissions, including the periodic burnings at the Fortress Rock dump. According to the Sanitary Landfill Report, the impacts of the dump burnings are small and "localized."[167] Certain wooden items and a small amount of paper are burned in the area near the Palmer Station heliport.[168]

---

[164] *Stuart* telex, note 162.

[165] Interview with Dr. *Jim Kilgroe*, Combustion Research/Municipal Waste Laboratory, EPA Office of Research and Development. (Hereinafter cited as *Kilgroe* interview.) According to letters on file dated 1 May and 11 September 1986, from *R. B. Thomson*, Director, Antarctic Division, Department of Science and Industrial Research, New Zealand, a similar incinerator has been used at a local hospital.

[166] *Schatz* interview, note 97.

[167] *Waldrip* Report, note 89.

[168] *Fowler* interviews, note 101.

4. *Retrograding of Waste*

The Code of Conduct recommends that batteries, harmful lubricating oils, plastics, rubber products, and waste containing isotopes be removed from the Treaty area.[169]

a) General Practice

The Australian Antarctic Division is in the process of installing large trash compactors at each station.[170] It is assumed that non-burnable solid waste will be compacted, and then containerized for return to Australia. The long-term charter of the Icebird provides for the possible return to Australia (RTA) of large quantities of waste by containerization. Containerization has two main advantages. First, it allows waste to be treated as unit cargo, and second, waste can be stored as it is generated or collected, and effectively contained against dispersal. Containerization allows for the maximum amount of waste to be shipped and makes for easy handling when backloading.[171]

Argentina's Marambio Base uses an industry-sized trash compactor for non-burnable wastes, which are baled and retrograded to Argentina.[172] Non-combustible solid waste at Argentina's Jubany Station is assembled in drums and removed from the area by ship.[173]

Non-burnable waste at China's Great Wall Station is transported out of the area, although it is unclear exactly how or where it is disposed of.[174]

Non-burnable solid waste is retrograded from West Germany's Georg von Neumayer Station in containers.[175] The West German Antarctic program's policy is to retrograde all harmful and non-burnable waste, although precise statistics are unavailable.[176]

At Syowa (Japan), non-biodegradable refuse is compacted and retrograded to Japan. Chemical wastes are removed from the Treaty area.

For several years (1972—77), New Zealand retrograded scrap metal, glass, plastic and other non-burnable waste material from Scott Base (See Table II). This waste was transported by sea in February and by outbound empty U.S. aircraft in October.[177] Recyclable materials were

---

169 See, in general, Code of Conduct, note 3.
170 *Bleasel* letter, note 94.
171 *Loc. cit.*
172 1983 US Inspection Report, note 131, 46.
173 *Loc. cit.*, 17.
174 *Loc. cit.*, 14.
175 *Loc. cit.*, 37.
176 *Hempel* letter, note 102.
177 1983 US Inspection Report, note 131, 28.

sold to manufacturers or recycling plants in Canterbury to raise funds for the Scott Base Social Club, while the remaining waste was sent to a Christchurch dump.[178]

As mentioned previously, in recent years, New Zealand has made increasing use of the Fortress Rock dump operated by the U.S. near McMurdo Station. At the same time, there has been a falling-off in the amounts of waste material being retrograded. This drop coincided with complaints from the U.S. Navy regarding the cargoes of crushed cans and smashed bottles being retrograded by New Zealand aboard U.S. aircraft, as well as difficulties with Christchurch dump administrators over the deposit of the waste.[179] This latter difficulty has been compounded by the Ministry of Agriculture and Fisheries (Agricultural Quarantine Service), which has classified waste from the Ross Dependency as "foreign" in origin. The Antarctic Division is currently negotiating with the MAF to ease the import restrictions on Antarctic waste.[180]

> Every endeavor has been made . . . to ensure that plastics, rubber products and batteries are returned to New Zealand. However, over the past two years stricter rules imposed by local authorities regarding importation of items into New Zealand and limited returning transportation are causing great difficulties. . . .[181]

Such resistance to the dumping of retrograded Antarctic waste in New Zealand has been persistent, as witnessed by the refusal of the municipal dump at Wellington to allow a recent West German research expedition (GANOVEX) to offload the garbage that had been carefully collected and containerized during its stay in the Antarctic.[182]

Empty fuel drums, building materials, old parts and supplies, old vehicles and batteries are returned to South Africa.[183] At the Sarie Marais field station, certain items are returned to SANAE for export to South Africa.[184]

Uruguay, because of the small size of its Antarctic operation, is able to retrograde all the non-burnable rubbish generated by its activities.[185]

Scrap metal is sent back to the USSR from Bellingshausen Station.[186]

---

178 *Monteath*, note 96.
179 *Ibid.*
180 *Geddes* letter, note 156.
181 Letter dated September 11, 1986, from *R. B. Thomson*, note 165.
182 See note 96.
183 1983 US Inspection Report, note 131, 34.
184 See note 107.
185 *Galarza* letter, see note 103.
186 1985 US Inspection Report, note 103, 13.

b) U.S. Practice

In response to the ASOC waste disposal survey, ***Dr. Peter Wilkniss*** of the U.S. National Science Foundation stated that:

> [W]aste such as tires, batteries, waste oils, and anti-freeze are returned to the United States for disposal . . . Waste disposal is carefully organized and repeatedly reviewed. . . .[187]

The U.S. program has, for the last several years, retrograded empty gas bottles, obsolete and waste oil, various other waste liquids, batteries, and tires by air to either New Zealand or the U.S.[188], but no statistics are available about what is returned, and how quantities of particular items, such as tires and batteries, compare to quantities shipped to Antarctica. There also is some doubt about compliance with the policy, based on the photographs taken by Greenpeace in February 1987 at McMurdo. Those photographs show all sorts of barrels and debris tumbling into the sea, including one vehicle chassis with at least six tires visible.

A primary difficulty associated with the retrogradation of materials from the Antarctic by air concerns the loading of the aircraft. Airborne materials have to be contained and securely stowed aboard aircraft in order to ensure safe operation of the plane. Likewise, an aircraft has to be balanced so as not to endanger its take-off and landing capabilities. Under Antarctic conditions, and given the manpower and equipment in place at McMurdo, for example, this is a difficult and time-consuming task. In addition, the airfield at McMurdo is an ice runway, not concrete, an added consideration when composing aircraft cargoes.[189]

A further point is that the Navy assigns priority status on outbound aircraft to items that must be repaired and returned to Antarctica. Although no comprehensive statistics are available covering the composition of outbound cargoes and space utilization, the impression is given that the Navy places highest priority on fulfilling its supply and maintenance support missions, and schedules its aircraft and other vessels and their cargoes accordingly.

Field camps in the Dry Valleys retrograde all waste, which then is disposed of as discussed above, depending on which station it is taken

---

[187] Letter from *Peter Wilkniss*, Director, Department of Polar Programs, National Science Foundation, on file.

[188] See, in general, U. S. Navy, Report of Operation Deepfreeze 86. Greenpeace's recent Antarctic expedition photographed a number of tires at the McMurdo dump, in a pile of rubbish that is falling into the sea. (Photographs on file at Greenpeace International, Washington, D. C.) According to NSF spokespersons, tires and batteries sometimes are put in the wrong place at the dump, but are recovered and retrograded as a matter of policy.

[189] *Schatz* interview, note 97.

to. Camps in the snowfields or glacial areas follow different practices depending on their size. Large camps generally bury their waste in snow pits. Smaller field parties will retrograde solid waste but dispose of liquid waste in snow pits.[190]

IV. The Beginnings of a Model Program

1. *Observations*

The combined strategy of compacting and retrograding wastes to the country of origin and installing effective sewage treatment facilities may form the beginnings of a model waste disposal program. High-temperature incinerators, if proven effective outside the Antarctic, could play a major role in a responsible program, but only on the conditions that (1) no hazardous or potentially hazardous materials such as plastics are allowed to be burned, and (2) that a careful effluent monitoring program is carried out.

Bearing in mind the cooperative mandate of the Antarctic Treaty, it would make sense for the ATCPs to convene a meeting of national Antarctic program managers, logisticians and waste management experts to discuss their respective situations, to evaluate model elements of existing programs, and to develop a long-term regional plan for waste management, and for the monitoring of the effects of each waste disposal program.

The inadequate response by governments to the SCAR panel's survey points out the need to increase the amount and kind of information being collected by ATCPs on the activities of their national Antarctic programs. Such information should be included in the exchanges of information called for by the Antarctic Treaty. Future inspection teams should include observers with the professional background to gather data on waste disposal procedures currently being employed, as well as to make on-site judgments on the environmental effects.

2. *Recommendations*

The following recommendations are put forward as a preliminary framework for developing a comprehensive waste management policy for the Antarctic:

1. The existing Code of Conduct should be adopted in the appropriate way by all member states of the Antarctic Treaty that were not ATCPs when it was originally adopted.

---

[190] *Fowler* interviews, note 101.

2. Every Treaty member should, if it has not already done so, enact binding waste handling and disposal regulations that are consistent with or stronger than the Code of Conduct and applicable Agreed Measures, covering all aspects of its program, and also take steps to ensure that the necessary equipment and procedures are in place to assure compliance.

3. A new Code of Conduct should be prepared by the ATCPs, based on input from biological scientists and logisticians in national programs, SCAR, IUCN and other interested organizations, that addresses all current waste disposal issues. The new code should include performance and monitoring criteria, a commitment to regularly keep each other informed about impacts of particular practices, and an obligation to progressively refine the Code in the light of new information and technology. It should be given a more binding quality, perhaps as a new Agreed Measure.

4. Ocean disposal, incineration or burial of plastics, in whatever form, should be banned within the Antarctic Treaty area and the CCAMLR area, as an Agreed Measure under the Treaty and as a conservation measure under CCAMLR.

5. To the maximum extent possible, the initial generation of "waste materials" should be minimized. This can be accomplished only if each national Antarctic program adopts this as a policy, and then takes firm steps to systematically review and reconsider what is taken to Antarctica, how it is packaged, and how it may be used again either in its program or some other Antarctic program.

6. To the maximum extent possible, materials should be re-used or recycled (in Antarctica where possible, or in the country of origin). This would include the re-using of packing boxes and crates, fuel drums, machinery (either given/sold to other countries in the area, or returned to the country of origin), and the recycling of glass, metals, paper products, chemicals, etc.

7. To the maximum extent possible, all waste products should be retrograded to the country of origin, or to another country if that is more logical and cost-effective, and disposed of by appropriate methods. All stations should use efficient trash compactors, to ease removal. Although the removal of wastes will be more expensive than local disposal, particularly in the short run, this cost must be regarded as the price of operating in the Antarctic, given the goal of providing maximum protection to its pristine environment. Logic dictates that this option is technically feasible, as all material that is brought down to the Antarctic leaves empty ship or plane space on the return trip that could be filled with waste materials.

8. Every base should establish a regular program of monitoring all effluents and point sources of water and air pollution, to establish a record of what actually is going on. This data should be related to regular scientific monitoring of various ecosystem indicators, including measurements of air and water quality and of contamination of various organisms in the region surrounding the facility.

9. Where bases or facilities are in close proximity, a cooperative approach should be employed to make best use of each facility's equipment and logistics capabilities, bearing in mind the timing of vessels and aircraft.

10. There should be agreement at an ATCM on a general program of cleaning up Antarctica. Given that some portion of the accumulated wastes of the past thirty years can be removed, an Antarctic clean-up may initially require the dedication of additional ships specifically for that purpose. Areas such as McMurdo Bay should receive priority attention.

11. New technologies to incinerate wastes should be tested and perfected in the some country, not in the Antarctic. All incineration facilities that are installed should include monitoring equipment to measure precisely what contaminants are being produced and released to the environment, through whatever means.

12. State-of-the-art technology should be employed to ensure that sewage discharge does not cause adverse environmental impacts, with the caveat that the treatment process should not cause more problems than it solves. The possibility of using sewage as a source of energy for stations should be studied.

13. Because most stations use fuel oil to generate electric power, as well as for both land and air vehicles, it would make sense to erect small physical barriers to impede the spread of leaks into the surrounding areas and nearby bodies of water. No stations appear to have taken this step, or the more extensive measure of building large protective berms around their fuel tanks, to protect the local environment against the possibility of a massive oil leak.

3. The Energy Linkage

There are linkages between energy use, waste disposal and pollution that should be considered more carefully. It is apparent that few member governments have given serious thought to the long-term benefits of using alternative energies, such as wind and solar power and biomass.

The ATCPs should commission SCAR or some other appropriate body to conduct an energy study of existing and projected levels of energy use for the next ten years, and an analysis of how alternative energies could be employed, bearing in mind the benefits of possible reductions in air pollution, number of containers devoted to transporting oil, and waste to be disposed of. This study should consider the inter-relationships of waste and energy using a time frame of at least 25 years.

The USSR uses three wind-driven electric generators installed at Novolazarevskaya Station in 1982. These generators are driven by two-bladed propellers with a total wing span of four meters. Each generator produces 3.5 KW at a constant speed of 109 revolutions per minute. Automatic controls keep the blades aligned to the wind and adjust propeller pitch to produce a constant output despite variations in wind velocity. The power thus generated is used to heat the buildings and reportedly was adepuate to the task in even the coldest months of 1982.[191] Such alternative sources of energy should be investigated for all bases and research stations.

The NSF has in the past considered and rejected solar power as an alternative, cleaner source of energy for the USAP. The stated reasons for the NSF rejection include the need for "massive" construction, and the use of batteries and acids required by solar systems.[192] The study was not made public for review and comment. An energy audit conducted at McMurdo in 1984 concluded that: "Over the years, little or no consideration has been given to energy conservation" and recommended that a "conservation program be initiated for all stations or areas. . . ."

---

[191] 1983 US Inspection Report, note 131, 30.
[192] *Schatz* interview, note 97.

Appendix

Code of Conduct for Antarctic Expeditions and Station Activities

1. Waste disposal

The following are recommended procedures:

(a) Solid Waste

(i) Non-combustible, including chemicals (except batteries). These materials may be disposed of at sea either in deep water or, if this is not possible, at specified sites in shallow water.

(ii) Batteries should be removed from the Antarctic Treaty Area.

(iii) Combustibles

— Wood, wood products and paper should be incinerated, the ash being disposed of at sea.

— Lubricating oils may be burnt except those containing harmful additives which should be removed from the Antarctic Treaty Area.

— Carcasses and materials associated with imported experimental animals should be incinerated.

— All plastics and rubber products should be removed from the Antarctic Treaty Area.

(b) Liquid Waste

(i) Human waste, garbage and laundry effluents should, where possible, be macerated and be flushed into the sea.

(ii) Large quantities of photographic liquids should be treated for the recovery of silver and the residue should be flushed into the sea.

(c) The above procedures are recommended for coastal stations. Field sites supported from coastal stations should, where feasible, use the facilities of their supporting station. Inland stations should concentrate waste in deep pits. Except as stated for inland stations, waste should not be buried.

(d) Waste containing radio-isotopes should be removed from the Antarctic Treaty Area.

(e) Every effort should be made to reduce the plastic packaging of products imported into the Antarctic Treaty Area.

(f) If possible the use of leaded fuels or fuels containing ethylene bromide and ethylene chloride should be avoided.

(g) When incinerators are used it is desirable to monitor effluents.

Source: Recommendation VIII-11, Antarctic Treaty, REPORT OF THE EIGHTH CONSULTATIVE MEETING (Oslo: June 1975).

Table I

ATCP	MARPOL	DUMPING	LOSC
Argentina	—	A	S
Australia	—	—	S
Belgium	—	—	S
Brazil	—	A	S
Chile	—	A	S
China	—	—	S
France	R	R*	S
FRG	—	A	—
Japan	—	A	S
New Zealand	—	R	S
Norway	R	R	S
Poland	—	A	S
South Africa	—	A	S
United Kingdom	—	R*	—
United States	—	R	—
U.S.S.R.	—	R*	S
Uruguay	—	—	S
Total = 18	2	13	15

A = Acceded
R = Ratified
R* = Ratified the annex only
S = Signatory

Source: Multilateral Treaties Deposited with the Secretary-General, UN Doc. ST/LEG/SER. E/3. Treaties in Force, U. S. Dept. of State.

Table II

NEW ZEALAND WASTE RETROGRADATION: 1972—1977
(In Kilograms)

Year	Scrap Metal	Glass	Plastic	Other
1972—73	300	60	—	—
1973—74	500	60	—	—
1974—75	850	320	190	250
1975—76	2800	700	160	350
1976—77	3280	600	460	—

Source: *Monteath, Colin,* Waste Not Left Behind at Scott Base, Antarctic (September 1977), 101.

Comment:
Waste Disposal: Need for Further Regulation?

*Roberto Puceiro Ripoll**

In order to examine the problem of waste disposal in the Antarctic Treaty System, we must first study its regulations, general implications and its present realities. I hope I am able to do so, to some extent, from a juridical point of view, though I do not forget — it has been wrongly said that lawyers are always more ready to get a man into trouble than out of it.

Mr. *Barnes* has kindly shown us, in a very complete way, the different facets of this topic and the need for its constant polishing and care. The Agenda for the next Antarctic Treaty Consultative Meeting includes once again the subject of waste disposal, and this shows us that the states are worried about it to some extent. Do they consider that the existing regulation is now insufficient, or that it is not properly and effectively applied?

The Consultative Parties have been especially careful in taking general, yet concrete and realistic, measures related to the preservation of man's impact on the Antarctic environment.

The philosophy of these general measures arise from the very principles ruling the matter, and are expressed in different Recommendations of the System. We can summarize them as follows:

a) the ecosystem of the Antarctic Treaty Area is vulnerable to human interference;

b) the Antarctic derives much of its scientific importance from its uncontaminated and relatively undisturbed condition;

c) in considering measures for a wise use and protection of the Antarctic environment, the states shall act in accordance with their responsibility for ensuring that such measures are consistent with the interests of all mankind;

d) no act or activity having an inherent tendency to modify the environment over wide areas within the Antarctic Treaty Area should be undertaken unless appropriate steps have first been taken;

* Dr. *Roberto Puceiro Ripoll*, Legal Adviser, Uruguayan Antarctic Institute, Montevideo, Uruguay. The opinions expressed in this volume are the personal views of their authors only.

e) environmental assessment procedures should not prejudice one of the fundamental principles of the Antarctic Treaty providing for freedom of scientific investigation, and such procedures should not encroach upon nor prejudice provisions for the protection of the environment, nor the conservation of living resources.

Specifically related with waste disposal, the first major step is Recommendation VIII-11, which recommends to Governments that "[t]o the greatest extent feasible they observe the code of conduct annexed to this Recommendation at their stations and for their activities within the Antarctic Treaty Area."

This "Code of Conduct for Antarctic Expeditions and Station Activities" was drawn up by the Scientific Committee on Antarctic Research (SCAR) recommending procedures on different matters, waste disposal being one of them. We have recommendations and procedures on this subject, indicating the method of eliminating or removing different solid and liquid wastes from the Antarctic Treaty Area. Some states thought that the Recommendation should have been stronger, and the problem was so treated at further Consultative Meetings.

In many cases the Treaty Parties have introduced environmental protection controls to their scientific programmes and associated logistic activities, according to, and in some cases exceeding, standards established in the Code.

The second step is Recommendation XII-4. It recommends to the Governments that they seek the advice of their respective Antarctic operating agencies as to any problem which they have experienced in implementing the Code of Conduct for Antarctic Expeditions and Station Activities, and the desirability and feasibility of revising that Code.

The third step is Recommendation XIII-4, that is, specifically regarding waste disposal, recommending to the Governments that through their National Antarctic Committees they invite SCAR, using all resources available to it, to undertake a comprehensive review of the waste disposal aspects of the Annex to Recommendation VIII-11 and, giving due consideration to the need for avoiding detrimental effects on neighbouring or associated ecosystems outside the Antarctic Treaty Area and to considerations of cost effectiveness, to offer:

1) scientific advice regarding waste disposal procedures and standards that it is desirable to achieve at coastal and inland stations and field camps;

2) advice regarding the logistic feasibility of such procedures, bearing in mind Antarctic operational circumstances, including

variations in the number of personnel between stations, operational and logistic difficulties, and local circumstances;

3) such other advice as seems to SCAR to be relevant to waste disposal procedures.

The reasons why the State Parties encouraged the re-examination and revision of the subject of waste disposal were: the renewed recognition of its great importance; the eventual use in the area of new, environmentally damaging, substances; the existence of new methods of eliminating and removing waste disposal; and, last but not least, that changes have occurred in the perception of what constitutes pollution and its analytical techniques.

Taking into account Recommendation XIII-4, SCAR decided upon the establishment of a Panel of Experts on Waste Disposal to study the problem and to inform SCAR. The Panel then agreed on the following Terms of Reference:

— Assess whether present waste disposal procedures, including mechanical plant emissions at stations, field camps and on ships are, or are likely to be, harmful to the environment;
— In the event of waste disposal procedures causing environmental impacts, identify procedures that contribute to impacts;
— Review, and if necessary, make recommendations to amend the existing Code of Conduct on waste disposal; and
— Advise on monitoring studies to assess environmental impacts associated with waste at stations and field camps.

The Panel has requested vast information from national Antarctic operators on waste disposal so as to be able to make its report. It has previously consulted scientists to identify waste disposal procedures currently used in the Antarctic that contribute to environmental impacts, and to recommend monitoring studies to assess those impacts. At this moment the final report is being considered by SCAR.

Some State Parties, on the other hand, think that the existing Code of Conduct should be substituted by "Waste Disposal Objectives." Unfortunately, we are not yet aware of the Panel report and we cannot anticipate SCAR's advice. But by analyzing the elements involved, the ruling principles and the evolution process, we can make some considerations.

In general, we can state that activities in the Antarctic area have increased in diversity and importance and this has shown the necessity of developing and implementing more precise plans for Antarctic environment conservation. As more states become interested in scientific research, living marine and mineral resources activities and new activities, as the recent expansion of tourism, the potential growth in impacts in the zone will require more systematic and precise attention. For example, most of the environmental impact associated with scientific activities result from research stations and their logistic supports, which may be areas of great impact, especially in pollution through waste disposal. And this situation can become worse, as new establishments are opened, bases and stations and other facilities are extended, personnel and visitors increase and new materials are used.

Moreover, all entvironmental impacts can of course, in many cases, affect not only the activities site and its surroundings, but also ecosystems near and far. The Antarctic Treaty System does not turn its back on the protection of Antarctic environment, but faces it directly in different ways.

This is an old as well as a present situation. For example, the important problems of the Antarctic mineral resources regime which is being negotiated, refer continually, direct and indirectly, to the protection of the Antarctic environment, mainly through its institutional organization and special principles, which include requirements for the determination of the acceptability of mineral activities, environmental assessments, liability for damage and the application of proper technology and safety standards in developing mineral activities.

In order to have some final reflections on this matter, we must leave now aside the concrete problem of the necessity of reforming and improving the existing Code of Conduct on waste disposal, because we need actual and present information for that. And this task is in process. Yet we can have some reflections, some fluent and scattered thoughts in other aspects.

The measures regulating waste disposal problems are preventive, and of a directed management nature, but offer neither a means of prompt and effective control nor fluent information. A first measure in this regard could be to try to increase permanently the kind and amount of information available on waste disposal and its actual impact in Antarctica. More complete and renewed information of national practices and experiences could allow actual enforcement of standing conservation rules, and help to detect unknown negative effects in Antarctic activities deriving from waste disposal. To that end, we can use some different means of information and control, such as the exchange of information according to the Antarctic Treaty and national reports to SCAR, inspections developed by official observers in accordance with the Antarctic Treaty, and environmental reports produced by State Parties on eventual waste disposal impacts.

Let me now divert your attention to a simple but illustrative example about national reports or assessments, related to my country. First of all, in the Memorandum attached to the notification made by the Uruguayan Government when applying for Consultative Status, it stated that while aware of the need of avoiding redundancy in scientific efforts, the Uruguayan Antarctic Institute believed that concentration of human activity in Antarctica, which is virtually unique in it, would itself offer opportunities for research relevant to questions of environmental impact analysis. In a second instance, and in carrying out these ideas, in 1985 Uruguay started a monitoring program on environment. The researching program is developed on King George Island in a 12 km^2 area, and is directed to a survey of the Enterobactereacea family. The samples are taken from shore and interior waters, soil and fauna. Thus, five families and eighteen species have been isolated. The program points to a select and appropriate index to be used in such area, once a complete relationship of the enterobacteria present in the area has been obtained, and their adaptation and survival capacity in the environment, including winter time, as well as their sources, have been studied. This project then will allow, in the future, the measurement of the incidence of waste disposal in this Antarctic environmental area. This reveals that newcomer states are also aware of the great importance of the subject, and they therefore care about it and work effectively on it.

Coming back to information and control, we stated the necessity of implementing more effective and expeditious measures for accomplishing them. To that effect, we consider that regulation arising from the existing, or future, Code of Conduct on waste disposal may be effective, not only by the quality of its rules but because it is known to exist and is enforced. Responsibility for enforcing the Agreed Measures on the subject lies with all the Antarctic Treaty Parties with respect to their nationals.

Therefore, formal reports by State Parties on their efforts to implement and ensure compliance with existing rules, legislative or enforcement actions, are desired.

We know that some states may not be very inclined to give this kind of information, as a defending position and natural reaction. However, this information is vital to reach final conclusions. It would also be desirable to look for a method of extending the application of measures on waste disposal to all states, organizations and individuals developing activities in Antarctica, including non-governmental activities.

At this stage, we could try to essay an answer to the original question. Does waste disposal need further regulation? We do not know yet. We can detect strong feelings among some State Parties that the subject must be adapted to new realities, but we do not yet know them precisely.

However, every new measure must be idealistic but also realistic and actually applicable. In deciding this subject we must think that theoretical solutions are not proper: "*Ce qui est vrai à la lampe n'est pas toujours vrai au soleil.*" Moreover, the improvements of the existing regime on waste disposal not only must include rules of recommendations and procedures but also some effective and special measures to assure the compliance with these rules. The Antarctic Treaty System has some *fiat* in his soul, and we trust it can, by itself, create a proper and harmonious small universe for the benefit of the whole Planet.

Comment

*Sudhir Chopra**

Human activity has now worked significant changes on the global scale, within the span of a few human generations: the burning of fossil fuels, for example, is injecting carbon dioxide into the atmosphere at unprecedented rates. The atmospheric concentrations of this gas has increased by nearly 25 % since the industrial revolution, and by over 10 % since 1958 alone. At this rate it will double within a century. Carbon dioxide-produced "greenhouse" effects and the present rate of increase of atmospheric carbon dioxide will produce, according to climate predictions prepared by NASA, an average global increase of at least two degrees centigrade in surface temperature during the next century. This will be an increase comparable to that experienced during the last Ice Age, that of 18,000 years ago. So what happened in 18,000 years we plan to do in the next hundred years.

Together with mild shifts in precipitation there are also a number of other green-house gases, including fluorocarbons and tropospheric ozone. Although the concentrations of these is presently much less than that of carbon dioxide, they are raising the effect much more rapidly. Molecule for molecule the fluoro-carbons produce 10,000 times the green-house effect as carbon dioxide, in addition to depleting the stratospheric ozone. Only one nation referred to Antarctica at the UNEP negotiations dealing with the protocol on the ozone layer. Originally studies of the green-house effects were not taken seriously; I personally refer to one of 1978 produced by Dr. *Mercer* at Ohio State University, which predicted a two-to-four degree centigrade rise in temperature, consequently resulting in the melting of west Antarctica. There are some other later studies, I am not aware, perhaps you might be, of whether they were taken seriously. Now, these reports are entirely separate from the other issues raised, such as the implications of dust, which together with the reduced reflection of sunlight will also increase the temperature of the geosphere. Geosphere and biosphere are two separate things and the temperature increase is taking place in both of them.

As *Finn Sollie* suggested, the continent will rise if the ice melts; he was very correct, and as a matter of fact about a year back I called

* Mr. *Sudhir K. Chopra*, LL.M., Antarctica Interest Group, Washington, D. C.

the California Institute of Technology and MIT, and I asked what would happen if the West Antarctic ice sheet melted. They said that the continent will rise and then that the water level will rise. The third thing they suggested was that it might even deflect the Earth's axis. And they went on to say, that if the Antarctic continent raises itself, the other continents have to adjust, quite simply. I do not know what that means, but if it does, perhaps it has very serious consequences. And how long it will be before we know that what we are doing can cause all that, that human activity can result in those kinds of consequences, may be one or two hundred years — but that is a very short time compared to 18,000 years for a rise of two degrees centigrade.

A related problem is that SCAR has not coordinated itself with the newly-created committees of ICSA. I think it is time that both the SCAR and the ATCPs take the results of these studies seriously, because it will be the first time that studies like this will be coordinated, and some kind of concrete results can be expected in the near future. Thank you very much.

Panel Discussion

Participants: *Patricia Birnie**
*Rahmatullah Khan***
*Ian Nicholson****
*Nicolas Mettra*****
*Roger Wilson******

L. Kappen, Chairman:

Well now, I want to invite the panelists, Dr. *Patrica Birnie*, Prof. *Kahn*, Mr. *Nicholson*, Mr. *Mettra* and Mr. *Wilson*. Please come to the table — I will go off. With respect to the time, I would ask you to keep to small statements, I mean about 10 minutes, everybody. Is that agreed? Then we shall almost be on time.

P. Birnie:

We heard today a great deal about the climate and biology of Antarctica and *Professor Friedmann* — whose extremely interesting and lively presentation this afternoon I very much enjoyed — drew attention to the fact that every visit in some way diminishes Antarctica. We have also had a number of interesting papers today about the present jurisdictional situation in Antarctica, in relation to some of the uses that are taking place. In *Professor Friedmann*'s case it was the question of scientific research and the problems that are generated there. In other papers we have heard about problems relating to the ambiguities concerning the status of ice, the problems generated by the ambiguities about the aerial situation — by that I mean the air space, not the scope of the Treaty — and the lack of any kind of coordinated air traffic control system. We have heard about the problems this afternoon of tourism and waste disposal. Again, attention has been drawn in the case of tourism to the problems of confusion of terminology, of jurisdictional application, the bases of jurisdiction; in the case of waste we have heard

---

* Dr. *Patricia Birnie*, London School of Economics and Political Science, U. K.

** Prof. *Rahmatullah Khan*, Jawaharlal Nehru University, New Delhi, India.

*** *Ian E. Nicholson*, Assistant Secretary, Treaties and Sea Law Branch, Department of Foreign Affairs and Trade, Canberra, Australia.

**** *Nicolas Mettra*, Direction des Affaires Juridiques, Ministère des Affaires Etrangères, Paris, France.

***** *Roger Wilson*, Political Coordinator, Antarctic Campaign, Greenpeace International, U. K.

The opinions expressed in this volume are the personal views of their authors only.

about the problems of enforcement in particular and some of the gaps in the Recommendations in relation to what is actually happening and the techniques available for disposing of waste. This leads me to consider that we already have what we refer to frequently as "constructive ambiguity." We might also have a certain amount of destructive apathy going on at the moment, since the ambiguities are generating an unwillingness to deal with some of these problems because of the difficulties of raising difficult jurisdictional questions, particularly the problem of enforcement, which seems to be acute in relation to many of the problems that we have heard about today.

Another point I wanted to make was that Antarctica may be outside the Law of the Sea Convention, as *Professor Mangone* illustrated in his paper, but it is not outside the world system, either ecologically or as a matter of international law. I have found extremely interesting — and I congratulate *Rüdiger Wolfrum* on his choice of papers this time in this respect — how very much the papers have inter-related every day, each day inter-relating within itself and also inter-relating with the other days. With regard to the question of the world system, I was interested in a point that was just made by the last speaker, concerning not only how what is going on in the outside world affects Antarctica, but also how what is going on in Antarctica itself as possibly having an effect on the outside world. This leads me to remind you about a paper that was given by Mr. *Hajost*, in which he outlined the international treaties and international organizations that already exist and which have some effect on Antarctica. I think it would be extremely useful at some future conference if we could perhaps explore some of these lines, if we could in fact hear more about the effect on the Antarctic System of these treaties: the inter-relationship of the outside treaties with Antarctica; which of the Antarctic Treaty States are parties to these other treaties, what their policies are within them and so on.

There has been much praise for the aims of the Convention, including international cooperation, freedom of scientific research, peaceful uses and so on, and we have in fact had a number of indications concerning where perhaps more coordination and cooperation are required to meet the aims of the Convention. I think papers we have had this afternoon indicate that much more could be done in these particular fields.

I personally consider that the lack of any kind of secretariat, whether it is a modest one or a less modest one, does affect the effectiveness of the System; for example, in the case of enforcement, there does not seem to be any kind of effective way of collecting the numerous complaints about the working of and gaps in the System except at meetings like this. For example, in the Whaling Commission, which I keep quoting to you, they are able to have an infraction sub-committee, which receives and discusses reports of infractions: thus, something can be said about them. These comments are reported back to the governments concerned. No international action is taken on them, but it does alert the states concerned to their failures to meet the standards and recommendations. I think perhaps this question of the secretariat is not really appropriate to discuss further today, but as I have now mentioned it, I would suggest that the question merits further papers, perhaps — if there has been no secretariat established by the next time there is a conference of this kind — on the various models that do exist, because there is a vast range internationally of different kinds of secretariats. One that I am particularly familiar with is the one that serves the Oslo and Paris Commissions and is a very modest affair, but nonetheless is able to circulate papers, deal with the infractions reports under those Conventions, collect a great deal of centralised information and sometimes organize joint meetings of these two Commissions, both with themselves and with other bodies, as well as servicing separate meetings.

I do not think that I have any more to say; I do not want to take up more time because other people are speaking, but I would like again to congratulate the organizers of the conference on their success in interrelating these problems and highlighting the gaps in the System and the possible way forward. Mr. *Khan*.

Mr. Khan:

Thank you very much. First, I take this opportunity to congratulate *Professor Wolfrum* and the Institute of International Law for holding such a fabulously organized conference with such a lovely inter-disciplinary orientation. I must express my gratitude for having been invited to this conference. My comments today relate to several issues, not necessarily limited to the presentations we have heard today.

Going back to the presentations we have heard in the last two or three days, my general comment is this: that the Antarctic Treaty System, if you look at the various provisions and the background in which it was drawn up, represents the triumph of the scientific curiosity of mankind over the instinct to grab territories, the acquisitive instinct of states for more territory. This scientific curiosity has been solely responsible for whatever success that the Treaty System achieved over a long period of time, more than 25 years. Having said that, I would not like to minimize the difficulties that this Treaty System has confronted of late. It has been demonstrated very ably in this symposium itself by various speakers that the Treaty System has confronted some intractable problems, some that Dr. *Birnie* mentioned in her presentation on the first day, such as the inter-relationship between the Law of the Sea Convention and the problem of jurisdiction arising out of Article IV of the Treaty.

Other problems have been identified by various other speakers, such as the non-existence of a comprehensive arrangement to deal with the problem of waste, the problem of air traffic, and several others. The latest and most difficult problem that has confronted the Antarctic Treaty System, in my view, is the problem of sharing the resources. This problem has become so acute that it has led to very combatative, confrontational posturing by states as well as scholars and we have witnessed some posturing here in this symposium also. I regret that this kind of posturing has been taken, hard lines have been drawn. I do not see why such hard, rigid lines ought to be taken in a symposium of this nature.

There are indications, however, amongst the statesmen and the politicians and the diplomats, of greater foresight and vision than unfortunately demonstrated by scholars. And this very vision and foresight of the statesmen has been responsible for tackling more intractable problems, like drawing up a new regime for five-eighths of the planet Earth, which was done recently —- I am referring to the new Law of the Sea Convention. If five-eights of this planet could be brought under some kind of an international regime — which admittedly has not come into effect until now — but if such a massive effort could be undertaken and successfully concluded I do not understand why one-fifth of the globe, which is occupied by Antarctica, cannot be subjected to a new international regime, given, of course, good-will and foresight.

These are two commodities which seem to be in short supply, but I am sure that such a regime would emerge, maybe in a fragmentary manner, as supplementary legislation involving mineral resources, the environmental issues and later, governing air traffic and so on. That would be the most desirable trend in the evolution of a fuller and more equitable and more just international order for the Antarctic continent. Thank you.

I. Nicholson:

I, too, have been struck, like *Pat Birnie*, by the rubbing together hereof the disciplines and the beneficial effects that has had during the course of this seminar. It certainly helps to broaden the perspective we each have arising from our different backgrounds. But, if I may, I will confine myself largely to *Professor Boczek*'s paper because he took the risk of taking my paper of two years ago further. I am delighted that he did that but I must admit to not being entirely happy with a couple of the directions in which he took it. Let me take a few points specifically.

First, although I do not think he mentioned it in the presentation, in case it remains in the printed paper, I might mention that I could not agree with the suggestion that the minerals convention is not so urgent or complex as a regime for tourism. One of the thoughts that struck me as we proceeded through our various subjects during Antarctic Challenge III was that it was even more urgent now to finish the minerals regime, because there are so many other things requiring attention which almost certainly will not get it, until we can take the minerals question off the agenda of senior Antarctic policy people. I have in mind such matters as air traffic, tourism, waste disposal, ice and so on. I was particularly stimulated by the paper on ice: the suggestions contained in it are extremely valuable.

I think we need to take a pragmatic approach as administrators, in dealing with problems primarily when we have to; it is very valuable, on the other hand, to have the academic contributions of people free to see the subject as a whole and to investigate inter-relationships across the board. But I would suggest that, in Antarctica in particular, there is a need for us to be unusually innovative and not to be too tightly bound by analogies developed for other parts of the world. That leads me to pick up a very important point raised by *Professor Boczek*, and to some comments made by *Mr. Hajost*.

First, the proposition that Antarctic waters from the very coastlines must be considered high seas and have no territorial sea or other maritime zones; I not only reject that absolutely on the ground of a Claimant position in Antarctica, from the point-of-view of a country exercising sovereignty there, but also in terms of world solutions. I think it makes no sense. We could reach that sort of ridiculous conclusion only by misapplying an analogy, or searching for an analogy which is not there. The fact that in some treaties, in some perceptions, sovereignty in territory gives rise to offshore areas says nothing about the right solution, I suggest, in Antarctica, which depends on the unique conditions of Antarctica. It depends more on the requirements of proper administration and navigation and protection of the environment and so on, as was so ably demonstrated when we looked at ice this morning. We are not bound by those elements developed for other parts of the world where sovereignty over the land is accepted by all when we come to consider what is appropriate for Antarctica. In this context it is important to note that the Law of the Sea Convention was not developed in contemplation of Antarctica, which was specifically put aside, excluded from consideration. Much of that Convention may well be relevant and applied in Antarctica, but that should not blind us to the fact that many elements in it are not appropriate, were not designed to fit Antarctica, and should not be applied there.

I think also, if I might say so, *Scott Hajost*'s analysis assumed a little too easily that international conventions which were not concluded in contemplation of application in Antarctica would apply, by looking narrowly at their terms. We must consider whether those treaties were made for Antarctica or not, both as a question of law, and as a question of fact and of common sense.

There was a point of lesser irritation, if I might also mention, in *Professor Boczek*'s analysis. That was the reference to the freedom of scientific research stopping us, if I understood him correctly, from regulating tourists, private visitors, adventurers and so on. We do indeed have a very adventurous and wealthy Australian scientist, *Dick Smith*, of whom you might have heard, who is full of bright ideas. I do not see the provision in the Antarctic Treaty relating to freedom of scientific research inhibiting the Antarctic Treaty Consultative Parties from either regulating that research or ensuring that people in other categories who might claim to be doing scientific research are in fact doing so.

In regard to the positive elements at the conclusion of *Professor Boczek*'s paper, I would make three points. First, the one at the beginning on the inconsistency of definitions: I think this is a positive reminder to all those of us who are here and will read the proceedings of this seminar, to lift our game in future and move away from some rather sloppy work. In regard to a consolidation of recommendations, I think that is timely. I am not sure we shall find someone to do it, unless *Professor Boczek* were to volunteer, until we can get minerals off our agenda. It certainly should be done as soon as possible. In regard to application to third countries and third parties, I think that the expansion of membership has, as you noted, certainly made a significant inroad into that problem.

The final point I would like to refer to is to take issue with *Professor Wolfrum*, something that I normally delight in. It may be that we do not disagree and that there is simply a semantic problem, or that I did not hear him exactly; I thought that his formulation yesterday was that the *common heritage* as a principle ran beyond the Law of the Sea Convention, Moon, Outer Space and so on. I would have problems with such a proposition; I would have less of a problem with a formulation along the lines of: that it would be prudent to acknowledge the general principle of *fairness and distributive justice*, both for its own intrinsic nature and in the interests of wider acceptability of action taken to expand the international framework of norms such as, of course, in the Antarctic Minerals Convention. And as I would always like to do, I should conclude by agreeing with *Professor Wolfrum* that, if that is what he means, this indeed will emerge as part of a successful Antarctic Treaty on minerals.

N. Mettra:

It is difficult to single out, from the varied and diverse topics dealt with today and in the limited span of time attributed to us in the panel, which element is one to react to specifically. Therefore, as I am a newcomer in the club of Antarctica, I would like to convey more a general feeling of common sense than detailed comments.

First, about the resource regime, the negotiation of which was the issue yesterday: we were talking about these negotiations as if they had already been concluded, and I was struck by the optimistic feeling conveyed by the speakers. I wonder, there is a saying in French that we must not serve the skin of the bear, before the bear is killed, and I think, we must always keep an eye on the fact that until negotiation is ended everything can happen. I think we must keep that in mind, because we *cannot* be sure of what will happen — this is only a common-sense remark.

Another point I would like to stress is the fruitful concept of *constructive ambiguity*, which was put forth yesterday and recalled by Ms. *Birnie* a few minutes ago. This concept of *constructive ambiguity* is not a satisfactory one because it leaves people frustrated and far away from the great expectations laid upon Antarctica, the issues dealt with in Antarctica. It does not answer, really, clear-cut positions. Yet, thinking of yesterday's interventions this concept of constructive ambiguity, although it is unsatisfactory, might be a sort of solution. It appears that the interventions of the speakers of today have clearly put forth the operability of the concept.

I would take up, for instance, the example of air traffic. The conclusions of the speech delivered by *Professor Francisco Orrego Vicuña* on air traffic are, in my view, one example of this concept. First of all, after this speech it was, I think, clearly recognized that the air traffic in the area will keep growing in the coming years, and that the need to provide a facility or kind of facilities must be now answered. But, as *Professor Orrego* clearly stated, the only way out of the existing vacuum must originate from some kind of international regime put forth by the parties concerned. I do not know if I make myself clearly understood. This need for an international regime is clearly felt, but now how shall we put it into force? And this is the starting point of negotiations and of, let us say, the sharing of interests which are often contradictory. But I think that the Antarctic Treaty System provides a unique forum and a unique framework to start thinking about and putting into effect such a regime, which is felt as a need, and would be clearly more needed in the years to come. That was an example which I wanted to single out. It is obviously very difficult to have clear-cut answers and every one of the speakers did stress this fact: that we are always in a grey zone — which allows us to go further and to progress. And that, I think, is the main lesson of the symposium. Thank you.

R. Wilson:

I, too, have been very impressed with the quality of the papers which we have had this afternoon, and this morning in particular. I would like to be able to comment in rather more depth on some of them than I have the time to, unfortunately. But I will confine myself to making comments primarily on *Professor Boczek's* paper, which I found very comprehensive. He assures me that 90 % of it was not delivered, and I look forward to seeing the whole. However, even that 10 % which he did manage to deliver went by me, as a non-lawyer, rather fast, and I hope you will forgive me if I use words rather loosely and not in the strict legal sense.

I should start by just giving you some background to the Greenpeace Expedition to the Antarctic, which is clearly one of the non-governmental expeditions which is of concern when we start talking about non-governmental expeditions. In fact, there have been two expeditions. In 1985/86 and in 1986/87, and currently planning is taking place for a third expedition to take place in the coming southern summer.

In the most recent summer season, there was a four-person base established on Ross Island, and there are at this moment four people over-wintering at that base, who will be picked up by our ship in the coming southern summer. The Greenpeace organization was founded in Canada, and is legally a Dutch non-profit "*Stichting*," though its head office is in the United Kingdom. It has offices in seventeen countries, world-wide. Its vessels are of various nationalities, with the vessel dedicated to the Antarctic, the *Greenpeace*, being registered under the United States flag, though its present "home" port is Auckland, New Zealand.

The point of departure on our first expedition was effectively Germany, and the ship transited via the Netherlands, Curaçao, Panama, New Zealand and Australia, before making its final departure for Antarctica. In the most recent summer season, the voyage was rather simpler, being merely a trip from New Zealand to Antarctica and back. On board the ship there were two helicopters, one of which was New Zealand-registered and one of which was United States-registered. The chief pilot was Australian, although he necessarily had both United States and New Zealand licenses. The base leader for the over-wintering team was a New Zealander, whereas the leader of the expedition itself was a citizen of the United Kingdom. Among the thirty-five people in total, I think that there were something on the order of eleven nationalities.

Many questions are raised by the wide spread of registrations and nationalities involved in our expedition, as to who in fact has jurisdiction and as a New Zealander living in the U.K., have obligations under U.K. law to provide information to the U.K. Government or to the New Zealand Government, or even to the Australian Government? Or did the organization under Dutch law have no responsibilities, or, because it was based in the United Kingdom, did it have responsibilities under U.K. law? Our legal advice was that the situation was too complex to even contemplate, and that the best solution would be provision of as much information to all Antarctic Treaty Parties, both Consultative Parties and Non-consultative Parties, without prejudice, which is in fact what we did, well before the 30 November deadline, I might add.

Particular interest also, though, attaches to the question of obligations of nationals and juridical persons under the control of Greenpeace, some of whom were residents or based in countries other than countries related to the Antarctic Treaty System. *Professor Boczek* suggested that it was logical to accept the *nationality* principle and I am not aware whether that has been tested and whether all international lawyers would necessarily accept that opinion — I am not contesting it, I just do not know.

There is a particular question which arose relatively recently which I would like to share with you, and that is a question relating to the Agreed Measures, under which the introduction of alien species into the Antarctic requires permission. In the specific circumstances, our German scientist needed the materials in the Antarctic; Germany had not at that stage ratified the Agreed Measures and so could not under German law require that an application was made (although I understand that in practice German citizens are encouraged to abide by the Agreed Measures). Did, under those circumstances, Dutch law apply to the organization as a whole, or U.K. law perhaps? We eventually came to the conclusion that since the base leader was responsible for what transpired on the base and since he was a New Zealander, that we should make an application under New Zealand law for him to import the particular alien species required. This was consequently done and approved, and I hope we have fulfilled any legal obligations that persons, natural or juridical, may have had. But it does illustrate the very complex nature of dealing with non-governmental expeditions especially where they may be multinational.

In respect to New Zealand law, my understanding is rather different from that of *Professor Boczek*. That may be at least in part due to my lack of legal training, and it may be the difference between asserting jurisdiction and claiming jurisdiction, and perhaps you will tell me if this is in fact the situation. But my understanding of the New Zealand Antarctica Act of, I think 1961, is that it at least claims jurisdiction over all New Zealanders anywhere in the Antarctic and over all persons in the New Zealand-claimed sector of the Antarctic. But that is, in effect, an aside.

I would like also to refer very briefly to the material presented by *Professor Orrego* relating to air traffic in the Antarctic. Again, it was a very interesting paper and I would support the clarification of the situation because on one occasion we found our helicopter operations in the Antarctic in a rather awkward situation. One of our helicopters had to take avoidance action in the air, when another machine appeared in the same location. This is possibly partly attributable to the policy of non-cooperation with non-governmental expeditions which some governments have adopted in the Antarctic in that neither pilot was aware of the fact that the other machine was in the area, in spite of the fact that both pilots had made their intentions known to the relevant authorities. Now, I am not intending to point the finger at anybody in particular over that situation, but merely to observe that air-traffic regulation or coordination of some description is very important, and secondly, that the policy of non-cooperation with non-governmental expeditions can be carried too far and that it may rebound with dangerous consequences.

I do not wish to comment in any depth on *Jim Barnes*' paper on waste disposal. However, I would say that it was of some surprise to members of the Greenpeace expedition that the extent of the problem in some of the areas they went to was as great as it was. We hope that in the coming Antarctic summer the Greenpeace expedition will be able to visit other locations, possibly in the Antarctic Peninsula area in addition, and we will be looking very closely at questions of waste disposal on that particular trip. Now that is not intended as a threat and I hope that we can deal with these issues in a manner which is constructive and which leads to better long-term solutions. However, I would say that if countries do wish to clean up their act in advance of our arrival, I for one would not be at all unhappy. Thank you.

L. Kappen, Chairman:

Well, thank you all for your statements.

General Discussion and Closing

L. Kappen, Chairman:

We have still a bit of time to open the general discussion. If you have any questions now to raise you are welcome to do so.

I. Friedmann:

I have a question to *Professor Boczek*. Who is paying for the costs of the rescue operations? Private, non-governmental expeditions do not have the capability to provide for their own rescue operations. They do not and cannot duplicate their resources. Only the big stations, which are big governmental operations, have reserve airplanes and reserve helicopters. Of course, commercial or private expeditions to Antarctica also take into consideration that in a certain percentage of cases emergencies must occur, but they rely on being rescued by governmental operations. Last year, the U. S. Antarctic Service did present a bill for such a rescue operation to one of the private expeditions. Are such bills valid? Are the private expeditions liable for the cost of such operations?

B. A. Boczek:

You are talking about the *Southern Quest* rescue. Now, according to U.S. practice the Government does not charge for the humanitarian emergency rescue. However, it does present a bill for transporting the rescued individuals from Antarctica — in this case, to New Zealand, and the individuals in question were presented with a bill for transportation from McMurdo to New Zealand. They were not charged at all for the rescue operation within Antarctica.

Of course, this is a very difficult problem because logically no expedition, whether national, public, or non-governmental can be sure that it is 100 % prepared for any emergency — and this is particularly true of a private expedition. So if you want to be absolutely logical you would simply say that no private expedition is ever adequately prepared for any emergency. As far as charges are concerned, they are not charged, at least, (by the United States) for the actual rescue but only for the transport from Antarctica to their homeland.

The opinions expressed in this volume are the personal views of their authors only.

L. Kappen, Chairman:

Thank you. Now, Mr. *Rebagliati*.

O. Rebagliati:

Thank you. Just a few remarks on non-governmental organizations in general. I think it is important that we recall that non-governmental organizations are subjects of internal law of national states; in fact they are legally analogous to a natural person, to a corporation, or to any other internal law institution. Now, if we consider that international relations from the point-of-view of international law is amongst states and other subjects of international law, we have to remember that relations relating to non-governmental organizations appertain to internal legislation, which in turn is being deferred by international law to their respective states or other subjects of international law. So if we make this clear, no dispute can arise in relation to the attitude which any state or other subject of international law can have towards non-governmental organizations. The dealings should be between the non-governmental organization and the state under which it is constituted, or under whose control it legally is bound.

It is not possible at all to alter the nature of international relations and international law, for we may be progressive in our minds, of course we have to be, we have to benefit from any positive contribution made by natural persons or other subjects of internal law. Nevertheless, we cannot equate the treatment, legally speaking, between states and other persons which are not subjects of international law. So, that being said, it is very clear that we cannot talk about an international duty or non-duty to cooperate with a non-governmental organization; myself, I would think that it is up to the discretion of any state to cooperate, to facilitate, to enhance. In fact, I think it is a very positive attitude if that state regards such a type of non-governmental organization as performing a positive role, and that is the widespread case. But, I could not judge at all from an international point-of-view the attitude of that sovereign state in relation to a non-governmental organization. It is a domestic question, a domestic jurisdiction question. We clearly have that perspective, that fortunately I think we cannot alter, and I say fortunately because, if we get into interfering into domestic jurisdiction — we have a very painful experience, particularly with newly-independent countries, and developing countries, which have suffered many times interference by other countries in their internal affairs, through different means. This occurs not only by violent means or economic means, there may be other, more subtle means. So, we have to bear in mind that the sovereignty and domestic jurisdiction of a state may be in play when calling for relationships between states and non-governmental organizations.

Having said that, I would like to claim that the attitude towards any non-governmental organization, either economically-orientated, producing butter, or environmentally-minded or philosophically-minded, favouring poetry, *any* kind of attitude relating to that is a clear domestic jurisdiction question, and we can only judge that under that focus. In sum, if we are going to consider the internal attitude of every state relating to non-governmental organizations, we are entering into the field which is beyond the realm of international relations as such. We can enter that field, but we have to be aware that we are not dealing with the same subject matter which poses to us an international community regulated by international law. Thank you.

S. Hajost:

Thank you. I do not have the U. S. policy on support of expeditions in front of me, and I have not had the opportunity to look at it for some time, but based on my recollection of it, I may have to disagree with *Professor Boczek* in his assessment. If I recall correctly, the United States reserves the right to seek, in accordance with international law and domestic law, recovery of all direct and indirect costs of any emergency search-and-rescue. When we were formulating that policy, the reference to international law was included because of the belief that for rescues at sea international law such as reflected in the Salvage Convention would not authorize the seeking of recompense for rescue "at sea," as compared to rescue "on land."

Second, I would like to respond to something *Ian Nicholson* said concerning my paper. I would just like to re-emphasize that my survey was indeed not intended to be definitive as far as the application of any particular agreement goes. I simply attempted to identify ones which from a global perspective seemed to be applicable to Antarctica.

I would like to take a moment to respond, for the record, to *Professor Lagoni*'s comments on my paper from way back on Tuesday, which I did not get a chance to respond to. He mentioned the General Assembly: I did include a reference to the General Assembly in my oral and written paper. He also made reference to the Civil Liability and FUND Conventions, that is, for oil pollution damage from ships, possibly applying. It is quite clear from the drafting that they apply exclusively to pollution damage in the land territory and the territorial sea. The 1984 Protocols, which are not yet in force, extended them to the EEZ, but the EEZ is definitely not an area beyond national jurisdiction.

He also made reference to the International Labour Organisation. In my written paper I did refer to two or three International Labour Organisation agreements which I did not refer to in my oral presentation — I am not yet convinced that the ILO is an organization that has a real direct interest in Antarctica, so I did not include that in my survey. He also made reference to the World Heritage Convention. We have had the opportunity in the U. S. to look at that agreement, and have come to the conclusion that with its specific references and link to territory, it could not be applicable in Antarctica, at least as drafted. And finally, he made reference to some Laws of War agreements. For obvious reasons, I think, I did not include any of those in my survey.

I would like to turn to another point that *Ian Nicholson* made. He categorically rejected the idea that high seas could extend all the way up to the Antarctic Coast, and he gave as one ground the view of the Claimant. I am not so clear as to the other grounds he gave and I would be very interested in any elaboration that might be added in this regard.

I shall wrap up with one last point. *Jim Barnes* asked a question yesterday on the Non-claimant perspective with respect to application of the minerals regime and offshore areas of Antarctica, and I think I might try and give a short answer, in addition to what *Professor Wolfrum* said yesterday. I think the first thing you would have to say is that the Non-claimants might not be in complete agreement on what the juridical basis would be for application of the Minerals Convention to the off-shore areas of Antarctica. You could run the gamut of those Non-claimants that have not signed the Law of the Sea Convention, saying there is no legal relevance of Part XI thereof and the International Sea-Bed Authority, and that the Antarctic Treaty Parties may agree to cooperate in managing mineral resources within the high seas areas within the scope of the Treaty. They could also take the view, as expressed by *Ian Nicholson*, that in a negotiation of the Law of the Sea Convention, there was no intention for Part XI to apply to the off-shore areas of Antarctica. They can also argue that since these is no consensus that the off-shore areas of Antarctica are beyond national jurisdiction, the Law of the Sea Convention's definition of the Area cannot apply in any event in this case. I do not believe the Non-claimants have to rely on any single one of these approaches. I think it is quite clear that the Non-claimants on the whole are satisfied with their juridical authority to conclude the Minerals Convention with respect to off-shore areas of Antarctica as well as on land. Thank you.

L. Kappen, Chairman:

Thank you. Well, *Mr. Heap.*

J. Heap:

Thank you, Mr. Chairman. I would just like to make a couple of small points, and then one rather more general point. The two small points relate to the paper given us by *Professor Boczek*. My understanding is that he said that the United Kingdom did not have legislation which related to visitors in the territory over which the United Kingdom asserts sovereignty in the Antarctic. This is not the case. We do have such legislation.

The second is to point out that some play has been made in the discussion on *Professor Boczek*'s paper about the problems that were raised by the *Southern Quest* sinking in Antarctica. I think it is fair to recall that there have in fact been two incidents in which private expeditions have been involved in rescue, and the other one was where the private expedition rescued four members of a national expedition. Perhaps the more general point that I want to make was actually raised in my mind very strongly by *Roger Wilson*'s graphic description of what seemed to be a jurisdictional nightmare. However, I am not sure that it is. There is a quite reasonable way out of many of the problems which he has posed. That is, of course, that the basis of jurisdiction over Greenpeace's expedition with its many people of different nationalities in the Antarctic, since it was in the Ross Dependency, should indeed be jurisdiction by New Zealand on the basis of its territorial claim. This leads me to reflect that there has been a presumption which has gone through today's sessions, perhaps because of the papers that have been read — but the natural order of things in Antarctica is to seek jurisdiction on the basis of nationality. I would like to suggest that that is an assertion which needs fairly careful scrutiny, and it needs to be scrutinized against the other possibility, which is that the natural way of doing things in the Antarctic is indeed on the basis of jurisdiction on the basis of territory. Thank you.

L. Kappen, Chairman:

Mr. Barnes, you are next on my list.

J. Barnes:

John (Heap) has picked up one of the points that I wanted to make, which is that there are examples of private expeditions rescuing and assisting government expeditions: I think that is an important point to put before the record. I believe that it was the Transglobe Expedition, was it not, *John*, the one you were referring to, which picked up some African researchers and saved their lives.

The second point I want to make is that we have this peculiar situation in Antarctica where many governments are operating and there are all these various theories about basis for jurisdiction and so forth, but we sometimes lose sight of the fact because of the "crazy" nature of the mixture of various theories, that governments in general have inherent responsibilities in certain respects, which are not to be withheld on a discriminatory basis. I would just toss out some of the ones that ought to be considered in that category, which should not be seen as the kind of assistance to private expeditions that many governments say that they are not going to provide. In my view, these would include basic things that the governments are always providing in territories which they are responsible for, which include provisions, basic information about safety to people in whichever guise they are operating in, like ice and weather information and so forth — mail service might be well included in this kind of class. I think you can distinguish things like providing fuel for people on private expeditions, or providing actual assistance, and exercising the other kind of normal powers, police powers, which states provide to all people operating in that area. I think it will be a step forward for the system as a whole if the governments did put together a method of making certain that that information is available to all people that happen to be in Antarctica, whatever their motive and whatever their background, be it government or non-government. Thank you.

L. Kappen, Chairman:

Now, *Mr. Berguño.*

J. Berguño:

Thank you, sir. I would like very much to say something which is generally addressed to *Professor Boczek*'s paper, and to the reaction and comments by the panel on that particular paper and on the question of the performance of the Consultative Parties with regard to expeditions, these non-governmental organizations, and other matters. I think a general picture of weakness or anarchy or *laissez-faire* emerges from that, which really does not do justice at all to what the Consultative Parties have done. The actual practice, of course, is related to the obligation of information which comes out from Article VII paragraph 4, I believe, and Article X, and the two have to be put together as a coherent interpretation, and as a coherent practice which has been followed. I think *Professor Boczek* at some point said that such a practice has not been carried out. We should look into the matter, because it is indeed a matter which is covered by the exchange of information. As to our compliance, I hope that there are no challenges to that, and we would want very much to have an impression if the performance of others in some way is lacking in this matter. But we also have to exercise this function within the bounds of common sense, and we have done so, trying to skirt the issue of jurisdiction as far as possible. I think this is something that we have to bear in mind. Article X has been exercised quite cogently and coherently by the Consultative Parties. Some of the new Consultative Parties know well that they were often approached on the matter. So I do not think the States Parties of the Treaty and the Consultative Parties in particular, have been found in any sense wanting on this matter.

Now, it is always said and it can always be said, about any organization, about any international system or sub-system, that there are weaknesses. The notion that comes out very strongly from some of the interventions here is that the system is not efficient, is not working, is not accomodating the new uses, while what we have as an example from the historic tradition of the Treaty is precisely the contrary demonstration. What we have seen is that the Treaty is, within the contemporary international system, as a sub-system, quite efficient. So I would agree with Mr. *Khan* when he says, "Let us apply the new internationalism," but the new internationalism is in fact the actual practice by the Parties of the Antarctic Treaty System, which is much richer and more resourceful than what we find in other areas of the world. We would very much like that the Antarctic Treaty System be completed by the Nuclear-Free-Zone in the Pacific, that such a Nuclear-Free-Zone be accepted by all. We would very much like that the LOS Convention be implemented and not remain as it is. We would like to expand the Antarctic Treaty, and to have cooperation in science and to have protection on an environmental and international cooperative basis on other areas of the Earth. I think that would be a very good challenge. So let us look with equity at what the Antarctic Treaty has done actually and what has been performed in other areas of the world, and let us say sincerely what the balance is.

Now, as to the question of jurisdiction, I think *John Heap* already made a very good point. But to make it more precise, I think the issue of jurisdiction as it has been developed in the Antarctic has been approached in a constructive and functional manner. I think there *Professor Boczek* was right when he expounded on the question of the constructive jurisdiction arising from the bases. That is one jurisdiction which is very appropriate, and I think when *Roger Wilson* explained the sort of problems a non-governmental expedition would have, he really not only illustrated the underlying complexities but he also, I hope not inadvertently, illustrated what the right approach was: to give information to every Party concerned. We in the Treaty System would know very well to whom we would address our request of information, because we address, as *Orlando (Rebagliati)* has said, states and not government expeditions. But when these non-governmental expeditions really wanted action on a matter which concerned a territorial area, they went to a territorial authority, precisely to the territorial authority of the base concerned. That makes sense, and that authority surely is the one which is apt to cope with questions like tourist and air expeditions. It looks from a functional approach, that in some cases nationality will indeed be appropriate, and nationality has been sanctioned within that framework of the base. But precisely on that functional basis, very often the territorial state will have, by geographical proximity or other reasons, a comparative advantage to enforce jurisdiction.

Finally, let me say one thing only which relates to the question of *common heritage:* this discussion between *Professor Wolfrum* and *Ian Nicholson* concerns, I think, on one side a question which I myself have a great difficulty in accepting, which is that the Antarctic Treaty zone is not to be understood to be under the authory of, or covered by, LOSC. I think that proposition is not at all sustainable, and without merit, because we do not have to go to the legislative history when the Convention itself makes no distinction. This is not to say that the Articles of the Law of the Sea Convention are applicable to the Antarctic in every possible case. It concerns the question of why we should look at the Antarctic in the framework of one part of the new international order, which is the word *heritage*, and not look at it as an integral part of the New International Economic Order. Our approach to the Minerals Regime comprises also some elements of the world *heritage* on one side, but certainly encompasses the basic elements of nationality, of state sovereignty over natural resources, the inherent protection, we feel, of our natural rights, our jurisdictional rights on land and sea, and of course of our claim. Thank you very much.

L. Kappen, Chairman:

Thank you. Now, Mr. *Davérède.*

A. Davérède:

Thank you very much, *Dr. Kappen.* I have a couple of points, actually, three. *Professor Bozcek* said that, if I understood well, the Parties had not been adequately informed on tourism activities in Antarctica. Speaking for my own country, I may reassure him that we have done so regularly on all our activities. In our plans and directives for our Antarctic activities we have directed the personnel in our scientific stations to accord the tourists the treatment they deserve according to the Recommendations, and to keep them advised on those rules and see that they do not get in trouble and all that.

The second point is in reference to what *Ian Nicholson* said, also about the Law of the Sea. *Ambassador Berguño* already referred to it in terms with which I agree. I have discussed it privately with *Ian Nicholson*. I do not have to re-state these views, but we think that as the Law of the Sea Convention is not still in force, up to a certain point we should not be discussing whether it applies or not to Antarctica. For the time being it does not apply to any part of the world, except where it is already part of customary law, and as such we think that it is applicable to our territory in Antarctica. Of course those that do not recognize our claims, or our exertion of sovereignty in Antarctica, I should rather say, are free to think that it is not applicable.

The third point was, also if I understood well, in reference to Dr. *Birnie*'s statement that it would be very useful to create a secretariat of the Treaty, because then we would have somebody checking infractions in questions such as disposal of waste. Well, I know that some other people have the same function in mind for a possible secretariat. We think that it would be very very dangerous to attribute such a capacity to an international official. We think that it would be a matter that would raise frictions, unnecessary frictions, and that we already have within the Treaty, once again, the necessary information and the necessary tools to carry out such activities. It is foreseen that the Consultative Parties can name observers to see to it that the provisions of the Treaty are being carried out. In addition, if such a function would be carried out by a secretariat, of course it could not be just, as I think *Ian Nicholson* remarked, a person, a personal computer and a file. We would need plenty of inspectors all over Antarctica. We can imagine how many there would be in a territory that is one and one-half times the United States territory. I think we would really be in trouble if we would give such a function to a secretariat. Thank you.

P. Birnie:

Could I just make a correction there? I think, I was slightly misunderstood, because all I was indicating was that if there was a secretariat, that would facilitate the circulation of things like reports on infractions, or observations or whatever. I was not suggesting that the secretariat had a role in actually enforcing these, merely that the reports could be circulated to the states concerned, which was the practice in that other organization I gave as an example.

L. Kappen, Chairman:

Three remain still, and then I would like to close the discussion. First, Mr. *Koch*.

J. Koch:

Thank you, Mr. Chairman. I have a short question to Mr. *Khan*. He made a reference to sharing of resources. Could he explain what he means by that, and does this include also the sharing of responsibilities to develop the resources and to share the risks inherent in the development of resources? Thank you.

R. Khan:

Very briefly, I do agree that the concept of sharing of resources carries with it the responsibility to develop and manage the resources. Since the non-parties to the Treaty have not had any opportunity until now to develop the resources, and since the Consultative Parties to the Treaty have had the opportunity, an equitable formula of sharing could be worked out. If you have had investments earlier for a long period of time, then you probably would deserve a greater share. Some such formula could be worked out, as has been done with the mineral resources of the sea-bed. This might look far-fetched, but it is much more constructive to think about it now: fifty years hence it will become terribly difficult to work out a formula for sharing the resources. Thank you.

L. Kappen, Chairman:

Thank you, Mr. *Khan*. Well, Mr. *Roncagliolo*.

N. Roncagliolo:

I would like to refer to the excellent presentations of Mr. *Barnes* and Dr. *Puceiro Ripoll* about waste disposal. It is evident, that the need of further measures to improve the management of waste disposal is not far from being a serious problem. This suggests to me two thoughts. If logistic support of the scientific research already produces these kinds of waste disposal problems, we can anticipate the degree of difficulties that would be present when we begin exploration and exportation of oil and mineral resources, because of the serious ecological risks it implies. And of course the negative implications to neighbour eco-systems, such as the South Pacific areas, as I mentioned yesterday afternoon and as already mentioned by other participants, must be considered.

My second remark is also in relation to the problem of scientific stations. The situation, as Dr. *Puceiro* already mentioned, should release the Antarctic Consultative countries not only to improve environmental regulation, but I think also to promote some solution to the proliferation of stations. One solution could be promoting the common use of scientific facilities, in order to avoid the proliferation of the use of facilities by single states. Thank you.

L. Kappen, Chairman:

Thank you. Now, Mr. *Koroma*.

A. Koroma:

Thank you, Mr. Chairman. Mr. Chairman, I too, agree that the discussions today have been very constructive and useful and indeed I think that they have helped the symposium achieve its original objective. So again, I would like to congratulate *Professor Wolfrum* and the Institute for organizing this symposium. Indeed, as *Professor Mangone* said this morning, and not too long ago as Mr. *Khan* said, ingenuity is capable of providing solutions to the most difficult problems, after all we have seen that when the UNCLOS negotiations started some states were claiming territorial seas to the tune of 200 miles. The Law of the Sea Convention was able to reduce this eventually to 12 miles. It also created a new regime, that of the Exclusive Economic Zone, in which states are allowed to exercise sovereign rights over living resources but at the same time guarantee innocent or transit passage for non-coastal states. Equally so, on the sea-bed, the Law of the Sea Convention created two regimes, one for the Enterprise and the one for private operators who may be disposed to operate in that Area. These are substantial areas. They go to show where there is good will and willingness on the part of states, solutions can be found to difficult problems.

I am trying to say that the question of Antarctica could be resolved by having an open mind. In my presentation yesterday, I referred to the fact that within the framework of the Minerals Regime of the Law of the Sea Convention, reference has been made to the fact that in the exploitation of the resources of minerals, the interest of mankind should not be prejudiced. That in itself is important. I do not think that there is one set of solutions: every possibility which is feasible should be looked into, should be examined. In that way we can find solutions even to difficult problems.

Turning now to problems, to an issue which has been debated or discussed this morning — that of the relationship of the Law of the Sea Convention to Antarctica, or its applicability: I think the point has to be made here; I know Australia was one of the leading negotiators of the Law of the Sea Convention. The point about the relationship or applicability of the Convention to Antarctica, or the exclusion of Antarctica from the negotiations at that moment in time was not that the provisions of the Convention would not eventually apply to Antarctica. It was said at the Conference that to have taken on both issues at the same time would unduly have prolonged the negotiations; in the event, it turned out that the negotiations of the Law of the Sea Convention took much longer than was anticipated, but it was not the intent that the Law of the Sea Convention provisions would not apply to Antarctica. In any case I was not privy to the submissions made by Mr. *Hajost* in his presentation here earlier in the week, but whatever those views might be, I think that it ought to be pointed out that the Secretary-General of the United Nations, who is expected to be neutral and impartial, has stated in his study on Antarctica that the Law of the Sea Convention does apply to Antarctica. In fact, if this interpretation is not accepted, it is conceivable that the matter will eventually have to be referred to the International Court of Justice. Of course, it can be argued, as someone just stated, that the Law of the Sea Convention has not yet come into force. Therefore it cannot be said to apply to Antarctica. And then of course, we can fall back to customary international law. But as I see it, if the interpretation is not accepted that the Convention applies to Antarctica, it could be a matter for the International Court of Justice. When the LOS Convention comes into force, the Sea-Bed Disputes Chamber will eventually come into being as well, then the matter could also be raised before the International Tribunal for the Law of the Sea. So these are new challenges; I am not suggesting that there should be, or should not be, an Antarctic Challenge IV, but these are matters which could occupy future symposiums like these or future meetings like these. Thank you.

L. Kappen, Chairman:

Thank you very much, Mr. *Koroma*, for raising new ideas for the next and future meetings; I think there is a lot of matter to discuss, maybe tonight or in the next meeting, and now I would like to give way to our President to make concluding remarks and close this session. Thank you all for speaking and taking part in the discussions.

R. Wolfrum:

Thank you, Mr. *Kappen*. Before I release you to what has been referred to in Antarctic Challenge II as the "Survivor's Party," a quite fair expression, invented by *Scott* (*Hajost*), let me just try to draw some conclusions.

In my opening remarks, I started by indicating that this symposium is meant to serve two purposes. I, at least, have learned quite a lot, and each of you may judge whether this is true for her or himself as well.

Second, the intention of this symposium is to provide for a better understanding of what I would refer to as different schools of thought. I would rather refrain from speaking of groups, or interests. Some of them I would like to mention, without trying to be exhaustive. We have heard those who would like to preserve the dominant role of the Antarctic Treaty Consultative Parties; that has been objected to by others, arguing that a stronger role should be played by the United Nations. The underlying question was as to whether the United Nations or the Antarctic Treaty Consultative Parties offer the best assurance that Antarctica is used for the benefit of mankind as a whole. Furthermore, some of you have endorsed the claims to parts of Antarctica whereas others have objected thereto. It is impossible to solve the underlying problem and, perhaps, it is even unnecessary. Article IV of the Antarctic Treaty, which has been mentioned quite frequently, provides a solution which makes a close cooperation among the Antarctic Treaty Consultative Parties mandatory, and is evidence to the fact that territorial problems may be solved not only by territorial assignment.

Further, this symposium is meant to provide for a better understanding between science and law. It should be taken into account that a legal regime on Antarctica has to respond to scientific findings as well as to preserve Antarctic research. I am particularly grateful to the scientists who are still amongst us.

If I may summarize my basic feeling on the outcome of this symposium, I would like to indicate that, compared to the discussion we had in Antarctic Challenge II, the controversies have been mitigated to a certain degree: the discussion in Antarctic Challenge II was definitely more controversial than it was here. I do not want to go into any detail; however, I would like to indicate that although it has been argued that the United Nations should play a more dominant role with respect to Antarctica, the idea was raised that the interest of mankind could be equally served in a substantive manner, perhaps not involving the United Nations but by making sure that the coming regime concerning mineral resources provides for *distributive justice*. To that extent, I would endorse to what has been said by *Ian (Nicholson)*. It is important for the Antarctic Treaty Consultative Parties to make sure that fairness and *distributive justice* are reflected in a coming regime concerning the use of Antarctic mineral resources.

I hope that these slight indications of harmonization will prevail in the coming negotiations concerning Antarctica — wherever they take place, be it the negotiations on the mineral resources, the negotiations in the Consultative Meetings, or in the United Nations.

As to the final question, addressed in his usual very elegant manner by *Arthur Watts*, as to whether we are willing to organize Antarctic Challenge IV, neither Mr. *Hempel* nor myself are inclined to commit ourselves here and now. However, I have taken it into account that some of you were good enough to propose new topics to us and even new presentations. We shall have our discussion internally, and I will ask you during the coming months, whether you are really willing to participate actively in Antarctic Challenge IV.

Let me end by thanking you all, not only for coming to Kiel, a place which is sometimes raining, windy, cold or warm, (we had all of these in five days), but for following so attentively our deliberations, and taking a very active and constructive part in the discussions.*

B. A. Boczek:

My remarks concerning the exchange of information relating to tourist and non-governmental expeditions in no way imply any fundamental weakness or "anarchy" of the Antarctic system. They only indicate, on the basis of Mr. *Nicholson*'s statement in Antarctic Challenge II, page 196, that in *some* cases such information exchange is incomplete. Reading my paper *in extenso* will no doubt dispel any misunderstandings that might arise in this respect.

As far as the U. S. policy concerning the costs for humanitarian assistance are concerned, my information is based on the text of the relevant U. S. regulations published in the Antarctic Journal of the United States of March 1986.

Concerning United Kingdom jurisdiction, I would like to reiterate that the United Kingdom does not assert jurisdiction over non-nationals in its claimed Antarctic territory.

* The following comment was later submitted in writing — *Ed.*

Deep Sea Drilling in the Ice-Covered Arctic: Scientific, Environmental, Technical and Political Challenge

or

THE CALL FOR C.O.N.D.

Jörn Thiede, Leonard Johnson**, Yngve Kristoffersen***, Steven Blasco****, Lawrence Mayer******

Table of Contents

* *Jörn Thiede*, GEOMAR, Forschungszentrum für Marine Geowissenschaften, Kiel, F. R. G.

** *Leonard Johnson*, Geophysical Sciences, Office of Naval Research, Arlington, VA, U.S.A.

*** *Yngve Kristoffersen*, Jordskjelvstasjonen, Universitetet i Bergen, Norway.

**** *Steven Blasco*, Geological Survey of Canada, Dartmouth, N.S., Canada.

***** *Lawrence Mayer*, Department of Oceanography, Dalhousie University, Halifax, N.S., Canada.

Abstract

The Arctic Ocean is the last major deep-sea basin of the world's ocean which has yet to be drilled for scientific purposes. However, without the type of geological information which can be collected by the means of deep-sea drilling one will not be able to resolve the basic questions of the geological nature of the Arctic deep-sea floors, of the long-term history of its depositional environment, and of its paleoceanographic history. Insight into nature and properties of the Arctic deep-sea floors are also needed to resolve the geological history of the adjacent continents, to assess their potential for mineral resources, and to make progress in forecasting the long-term history of the northern hemispheric climate.

Despite the very complex technology and despite the environmental hazards, recent assessments suggest that Arctic deep-sea drilling is technologically feasible. A large international and interdisciplinary effort is therefore proposed to organize a major expedition into the deep Arctic, with deep-sea drilling from a drifting platform as its central scientific experiment, but with the potential for participation of many other polar scientific disciplines. Considering the magnitude of the organizational and scientific challenge, it seems important to start preparations now for an expedition in the 'nineties. With this scientific enterprise, it is also proposed to commemorate the centennial of the great polar explorer *F. Nansen*'s *FRAM* drift during which the deep-sea nature of the Arctic basins was first recognized.

I. Introduction: Why drill the deep Arctic for science?

The Arctic Ocean has not lost much of its mystery ever since *F. Nansen*, almost a hundred years ago, designed his special ice-going research vessel *FRAM*, to prove that the Arctic ice cover was moving in a predictable way. When these courageous men left their home country they had no idea that the ice would carry them and their ship from the wide and relatively shallow-shelf seas which accompany the Eurasian coastlines, out into a part of the Arctic seas, with water depths of several thousand meters. It is moving to read, in these days of versatile and well-equipped modern research vessels, how *Nansen* and his men had to bring ropes out into the ice, to unwind its strands, in order to obtain sufficiently long sounding cables once they had detected that they could not reach the sea floor anymore. Anyway, *Nansen* was quick in catching on the these soundings, and after the successful completion of his expedition he published the first map of the Arctic with its contiguous deep-sea basins. He also succeeded in collecting the first samples from the Arctic deep-sea floor (*Böggild*, 1906).

Since these early days of Arctic deep-sea geoscientific exploration much progress has been achieved. The gross bathymetry of the Arctic deep-sea basins has been surveyed and made available to the public in reasonable detail (*Figures 1 and 4*). Interpretations of geophysical data, in harmony with the theory of sea floor spreading, have resolved the problem of the presence of oceanic crust under the basinal structures of the Arctic Ocean (*Figure 1*). Numerous sediment cores have given

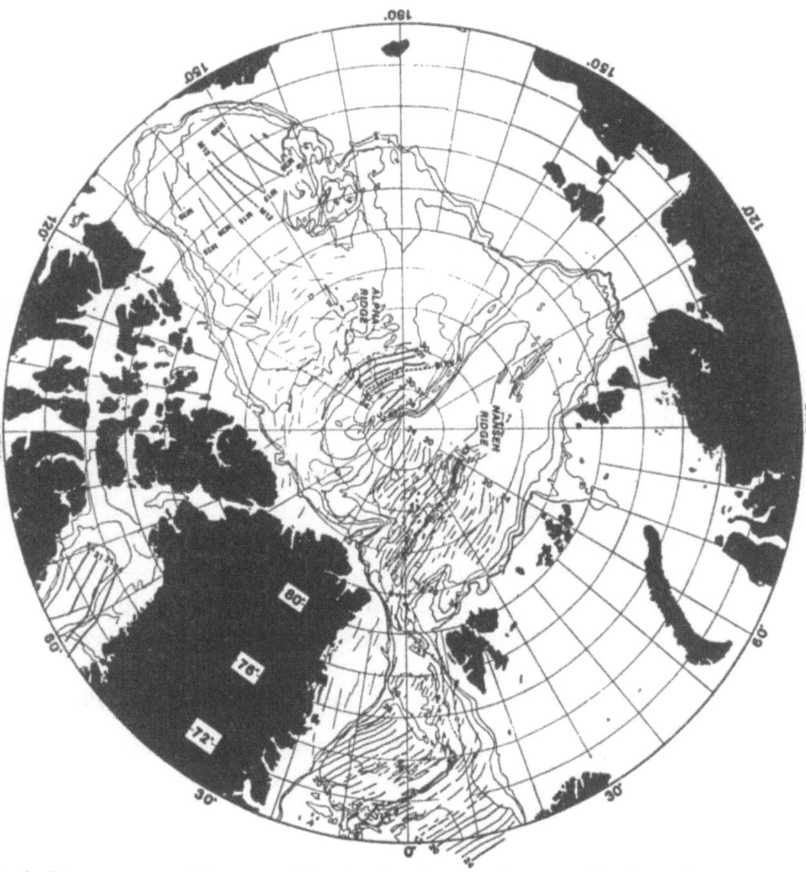

Fig. 1: Linear magnetic anomalies in the Arctic deep-sea basins; they mark the extent of basins with true oceanic crust and give an idea of the age of the Arctic deep-sea floors. Ages and nature of major structural highs remain unknown (from *Taylor et al.*, 1981).

some insight into the evolution of the Arctic marine paleoenvironments and of the paleoclimate of the northern hemisphere (*Figure 2*). Exploration for mineral resources, especially hydrocarbons in the Arctic shelf seas and in the adjacent land regions, have provided much detail on the geological evolution of this area (*Grantz, Johnson* & *Sweeney*, 1987, in press).

Why would it then be important to go to the (certainly major) expense and to organize the complex effort of an expedition to carry out deep-sea drilling in the permanently ice-covered Arctic? In this paper we will attempt to list some of the major unsolved scientific problems of a geological nature, and suggest that these can only be solved adequately through sampling the entire stratigraphy of both the sedimentary sequences covering the Arctic deep-sea floors as well as the underlying basement of most of the major structural units. It can easily be shown that such results would reach in their impact far beyond the regional boundaries of the Arctic deep-sea basins. They would be of truly global importance, and progress in some areas of geological research is actually entirely dependent on the availability of such data.

There is no question that the organization, preparation and execution of an expedition to carry out deep-sea drilling in the permanently ice-covered waters of the Arctic faces formidable problems for scientific, technical, environmental, financial and political reasons. We are trying to discuss some of these problems, suggesting that they can be solved.

Finally, we are proposing the preparation of a large-scale interdisciplinary and international expedition to harvest Arctic data in a wide variety of scientific disciplines in the permanently ice-covered deep-sea basins of the northern polar ocean. If successful, the results of this expedition would mean enormous scientific rewards and progress in almost all disciplines of polar science; they would be truly worthy of celebrating the centennial of the great first *FRAM*-expedition under *F. Nansen*'s leadership. This expedition should then be called C.O.N.D. (**C***entennial* **o***f* **N***ansen*'s **D***rift*), and mounted during the years 1993—1996.

II. On the Geological Properties of the Arctic Deep-Sea Floors

In this chapter, we will point to a number of specific geological properties of the Arctic deep-sea floors, which can only be described adequately after successful Arctic deep-sea drilling. Up-dated and in-depth discussions of the geological structure based on presently available data is accessible elsewhere in the scientific literature. A comprehensive documentation of this literature can be found in *Grantz, Johnson* & *Sweeney*, 1987 (in press).

1. Bathymetry of the Arctic Deep-Sea Floors

Since the early days of *F. Nansen*, almost 100 years ago, much progress has been achieved in describing the gross trends of the bathymetry of the Arctic. The dominant share of the new bathymetric data (*Figures*

1 and 4) have been collected along submarine tracks. Scientific expeditions, using mostly ice islands as their platforms, have also contributed significant amounts of data, so that modern bathymetric charts could be published depicting a great deal of regional detail (*Gorshkov*, 1983; GEBCO, 1979).

It is now clear that the Arctic deep-sea basins are subdivided into a number of sub-basins by major trans-Arctic structural highs, such as the Lomonosov and the Alpha-Mendeleev ridges. The deep-sea basins, between the ridges and between the continental margins and these ridges, reveal the typical morphologic features of true ocean floors, and the dispute about their continental or oceanic nature has been resolved after lineated "sea-floor spreading type" magnetic anomalies have been found under part of the Canada basin, presumably under the Makarov basin, and unequivocally under the Eurasian basin. With the exception of some of the marginal plateaus (Chukchi Plateau, Morris Jesup Rise, Yermak Plateau) the physiographic limits of the shallow shelf sea surrounding the Arctic deep-sea basins are reasonably well constrained, although much more bathymetric detail would be desirable in specific areas of the Arctic. This applies in particular to the intersection of the active mid-ocean ridge with the Siberian continental margins. Additional bathymetric data from the Arctic will also be needed from the immediate vicinity of any drill sites.

For the purpose of Arctic deep-sea drilling, it would be desirable to locate the boundary between continental and oceanic crust much more precisely than possible by means of bathymetric data. Detailed bathymetric surveys will also be needed to assess source areas and transport paths of many of the turbidite deposits which are known to cover important sectors of the Arctic deep-sea basins, *e.g.*, in the Canada Basin and the Eurasian Basin north of Svalbard.

2. *Age and Nature of the Major Structural Units*

With the exception of some of the Arctic deep-sea basins where linear magnetic anomalies have been found (*Figure 1*), little is known about the age and nature of the major structural units of the Arctic. The "sea-floor spreading type" linear magnetic anomalies suggest a Late Paleocene-modern age of the Eurasian basin, a Late Cretaceous and possible Paleocene age for the Makarov Basin, and a possibly Late Jurassic to Early Cretaceous age for the Canada Basin. While the interpretation of magnetic anomalies is clear in the Eurasian Basin, only deep-sea drilling could confirm the presently accepted interpretations for the Makarov and Canada basins. The confirmation of these interpretations for the two latter basins would also be of utmost importance for our understanding of the tectonic and paleogeographic evolution of the early Arctic deep basins and the positions and movements of the adjacent continents relative to each other.

Only deep-sea drilling, through the overlying sediment cover and into the basement rocks, will allow us to resolve the mysteries of age and nature of the structural highs and marginal plateaus of the Arctic Ocean. Alpha Ridge is an underwater mountain system comparable to the Alps in size. With the exception of *one*, poorly preserved sample of weathered tholeiitic basalt, which has been collected by the Canadian CESAR-Expedition, some sediment cores collected by the T-3 and CESAR expeditions (*Figure 2*) of the Late Cretaceous ages (offering an idea of the minimum age of this structural high) and a variety of ambiguous geophysical data, nothing is known about the age and origin (probably volcanic) of this important ridge system. Based on its physiography and geophysical data, the Lomonosov Ridge seems to represent a strange sliver or series of blocks, consisting mostly of continental crust which was part of the Eurasian Arctic continental margin up to the moment when the mid-ocean ridge propagated into this area from the Norwegian-Greenland Sea, during Late Paleocene time (55—56 Ma). Nothing is known about the nature of the Chukchi Plateau. Circumstantial geophysical evidence suggests a volcanic origin for the Yermak Plateau and its "sister" structure north of Greenland, the Morris-Jesup Rise. The nature of the crust under the Lincoln Sea, under the intersections of the major trans-Arctic ridges with the continental margins, as well as under the intersection of the active mid-ocean ridge with the Asian continental margin off the Lena, are of great geological interest; they cannot be determined without deep drilling techniques.

3. *Evolution of the Paleoenvironment, Paleogeography and Paleobathymetry*

It is clear from the available data that the paleogeographic evolution of the Arctic deep-sea basins can be reconstructed with reasonable certainty, provided the interpretations of the magnetic anomalies are correct. We have to assume that both continental margins surrounding the Arctic and the trans-Arctic rises have undergone subsidence since their time of formation, as observed in many other parts of the world ocean; the amount of the subsidence, however, can only be estimated with reasonable precision if the nature and age of their basement rocks are established. The few Upper Cretaceous and Paleogene cores which have been collected hitherto do suggest that the individual Arctic sub-basins were quite isolated from each other; the contents of terrestrial plant debris found in Upper Cretaceous organic rich black shale on the flank of Alpha Ridge could even mean that this rise rose as a large land mass or an island chain above sea level only 70—80 Ma. The physiographic evolution of seaways connecting the deep Arctic basins with the Atlantic and Pacific Oceans is poorly constrained, with the exception of Fram Strait.

The linear magnetic anomalies found under the Arctic deep-sea basins have allowed documentation of the existence of a major ocean basin for the past 120—150 my. However, if trying to reconstruct the temporal evolution of paleoenvironmental changes which have affected this ocean basin, the scarce and fragmentary sediment record available through

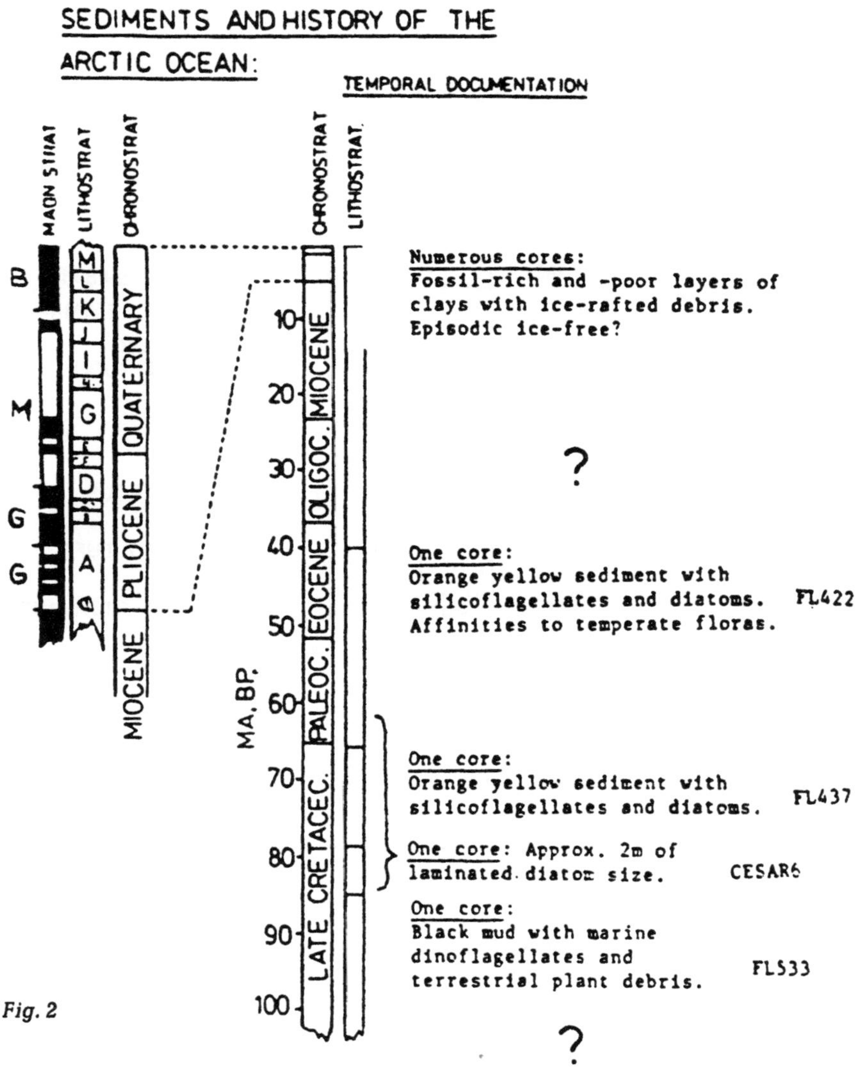

Fig. 2

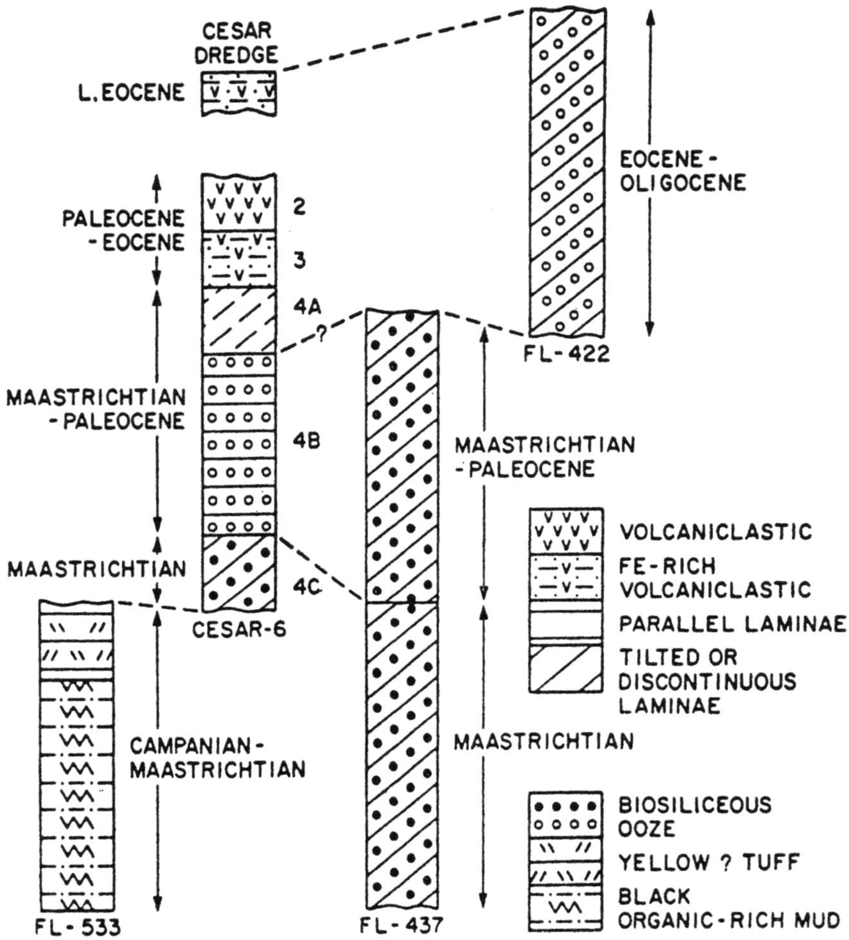

Fig. 2 (cont'd): Ages and composition of Arctic deep-sea sediment cores (after *Mudie et al.*, 1986).

sampling the Arctic Ocean with conventional methods is a major obstacle for any progress. In *Figure 2* the available evidence has been compiled and plotted against time. It is clear that no samples at all are available to document the properties of the deep Arctic depositional environments for the earliest 40—60 my.

The time span from roughly 80—40 Ma can only be described by means of four short sediment cores. However, they do suggest that the Arctic Ocean during that time span was fully marine, relatively warm, with highly productive surface water masses and stagnant, oxygen-deficient bottom waters. If better and more complete sample materials were available they could be used to study the oceanographic properties of a "warm" (ice-free) polar ocean, which has no modern analog. Depositional environments leading to the formation of organic rich black shales are also of high industrial interest, because under certain geological boundary conditions they can lead to the formation of source rocks for hydrocarbons.

Sometime between 40 and roughly 2—3 Ma, the northern hemisphere climate cooled sufficiently that an ice-cover developed. We have no idea when this paleoclimatic event happened, which is so important for our own living circumstances. It is quite clear that a key for its understanding has to be sought in the pelagic sediments of the Arctic deep-sea basins.

The youngest part of the sampled sediment sections which can be studied in several hundred cores from the central and eastern Arctic basins documents the paleoclimatic variability of the glaciated Arctic. The revised dating of these stratigraphic intervals (G. *Jones*, 1987 personal communication) suggests that the Arctic ice cover has existed for at least the past 2.5 — 3 my. Lithologic changes of the cored sediment sections suggest that the nature of the existing ice cover and sediment transport to the Arctic varied considerably and repeatedly in much the same way. The details of this variabilty, and of the Arctic Ocean's response to the Late Cenozoic climatic fluctuations which can be documented so well in lower latitudes, have yet to be resolved.

A solution for these processes has to be sought in the Arctic deep-sea basin with its unique sediment record of a cold, glaciated deep-sea basin in polar position; this can only be adequately achieved through a careful and well-designed strategy of deep-sea drilling.

III. Feasibility of Arctic Deep-Sea Drilling

Now that we have looked at some of the exciting scientific reasons why Arctic deep-sea drilling would be important, we will attempt to discuss a number of boundary conditions which will have to be considered when planning the complex operations of Arctic deep-sea drilling. They will have to touch upon scientific, technical, environmental, financial and political aspects and — at this stage — cannot be considered complete by any means.

1. *Technical Feasibility: Choice of Platforms, Drilling Techniques*

The desirability of Arctic deep-sea drilling has been discussed for more than a decade, first under the auspices of the Deep-Sea Drilling Project (DSDP), more recently of the Ocean Drilling Program (ODP).

Both drill ships employed by these projects, first the *GLOMAR CHALLENGER*, more recently the *JOIDES RESOLUTION*, have already drilled successfully in ice-infested waters. However, during these attempts it also became quite clear that these vessels which are not ice-capable would not be permitted to enter permanently ice-covered waters. The question of how deep-sea drilling could be carried out in ice-covered waters has lingered on unresolved for some time until late 1986 when international scientific organisations (IUGG-ICL, IUGS-CMG, SCOR WG 82) called for a workshop (in Halifax) to assess the technical feasibility of Arctic deep-sea drilling.

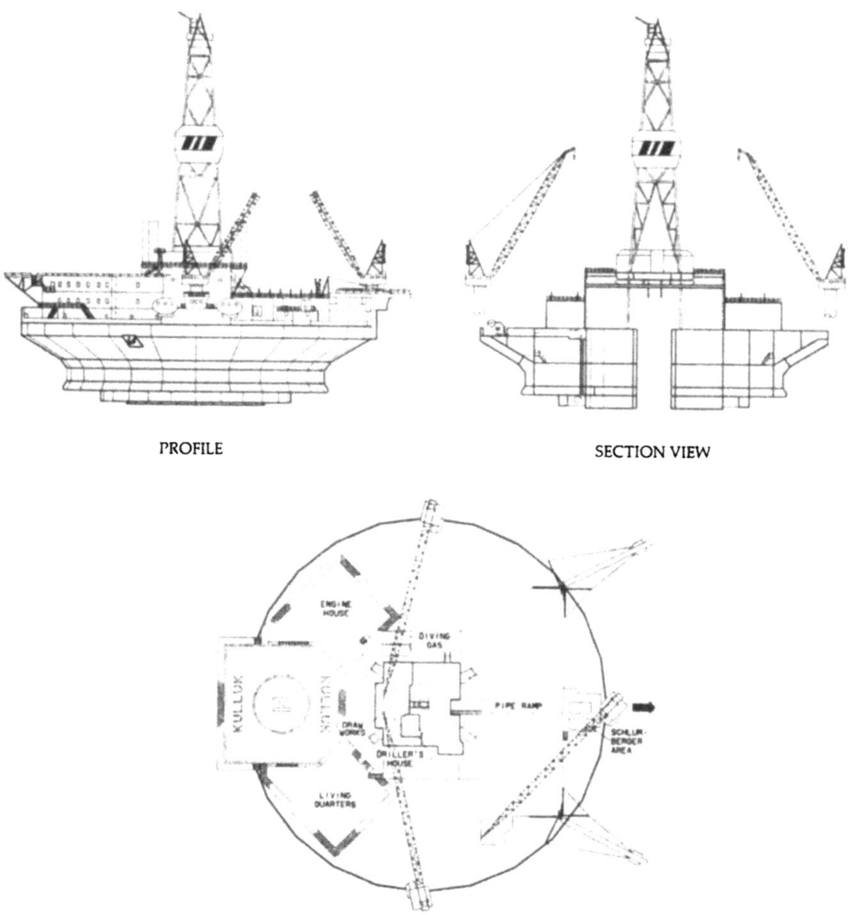

Fig. 3: Semisubmersible drilling platform of the Kulluk-type which has been used for Arctic shelf drilling and which is being considered for Arctic deep-sea drilling (from company prospect).

With the help of industry personnel with many years experience from high Arctic hydrocarbon exploration, it could quickly be shown that such drilling would be very costly, very complicated, but technically feasible. It could actually be shown that a variety of options existed (*Table 1*) which are discussed in detail in the workshop report from this Halifax meeting. In *Figure 3* we have illustrated one of the potential platforms, a semisubmersible conically-shaped circular drilling platform, which has the capability to withstand the lateral ice pressures to be expected and which would have to follow the path of the pack-ice drift passively drifting. Because of the long-term uncertainties of this drift it was also clear that it would be preferable to make use of an ice-breaker with the capability to relocate at will and to search for the selected drilling sites. Much future work will have to be invested into the proper selection of a platform suitable for Arctic deep-sea drilling. As long as this project is mainly concerned with basic science, the high costs (up to 200 mill. dollars) will be prohibitive to the construction of a specially designed new platform.

Regardless which platform is chosen, finally, one will have to cope with the usually slow, but variable movements of the Arctic ice cover, which is reasonably well understood after several decades of monitoring ice station movements and which had been predicted and proven early by *F. Nansen*. The water depths to be drilled in will range from 1000—4000 m, allowing for some (limited) lateral drift of the drilling platform. The relatively thin sediment sequences (estimated 500—1000 m) above the Arctic basement can be penetrated within a few days, if the efficacy of the platform is close to that of the *JOIDES RESOLUTION*. If the ice moves too fast, drilling would have to be suspended or stratigraphic sections would have to be pieced together from stratigraphically overlapping sections obtained along the drift path by stepwise extending the penetration.

In terms of coring techniques the workshop participants agreed that continuous coring, using the riserless techniques developed by ODP, could be adopted to any of the drilling platforms considered. They would not require re-entering capability, but would be single-bit holes penetrating the entire sedimentary section up to 50 m into the underlying basement.

Logistic requirements would be complicated and difficult to fulfill. Operations would have to be subdivided into legs of some 2—3 months in duration. In between these periods the personnel would have to be exchanged (probably by aircraft) and supplies and spares would have to be replenished.

The complexity of the drilling operations will require the establishment of an extensive, capable, and dependable logistic network to keep the operations going. Since most of the time the drilling platform would be located in regions which are only accessible with difficulties, it is evident that it should also offer space to experiments from many other polar research disciplines such as marine biology, physical oceanography, meteorology, geophysics, geochemistry, *etc.* It is presently considered mandatory that the entire expedition is interdisciplinary in nature, even though the geoscientific investigations will receive the most emphasis.

2. *Scientific Feasibility: the Problem of Site Surveying; Drilling Targets*

Figure 4 illustrates the distribution over the entire Arctic Ocean of locations addressing selected scientific targets (a listing of these targets is to be found in the Halifax Workshop 1986 report, (*cf. Blasco et al.*, 1987). Existing data have already permitted identification of the areas with the highest priority for deep-sea drilling in the permanently ice-covered Alpha Ridge in the central Arctic where all pre-Neogene sediment cores have been obtained.

Sites in seasonally ice-free marginal Arctic regions can probably be drilled by conventional means of deep-sea drilling, *e. g.* by means of the *JOIDES RESOLUTION*. Sites in the shallow-shelf seas of peri-Arctic realm can be drilled by a variety of techniques which have been proven and which are not the subject of this paper (for details see Halifax Workshop 1986 report).

Site surveying of the proposed drill sites poses major problems, both for survey before and after the drilling. If areas without adequate data are selected, new seismic lines have to be collected, which can be done in a number of ways:

a) Gimbaled geophones can be dragged over the ice achieving sufficient coupling during stopping. Using this method a skidoo can tow the geophones, stopping every 50 m to drill a hole for a 1 pound dynamite charge. It is estimated that 100 km a week could be covered.

b) Source and hydrophone array could be towed from ship; it would be most practical to use a submarine which, however, is unlikely to be made available. Preliminary studies suggest that submarine drones are promising, and preliminary engineering studies are under way.

c) Arrays of hydrophones or sonobuoys could be deployed symmetrically around the drilling platform, which would support the sound source.

d) Marginal regions such as the Yermak Plateau might be accessible for conventional research vessels during years of optimal ice conditions.

Numbers on this map mark proposed sites for scientific drilling in the Arctic Ocean. (From Office of Naval Research)

Fig. 4: **Preliminary proposals for potential locations of scientific interest for Arctic deep drilling, as developed by Halifax workshop, Dec. 1986 on Arctic Drilling Technology (from *Blacos et al.*, 1987).**

3. *Environmental Protection*

The planned operations (here only considered for the Arctic deep-sea basins and not for shallow peri-Arctic shelf seas) will have to satisfy several aspects of protecting the environment.

First, the entire suite of activities will have to be carried out with minimal disturbance of the natural environment; that this can be done to a certain degree has been successfully demonstrated by the ice-island stations, which in part have been occupied for many consecutive years by researchers from both eastern and western countries.

Second, the selected site must satisfy the scrutiny-of-safety review, involving the best scientific and technical knowledge such as is presently represented in *JOIDES* and *ODP* Safety Panels, as well as any national safety regulations, before approval for drilling can be granted. The type of drilling will be riserless, as is usually employed for sampling deep-sea sections of pelagic sediments.

4. *Financial Feasibility*

Before the final selection of a drilling platform, it will be impossible to accurately assess the financial requirements of the planned operations, which will have to include the scientific evaluation of the collected samples and data. In *Table 1* we have listed some rough estimates for costs of the individual platforms as obtained from various sources. It is clear that Arctic deep-sea drilling will be very costly, on the order of the funds needed for the Ocean Drilling Program (ODP), that is to say 30—50 million dollars per year (excluding capital investment). Presently, we do not expect to find one single country which would be willing to cover these costs, but we are aiming rather at a consortium of circum-Arctic and Sub-Arctic countries (possibly including industry and international organizations).

5. *Political Feasibility*

The political situation of the countries bordering the Arctic Ocean itself, and differences in opinion about the validity of their claims to the economic zones adjacent to the shelf regions is complex, as can easily be illustrated by *Figures* 5 and 6. Different, and possibly unresolved, regional claims might exist in other parts of the Arctic Ocean. The possibilities of scientific ventures such as deep-sea drilling mounted jointly by eastern and western countries have recently been complicated by the rejection of the USSR from ODP membership.

The scientific exploration of the central Arctic with operations as complex and dangerous as deep-sea drilling in permanently ice-covered waters cannot be achieved without the active participation and assistance of all major potential partners. It will be of utmost importance to find or build a scientific organization acceptable to all partners involved.

IV. Call for a Large International, Interdisciplinary Expedition to Explore the Nature of the Deep Arctic: C. O. N. D. — Centennial of F. Nansen's Drift 1893—1896

The unique scientific opportunities of exploring the natural properties of the sea floors under the permanent ice cover of the Arctic are presently

Fig. 5: **Examples of political complications to be expected in obtaining licenses for Arctic deep-sea drilling close to the continental margins, (after CIA, 1978).**

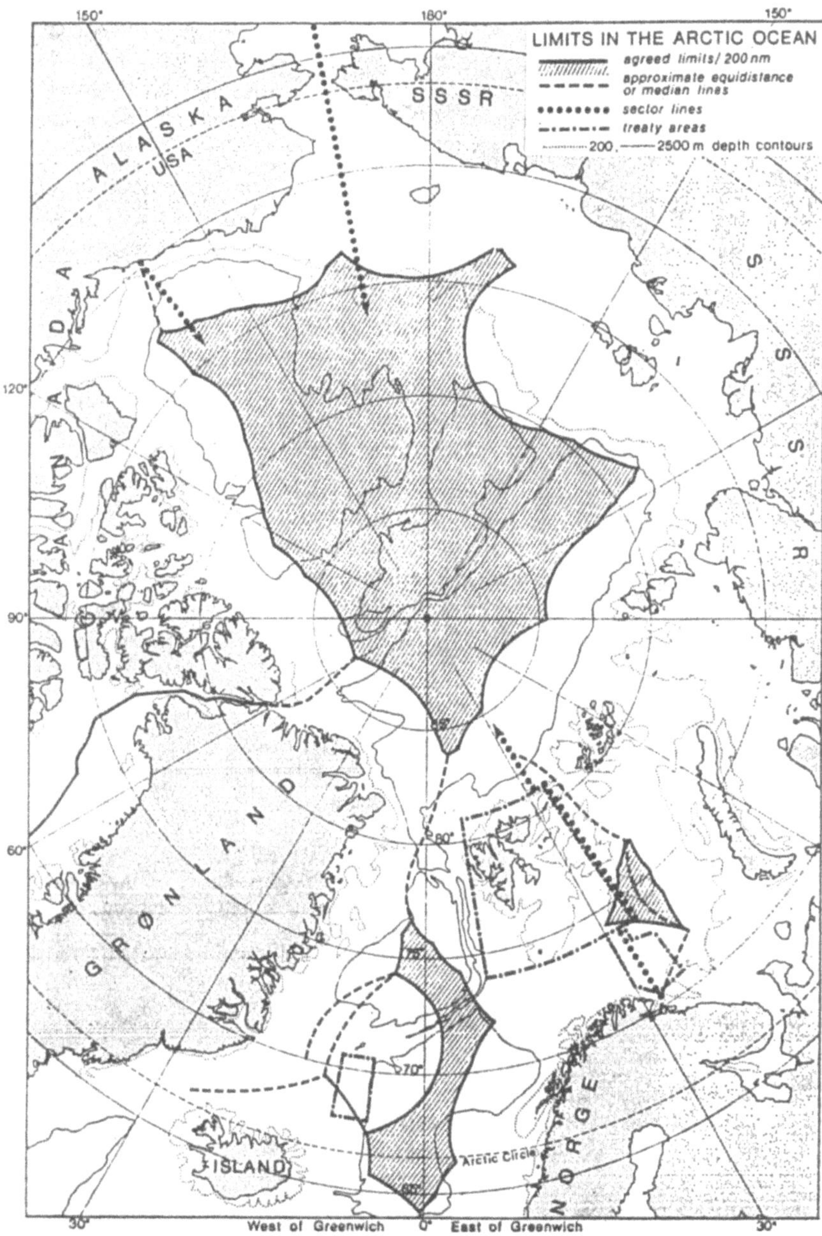

Fig. 6: **Examples of political complications to be expected in obtaining licenses for Arctic deep-sea drilling close to the continental margins, (from *Jenisch*, 1985).**

under intensive discussion. Plans for Arctic deep-sea drilling are pursued by a number of different groups with different scientific objectives; they have been presented as a concerted effort for the first time during COSOD II (Conference on Scientific Ocean Drilling, Strasbourg July 1987). There is also no question that the planning of Arctic deep-sea drilling will have to rely heavily on the expertise of the Ocean Drilling Program (ODP) and its advisory structure; ODP and its predecessor, the Deep-Sea Drilling Project (DSDP), combine many of the world's experts on deep-sea drilling. One will also have to seek close cooperation with the oil companies with experience in Arctic exploration.

However, because of a variety of reasons, none of the existing organizations will in all likelihood promote these plans strongly enough so that Arctic deep-sea drilling can become a reality. Plans are therefore underway to organize a new effort aiming at the organization of a large international, interdisciplinary expedition to explore the nature of the deep Arctic. It will have to fulfill the following requirements:

1. The most exciting and the most complex as well as costly element of this effort will consist of the exploration of the geological structure of the Arctic deep-sea floors. The possibility of Arctic deep-sea drilling as the operational and scientific centerpiece of this effort is a *conditio sine qua non.*

2. The long duration of the drilling effort, the powerful logistic apparatus which will have to be organized and financed, as well as the remoteness of the areas will result in unique research opportunities for other polar science disciplines as well. The effort should be interdisciplinary.

3. The nature and shape of the Arctic Ocean and its continental margins, the location of the scientific targets with the highest priorities, as well as the complex and dangerous operations in an environment hostile to man will require the active participation of all circum-Arctic and Sub-Arctic countries.

4. The global impact of the geological evolution and of many natural properties of the modern Arctic will hopefully make it attractive to a number of powerful non-Arctic countries and major, world-wide operating oil companies to contribute to this effort, on the scientific, organisational, technical and financial level. It might also be of interest to a number of international organizations.

5. New and major scientific enterprises should carry an easily identifiable symbol. Why should we not devote this expedition to the memories of *F. Nansen*, the great Norwegian Polar Explorer, who prepared, organized and executed the well-known *FRAM* expedition to the Arctic Ocean during 1893—1896? He was truly interdisciplinary, as

a biologist he also brought with him the first sediment samples from the Arctic deep-sea floors, and made important scientific contributions to geography, geology, oceanography and biology. He was daring and courageous, and truly international. The centennial of the first *FRAM* expedition would come during 1993—1996, which would allow about 5 years for preparations, barely enough for a scientific effort of the complexity and magnitude of deep-sea drilling in the permanently ice-covered Arctic.

It is our proposal that the scientific community joins forces to start preparations for an expedition to the Arctic with the aim to explore the natural properties of some of the least known, most hostile regions of our globe. **C. O. N. D.** would also celebrate the **C**entennial**o**f **N**ansen's **D**rift.

Acknowledgements

A major part of these opinions have been formulated during a workshop on the TECHNICAL FEASIBILITY OF ARCTIC DEEP-SEA DRILLING held in Halifax during December 1986 (sponsored by the ICL Subcommittee on the Arctic and by the IUGS Commission for Marine Geology). *J. Thiede* also benefitted from discussion with his fellow geoscientists during a sabbatical term spent at the University of Bergen in Spring 1987. Part of this study has been supported by ONR grant no. N00014-85-G-0124. It represents part of the activities of SCOR WG 82.

TABLE 1

Platform	Capability Coring	Other	Cost Appro.	Limitations
A. Bottom Coupled	continuous if ODP technology used	deep holes possible limited to one hole	1 m per day	very high cost 60 m maximum depth of water
B. Ice (thickened)	continuous if ODP technology is used in existing rigs	deep holes possible	21—23 m per core	limited mobility via air high logistic and support cost summer operations might be difficult
C. Drill ship	continuous if ODP technology is used in existing ships	most reasonable in both cost and in reaching science objectives limited mobility	30—60 m per year with ice breaker	require ice breaker support rounded hull to minimize ice pressures
D. Shallow drilling	continuous	*ship ice or* land mounted	8,500 a day	depth limited (60 m) 120 m core length
E. Frozen in barge	continuous if ODP technology is used	deep holes possible	40 m per year without ice breaker	lack of mobility unless round hull is used subject to ice crushing ice breaker escort required
F. ODP	continuous with well logging		32.5 m per year	cannot work in even loose ice
G. Canadian Class 8	continuous	maximum depth of about 150 m	?	will be capable of steaming to any part of the Arctic.

Table 1: Characteristics of drilling platforms which can be used for Arctic deep drilling (from Halifax workshop, Dec. 1986 on Arctic Drilling Technology).

REFERENCES

BLASCO, S., JOHNSON, G. L., MAYER, L. and J. THIEDE (1987),
In the Arctic: Drilling will reveal important changes, in: Geotimes August 1987, 8—9.

BÖGGILD, O. B. (1906),
On the bottom deposits of the North Polar Sea, in: Norwegian North Polar Expedition, 1893—1896, Sci. Res. 5, 1—62.

CIA (Central Intelligence Agency) (1978),
Polar Regions Atlas. 66 pp., Washington.

GEBCO (General Bathymetric Chart of the Ocean) (1979),
Arctic Ocean Sheet, Ottawa.

GORSHKOV, S. G. (1983),
World Ocean Atlas, Arctic Ocean, Vol. 3, (Pergamon Press) Oxford.

GRANTZ, A., JOHNSON, G. L. and W. SWEENEY (eds.) (1987),
The Arctic Ocean Region, in: Geol. Soc. Amer. DNAG, vol. L, in press.

JENISCH, U. (1985),
Sovereign rights in the Arctic: Maritime policies and practices after UNCLOS III, in: GYIL, vol. 28, 297—321.

MUDIE, P. J., STOFFYN-EGLI, P. and N. A. VAN WAGONER (1986),
Geological constraints for tectonic models of the Alpha Ridge, in: J. Geodyn. 6, 215—236.

NANSEN, F. (1904),
The bathymetrical features of the North Polar Seas, with a discussion of the continental shelves and previous oscillations of the shore line, in: Norwegian North Polar Expedition 1893—1896, Sci. Res. 4 (13), 232 pp.

TAYLOR, P. T., KOVACS, L. C., VOGT, P. R. and G. L. JOHNSON (1981),
Detailed aeromagnetic investigations of the Arctic basin, 2. J. Geophys. Res. 86 (B 7), 6323—6333.

List of Participants

ADELUNG, DIETER	Prof. Dr., Institut für Meereskunde — Meereszoologie — Universität Kiel, Olshausenstraße 40, 2300 Kiel, FRG.
AUGSTEIN, ERNST	Prof. Dr., Alfred-Wegener-Institut für Polar- und Meeresforschung, Columbus Center, 2850 Bremerhaven, FRG.
BARNES, JAMES NEIL	Executive Director, The Antarctica Project, 218 D Street, S.E., Washington, D.C. 20003, U.S.A.
BEHRENDT, JOHN C.	Dr., U.S. Department of the Interior, Geological Survey, Denver Federal Center MS 903, Box 25046, Denver, Colorado 80225, U.S.A.
BERGUÑO, JORGE	Ambassador of Chile, 56 Sparks Street, Suite 891, Ottawa, Ontario KIP 5A9, Canada.
BIRNIE, PATRICIA W.	Prof. Dr., London School of Economics and Political Science, Houghton Street, London WC2 2AE, U. K.
BOCKSLAFF, KLAUS	Dr., Dorf 9, 2300 Kiel 17, FRG.
BOCZEK, BOLESLAW ADAM	Prof., Kent State University, Kent, Ohio 44242, U.S.A.
BØLSET, NILS	Special Adviser, Ministry of Foreign Affairs, Oslo, Norway.
BRAMMER, SILKE	Wilhelm-Lobsien Weg 10, 2300 Kiel 17, FRG.
BUNGENSTOCK, HERWALD	Prof. Dr., Regierungsdirektor, Bundesministerium für Forschung und Technologie, Heinemannstraße 2, 5300 Bonn 2, FRG.
BURHENNE, WOLFGANG E.	Dr., Chairman, IUCN Commission of Environmental Policy, Law and Administration; Interparlementarian Working Group, PF 01 10, Bundeshaus, Adenauerallee 214, 5300 Bonn 1, FRG.
CHOPRA, SUDHIR K.	LL.M., Antarctica Interest Group, 8644 W. Golf Road, Apt. A-3, Des Plaines, IL 600016, U.S.A.

DAVÉRÈDE, ALBERTO L.	Dr., Minister Plenipotentiary, Director-General of Antarctica, Ministry of Foreign Affairs and Worship, Reconguista 1088, 1003 Buenos Aires, Argentina.
DELBRÜCK, JOST	Prof. Dr., LL.M. (Indiana), Direktor des Instituts für Internationales Recht, Rektor der Christian-Albrechts-Universität zu Kiel, Olshausenstraße 40—60, 2300 Kiel 1, FRG.
DICKE, KLAUS	Dr., Institut für Internationales Recht, Olshausenstraße 40—60, 2300 Kiel 1, FRG.
FRIEDMANN, E. IMRE	Prof. Dr., Department of Biological Science, Florida State University, Tallahassee, FL 32306, U.S.A.
FÜTTERER, DIETER KARL	Prof. Dr., Alfred-Wegener-Institut für Polar- und Meeresforschung, Columbus Center, 2850 Bremerhaven, FRG.
GIERMANN, GÜNTER	Dr., Alfred-Wegener-Institut für Polar- und Meeresforschung, Columbus Center, 2850 Bremerhaven, FRG.
GIRET, ANDRÉ R.	Dr., Chef des Expeditions Polaires Françaises, 47 Avenue du Marechal Fryolle, Paris 75116, France.
GOLITSYN, VLADIMIR	Senior Legal Officer, and Special Assistant to the Under-Secretary-General for Legal Affairs, United Nations Secretariat, Room 201 i, New York, NY 10017, U.S.A.
GRÖNBERG, TOM	Ambassador, Deputy Director of the Legal Department, Ministry of Foreign Affairs, Erottajankatz 19 B, 00130 Helsinki, Finland.
HAFNER, GERHARD	Dr., Universitäts Dozent, Institut für Völkerrecht und Internationale Beziehungen, Universitätsstraße 2, A-1090 Wien, Austria.
HAJOST, SCOTT A.	Legal Adviser, Office for Environmental Sciences, United States Department of State, 2201 C Street, N.W., Washington, D.C. 20520, U.S.A.
HARDERS, J. ENNO	Institut für Internationales Recht, Olshausenstr. 40—60, 2300 Kiel 1, FRG.

HARON, MOHAMED	High Commissioner for Malaysia, Malaysian High Commission, 50-M, Satya Marg, Chanakyapuri, New Delhi - 110021, India.
HEAP, JOHN A.	Dr., Polar Regions Section, Foreign and Commonwealth Office, London, S.W. 1A 2AH, Great Britain.
HEINZ, URSULA	Dr., Institut für Internationales Recht, Olshausenstraße 40—60, 2300 Kiel 1, FRG.
HEMPEL, GOTTHILF	Prof. Dr., Direktor, Alfred-Wegener-Institut für Polar- und Meeresforschung, Columbus Center, 2850 Bremerhaven, FRG.
HENDRY, IAN D.	Legal Adviser, Foreign and Commonwealth Office, London SW 1A 2AH, Great Britain.
HOEL, ALF HÅKON	Research Fellow, Fridtjof Nansens Institut, Polhodga, Fridtjof Nansens vei 17, N - 1324 Lysaker, Norway.
HUBOLD, GERD	Dr., Institut für Polarökologie, Leibnizstraße 11, Universität Kiel, 2300 Kiel FRG.
JACOBSSON, MARIE	First Secretary, Swedish Foreign Ministry, Töysta Marestangen 2, Stockholm, Sweden.
JAHN-KOCH, INGRID L.	LL.M. (American University), Mönkemöllerstr. 43, 5300 Bonn, FRG.
JENISCH, UWE	Dr., Ministerialrat, Ministerium für Wirtschaft und Verkehr des Landes Schleswig-Holstein, Düsternbrooker Weg 94—100, 2300 Kiel, FRG.
JOHNSON, JUDITH C.	Co-ordinator, Secretariat of the Convention on the Conservation of Migratory Species of Wild Animals, United Nations Environment Programme, Ahrstr. 45, 5300 Bonn 2, FRG.
JØRGENSEN-DAHL, ARNFINN	Dr., Fridtjof Nansens Institut, Polhogda, Fridtjof Nansens vei 17, N-1324 Lysaker, Norway.
JOYNER, CHRISTOPHER C.	Prof. Dr., Department of Political Science, George Washington University, Washington, D.C., 20052, U.S.A.
KÄDE, ANDREAS	Obersdorf 21, 7024 Filderstadt 4, FRG.

KAPPEN, LUDGER	Prof. Dr., Direktor, Botanisches Institut der Universität Kiel, Olshausenstraße 40—60, 2300 Kiel, FRG.
KERN, STEFAN	Bundesministerium für Forschung und Technologie, Heinemannstr. 2, 5300 Bonn 2, FRG.
KHAN, RHAMATULLA	Professor of International Law, Jawaharlal Nehru University, New Delhi 110067, India.
KIILU, RAPHAEL M.	Ambassador, Permanent Mission of Kenya to the United Nations, United Nations Plaza, Room 486, New York, N.Y. 10017, U.S.A.
KIRNDÖRFER, JÜRGEN-GEORG	Norddeutscher Rundfunk, Wall 68-74, 2300 Kiel 1, FRG.
KOCH, JOACHIM	Regional Direktor, Bundesministerium für Wirtschaft, Villemombler Str. 76, 5300 Bonn, FRG.
KÖNIG, DORIS	M.C.L. (University of Miami), Bismarckstr. 46, 2000 Hamburg 2, FRG.
KOROMA, ABDUL G.	Ambassador, Embassy of Sierra Leone, 410 Avenue de Tervuren, B- 1150 Brussels, Belgium.
KOSCHORRECK, WILFRIED	Ministerialrat, Bundesministerium der Finanzen, Graurheindorferstr. 108, 5300 Bonn 1, FRG.
KOSKE, PETER	Prof. Dr., Institut für Angewandte Physik, Universität Kiel, Olshausenstraße 40—60, 2300 Kiel, FRG.
LAGONI, RAINER	Prof. Dr., LL.M. (Columbia), Institut für Seerecht, Universität Hamburg, Schlüterstr. 28, 2000 Hamburg 13, FRG.
LI, SONG	Deputy Division Chief, Department of Treaty and Law, Ministry of Foreign Affairs, Beijing, People's Republic of China.
LUDWIG, REGINE	Werwarthstraße 6, 1000 Berlin 45, FRG.
MANGONE, GERARD J.	Prof. Dr., Director, Center for the Study of Marine Policy; H. Rodney Sharp Professor of International Law, Univ. of Delware, Robinson Hall 301, Newark, Delaware 19711, U.S.A.
MAQUIEIRA, CRISTIAN	Counsellor, Permanent Mission of Chile to the United Nations, Fourth Floor, 809 United Nations New York, NY 10017, U.S.A.

MESSER, KURT	Dr., Vortragender Legationsrat I, Auswärtiges Amt, Adenauerallee 99—103, 5300 Bonn, FRG.
METTRA, NICOLAS	Direction des Affairs Juridiques, Ministère des Affaires Étrangères, 37 Quai d'Orsay, 75 007 Paris, France.
MÜLLER, REINHARD	Prof. Dr., Martin-Luther-Universität, Halle-Wittenberg, August-Bebel-Str. 13 und 50, 4010 Halle (Saale), GDR.
MUÑOZ SECA, ALFONSO	Deputy Director General of Terrestrial, Maritime and Aerial Cooperation, Ministry of Foreign Affairs, José Abascal 41, Madrid, Spain.
NICHOLSON, IAN E.	Ambassador of Australia, Australian Embassy, Sergels Torg 12, Stockholm, Sweden.
OCAMPO-FRIEDMANN, ROSELI	Prof. Dr., Department of Biology, Florida A&M University, Tallahassee, FL 32307, U.S.A.
ORREGO VICUÑA, FRANCISCO	Prof., School of Law and Institute of International Studies, University of Chile, Condell 249, Santiago, Chile.
PUCEIRO RIPOLL, ROBERTO	Dr., Legal Adviser, Goes 2352, Montevideo, Uruguay.
PUNUNGWE, GIFT	Permanent Mission of Zimbabwe to the United Nations, 19 East 47th Street, New York, N.Y. 10017, U.S.A.
QUILTY, PATRICK G.	Dr., Department of the Arts, Sport, the Environment, Tourism and Territories, Antarctic Division, Channel Highway, Kingston, Tasmania 7150, Australia.
RAJAN, H. P.	Principal Scientific Officer, Government of India, Department of Ocean Development, Mahasagar Bhavan Block 12, CGP Complex Lodi Road, New Delhi 110003, India.
REBAGLIATI, ORLANDO R.	Dr., Minister Plenipotentiary, Cónsul General de la Argentina, Casilla 126 V. Valparaiso, Chile.
ROLLE, BRITTA	Dipl. Biol., Greenpeace Deutschland, Haus der Seefahrt, Hohe Brücke 1, 2000 Hamburg 11, FRG.
RONCAGLIOLO, NICOLAS	Consulado General del Peru, San Martin No. 220, Casilla Postal 17, Arica, Chile.

ROSENBERG, JÖRN — Gudenauer Weg 134—136, 5300 Bonn-Ippendorf, FRG.

SAHRHAGE, DIETRICH — Prof. Dr., Leitender Direktor, Institut für Seefischerei, Bundesforschungsanstalt für Fischerei, Palmaille 9, 2000 Hamburg 50, FRG.

SANDER, KIRSTEN — Hegnshusene 125, 2700 Bronshoj, Denmark.

SCULLY, R. TUCKER — Director of the Office of Ocean and Polar Affairs, Bureau of Oceans and International Environmental and Scientific Affairs, U.S. Dept. of State, Washington D.C. 20520, U.S.A.

SOLA, JUAN V. — Dr., National Director of the Argentine Antarctic Institute, Ministry of Defence, Buenos Aires, Argentina.

SOLLIE, FINN — Director, Group Perspectives Group for Northerly Regions, Ullervein 38, N - 0381 Oslo 3, Norway.

SUCHOD, MICHEL — Direction des Affaires Juridiques, Ministère des Affaires Étrangères, 37 Quai d'Orsay 75 007 Paris, France.

SÜVERKRÜP, FRITZ — Dr., Vors. der Industrie- und Handelskammer zu Kiel, Lorentzendamm 24, 2300 Kiel 1, FRG.

TESSENSOHN, FRANZ — Dr., Leiter der Forschungsgruppe Antarktis, Bundesanstalt für Geowissenschaft und Rohstoffe, Stilleweg 2, 3000 Hannover 51, FRG.

THEUTENBERG, BO JOHNSON — Legal Adviser, Ministry of Foreign Affairs, Box 1612, S - 10323 Stockholm, Sweden.

VIALL, JOHN D. — Chief Legal Adviser, Department of Foreign Affairs, 1601 H. F. Verwoerd Bldg., Capetown, 8001, Republic of South Africa.

WATTS, ARTHUR — Deputy Legal Adviser, Foreign and Commonwealth Office, London, SW1A 2AH, Great Britain.

WILSON, ROGER — Political Co-ordinator, Antarctic Campaign, Greenpeace International, 25—26 High Street, Lewes, East Sussex BN7 2LU, Great Britain.

WOLFRUM, RÜDIGER — Prof. Dr., Direktor des Instituts für Internationales Recht an der Universität Kiel, Olshausenstraße 40—60, 2300 Kiel 1, FRG.

WOOLCOTT, RICHARD A.	Ambassador, Permanent Mission of Australia to the United Nations, 885 Second Avenue 16th Floor, New York, NY 10017, U.S.A.
WRIESSNIG, THOMAS	Legationsrat, Auswärtiges Amt, Adenauer Allee 99—103, 5300 Bonn.

MIX
Papier aus verantwortungsvollen Quellen
Paper from responsible sources
FSC® C105338

Printed by Libri Plureos GmbH
in Hamburg, Germany